# AZ GREAT BRITAIN

## and Northern Ireland

EDITION 2 2020

Copyright © Geographers' A-Z Map Company Ltd.

www. /az.co.uk

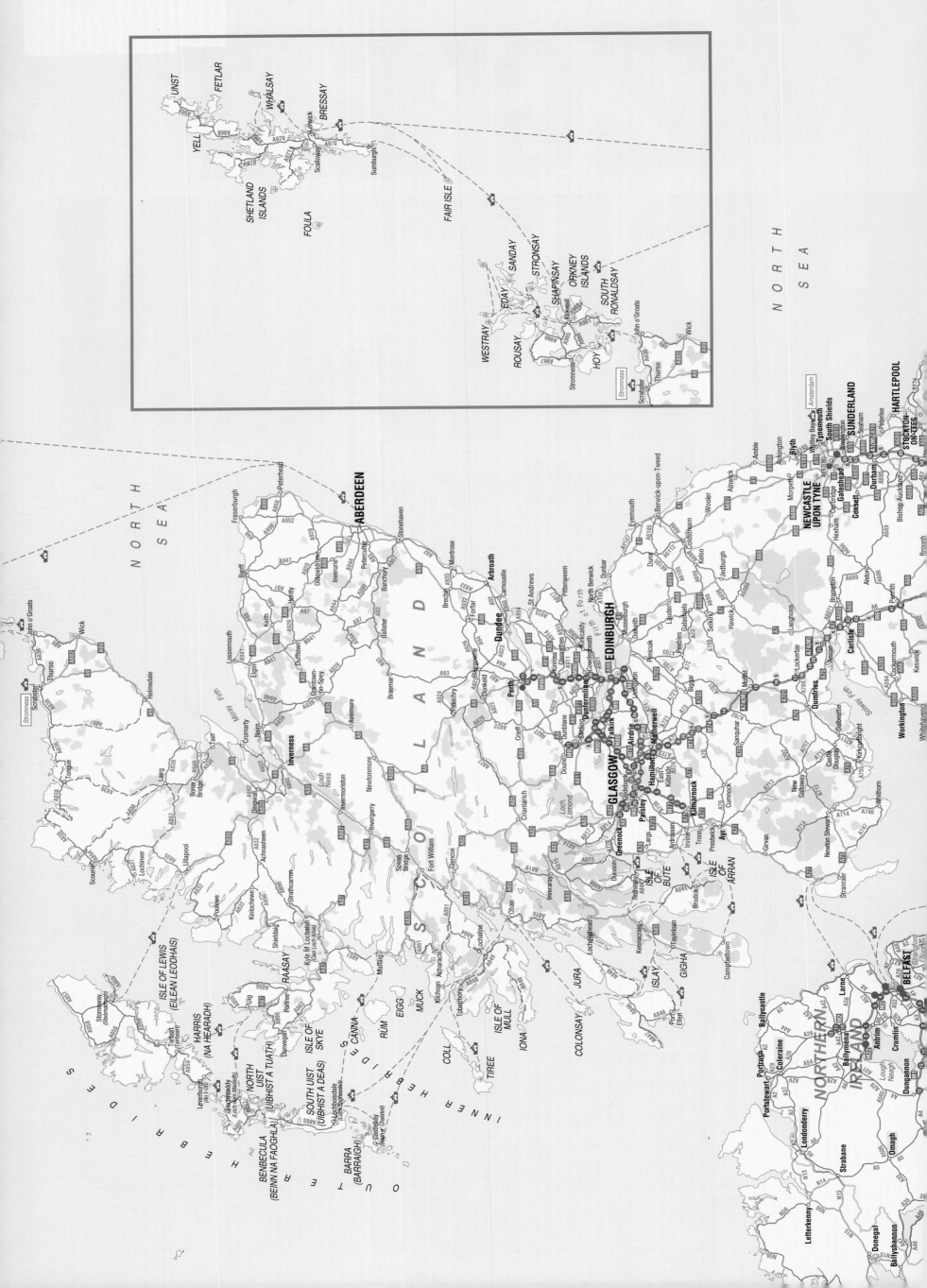

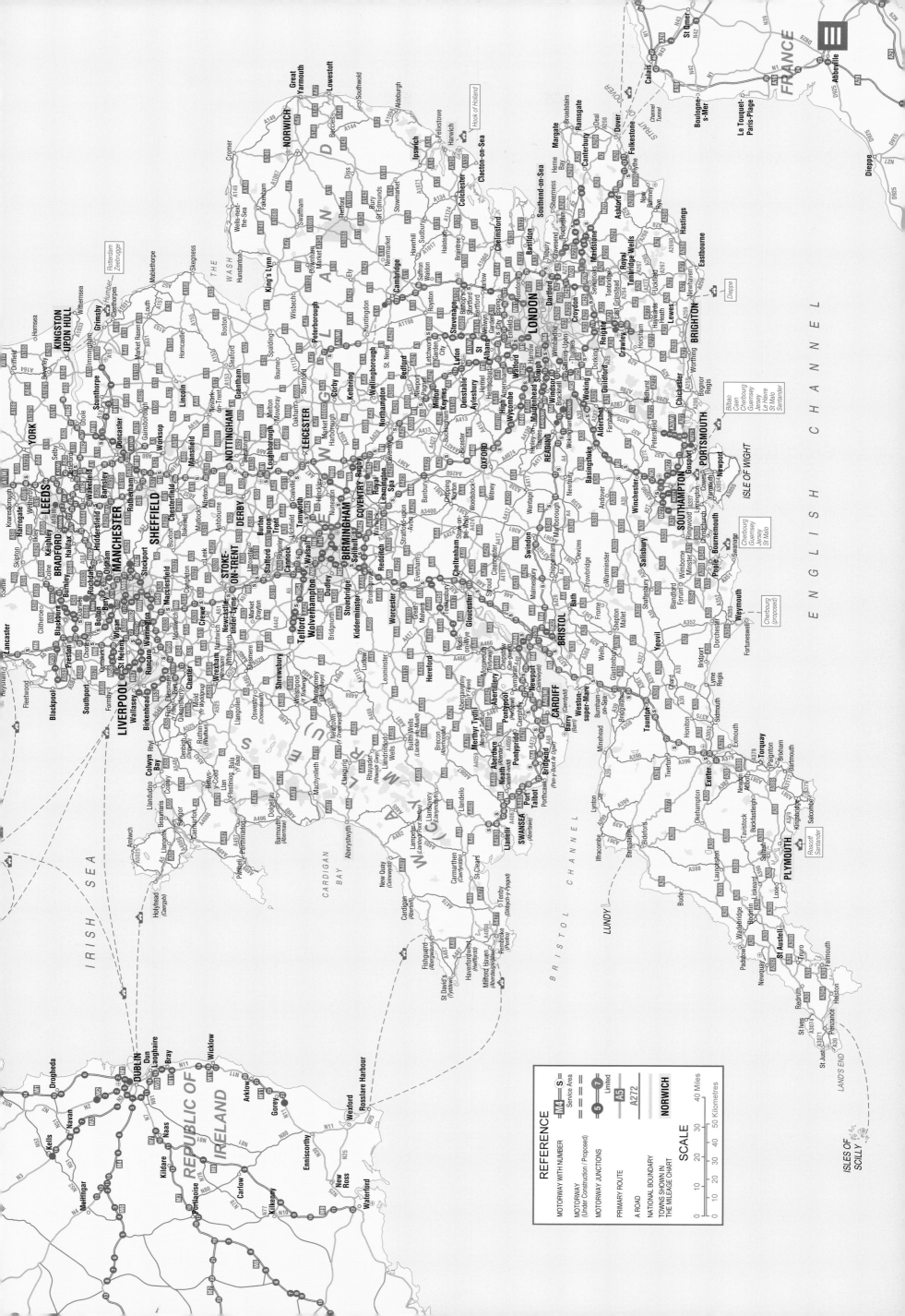

This chart shows the distance in miles and journey time between two cities or towns in Great Britain. Each route has been calculated using a combination of motorways, primary routes and other major roads. This is normally the quickest, though not always the shortest route.

Average journey times are calculated whilst driving at the maximum speed limit. These times are approximate and do not include traffic congestion or convenience breaks.

To find the distance and journey time between two cities or towns, follow a horizontal line and vertical column until they meet each other.

For example, the 285 mile journey from London to Penzance is approximately 4 hours and 59 minutes.

## Northern Ireland

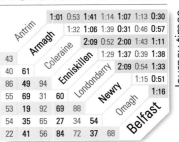

Journey times

Distance in miles

Belfast to London = 440m / 9:46h (excluding ferry)
Belfast to Glasgow = 104m / 4:46h (excluding ferry)

## Great Britain

Journey times

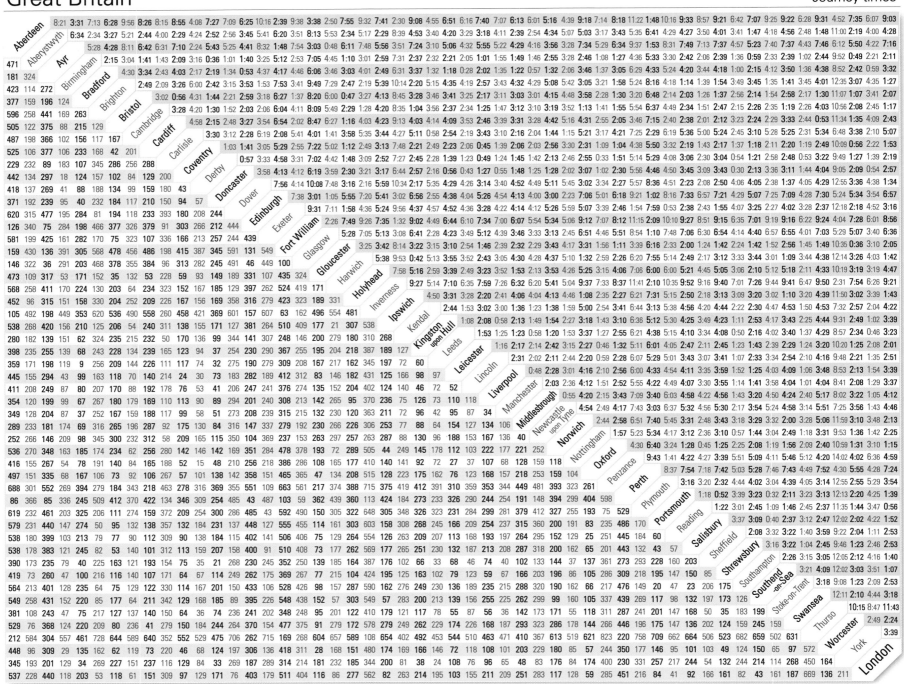

Distance in miles

## Scales to Map Pages

**BRITAIN**
1:221,760 = 3.5 miles to 1 inch (2.54 cm)
2.2 km to 1 cm

**NORTHERN IRELAND**
1:380,160 = 6 miles to 1 inch (2.54 cm)
3.8 km to 1 cm

# Limited Interchange Motorway Junctions

Limited Interchange Motorway Junctions are shown on the mapping pages by red junction indicators 2

## Junction M1

| Junction | Direction | Restriction |
|---|---|---|
| 2 | Northbound<br>Southbound | No exit, access from A1 only<br>No access, exit to A1 only |
| 4 | Northbound<br>Southbound | No exit, access from A41 only<br>No access, exit to A41 only |
| 6a | Northbound<br>Southbound | No exit, access from M25 only<br>No access, exit to M25 only |
| 17 | Northbound<br>Southbound | No access, exit to M45 only<br>No exit, access from M45 only |
| 19 | Northbound<br>Southbound | Exit to M6 only, access from A14 only<br>Access from M6 only, exit to A14 only |
| 21a | Northbound<br>Southbound | No access, exit to A46 only<br>No exit, access from A46 only |
| 24a | Northbound<br>Southbound | No exit<br>Access from A50 only |
| 35a | Northbound<br>Southbound | No access, exit to A616 only<br>No exit, access from A616 only |
| 43 | Northbound<br>Southbound | Exit to M621 only<br>Access from M621 only |
| 48 | Eastbound<br>Westbound | Exit to A1(M) northbound only<br>Access from A1(M) southbound only |

## Junction M2

| Junction | Direction | Restriction |
|---|---|---|
| 1 | Eastbound<br>Westbound | Access from A2 eastbound only<br>Exit to A2 westbound only |

## Junction M3

| Junction | Direction | Restriction |
|---|---|---|
| 8 | Eastbound<br>Westbound | No exit, access from A303 only<br>No access, exit to A303 only |
| 10 | Northbound<br>Southbound | No access from A31<br>No exit to A31 |
| 13 | Southbound | No access from A335 to M3 leading to M27 Eastbound |

## Junction M4

| Junction | Direction | Restriction |
|---|---|---|
| 1 | Eastbound<br>Westbound | Exit to A4 eastbound only<br>Access from A4 westbound only |
| 21 | Eastbound<br>Westbound | No exit to M48<br>No access from M48 |
| 23 | Eastbound<br>Westbound | No access from M48<br>No exit to M48 |
| 25 | Eastbound<br>Westbound | No exit<br>No access |
| 25a | Eastbound<br>Westbound | No exit<br>No access |
| 29 | Eastbound<br>Westbound | No exit, access from A48(M) only<br>No access, exit to A48(M) only |
| 38 | Westbound | No access, exit to A48 only |
| 39 | Eastbound<br>Westbound | No access or exit<br>No exit, access from A48 only |
| 42 | Eastbound<br>Westbound | No access from A48<br>No exit to A48 |

## Junction M5

| Junction | Direction | Restriction |
|---|---|---|
| 10 | Northbound<br>Southbound | No exit, access from A4019 only<br>No access, exit to A4019 only |
| 11a | Southbound | No exit to A417 westbound |
| 18a | Northbound<br>Southbound | No access from M49<br>No exit to M49 |

## Junction M6

| Junction | Direction | Restriction |
|---|---|---|
| 3a | Eastbound<br>Westbound | No exit to M6 Toll<br>No access from M6 Toll |
| 4 | Northbound<br><br>Southbound | No exit to M42 northbound<br>No access from M42 southbound<br>No exit to M42<br>No access from M42 southbound |
| 4a | Northbound<br>Southbound | No exit, access from M42 southbound only<br>No access, exit to M42 only |
| 5 | Northbound<br>Southbound | No access, exit to A452 only<br>No exit, access from A452 only |
| 10a | Northbound<br>Southbound | No access, exit to M54 only<br>No exit, access from M54 only |
| 11a | Northbound<br>Southbound | No exit to M6 Toll<br>No access from M6 Toll |
| 20 | Northbound<br>Southbound | No exit to M56 eastbound<br>No access from M56 westbound |
| 24 | Northbound<br>Southbound | No exit, access from A58 only<br>No access, exit to A58 only |
| 25 | Northbound<br>Southbound | No access, exit to A49 only<br>No exit, access from A49 only |
| 30 | Northbound<br>Southbound | No exit, access from M61 northbound only<br>No access, exit to M61 southbound only |
| 31a | Northbound<br>Southbound | No access, exit to B6242 only<br>No exit, access from B6242 only |
| 45 | Northbound<br>Southbound | No access onto A74(M)<br>No exit from A74(M) |

## Junction M6 Toll

| Junction | Direction | Restriction |
|---|---|---|
| T1 | Northbound<br>Southbound | No exit<br>No access |
| T2 | Northbound<br>Southbound | No access or exit<br>No access |
| T5 | Northbound<br>Southbound | No exit<br>No access |
| T7 | Northbound<br>Southbound | No access from A5<br>No exit |
| T8 | Northbound<br>Southbound | No exit to A460 northbound<br>No exit |

## Junction M8

| Junction | Direction | Restriction |
|---|---|---|
| 6 | Eastbound<br>Westbound | No exit, access only<br>No access, exit only |
| 6a | Eastbound<br>Westbound | No access, exit only<br>No exit, access only |
| 7 | Eastbound<br>Westbound | No access, exit only<br>No exit, access only |
| 7a | Eastbound<br><br>Westbound | No exit, access from A725<br>Northbound only<br>No access, exit to A725<br>Southbound only |
| 8 | Eastbound<br>Westbound | No exit to M73 northbound<br>No access from M73 southbound |
| 9 | Eastbound<br>Westbound | No access, exit only<br>No exit, access only |
| 13 | Eastbound<br>Westbound | No access from M80 southbound<br>No exit to M80 northbound |
| 14 | Eastbound<br>Westbound | No access, exit only<br>No exit, access only |
| 16 | Eastbound<br>Westbound | No exit, access only<br>No access, exit only |
| 17 | Eastbound<br>Westbound | No exit, access from A82 only<br>No access, exit to A82 only |
| 18 | Westbound | No exit, access only |
| 19 | Eastbound<br>Westbound | No exit to A814 eastbound<br>No access from A814 westbound |
| 20 | Eastbound<br>Westbound | No exit, access only<br>No access, exit only |
| 21 | Eastbound<br>Westbound | No access, exit only<br>No exit, access only |
| 22 | Eastbound<br>Westbound | No exit, access from M77 only<br>No access, exit to M77 only |
| 23 | Eastbound<br>Westbound | No exit, access from B768 only<br>No access, exit to B768 only |
| 25 | Eastbound &<br>Westbound | Access from A739 southbound only<br>Exit to A739 northbound only |
| 25a | Eastbound<br>Westbound | Access only<br>Exit only |
| 28 | Eastbound<br>Westbound | No exit, access from airport only<br>No access, exit to airport only |
| 29a | Eastbound<br>Westbound | No exit, access only<br>No access, exit only |

## Junction M9

| Junction | Direction | Restriction |
|---|---|---|
| 2 | Northbound<br>Southbound | No exit, access from B8046 only<br>No access, exit to B8046 only |
| 3 | Northbound<br>Southbound | No access, exit to A803 only<br>No exit, access from A803 only |
| 6 | Northbound<br>Southbound | No exit, access only<br>No access, exit to A905 only |
| 8 | Northbound<br>Southbound | No access, exit to M876 only<br>No exit, access from M876 only |

## Junction M11

| Junction | Direction | Restriction |
|---|---|---|
| 4 | Northbound<br>Southbound | No exit, access from A406 eastbound only<br>No access, exit to A406 westbound only |
| 5 | Northbound<br>Southbound | No access, exit to A1168 only<br>No exit, access from A1168 only |
| 8a | Northbound<br>Southbound | No access, exit only<br>No exit, access only |
| 9 | Northbound<br>Southbound | No access, exit only<br>No exit, access only |
| 13 | Northbound<br>Southbound | No access, exit only<br>No exit, access only |
| 14 | Northbound<br><br>Southbound | No access from A428 eastbound<br>No exit to A428 westbound<br>No exit, access from A428 eastbound only |

## Junction M20

| Junction | Direction | Restriction |
|---|---|---|
| 2 | Eastbound<br><br>Westbound | No access, exit to A20 only<br>(access via M26 Junction 2a)<br>No exit, access only (exit via M26 Jun.2a) |
| 3 | Eastbound<br>Westbound | No exit, access from M26 eastbound only<br>No access, exit to M26 westbound only |
| 10 | Eastbound<br>Westbound | No access, exit only<br>No exit, access only |
| 11a | Eastbound<br>Westbound | No access from Channel Tunnel<br>No exit to Channel Tunnel |

## Junction M23

| Junction | Direction | Restriction |
|---|---|---|
| 7 | Northbound<br>Southbound | No exit to A23 southbound<br>No access from A23 northbound |

## Junction M25

| Junction | Direction | Restriction |
|---|---|---|
| 5 | Clockwise<br>Anti-clockwise | No exit to M26 eastbound<br>No access from M26 westbound |
| Spur to A21 | Northbound<br>Southbound | No exit to M26 eastbound<br>No access from M26 westbound |
| 19 | Clockwise<br>Anti-clockwise | No access, exit only<br>No exit, access only |
| 21 | Clockwise &<br>Anti-clockwise | No exit to M1 southbound<br>No access from M1 northbound |
| 31 | Northbound<br>Southbound | No access, exit only (access via Jun.30)<br>No exit, access only (exit via Jun.30) |

## M26

**Junction with M25** (M25 Jun.5)

| Direction | Restriction |
|---|---|
| Eastbound | No access from M25 clockwise or spur from A21 northbound |
| Westbound | No exit to M25 anti-clockwise or spur to A21 southbound |

**Junction with M20** (M20 Jun.3)

| Direction | Restriction |
|---|---|
| Eastbound | No exit to M20 westbound |
| Westbound | No access from M20 eastbound |

## Junction M27

| Junction | Direction | Restriction |
|---|---|---|
| 4 | Eastbound &<br>Westbound | No exit to A33 southbound (Southampton)<br>No access from A33 northbound |
| 10 | Eastbound<br>Westbound | No exit, access from A32 only<br>No access, exit to A32 only |

## Junction M40

| Junction | Direction | Restriction |
|---|---|---|
| 3 | North-Westbound<br>South-Eastbound | No access, exit to A40 only<br>No exit, access from A40 only |
| 7 | N.W bound<br>S.E bound | No access, exit only<br>No exit, access only |
| 13 | N.W bound<br>S.E bound | No access, exit only<br>No exit, access only |
| 14 | N.W bound<br>S.E bound | No exit, access only<br>No access, exit only |
| 16 | N.W bound<br>S.E bound | No exit, access only<br>No access, exit only |

## Junction M42

| Junction | Direction | Restriction |
|---|---|---|
| 1 | Eastbound<br>Westbound | No exit<br>No access |
| 7 | Northbound<br>Southbound | No access, exit to M6 only<br>No exit, access from M6 northbound only |
| 8 | Northbound<br>Southbound | No exit, access from M6 southbound only<br>Exit to M6 nothbound only<br>Access from M6 southbound only |

## M45

**Junction with M1** (M1 Jun.17)

| Direction | Restriction |
|---|---|
| Eastbound | No exit to M1 northbound |
| Westbound | No access from M1 southbound |

**Junction with A45 east of Dunchurch**

| Direction | Restriction |
|---|---|
| Eastbound | No access, exit to A45 only |
| Westbound | No exit, access from A45 northbound only |

## M48

**Junction with M4** (M4 Jun.21)

| Direction | Restriction |
|---|---|
| Eastbound | No exit to M4 westbound |
| Westbound | No access from M4 eastbound |

**Junction with M4** (M4 Jun.23)

| Direction | Restriction |
|---|---|
| Eastbound | No access from M4 westbound |
| Westbound | No exit to M4 eastbound |

## Junction M53

| Junction | Direction | Restriction |
|---|---|---|
| 11 | Northbound &<br>Southbound | No access from M56 eastbound,<br>no exit to M56 westbound |

## Junction M56

| Junction | Direction | Restriction |
|---|---|---|
| 1 | Eastbound<br><br>S.E bound<br>Westbound | No exit to M60 N.W bound<br>No exit to A34 southbound<br>No access from A34 northbound<br>No access from M60 |
| 2 | Eastbound<br>Westbound | No exit, access from A560 only<br>No access, exit to A560 only |
| 3 | Eastbound<br>Westbound | No access, exit only<br>No exit, access only |
| 4 | Eastbound<br>Westbound | No exit, access only<br>No access, exit only |
| 7 | Westbound | No access, exit only |
| 8 | Eastbound<br>Westbound | No access or exit<br>No exit, access from A556 only |
| 9 | Eastbound<br>Westbound | No access from M6 northbound<br>No exit to M60 southbound |
| 10a | Northbound<br>Southbound | No exit, access only<br>No access, exit only |
| 15 | Eastbound<br>Westbound | No exit to M53<br>No access from M53 |

## Junction M57

| Junction | Direction | Restriction |
|---|---|---|
| 3 | Northbound<br>Southbound | No exit, access only<br>No access, exit only |
| 5 | Northbound<br>Southbound | No exit, access from A580 westbound only<br>No access, exit to A580 eastbound only |

## Junction M60

| Junction | Direction | Restriction |
|---|---|---|
| 2 | N.E bound<br>S.W bound | No access, exit to A560 only<br>No exit, access from A560 only |
| 3 | Eastbound<br>Westbound | No access from A34 southbound<br>No exit to A34 northbound |
| 4 | Eastbound<br><br>Westbound | No exit to M56 S.W bound<br>No exit to A34 northbound<br>No access from A34 southbound<br>No access from M56 eastbound |
| 5 | N.W bound<br>S.E bound | No access from or exit to A5103 southbound<br>No access from or exit to A5103 northbound |
| 14 | Eastbound<br><br>Westbound | No exit to A580<br>No access from A580 westbound<br>No exit to A580 eastbound<br>No access from A580 |
| 16 | Eastbound<br>Westbound | No exit, access from A666 only<br>No access, exit to A666 only |
| 20 | Eastbound<br>Westbound | No access from A664<br>No exit to A664 |
| 22 | Westbound | No access from A62 |
| 25 | S.W bound | No access from A560 / A6017 |
| 26 | N.E bound | No access or exit |
| 27 | N.E bound<br>S.W bound | No access, exit only<br>No exit, access only |

## Junction M61

| Junction | Direction | Restriction |
|---|---|---|
| 2&3 | N.W bound<br>S.E bound | No access from A580 eastbound<br>No exit to A580 westbound |

**Junction with M6** (M6 Jun.30)

| Direction | Restriction |
|---|---|
| N.W bound | No exit to M6 southbound |
| S.E bound | No access from M6 northbound |

## Junction M62

| Junction | Direction | Restriction |
|---|---|---|
| 23 | Eastbound<br>Westbound | No access, exit to A640 only<br>No exit, access from A640 only |

## Junction M65

| Junction | Direction | Restriction |
|---|---|---|
| 9 | N.E bound<br>S.W bound | No access, exit to A679 only<br>No exit, access from A679 only |
| 11 | N.E bound<br>S.W bound | No exit, access only<br>No access, exit only |

## Junction M66

| Junction | Direction | Restriction |
|---|---|---|
| 1 | Northbound<br>Southbound | No access, exit to A56 only<br>No exit, access from A56 only |

## Junction M67

| Junction | Direction | Restriction |
|---|---|---|
| 1 | Eastbound<br>Westbound | Access from A57 eastbound only<br>Exit to A57 westbound only |
| 1a | Eastbound<br>Westbound | No access, exit to A6017 only<br>No exit, access from A6017 only |
| 2 | Eastbound<br>Westbound | No exit, access from A57 only<br>No access, exit to A57 only |

## Junction M69

| Junction | Direction | Restriction |
|---|---|---|
| 2 | N.E bound<br>S.W bound | No exit, access from B4669 only<br>No access, exit to B4669 only |

## Junction M73

| Junction | Direction | Restriction |
|---|---|---|
| 1 | Southbound | No exit to A721 eastbound |
| 2 | Northbound<br><br>Southbound | No access from M8 eastbound<br>No exit to A89 eastbound<br>No exit to M8 westbound<br>No access from A89 westbound |
| 3 | Northbound<br>Southbound | No exit to A80 S.W bound<br>No access from A80 N.E bound |

## Junction M74

| Junction | Direction | Restriction |
|---|---|---|
| 1 | Eastbound<br>Westbound | No access from M8 Westbound<br>No exit to M8 Westbound |
| 3 | Eastbound<br>Westbound | No exit<br>No access |
| 7 | Northbound<br>Southbound | No exit, access from A72 only<br>No access, exit to A72 only |
| 9 | Northbound<br>Southbound | No access or exit<br>No access, exit to B7078 only |
| 10 | Southbound | No exit, access from B7078 only |
| 11 | Northbound<br>Southbound | No exit, access from B7078 only<br>No access, exit to B7078 only |
| 12 | Northbound<br>Southbound | No access, exit to A70 only<br>No exit, access from A70 only |

## Junction M77

**Junction with M8** (M8 Jun.22)

| Direction | Restriction |
|---|---|
| Northbound | No exit to M8 westbound |
| Southbound | No access from M8 eastbound |

| Junction | Direction | Restriction |
|---|---|---|
| 4 | Northbound<br>Southbound | No exit<br>No access |
| 6 | Northbound<br>Southbound | No exit to A77<br>No access from A77 |
| 7 | Northbound | No access from A77<br>No exit to A77 |

## Junction M80

| Junction | Direction | Restriction |
|---|---|---|
| 1 | Northbound<br>Southbound | No access from M8 westbound<br>No exit to M8 eastbound |
| 4a | Northbound<br>Southbound | No access<br>No exit |
| 6a | Northbound<br>Southbound | No exit<br>No access |
| 8 | Northbound<br>Southbound | No access from M876<br>No exit to M876 |

## Junction M90

| Junction | Direction | Restriction |
|---|---|---|
| 1 | Northbound<br>Southbound | No exit<br>No Access from A90 |
| 2a | Northbound<br>Southbound | No access, exit to A92 only<br>No exit, access from A92 only |
| 7 | Northbound<br>Southbound | No exit, access from A91 only<br>No access, exit to A91 only |
| 8 | Northbound<br>Southbound | No access, exit to A91 only<br>No exit, access from A91 only |
| 10 | Northbound<br><br>Southbound | No access from A912<br>Exit to A912 northbound only<br>No exit to A912<br>Access from A912 southbound only |

## Junction M180

| Junction | Direction | Restriction |
|---|---|---|
| 1 | Eastbound<br>Westbound | No access, exit only<br>No exit, access from A18 only |

## Junction M606

| Junction | Direction | Restriction |
|---|---|---|
| 2 | Northbound | No access, exit only |

## Junction M621

| Junction | Direction | Restriction |
|---|---|---|
| 2a | Eastbound<br>Westbound | No exit, access only<br>No access, exit only |
| 4 | Southbound | No exit |
| 5 | Northbound<br>Southbound | No access, exit to A61 only<br>No exit, access from A61 only |
| 6 | Northbound<br>Southbound | No exit, access only<br>No access, exit only |
| 7 | Eastbound<br>Westbound | No access, exit only<br>No exit, access only |
| 8 | Northbound<br>Southbound | No access, exit only<br>No exit, access only |

## Junction M876

**Junction with M80** (M80 Jun.5)

| Direction | Restriction |
|---|---|
| N.E bound | No access from M80 southbound |
| S.W bound | No exit to M80 northbound |

**Junction with M9** (M9 Jun.8)

| Direction | Restriction |
|---|---|
| N.E bound | No exit to M9 northbound |
| S.W bound | No access from M9 southbound |

## Junction A1(M)

**Hertfordshire Section**

| Junction | Direction | Restriction |
|---|---|---|
| 2 | Northbound<br>Southbound | No access, exit only<br>No exit, access from A1001 only |
| 3 | Southbound | No access, exit only |
| 5 | Northbound<br>Southbound | No exit, access only<br>No access or exit |

**Cambridgeshire Section**

| Junction | Direction | Restriction |
|---|---|---|
| 14 | Northbound<br>Southbound | No exit, access only<br>No access, exit only |

**Leeds Section**

| Junction | Direction | Restriction |
|---|---|---|
| 40 | Southbound | Exit to A1 southbound only |
| 43 | Northbound<br>Southbound | Access from M1 eastbound only<br>Exit to M1 westbound only |

**Durham Section**

| Junction | Direction | Restriction |
|---|---|---|
| 57 | Northbound<br>Southbound | No access, exit to A66(M) only<br>No exit, access from A66(M) |
| 65 | Northbound<br><br>Southbound | Exit to A1 N.W bound and to A194(M) only<br>Access from A1 S.E bound and from A194(M) only |

## Junction A3(M)

| Junction | Direction | Restriction |
|---|---|---|
| 4 | Northbound<br>Southbound | No access, exit only<br>No exit, access only |

## Aston Expressway A38(M)

**Junction with Victoria Road, Aston**

| Direction | Restriction |
|---|---|
| Northbound | No exit, access only |
| Southbound | No access, exit only |

## Junction A48(M)

**Junction with M4** (M4 Jun.29)

| Direction | Restriction |
|---|---|
| N.E bound | Exit to M4 eastbound only |
| S.W bound | Access from M4 westbound only |

| Junction | Direction | Restriction |
|---|---|---|
| 29a | N.E bound<br>S.W bound | Access from A48 eastbound only<br>Exit to A48 westbound only |

## Mancunian Way A57(M)

**Junction with A34 Brook Street, Manchester**

| Direction | Restriction |
|---|---|
| Eastbound | No access, exit to A34 Brook Street, southbound only |
| Westbound | No exit, access only |

## Leeds Inner Ring Road A58(M)

**Junction with Park Lane / Westgate**

| Direction | Restriction |
|---|---|
| Southbound | No access, exit only |

## Leeds Inner Ring Road A64(M) (continuation of A58(M))

**Junction with A58 Clay Pit Lane**

| Direction | Restriction |
|---|---|
| Eastbound | No access |
| Westbound | No exit |

## A66(M)

**Junction with A1(M)** (A1(M) Jun.57)

| Direction | Restriction |
|---|---|
| N.E bound | Access from A1(M) northbound only |
| S.W bound | Exit to A1(M) southbound only |

## Junction A74(M)

| Junction | Direction | Restriction |
|---|---|---|
| 18 | Northbound<br>Southbound | No access<br>No exit |

## Newcastle Central Motorway A167(M)

**Junction with Camden Street**

| Direction | Restriction |
|---|---|
| Northbound | No exit, access only |
| Southbound | No access or exit |

## A194(M)

**Junction with A1(M)** (A1(M) Jun.65) **and A1 Gateshead Western By-Pass**

| Direction | Restriction |
|---|---|
| Northbound | Access from A1(M) only |
| Southbound | Exit to A1(M) only |

# Northern Ireland

## Junction M1

| Junction | Direction | Restriction |
|---|---|---|
| 3 | Northbound<br>Southbound | No exit, access only<br>No access, exit only |
| 7 | Westbound | No access, exit only |

## Junction M2

| Junction | Direction | Restriction |
|---|---|---|
| 2 | Eastbound<br>Westbound | No access to M5 northbound<br>No exit to M5 southbound |

## Junction M5

| Junction | Direction | Restriction |
|---|---|---|
| 2 | Northbound<br>Southbound | No access from M2 eastbound<br>No exit to M2 westbound |

## Reference

**Motorway**
Autoroute
Autobahn

**Motorway Under Construction**
Autoroute en construction
Autobahn im Bau

**Motorway Proposed**
Autoroute prévue
Geplante Autobahn

**Motorway Junctions with Numbers**
Unlimited Interchange
Limited Interchange

Autoroute échangeur numéroté
Echangeur complet
Echangeur partiel

Autobahnanschlußstelle mit Nummer
Unbeschränkter Fahrtrichtungswechsel
Beschränkter Fahrtrichtungswechsel

**Motorway Service Area** (with fuel station)
with access from one carriageway only

Aire de services d'autoroute (avec station service)
accessible d'un seul côté
Rastplatz oder Raststätte (mit tankstelle)
Einbahn

**Major Road Service Area** (with fuel station) with 24 hour facilities
Primary Route          Class A Road
Aire de services sur route prioritaire (avec station service) Ouverte 24h sur 24
Route à grande circulation          Route de type A
Raststätte (mit tankstelle) Durchgehend geöffnet
Hauptverkehrsstraße          A- Straße

**Major Road Junctions**    Detailed
Jonctions grands routiers    Détaillé
Hauptverkehrsstraße Kreuzungen  Ausführlich
                    Other  Autre  Andere

**Truckstop** (selection of)
Sélection d'aire pour poids lourds
Auswahl von Fernfahrerrastplatz

**Primary Route**
Route à grande circulation
Hauptverkehrsstraße

**Primary Route Junction with Number**
Echangeur numéroté
Hauptverkehrsstraßenkreuzung mit Nummer

**Primary Route Destination**
Route prioritaire, direction
Hauptverkehrsstraße Richtung

**Dual Carriageways** (A & B roads)
Route à double chaussées séparées (route A & B)
Zweispurige Schnellstraße (A- und B- Straßen)

**Class A Road**
Route de type A
A-Straße

**Class B Road**
Route de type B
B-Straße

**Narrow Major Road** (passing places)
Route prioritaire étroite (possibilité de dépassement)
Schmale Hauptverkehrsstaße (mit Überholmöglichkeit)

**Major Roads Under Construction**
Route prioritaire en construction
Hauptverkehrsstaße im Bau

**Major Roads Proposed**
Route prioritaire prévue
Geplante Hauptverkehrsstaße

**Gradient 1:7** (14%) **& steeper**
(descent in direction of arrow)
Pente égale ou supérieure à 14% (dans le sens de la descente)
14% Steigung und steiler (in Pfeilrichtung)

**Toll**
Barrière de péage
Gebührenpflichtig

**Dart Charge**
www.gov.uk/pay-dartford-crossing-charge

**Park & Ride**
Parking avec Service Navette
Parken und Reisen

**Mileage between markers**
Distence en miles entre les flèches
Strecke zwischen Markierungen in Meilen

**Airport**
Aéroport
Flughafen

**Airfield**
Terrain d'aviation
Flugplatz

**Heliport**
Héliport
Hubschrauberlandeplatz

**Ferry**          Bac          Fähre
(vehicular, sea)  (véhicules, mer)  (auto, meer)
(vehicular, river)  (véhicules, rivière)  (auto, fluß)
(foot only)      (piétons)      (nur für Personen)

**Railway and Station**
Voie ferrée et gare
Eisenbahnlinie und Bahnhof

**Level Crossing and Tunnel**
Passage à niveau et tunnel
Bahnübergang und Tunnel

**River or Canal**
Rivière ou canal
Fluß oder Kanal

**County or Unitary Authority Boundary**
Limite de comté ou de division administrative
Grafschafts- oder Verwaltungsbezirksgrenze

**National Boundary**
Frontière nationale
Landesgrenze

**Built-up Area**
Agglomération
Geschloßene Ortschaft

**Town, Village or Hamlet**
Ville, Village ou hameau
Stadt, Dorf oder Weiler

**Wooded Area**
Zone boisée
Waldgebiet

**Spot Height in Feet**
Altitude (en pieds)
Höhe in Fuß

**Relief above 400'** (122m)
Relief par estompage au-dessus de 400' (122m)
Reliefschattierung über 400' (122m)

**National Grid Reference** (kilometres)
Coordonnées géographiques nationales (Kilomètres)
Nationale geographische Koordinaten (Kilometer)

**Page Continuation**
Suite à la page indiquée
Seitenfortsetzung

## Tourist Information

**Abbey, Church, Friary, Priory**
Abbaye, église, monastère, prieuré
Abtei, Kirche, Mönchskloster, Kloster

**Animal Collection**
Ménagerie
Tiersammlung

**Aquarium**
Aquarium
Aquarium

**Arboretum, Botanical Garden**
Jardin Botanique
Botanischer Garten

**Aviary, Bird Garden**
Volière
Voliere

**Battle Site and Date**
Champ de bataille et date
Schlachtfeld und Datum

**Blue Flag Beach**
Plage Pavillon Bleu
Blaue Flagge Strand

**Bridge**
Pont
Brücke

**Butterfly Farm**
Ferme aux Papillons
Schmetterlingsfarm

**Castle** (open to public)
Château (ouvert au public)
Schloß / Burg (für die Öffentlichkeit zugänglich)

**Castle with Garden** (open to public)
Château avec parc (ouvert au public)
Schloß mit Garten (für die Öffentlichkeit zugänglich)

**Cathedral**
Cathédrale
Kathedrale

**Cidermaker**
Cidrerie (fabrication)
Apfelwein Hersteller

**Country Park**
Parc régional
Landschaftspark

**Distillery**
Distillerie
Brennerei

**Farm Park, Open Farm**
Park Animalier
Bauernhof Park

**Fortress, Hill Fort**
Château Fort
Festung

**Garden** (open to public)
Jardin (ouvert au public)
Garten (für die Öffentlichkeit zugänglich)

**Historic Building** (open to public)
Monument historique (ouvert au public)
Historisches Gebäude (für die Öffentlichkeit zugänglich)

**Historic Building with Garden** (open to public)
Monument historique avec jardin (ouvert au public)
Historisches Gebäude mit Garten (für die Öffentlichkeit zugänglich)

**Horse Racecourse**
Hippodrome
Pferderennbahn

**Industrial Monument**
Monument Industrielle
Industriedenkmal

**Leisure Park, Leisure Pool**
Parc d'Attraction, Loisirs Piscine
Freizeitpark, Freizeit pool

**Lighthouse**
Phare
Leuchtturm

**Mine, Cave**
Mine, Grotte
Bergwerk, Höhle

**Monument**
Monument
Denkmal

**Motor Racing Circuit**
Circuit Automobile
Automobilrennbahn

**Museum, Art Gallery**
Musée
Museum, Galerie

**National Park**
Parc national
Nationalpark

**National Trail**
Sentier national
Nationaler weg

**National Trust Property**
National Trust Property
National Trust- Eigentum

**Natural Attraction**
Attraction Naturelle
Natürliche Anziehung

**Place of Interest**          Craft Centre •
Site, curiosité
Sehenswürdigkeit

**Prehistoric Monument**
Monument Préhistorique
Prähistorische Denkmal

**Railway, Steam or Narrow Gauge**
Chemin de fer, à vapeur ou à voie étroite
Eisenbahn, Dampf- oder Schmalspurbahn

**Roman Remains**
Vestiges Romains
Römischen Ruinen

**Theme Park**
Centre de loisirs
Vergnügungspark

**Tourist Information Centre**
Office de Tourisme
Touristeninformationen

**Viewpoint**          (360 degrees)
Vue panoramique    (360 degrés)
Aussichtspunkt      (360 Grade)

                    (180 degrees)
                    (180 degrés)
                    (180 Grade)

**Vineyard**
Vignoble
Weinberg

**Visitor Information Centre**
Centre d'information touristique
Besucherzentrum

**Wildlife Park**
Réserve de faune
Wildpark

**Windmill**
Moulin à vent
Windmühle

**Zoo or Safari Park**
Parc ou réserve zoologique
Zoo oder Safari-Park

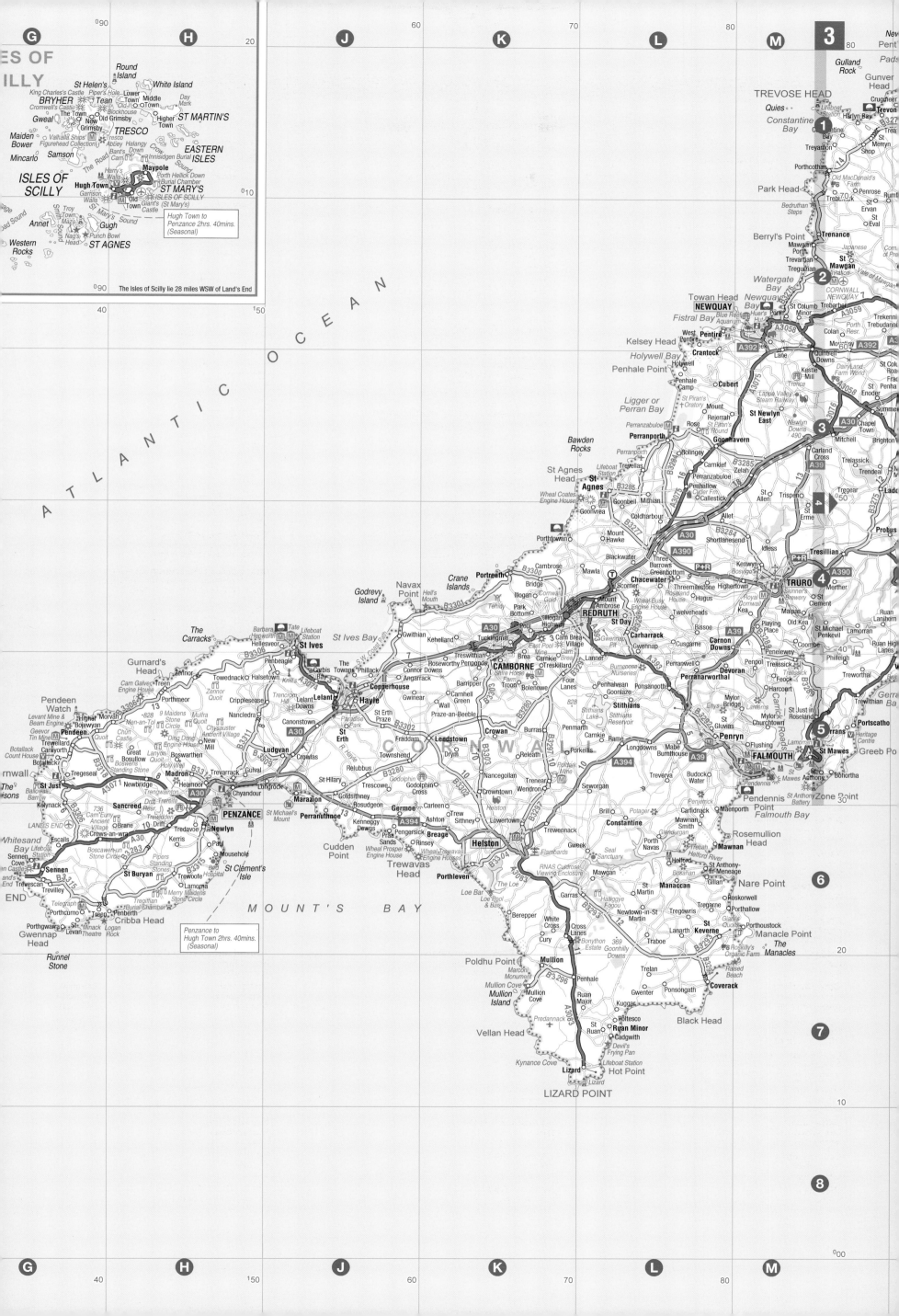

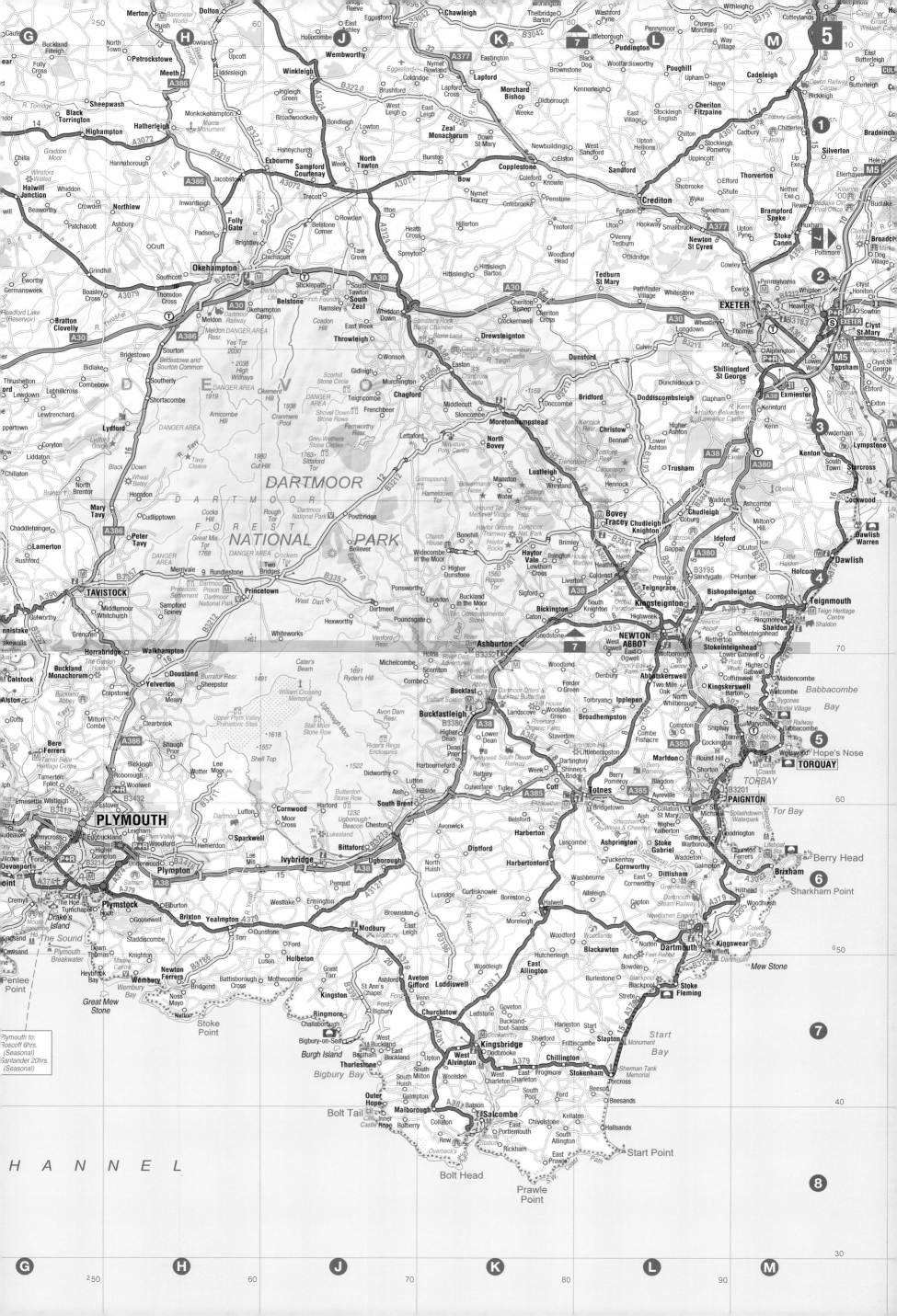

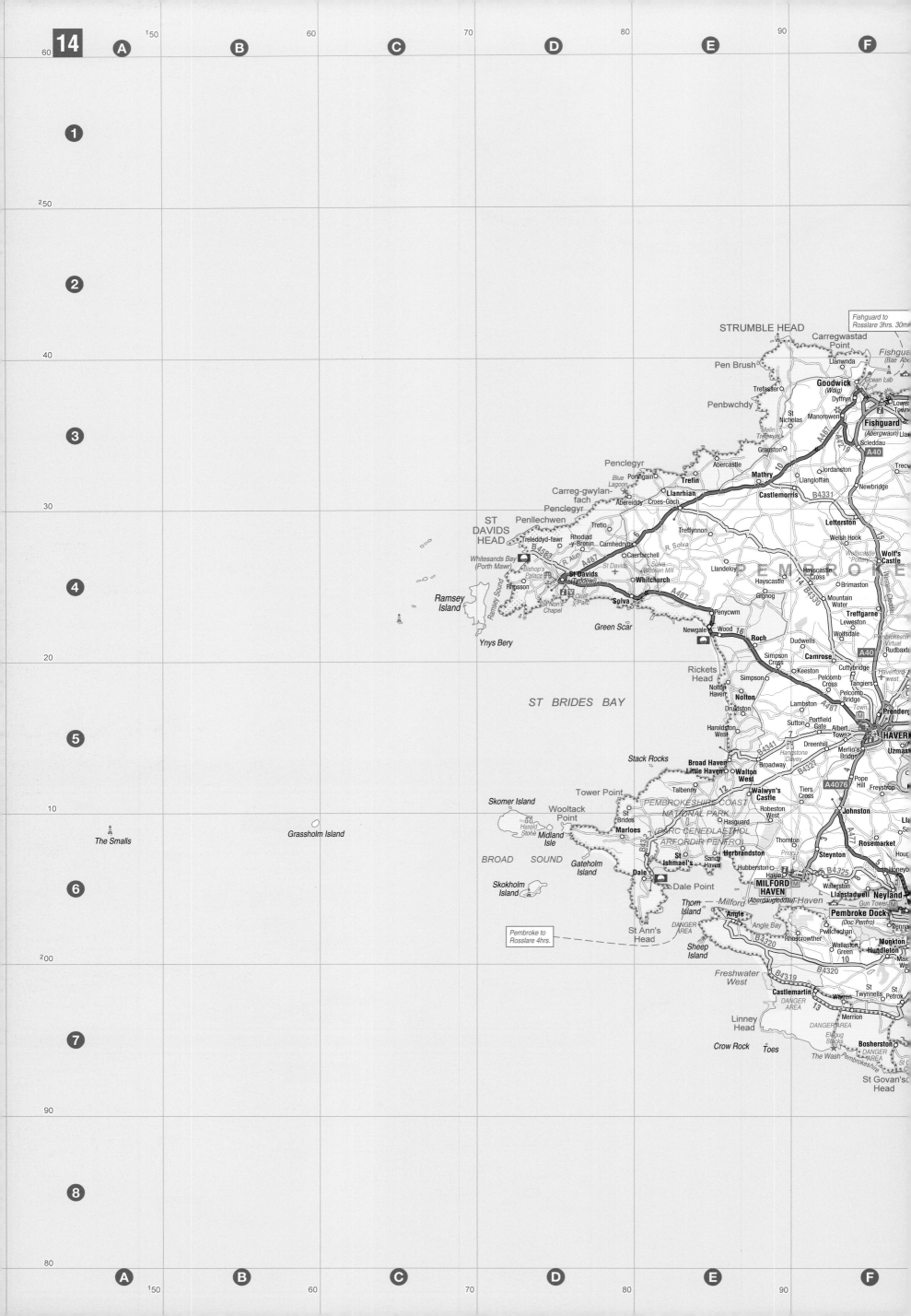

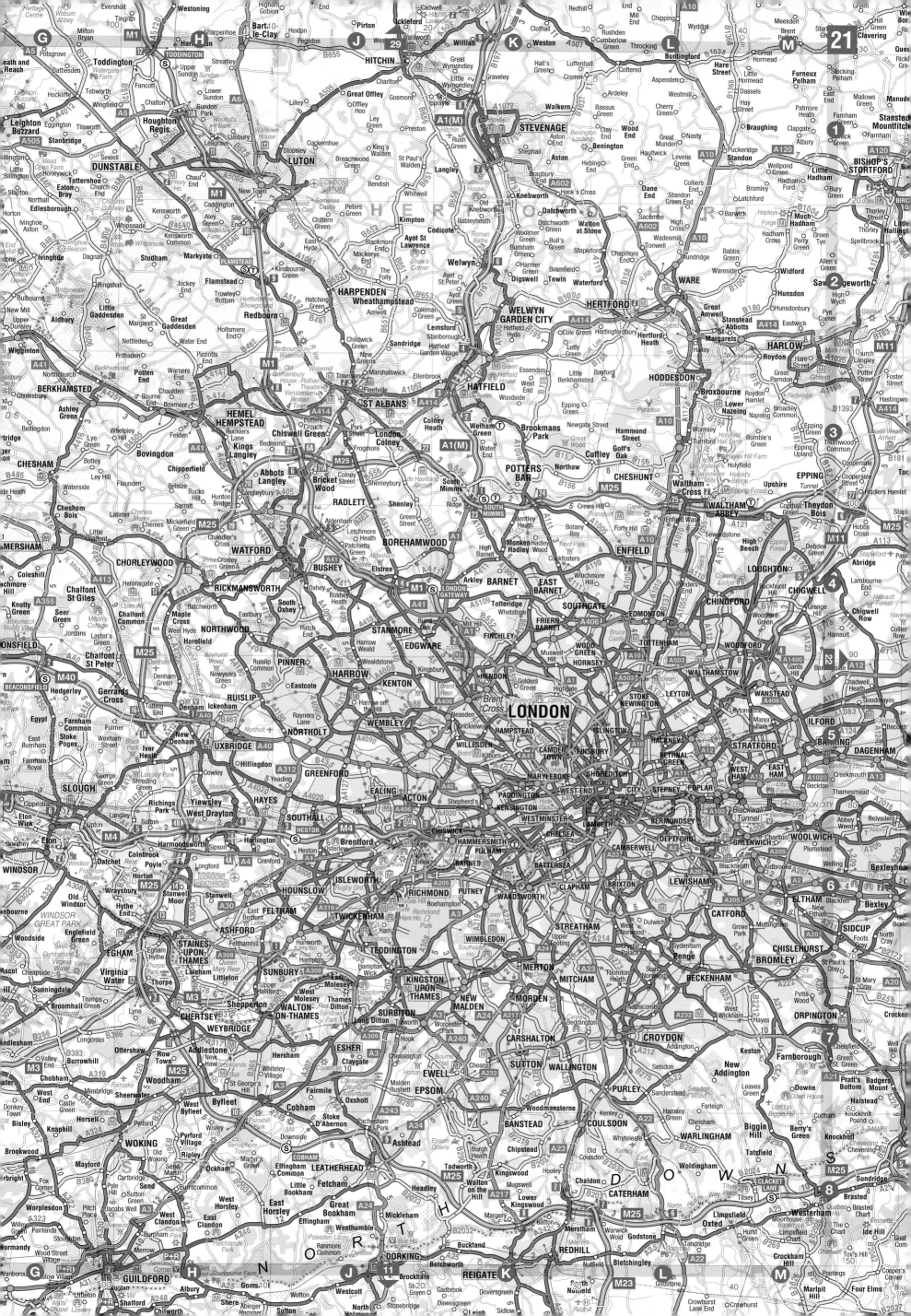

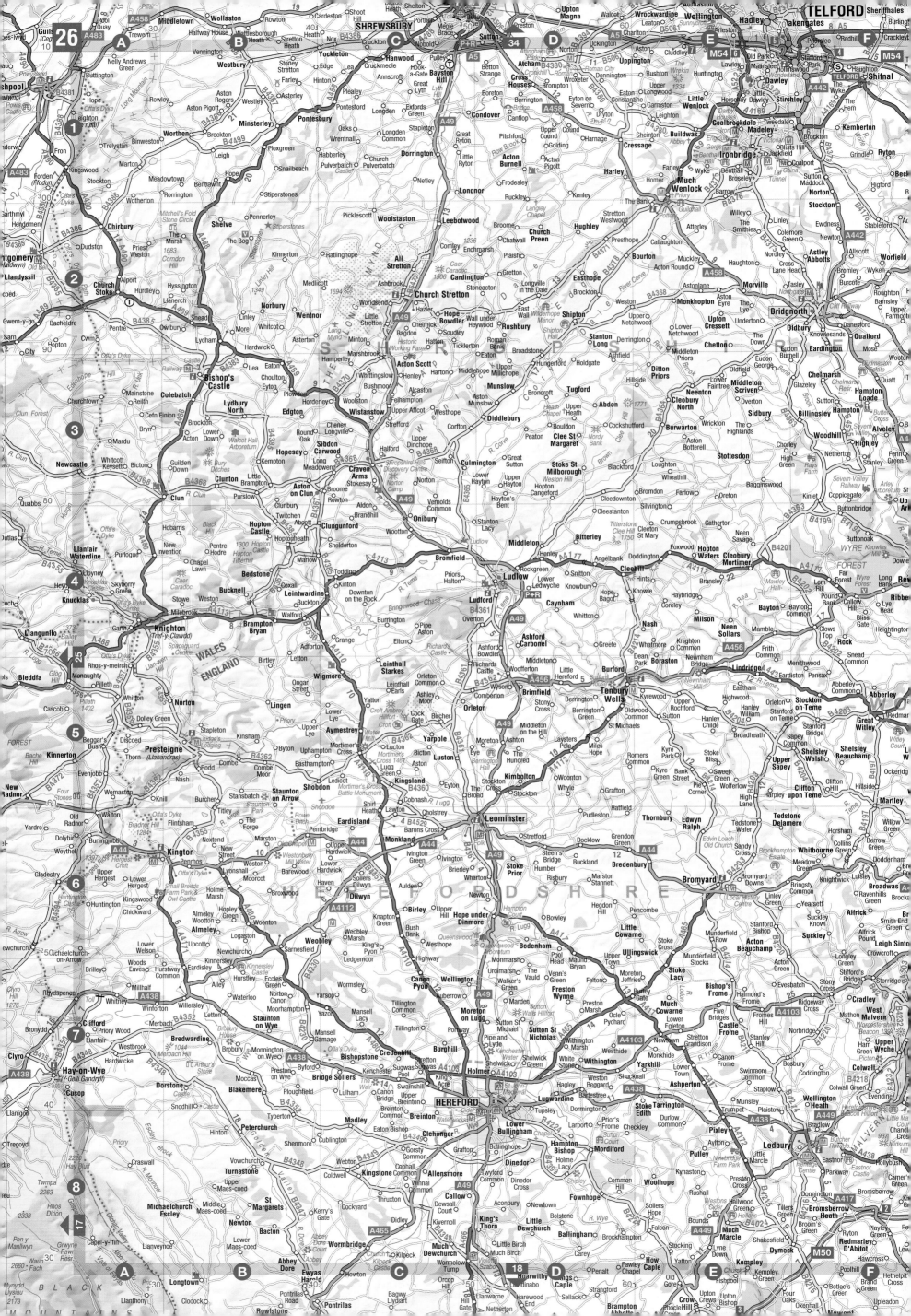

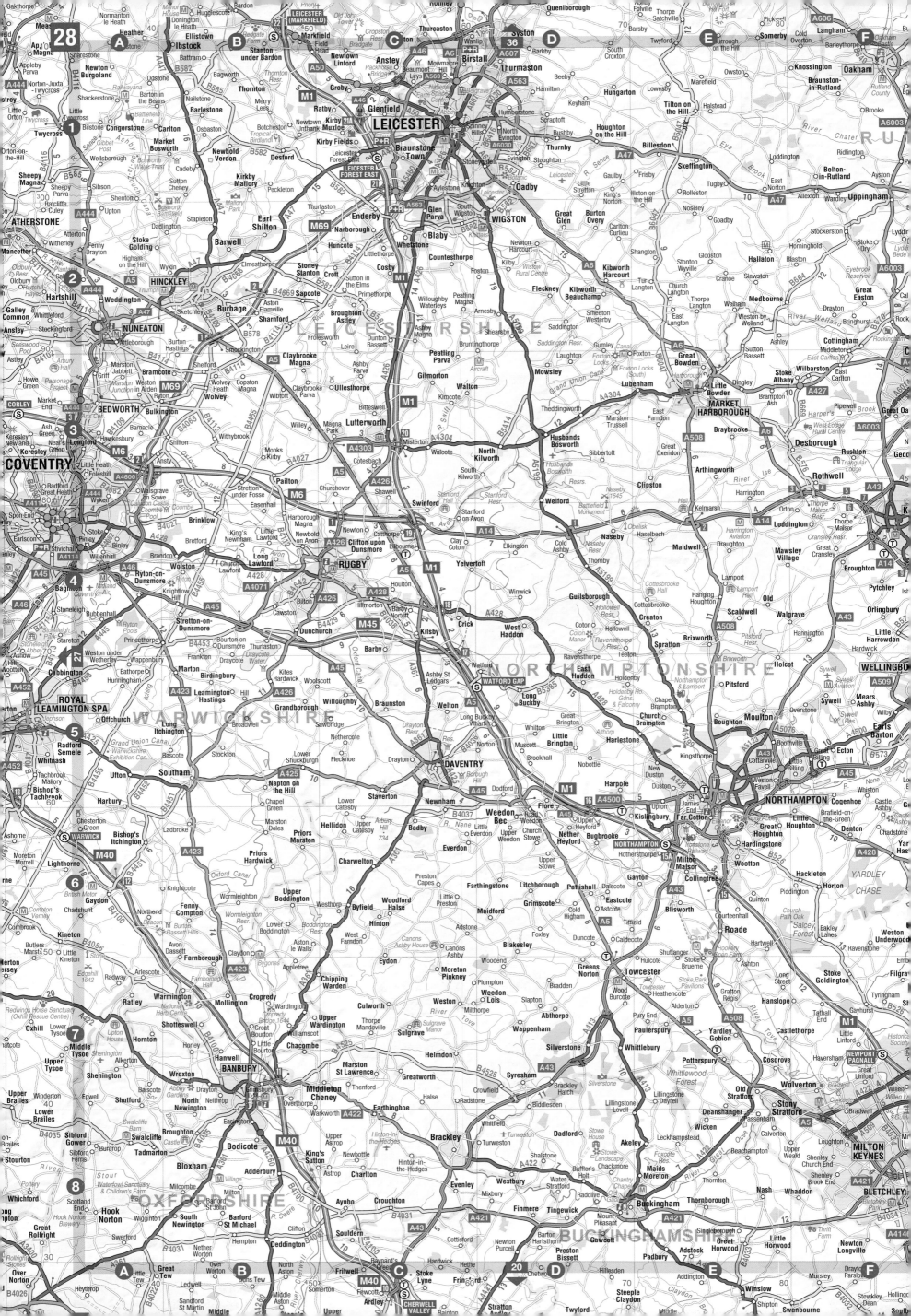

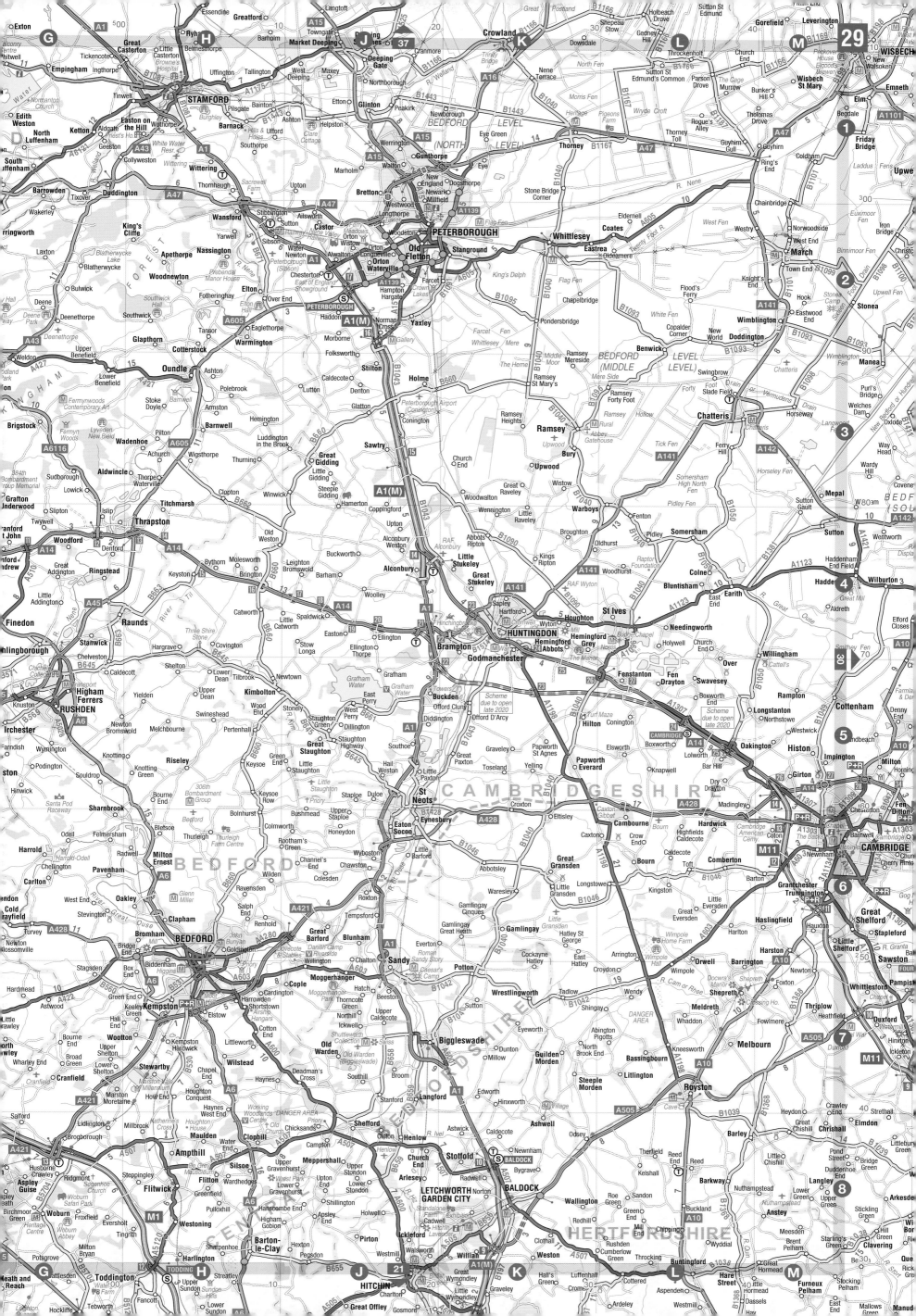

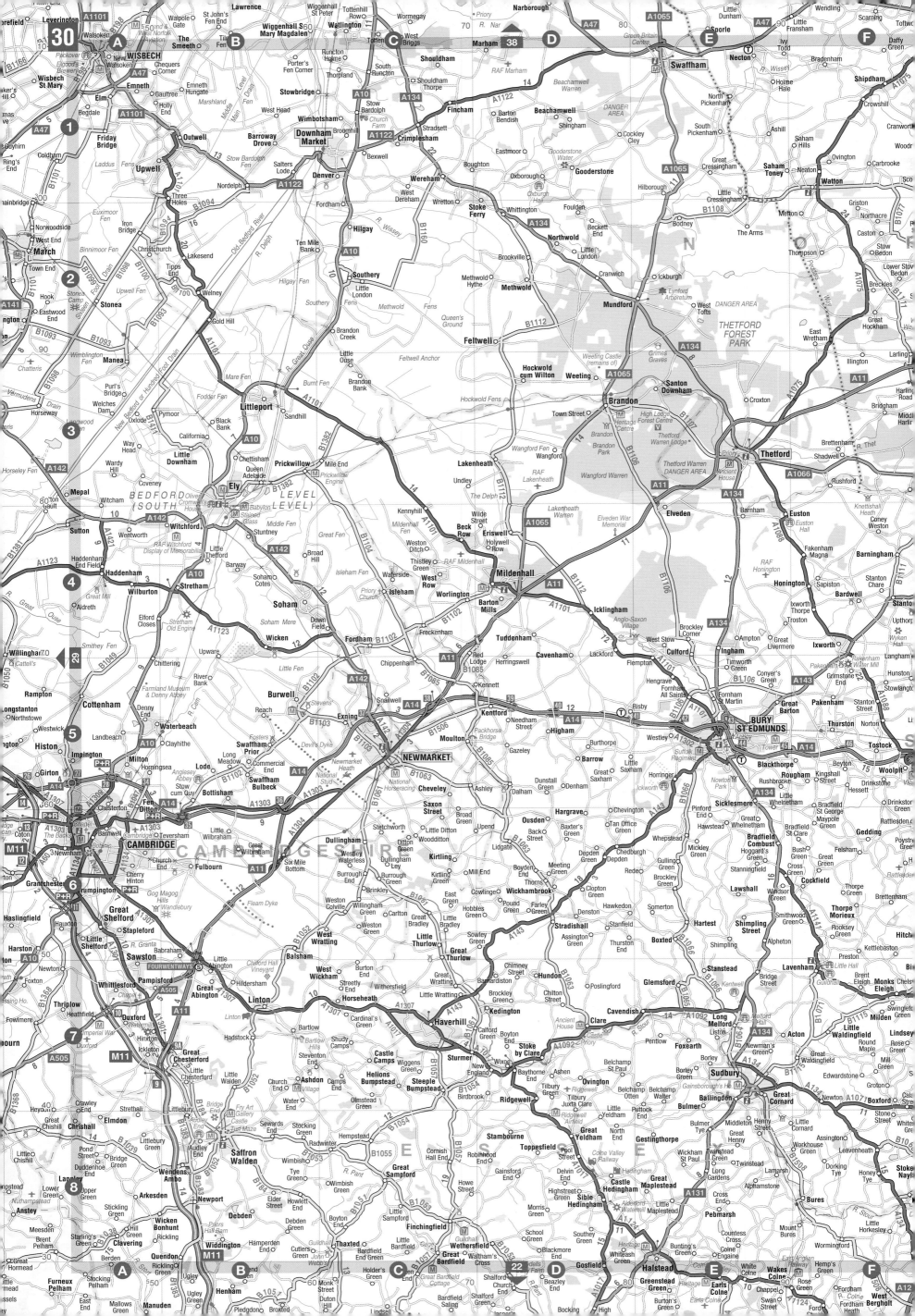

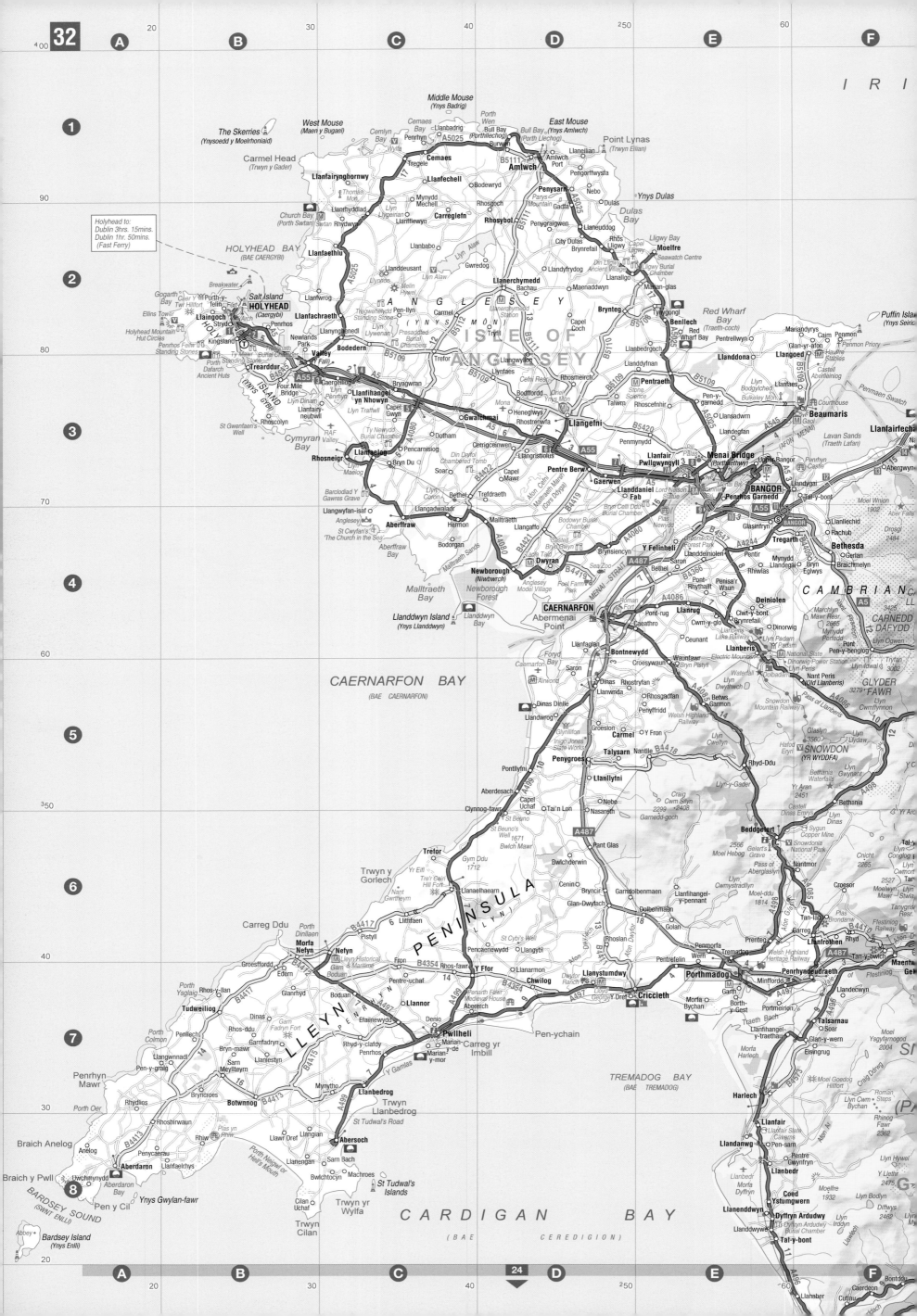

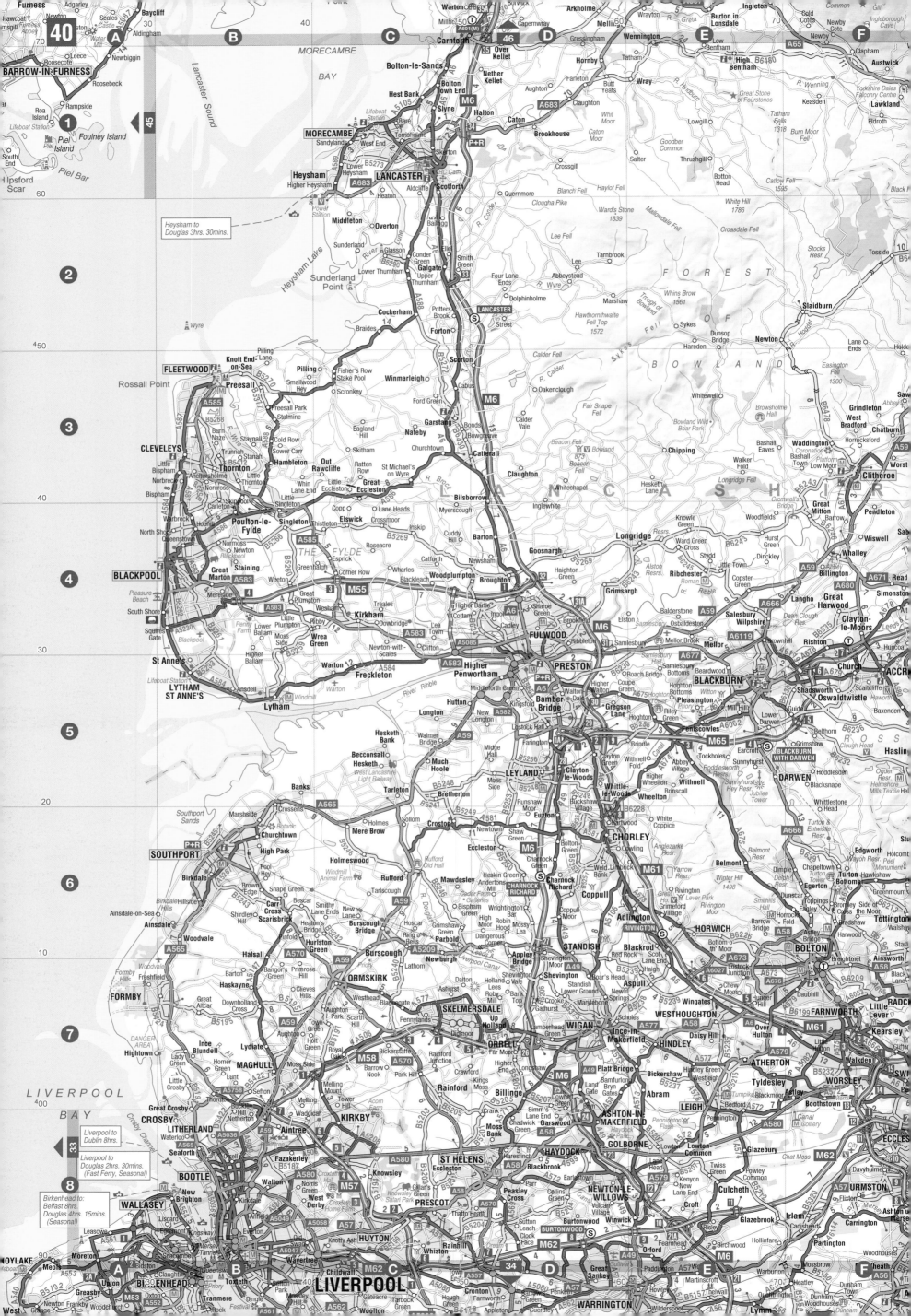

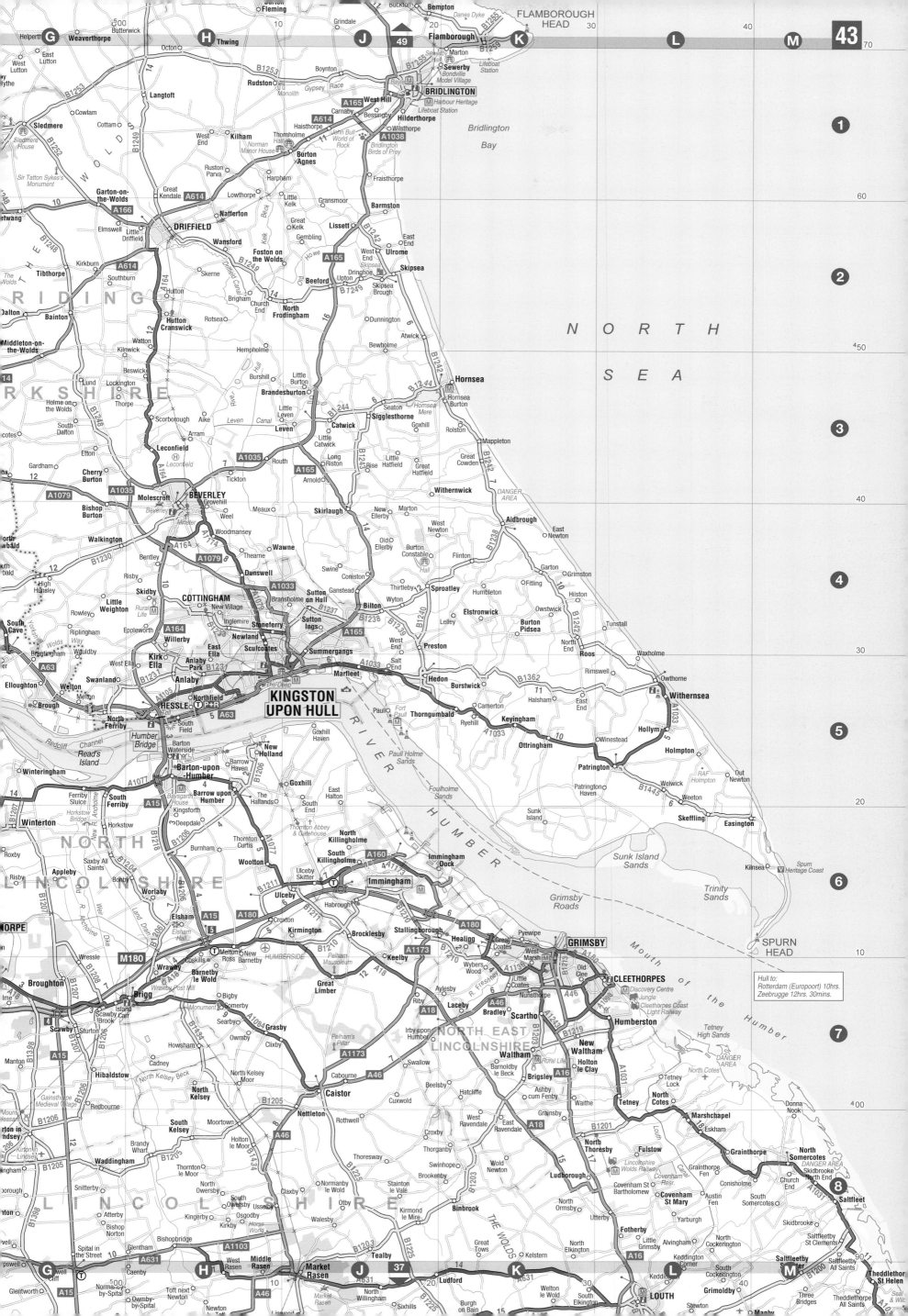

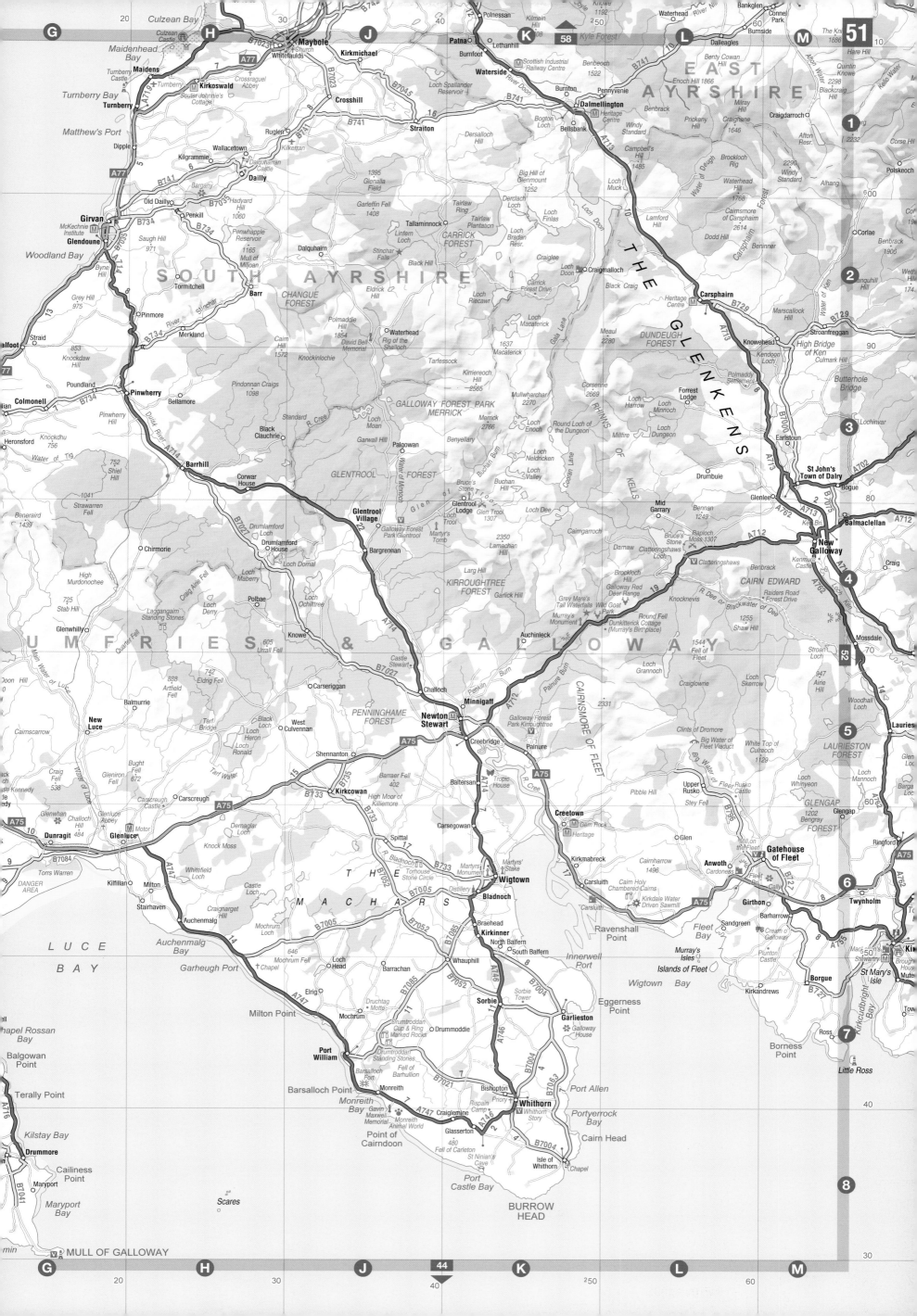

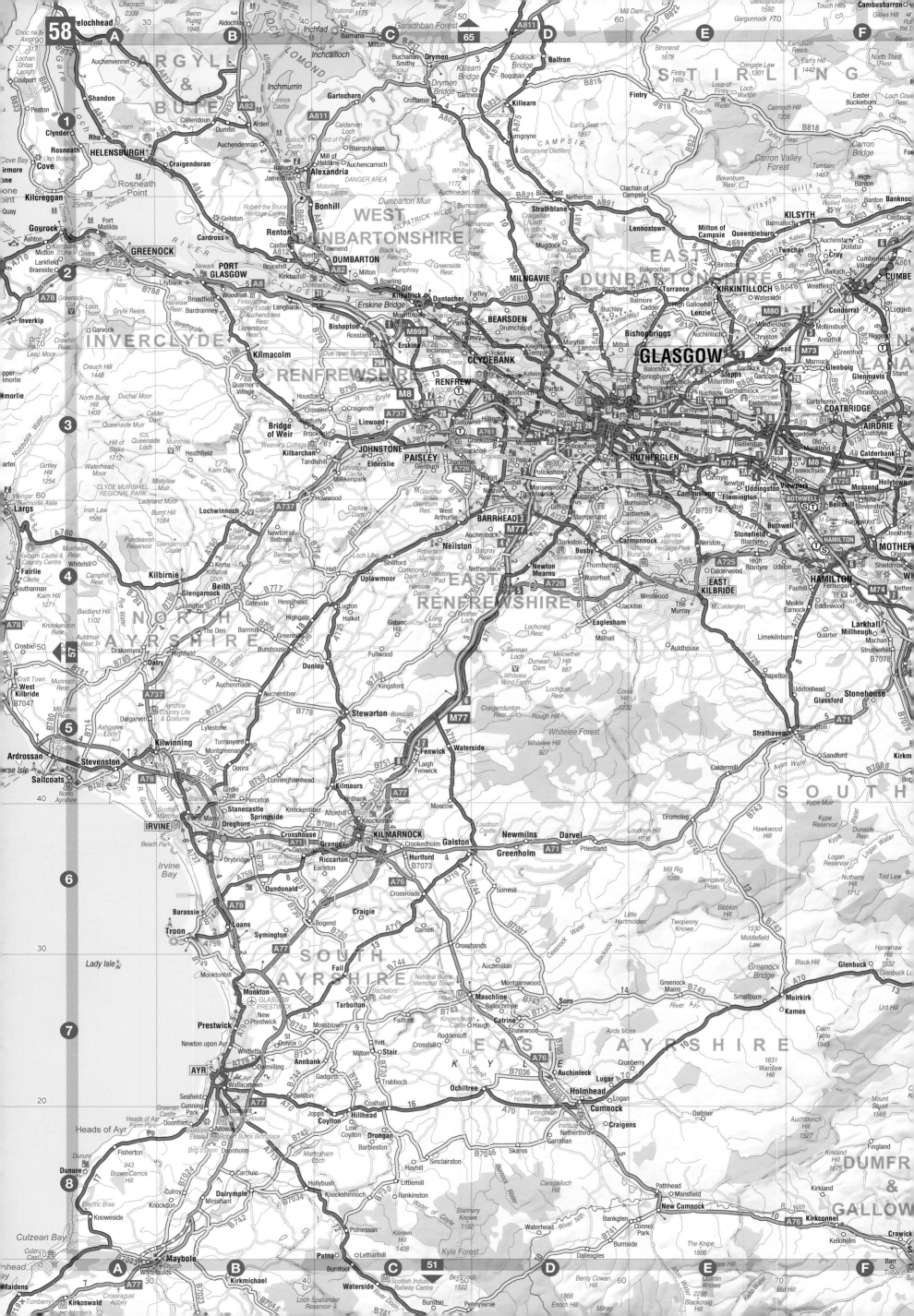

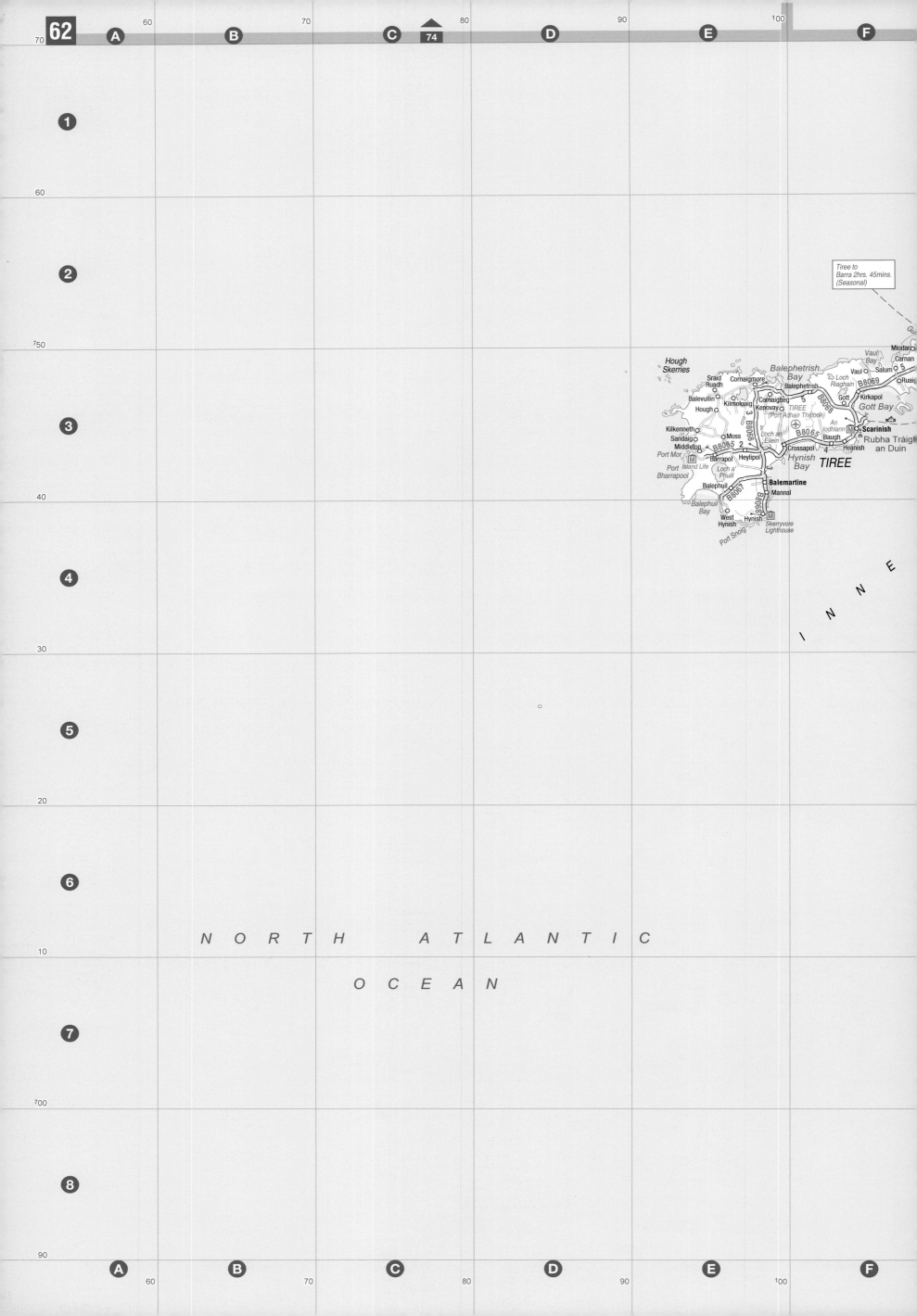

**1**

60

**2**

⁷50

Tiree to
Barra 2hrs. 45mins.
(Seasonal)

Hough
Skerries

Miodar
Carnan
Vaul
Bay
Vaul
Salum
Ruaig

Balephetrish
Bay
Sraid
Ruadh
Cornaigmore
Balephetrish
Loch
Riaghain
B8069

**3**

Balevullin
Kilmoluaig
Cornaigbeg
Kenovay
TIREE
(Port Adhair Thiriodh)
An
Iodhlann
Gott
Kirkapol
Gott Bay

Hough
Kilkenneth
Sandaig
Moss
Loch an
Eilein
Scarinish
Baugh
Rubha Tràigh
an Duin

Middleton
Port Mor
Barrapol
Loch a'
Phuill
Crossapol
Heanish

40
Port
Bharrapool
Island Life
Heylipol
Hynish
Bay
TIREE

Balephuil
Balemartine
Mannal

**4**

Balephuil
Bay
West
Hynish
Hynish
Port Snoig
Skerryvore
Lighthouse

30

I   N   N   E

**5**

20

**6**

N   O   R   T   H     A   T   L   A   N   T   I   C

10

O   C   E   A   N

**7**

⁷00

**8**

90

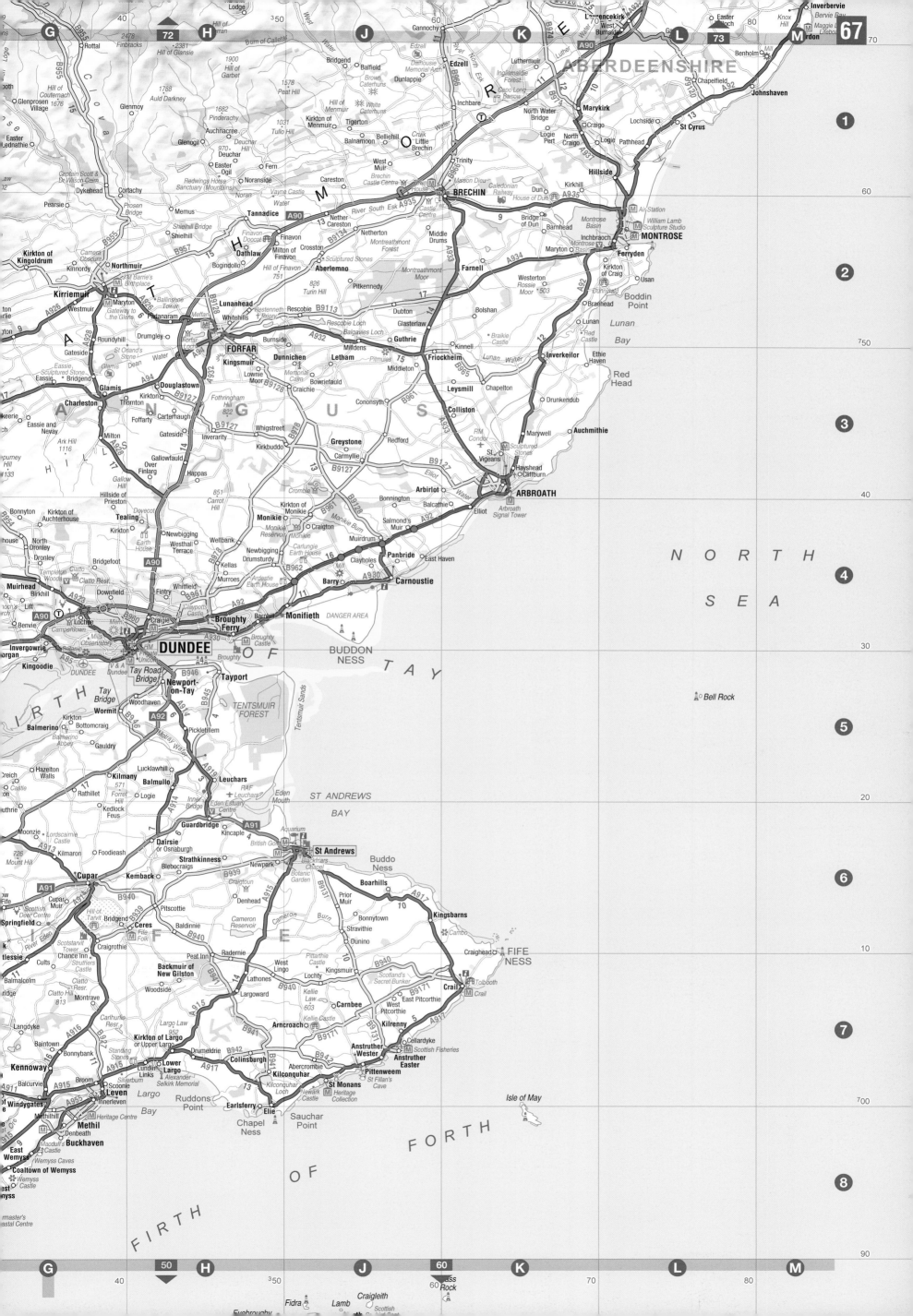

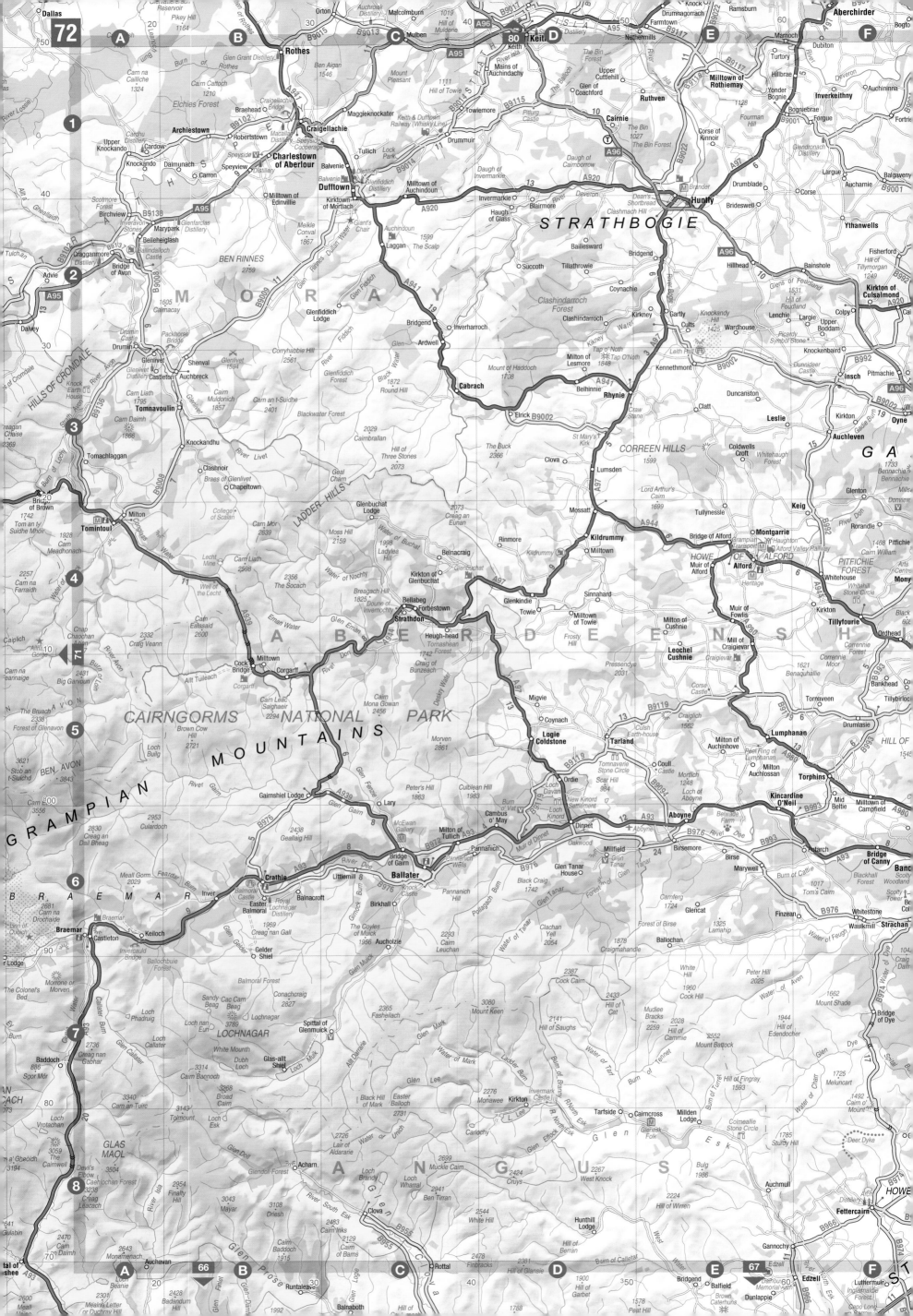

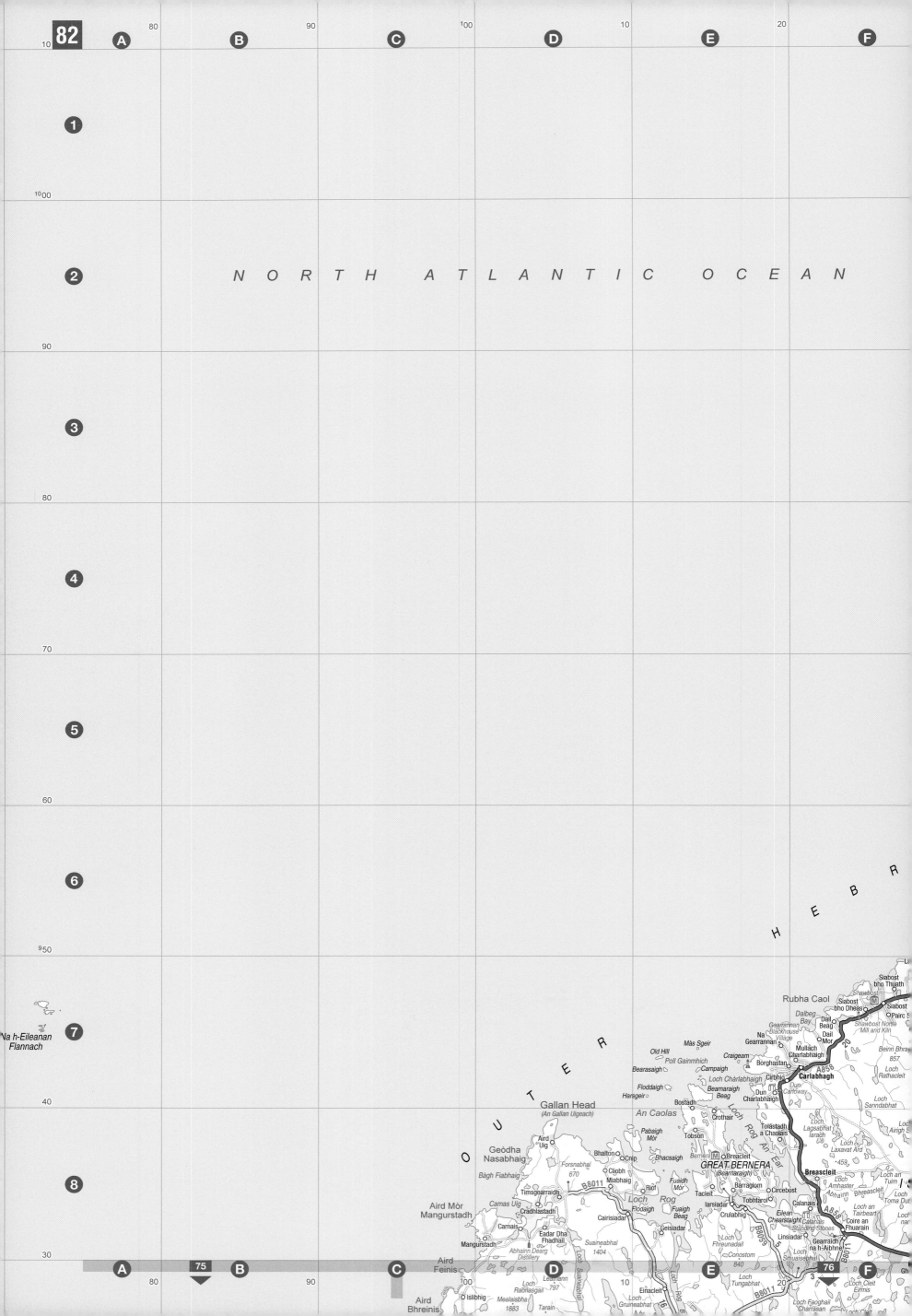

N O R T H   A T L A N T I C   O C E A N

Na h-Eileanan
Flannach

H E B R

Rubha Caol

Siabost
bho Thuath
Shawbost
Siabost
bho Dheas
Pairc S
Dalbeg
Beag
Gearrannan
Blackhouse
Village
Dail
Beag
Shawbost Norse
Mill and Kiln
Old Hill
Màs Sgeir
Na
Gearrannan
Dail
Mòr
Beinn Bhra
857
Poll Gainmhich
Mullach
Charlabhaigh
Craigeam
Borghastan
Bearasaigh
Campaign
Loch Chàrlabhaigh
Cirbhig
Carlabhagh
Loch
Rathacleit
Floddaigh
Harsgeir
Bearnaraigh
Beag
Dun
Carloway
A858
Loch
Sanndabhat
Gallan Head
(An Gallan Uigeach)
An Caolas
Bostadh
Dun
Charlabhaigh
Loch
Airigh
Crothair
Tolàstadh
a Chaolais
Lagsabhat
Iarach
Pabaigh
Mòr
Tobson
Loch
Rog
An
Aird
Geòdha
Nasabhaig
Uig
Bhalton
Cnip
Bhacsaigh
Breacleit
Loch
Laxavat Ard
Bàgh Fiabhaig
Cliobh
Miabhaig
Bernera
Breascleit
GREAT BERNERA
(Bearnaraigh)
·459
Forsnabhal
670
Fuaidh
Mòr
Loch an
Tuim
Aird Mòr
Mangurstadh
Camas Uig
Cradhlastadh
Timsgearraidh
B8011
Loch
Rog
Flòdaigh
Tacleit
Tobhtarol
Circebost
Breascleit
Loch
Amhaster
Bhreascleit
Loch
Toma Dut
Carnais
Eadar Dha
Fhadhail
Fuaigh
Beag
Iarsiadar
Crulabhig
Calanais
Loch an
Tairbeart
Loch
Cairisiadar
Suaineabhal
1404
Calanais
Standing Stones
Coire an
Fhuarain
Mangurstadh
Abhainn Dearg
Distillery
Geisiadar
Linsiadar
A858
Gearraidh
na h-Aibhne
Aird
Feinis
Leathann
797
Loch
Fhreunadail
Conostom
840
Loch
Sruaisebhal
B8059
Aird
Bhreinis
Loch
Raonasgail
Islibhig
Mealaisbha
1883
Tarain
Eiñacleit
Loch
Gruineabhat
Loch
Tungabhat
B8011
Loch Cleit
Eirmis
Loch Faoghail
Charrasan

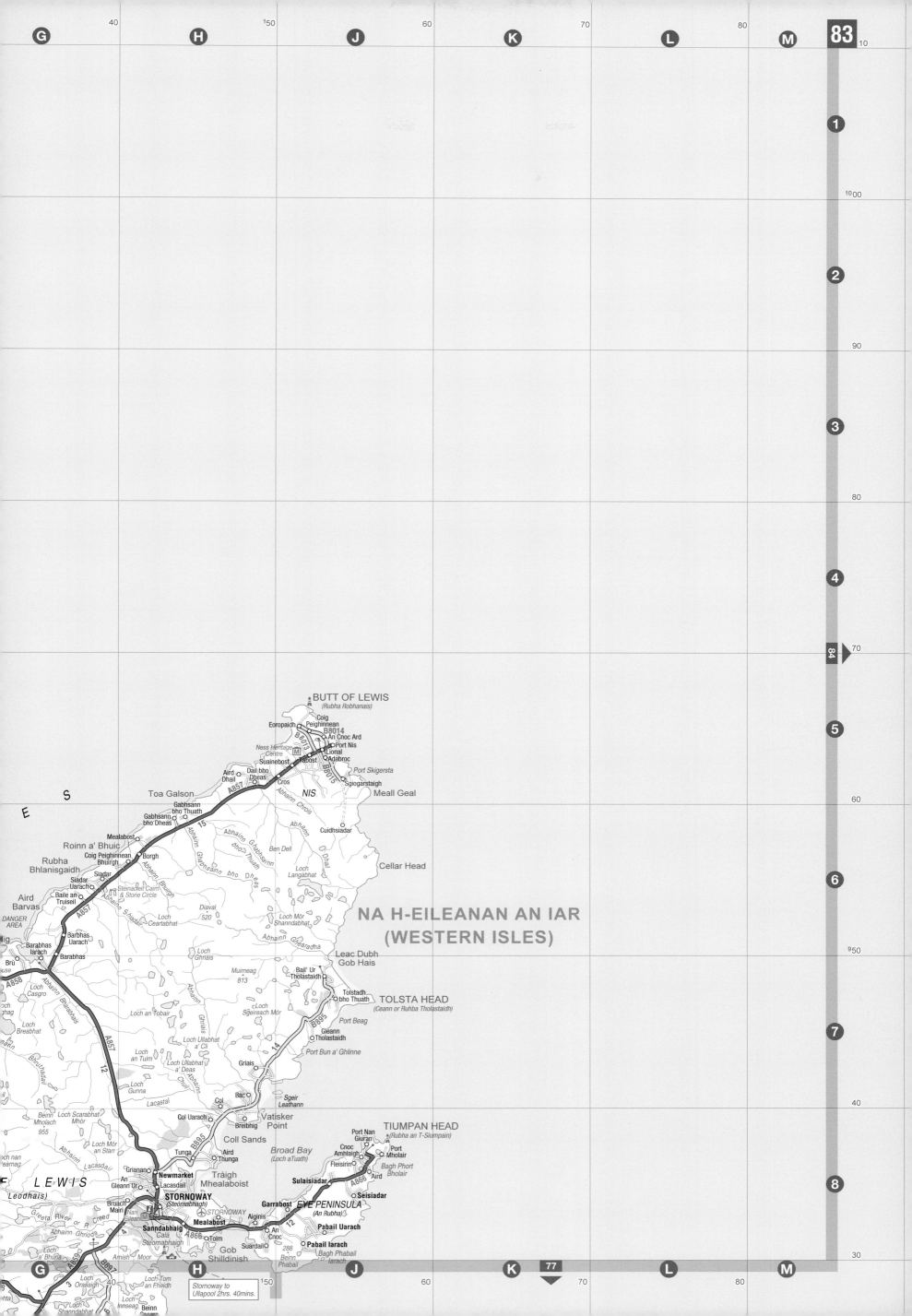

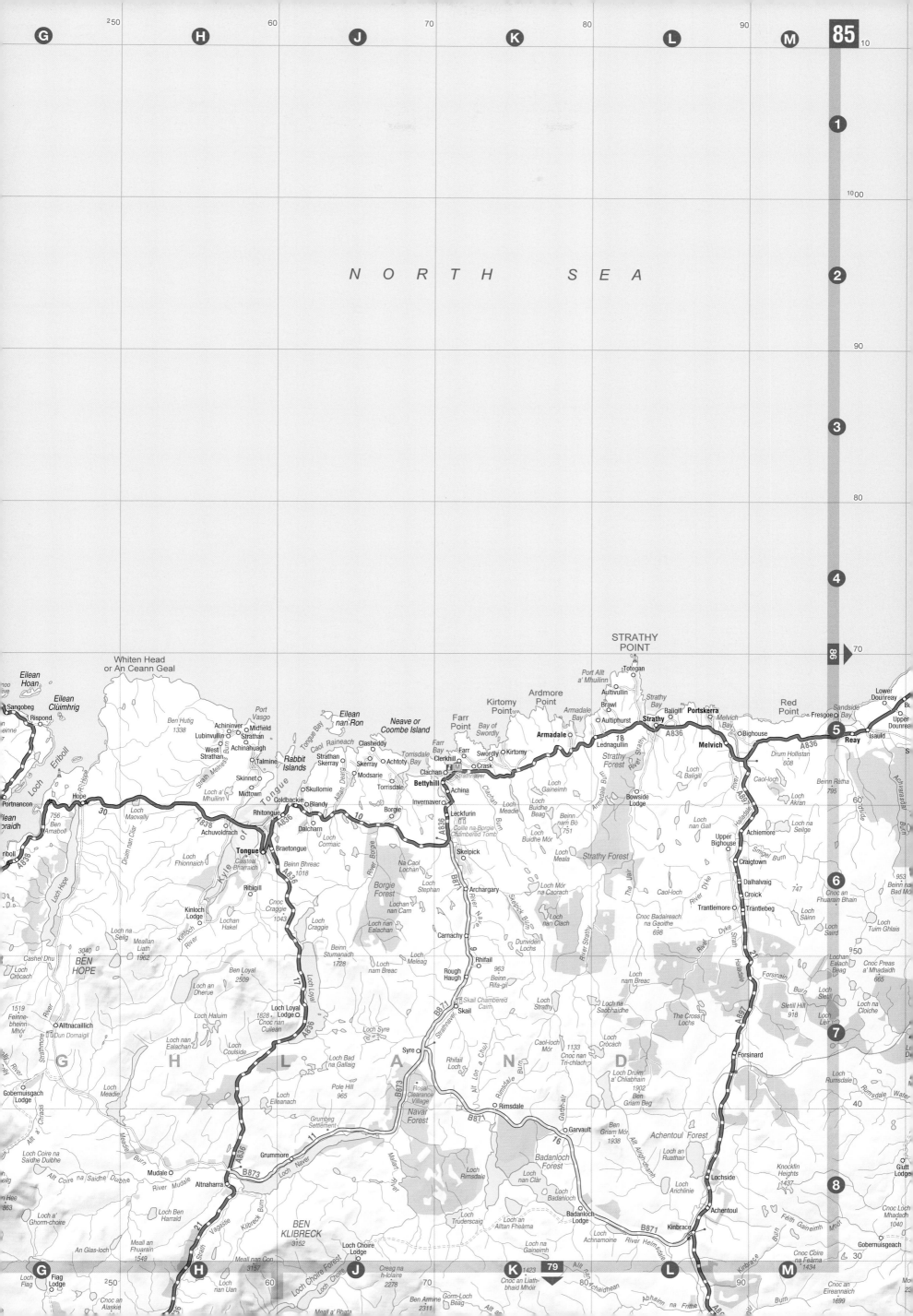

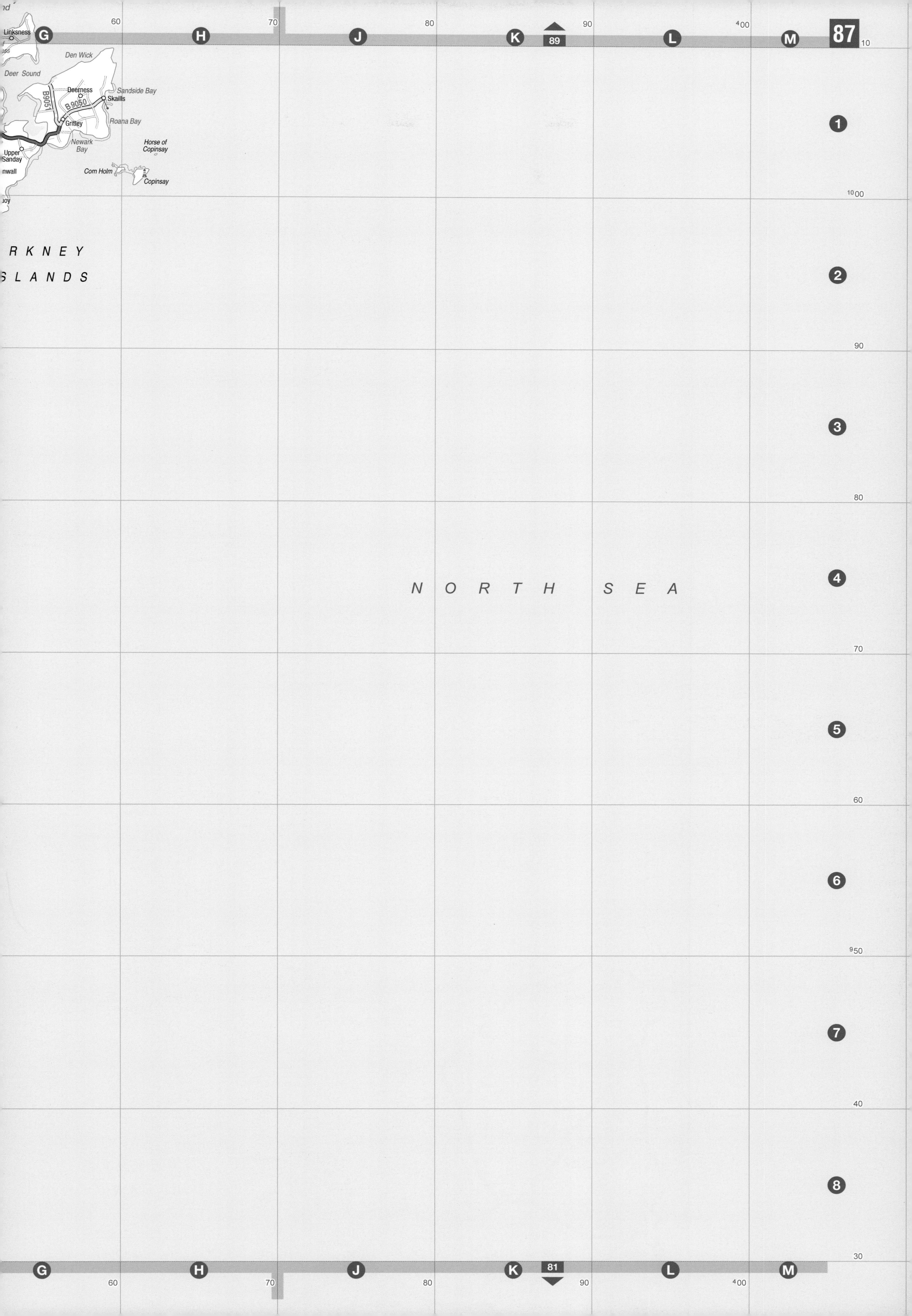

Linksness

Den Wick

Deer Sound

Deerness
Sandside Bay
B9051
B 9050
Skaills
Gritley
Roana Bay
Newark
Bay
Horse of
Copinsay
Upper
Sanday
nwall
Corn Holm
oy
Copinsay

**1**

10 00

**R K N E Y**

**S L A N D S**

**2**

90

**3**

80

**4**

N O R T H    S E A

70

**5**

60

**6**

9 50

**7**

40

**8**

30

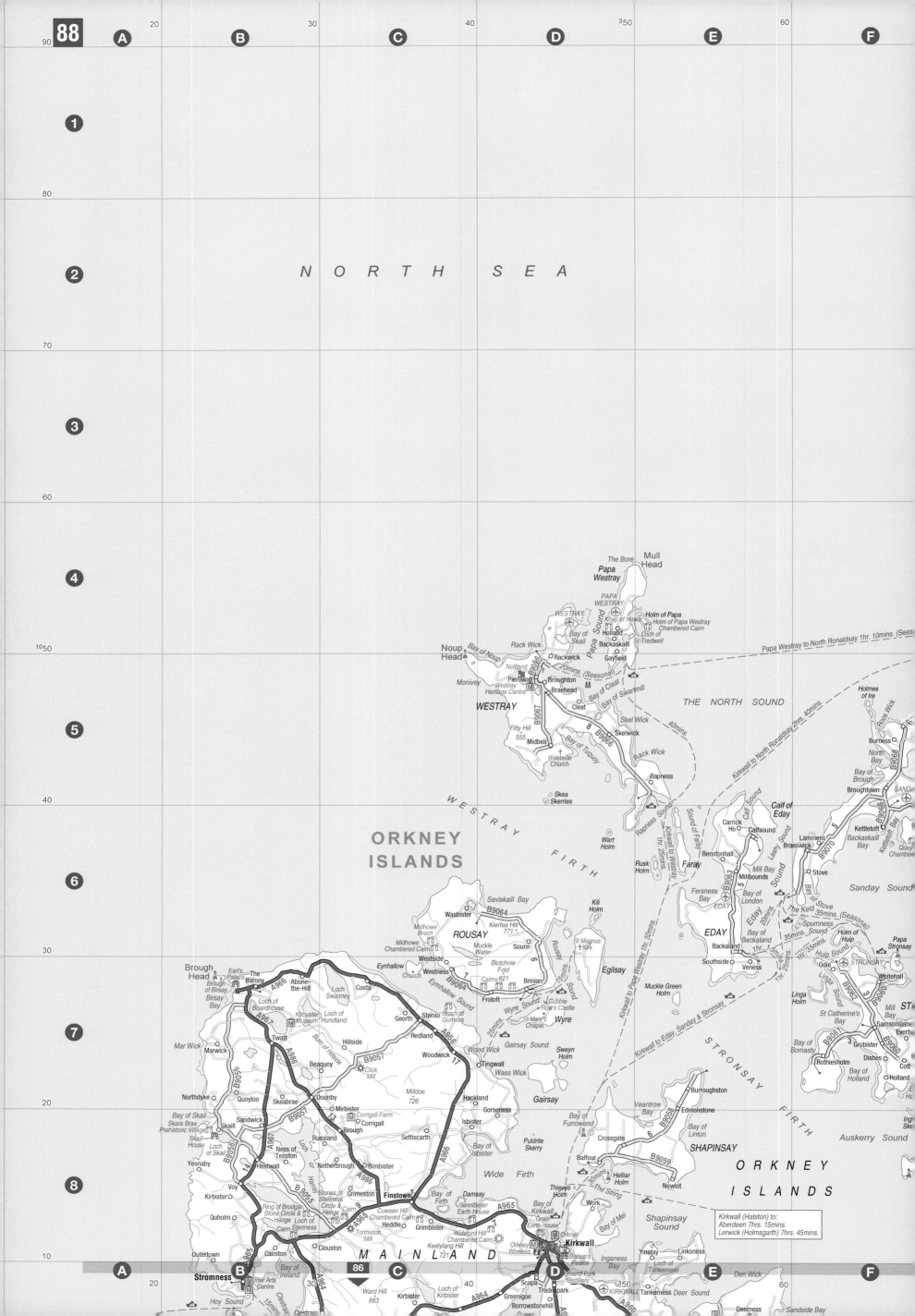

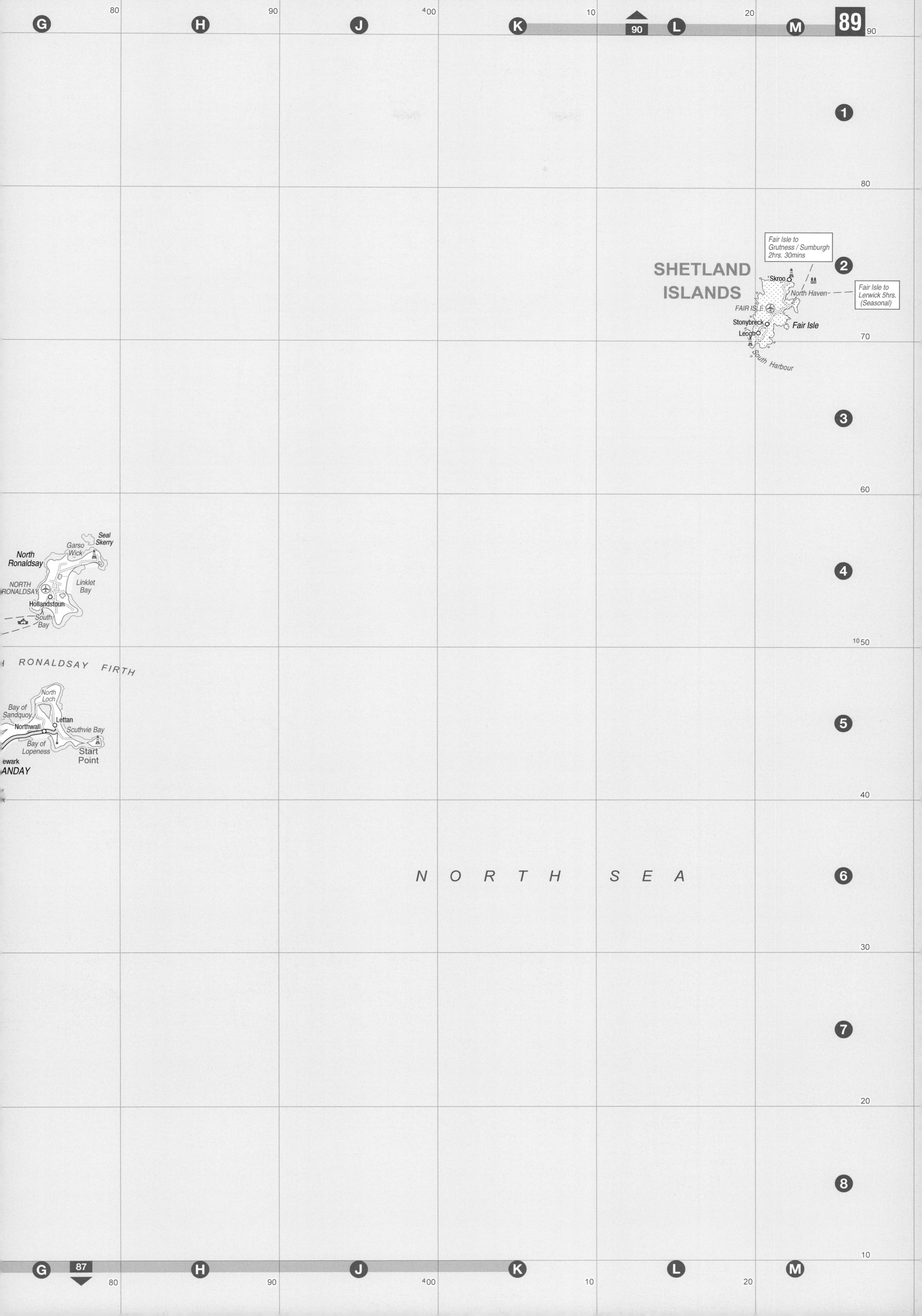

1

80

**SHETLAND
ISLANDS**

Fair Isle to
Grutness / Sumburgh
2hrs. 30mins

2

Skroo

North Haven

FAIR ISLE

Fair Isle to
Lerwick 5hrs.
(Seasonal)

Stonybreck

Leogh   Fair Isle

70

*South Harbour*

3

60

Seal
Skerry

Garso
Wick

**North
Ronaldsay**

NORTH
RONALDSAY

Linklet
Bay

4

Hollandstoun

South
Bay

10 50

H RONALDSAY FIRTH

North
Loch

Bay of
Sandquoy

Lettan

Northwall

Scuthvie Bay

Bay of
Lopeness

Start
Point

5

ewark

ANDAY

40

N   O   R   T   H    S   E   A

6

30

7

20

8

10

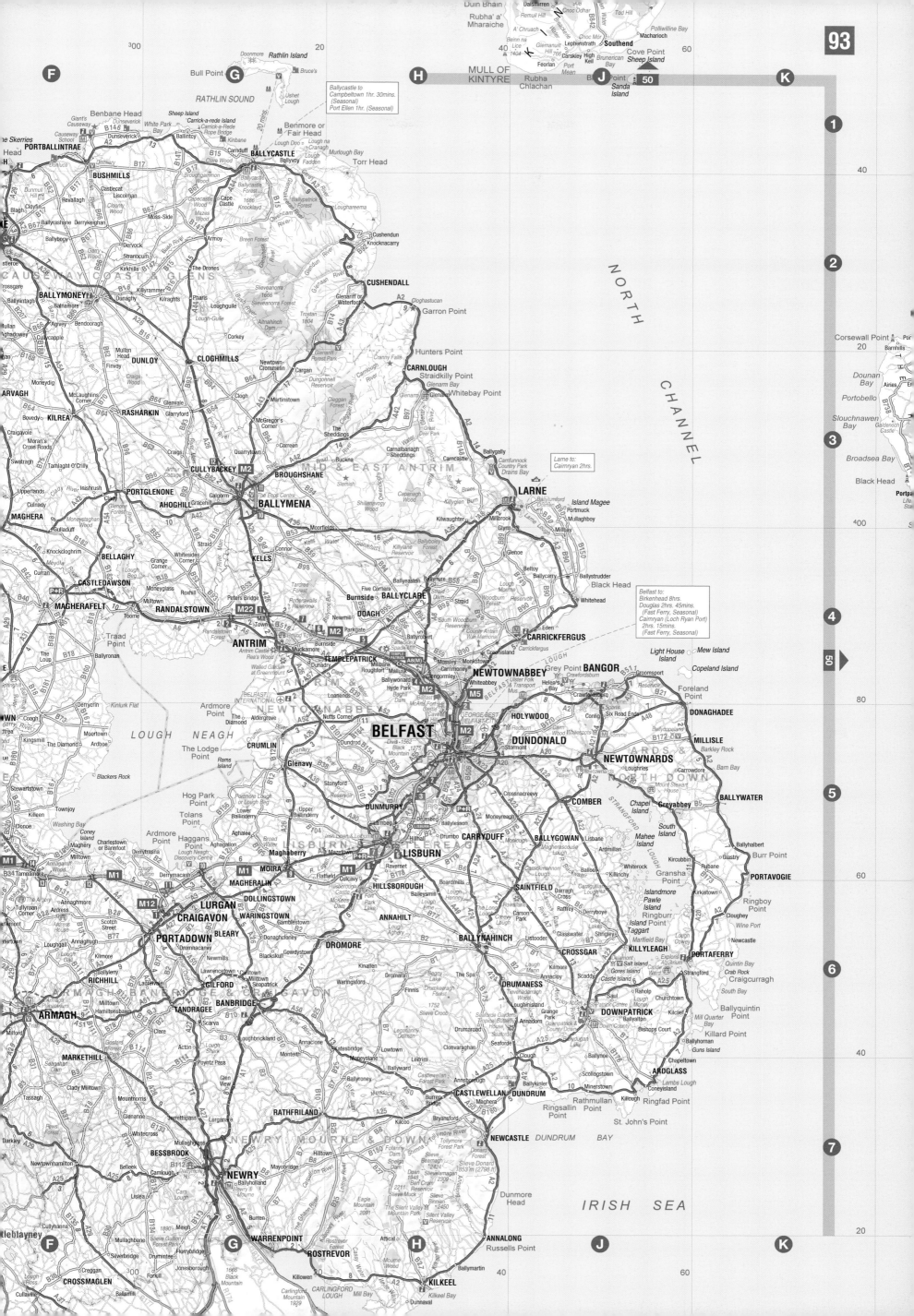

# INDEX TO CITIES, TOWNS, VILLAGES, HAMLETS, LOCATIONS & AIRPORTS

(1) A strict alphabetical order is used e.g. An Dùnan follows Andreas but precedes Andwell.

(2) The map reference given refers to the actual map square in which the town spot or built-up area is located and not to the place name.

(3) Major towns and destinations are shown in bold, i.e. **Aberdeen**. *Aber* . . . . 5J **73**

(4) Where two or more places of the same name occur in the same County or Unitary Authority, the nearest large town is also given; e.g. Achiemore. *High* nr. Durness . . . .5F **84** indicates that Achiemore is located in square 5F on page **84** and is situated near Durness in the Unitary Authority of Highland.

(5) Only one reference is given although due to page overlaps the place may appear on more than one page.

## COUNTIES and UNITARY AUTHORITIES with the abbreviations used in this index

Aberdeen : *Aber*
Aberdeenshire : *Abers*
Angus : *Ang*
Antrim & Newtownabbey : *Ant*
Ards & North Down : *Ards*
Argyll & Bute : *Arg*
Armagh, Banbridge & Craigavon : *Arm*
Bath & N E Somerset : *Bath*
Bedford : *Bed*
Belfast : *Bel*
Blackburn with Darwen : *Bkbn*
Blackpool : *Bkpl*
Blaenau Gwent : *Blae*
Bournemouth : *Bour*
Bracknell Forest : *Brac*
Bridgend : *B'end*
Brighton & Hove : *Brig*
Bristol : *Bris*
Buckinghamshire : *Buck*
Caerphilly : *Cphy*
Cambridgeshire : *Cambs*
Cardiff : *Card*
Carmarthenshire : *Carm*
Causeway Coast & Glens : *Caus*
Central Bedfordshire : *C Beds*
Ceredigion : *Cdgn*
Cheshire East : *Ches E*
Cheshire West & Chester : *Ches W*
Clackmannanshire : *Clac*
Conwy : *Cnwy*
Cornwall : *Corn*
Cumbria : *Cumb*
Darlington : *Darl*
Denbighshire : *Den*
Derby : *Derb*
Derbyshire : *Derbs*
Derry & Strabane : *Derr*
Devon : *Devn*
Dorset : *Dors*
Dumfries & Galloway : *Dum*
Dundee : *D'dee*
Durham : *Dur*
East Ayrshire : *E Ayr*
East Dunbartonshire : *E Dun*
East Lothian : *E Lot*
East Renfrewshire : *E Ren*
East Riding of Yorkshire : *E Yor*
East Sussex : *E Sus*
Edinburgh : *Edin*
Essex : *Essx*
Falkirk : *Falk*
Fermanagh & Omagh : *Ferm*
Fife : *Fife*
Flintshire : *Flin*
Glasgow : *Glas*
Gloucestershire : *Glos*
Greater London : *G Lon*
Greater Manchester : *G Man*
Gwynedd : *Gwyn*
Halton : *Hal*
Hampshire : *Hants*
Hartlepool : *Hart*
Herefordshire : *Here*
Hertfordshire : *Herts*
Highland : *High*
Inverclyde : *Inv*
Isle of Anglesey : *IOA*
Isle of Man : *IOM*
Isle of Wight : *IOW*
Isles of Scilly : *IOS*
Kent : *Kent*
Kingston upon Hull : *Hull*
Lancashire : *Lanc*
Leicester : *Leic*
Leicestershire : *Leics*
Lincolnshire : *Linc*
Lisburn & Castlereagh : *Lis*
Luton : *Lutn*
Medway : *Medw*
Merseyside : *Mers*
Merthyr Tydfil : *Mer T*
Mid & East Antrim : *ME Ant*
Middlesbrough : *Midd*
Midlothian : *Midl*
Mid Ulster : *M Ulst*
Milton Keynes : *Mil*
Monmouthshire : *Mon*
Moray : *Mor*
Neath Port Talbot : *Neat*
Newport : *Newp*
Newry, Mourne & Down : *New M*
Norfolk : *Norf*
Northamptonshire : *Nptn*
North Ayrshire : *N Ayr*
North East Lincolnshire : *NE Lin*
North Lanarkshire : *N Lan*
North Lincolnshire : *N Lin*
North Somerset : *N Som*
Northumberland : *Nmbd*
North Yorkshire : *N Yor*
Nottingham : *Nott*
Nottinghamshire : *Notts*
Orkney : *Orkn*
Oxfordshire : *Oxon*
Pembrokeshire : *Pemb*
Perth & Kinross : *Per*
Peterborough : *Pet*
Plymouth : *Plym*
Poole : *Pool*
Portsmouth : *Port*
Powys : *Powy*
Reading : *Read*
Redcar & Cleveland : *Red C*
Renfrewshire : *Ren*
Rhondda Cynon Taff : *Rhon*
Rutland : *Rut*
Scottish Borders : *Bord*
Shetland : *Shet*
Shropshire : *Shrp*
Slough : *Slo*
Somerset : *Som*
Southampton : *Sotn*
South Ayrshire : *S Ayr*
Southend-on-Sea : *S'end*
South Gloucestershire : *S Glo*
South Lanarkshire : *S Lan*
South Yorkshire : *S Yor*
Staffordshire : *Staf*
Stirling : *Stir*
Stockton-on-Tees : *Stoc T*
Stoke-on-Trent : *Stoke*
Suffolk : *Suff*
Surrey : *Surr*
Swansea : *Swan*
Swindon : *Swin*
Telford & Wrekin : *Telf*
Thurrock : *Thur*
Torbay : *Torb*
Torfaen : *Torf*
Tyne & Wear : *Tyne*
Vale of Glamorgan, The : *V Glam*
Warrington : *Warr*
Warwickshire : *Warw*
West Berkshire : *W Ber*
West Dunbartonshire : *W Dun*
Western Isles : *W Isl*
West Lothian : *W Lot*
West Midlands : *W Mid*
West Sussex : *W Sus*
West Yorkshire : *W Yor*
Wiltshire : *Wilts*
Windsor & Maidenhead : *Wind*
Wokingham : *Wok*
Worcestershire : *Worc*
Wrexham : *Wrex*
York : *York*

## INDEX

### A

**Column 1 (left edge, partially cut off)**

...by. Linc ....2K 37
...ley. Shrp ....1B 26
...thorn. Shrp ....2B 26
...all. Oxon ....2L 19
... Leigh. Oxon ....2M 19
... High ....4H 79
...ley. G Man ....7F 40
...by. Shrp ....8D 34
... Warw ....3M 27
...y. Worc ....5F 26
...y Abbotts. Shrp ....2F 26
...y Bridge. G Man ....8F 41
...y Cross. Worc ....5G 27
...y. Ches W ....2D 34
...n. Derbs
...nr. Hope ....1K 35
...nr. Sudbury ....6K 35
...la. Flin ....3B 34
...n. Here ....5C 26
...y. Herts ....2C 20
...n. Shrp
...nr. Bridgnorth ....2G 27
...nr. Wem ....7D 34
...n. S Yor ....1B 36
...y. Staf ....5F 34
...y. Telf ....1E 27
...W Mid ....2J 27
... Abbotts. Staf ....1E 20
... Botterell. Shrp ....3E 26
...n-by-Stone. Staf ....6H 35
... Cantlow. Warw ....6K 27
...n Clinton. Buck ....1E 18
... Crews. Here ....1E 18
...s End. Herts ....1K 21
...s Eyre. Shrp ....2E 26
...n Fields. Worc ....5H 27
... Flamville. Leics ....2B 28
...n Ingham. Here ....1E 18
...n juxta Mondrum.
...Ches E ....4E 34
...lane. Shrp ....2E 26
... the Walls. Nptn ....6B 28
...n Magna. Glos ....8K 27
...n Munslow. Shrp ....3D 26
...on Carrant. Glos ....8H 27
...n on Clun. Shrp ....3B 26
...on-Trent. Derbs ....7B 36
...n Pigott. Shrp ....1B 26
...n Rogers. Shrp ....1B 26
...n Rowant. Oxon ....4E 20
...n Sandford. Buck ....3E 20
...n Somerville. Worc ....8J 27
...n Subedge. Glos ....7K 27
...n Tirrold. Oxon ....5C 20
...rby. Linc ....6H 37
...rdby. Linc ....1D 26
...n. Shrp ....1D 26
...Lench. Worc ....6J 27
...hampton. Dors ....6F 8
...ngton. S Lan ....4J 31
...ney. Som ....3B 8
...ton. Linc
...ale. Leics ....2A 28
...l. New M ....7H 93
...borough. Norf ....2G 31
...borough. Warw ....2G 31
...ridge. Nor ....8H 39
...k. E Yor ....2J 43
...row. Here ....7C 26
...urn. Linc ....3G 37
...nr. Alfreton ....6F 17
...evan. Ang ....1E 66
...Mor ....6C 28
...enback. E Ren ....8C 73
...enbrack. Pover ....1E 66
...enbreck. Arg ....1K 57
...encairn. Dum
...nr. Dalbeattie ....6B 52
...nr. Dumfries ....3D 52
...encarroch. W Dun ....1K 58
...encrow. Bord ....3F 60
...endenman. Arg ....1B 58
...endinny. Midl ....3L 59
...engray. S Lan ....4H 59
...enhalrig. Mor ....5G 79
...enheath. S Lan ....5G 59
...enlochan. Arg ....2J 57
...enmanna. Dum ....6H 51
...entiber. N Ayr ....5B 58
...envennel. Arg ....7E 64
...endrain. Arg ....1F 72
...inina. Abers ....1F 72
...nleck. Dum ....4H 51
...nloch. N Lan ....2E 58
...nstarry. N Lan ....2F 58
...even. Abers ....1F 72
...ochan. S Lan ....6G 59
...millan. E Ayr ....7D 58
...e. S Lan ....4J 59
...nailie. Fife ....7F 66
...multi. Ang ....8E 72
...hafree. Per ....4B 66
...nagallin. Abers ....1J 73
...olzie. Abers ....6C 72
...eddie. Abers ....1E 73
...erarder. Per ....6C 66
...eraw. High ....5D 70
...erderran. Fife ....8F 66
...erhouse. Arg ....4G 67
...ermuchty. Fife ....6F 66
...erneled. High ....8E 78
...ertool. Fife ....3E 69
...angill. High ....5K 85
...Stir ....5K 86
...nshaw. G Man ....8H 41
...ley. Staf ....5E 34
...Ches E ....5E 34
...Essx ....7B 30
...Abers ....7F 80
...ine. M Ulst ....6D 92
...ertree. Cumb ....8G 53
...nacloy. M Ulst ....7L 93
...ton. Lan
...ton. Lancaster ....1D 40
...ton. Ormskirk
...ton. S Yor ....1B 36
...ton. Wilts ....8B 18
...ton Park. Lan ....8K 79
...sh. High ....8B 78
...earg. High ....7A 78
...urnish. High ....6D 78
...pucknall. Derbs ....3D 36
...High ....5K 77
...nbarg. High ....5L 77
...hnuish Inn. High ....6D 78
...hucknell. Derbs ....3D 36

Aust. S Glo ....5D 18
Austerfield. S Yor ....8D 42
Austin Fen. Linc ....8L 43
Austrey. Warw ....1L 27
Austwick. N Yor ....1F 40
Authorpe. Linc ....1M 37
Authorpe Row. Linc ....2B 38
Avebury. Wilts ....7K 19
Avebury Trusloe. Wilts ....7J 19
Aveley. Thur ....5B 22
Avening. Glos ....4G 19
Averham. Notts ....4E 36
Aveton Gifford. Devn ....7J 5
Avielochan. High ....4K 71
Avielmore. High ....4J 71
Avington. Hants ....2C 10
Avoch. High ....8H 79
Avon. Hants ....6K 9
Avonbridge. Falk ....2G 59
Avon Dassett. Warw ....6B 28
Avonmouth. Bris ....6K 5
Avonwick. Devn ....6K 5
Y Bala. Gwyn ....7J 33
nr. Cannich ....2E 70
nr. Loch Ness ....3E 70
Awbridge. Hants ....3B 10
Awkley. S Glo ....5B 18
Awliscombe. Devn ....5L 7
Awre. Glos ....3F 18
Awsworth. Notts ....5B 36
Axbridge. Som ....8C 18
Axford. Hants ....1D 10
Axford. Wilts ....7L 19
Axminster. Devn ....6B 8
Axmouth. Devn ....6A 8
Aycliffe Village. Dur ....3L 47
Aydon. Nmbd ....5D 54
Aykley Heads. Dur ....7F 54
Aylburton. Glos ....3E 18
Aylburton Common. Glos ....3E 18
Ayle. Nmbd ....7M 53
Aylesbeare. Devn ....6K 7
Aylesbury. Buck ....2F 20
Aylesby. N E Lin ....7K 43
Aylescott. Devn ....4F 6
Aylesford. Kent ....8D 22
Aylesham. Kent ....8J 23
Aylestone. Leic ....1C 28
Aylmerton. Norf ....6H 39
Aylsham. Norf ....7H 39
Aylton. Here ....8E 26
Aylworth. Glos ....1K 19
Aymestrey. Here ....5C 26
Aynho. Nptn ....8C 28
Ayot Green. Herts ....2K 21
Ayot St Lawrence. Herts ....2J 21
Ayot St Peter. Herts ....2K 21
Ayr. S Ayr ....7B 58
Ayres of Selivoe. Shet ....3C 90
Ayreville. Torb ....5L 5
Aysgarth. N Yor ....7J 47
Ayshford. Devn ....4K 7
Ayside. Cumb ....7B 46
Ayston. Rut ....1F 28
Ayton. Bord ....3G 61
Aywick. Shet ....5K 91
Azerley. N Yor ....8L 47

**B**

Babbacombe. Torb ....5M 5
Babbinswood. Shrp ....6B 34
Babbs Green. Herts ....2L 21
Babcary. Som ....3D 8
Babel. Carm ....1H 17
Babell. Flin ....3L 33
Babingley. Norf ....7C 38
Bablock Hythe. Oxon ....3B 20
Babraham. Cambs ....6B 30
Babworth. Notts ....1D 36
Bac. W Isl ....7H 83
Bachau. IOM ....6D 44
Bacheldre. Powy ....3M 25
Bachymbyd Fawr. Den ....4K 33
Backaland. Orkn ....6D 88
Backaskaill. Orkn ....4D 88
Backbarrow. Cumb ....7B 46
Backe. Carm ....5J 15
Backfolds. Abers ....8K 81
Backford. Ches W ....2C 34
Backford Green. Norf ....4F 22
Backhill. Abers
nr. Castletown ....7B 44
nr. Kirk Michael ....6C 44
Backies. High ....3J 79
Backmuir of New Gilston.
Fife ....7H 67
Back of Keppoch. High ....7J 69
Back Street. Suff ....6D 30
Backwell. N Som ....7C 18
Backworth. Tyne ....4G 55
Bacon End. Essx ....2C 22
Baconsthorpe. Norf ....6H 39
Bacton. Here ....8B 26
Bacton. Norf ....6K 39
Bacton. Suff ....5G 31
Bacton Green. Norf ....5G 31
Bacup. Lanc ....5G 41
Badachonacher. High ....6G 79
Badachro. High ....6J 77
Badanloch Lodge. High ....8K 85
Badavanich. High ....8B 78
Badbury. Swin ....5K 19
Badby. Nptn ....6C 28
Badcall. High ....6E 84
Badcaul. High ....4H 77
Baddeley Green. Stoke ....4H 35
Baddesley Clinton. W Mid ....4K 27
Baddesley Ensor. Warw ....1L 27
Baddidarach. High ....1A 78
Baddoch. Abers ....7M 71
Badenscallie. High ....3A 78
Badenscoth. Abers ....2G 73
Badentarbat. High ....2M 77
Badgall. Corn ....7B 6
Badgers Mount. Kent ....7A 22
Badgeworth. Glos ....2H 19
Badgworth. Som ....8B 18
Badicaul. High ....3J 69
Badingham. Suff ....5K 31
Badlesmere. Kent ....8G 23
Badlipster. High ....7D 86
Badluarach. High ....4L 77
Badminton. S Glo ....5G 19
Badnaban. High ....1A 78
Badnabay. High ....7E 84
Badnagie. High ....8C 86
Badnellan. High ....3J 79
Badninish. High ....4H 79
Badrallach. High ....4L 77
Badsey. Worc ....7J 27
Badshot Lea. Surr ....1F 10
Badsworth. W Yor ....6B 42
Badwell Ash. Suff ....5F 30
Bae Cinmel. Cnwy ....2J 33
Bae Colwyn. Cnwy ....3H 33
Bae Penrhyn. Cnwy ....2H 33
Bagby. N Yor ....7B 48
Bag Enderby. Linc ....2L 37
Bagendon. Glos ....3J 19
Bagginswood. Shrp ....3E 26
Bàgh a Chàise. W Isl ....6A 76
Bagh a' Chaisteil. W Isl ....6J 57
Bagham. Kent ....8G 23
Bagh Mòr. W Isl ....8D 74
Bagh Shiarabhagh. W Isl ....5D 74
Bagillt. Flin ....3M 33
Baginton. Warw ....4M 27
Baglan. Neat ....5G 17
Bagley. Shrp ....7C 34
Bagley. Som ....1C 8
Bagnall. Staf ....4H 35
Bagnor. W Ber ....7B 20
Bagshot. Surr ....7G 21
Bagshot. Wilts ....7M 19
Bagstone. S Glo ....5E 18
Bagthorpe. Norf ....6D 38
Bagthorpe. Notts ....4B 36
Bagworth. Leics ....1B 28
Bagwy Llydiart. Here ....1C 18
Baildon. W Yor ....4K 41
Baildon Green. W Yor ....4K 41
Baile. W Isl ....5J 75
Baile Ailein. W Isl ....1D 76
Baile an Truiseil. W Isl ....6G 83
Baile Boidheach. Arg ....2G 57
Bailemeonach. Arg ....3A 64
Baile Mhanaich. W Isl ....8J 75
Baile Mhartainn. W Isl ....6H 75
Baile MhicPhail. W Isl ....5H 75
Baile Mòr. Arg ....5H 63

Baile nan Cailleach. W Isl ....8J 75
Baile Raghaill. W Isl ....7J 75
Bailey Green. Hants ....3D 10
Baileyhead. Cumb ....3K 53
Bailiesward. Abers ....2D 72
Baillieston. Glas ....3E 58
Bailrigg. Lanc ....2C 40
Bail Uachdraich. W Isl ....7K 75
Bail' Ur Tholastaidh. W Isl ....7J 83
Bainbridge. N Yor ....6H 47
Bainsford. Falk ....1G 59
Bainshole. Abers ....2F 72
Bainton. E Yor ....2G 43
Bainton. Oxon ....1C 20
Bainton. Pet ....1H 29
Baintown. Fife ....7G 67
Baker Street. Thur ....5C 22
Bakewell. Derbs ....3L 35
Bala. Gwyn ....7J 33
Balachuish. High ....1F 70
Balbeg. High
nr. Cannich ....2E 70
nr. Loch Ness ....3E 70
Balbeggie. Per ....5E 66
Balblair. High
nr. Bonar Bridge ....4F 78
nr. Invergordon ....7H 79
nr. Inverness ....1F 70
Balby. S Yor ....7C 42
Balcathie. Ang ....4K 67
Balchladich. High ....8C 84
Balchraggan. High ....1F 70
Balchrick. High ....6D 84
Balcombe. W Sus ....2L 11
Balcombe Lane. W Sus ....2L 11
Balcurvie. Fife ....7G 67
Baldersby. N Yor ....8A 48
Baldersby St James. N Yor ....8A 48
Balderstone. Lanc ....4E 40
Balderton. Ches W ....3B 34
Balderton. Notts ....4F 36
Baldinnie. Fife ....6H 67
Baldock. Herts ....8K 29
Baldrine. IOM ....6D 44
Baldslow. E Sus ....4E 12
Baldwin. IOM ....6C 44
Baldwinholme. Cumb ....6H 53
Baldwin's Gate. Staf ....5F 34
Bale. Norf ....6G 39
Balearn. Abers ....8K 81
Balemartine. Arg ....3E 62
Balephetrish. Arg ....3E 62
Balephuil. Arg ....3E 62
Balerno. Edin ....3K 59
Balevullin. Arg ....3E 62
Balfield. Ang ....1J 67
Balfour. Orkn ....7D 88
Balfron. Stir ....1D 58
Balgaveny. Abers ....1F 72
Balgonar. Fife ....8D 66
Balgowan. High ....6G 71
Balgown. High ....7E 76
Balgonar. Fife ....8D 66
Balgy. High ....8K 77
Balhalgardy. Abers ....3G 73
Baliasta. Shet ....3L 91
Baligill. High ....5L 85
Balintore. Ang ....2F 66
Balintore. High ....6J 79
Balintraid. High ....6H 79
Balk. N Yor ....7B 48
Balkeerie. Ang ....3G 67
Balkholme. E Yor ....5E 42
Ball. Shrp ....7B 34
Ballabeg. IOM ....7B 44
Ballacannell. IOM ....6D 44
Ballacarnane Beg. IOM ....6C 44
Ballachulish. High ....1F 70
Ballagyr. IOM ....6B 44
Ballaleigh. IOM ....6C 44
Ballamodha. IOM ....7B 44
Ballantrae. S Ayr ....3F 50
Ballards Gore. Essx ....4F 22
Ballasalla. IOM
nr. Castletown ....7B 44
nr. Kirk Michael ....6C 44
Ballater. Abers ....6C 72
Ballaugh. IOM ....5C 44
Ballencrieff. E Lot ....2B 60
Ballencrieff Toll. W Lot ....2H 59
Ballentoul. Per ....1B 66
Ball Hill. Hants ....7B 20
Ballidon. Derbs ....4L 35
Balliemore. Arg
nr. Dunoon ....1K 57
nr. Oban ....5C 64
Ballieward. High ....2L 71
Ballig. Stir ....6B 44
Ballimore. Stir ....6K 65
Ballinamallard. Ferm ....6C 92
Ballindarragh. Ferm ....7E 92
Ballingdon. Suff ....7E 30
Ballinger Common. Buck ....3G 21
Ballingham. Here ....8D 26
Ballingry. Fife ....8E 66
Ballinluig. Per ....2C 66
Ballintoy. Caus ....1G 93
Ballintuim. Per ....2F 66
Balliveolan. Arg ....3C 64
Balloan. High ....3F 78
Balloch. Ang ....2G 67
Balloch. High ....1H 71
Balloch. N Lan ....2F 58
Balloch. W Dun ....1C 58
Ballochan. Abers ....6E 72
Ballochgair. Arg ....7G 57
Ballochmyle. E Ayr ....7D 58
Ballochroy. Arg ....4G 57
Balls Cross. W Sus ....3G 11
Ball's Green. E Sus ....2A 12
Ballyalton. New M ....7J 93
Ballybogy. Caus ....1F 93
Ballycassidy. Ferm ....6C 92
Ballyclare. Ant ....4H 93
Ballygally. ME Ant ....3J 93
Ballygowan. ME Ant ....6H 93
Ballygown. Arg ....3K 63
Ballygrant. Arg ....3C 56
Ballyhalbert. Ards ....5K 93
Ballyholland. New M ....7H 93
Ballykelly. Caus ....2E 92
Ballykinler. New M ....7J 93
Ballylesson. Lis ....5H 93
Ballymacorry. Derr ....5H 92
Ballymagorry. Derr ....3G 92
Ballymena. ME Ant ....3G 93
Ballymoney. Caus ....2F 93
Ballynahinch. New M ....6H 93
Ballynakilly. New M ....4H 93
Ballynoe. New M ....7J 93
Ballyrashane. Caus ....1F 93
Ballyristan. Caus ....2F 93
Ballyrobert. ME Ant ....4J 93
Ballyronan. M Ulst ....3G 93
Ballyscullion. ME Ant ....4F 93
Ballystrudder. ME Ant ....4J 93
Ballyvoy. Caus ....1G 93
Ballywalter. Ards ....5K 93
Ballyward. New M ....7H 93
Ballyweaton. Ant ....4H 93
Balmacara. High ....3K 69
Balmaclellan. Dum ....4A 52
Balmacneil. Per ....2C 66
Balmacqueen. High ....6E 76
Balmaha. Stir ....8J 65
Balmalcolm. Fife ....7G 67
Balmalloch. N Lan ....2E 58
Balmeanach. High ....1G 69
Balmedie. Abers ....4J 73
Balmerino. Fife ....5G 67
Balmerlawn. Hants ....5A 10
Balmore. E Dun ....2D 58
Balmore. High ....1D 68
Balmullo. Fife ....5H 67
Balmurrie. Dum ....5H 51
Balnaboth. Ang ....1G 67

Balnabruaich. High ....6H 79
Balnabruich. High ....1A 80
Balnacoil. High ....2J 79
Balnacra. High ....1L 69
Balnacroft. Abers ....6B 72
Balnageith. Mor ....8L 79
Balnaglaic. High ....2E 70
Balnagrantach. High ....2E 70
Balnaguard. Per ....2C 66
Balnahard. Arg ....8K 63
Balnain. High ....2E 70
Balnakeil. High ....5F 84
Balnaknock. High ....7F 76
Balnamoon. Ang ....1J 67
Balnamoon. Abers ....8J 81
Balnamore. Caus ....2F 93
Balnapaling. High ....7H 79
Balornock. Glas ....3E 58
Balquhidder. Stir ....5K 65
Balsall. W Mid ....4L 27
Balsall Common. W Mid ....4L 27
Balscote. Oxon ....7A 28
Balsham. Cambs ....6B 30
Balstonia. Thur ....5C 22
Baltasound. Shet ....3L 91
Balterley. Staf ....4F 34
Baltersan. Dum ....5K 51
Balthangie. Abers ....8H 81
Balvaird. High ....8G 79
Balvaird. Per ....6E 66
Balvenie. Mor ....1C 72
Balvicar. Arg ....6B 64
Balvraid. Arg ....4K 69
Balvraid Lodge. High ....2J 71
Bamber Bridge. Lanc ....5D 40
Bamber's Green. Essx ....1B 22
Bamburgh. Nmbd ....6J 61
Bamford. Derbs ....1L 35
Bamfurlong. G Man ....7D 40
Bampton. Cumb ....4D 46
Bampton. Devn ....3J 7
Bampton. Oxon ....3M 19
Bampton Grange. Cumb ....4D 46
Banavie. High ....8B 70
The Banarby. Orkn ....7B 88
Banbury. Oxon ....7B 28
Bancffosfelen. Carm ....5L 15
Banchory. Abers ....6F 72
Banchory-Devenick. Abers ....5J 73
Bancycapel. Carm ....5L 15
Bancyfelin. Carm ....1G 57
Banc-y-ffordd. Carm ....3K 15
Banff. Abers ....7F 80
Bangor. Ards ....4J 93
Bangor. Gwyn ....3E 32
Bangor-is-y-coed. Wrex ....5B 34
Bangors. Corn ....6B 6
Bangor's Green. Lanc ....7B 40
Banham. Norf ....3G 31
Bank. Hants ....5L 9
Bankend. Dum ....5E 52
Bankfoot. Per ....4D 66
Bankglen. E Ayr ....8E 58
Bankhead. Aber ....4H 73
Bankhead. S Lan ....5G 59
Bank Newton. N Yor ....2H 41
Banknock. Falk ....2F 58
Banks. Cumb ....5K 53
Banks. Lanc ....5B 40
Bankshill. Dum ....3F 52
Bank Street. Worc ....5E 26
Bank Top. Lanc ....7D 40
Banners Gate. W Mid ....2J 27
Banningham. Norf ....7J 39
Banniskirk. High ....6C 86
Bannister Green. Essx ....1C 22
Bannockburn. Stir ....8B 66
Banstead. Surr ....8K 21
Bantham. Devn ....7J 5
Banton. N Lan ....2F 58
Banwell. N Som ....8B 18
Banyard's Green. Suff ....4K 31
Bapchild. Kent ....7F 22
Bapton. Wilts ....2H 9
Barabhas. W Isl ....6G 83
Barabhas Iarach. W Isl ....7G 83
Barabhas Uarach. W Isl ....6G 83
Baramore. High ....8H 69
Barassie. S Ayr ....6B 58
Barbaraville. High ....6H 79
Barber Booth. Derbs ....1K 35
Barber Green. Cumb ....7B 46
Barbhas Uarach. W Isl ....6G 83
Barbieston. S Ayr ....8C 58
Barbon. Cumb ....7E 46
Barbourne. Worc ....6G 27
Barbridge. Ches E ....4E 34
Barbrook. Devn ....1G 7
Barby. Nptn ....4C 28
Barby Nortoft. Nptn ....4C 28
Barcaldine. Arg ....3D 64
Barcheston. Warw ....7L 27
Barclose. Cumb ....5J 53
Barcombe. E Sus ....4M 11
Barcombe Cross. E Sus ....4M 11
Barden. N Yor ....6K 47
Barden Scale. N Yor ....2J 41
Bardfield End Green. Essx ....8C 30
Bardfield Saling. Essx ....1C 22
Bardister. Shet ....6H 91
Bardnabeyne. High ....4H 79
Bardney. Linc ....3J 37
Bardon. Leics ....8B 36
Bardon Mill. Nmbd ....5A 54
Bardowie. E Dun ....2D 58
Bardrainney. Inv ....2B 58
Bardsea. Cumb ....8B 46
Bardsey. W Yor ....3A 42
Bardsley. G Man ....7H 41
Bardwell. Suff ....4F 30
Bare. Lanc ....1C 40
Bareless. Nmbd ....6G 61
Barewood. Here ....6B 26
Barford. Hants ....2F 10
Barford. Norf ....1H 31
Barford. Warw ....5L 27
Barford St John. Oxon ....8B 28
Barford St Martin. Wilts ....2J 9
Barford St Michael. Oxon ....8B 28
Barfrestone. Kent ....8J 23
Bargeddie. N Lan ....3E 58
Bargod. Cphy ....5L 17
Bargoed. Cphy ....5L 17
Bargrennan. Dum ....4J 51
Barham. Cambs ....4J 29
Barham. Kent ....8J 23
Barham. Suff ....6H 31
Barharrow. Dum ....6A 52
Bar Hill. Cambs ....5L 29
Barholm. Linc ....8H 37
Barkby. Leics ....1D 28
Barkestone-le-Vale. Leics ....6E 36
Barkham. Wok ....7E 20
Barking. G Lon ....5M 21
Barking. Suff ....6G 31
Barkingside. G Lon ....5A 22
Barking Tye. Suff ....6G 31
Barkisland. W Yor ....6J 41
Barkston. Linc ....5G 37
Barkston Ash. N Yor ....4B 42
Barkway. Herts ....8L 29
Barlanark. Glas ....3E 58
Barlaston. Staf ....6G 35
Barlavington. W Sus ....4G 11
Barlborough. Derbs ....2B 36
Barlby. N Yor ....4C 42
Barlestone. Leics ....1B 28
Barley. Herts ....8L 29
Barley. Lanc ....3G 41
Barley Mow. Tyne ....6F 54
Barleythorpe. Rut ....1F 28
Barling. Essx ....5F 22
Barlings. Linc ....2H 37
Barlow. Derbs ....2A 36
Barlow. N Yor ....5D 42
Barlow. Tyne ....5E 54
Barmby Moor. E Yor ....3E 42
Barmby on the Marsh.
E Yor ....5D 42
Barmer. Norf ....6E 38
Barming. Kent ....8D 22
Barming Heath. Kent ....8D 22
Barmoor. Nmbd ....6G 61
Barmouth. Gwyn ....1F 24

**Column 5**

Barmpton. Darl ....4M 47
Barmston. E Yor ....2J 43
Barmulloch. Glas ....3E 58
Barnack. Pet ....1H 29
Barnacle. Warw ....3A 28
Barnard Castle. Dur ....4J 47
Barnard Gate. Oxon ....2B 20
Barnardiston. Suff ....7D 30
Barnbarroch. Dum ....6C 52
Barnburgh. S Yor ....7B 42
Barnby. Suff ....3L 31
Barnby Dun. S Yor ....7D 42
Barnby in the Willows. Notts ....4F 36
Barnby Moor. Notts ....1D 36
Barnes. G Lon ....6K 21
Barnes Street. Kent ....1C 12
Barnet. G Lon ....4K 21
Barnetby le Wold. N Lin ....7H 43
Barney. Norf ....6F 38
Barnham. Suff ....4E 30
Barnham. W Sus ....5G 11
Barnham Broom. Norf ....1G 31
Barnhead. Ang ....2K 67
Barnhill. D'dee ....4H 67
Barnhill. Mor ....8M 79
Barnhill. Per ....5E 66
Barnhills. Dum ....4E 50
Barningham. Dur ....4J 47
Barningham. Suff ....4F 30
Barnoldby le Beck. N E Lin ....7K 43
Barnoldswick. Lanc ....3G 41
Barns Green. W Sus ....3J 11
Barnsley. Glos ....3J 19
Barnsley. Shrp ....2F 26
Barnsley. S Yor ....7M 41
Barnstaple. Devn ....2E 6
Barnston. Essx ....2C 22
Barnston. Mers ....1A 34
Barnstone. Notts ....6E 36
Barnt Green. Worc ....4J 27
Barnton. Ches W ....2E 34
Barnwell. Nptn ....3H 29
Barnwood. Glos ....2G 19
Barons Cross. Here ....6C 26
The Barony. Orkn ....7B 88
Barr. Dum ....3C 52
Barr. S Ayr ....2H 51
Barra Airport. W Isl ....5C 74
Barrachan. Dum ....7J 51
Barraglom. W Isl ....8D 82
Barrahormid. Arg ....1G 57
Barrapol. Arg ....3E 62
Barras. Cumb ....4G 47
Barrasford. Nmbd ....4C 54
Barravullin. Arg ....7C 64
Barregarrow. IOM ....6C 44
Barrhead. E Ren ....4D 58
Barrhill. S Ayr ....3H 51
Barri. V Glam ....8L 17
Barrington. Cambs ....7L 29
Barrington. Som ....4B 8
Barripper. Corn ....5K 3
Barrmill. N Ayr ....5B 58
Barrock. High ....4D 86
Barrow. Lanc ....4F 40
Barrow. Rut ....8F 36
Barrow. Shrp ....1E 26
Barrow. Som ....2F 8
Barroway Drove. Norf ....1B 30
Barrow Bridge. G Man ....6E 40
Barrowburn. Nmbd ....8B 60
Barrowby. Linc ....6F 36
Barrowcliff. N Yor ....7H 49
Barrowden. Rut ....1G 29
Barrowford. Lanc ....4G 41
Barrow Common. N Som ....7D 18
Barrowend. Buck ....6F 54
Barrowford. Lanc ....4G 41
Barrow Gurney. N Som ....7D 18
Barrow Haven. N Lin ....5H 43
Barrow Hill. Derbs ....2B 36
Barrow-in-Furness. Cumb ....8M 45
Barrow Nook. Lanc ....7C 40
Barrow's Green. Hal ....1D 34
Barrows Green. Cumb ....7D 46
Barrow Street. Wilts ....2G 9
Barrow upon Humber. N Lin ....5H 43
Barrow upon Soar. Leics ....8C 36
Barrow upon Trent. Derbs ....7A 36
Barry. Ang ....4J 67
Barry. V Glam ....8L 17
Barry Island. V Glam ....8L 17
Barsby. Leics ....1D 28
Barsham. Suff ....3K 31
Barston. W Mid ....4L 27
Bartestree. Here ....7D 26
Barthol Chapel. Abers ....2H 73
Bartholomew Green. Essx ....1D 22
Barthomley. Ches E ....4F 34
Barton. Cambs ....6M 29
Barton. Ches W ....4C 34
Barton. Cumb ....3D 46
Barton. Glos ....1K 19
Barton. Lanc
nr. Ormskirk ....7B 40
nr. Preston ....4D 40
Barton. N Som ....8B 18
Barton. N Yor ....5L 47
Barton. Oxon ....3D 20
Barton. Torb ....5M 5
Barton. Warw ....6K 27
Barton Bendish. Norf ....1D 30
Barton Gate. Staf ....8K 35
Barton Green. Staf ....8K 35
Barton Hartshorn. Buck ....8D 28
Barton Hill. Nmbd ....1E 42
Barton in Fabis. Notts ....6C 36
Barton in the Beans. Leics ....1A 28
Barton-le-Clay. C Beds ....8H 29
Barton-le-Street. N Yor ....8E 48
Barton-le-Willows. N Yor ....1E 42
Barton Mills. Suff ....4D 30
Barton on Sea. Hants ....6L 9
Barton-on-the-Heath. Warw ....8L 27
Barton St David. Som ....2D 8
Barton Seagrave. Nptn ....4F 28
Barton Stacey. Hants ....1B 10
Barton Town. Devn ....1F 6
Barton Turf. Norf ....7K 39
Barton-Under-Needwood.
Staf ....8K 35
Barton-upon-Humber. N Lin ....5H 43
Barton Waterside. N Lin ....5H 43
Barugh Green. S Yor ....7M 41
Barway. Cambs ....4B 30
Barwell. Leics ....2B 28
Barwick. Herts ....2L 21
Barwick. Som ....4D 8
Barwick in Elmet. W Yor ....4A 42
Baschurch. Shrp ....7C 34
Bascote. Warw ....5B 28
Basford Green. Staf ....4H 35
Bashall Eaves. Lanc ....3E 40
Bashall Town. Lanc ....3F 40
Bashley. Hants ....6L 9
Basildon. Essx ....5D 22
Basingstoke. Hants ....8D 20
Baslow. Derbs ....2L 35
Bason Bridge. Som ....1B 8
Bassaleg. Newp ....5A 18
Bassendean. Bord ....5D 60
Bassenthwaite. Cumb ....8G 53
Bassett. Sotn ....4B 10
Bassingbourn. Cambs ....7L 29
Bassingfield. Notts ....6D 36
Bassingham. Linc ....3G 37
Bassingthorpe. Linc ....7G 37
Bassus Green. Herts ....1L 21
Basta. Shet ....4K 91
Baston. Linc ....8H 37
Bastonford. Worc ....6G 27
Bastwick. Norf ....8L 39
Batchley. Worc ....5J 27
Batchworth. Herts ....4H 21
Batcombe. Dors ....5E 8
Batcombe. Som ....2E 8
Bate Heath. Ches E ....2E 34
Bath. Bath ....7F 18
Bathampton. Bath ....7F 18
Bathealton. Som ....3K 7
Batheaston. Bath ....7F 18
Bathford. Bath ....7F 18
Bathgate. W Lot ....3H 59
Bathley. Notts ....4E 36
Bathpool. Corn ....8B 6
Bathpool. Som ....3M 7
Bathville. W Lot ....3H 59
Bathway. Som ....8D 18
Batley. W Yor ....5L 41
Batsford. Glos ....8K 27
Batson. Devn ....8K 5
Battersby. N Yor ....5C 48
Battersea. G Lon ....6K 21
Battisborough Cross. Devn ....7J 5
Battisford. Suff ....6G 31
Battisford Tye. Suff ....6G 31
Battle. E Sus ....4D 12
Battle. Powy ....1K 17
Battleborough. Som ....8B 18
Battledown. Glos ....1H 19
Battlefield. Shrp ....8D 34
Battlesbridge. Essx ....4D 22
Battlesea Green. Suff ....4J 31
Battleton. Som ....3J 7
Battram. Leics ....1B 28
Battramsley. Hants ....6M 9
Batt's Corner. Surr ....1F 10
Bauds of Cullen. Mor ....7D 80
Baughton. Worc ....7G 27
Baughurst. Hants ....7C 20
Baulking. Oxon ....4M 19
Baumber. Linc ....2K 37
Baunton. Glos ....3J 19
Baverstock. Wilts ....2J 9
Bawburgh. Norf ....1H 31
Bawdeswell. Norf ....7G 39
Bawdrip. Som ....2B 8
Bawdsey. Suff ....7K 31
Bawsey. Norf ....8C 38
Bawtry. S Yor ....8D 42
Baxenden. Lanc ....5F 40
Baxterley. Warw ....2L 27
Baxter's Green. Suff ....6D 30
Bay. High ....8D 76
Baybridge. Hants ....3C 10
Baycliff. Cumb ....8A 46
Baydon. Wilts ....6L 19
Bayford. Herts ....3L 21
Bayford. Som ....3F 8
Bayles. Cumb ....7M 53
Baylham. Suff ....6H 31
Baynard's Green. Oxon ....1C 20
Bayston Hill. Shrp ....1C 26
Baythorne End. Essx ....7D 30
Bayton. Worc ....4E 26
Bayton Common. Worc ....4F 26
Bayworth. Oxon ....3C 20
Beach. S Glo ....6F 18
Beachampton. Buck ....8E 28
Beachamwell. Norf ....1D 30
Beachley. Glos ....4D 18
Beacon. Devn ....5L 7
Beacon End. Essx ....1F 22
Beacon Hill. Surr ....2F 10
Beacon's Bottom. Buck ....4E 20
Beaconsfield. Buck ....4G 21
Beacrabhaic. W Isl ....4C 76
Beadlam. N Yor ....7D 48
Beadnell. Nmbd ....7K 61
Beaford. Devn ....4E 6
Beal. Nmbd ....5H 61
Beal. N Yor ....5C 42
Bealsmill. Corn ....8C 6
Beam Hill. Staf ....7L 35
Beamhurst. Staf ....6J 35
Beaminster. Dors ....5C 8
Beamish. Dur ....6F 54
Beamond End. Buck ....4G 21
Beamsley. N Yor ....2J 41
Bean. Kent ....6B 22
Beanacre. Wilts ....7H 19
Beanley. Nmbd ....8H 61
Beaquoy. Orkn ....6C 88
Beardwood. Bkbn ....5E 40
Beare. Devn ....5J 7
Beare Green. Surr ....1J 11
Bearley. Warw ....5K 27
Bearpark. Dur ....7F 54
Bearsbridge. Nmbd ....6A 54
Bearsden. E Dun ....2D 58
Bearsted. Kent ....8D 22
Bearstone. Shrp ....6F 34
Bearwood. Pool ....6J 9
Bearwood. W Mid ....3J 27
Beattock. Dum ....1E 52
Beauchamp Roding. Essx ....2B 22
Beauchief. S Yor ....1M 35
Beaufort. Blae ....3L 17
Beaulieu. Hants ....5A 10
Beauly. High ....1F 70
Beaumaris. IOA ....3F 32
Beaumont. Cumb ....6H 53
Beaumont. Essx ....1H 23
Beaumont Hill. Darl ....4L 47
Beaumont Leys. Leic ....1C 28
Beausale. Warw ....4L 27
Beauvale. Notts ....5B 36
Beauworth. Hants ....3C 10
Beaworthy. Devn ....6D 6
Beazley End. Essx ....1D 22
Bebington. Mers ....1B 34
Bebside. Nmbd ....3F 54
Beccles. Suff ....3L 31
Becconsall. Lanc ....5C 40
Beckbury. Shrp ....1F 26
Beckenham. G Lon ....7L 21
Beckermet. Cumb ....4K 45
Beckermonds. N Yor ....7G 47
Beckett End. Norf ....2D 30
Beck Foot. Cumb ....6E 46
Beckfoot. Cumb
nr. Broughton in Furness ....6L 45
nr. Seascale ....4K 45
nr. Silloth ....7E 52
Beckford. Worc ....8H 27
Beckhampton. Wilts ....7J 19
Beck Hole. N Yor ....5F 48
Beckingham. Linc ....4F 36
Beckingham. Notts ....8E 42
Beckington. Som ....8G 19
Beckjay. Shrp ....4B 26
Beckley. E Sus ....3E 12
Beckley. Hants ....6L 9
Beckley. Oxon ....2C 20
Beck Row. Suff ....4C 30
Beck Side. Cumb
nr. Cartmel ....7B 46
nr. Ulverston ....6M 45
Beckside. Cumb ....7E 46
Beckton. G Lon ....5A 22
Beckwithshaw. N Yor ....2L 41
Becontree. G Lon ....5A 22
Bedale. N Yor ....7L 47
Bedburn. Dur ....8E 54
Bedchester. Dors ....4G 9
Beddau. Rhon ....6K 17
Beddgelert. Gwyn ....5E 32
Beddingham. E Sus ....5M 11
Beddington. G Lon ....7L 21
Bedfield. Suff ....5J 31
Bedford. Bed ....7H 29
Bedford. G Man ....8E 40
Bedham. W Sus ....3H 11
Bedhampton. Hants ....5E 10
Bedingfield. Suff ....5H 31
Bedingham Green. Norf ....2J 31
Bedlam. N Yor ....1L 41
Bedlar's Green. Essx ....1B 22
Bedlington. Nmbd ....3F 54
Bedlinog. Mer T ....4K 17
Bedminster. Bris ....6D 18
Bedmond. Herts ....3H 21
Bednall. Staf ....8H 35
Bedrule. Bord ....8C 60
Bedstone. Shrp ....4B 26
Bedwas. Cphy ....6L 17
Bedwell. Herts ....1K 21
Bedwellty. Cphy ....4L 17
Bedworth. Warw ....3A 28
Beeby. Leics ....1D 28
Beech. Hants ....2D 10
Beech. Staf ....6G 35
Beech Hill. W Ber ....7D 20
Beechingstoke. Wilts ....8J 19
Beedon. W Ber ....6B 20
Beeford. E Yor ....2J 43
Beeley. Derbs ....3L 35
Beelsby. N E Lin ....7K 43
Beenham. W Ber ....7C 20
Beeny. Corn ....2D 4
Beer. Devn ....7M 7
Beer. Som ....2C 8
Beercrocombe. Som ....3B 8

**Column 6**

Beer Hackett. Dors ....4E 8
Beesands. Devn ....7L 5
Beesby. Linc ....1A 38
Beeson. Devn ....7L 5
Beeston. C Beds ....7J 29
Beeston. Ches W ....4D 34
Beeston. Norf ....8F 38
Beeston. Notts ....6C 36
Beeston. W Yor ....4L 41
Beeston Regis. Norf ....5H 39
Beeswing. Dum ....5C 52
Beetham. Cumb ....8C 46
Beetham. Som ....4A 8
Beetley. Norf ....8F 38
Beffcote. Staf ....8G 35
Began. Card ....6M 17
Begbroke. Oxon ....2B 20
Begdale. Cambs ....1B 30
Begelly. Pemb ....6H 15
Beggar Hill. Essx ....3C 22
Beggar's Bush. Powy ....5A 26
Beggearn Huish. Som ....2K 7
Beguildy. Powy ....4L 25
Beighton. Norf ....1K 31
Beighton. S Yor ....1B 36
Beighton Hill. Derbs ....4L 35
Beith. N Ayr ....4B 58
Bekesbourne. Kent ....8H 23
Belaugh. Norf ....8J 39
Belbroughton. Worc ....4H 27
Belchalwell. Dors ....4F 8
Belchalwell Street. Dors ....5F 8
Belchamp Otten. Essx ....7E 30
Belchamp St Paul. Essx ....7D 30
Belchamp Walter. Essx ....7E 30
Belchford. Linc ....2K 37
Belcoo. Ferm ....7B 92
Belfast. Bel ....5J 93
Belfast City George Best Airport.
Bel ....5H 93
Belfast International Airport.
Ant ....4G 93
Belfatton. Abers ....8K 81
Belford. Nmbd ....6J 61
Belgrano. Cnwy ....3J 33
Belhaven. E Lot ....2D 60
Belhelvie. Abers ....4J 73
Belhinnie. Abers ....3D 72
Belladrum. High ....1F 70
Bellabeg. Abers ....4C 72
Bellaghy. M Ulst ....4F 93
Bellamore. S Ayr ....3H 51
Bellanaleck. Ferm ....7C 92
Bellanoch. Arg ....8C 64
Bellasize. E Yor ....5F 42
Bellaty. Ang ....2F 66
Bell Busk. N Yor ....2H 41
Belleau. Linc ....2M 37
Belleek. New M ....7H 93
Belleek. New M ....6A 92
Bellerby. N Yor ....6K 47
Bellerby Camp. N Yor ....6J 47
Bellever. Devn ....8F 6
Belle Vue. Cumb ....8F 52
Belle Vue. Shrp ....8C 34
Bellfield. S Lan ....5G 59
Belliehill. Abers ....1J 67
Bellingdon. Buck ....3G 21
Bellingham. Nmbd ....3B 54
Belloch. Arg ....6F 56
Bellochantuy. Arg ....6F 56
Bell's Cross. Suff ....6H 31
Bellshill. N Lan ....4F 58
Bellshill. Nmbd ....6J 61
Bellside. N Lan ....4G 59
Bellspool. Bord ....6K 59
Bellsquarry. W Lot ....3J 59
Bells Yew Green. E Sus ....2C 12
Belmaduthy. High ....8H 79
Belmesthorpe. Rut ....8H 37
Belmont. Bkbn ....6E 40
Belmont. S Ayr ....7B 58
Belmont. Shet ....3K 91
Belnacraig. Abers ....4C 72
Belnie. Linc ....6K 37
Belowda. Corn ....5B 4
Belper. Derbs ....5A 36
Belper Lane End. Derbs ....5M 35
Belph. Derbs ....2C 36
Belsay. Nmbd ....4E 54
Belside. S Lan ....4G 59
Belsize. Herts ....3H 21
Belstead. Suff ....7H 31
Belston. S Ayr ....7B 58
Belstone. Devn ....6F 6
Belstone Corner. Devn ....6F 6
Belthorn. Lanc ....5F 40
Beltinge. Kent ....7H 23
Beltoft. N Lin ....7F 42
Belton. Leics ....7B 36
Belton. Linc ....6G 37
Belton. Norf ....1L 31
Belton. N Lin ....7E 42
Belton-in-Rutland. Rut ....1F 28
Beltring. Kent ....1C 12
Belts of Collonach. Abers ....6F 72
Belvedere. G Lon ....6A 22
Belvoir. Leics ....6F 36
Bembridge. IOW ....7D 10
Bemersyde. Bord ....6C 60
Bemerton. Wilts ....2K 9
Bempton. E Yor ....8J 49
Benacre. Suff ....3M 31
Ben Alder Lodge. High ....8H 71
Ben Armine Lodge. High ....2F 78
Benbecula Airport. W Isl ....8J 75
Benbuie. Dum ....2B 52
Benchill. G Man ....1G 35
Benderloch. Arg ....4D 64
Bendish. Herts ....1J 21
Bendooragh. Caus ....2F 93
Bendronaig Lodge. High ....2M 69
Benenden. Kent ....2E 12
Benfieldside. Dur ....6D 54
Bengate. Norf ....7K 39
Bengeworth. Worc ....7J 27
Benhall Green. Suff ....5K 31
Benholm. Abers ....1M 67
Beningbrough. N Yor ....2C 42
Benington. Herts ....1K 21
Benington. Linc ....5L 37
Benington Sea End. Linc ....5M 37
Benllech. IOA ....2E 32
Benmore Lodge. High ....2D 78
Bennacott. Corn ....7C 6
Bennah. Devn ....7H 7
Bennecarrigan. N Ayr ....7J 57
Bennethead. Cumb ....3C 46
Benniworth. Linc ....1K 37
Benover. Kent ....1D 12
Benson. Oxon ....4D 20
Benston. Shet ....2E 90
Bentfield Green. Essx ....1A 22
Benthall. Shrp ....1E 26
Bentham. Glos ....2H 19
Bentlawnt. Shrp ....1B 26
Bentley. E Yor ....4H 43
Bentley. Hants ....1E 10
Bentley. Suff ....8H 31
Bentley. S Yor ....7C 42
Bentley. Warw ....2L 27
Bentley. W Mid ....2J 27
Bentley Heath. Herts ....4K 21
Bentley Heath. W Mid ....4K 27
Bentpath. Dum ....2H 53
Bents. W Lot ....3H 59
Bentworth. Hants ....1D 10
Benville. Dors ....5D 8
Benwick. Cambs ....2L 29
Beoley. Worc ....5J 27
Beoraidbeg. High ....6H 69
Bepton. W Sus ....4F 10
Berden. Essx ....1A 22
Bere Alston. Devn ....4G 5
Bere Ferrers. Devn ....5G 5
Berepper. Corn ....6K 3
Bere Regis. Dors ....6G 9
Bergh Apton. Norf ....1K 31
Berinsfield. Oxon ....4C 20
Berkeley. Glos ....4E 18
Berkhamsted. Herts ....3G 21
Berkley. Som ....1G 9

**Column 7**

Berkswell. W Mid ....4L 27
Bermondsey. G Lon ....6L 21
Bernera. High ....3K 69
Berner. Arg ....8F 64
Berrick Salome. Oxon ....4D 20
Berriedale. High ....1M 79
Berrier. Cumb ....3B 46
Berriew. Powy ....2L 25
Berrington. Nmbd ....5H 61
Berrington. Shrp ....1D 26
Berrington. Worc ....5D 26
Berrington Green. Worc ....5D 26
Berrington Law. Nmbd ....5G 61
Berrow. Som ....8B 18
Berrow Green. Worc ....6F 26
Berry Cross. Devn ....4D 6
Berry Down Cross. Devn ....1E 6
Berry Hill. Glos ....2D 18
Berry Hill. Pemb ....2G 15
Berryhillock. Mor ....7E 80
Berrynarbor. Devn ....1E 6
Berry Pomeroy. Devn ....5L 5
Berryscaur. Dum ....2F 52
Bersham. Wrex ....5B 34
Berthengam. Flin ....3L 33
Berwick. E Sus ....5B 12
Berwick Bassett. Wilts ....6K 19
Berwick Hill. Nmbd ....4E 54
Berwick St James. Wilts ....2J 9
Berwick St John. Wilts ....3H 9
Berwick St Leonard. Wilts ....2H 9
Berwick-upon-Tweed.
Nmbd ....4G 61
Berwyn. Den ....6L 33
Bescaby. Leics ....7F 36
Bescar. Lanc ....6B 40
Besford. Worc ....7H 27
Bessacarr. S Yor ....7D 42
Bessbrook. New M ....7G 93
Bessels Leigh. Oxon ....3B 20
Bessingby. E Yor ....1J 43
Bessingham. Norf ....6H 39
Best Beech Hill. E Sus ....2C 12
Besthorpe. Norf ....2G 31
Besthorpe. Notts ....3F 36
Bestwood Village. Notts ....5C 36
Beswick. E Yor ....3H 43
Betchworth. Surr ....8K 21
Bethania. Cdgn ....6E 24
Bethania. Gwyn
nr. Blaenau Ffestiniog ....5G 33
nr. Caernarfon ....5F 32
Bethel. Gwyn
nr. Bala ....7J 33
nr. Caernarfon ....4E 32
Bethel. IOA ....3C 32
Bethersden. Kent ....1F 12
Bethesda. Gwyn ....4F 32
Bethesda. Pemb ....5G 15
Bethlehem. Carm ....1F 16
Bethnal Green. G Lon ....5L 21
Betley. Staf ....5F 34
Betsham. Kent ....6C 22
Betteshanger. Kent ....8K 23
Bettiscombe. Dors ....6C 8
Bettisfield. Wrex ....6C 34
Betton. Shrp ....6E 34
Betton Strange. Shrp ....1D 26
Bettws. Brnd ....6L 17
Bettws. Newp ....4A 18
Bettws Bledrws. Cdgn ....7E 24
Bettws Cedewain. Powy ....3K 25
Bettws Gwerfil Goch. Den ....6K 33
Bettws Ifan. Cdgn ....2K 15
Bettws Newydd. Mon ....3B 18
Bettyhill. High ....5K 85
Betws. Carm ....3F 16
Betws Garmon. Gwyn ....5E 32
Betws-y-Rhos. Cnwy ....5G 33
Betws-yn-Rhos. Cnwy ....3J 33
Beulah. Cdgn ....2J 15
Beulah. Powy ....6J 25
Beul an Atha. Arg ....3D 56
Bevendean. Brig ....5L 11
Bevercotes. Notts ....2E 36
Beverley. E Yor ....4H 43
Beverston. Glos ....4G 19
Bevington. Glos ....4E 18
Bewaldeth. Cumb ....8G 53
Bewcastle. Cumb ....4K 53
Bewdley. Worc ....4F 26
Bewerley. N Yor ....1K 41
Bewholme. E Yor ....2J 43
Bexfield. Norf ....7G 39
Bexhill. E Sus ....5D 12
Bexley. G Lon ....6A 22
Bexleyheath. G Lon ....6A 22
Bexleyhill. W Sus ....3G 11
Bexwell. Norf ....1C 30
Beyton. Suff ....5F 30
Bhalton. W Isl ....8D 82
Bhatarsaigh. W Isl ....6C 74
Bibbington. Derbs ....2K 35
Bibury. Glos ....3K 19
Bicester. Oxon ....1C 20
Bickenhall. Som ....4A 8
Bickenhill. W Mid ....3K 27
Bicker. Linc ....6K 37
Bicker Bar. Linc ....6K 37
Bicker Gauntlet. Linc ....6K 37
Bickershaw. G Man ....7E 40
Bickerstaffe. Lanc ....7C 40
Bickerton. Ches E ....4D 34
Bickerton. Nmbd ....1C 54
Bickford. Staf ....8G 35
Bickington. Devn
nr. Barnstaple ....2E 6
nr. Newton Abbot ....8G 7
Bickleigh. Devn
nr. Plymouth ....5H 5
nr. Tiverton ....5J 7
Bickley. N Yor ....6G 49
Bickley Moss. Ches W ....5D 34
Bickmarsh. Worc ....7K 27
Bicknacre. Essx ....3D 22
Bicknoller. Som ....2L 7
Bicknor. Kent ....8E 22
Bickton. Hants ....4K 9
Bicton. Here ....5C 26
Bicton. Shrp
nr. Bishop's Castle ....3A 26
nr. Shrewsbury ....8C 34
Bicton Heath. Shrp ....8C 34
Bidborough. Kent ....1B 12
Biddenden. Kent ....2E 12
Biddenden Green. Kent ....1E 12
Biddenham. Bed ....7H 29
Biddestone. Wilts ....6G 19
Biddisham. Som ....8B 18
Biddlesden. Buck ....7D 28
Biddlestone. Nmbd ....1C 54
Biddulph. Staf ....4G 35
Biddulph Moor. Staf ....4H 35
Bideford. Devn ....3D 6
Bidford-on-Avon. Warw ....6J 27

**Column 8**

Bielby. E Yor ....3E 42
Bieldside. Aber ....5H 73
Bierley. IOW ....8C 10
Bierley. W Yor ....4K 41
Bierton. Buck ....2F 20
Bigbury. Devn ....7J 5
Bigbury-on-Sea. Devn ....7J 5
Bigby. Linc ....7H 43
Biggar. Cumb ....8L 45
Biggar. S Lan ....6J 59
Biggin. Derbs
nr. Hartington ....4K 35
nr. Hulland ....5L 35
Biggin. N Yor ....4C 42
Biggin Hill. G Lon ....8M 21
Biggleswade. C Beds ....7J 29
Bighouse. High ....5L 85
Bighton. Hants ....2D 10
Biglands. Cumb ....6G 53
Bignall End. Staf ....4G 35
Bignor. W Sus ....4G 11
Bigrigg. Cumb ....3K 45
Big Sand. High ....6H 77
Bigton. Shet ....5D 90
Bilberry. Corn ....5C 4
Bilborough. Notts ....5C 36
Bilbrook. Som ....1K 7
Bilbrook. Staf ....1G 27
Bilbrook. Som ....1K 7

Bilbrook—Broad Oak

Bilbrook. Staf 1G 27
Bilbrough. N Yor 3C 42
Bilbster. High 6D 86
Bilby. Notts 1D 36
Bildershaw. Dur 3L 47
Bildeston. Suff 7F 30
**Billericay**. Essx 4C 22
Billesdon. Leics 1E 28
Billesley. Warw 6K 27
Billingborough. Linc 6J 37
Billinge. Mers 7D 40
Billingford. Norf
nr. Dereham 7G 39
nr. Diss 4H 31
**Billingham**. Stoc T 3B 48
Billinghay. Linc 4J 37
Billingley. S Yor 7B 42
Billingshurst. W Sus 3H 11
Billingsley. Shrp 3F 26
Billington. C Beds 1G 21
Billington. Lanc 4F 40
Billington. Staf 7G 35
Billockby. Norf 8L 39
Billy Row. Dur 8E 54
Bilsborrow. Lanc 3D 40
Bilsby. Linc 2A 38
Bilsham. W Sus 5G 11
Bilsington. Kent 2G 13
Bilson Green. Glos 2E 18
Bilsthorpe. Notts 3D 36
Bilston. Midl 3L 59
Bilston. W Mid 2H 27
Bilstone. Leics 1A 28
Bilting. Kent 1G 13
Bilton. E Yor 4J 43
Bilton. Nmbd 8K 61
Bilton. N Yor 2M 41
Bilton. Warw 4B 28
Bilton in Ainsty. N Yor 3B 42
Bimbister. Orkn 8C 88
Binbrook. Linc 8K 43
Binchester. Dur 8F 54
Bincombe. Dors 7E 8
Bindal. High 5K 79
Binegar. Som 1E 8
Bines Green. W Sus 4J 11
Binfield. Brac 6F 20
Binfield Heath. Oxon 6E 20
Bingfield. Nmbd 4C 54
Bingham. Notts 6E 36
Bingham's Melcombe. Dors 5F 8
**Bingley**. W Yor 4K 41
Bings Heath. Shrp 8D 34
Binham. Norf 6F 38
Binley. Hants 8B 20
Binley. W Mid 4A 28
Binnegar. Dors 7G 9
Binniehill. Falk 2G 59
Binsoe. N Yor 8L 47
Binstead. IOW 6C 10
Binsted. Hants 1E 10
Binsted. W Sus 5G 11
Binton. Warw 6K 27
Bintree. Norf 7G 39
Binweston. Shrp 1B 26
Birch. Essx 2F 22
Birch. G Man 7G 41
Birchall. Staf 4H 35
Bircham Newton. Norf 6D 38
Bircham Tofts. Norf 6D 38
Birchanger. Essx 1B 22
Birchburn. N Ayr 7J 57
Birch Cross. Staf 6K 35
Bircher. Here 5C 26
Birch Green. Essx 2F 22
Birchgrove. Card 6L 17
Birchgrove. Swan 5G 17
Birch Heath. Ches W 3D 34
Birch Hill. Ches W 2D 34
Birchill. Devn 5B 8
Birchington. Kent 7J 23
Birchley Heath. Warw 2L 27
Birchmoor. Warw 1L 27
Birchmoor Green. C Beds 8G 29
Birchover. Derbs 3L 35
Birch Vale. Derbs 1J 35
Birchview. Mor 2A 72
**Birchwood**. Linc 3G 37
Birchwood. Som 4M 7
Birchwood. Warr 8E 40
Bircotes. Notts 8D 42
Birdbrook. Essx 7D 30
Birdham. W Sus 5F 10
Birdholme. Derbs 3A 36
Birdingbury. Warw 5B 28
Birdlip. Glos 2H 19
Birdsall. N Yor 1F 42
Birds Edge. W Yor 7L 41
Birds Green. Essx 3B 22
Birdsgreen. Shrp 3F 26
Birdsmoorgate. Dors 5B 8
Birdston. E Dun 2E 58
Birdwell. S Yor 7M 41
Birdwood. Glos 2F 18
Birgham. Bord 6E 60
Birichen. High 4H 79
Birkby. Cumb 8E 52
Birkby. N Yor 5M 47
Birkdale. Mers 6B 40
**Birkenhead**. Mers 1B 34
Birkenhills. Abers 1G 73
Birkenshaw. N Lan 3E 58
Birkenshaw. W Yor 5L 41
Birkhall. Abers 6C 72
Birkhill. Ang 4G 67
Birkholme. Linc 7G 37
Birkin. N Yor 5C 42
Birley. Here 6C 26
Birling. Kent 7C 22
Birling. Nmbd 1F 54
Birling Gap. E Sus 6B 12
Birlingham. Worc 7H 27
**Birmingham**. W Mid 3J 27
Birmingham Airport. W Mid 3K 27
Birnam. Per 3D 66
Birse. Abers 6E 72
Birsemore. Abers 6E 72
**Birstall**. Leics 1C 28
Birstall. W Yor 5L 41
Birstall Smithies. W Yor 5L 41
Birstwith. N Yor 2L 41
Birthorpe. Linc 6J 37
Birtle. G Man 6G 41
Birtley. Here 5B 26
Birtley. Nmbd 4B 54
Birtley. Tyne 6F 54
Birtsmorton. Worc 8G 27
Birts Street. Worc 8F 26
Bisbrooke. Rut 2F 28
Bisham. Wind 5F 20
Bishampton. Worc 6H 27
Bish Mill. Devn 3G 7
Bishop Auckland. Dur 3L 47
Bishopbridge. Linc 8H 43
**Bishopbriggs**. E Dun 2E 58
Bishop Burton. E Yor 4G 43
Bishopdown. Wilts 2K 9
Bishop Middleham. Dur 8G 55
Bishopmill. Mor 7B 80
Bishop Monkton. N Yor 1M 41
Bishop Norton. Linc 8G 43
Bishopsbourne. Kent 8H 23
Bishops Cannings. Wilts 7J 19
Bishop's Castle. Shrp 3B 26
Bishop's Caundle. Dors 4E 8
**Bishop's Cleeve**. Glos 1H 19
Bishops Court. New M 6J 93
Bishop's Down. Dors 4E 8
Bishop's Frome. Here 7E 26
Bishop's Green. Essx 2C 22
Bishop's Green. Hants 7C 20
Bishop's Hull. Som 3M 7
Bishop's Itchington. Warw 6A 28
Bishops Lydeard. Som 3L 7
Bishop's Norton. Glos 1G 19
Bishop's Nympton. Devn 3G 7
Bishop's Offley. Staf 7F 34
**Bishop's Stortford**. Herts 1A 22
Bishop's Sutton. Hants 2D 10
Bishop's Tachbrook. Warw 5M 27
Bishop's Tawton. Devn 2E 6
Bishopsteignton. Devn 8J 7
**Bishopstoke**. Hants 4B 10
Bishopston. Swan 6E 16
Bishopstone. Buck 2F 20
Bishopstone. E Sus 5A 12
Bishopstone. Here 7C 26
Bishopstone. Swin 5L 19
Bishopstone. Wilts 3J 9
Bishopstrow. Wilts 1G 9
Bishop Sutton. Bath 8D 18
Bishop's Waltham. Hants 4C 10
Bishops Wood. Staf 1G 27
Bishopswood. Som 4A 8
Bishopsworth. Bris 7D 18
Bishop Thornton. N Yor 1L 41
Bishopthorpe. York 3C 42
Bishopton. Darl 3A 48
Bishopton. Dum 7K 51
Bishopton. N Yor 8L 47
Bishopton. Ren 2C 58
Bishopton. Warw 6K 27
Bishop Wilton. E Yor 2E 42
Bishton. Newp 5B 18
Bishton. Staf 7J 35
Bisley. Glos 3H 19
Bisley. Surr 8G 21
Bispham. Bkpl 3B 40
Bispham Green. Lanc 6C 40
Bissoe. Corn 4L 3
Bisterne. Hants 5K 9
Bisterne Close. Hants 5L 9
Bitchfield. Linc 7G 37
Bittadon. Devn 1E 6
Bittaford. Devn 6J 5
Bittering. Norf 8F 38
Bitterley. Shrp 4D 26
Bitterne. Sotn 4B 10
Bitteswell. Leics 3C 28
Bitton. S Glo 7E 18
Bix. Oxon 5E 20
Bixter. Shet 2D 90
Blaby. Leics 2C 28
Blackawton. Devn 6L 5
Black Bank. Cambs 3B 30
Black Barn. Linc 7M 37
Blackborough. Devn 5K 7
Blackborough. Norf 8C 38
Blackborough End. Norf 8C 38
Black Bourton. Oxon 3L 19
Blackboys. E Sus 3B 12
Blackbrook. Derbs 5M 35
Blackbrook. Mers 8D 40
Blackbrook. Staf 6F 34
Blackbrook. Surr 1J 11
Blackburn. Abers 4H 73
**Blackburn**. Bkbn 5E 40
Blackburn. W Lot 3H 59
Black Callerton. Tyne 5E 54
Black Carr. Norf 2G 31
Black Clauchrie. S Ayr 3H 51
Black Corries. High 2G 65
Black Crofts. Arg 4D 64
Black Cross. Corn 5B 4
Blackden Heath. Ches E 2F 34
Blackditch. Oxon 3B 20
Black Dog. Devn 5H 7
Blackdog. Abers 4J 73
Blackdown. Dors 5B 8
Blackdyke. Cumb 6F 52
Blacker Hill. S Yor 7A 42
Blackfen. G Lon 6A 22
Blackfield. Hants 5B 10
Blackford. Cumb 5H 53
Blackford. Per 7B 66
Blackford. Shrp 3D 26
Blackford. Som
nr. Burnham-on-Sea 1C 8
nr. Wincanton 3E 8
Blackfordby. Leics 8M 35
Blackgang. IOW 8B 10
Blackhall. Edin 2L 59
Blackhall. Ren 3C 58
Blackhall Colliery. Dur 8H 55
Blackhall Mill. Tyne 6E 54
Blackhall Rocks. Dur 8H 55
Blackham. E Sus 2A 12
Blackheath. Essx 1G 23
Blackheath. G Lon 6L 21
Blackheath. Suff 4L 31
Blackheath. Surr 1H 11
Blackheath. W Mid 3H 27
Black Heddon. Nmbd 4D 54
Black Hill. Warw 6L 27
Blackhill. Abers 1K 73
Blackhill. High 8E 76
Blackhills. Abers 7J 81
Blackhills. High 8K 79
Blackjack. Linc 6K 37
Blackland. Wilts 7J 19
Black Lane. G Man 7F 40
Blackleach. Lanc 4C 40
Blackley. G Man 7G 41
Blackley. W Yor 6K 41
Blacklunans. Per 1E 66
Blackmill. B'end 6J 17
Blackmoor. G Man 7E 40
Blackmoor. Hants 2E 10
Blackmoor Gate. Devn 1F 6
Blackmore. Essx 3C 22
Blackmore End. Essx 8D 30
Blackmore End. Herts 2J 21
Black Mount. Arg 3G 65
Blackness. Falk 2J 59
Blacknest. Hants 1E 10
Blackney. Dors 6C 8
Blacknoll. Dors 7G 9
Black Notley. Essx 1D 22
Blacko. Lanc 3G 41
Black Pill. Swan 5F 16
**Blackpool**. Bkpl 4B 40
Blackpool. Devn 7L 5
Blackpool Corner. Dors 6B 8
Blackpool Gate. Cumb 4K 53
Blackridge. W Lot 3G 59
Blackrock. Arg 3C 56
Blackrock. Mon 3M 17
Blackrod. G Man 6E 40
Blackshaw. Dum 5E 52
Blackshaw Head. W Yor 5H 41
Blackshaw Moor. Staf 4J 35
Blackskull. Arm 6G 93
Blacksmith's Green. Suff 5H 31
Blacksnape. Bkbn 5F 40
Blackstone. W Sus 4K 11
Black Street. Suff 3M 31
Black Tar. Pemb 6F 14
Blackthorn. Oxon 2D 20
Blackthorpe. Suff 5F 30
Blacktoft. E Yor 5F 42
Blacktop. Aber 5H 73
Black Torrington. Devn 5D 6
Blacktown. Newp 5A 18
**Blackwall Tunnel**. G Lon 5L 21
Blackwater. Corn 4L 3
Blackwater. Hants 8F 20
Blackwater. IOW 7C 10
Blackwater. Som 4A 8
Blackwaterfoot. N Ayr 7H 57
Blackwatertown. Arm 6F 93
Blackwell. Darl 4L 47
Blackwell. Derbs
nr. Alfreton 4B 36
nr. Buxton 2K 35
Blackwell. Som 3K 7
Blackwell. Warw 7L 27
Blackwell. Worc 4H 27
**Blackwood**. Cphy 5L 17
Blackwood. Dum 3D 52
Blackwood. S Lan 5F 58
Blackwood Hill. Staf 4H 35
Blacon. Ches W 3B 34
Bladnoch. Dum 6K 51
Bladon. Oxon 2B 20
Blaenannerch. Cdgn 2J 15
Blaenau Dolwyddelan. Cnwy 5F 32
Blaenau Ffestiniog. Gwyn 6G 33
Blaenavon. Torf 3A 18
Blaenawey. Mon 2A 18
Blaen Celyn. Cdgn 1K 15
Blaen Clydach. Rhon 5J 17
Blaencwm. Rhon 5J 17
Blaendulais. Neat 4H 17
Blaenffos. Pemb 3H 15
Blaengarw. B'end 5J 17
Blaen-geuffordd. Cdgn 4F 24
Blaengwrach. Neat 4H 17
Blaengwynfi. Neat 5H 17
Blaenllechau. Rhon 5J 17
Blaenpennal. Cdgn 6F 24
Blaenplwyf. Cdgn 5E 24
Blaenporth. Cdgn 2J 15
Blaenrhondda. Rhon 4J 17
Blaenwaun. Carm 4J 15
Blaen-y-coed. Carm 4K 15
Blagdon. N Som 8D 18
Blagdon. Torb 5L 5
Blagdon Hill. Som 4M 7
Blagill. Cumb 7M 53
Blaguegate. Lanc 7C 40
Blaich. High 8M 69
Blain. High 1A 64
Blaina. Blae 4M 17
Blair Atholl. Per 1B 66
Blair Drummond. Stir 8M 65
Blairgowrie. Per 3E 66
Blairhall. Fife 1J 59
Blairingone. Per 8C 66
Blairlogie. Stir 8B 66
Blairmore. Abers 2D 72
Blairmore. Arg 1L 57
Blairmore. High 6D 84
Blairquhanan. W Dun 1C 58
Blaisdon. Glos 2F 18
Blakebrook. Worc 4G 27
Blakedown. Worc 4G 27
Blake End. Essx 1D 22
Blakemere. Here 7B 26
Blakeney. Glos 3E 18
Blakeney. Norf 5G 39
Blakenhall. Ches E 5F 34
Blakeshall. Worc 3G 27
Blakesley. Nptn 6D 28
Blanchland. Nmbd 6C 54
Blandford Camp. Dors 5H 9
Blandford Forum. Dors 5G 9
Blandford St Mary. Dors 5G 9
Bland Hill. N Yor 2L 41
Blandy. High 5J 85
Blanefield. Stir 2D 58
Blaney. Ferm 6B 92
Blankney. Linc 3H 37
**Blantyre**. S Lan 4E 58
Blarmachfoldach. High 1E 64
Blarnalearoch. High 4B 78
Blashford. Hants 5K 9
Blaston. Leics 2F 28
Blatchbridge. Som 1F 8
Blathaisbhal. W Isl 6K 75
Blatherwycke. Nptn 2G 29
Blawith. Cumb 7A 46
Blaxhall. Suff 6K 31
Blaxton. S Yor 7D 42
**Blaydon**. Tyne 5E 54
Bleadney. Som 1C 8
Bleadon. N Som 8B 18
Blean. Kent 7H 23
Bleary. Arm 6G 93
Bleasby. Linc 1J 37
Bleasby. Notts 5E 36
Bleasby Moor. Linc 1J 37
Blebocraigs. Fife 6H 67
Bleddfa. Powy 6M 25
Bledington. Glos 1L 19
Bledlow. Buck 3E 20
Bledlow Ridge. Buck 4E 20
Blencarn. Cumb 8L 53
Blencogo. Cumb 7F 52
Blendworth. Hants 4E 10
Blennerhasset. Cumb 7F 52
Bletchingdon. Oxon 2C 20
Bletchingley. Surr 8L 21
**Bletchley**. Mil 8F 28
Bletchley. Shrp 6E 34
Bletherston. Pemb 4G 15
Bletsoe. Bed 6H 29
Blewbury. Oxon 5C 20
Blickling. Norf 7H 39
Blidworth. Notts 4C 36
Blindburn. Nmbd 8F 60
Blindcrake. Cumb 8F 52
Blindley Heath. Surr 1L 11
Blindmoor. Som 4A 8
Blisland. Corn 4D 4
Blissford. Hants 4K 9
Bliss Gate. Worc 4F 26
Blists Hill. Telf 1E 26
Blisworth. Nptn 6E 28
Blithbury. Staf 7J 35
Blitterlees. Cumb 6F 52
Blockley. Glos 8K 27
Blofield. Norf 1K 31
Blofield Heath. Norf 8K 39
Blo' Norton. Norf 4G 31
Bloomfield. Bord 7C 60
Blore. Staf 5K 35
Blount's Green. Staf 6J 35
Bloxham. Oxon 8B 28
Bloxholm. Linc 4H 37
Bloxwich. W Mid 1H 27
Bloxworth. Dors 6G 9
Blubberhouses. N Yor 2K 41
Blue Anchor. Som 1K 7
Blue Anchor. Swan 5E 16
Blue Bell Hill. Kent 7D 22
Blue Row. Essx 2G 23
Bluetown. Kent 8F 22
Blundeston. Suff 2M 31
Blunham. C Beds 6J 29
Blunsdon St Andrew. Swin 5K 19
Bluntington. Worc 4G 27
Bluntisham. Cambs 4L 29
Blunts. Corn 5F 4
Blurton. Stoke 5G 35
Blyborough. Linc 8G 43
Blyford. Suff 4L 31
Blymhill. Staf 8G 35
Blymhill Lawns. Staf 8G 35
**Blyth**. Nmbd 3G 55
Blyth. Notts 1D 36
Blyth. Bord 5K 59
Blyth Bank. Bord 5K 59
Blyth Bridge. Bord 5K 59
Blythburgh. Suff 4L 31
The Blythe. Staf 7J 35
Blythe Bridge. Staf 5H 35
Blythe Marsh. Staf 5H 35
Blyton. Linc 8F 42
Boardmills. Lis 6H 93
Boarhills. Fife 6J 67
Boarhunt. Hants 5D 10
Boar's Head. G Man 7D 40
Boarshead. E Sus 2B 12
Boars Hill. Oxon 3B 20
Boarstall. Buck 2D 20
Boasley Cross. Devn 6E 6
Boath. High 6F 78
Boat of Garten. High 4K 71
Bobbing. Kent 7E 22
Bobbington. Staf 2G 27
Bobbingworth. Essx 3B 22
Bocaddon. Corn 6D 4
Bocking. Essx 1D 22
Bocking Churchstreet. Essx 1D 22
Boddam. Abers 1L 73
Boddam. Shet 6D 90
Boddington. Glos 1G 19
Bodedern. IOA 2C 32
Bodelwyddan. Den 3K 33
Bodenham. Here 6D 26
Bodenham. Wilts 3K 9
Bodewryd. IOA 1C 32
Bodfari. Den 3K 33
Bodffordd. IOA 3D 32
Bodham. Norf 5H 39
Bodiam. E Sus 3D 12
Bodicote. Oxon 8B 28
Bodieve. Corn 4B 4
Bodinnick. Corn 6D 4
Bodle Street Green. E Sus 4C 12
**Bodmin**. Corn 5C 4
Bodnant. Cnwy 3H 33
Bodney. Norf 2E 30
Bodorgan. IOA 4C 32
Bodrane. Corn 5E 4
Bodsham. Kent 1H 13
Boduan. Gwyn 7C 32
Bodymoor Heath. Warw 2K 27
The Bog. Shrp 2B 26
Bogallan. High 8G 79
Bogbrae Croft. Abers 2K 73
Bogend. S Ayr 6B 58
Boghall. Midl 3L 59
Boghall. W Lot 3H 59
Boghead. S Lan 5F 58
Bogindollo. Ang 2H 67
Bogmoor. Mor 7C 80
Bogniebrae. Abers 1E 72
**Bognor Regis**. W Sus 6G 11
Bograxie. Abers 4G 73
Bogside. N Lan 4G 59
Bogton. Abers 8F 80
Bogue. Dum 3M 51
Bohenie. High 7C 70
Bohortha. Corn 8A 4
Boirseam. W Isl 5B 76
Bokiddick. Corn 5C 4
Bolam. Dur 3K 47
Bolam. Nmbd 3D 54
Bolberry. Devn 8J 5
Bold Heath. Mers 1D 34
**Boldon**. Tyne 5G 55
Boldon Colliery. Tyne 5G 55
Boldre. Hants 6M 9
Boldron. Dur 4J 47
Bole. Notts 1E 36
Bolehall. Staf 1L 27
Bolehill. Derbs 4L 35
Bolenowe. Corn 5K 3
Boleside. Bord 6B 60
Bolham. Devn 4J 7
Bolham Water. Devn 4L 7
Bolingey. Corn 3L 3
Bollington. Ches E 2H 35
Bolney. W Sus 3K 11
Bolnhurst. Bed 6H 29
Bolshan. Ang 2K 67
**Bolsover**. Derbs 2B 36
Bolsterstone. S Yor 8L 41
Bolstone. Here 8D 26
Boltachan. Per 2B 66
Boltby. N Yor 7B 48
Bolton. Cumb 3E 46
Bolton. E Lot 2C 60
Bolton. E Yor 2E 42
**Bolton**. G Man 7F 40
Bolton. Nmbd 8J 61
Bolton Abbey. N Yor 2J 41
Bolton-by-Bowland. Lanc 3F 40
Boltonfellend. Cumb 5J 53
Boltongate. Cumb 7G 53
Bolton Green. Lanc 6D 40
Bolton-le-Sands. Lanc 1C 40
Bolton Low Houses. Cumb 7G 53
Bolton New Houses. Cumb 7G 53
Bolton-on-Swale. N Yor 6L 47
Bolton Percy. N Yor 3C 42
Bolton Town End. Lanc 1C 40
Bolton upon Dearne. S Yor 7B 42
Bolton Wood Lane. Cumb 7G 53
Bolventor. Corn 8A 6
Bomarsund. Nmbd 3F 54
Bomere Heath. Shrp 8C 34
Bonar Bridge. High 4G 79
Bonawe. Arg 4E 64
Bonby. N Lin 6H 43
Boncath. Pemb 3J 15
Bonchester Bridge. Bord 8C 60
Bonchurch. IOW 8C 10
Bond End. Staf 8K 35
Bondleigh. Devn 5F 6
Bonds. Lanc 3C 40
Bonehill. Devn 8G 7
Bonehill. Staf 1K 27
**Bo'ness**. Falk 1H 59
Boney Hay. Staf 8J 35
Bonham. Wilts 2F 8
**Bonhill**. W Dun 2B 58
Boningale. Shrp 1G 27
Bonjedward. Bord 7D 60
Bonkle. N Lan 4G 59
Bonnanaboigh. Caus 3E 92
Bonnington. Ang 4J 67
Bonnington. Edin 3K 59
Bonnington. Kent 2G 13
Bonnybank. Fife 7G 67
**Bonnybridge**. Falk 1G 59
Bonnykelly. Abers 8H 81
**Bonnyrigg**. Midl 3M 59
Bonnyton. Ang 4G 67
Bonnytown. Fife 6J 67
Bonsall. Derbs 4L 35
Bont. Mon 2B 18
Bontddu. Gwyn 1F 24
Bont Dolgadfan. Powy 2H 25
Y Bont-Faen. V Glam 7J 17
Bontgoch. Cdgn 4F 24
Bonthorpe. Linc 2A 38
Bont Newydd. Gwyn 6G 33
Bont-newydd. Cnwy 3K 33
Bontnewydd. Cdgn 6F 24
Bontnewydd. Gwyn 4D 32
Bontuchel. Den 5K 33
Bonvilston. V Glam 7K 17
Bon-y-maen. Swan 5F 16
Booker. Buck 4F 20
Booley. Shrp 7D 34
Boorley Green. Hants 4C 10
Boosbeck. Red C 4D 48
Boot. Cumb 4L 45
Booth. W Yor 5J 41
Boothby Graffoe. Linc 4G 37
Boothby Pagnell. Linc 6G 37
Booth Green. Ches E 1H 35
Booth of Toft. Shet 6J 91
Boothstown. G Man 7F 40
Boothville. Nptn 5E 28
Bootle. Cumb 6L 45
**Bootle**. Mers 8B 40
Booton. Norf 7H 39
Booze. N Yor 5J 47
Boquhan. Stir 1D 58
Boraston. Shrp 4E 26
Borden. Kent 7E 22
Borden. W Sus 3F 10
Bordlands. Bord 5K 59
Bordley. N Yor 1H 41
**Bordon**. Hants 2E 10
Boreham. Essx 3D 22
Boreham. Wilts 1G 9
Boreham Street. E Sus 4C 12
**Borehamwood**. Herts 4J 21
Boreland. Dum 2F 52
Boreston. Devn 6K 5
Borestone Brae. Stir 8A 66
Boreton. Shrp 1D 26
Borgh. W Isl
on Barra 5C 74
on Benbecula 8J 75
on Berneray 5L 75
on Isle of Lewis 6H 83
Borghasdal. W Isl 5B 76
Borghastan. W Isl 7E 82
Borgh na Sgiotaig. High 6E 76
Borgie. High 6J 85
Borgue. Dum 7M 51
Borgue. High 1M 79
Borley. Essx 7E 30
Borley Green. Essx 7E 30
Borley Green. Suff 5F 30
Borlum. High 3F 70
Bornais. W Isl 3D 74
Bornesketaig. High 6E 76
Boroughbridge. N Yor 1A 42
Borough Green. Kent 8C 22
Borreraig. High 8C 76
Borrobol Lodge. High 1J 79
Borrodale. High 1C 68
Borrowash. Derbs 6B 36
Borrowby. N Yor
nr. Northallerton 7B 48
nr. Whitby 4E 48
Borrowston. High 7E 86
Borrowstonehill. Orkn 1F 86
Borrowstoun. Falk 1H 59
Borstal. Medw 7D 22
Borth. Cdgn 4F 24
Borthwick. Midl 4A 60
Borth-y-Gest. Gwyn 7E 32
Borve. High 1F 68
Borwick. Lanc 8D 46
Bosbury. Here 7E 26
Boscastle. Corn 2C 4
Boscombe. Bour 6K 9
Boscombe. Wilts 2L 9
Boscoppa. Corn 6C 4
Bosham. W Sus 5F 10
Bosherston. Pemb 7F 14
Bosley. Ches E 3H 35
Bossall. N Yor 1E 42
Bossiney. Corn 3C 4
Bossingham. Kent 1H 13
Bossington. Som 1H 7
Bostadh. W Isl 7E 82
Bostock Green. Ches W 3E 34
**Boston**. Linc 5L 37
Boston Spa. W Yor 3B 42
Boswarthen. Corn 5H 3
Boswinger. Corn 7B 4
Botallack. Corn 5G 3
Botany Bay. G Lon 4K 21
Botcheston. Leics 1B 28
Botesdale. Suff 4G 31
Bothal. Nmbd 3F 54
Bothampstead. W Ber 6C 20
Bothamsall. Notts 2D 36
Bothel. Cumb 8F 52
Bothenhampton. Dors 6C 8
Bothwell. S Lan 4F 58
Botley. Buck 3G 21
Botley. Hants 4C 10
Botley. Oxon 3B 20
Botloe's Green. Glos 1F 18
Botolph Claydon. Buck 1E 20
Botolphs. W Sus 5J 11
Bottacks. High 7E 78
Bottesford. Leics 6F 36
Bottesford. N Lin 7F 42
Bottisham. Cambs 5B 30
Bottlesford. Wilts 8K 19
Bottomcraig. Fife 5G 67
Bottom o' th' Moor. G Man 6E 40
Botton. N Yor 5D 48
Botton Head. Lanc 1E 40
Bottreaux Mill. Devn 3H 7
Botus Fleming. Corn 5G 5
Botwnnog. Gwyn 7B 32
Bough Beech. Kent 1A 12
Boughrood. Powy 1L 17
Boughspring. Glos 4D 18
Boughton. Norf 1C 30
Boughton. Nptn 5E 28
Boughton. Notts 3D 36
Boughton Aluph. Kent 1G 13
Boughton Green. Kent 8D 22
Boughton Lees. Kent 1G 13
Boughton Malherbe. Kent 1E 12
Boughton Monchelsea. Kent 8D 22
Boughton under Blean. Kent 8G 23
Boulby. Red C 4E 48
Bouldnor. IOW 7A 10
Bouldon. Shrp 3D 26
Boulmer. Nmbd 8K 61
Boulston. Pemb 5F 14
Boultham. Linc 3G 37
Boulton. Derb 6A 36
Boundary. Staf 5H 35
Bounds. Here 8E 26
Bourn. Cambs 6L 29
Bournbrook. W Mid 3J 27
Bourne. Linc 7H 37
The Bourne. Surr 1F 10
Bourne End. Bed 5H 29
Bourne End. Buck 5F 20
Bourne End. C Beds 7G 29
Bourne End. Herts 3H 21
**Bournemouth**. Bour 6J 9
Bournemouth Airport. Dors 6K 9
Bournes Green. Glos 3H 19
Bournes Green. S'end 5F 22
Bournheath. Worc 4H 27
Bournmoor. Dur 6G 55
Bournville. W Mid 3J 27
Bourton. Dors 2F 8
Bourton. N Som 7B 18
Bourton. Oxon 5L 19
Bourton. Shrp 2D 26
Bourton. Wilts 7J 19
Bourton on Dunsmore. Warw 4B 28
Bourton-on-the-Hill. Glos 8K 27
Bourton-on-the-Water. Glos 1K 19
Bousd. Arg 1H 63
Bousta. Shet 2C 90
Boustead Hill. Cumb 6G 53
Bouth. Cumb 7B 46
Bouthwaite. N Yor 8K 47
Boveney. Buck 6G 21
Boveridge. Dors 4J 9
Boverton. V Glam 8J 17
Bovey Tracey. Devn 8H 7
Bovingdon. Herts 3H 21
Bovingdon Green. Buck 5F 20
Bovinger. Essx 3B 22
Bovington Camp. Dors 7G 9
Bow. Devn 5G 7
Bowbank. Dur 3H 47
Bow Brickhill. Mil 8G 29
Bowbridge. Glos 3G 19
Bowburn. Dur 8G 55
Bowcombe. IOW 7B 10
Bowd. Devn 7L 7
Bowden. Devn 7L 5
Bowden. Bord 6C 60
Bowden Hill. Wilts 7H 19
Bowdens. Som 3C 8
Bowderdale. Cumb 5E 46
Bowdon. G Man 1F 34
Bower. Nmbd 3A 54
Bowerchalke. Wilts 3J 9
Bowerhill. Wilts 7H 19
Bower Hinton. Som 4C 8
Bowermadden. High 5D 86
Bowers. Staf 6G 35
Bowers Gifford. Essx 5D 22
Bowershall. Fife 8D 66
Bowertower. High 5D 86
Bowes. Dur 4H 47
Bowgreave. Lanc 3C 40
Bowhousebog. N Lan 4G 59
Bowithick. Corn 7A 6
Bowland Bridge. Cumb 7C 46
Bowlees. Dur 3H 47
Bowley. Here 6D 26
Bowlhead Green. Surr 2G 11
Bowling. W Dun 2C 58
Bowling. W Yor 4K 41
Bowling Bank. Wrex 5B 34
Bowling Green. Worc 6G 27
Bowlish. Som 1E 8
Bowmanstead. Cumb 6B 46
Bowmore. Arg 4C 56
Bowness-on-Solway. Cumb 5G 53
Bowness-on-Windermere. Cumb 6C 46
Bow of Fife. Fife 6G 67
Bowriefauld. Ang 3J 67
Bowscale. Cumb 8H 53
Bowsden. Nmbd 5G 61
Bowside Lodge. High 5L 85
Bowston. Cumb 6C 46
Bow Street. Cdgn 4F 24
Bowthorpe. Norf 1H 31
Box. Glos 3G 19
Box. Wilts 7G 19
Boxbush. Glos 1E 18
Box End. Bed 7H 29
Boxford. Suff 7F 30
Boxford. W Ber 6B 20
Boxgrove. W Sus 5G 11
Box Hill. Wilts 7G 19
Boxley. Kent 8D 22
Boxmoor. Herts 3H 21
Box's Shop. Corn 5B 6
Boxted. Essx 8F 30
Boxted. Suff 6E 30
Boxted Cross. Essx 8G 31
Boxworth. Cambs 5L 29
Boxworth End. Cambs 5L 29
Boyden End. Suff 6D 30
Boyden Gate. Kent 7J 23
Boylestone. Derbs 6K 35
Boylestonfield. Derbs 6K 35
Boyndie. Abers 7F 80
Boynton. E Yor 1J 43
Boys Hill. Dors 4E 8
Boythorpe. Derbs 3A 36
Boyton. Corn 6C 6
Boyton. Suff 7K 31
Boyton. Wilts 2H 9
Boyton Cross. Essx 3C 22
Boyton End. Essx 8C 30
Boyton End. Suff 7D 30
Bozeat. Nptn 6G 29
Braaid. IOM 7C 44
Braal Castle. High 6C 86
Brabling Green. Suff 5J 31
Brabourne. Kent 1H 13
Brabourne Lees. Kent 1G 13
Brabster. High 5E 86
Bracadale. High 2E 68
Bracara. High 6J 69
Braceborough. Linc 8H 37
Bracebridge. Linc 3G 37
Bracebridge Heath. Linc 3G 37
Braceby. Linc 6H 37
Bracewell. Lanc 3G 41
Brackenber. Cumb 4F 46
Brackenfield. Derbs 4A 36
Brackenlands. Cumb 7G 53
Brackenthwaite. Cumb 7G 53
Brackenthwaite. N Yor 2L 41
Brackla. B'end 7J 17
Brackla. High 8J 79
Bracklesham. W Sus 6F 10
Brackletter. High 7B 70
Brackley. Nptn 8C 28
Brackley Hatch. Nptn 7D 28
Brackloch. High 1B 78
**Bracknell**. Brac 7F 20
Braco. Per 7B 66
Bracobrae. Mor 8E 80
Bracon. N Lin 7E 42
Bracon Ash. Norf 2H 31
Bradbourne. Derbs 4L 35
Bradbury. Dur 3M 47
Bradda. IOM 7A 44
Bradden. Nptn 7D 28
Bradenham. Buck 4F 20
Bradenham. Norf 1F 30
Bradenstoke. Wilts 6J 19
Bradfield. Essx 8H 31
Bradfield. Norf 6J 39
Bradfield. W Ber 6D 20
Bradfield Combust. Suff 6E 30
Bradfield Green. Ches E 4E 34
Bradfield Heath. Essx 1H 23
Bradfield St Clare. Suff 6F 30
Bradfield St George. Suff 5F 30
Bradford. Derbs 3L 35
Bradford. Devn 5D 6
Bradford. Nmbd 6J 61
**Bradford**. W Yor 4K 41
Bradford Abbas. Dors 4D 8
Bradford Barton. Devn 4H 7
Bradford Leigh. Wilts 7G 19
Bradford-on-Avon. Wilts 7G 19
Bradford-on-Tone. Som 3L 7
Bradford Peverell. Dors 6E 8
Bradiford. Devn 2E 6
Brading. IOW 7D 10
Bradley. Ches W 2D 34
Bradley. Derbs 5L 35
Bradley. Glos 4F 18
Bradley. Hants 1D 10
Bradley. NE Lin 7K 43
Bradley. N Yor 7J 47
Bradley. Staf 8G 35
Bradley. W Mid 2H 27
Bradley. W Yor 5K 41
Bradley. Wrex 4B 34
Bradley Cross. Som 8C 18
Bradley Green. Ches W 5D 34
Bradley Green. Som 2A 8
Bradley Green. Warw 1L 27
Bradley Green. Worc 5H 27
Bradley in the Moors. Staf 5J 35
Bradley Mount. Ches E 2H 35
Bradley Stoke. S Glo 5E 18
Bradlow. Here 8F 26
Bradmore. Notts 6C 36
Bradmore. W Mid 2G 27
Bradninch. Devn 5K 7
Bradnop. Staf 4J 35
Bradpole. Dors 6C 8
Bradshaw. G Man 6F 40
Bradstone. Devn 7C 6
Bradwall Green. Ches E 3F 34
Bradway. S Yor 1M 35
Bradwell. Derbs 1K 35
Bradwell. Essx 1E 22
Bradwell. Mil 8F 28
Bradwell. Norf 1M 31
Bradwell-on-Sea. Essx 3G 23
Bradwell Waterside. Essx 3F 22
Bradworthy. Devn 4C 6
Brae. High 5K 77
Brae. Shet 1D 90
Braeantra. High 6F 78
Braefield. High 2E 70
Braefindon. High 8G 79
Braegrum. Per 5D 66
Braehead. Ang 2K 67
Braehead. Dum 6K 51
Braehead. Mor 1B 72
Braehead. Orkn 5D 88
Braehead. S Lan
nr. Coalburn 6G 59
nr. Forth 4H 59
Braehoulland. Shet 6G 91
Braemar. Abers 6A 72
Braemore. High
nr. Dunbeath 8B 86
nr. Ullapool 6B 78
Brae of Achnahaird. High 2M 77
Brae Roy Lodge. High 6D 70
Braeside. Abers 2J 73
Braeside. Inv 2M 57
Braes of Coul. Ang 2F 66
Braeswick. Orkn 6F 88
Braetongue. High 6H 85
Braeval. Stir 7K 65
Braevallich. Arg 7D 64
Braewick. Shet 2D 90
Brafferton. Darl 3L 47
Brafferton. N Yor 8B 48
Brafield-on-the-Green. Nptn 6F 28
Bragar. W Isl 7F 82
Bragbury End. Herts 1K 21
Bragleenbeg. Arg 5D 64
Braichmelyn. Gwyn 4F 32
Braides. Lanc 2C 40
Braidwood. S Lan 5G 59
Braigo. Arg 3B 56
Brailsford. Derbs 5L 35
**Braintree**. Essx 1D 22
Braiseworth. Suff 4H 31
Braishfield. Hants 3A 10
Braithwaite. Cumb 2M 45
Braithwaite. S Yor 6D 42
Braithwaite. W Yor 3J 41
Braithwell. S Yor 8C 42
Brakefield Green. Norf 1G 31
Bramber. W Sus 4J 11
Brambridge. Hants 3B 10
Bramcote. Notts 6C 36
Bramcote. Warw 3B 28
Bramdean. Hants 3D 10
Bramerton. Norf 1J 31
Bramfield. Herts 2K 21
Bramfield. Suff 4K 31
Bramford. Suff 7H 31
**Bramhall**. G Man 1G 35
Bramham. W Yor 3B 42
Bramhope. W Yor 3L 41
Bramley. Hants 8D 20
Bramley. S Yor 8B 42
Bramley. Surr 1H 11
Bramley. W Yor 4L 41
Bramley Green. Hants 8D 20
Bramley Head. N Yor 2K 41
Bramley Vale. Derbs 3B 36
Bramling. Kent 8J 23
Brampford Speke. Devn 6J 7
Brampton. Cambs 4K 29
Brampton. Cumb
nr. Appleby-in-Westmorland 3E 46
nr. Carlisle 5K 53
Brampton. Linc 2F 36
Brampton. Norf 7J 39
Brampton. S Yor 7B 42
Brampton. Suff 3L 31
Brampton Abbotts. Here 1E 18
Brampton Ash. Nptn 3E 28
Brampton Bryan. Here 4B 26
Brampton en le Morthen. S Yor 1B 36
Bramshall. Staf 6J 35
Bramshaw. Hants 4L 9
Bramshill. Hants 7E 20
Bramshott. Hants 2F 10
Branault. High 1L 63
Brancaster. Norf 5D 38
Brancaster Staithe. Norf 5D 38
Brancepeth. Dur 8F 54
Branch End. Nmbd 5D 54
Branchill. Mor 8L 79
Brand End. Linc 5L 37
Branderburgh. Mor 6B 80
Brandesburton. E Yor 3J 43
Brandeston. Suff 5J 31
Brand Green. Glos 1F 18
Brandhill. Shrp 4C 26
Brandis Corner. Devn 5D 6
Brandish Street. Som 1J 7
Brandiston. Norf 7H 39
Brandon. Dur 8F 54
Brandon. Linc 5G 37
Brandon. Nmbd 8H 61
Brandon. Suff 3D 30
Brandon. Warw 4B 28
Brandon Bank. Cambs 3C 30
Brandon Creek. Norf 2C 30
Brandon Parva. Norf 1G 31
Brandsby. N Yor 8C 48
Brandy Wharf. Linc 8H 43
Brane. Corn 6H 3
Bran End. Essx 1C 22
Branksome. Pool 6J 9
Bransbury. Hants 1B 10
Bransby. Linc 2F 36
Branscombe. Devn 7L 7
Bransford. Worc 6F 26
Bransgore. Hants 6K 9
Bransholme. Hull 4J 43
Bransley. Shrp 4E 26
Branston. Leics 7F 36
Branston. Linc 3H 37
Branston. Staf 7L 35
Branston Booths. Linc 3H 37
Branstone. IOW 7C 10
Bransty. Cumb 3J 45
Brant Broughton. Linc 4G 37
Brantham. Suff 8H 31
Branthwaite. Cumb
nr. Caldbeck 8G 53
nr. Workington 2K 45
Brantingham. E Yor 5G 43
Branton. Nmbd 8H 61
Branton. S Yor 7D 42
Branton Green. N Yor 1B 42
Branxholme. Bord 8B 60
Branxton. Nmbd 6F 60
Brassington. Derbs 4L 35
Brasted. Kent 8A 22
Brasted Chart. Kent 8A 22
The Bratch. Staf 2G 27
Brathens. Abers 6F 72
Bratoft. Linc 3A 38
Brattleby. Linc 1G 37
Bratton. Som 1J 7
Bratton. Telf 8E 34
Bratton. Wilts 8H 19
Bratton Clovelly. Devn 6D 6
Bratton Fleming. Devn 2F 6
Bratton Seymour. Som 3E 8
Braughing. Herts 1L 21
Braulen Lodge. High 2C 70
Braunston. Nptn 5C 28
Braunstone Town. Leics 1C 28
Braunston-in-Rutland. Rut 1F 28
Braunton. Devn 2D 6
Brawby. N Yor 8E 48
Brawl. High 5L 85
Brawlbin. High 6B 86
Bray. Wind 6G 21
Braybrooke. Nptn 3E 28
Brayford. Devn 2F 6
Bray Shop. Corn 8C 6
Braystones. Cumb 4K 45
Brayton. N Yor 4D 42
Bray Wick. Wind 6F 20
Brazacott. Corn 6B 6
Brea. Corn 4K 3
Breach. W Sus 5E 10
Breachwood Green. Herts 1J 21
Breacleit. W Isl 8E 82
Breaden Heath. Shrp 6C 34
Breadsall. Derbs 5A 36
Breadstone. Glos 3F 18
Breage. Corn 6K 3
Breakachy. High 1E 70
Breakish. High 3H 69
Bream. Glos 3E 18
Breamore. Hants 4K 9
Bream's Meend. Glos 3E 18
Brean. Som 8A 18
Breanais. W Isl 1A 76
Brearton. N Yor 1M 41
Breascleit. W Isl 8F 82
Breaston. Derbs 6B 36
Brecais Àrd. High 3H 69
Brecais Iosal. High 3H 69
Brechfa. Carm 3M 15
Brechin. Ang 2K 67
Breckles. Norf 2F 30
Brecon. Powy 2K 17
**Bredbury**. G Man 8H 41
Brede. E Sus 4E 12
Bredenbury. Here 6E 26
Bredfield. Suff 6J 31
Bredgar. Kent 7E 22
Bredhurst. Kent 7D 22
Bredicot. Worc 6H 27
Bredon. Worc 8H 27
Bredon's Norton. Worc 8H 27
Bredwardine. Here 7B 26
Breedon on the Hill. Leics 7B 36
Breibhig. W Isl
on Barra 6C 74
on Isle of Lewis 8H 83
Breich. W Lot 3H 59
Breightmet. G Man 7F 40
Breighton. E Yor 4E 42
Breinton. Here 8C 26
Breinton Common. Here 8C 26
Breiwick. Shet 3E 90
Brelston Green. Here 1D 18
Bremhill. Wilts 6H 19
Brenachie. High 6H 79
Brenchley. Kent 1C 12
Brendon. Devn 1G 7
**Brent Cross**. G Lon 5K 21
Brent Eleigh. Suff 7F 30
**Brentford**. G Lon 6J 21
Brentingby. Leics 8E 36
Brent Knoll. Som 8B 18
Brent Pelham. Herts 8M 29
**Brentwood**. Essx 4B 22
Brenzett. Kent 3G 13
Brereton. Staf 8J 35
Brereton Cross. Staf 8J 35
Brereton Green. Ches E 3F 34
Brereton Heath. Ches E 3G 35
Bressingham. Norf 3G 31
Bretby. Derbs 7L 35
Bretford. Warw 4B 28
Bretforton. Worc 7J 27
Bretherdale Head. Cumb 5D 46
Bretherton. Lanc 5C 40
Brettabister. Shet 2E 90
Brettenham. Norf 3F 30
Brettenham. Suff 6F 30
Bretton. Flin 3B 34
Bretton. Pet 1J 29
Brewlands Bridge. Ang 1E 66
Brewood. Staf 1G 27
Briantspuddle. Dors 6G 9
Bricket Wood. Herts 3J 21
Bricklehampton. Worc 7H 27
Bride. IOM 4D 44
Bridekirk. Cumb 8F 52
Bridell. Pemb 2H 15
Bridestowe. Devn 7E 6
Brideswell. Abers 2E 72
Bridford. Devn 7H 7
Bridge. Corn 4K 3
Bridge. Kent 8H 23
Bridge. Som 5B 8
Bridge End. Bed 6H 29
Bridge End. Cumb
nr. Broughton in Furness 5M 45
nr. Dalston 7H 53
Bridge End. Linc 6J 37
Bridge End. Shet 4D 90
Bridgefoot. Ang 4G 67
Bridgefoot. Cumb 2K 45
Bridge Green. Essx 8A 30
Bridgehampton. Som 3D 8
Bridge Hewick. N Yor 8M 47
Bridgehill. Dur 6D 54
Bridgemary. Hants 5C 10
Bridgemere. Ches E 5F 34
Bridgemont. Derbs 1J 35
Bridgend. Abers
nr. Huntly 2E 72
nr. Peterhead 2K 73
Bridgend. Ang
nr. Brechin 1J 67
nr. Kirriemuir 3G 67
Bridgend. Arg
nr. Lochgilphead 8C 64
on Islay 3C 56
**Bridgend**. B'end 6J 17
Bridgend. Cumb 4B 46
Bridgend. Devn 7H 5
Bridgend. Fife 6G 67
Bridgend. High 8D 78
Bridgend. Mor 2C 72
Bridgend. Per 5E 66
Bridgend. W Lot 2J 59
Bridgend of Lintrathen. Ang 2
Bridgeness. Falk 1
Bridge of Alford. Abers 4
Bridge of Allan. Stir 8
Bridge of Avon. Mor 2
Bridge of Awe. Arg 5
Bridge of Balgie. Per 3
Bridge of Brown. High 3
Bridge of Cally. Per 2
Bridge of Canny. Abers 6
Bridge of Dee. Dum 5
Bridge of Don. Aber 4
Bridge of Dun. Ang 2
Bridge of Dye. Abers 7
Bridge of Earn. Per 6
Bridge of Ericht. Per 2
Bridge of Feugh. Abers 6
Bridge of Gairn. Abers 6
Bridge of Gaur. Per 2
Bridge of Muchalls. Abers 6
Bridge of Oich. High 5
Bridge of Orchy. Arg 4
Bridge of Walls. Shet 2
Bridge of Weir. Ren 3
Bridge Reeve. Devn
Bridgerule. Devn
Bridge Sollers. Here 7
Bridge Street. Suff 7
Bridge Town. Warw 6
Bridgetown. Devn
Bridgetown. Som
Bridge Trafford. Ches W 2
Bridgeyate. S Glo 6
Bridgham. Norf 3
**Bridgnorth**. Shrp 2
Bridgtown. Staf 1
**Bridgwater**. Som
**Bridlington**. E Yor 1
**Bridport**. Dors
Bridstow. Here 1
**Brierfield**. Lanc 4
Brierley. Glos 2
Brierley. Here 6
Brierley. S Yor 6
Brierley Hill. W Mid 3
Brierton. Hart 8
Briestfield. W Yor 6
Brigg. N Lin 7
Briggate. Norf 7
Briggswath. N Yor 5
Brigham. Cumb 8
Brigham. E Yor 2
**Brighouse**. W Yor 5
Brighstone. IOW 7
Brightgate. Derbs 4
Brighthampton. Oxon 3
Brightholmlee. S Yor 8
Brightley. Devn
Brightling. E Sus 3
Brightlingsea. Essx 2
**Brighton**. Brig 5
Brighton. Corn
Brighton Hill. Hants 1
Brightons. Falk 2
Brightwalton. W Ber 6
Brightwalton Green. W Ber 6
Brightwell. Suff 7
Brightwell Baldwin. Oxon 4
Brightwell-cum-Sotwell. Oxon 4
Brigmerston. Wilts
Brignall. Dur 4
Brig o' Turk. Stir 7
Brigsley. NE Lin 7
Brigsteer. Cumb 7
Brigstock. Nptn 3
Brill. Buck 2
Brill. Corn
Brilley. Here 7
Brimaston. Pemb 4
Brimfield. Here 5
Brimington. Derbs 2
Brimley. Devn
Brimpsfield. Glos 2
Brimpton. W Ber 7
Brims. Orkn 3
Brimscombe. Glos 3
Brimstage. Mers 1
Brincliffe. S Yor 1
Brind. E Yor 4
Brindister. Shet
nr. West Burrafirth 2
nr. West Lerwick 4
Brindle. Lanc 5
Brindley. Ches E 4
Brindley Ford. Stoke 4
Brineton. Staf 8
Bringhurst. Leics 2
Bringsty Common. Here 6
Brington. Cambs 4
Brinian. Orkn 7
Briningham. Norf 6
Brinkhill. Linc 2
Brinkley. Cambs 6
Brinklow. Warw 4
Brinkworth. Wilts 5
Brinscall. Lanc 5
Brinscombe. Som 8
Brinsley. Notts 5
Brinsworth. S Yor 1
Brinton. Norf 6
Brisco. Cumb 6
Brisley. Norf 7
Brislington. Bris 6
Brissenden Green. Kent 2
**Bristol**. Bris 6
Bristol Airport. N Som 7
Briston. Norf 6
Britannia. Lanc 5
Britford. Wilts
Brithdir. Cphy 4
Brithdir. Cdgn 2
Brithdir. Gwyn 1
Briton Ferry. Neat 5
Britwell Salome. Oxon 4
**Brixham**. Torb 6
Brixton. Devn
**Brixton**. G Lon 6
Brixton Deverill. Wilts
Brixworth. Nptn 4
Brize Norton. Oxon 3
The Broad. Here 5
Broad Alley. Worc 5
Broad Blunsdon. Swin 4
Broadbottom. G Man 8
Broadbridge. W Sus 5
Broadbridge Heath. W Sus 2
Broad Campden. Glos 8
Broad Chalke. Wilts
Broadclyst. Devn
Broadfield. Inv 2
Broadfield. Pemb 6
Broadfield. W Sus 2
Broadford. High 3
Broadford Bridge. W Sus 3
Broadgate. Cumb 6
Broad Green. Cambs 6
Broad Green. C Beds 7
Broad Green. Worc
nr. Bromsgrove 4
nr. Worcester 6
Broad Haven. Pemb 5
Broadhaven. High 6
Broad Heath. Staf 7
Broadheath. G Man 1
Broadheath. Worc 5
Broadheath Common. Worc 6
Broadhembury. Devn
Broadhempston. Devn
Broad Hill. Cambs 4
Broad Hinton. Wilts 6
Broadholme. Derbs 5
Broadholme. Linc 2
Broadlay. Carm 6
Broad Laying. Hants 7
Broadley. Lanc 6
Broadley. Mor 7
Broadley Common. Essx 3
Broad Marston. Worc 7
Broadmayne. Dors
Broadmere. Hants 1
Broadmoor. Pemb 6
Broad Oak. Carm 2
Broad Oak. Cumb 5
Broad Oak. Devn
Broad Oak. Dors
Broad Oak. E Sus
nr. Hastings 4
nr. Heathfield 3

d Oak. Here 1C 18
d Oak. Kent 7H 23
doak. Dors 6C 8
doak. Glos 2E 18
doak. Hants 4C 10
drashes. Mor 8D 80
dsea. Abers 7J 81
d's Green. Essx 2C 22
dshard. Som 4C 8
dstairs. Kent 7K 23
dstone. Pool 6J 9
dstone. Shrp 3D 26
d Street. E Sus 4E 12
d Street. Kent
nr. Ashford 1H 13
nr. Maidstone 8E 22
d Street Green. Essx 3E 22
d Town. Wilts 6J 19
dwas. Worc 6F 26
dwath. Cumb 6J 53
dway. Carm
nr. Kidwelly 6K 15
nr. Laugharne 6J 15
dway. Pemb 5E 14
dway. Som 4B 8
dway. Suff 4K 31
dway. Worc 8J 27
dwell. Glos
nr. Cinderford 2D 18
nr. Stow-on-the-Wold 1L 19
dwell. Oxon 3L 19
dwell. Warw 5B 28
dwell House. Nmbd 6C 54
dwey. Dors 7E 8
dwindsor. Dors 5C 8
dwoodkelly. Devn 5F 6
dwoodwidger. Devn 7D 6
'an. High 1E 70
ury. Here 7B 26
el. High 1G 69
aghboy. Caus 3F 93
amin. Worc 6F 26
bridge. Hants 4D 10
dish. Norf 4J 31
encote. Worc 4G 27
enhurst. Hants 5L 9
etsbrae. S Lan 6G 59
ford Street. Suff 5H 31
hall. Nptn 5D 28
ham. Surr 1J 11
hampton. Glos
nr. Bishop's Cleeve 1H 19
nr. Sevenhampton 1J 19
hampton. Here 8D 26
hill. Bord 7A 60
holes. W Yor 6K 41
hurst. Hants 5C 10
lesby. Linc 6J 43
ley. N Som 7C 18
ley Corner. Suff 4E 30
ley Green. Suff
nr. Bury St Edmunds 7D 30
nr. Haverhill 6E 30
leymoor. Cumb 8J 53
moor. W Mid 3H 27
ton. Shrp
nr. Bishop's Castle 3B 26
nr. Madeley 1F 26
nr. Much Wenlock 2D 26
nr. Pontesbury 1B 26
ton. Staf 6G 35
ton. Telf 8F 34
weir. Glos 3D 18
worth. Glos 2G 19
on. Staf 8H 35
ck. N Ayr 6K 57
e. Mor 8K 79
esord. Abers 8E 80
worth. S Yor 7C 42
ig. High 7F 76
orough. C Beds 8G 29
nborough. Wilts 5H 19
n Cross. Ches E 2G 35
oorough. Mers 1B 34
don. Shrp 3E 26
e. Suff 4H 31
e Street. Suff 4H 31
eswell. Suff 6K 31
field. Cumb 7F 52
field. Shrp 4C 26
ford. W Mid 2K 27
ham. Bed 6H 29
ham. Wilts 7H 19
ley. G Lon 7M 21
ley. Herts 1M 21
ley. Shrp 2F 26
ley Cross. G Man 6F 40
ley Green. Kent 2F 12
ley Wood. Staf 7K 35
pton. Medw 7D 22
pton. N Yor
nr. Northallerton 6A 48
nr. Scarborough 7G 49
pton. Shrp 1D 26
pton-on-Swale. N Yor 6L 47
pton Ralph. Som 2K 7
pton Regis. Som 2J 7
sash. Here 1E 18
sberrow. Glos 8F 26
sberrow Heath. Glos 8F 26
sgrove. Worc 4H 27
stead Heath. Staf 8F 34
yard. Here 6E 26
yard Downs. Here 6E 26
ber. Gwyn 7G 33
roft. Shrp 3D 26
est. Cdgn 2K 15
wyn. Cdgn 2J 15
ngton. Wrex 6C 34
ys. Powy 1L 17
ant. Cdgn 6F 24
ydd Arms. Carm 4L 15
dd. Powy 8M 25
garth. Shrp 6A 34
. Carm 6J 15
. Hants
nr. Cadnam 4L 9
nr. Romsey 3M 9
. IOW 7A 10
. Kent 1G 13
. Surr
nr. Guildford 1H 11
nr. Haslemere 2G 11
e. Norf 2J 31
e. Rut 1F 28
eborough. Ferm 6C 92
enby. Linc 8K 43
End. Worc 7G 27
end. Glos 3E 18
field. Lanc 4D 40
field. Ren 3C 58
house. Lanc 1D 40
house. S Yor 1C 36
house Green. Ches E 3G 35
houses. Staf 5H 35
hurst. Mers 1B 34
land. Kent 3F 12
lands. G Man 8F 40
lands. Shrp 5D 34
mans Park. Herts 3K 21
s. Powy 3L 25
sby. Leics 8D 36
s Green. W Sus 3J 11
Street. Essx 4B 22
Street. Kent 2F 12
Street. W Sus 3L 11
thorpe. Glos 2G 19
ville. Norf 2D 30
wood. Surr 8G 21
n. C Beds 7J 29
n. Fife 7G 67
n. Warw 6J 27
ne. Norf 2K 31
ne. Shrp
nr. Cardington 2D 26
nr. Craven Arms 3C 26
ne. Worc 4H 27
nedge. Warr 1F 34
nend. Abers 4G 73
ner's Corner. W Sus 3J 11
nfield. Abers 2J 73
nfield. Essx 2D 22
nfield. Kent
nr. Herne Bay 7H 23
nr. Maidstone 8E 22
nfield. Som 2M 7
nfleet. E Yor 5F 42
n Green. Norf 7F 38
nhall. Ches E 5E 34
Broomhall. Wind 7G 21
Broomhaugh. Nmbd 5D 54
Broom Hill. Dors 5J 9
Broom Hill. Worc 4H 27
Broomhill. High
nr. Grantown-on-Spey 3K 71
nr. Invergordon 6H 79
Broomhill. Norf 1C 30
Broomhill. S Yor 7B 42
Broomhillbank. Dum 2F 52
Broomholm. Norf 6K 39
Broomlands. Dum 1E 52
Broomley. Nmbd 5D 54
Broom of Moy. Mor 8L 79
Broompark. Dur 7F 54
Broom's Green. Glos 8F 26
Brora. High 3K 79
Broseley. Shrp 1E 26
Brotherhouse Bar. Linc 8K 37
Brotheridge Green. Worc 7G 27
Brotherlee. Dur 8C 54
Brothertoft. Linc 5K 37
Brotherton. N Yor 5B 42
Brotton. Red C 4D 48
Broubster. High 5B 86
Brough. Cumb 4F 46
Brough. Derbs 1K 35
Brough. E Yor 5G 43
Brough. High 4D 86
Brough. Notts 4F 36
Brough. Orkn
nr. Finstown 8C 88
nr. St Margaret's Hope 3F 86
Brough. Shet
nr. Benston 2E 90
nr. Booth of Toft 6J 91
on Bressay 3F 90
on Whalsay 1F 90
Broughall. Shrp 5D 34
Brougham. Cumb 3D 46
Brough Lodge. Shet 4K 91
Broughshane. ME Ant 3G 93
Brough Sowerby. Cumb 4F 46
Broughton. Cambs 4K 29
Broughton. Flin 3B 34
Broughton. Hants 2M 9
Broughton. Lanc 4D 40
Broughton. Mil 8F 28
Broughton. Nptn 4F 28
Broughton. N Lin 7G 43
Broughton. N Yor
nr. Malton 8E 48
nr. Skipton 2H 41
Broughton. Orkn 5D 88
Broughton. Oxon 8B 28
Broughton. Bord 6K 59
Broughton. Staf 6F 34
Broughton. V Glam 7J 17
Broughton Astley. Leics 2C 28
Broughton Beck. Cumb 7A 46
Broughton Cross. Cumb 8E 52
Broughton Gifford. Wilts 7G 19
Broughton Green. Worc 5H 27
Broughton Hackett. Worc 6H 27
Broughton in Furness. Cumb 6M 45
Broughton Mills. Cumb 5M 45
Broughton Moor. Cumb 8E 52
Broughton Park. G Man 7G 41
Broughton Poggs. Oxon 3L 19
Broughtown. Orkn 5F 88
Broughty Ferry. D'dee 4H 67
Browland. Shet 2C 90
Brownbread Street. E Sus 4C 12
Brown Candover. Hants 2C 10
Brown Edge. Lanc 6B 40
Brown Edge. Staf 4H 35
Brownhill. Bkbn 4E 40
Brownhill. Shrp 7C 34
Brownhills. Shrp 6E 34
Brownhills. W Mid 1J 27
Brown Knowl. Ches W 4C 34
Brownlow. Ches E 3G 35
Brownlow Heath. Ches E 3G 35
Brown's Green. W Mid 2J 27
Brownshill. Glos 3G 19
Brownston. Devn 6J 5
Brownstone. Devn 5G 7
Browston Green. Norf 1L 31
Broxa. N Yor 6G 49
Broxbourne. Herts 3L 21
Broxburn. E Lot 2D 60
Broxburn. W Lot 2J 59
Broxholme. Linc 2G 37
Broxted. Essx 1B 22
Broxton. Ches W 4C 34
Broxwood. Here 6B 26
Broyle Side. E Sus 4A 12
Brù. W Isl 7G 83
Bruach Mairi. W Isl 8H 83
Bruairnis. W Isl 5D 74
Bruan. High 8E 86
Bruar Lodge. Per 8J 71
Brucehill. W Dun 2B 58
Brucklay. Abers 8J 81
Bruera. Ches W 3C 34
Bruern Abbey. Oxon 1L 19
Bruichladdich. Arg 3B 56
Bruisyard. Suff 5K 31
Bruisyard Street. Suff 5K 31
Brund. Staf 3K 35
Brundall. Norf 1K 31
Brundish. Norf 2K 31
Brundish. Suff 5J 31
Brundish Street. Suff 4J 31
Brunery. High 8J 69
Brunswick Village. Tyne 4F 54
Brunthwaite. W Yor 3J 41
Bruntingthorpe. Leics 2D 28
Brunton. Fife 5G 67
Brunton. Nmbd 7K 61
Brunton. Wilts 8L 19
Brushford. Devn 5F 6
Brushford. Som 3J 7
Brusta. W Isl 5L 75
Bruton. Som 2E 8
Bryansford. New M 7H 93
Bryanston. Dors 5G 9
Bryant's Bottom. Buck 4F 20
Brydekirk. Dum 4F 52
Brymbo. Cnwy 3H 33
Brymbo. Wrex 4A 34
Brympton D'Evercy. Som 4D 8
Bryn. Carm 6M 15
Bryn. G Man 7D 40
Bryn. Neat 5H 17
Bryn. Shrp 3A 26
Brynamman. Carm 3G 17
Brynberian. Pemb 3H 15
Brynbryddan. Neat 5G 17
Bryncae. Rhon 6J 17
Bryncethin. B'end 6J 17
Bryncir. Gwyn 6D 32
Bryncoch. Neat 5G 17
Bryncroes. Gwyn 7B 32
Bryncrug. Gwyn 2F 24
Bryn Du. IOA 3C 32
Bryn Eden. Gwyn 8G 33
Bryn Eglwys. Gwyn 4F 32
Bryneglwys. Den 6L 33
Brynford. Flin 3L 33
Bryn Gates. G Man 7D 40
Bryn Golau. Rhon 6K 17
Bryngwran. IOA 3C 32
Bryngwyn. Mon 3B 18
Bryngwyn. Powy 8L 25
Bryn-henllan. Pemb 3G 15
Brynhoffnant. Cdgn 1K 15
Bryn-llwyn. Den 2K 33
Brynllywarch. Powy 4L 25
Bryn-mawr. Gwyn 7B 32
Brynmawr. Blae 3L 17
Brynmenyn. B'end 6J 17
Brynmill. Swan 5F 16
Brynna. Rhon 6J 17
Brynrefail. Gwyn 4E 32
Brynrefail. IOA 2D 32
Brynsadler. Rhon 6K 17
Bryn-Saith Marchog. Den 5K 33
Brynsiencyn. IOA 4D 32
Brynteg. IOA 2D 32
Brynteg. Wrex 4B 34
Brynygwenyn. Mon 2B 18
Bryn-y-maen. Cnwy 3H 33
Buaile nam Bodach. W Isl 5D 74
Bualintur. High 3F 68
Bubbenhall. Warw 4A 28
Bubwith. E Yor 4E 42
Buccleuch. Bord 8M 59
Buchanan Smithy. Stir 1C 58
Buchanhaven. Abers 1L 73
Buchanty. Per 5C 66
Buchany. Stir 7M 65
Buchley. E Dun 2D 58
Buchlyvie. Stir 8K 65
Buckabank. Cumb 7H 53
Buckden. Cambs 5J 29
Buckden. N Yor 8H 47
Buckenham. Norf 1K 31
Buckerell. Devn 5L 7
Buckfast. Devn 5K 5
Buckfastleigh. Devn 5K 5
Buckhaven. Fife 8G 67
Buckholm. Bord 6B 60
Buckholt. Here 2D 18
Buckhorn Weston. Dors 3F 8
Buckhurst Hill. Essx 4M 21
Buckie. Mor 7D 80
Buckingham. Buck 8D 28
Buckland. Buck 2F 20
Buckland. Glos 8J 27
Buckland. Here 6D 26
Buckland. Herts 8L 29
Buckland. Kent 1K 13
Buckland. Oxon 4M 19
Buckland. Surr 8K 21
Buckland Brewer. Devn 3D 6
Buckland Common. Buck 3G 21
Buckland Dinham. Som 8F 18
Buckland Filleigh. Devn 5D 6
Buckland in the Moor. Devn 8G 7
Buckland Monachorum. Devn 5G 5
Buckland Newton. Dors 5E 8
Buckland Ripers. Dors 7E 8
Buckland St Mary. Som 4A 8
Buckland-tout-Saints. Devn 7K 5
Bucklebury. W Ber 6C 20
Bucklegate. Linc 6L 37
Buckleigh. Devn 3D 6
Buckler's Hard. Hants 6B 10
Bucklesham. Suff 7J 31
Buckley. Flin 3A 34
Buckley Green. Warw 5K 27
Buckley Hill. Mers 8B 40
Bucklow Hill. Ches E 1F 34
Buckminster. Leics 7F 36
Bucknall. Linc 3J 37
Bucknall. Stoke 5H 35
Bucknell. Oxon 1C 20
Bucknell. Shrp 4B 26
Buckpool. Mor 7D 80
Bucksburn. Aber 5H 73
Buck's Cross. Devn 3C 6
Bucks Green. W Sus 2H 11
Buckshaw Village. Lanc 5D 40
Bucks Hill. Herts 3H 21
Bucks Horn Oak. Hants 1F 10
Buck's Mills. Devn 3C 6
Buckton. E Yor 8J 49
Buckton. Here 4B 26
Buckton. Nmbd 6H 61
Buckton Vale. G Man 7H 41
Buckworth. Cambs 4J 29
Budby. Notts 3D 36
Bude. Corn 5B 6
Budge's Shop. Corn 6F 4
Budlake. Devn 5J 7
Budle. Nmbd 6J 61
Budleigh Salterton. Devn 7K 7
Budock Water. Corn 5L 3
Buerton. Ches E 5E 34
Buffler's Holt. Buck 8D 28
Bugbrooke. Nptn 6D 28
Buglawton. Ches E 3G 35
Bugle. Corn 6C 4
Bugthorpe. E Yor 2E 42
Buildwas. Shrp 1E 26
Builth Road. Powy 7K 25
Builth Wells. Powy 7K 25
Bulbourne. Herts 2G 21
Bulby. Linc 7H 37
Bulcote. Notts 5D 36
Buldoo. High 5A 86
Bulford. Wilts 1K 9
Bulford Camp. Wilts 1K 9
Bulkeley. Ches E 4D 34
Bulkington. Warw 3A 28
Bulkington. Wilts 8H 19
Bulkworthy. Devn 4C 6
Bullamoor. N Yor 6A 48
Bull Bay. IOA 1D 32
Bullbridge. Derbs 4A 36
Bullgill. Cumb 8E 52
Bull Hill. Hants 6M 9
Bullinghope. Here 8D 26
Bull's Green. Herts 2K 21
Bullwood. Arg 2L 57
Bulmer. Essx 7E 30
Bulmer. N Yor 1D 42
Bulmer Tye. Essx 8E 30
Bulphan. Thur 5C 22
Bulverhythe. E Sus 5D 12
Bulwark. Abers 1J 73
Bulwell. Nott 5C 36
Bulwick. Nptn 2G 29
Bumble's Green. Essx 3M 21
Bun Abhainn Eadarra. W Isl 3C 76
Bunacaimb. High 7H 69
Bun a' Mhuillinn. W Isl 4D 74
Bunarkaig. High 7B 70
Bunbury. Ches E 4D 34
Bunchrew. High 1G 71
Bundalloch. High 3K 69
Buness. Shet 3L 91
Bunessan. Arg 5J 63
Bungay. Suff 3K 31
Bunkegivie. High 4F 70
Bunker's Hill. Cambs 1M 29
Bunker's Hill. Suff 1M 31
Bunkers Hill. Linc 4K 37
Bunloit. High 3F 70
Bunnahabhain. Arg 2D 56
Bunny. Notts 7C 36
Bunoich. High 5D 70
Bunree. High 1E 64
Bunroy. High 7C 70
Buntait. High 2E 70
Buntingford. Herts 1L 21
Bunting's Green. Essx 8E 30
Bunwell. Norf 2H 31
Burbage. Derbs 2J 35
Burbage. Leics 2B 28
Burbage. Wilts 7L 19
Burcher. Here 5B 26
Burchett's Green. Wind 5F 20
Burcombe. Wilts 2J 9
Burcot. Oxon 4C 20
Burcot. Worc 4H 27
Burcote. Shrp 2F 26
Burcott. Buck 1F 20
Burcott. Som 1D 8
Burdale. N Yor 1F 42
Burdrop. Oxon 8A 28
Bures. Suff 8F 30
The Burf. Worc 5G 27
Burford. Oxon 2L 19
Burford. Shrp 5D 26
Burg. Arg 3J 63
Burgate Great Green. Suff 4G 31
Burgate Little Green. Suff 4G 31
Burgess Hill. W Sus 4L 11
Burgh. Suff 6J 31
Burgh by Sands. Cumb 6H 53
Burgh Castle. Norf 1L 31
Burghclere. Hants 7B 20
Burghead. Mor 7M 79
Burghfield. W Ber 7D 20
Burghfield Common. W Ber 7D 20
Burghfield Hill. W Ber 7D 20
Burgh Heath. Surr 8K 21
Burghill. Here 7C 26
Burgh le Marsh. Linc 3B 38
Burgh Muir. Abers 4G 73
Burgh next Aylsham. Norf 7J 39
Burgh on Bain. Linc 1K 37
Burgh St Margaret. Norf 8L 39
Burgh St Peter. Norf 2L 31
Burghwallis. S Yor 6C 42
Burham. Kent 7D 22
Buriton. Hants 3E 10
Burland. Ches E 4E 34
Burland. Shet 4D 90
Burlawn. Corn 5B 4
Burleigh. Glos 3G 19
Burleigh. Wind 6F 20
Burlescombe. Devn 4K 7
Burleston. Dors 6F 8
Burlestone. Devn 7L 5
Burley. Hants 5L 9
Burley. Rut 8F 36
Burley. W Yor 4L 41
Burleydam. Ches E 5E 34
Burley Gate. Here 7D 26
Burley in Wharfedale. W Yor 3K 41
Burley Street. Hants 5L 9
Burley Woodhead. W Yor 3K 41
Burlingjobb. Powy 6A 26
Burlington. Shrp 8F 34
Burlton. Shrp 7C 34
Burmantofts. W Yor 4M 41
Burmarsh. Kent 2H 13
Burmington. Warw 8L 27
Burn. N Yor 5C 42
Burnage. G Man 8G 41
Burnaston. Derbs 6L 35
Burnbanks. Cumb 4D 46
Burnby. E Yor 3F 42
Burncross. S Yor 8M 41
Burneside. Cumb 6D 46
Burness. Orkn 5F 88
Burneston. N Yor 7M 47
Burnett. Bath 7E 18
Burnfoot. E Ayr 1K 51
Burnfoot. Per 7C 66
Burnfoot. Bord
nr. Hawick 8C 60
nr. Roberton 8B 60
Burngreave. S Yor 1A 36
Burnham. Buck 5G 21
Burnham. N Lin 6H 43
Burnham Deepdale. Norf 5E 38
Burnham Green. Herts 2K 21
Burnham Market. Norf 5E 38
Burnham Norton. Norf 5E 38
Burnham-on-Crouch. Essx 4F 22
Burnham-on-Sea. Som 1B 8
Burnham Overy Staithe. Norf 5E 38
Burnham Overy Town. Norf 5E 38
Burnham Thorpe. Norf 5E 38
Burnhaven. Abers 1L 73
Burnhead. Dum 2C 52
Burnhervie. Abers 4G 73
Burnhill Green. Staf 1F 26
Burnhope. Dur 7E 54
Burnhouse. N Ayr 4B 58
Burniston. N Yor 6H 49
Burnlee. W Yor 7K 41
Burnley. Lanc 4G 41
Burnmouth. Bord 3G 61
Burn Naze. Lanc 3B 40
Burn of Cambus. Stir 7M 65
Burnopfield. Dur 6E 54
Burnsall. N Yor 1J 41
Burnside. Ang 2J 67
Burnside. Ant
nr. Antrim 4G 93
nr. Ballyclare 4H 93
Burnside. E Ayr 8D 58
Burnside. Per 7E 66
Burnside. Shet 6G 91
Burnside. S Lan 4E 58
Burnside. W Lot
nr. Broxburn 2J 59
nr. Winchburgh 2J 59
Burntcommon. Surr 8H 21
Burnt Heath. Essx 1G 23
Burntheath. Derbs 6L 35
Burnt Hill. W Ber 6C 20
Burnt Houses. Dur 3K 47
Burntisland. Fife 1L 59
Burnt Oak. G Lon 4K 21
Burnton. E Ayr 1K 51
Burntstalk. Norf 6D 38
Burntwood. Staf 1J 27
Burntwood Green. Staf 1J 27
Burnt Yates. N Yor 1L 41
Burnwynd. Edin 3K 59
Burpham. Surr 8H 21
Burpham. W Sus 5H 11
Burradon. Nmbd 1C 54
Burradon. Tyne 4F 54
Burrafirth. Shet 2L 91
Burragarth. Shet 3K 91
Burras. Corn 5K 3
Burraton. Corn 6G 5
Burravoe. Shet
nr. North Roe 5H 91
on Mainland 1D 90
on Yell 6K 91
Burray Village. Orkn 2F 86
Burrells. Cumb 4E 46
Burrelton. Per 4E 66
Burren. New M 7G 93
Burren Bridge. New M 7H 93
Burridge. Hants 4C 10
Burridge. Som 5B 8
Burrigill. High 8D 86
Burrill. N Yor 7L 47
Burringham. N Lin 7F 42
Burrington. Devn 4F 6
Burrington. Here 4C 26
Burrington. N Som 8C 18
Burrough End. Cambs 6C 30
Burrough Green. Cambs 6C 30
Burrough on the Hill. Leics 8E 36
Burroughston. Orkn 7E 88
Burrow. Devn 7K 7
Burrow. Som 1J 7
Burrowbridge. Som 3B 8
Burrowhill. Surr 7G 21
Burry. Swan 7L 15
Burry Green. Swan 7L 15
Burry Port. Carm 6L 15
Burscough. Lanc 6C 40
Burscough Bridge. Lanc 6C 40
Bursea. E Yor 4F 42
Burshill. E Yor 3H 43
Bursledon. Hants 5B 10
Burslem. Stoke 5G 35
Burstall. Suff 7G 31
Burstock. Dors 5C 8
Burston. Devn 5G 7
Burston. Norf 3H 31
Burston. Staf 6H 35
Burstow. Surr 1L 11
Burstwick. E Yor 5K 43
Burtersett. N Yor 7G 47
Burtholme. Cumb 5K 53
Burthorpe. Suff 5D 30
Burthwaite. Cumb 7J 53
Burtle. Som 1C 8
Burtoft. Linc 6K 37
Burton. Ches W
nr. Kelsall 3D 34
nr. Neston 2B 34
Burton. Dors
nr. Christchurch 6K 9
nr. Dorchester 6E 8
Burton. Nmbd 6J 61
Burton. Pemb 6F 14
Burton. Som 1L 7
Burton. Wilts
nr. Chippenham 6G 19
nr. Warminster 2G 9
Burton. Wrex 4B 34
Burton Agnes. E Yor 1J 43
Burton Bradstock. Dors 7C 8
Burton-by-Lincoln. Linc 2G 37
Burton Coggles. Linc 7G 37
Burton Constable. E Yor 4J 43
Burton Corner. Linc 5L 37
Burton End. Cambs 7C 30
Burton End. Essx 1B 22
Burton Fleming. E Yor 8H 49
Burton Green. Warw 4L 27
Burton Green. Wrex 4B 34
Burton Hastings. Warw 3B 28
Burton-in-Kendal. Cumb 8D 46
Burton in Lonsdale. N Yor 8E 46
Burton Joyce. Notts 5D 36
Burton Latimer. Nptn 4G 29
Burton Lazars. Leics 8E 36
Burton Leonard. N Yor 1M 41
Burton on the Wolds. Leics 7C 36
Burton Overy. Leics 2D 28
Burton Pedwardine. Linc 5J 37
Burton Pidsea. E Yor 4K 43
Burton Salmon. N Yor 5B 42
Burton's Green. Essx 1E 22
Burton Stather. N Lin 6F 42
Burton upon Stather. N Lin 6F 42
Burton upon Trent. Staf 7L 35
Burton Wolds. Leics 7D 36
Burtonwood. Warr 8D 40
Burwardsley. Ches W 4D 34
Burwarton. Shrp 3E 26
Burwash. E Sus 3C 12
Burwash Common. E Sus 3C 12
Burwash Weald. E Sus 3C 12
Burwell. Cambs 5B 30
Burwell. Linc 2L 37
Burwen. IOA 1D 32
Burwick. Orkn 3F 86
Bury. Cambs 3K 29
Bury. G Man 6G 41
Bury. Som 3J 7
Bury. W Sus 4H 11
Burybank. Staf 6G 35
Bury End. Worc 8J 27
Bury Green. Herts 1A 22
Bury St Edmunds. Suff 5E 30
Burythorpe. N Yor 1E 42
Busbridge. Surr 1G 11
Busby. E Ren 4D 58
Busby. Per 5D 66
Buscot. Oxon 4L 19
Bush. Corn 5B 6
The Bush. M Ulst 5F 93
Bush Bank. Here 6C 26
Bushbury. W Mid 1H 27
Bushby. Leics 1D 28
Bushey. Dors 7H 9
Bushey. Herts 4J 21
Bushey Heath. Herts 4J 21
Bush Green. Norf
nr. Attleborough 2G 31
nr. Harleston 3J 31
Bush Green. Suff 6F 30
Bushley. Worc 8G 27
Bushley Green. Worc 8G 27
Bushmead. Bed 5J 29
Bushmills. Caus 1F 93
Bushmoor. Shrp 3C 26
Bushton. Wilts 6J 19
Bushy Common. Norf 8F 38
Busk. Cumb 7L 53
Buslingthorpe. Linc 1H 37
Bussage. Glos 3G 19
Bussex. Som 2B 8
Busta. Shet 1D 90
Butcher's Cross. E Sus 3B 12
Butcombe. N Som 7D 18
Bute Town. Cphy 4L 17
Butleigh. Som 2D 8
Butleigh Wootton. Som 2D 8
Butlers Marston. Warw 7M 27
Butley. Suff 6K 31
Butley High Corner. Suff 7K 31
Butlocks Heath. Hants 5B 10
Butterburn. Cumb 4L 53
Buttercrambe. N Yor 2E 42
Butterknowle. Dur 3K 47
Butterleigh. Devn 5J 7
Buttermere. Cumb 3L 45
Buttermere. Wilts 7M 19
Buttershaw. W Yor 5K 41
Butterstone. Per 3D 66
Butterton. Staf
nr. Leek 4J 35
nr. Stoke-on-Trent 5G 35
Butterwick. Dur 3A 48
Butterwick. Linc 5L 37
Butterwick. N Yor
nr. Malton 8E 48
nr. Weaverthorpe 8G 49
Butteryhaugh. Nmbd 2L 53
Butt Green. Ches E 4E 34
Buttington. Powy 1A 26
Buttonbridge. Shrp 4F 26
Buttonoak. Shrp 4F 26
Buttsash. Hants 5B 10
Butt's Green. Essx 3D 22
Butt Yeats. Lanc 1D 40
Buxhall. Suff 6G 31
Buxted. E Sus 3A 12
Buxton. Derbs 2J 35
Buxton. Norf 7J 39
Buxworth. Derbs 1J 35
Bwcle. Flin 3A 34
Bwlch. Powy 2L 17
Bwlchderwin. Gwyn 6D 32
Bwlchgwyn. Wrex 4A 34
Bwlch-Llan. Cdgn 7E 24
Bwlchnewydd. Carm 4K 15
Bwlchtocyn. Gwyn 8C 32
Bwlch-y-cibau. Powy 1L 25
Bwlchyddar. Powy 8L 33
Bwlch-y-fadfa. Cdgn 2L 15
Bwlch-y-ffridd. Powy 3K 25
Bwlch y Garreg. Powy 3K 25
Bwlch-y-groes. Pemb 3J 15
Bwlch-y-sarnau. Powy 5K 25
Bybrook. Kent 1G 13
Byermoor. Tyne 6E 54
Byers Garth. Dur 7G 55
Byers Green. Dur 8F 54
Byfield. Nptn 6C 28
Byfleet. Surr 7H 21
Byford. Here 7B 26
Bygrave. Herts 8K 29
Byker. Tyne 5F 54
Byland Abbey. N Yor 8C 48
Bylchau. Cnwy 4J 33
Byley. Ches W 3F 34
Bynea. Carm 7M 15
Byram. N Yor 5B 42
Byrness. Nmbd 1A 54
Bystock. Devn 7K 7
Bythorn. Cambs 4H 29
Byton. Here 5B 26
Bywell. Nmbd 5D 54
Byworth. W Sus 3G 11


## C


Cabharstadh. W Isl 2E 76
Cabourne. Linc 7J 43
Cabrach. Arg 3D 56
Cabrach. Mor 3C 72
Cabragh. M Ulst 5E 92
Cabus. Lanc 3C 40
Cadbury. Devn 5J 7
Cadder. E Dun 2E 58
Caddington. C Beds 2H 21
Caddonfoot. Bord 6B 60
Cadeby. Leics 1B 28
Cadeby. S Yor 7C 42
Cadeleigh. Devn 5J 7
Cade Street. E Sus 3C 12
Cadgwith. Corn 7L 3
Cadham. Fife 7F 66
Cadishead. G Man 8F 40
Cadle. Swan 5F 16
Cadley. Lanc 4D 40
Cadley. Wilts
nr. Ludgershall 8L 19
nr. Marlborough 7L 19
Cadmore End. Buck 4E 20
Cadnam. Hants 4L 9
Cadney. N Lin 7H 43
Cadole. Flin 4M 33
Cadoxton-juxta-Neath. Neat 5G 17
Cadwell. Herts 8J 29
Cadwst. Den 7K 33
Caeathro. Gwyn 4E 32
Caehopkin. Powy 3H 17
Caenby. Linc 1H 37
Caerau. B'end 5H 17
Caerau. Card 7L 17
Cae'r-bont. Powy 3H 17
Cae'r-bryn. Carm 3E 16
Caerdeon. Gwyn 1F 24
Caerdydd. Card 7L 17
Caerfarchell. Pemb 4D 14
Caerffili. Cphy 6L 17
Caerfyrddin. Carm 5L 15
Caergeiliog. IOA 3C 32
Caergwrle. Flin 4B 34
Caergybi. IOA 2B 32
Caerlaverock. Per 6B 66
Caerleon. Newp 4B 18
Caerlleon. Carm 4J 15
Caerllion. Newp 4B 18
Caernarfon. Gwyn 4D 32
Caerphilly. Cphy 6L 17
Caersws. Powy 3K 25
Caerwedros. Cdgn 1K 15
Caerwent. Mon 4C 18
Caerwys. Flin 3L 33
Caim. IOA 2F 32
Caio. Carm 1F 16
Cairinis. W Isl 7K 75
Cairisiadar. W Isl 8D 82
Cairminis. W Isl 5B 76
Cairnbaan. Arg 8C 64
Cairnbulg. Abers 7K 81
Cairncross. Ang 8D 72
Cairndow. Arg 6F 64
Cairness. Abers 7K 81
Cairneyhill. Fife 1J 59
Cairngarroch. Dum 7F 50
Cairnhill. Abers 2F 72
Cairnie. Abers 1D 72
Cairnorrie. Abers 1H 73
Cairnryan. Dum 5F 50
Cairston. Orkn 8B 88
Caister-on-Sea. Norf 8M 39
Caistor. Linc 7J 43
Caistor St Edmund. Norf 1J 31
Caistron. Nmbd 1C 54
Cakebole. Worc 4G 27
Calais Street. Suff 7F 30
Calanais. W Isl 8F 82
Calbost. W Isl 2F 76
Calbourne. IOW 7B 10
Calceby. Linc 2L 37
Calcot. Glos 2J 19
Calcot Row. W Ber 6D 20
Calcott. Kent 7H 23
Calcott. Shrp 8C 34
Caldback. Shet 3L 91
Caldbeck. Cumb 8H 53
Caldbergh. N Yor 7J 47
Caldecote. Cambs
nr. Cambridge 6L 29
nr. Peterborough 3J 29
Caldecote. Herts 8K 29
Caldecote. Nptn 6D 28
Caldecote. Warw 2A 28
Caldecott. Nptn 5G 29
Caldecott. Oxon 4B 20
Caldecott. Rut 2F 28
Calderbank. N Lan 3F 58
Calder Bridge. Cumb 4K 45
Calderbrook. G Man 6H 41
Caldercruix. N Lan 3G 59
Calder Grove. W Yor 6M 41
Calder Mains. High 6B 86
Caldermill. S Lan 5E 58
Calder Vale. Lanc 3D 40
Calderwood. S Lan 4E 58
Caldicot. Mon 5C 18
Caldwell. Derbs 8L 35
Caldwell. N Yor 4K 47
Caldy. Mers 2M 33
Calebrack. Cumb 8H 53
Caledon. M Ulst 6E 92
Calf Heath. Staf 1H 27
Calford Green. Suff 7C 30
Calfsound. Orkn 6E 88
Calgary. Arg 2J 63
Califer. Mor 8L 79
California. Cambs 3B 30
California. Falk 2H 59
California. Norf 8M 39
California. Suff 7H 31
Calke. Derbs 7A 36
Callakille. High 8H 77
Callaly. Nmbd 1D 54
Callander. Stir 7L 65
Callaughton. Shrp 2E 26
Callendoun. Arg 1B 58
Callestick. Corn 3L 3
Calligarry. High 5H 69
Callington. Corn 5F 4
Callingwood. Staf 7K 35
Callow. Here 8C 26
Callowell. Glos 3G 19
Callow End. Worc 7G 27
Callow Hill. Wilts 5J 19
Callow Hill. Worc
nr. Bewdley 4F 26
nr. Redditch 5J 27
Calmore. Hants 4M 9
Calmsden. Glos 3J 19
Calne. Wilts 6H 19
Calow. Derbs 2B 36
Calshot. Hants 5B 10
Calstock. Corn 5G 5
Calstone Wellington. Wilts 7J 19
Calthorpe. Norf 6H 39
Calthorpe Street. Norf 7L 39
Calthwaite. Cumb 7J 53
Calton. N Yor 2H 41
Calton. Staf 4K 35
Calveley. Ches E 4D 34
Calver. Derbs 2L 35
Calverhall. Shrp 6E 34
Calverleigh. Devn 4J 7
Calverley. W Yor 4L 41
Calvert. Buck 1D 20
Calverton. Mil 8E 28
Calverton. Notts 5D 36
Calvine. Per 1B 66
Calvo. Cumb 6F 52
Cam. Glos 4F 18
Camaghael. High 8B 70
Camas-luinie. High 3L 69
Camasnacroise. High 2C 64
Camastianavaig. High 2G 69
Camasunary. High 4G 69
Camault Muir. High 1F 70
Camb. Shet 4K 91
Camber. E Sus 4F 12
Camberley. Surr 7F 20
Camberwell. G Lon 6L 21
Camblesforth. N Yor 5D 42
Cambo. Nmbd 3D 54
Cambois. Nmbd 3G 55
Camborne. Corn 5K 3
Cambourne. Cambs 6L 29
Cambridge. Cambs 6A 30
Cambridge. Glos 3F 18
Cambrose. Corn 4K 3
Cambus. Clac 8B 66
Cambusbarron. Stir 8A 66
Cambuskenneth. Stir 8B 66
Cambuslang. S Lan 3E 58
Cambusnethan. N Lan 4G 59
Cambus o' May. Abers 6D 72
Camden Town. G Lon 5K 21
Cameley. Bath 8E 18
Camelford. Corn 3D 4
Camelon. Falk 1G 59
Camelsdale. W Sus 2F 10
Camer's Green. Worc 8F 26
Camerton. Bath 8E 18
Camerton. Cumb 8E 52
Camerton. E Yor 5K 43
Camghouran. Per 2K 65
Camlough. New M 7G 93
Cammachmore. Abers 6J 73
Cammeringham. Linc 1G 37
Camore. High 4H 79
The Camp. Glos 3H 19
Campbelton. N Ayr 4L 57
Campbeltown. Arg 7G 57
Campbeltown Airport. Arg 7F 56
Cample. Dum 2C 52
Campmuir. Per 4F 66
Campsall. S Yor 6C 42
Campsea Ashe. Suff 6K 31
Camps End. Cambs 7C 30
Campsey. Derr 2D 92
Campton. C Beds 8J 29
Camptoun. E Lot 2C 60
Camptown. Bord 8D 60
Camrose. Pemb 4F 14
Camserney. Per 3B 66
Camster. High 7D 86
Camus Croise. High 4H 69
Camuscross. High 4H 69
Camusdarach. High 6H 69
Camusnagaul. High
nr. Fort William 8A 70
nr. Little Loch Broom 5A 78
Camus Park. Derr 4C 92
Camusteel. High 1J 69
Camusterrach. High 1J 69
Camusvrachan. Per 3L 65
Canada. Hants 4L 9
Canadia. E Sus 4D 12
Canaston Bridge. Pemb 5G 15
Candlesby. Linc 3A 38
Candle Street. Suff 4G 31
Candy Mill. S Lan 5J 59
Cane End. Oxon 6D 20
Canewdon. Essx 4F 22
Canford Cliffs. Pool 7J 9
Canford Heath. Pool 6J 9
Canford Magna. Pool 6J 9
Cangate. Norf 8K 39
Canham's Green. Suff 5G 31
Canholes. Derbs 2J 35
Canisbay. High 4E 86
Canley. W Mid 4M 27
Cann. Dors 3G 9
Cann Common. Dors 3G 9
Cannich. High 2D 70
Cannington. Som 2A 8
Cannock. Staf 8H 35
Cannock Wood. Staf 8J 35
Canonbie. Dum 4H 53
Canon Bridge. Here 7C 26
Canon Frome. Here 7E 26
Canon Pyon. Here 7C 26
Canons Ashby. Nptn 6C 28
Canonstown. Corn 5J 3
Canterbury. Kent 8H 23
Cantley. Norf 1K 31
Cantley. S Yor 7D 42
Cantlop. Shrp 1D 26
Canton. Card 7L 17
Cantray. High 1H 71
Cantraybruich. High 1H 71
Cantraywood. High 1H 71
Cantsdam. Fife 8E 66
Cantsfield. Lanc 8E 46
Canvey Island. Essx 5D 22
Canwick. Linc 3G 37
Canworthy Water. Corn 6B 6
Caol. High 8B 70
Caolas. Arg 3F 62
Caolas. W Isl 6C 74
Caolas Liubharsaigh. W Isl 1E 74
Caolas Scalpaigh. W Isl 4D 76
Caolas Stocinis. W Isl 4C 76
Caol Ila. Arg 2D 56
Caol Loch Ailse. High 3J 69
Caol Reatha. High 3J 69
Capel. Kent 1C 12
Capel. Surr 1J 11
Capel Bangor. Cdgn 4F 24
Capel Betws Lleucu. Cdgn 7F 24
Capel Coch. IOA 2D 32
Capel Curig. Cnwy 5G 33
Capel Cynon. Cdgn 2K 15
Capel Dewi. Carm 4L 15
Capel Dewi. Cdgn
nr. Aberystwyth 4F 24
nr. Llandysul 2L 15
Capel Garmon. Cnwy 5H 33
Capel Green. Suff 7K 31
Capel Gwyn. IOA 3C 32
Capel Gwynfe. Carm 2G 17
Capel Hendre. Carm 3E 16
Capel Isaac. Carm 2E 16
Capel Iwan. Carm 3J 15
Capel-le-Ferne. Kent 2J 13
Capel Llanilltern. Card 7K 17
Capel Mawr. IOA 3D 32
Capel Newydd. Pemb 3J 15
Capel St Andrew. Suff 7K 31
Capel St Mary. Suff 8G 31
Capel Seion. Carm 5M 15
Capel Seion. Cdgn 5F 24
Capel Uchaf. Gwyn 6D 32
Capel-y-ffin. Powy 8A 26
Capenhurst. Ches W 2B 34
Capernwray. Lanc 8D 46
Capheaton. Nmbd 3D 54
Cappagh. M Ulst 5E 92
Cappercleuch. Bord 7L 59
Capplegill. Dum 1F 52
Capton. Devn 6L 5
Capton. Som 2K 7
Caputh. Per 4D 66
Caradon Town. Corn 8B 6
Carbis Bay. Corn 5J 3
Carbost. High
nr. Loch Harport 2E 68
nr. Portree 1F 68
Carbrook. S Yor 1A 36
Carbrooke. Norf 1F 30
Carburton. Notts 2D 36
Carcluie. S Ayr 8B 58
Car Colston. Notts 5E 36
Carcroft. S Yor 7C 42
Cardenden. Fife 8F 66
Cardeston. Shrp 8B 34
Cardewlees. Cumb 6H 53
Cardiff. Card 7L 17
Cardiff Airport. V Glam 8K 17
Cardigan. Cdgn 2H 15
Cardinal's Green. Cambs 7C 30
Cardington. Bed 7H 29
Cardington. Shrp 2D 26
Cardinham. Corn 5D 4
Cardno. Abers 7J 81
Cardow. Mor 1A 72
Cardross. Arg 2B 58
Cardurnock. Cumb 6F 52
Careby. Linc 8H 37
Careston. Ang 1J 67
Carew. Pemb 6G 15
Carew Cheriton. Pemb 6G 15
Carew Newton. Pemb 6G 15
Carey. Here 8D 26
Carfin. N Lan 4F 58
Carfrae. Bord 4C 60
Cargan. ME Ant 3G 93
Cargate Green. Norf 8K 39
Cargenbridge. Dum 4D 52
Cargill. Per 4E 66
Cargo. Cumb 6H 53
Cargreen. Corn 5G 5
Carham. Nmbd 6F 60
Carhampton. Som 1K 7
Carharrack. Corn 4L 3
Carie. Per
nr. Loch Rannah 2L 65
nr. Loch Tay 4L 65
Carisbrooke. IOW 7B 10
Cark. Cumb 8B 46
Carkeel. Corn 5G 5
Carlabhagh. W Isl 7F 82
Carland Cross. Corn 3M 3
Carlbury. Darl 4L 47
Carlby. Linc 8H 37
Carlecotes. S Yor 7K 41
Carleen. Corn 6K 3
Carlesmoor. N Yor 8K 47
Carleton. Cumb
nr. Carlisle 6J 53
nr. Egremont 4K 45
nr. Penrith 3D 46
Carleton. Lanc 3B 40
Carleton. N Yor 3H 41
Carleton. W Yor 5B 42
Carleton Forehoe. Norf 1G 31
Carleton Rode. Norf 2H 31
Carleton St Peter. Norf 1K 31
Carlidnack. Corn 6L 3
Carlingcott. Bath 8E 18
Carlin How. Red C 4E 48
Carlisle. Cumb 6J 53
Carloonan. Arg 6E 64
Carlops. Bord 4K 59
Carlton. Bed 6G 29
Carlton. Cambs 6C 30
Carlton. Leics 1A 28
Carlton. N Yor
nr. Helmsley 7D 48
nr. Middleham 7J 47
nr. Selby 5D 42
Carlton. Notts 5D 36
Carlton. S Yor 6A 42
Carlton. Stoc T 3A 48
Carlton. Suff 5K 31
Carlton. W Yor 5M 41
Carlton Colville. Suff 2M 31
Carlton Curlieu. Leics 2D 28
Carlton Husthwaite. N Yor 8B 48
Carlton in Cleveland. N Yor 5C 48
Carlton in Lindrick. Notts 1C 36
Carlton-le-Moorland. Linc 4G 37
Carlton Miniott. N Yor 7A 48
Carlton-on-Trent. Notts 3F 36
Carlton Scroop. Linc 5G 37
Carluke. S Lan 4G 59
Carlyon Bay. Corn 6C 4
Carmarthen. Carm 5L 15
Carmel. Carm 3E 16
Carmel. Flin 3L 33
Carmel. Gwyn 5D 32
Carmel. IOA 2C 32
Carmichael. S Lan 6H 59
Carmunnock. Glas 4E 58
Carmyle. Glas 3E 58
Carmyllie. Ang 3J 67
Carnaby. E Yor 1J 43
Carnach. High
nr. Lochcarron 3M 69
nr. Ullapool 4M 77
Carnach. Mor 1L 71
Carnach. W Isl 4D 76
Carnachy. High 6K 85
Carnain. Arg 3C 56
Carnais. W Isl 8D 82
Carnan. Arg 3F 62
Carnan. W Isl 1D 74
Carnbee. Fife 7J 67
Carnbo. Per 7D 66
Carn Brea Village. Corn 4K 3
Carndu. High 3K 69
Carnduff. Caus 1G 93
Carne. Corn 8B 4
Carnell. S Ayr 6C 58
Carnforth. Lanc 8D 46
Carn-gorm. High 3L 69
Carnhedryn. Pemb 4E 14
Carnhell Green. Corn 5K 3
Carnie. Abers 5H 73
Carnkie. Corn
nr. Falmouth 5L 3
nr. Redruth 5K 3
Carnkief. Corn 3L 3
Carnlough. ME Ant 3H 93
Carnmoney. Ant 4H 93
Carno. Powy 3J 25
Carnock. Fife 1J 59
Carnon Downs. Corn 4L 3
Carnoustie. Ang 4J 67
Carnteel. M Ulst 6E 92
Carntyne. Glas 3E 58
Carnwath. S Lan 5H 59
Carnyorth. Corn 5G 3
Carol Green. W Mid 4L 27
Carpalla. Corn 6B 4
Carperby. N Yor 7J 47
Carradale. Arg 6H 57
Carragraich. W Isl 4C 76
Carrbridge. High 3K 71
Carr Cross. Lanc 6B 40
Carreglefn. IOA 2C 32
Carrhouse. N Lin 7E 42
Carrick Castle. Arg 8F 64
Carrickfergus. ME Ant 4J 93
Carrick Ho. Orkn 6E 88
Carrickmore. Ferm 5E 92
Carriden. Falk 1J 59
Carrington. G Man 8F 40
Carrington. Linc 4L 37
Carrington. Midl 3M 59
Carrog. Cnwy 6G 33
Carrog. Den 6L 33
Carron. Falk 1G 59
Carron. Mor 1B 72
Carronbridge. Dum 2C 52
Carronshore. Falk 1G 59
Carrowclare. Caus 2E 92
Carrowdore. Ards 5J 93
Carrow Hill. Mon 4C 18
Carr Shield. Nmbd 7B 54
Carrutherstown. Dum 4F 52
Carr Vale. Derbs 3B 36
Carrville. Dur 7G 55
Carryduff. Lis 5H 93
Carsaig. Arg 5L 63
Carscreugh. Dum 5H 51
Carsegowan. Dum 6K 51
Carse House. Arg 3G 57
Carseriggan. Dum 5J 51
Carsethorn. Dum 6D 52
Carshalton. G Lon 7K 21
Carsington. Derbs 4L 35
Carskiey. Arg 1B 50
Carsluith. Dum 6K 51
Carson Park. New M 6J 93
Carsphairn. Dum 2L 51
Carstairs. S Lan 5H 59
Carstairs Junction. S Lan 5H 59
Cartbridge. Surr 8H 21
Carterhaugh. Ang 3H 67
Carter's Clay. Hants 3M 9
Carterton. Oxon 3L 19
Carterway Heads. Nmbd 6D 54
Carthew. Corn 6C 4
Carthorpe. N Yor 7M 47
Cartington. Nmbd 1D 54
Cartland. S Lan 5G 59
Cartmel. Cumb 8B 46
Cartmel Fell. Cumb 7C 46
Cartworth. W Yor 7K 41
Carwath. Cumb 7H 53
Carway. Carm 6L 15
Carwinley. Cumb 4J 53
Cascob. Powy 6M 25
Cas-gwent. Mon 4D 18
Cash Feus. Fife 7F 66
Cashlie. Per 3J 65
Cashmoor. Dors 4H 9
Cas-Mael. Pemb 4G 15
Casnewydd. Newp 5B 18
Cassington. Oxon 2B 20
Cassop. Dur 8G 55
Castell. Cnwy 4G 33
Castell. Den 4L 33
Castell Hendre. Pemb 4G 15
Castell-Nedd. Neat 5G 17
Castell Newydd Emlyn. Carm 2K 15
Castell-y-bwch. Torf 4A 18
Casterton. Cumb 8E 46
Castle. Som 1D 8
Castle Acre. Norf 8E 38
Castle Ashby. Nptn 6F 28
Castlebay. W Isl 6C 74
Castle Bolton. N Yor 6J 47
Castle Bromwich. W Mid 3K 27
Castle Bytham. Linc 8G 37
Castlebythe. Pemb 4G 15
Castle Caereinion. Powy 2L 25
Castle Camps. Cambs 7C 30
Castle Carrock. Cumb 6K 53
Castle Cary. Som 2E 8
Castlecary. N Lan 2F 58
Castlecaulfield. M Ulst 5E 92
Castle Combe. Wilts 6G 19
Castlecraig. High 7J 79
Castledawson. M Ulst 4F 93
Castlederg. Derr 4C 92
Castle Donington. Leics 7B 36
Castle Douglas. Dum 5B 52
Castle Eaton. Swin 4K 19
Castle Eden. Dur 8H 55
Castleford. W Yor 5B 42
Castle Frome. Here 7E 26
Castle Green. Surr 7G 21
Castle Green. Warw 4L 27
Castle Gresley. Derbs 8L 35
Castle Heaton. Nmbd 5G 61
Castle Hedingham. Essx 8D 30
Castle Hill. Kent 1C 12
Castle Hill. Suff 7H 31
Castlehill. Per 4F 66
Castlehill. S Lan 4G 59
Castlehill. W Dun 2B 58
Castle Kennedy. Dum 6G 51
Castle Lachlan. Arg 8E 64
Castlemartin. Pemb 7F 14
Castlemilk. Glas 4E 58
Castlemorris. Pemb 3F 14
Castlemorton. Worc 8F 26
Castle O'er. Dum 2G 53
Castle Park. N Yor 4F 48
Castlerigg. Cumb 3A 46
Castle Rising. Norf 7C 38
Castlerock. Caus 2E 92
Castleroe. Caus 2F 93
Castleside. Dur 7D 54
Castlethorpe. Mil 7E 28
Castleton. Abers 6A 72
Castleton. Arg 1H 57
Castleton. Derbs 1K 35
Castleton. G Man 6G 41
Castleton. Mor 3A 72
Castleton. Newp 5A 18
Castleton. N Yor 5D 48
Castleton. Per 6C 66
Castletown. Cumb 8K 53
Castletown. Dors 8E 8
Castletown. High 5C 86
Castletown. IOM 8B 44
Castletown. Tyne 6G 55
Castlewellan. New M 7H 93
Castley. N Yor 3L 41
Caston. Norf 2F 30
Castor. Pet 2J 29
Caswell. Swan 6E 16

pton. *Wilts* 8K 19
pton Abbas. *Dors* 4G 9
pton Abdale. *Glos* 2J 19
pton Bassett. *Wilts* 6J 19
pton Beauchamp.
*Oxon* 5L 19
pton Bishop. *Som* 8B 18
pton Chamberlayne.
*Wilts* 3J 9
pton Dando. *Bath* 7E 18
pton Dundon. *Som* 2C 8
pton Greenfield. *S Glo* 5D 18
pton Martin. *Bath* 8D 18
pton Pauncefoot. *Som* 3E 8
pton Valence. *Dors* 6D 8
rie. *Fife* 1J 59
rie. *Per* 5A 66
glen. *High* 1E 64
hra. *Arg* 1K 57
hra. *High* 3K 69
er Green. *Lanc* 2C 40
erton. *Worc* 8H 27
icote. *Glos* 1K 19
orrat. *N Lan* 2F 58
over. *Shrp* 1C 26
yhurst. *W Sus* 3J 11
yisland. *New M* 7J 93
ysthorpe. *N Yor* 8E 48
ythorpe. *N Yor* 2A 42
y Weston. *Suff* 4F 30
ord. *Hants* 2F 10
don's Shop. *Corn* 8B 6
erstone. *Leics* 1A 28
ham. *Norf* 7D 38
**leton**. *Ches E* 3G 35
l-y-wal. *Gwyn* 6G 33
resbury. *N Som* 7C 18
reve. *Staf* 8H 35
am. *S Glo* 6E 18
aval. *Mor* 8K 79
gsby. *Linc* 4K 37
gton. *Cambs*
nr. Fenstanton 5L 29
nr. Sawtry 3J 29
**sbrough**. *S Yor* 8C 42
by. *Arg* 3B 56
holme. *Linc* 8M 43
ton. *Cumb* 6B 46
ton. *E Yor* 4J 43
ton Cold. *N Yor* 2H 41
tone. *N Yor* 1H 41
. *Ards* 5J 93
**ah's Quay**. *Flin* 2A 34
el. *Arg* 4D 64
el Park. *E Ayr* 8E 58
sta. *High* 6F 76
or. *ME Ant* 4G 93
or Downs. *Corn* 5J 3
ck. *Wilts* 8J 19
n Bridge. *High* 8F 78
nley. *N Yor* 3H 41
nsyth. *Ang* 3J 67
rdan. *High* 2G 69
all. *Staf* 5H 35
**ett**. *Dur* 6E 54
able Burton. *N Yor* 6K 47
antine. *Corn* 6L 3
antine Bay. *Corn* 4A 4
n. *High* 8E 78
llich. *High* 6G 79
y. *Cnwy* 3G 33
er. *Kent* 7F 22
er's Green. *Suff* 5E 30
en. *E Sus* 5D 12
*IOM* 7C 44
oury. *Devn* 5D 6
oury Wick. *Devn* 5C 6
nam. *Wind* 5F 20
nam Dean. *Wind* 5F 20
nam Rise. *Wind* 5F 20
nill. *Worc* 6J 27
ey. *Suff* 4K 31
ey. *Worc* 3G 27
ey Green. *Oxon* 4D 20
ney. *Abers* 6H 73
sbridge. *E Sus* 4M 11
sey Green. *Worc* 5H 27
shill. *Staf* 5H 35
smill Green. *Essx* 3C 22
**stown**. *M Ulst* 5F 93
am. *W Sus* 3J 11
ag. *Medw* 6D 22
ag Street. *Medw* 6D 22
be. *Corn*
nr. Bude 4B 6
nr. St Austell 6B 4
nr. Truro 4M 3
be. *Devn*
nr. Sidmouth 6L 7
nr. Teignmouth 8J 7
be. *Glos* 4F 18
be. *Hants* 3D 10
be. *Wilts* 8K 19
be Bissett. *Wilts* 3K 9
be Hill. *Glos* 1G 19
be Keynes. *Dors* 7G 9
bes. *W Sus* 5J 11
ersale. *Essx* 3A 22
ersale Street. *Essx* 3A 22
er's Corner. *Kent* 1A 12
er Street. *Kent* 8K 23
am. *W Sus* 4H 11
der Corner. *Cambs* 2L 29
ck. *Suff* 7H 31
rd. *Essx* 1F 22
rd Green. *Essx* 1F 22
ove. *N Yor* 1M 41
er. *Shet* 6J 91
*Bed* 7J 29
y. *Dur* 3J 47
w Dale. *Derbs* 2K 35
anthorpe. *York* 3C 42
*Lanc* 4C 40
thorne. *Corn* 5B 6
nhall. *Ches E* 4F 34
nhall. *Staf* 8H 35
nhall Moss. *Ches E* 4F 34
rhouse. *Corn* 5J 3
cegate. *Shrp* 3F 26
ngford. *Cambs* 3J 29
estone. *Devn* 5G 7
ll. *Lanc* 6D 40
ll Moor. *Lanc* 6D 40
le. *W Sus* 3J 11
aw Holm. *Bord* 3J 53
er Green. *Lanc* 4E 40
on Magna. *Warw* 3B 28
Green. *Warw* 5K 27
all Green. *Essx* 3M 21
Heath. *W Mid* 4K 27
Hewick. *N Yor* 8M 47
ll. *Dur* 7B 54
orne. *W Sus* 2L 11
iney. *Shrp* 6C 34
Green. *Norf* 6F 38
horne. *Hants* 4M 9
dge. *Nmbd* 5C 54
. *Nptn* 3F 28
Glen. *Linc* 7G 37
n. *N Ayr* 6K 57
y. *Shrp* 4E 26
*Som* 4M 7
Castle. *Dors* 7H 9
Mullen. *Dors* 6H 9
n. *Shrp* 3C 26
ff. *Abers* 5B 72
mpton. *Hants* 3D 10
y. *Caus* 2G 93
. *Dum* 2A 52
nau. *Neat* 5G 17
. *Warw* 3M 27
Ash. *Warw* 3L 27
Moor. *Warw* 3L 27
ston. *S Lan* 6J 59
a. *IOM* 6D 44
gbeg. *Arg* 3E 62
gmore. *Arg*
n Coll 1H 63
n Tiree 3E 62
Row. *Lanc* 4C 40
y. *Cumb* 5L 45
orth. *Dur* 8G 55
ill. *Abers* 8E 80
ill. *High* 4F 78
ill-on-Tweed. *Nmbd* 6F 60
olme. *W Yor* 5H 41
h Hall End. *Essx* 8C 30
uoy. *Orkn* 1G 87
ggs. *Dur* 7B 54
Cornsay. *Dur* 7E 54
Cornsay Colliery. *Dur* 7E 54
Corntown. *High* 8F 78
Corntown. *V Glam* 7J 17
Cornwall Airport Newquay.
*Corn* 5A 4
Cornwell. *Oxon* 1L 19
Cornwood. *Devn* 6J 5
Cornworthy. *Devn* 6L 5
Corpach. *High* 8A 70
Corpusty. *Norf* 7H 39
Corra. *Dum* 5C 52
Corran. *High*
nr. Arnisdale 1E 64
nr. Fort William 5K 69
Corrany. *IOM* 6D 44
Corribeg. *High* 8L 69
Corrie. *N Ayr* 5K 57
Corrie Common. *Dum* 3G 53
Corriecravie. *N Ayr* 7J 57
Corriekinloch. *High* 1D 78
Corriemoillie. *High* 7D 78
Corrievarkie Lodge. *Per* 8F 70
Corrievorrie. *High* 3H 71
Corrigall. *Orkn* 8C 88
Corrimony. *High* 2D 70
Corringham. *Linc* 8F 42
**Corringham**. *Thur* 5D 22
Corris. *Gwyn* 2G 25
Corris Uchaf. *Gwyn* 2G 25
Corrour Shooting Lodge.
*High* 1J 65
Corry. *High* 3H 69
Corrybrough. *High* 3J 71
Corrygills. *N Ayr* 6K 57
Corry of Ardnagrask. *High* 1F 70
Corsback. *High*
nr. Dunnet 4D 86
nr. Halkirk 6D 86
Corscombe. *Dors* 5D 8
Corse. *Abers* 1F 72
Corse. *Glos* 1F 18
Corsehill. *Abers* 8J 81
Corse Lawn. *Worc* 8G 27
Corse of Kinnoir. *Abers* 1E 72
**Corsham**. *Wilts* 6G 19
Corsley. *Wilts* 1G 9
Corsley Heath. *Wilts* 1G 9
Corsock. *Dum* 4B 52
Corston. *Bath* 7E 18
Corston. *Wilts* 5H 19
Corstorphine. *Edin* 2L 59
Cortachy. *Ang* 2G 67
Corton. *Suff* 2M 31
Corton. *Wilts* 1H 9
Corton Denham. *Som* 3E 8
Corwar House. *S Ayr* 3H 51
Corwen. *Den* 6K 33
Coryates. *Dors* 7E 8
Coryton. *Devn* 7D 6
Coryton. *Thur* 5D 22
Cosby. *Leics* 2C 28
Coscote. *Oxon* 5C 20
Coseley. *W Mid* 2H 27
Cosgrove. *Nptn* 7E 28
Cosham. *Port* 5D 10
Cosheston. *Pemb* 6G 15
Coskills. *N Lin* 6H 43
Cosmeston. *V Glam* 8L 17
Cossall. *Notts* 5B 36
Cossington. *Leics* 8D 36
Cossington. *Som* 1B 8
Costa. *Orkn* 7C 88
Costessey. *Norf* 8H 39
Costock. *Notts* 7C 36
Coston. *Leics* 7F 36
Coston. *Norf* 1G 31
Cote. *Oxon* 3A 20
Cotebrook. *Ches W* 3D 34
Cotehill. *Cumb* 6J 53
Cotes. *Cumb* 7C 46
Cotes. *Leics* 7C 36
Cotes. *Staf* 6G 35
Cotesbach. *Leics* 3C 28
Cotes Heath. *Staf* 6G 35
Cotford St Luke. *Som* 3L 7
Cotgrave. *Notts* 6D 36
Cothal. *Abers* 4H 73
Cotham. *Notts* 5E 36
Cothelstone. *Som* 2L 7
Cotheridge. *Worc* 6F 26
Cotherstone. *Dur* 4J 47
Cothill. *Oxon* 4B 20
Cotland. *Mon* 3D 18
Cotleigh. *Devn* 5M 7
Cotmanhay. *Derbs* 5B 36
Coton. *Cambs* 6M 29
Coton. *Nptn* 4D 28
Coton. *Staf*
nr. Gnosall 7G 35
nr. Stone 6H 35
nr. Tamworth 1K 27
Coton Clanford. *Staf* 7G 35
Coton Hayes. *Staf* 6H 35
Coton Hill. *Shrp* 8C 34
Coton in the Clay. *Staf* 7K 35
Coton in the Elms. *Derbs* 8L 35
Cotonwood. *Shrp* 6D 34
Cotonwood. *Staf* 7G 35
Cott. *Devn* 5K 5
Cott. *Orkn* 7F 88
Cottam. *E Yor* 1G 43
Cottam. *Lanc* 4D 40
Cottam. *Notts* 2F 36
Cottartown. *High* 2L 71
Cottarville. *Nptn* 5E 28
Cottenham. *Cambs* 5A 30
Cotterdale. *N Yor* 6G 47
Cottered. *Herts* 1L 21
Cotterstock. *Nptn* 2H 29
Cottesbrooke. *Nptn* 4E 28
Cottesmore. *Rut* 8G 37
Cotteylands. *Devn* 4J 7
Cottingham. *E Yor* 4H 43
Cottingham. *Nptn* 2F 28
Cottingley. *W Yor* 4K 41
Cottisford. *Oxon* 8C 28
Cotton. *Staf* 5J 35
Cotton. *Suff* 5G 31
Cotton End. *Bed* 7H 29
Cottown. *Abers* 1H 73
Cotts. *Devn* 5G 5
Cotwalton. *Staf* 6H 35
Couch's Mill. *Corn* 6D 4
Coughton. *Here* 1D 18
Coughton. *Warw* 5J 27
Coulags. *High* 1L 69
Coulby Newham. *Midd* 4C 48
Coulderton. *Cumb* 4J 45
Coulin Lodge. *High* 8M 77
Coull. *Abers* 5E 72
Coulport. *Arg* 1M 57
**Coulsdon**. *G Lon* 8K 21
Coulston. *Wilts* 8H 19
Coulter. *S Lan* 6J 59
Coultings. *Som* 1M 7
Coulton. *N Yor* 8D 48
Cound. *Shrp* 1D 26
Coundon. *Dur* 3L 47
Coundon Grange. *Dur* 3L 47
Countersett. *N Yor* 7H 47
Countess. *Wilts* 1K 9
Countess Cross. *Essx* 8E 30
Countesthorpe. *Leics* 2C 28
Countisbury. *Devn* 1G 7
Coupar Angus. *Per* 3F 66
Coupe Green. *Lanc* 5D 40
Coupland. *Cumb* 4F 46
Coupland. *Nmbd* 6G 61
Cour. *Arg* 5H 57
Courance. *Dum* 2E 52
Court-at-Street. *Kent* 2G 13
Courteachan. *High* 6H 69
Courteenhall. *Nptn* 6E 28
Court Henry. *Carm* 2E 16
Courtsend. *Essx* 4G 23
Courtway. *Som* 2M 7
Cousland. *Midl* 3A 60
Cousley Wood. *E Sus* 2C 12
Coustonn. *Arg* 2K 57
Cove. *Arg* 1M 57
Cove. *Devn* 4J 7
Cove. *Hants* 8F 20
Cove. *High* 4K 77
Cove. *Bord* 2E 60
Cove Bay. *Aber* 5J 73
Covehithe. *Suff* 3M 31
Coven. *Staf* 1H 27
Coveney. *Cambs* 3A 30
Covenham St Bartholomew.
*Linc* 8L 43
Covenham St Mary. *Linc* 8L 43
Coven Heath. *Staf* 1H 27
**Coventry**. *W Mid* 4M 27
Coverack. *Corn* 7L 3
Coverham. *N Yor* 7K 47
Covesea. *Mor* 6A 80
Covingham. *Swin* 5K 19
Covington. *Cambs* 4H 29
Covington. *S Lan* 6H 59
Cowan Bridge. *Lanc* 8E 46
Cowan Head. *Cumb* 6C 46
Cowbar. *Red C* 4E 48
Cowbeech. *E Sus* 4C 12
Cowbit. *Linc* 8K 37
Cowbridge. *V Glam* 7J 17
Cowden. *Kent* 1A 12
**Cowdenbeath**. *Fife* 8E 66
Cowdenburn. *Bord* 4L 59
Cowdenend. *Fife* 8E 66
Cowers Lane. *Derbs* 5M 35
**Cowes**. *IOW* 6B 10
Cowesby. *N Yor* 7B 48
Cowfold. *W Sus* 3K 11
Cowfords. *Mor* 7C 80
Cowgill. *Cumb* 7F 46
Cowie. *Abers* 7H 73
Cowie. *Stir* 1G 59
Cowlam. *E Yor* 1G 43
Cowley. *Devn* 6J 7
Cowley. *Glos* 2H 19
Cowley. *G Lon* 5H 21
Cowley. *Oxon* 3C 20
Cowley. *Staf* 8G 35
Cowleymoor. *Devn* 4J 7
Cowling. *Lanc* 6D 40
Cowling. *N Yor*
nr. Bedale 7L 47
nr. Glusburn 3H 41
Cowlinge. *Suff* 6D 30
Cowmes. *W Yor* 6K 41
Cowpe. *Lanc* 5G 41
Cowpen. *Nmbd* 3F 54
Cowpen Bewley. *Stoc T* 3B 48
Cowplain. *Hants* 4D 10
Cowshill. *Dur* 7B 54
Cowslip Green. *N Som* 7C 18
Cowstrandburn. *Fife* 8D 66
Cowthorpe. *N Yor* 2B 42
Coxall. *Here* 4B 26
Coxbank. *Ches E* 5E 34
Coxbench. *Derbs* 5A 36
Cox Common. *Suff* 3L 31
Coxford. *Norf* 7E 38
Cox Green. *Surr* 2H 11
Cox Green. *Tyne* 6G 55
Coxgreen. *Staf* 3G 27
Coxheath. *Kent* 8D 22
Coxhoe. *Dur* 8G 55
Coxley. *Som* 1D 8
Coxwold. *N Yor* 8C 48
Coychurch. *B'end* 6J 17
Coylton. *S Ayr* 8C 58
Coylumbridge. *High* 4K 71
Coynach. *Abers* 5D 72
Coynachie. *Abers* 2D 72
Coytrahen. *B'end* 6H 17
Crabbs Cross. *Worc* 5J 27
Crabgate. *Norf* 7G 39
Crab Orchard. *Dors* 5J 9
Crabtree. *W Sus* 3K 11
Crabtree Green. *Wrex* 5B 34
Crackaig. *High* 2K 79
Crackenthorpe. *Cumb* 3E 46
Crackington Haven. *Corn* 2D 4
Crackley. *Staf* 4G 35
Crackley. *Warw* 4L 27
Crackleybank. *Shrp* 8F 34
Crackpot. *N Yor* 6H 47
Cracoe. *N Yor* 1H 41
Craddock. *Devn* 4K 7
Cradhlastadh. *W Isl* 8D 82
Cradley. *Here* 7F 26
Cradley. *W Mid* 3H 27
Cradoc. *Powy* 1K 17
Crafthole. *Corn* 6F 4
Crafton. *Buck* 2F 20
Cragabus. *Arg* 5C 56
Crag Foot. *Lanc* 8C 46
Craggan. *High* 3L 71
Cragganmore. *Mor* 2A 72
Cragganvallie. *High* 2F 70
Craggie. *High* 2J 79
Craggiemore. *High* 2H 71
Cragg Vale. *W Yor* 5J 41
Craghead. *Dur* 6F 54
Crai. *Powy* 2H 17
Craichie. *Ang* 3J 67
Craig. *Arg* 4E 64
Craig. *Dum* 4A 52
Craig. *High*
nr. Achnashellach 1M 69
nr. Lower Diabaig 7J 77
nr. Stromeferry 2K 69
Craiganour Lodge. *Per* 2L 65
**Craigavon**. *Arm* 6G 93
Craigbrack. *Arg* 8F 64
Craig-Cefn-Parc. *Swan* 4F 16
Craigdallie. *Per* 5F 66
Craigdam. *Abers* 2H 73
Craigdarragh. *Derr* 3D 92
Craigdarroch. *E Ayr* 1M 51
Craigdarroch. *High* 8E 78
Craigdhu. *High* 1E 70
Craigearn. *Abers* 4G 73
Craigellachie. *Mor* 1B 72
Craigend. *Per* 5E 66
Craigendoran. *Arg* 1B 58
Craigends. *Ren* 3C 58
Craigenputtock. *Dum* 3B 52
Craigens. *E Ayr* 8D 58
Craighall. *Edin* 2K 59
Craighead. *Fife* 6K 67
Craighouse. *Arg* 3E 56
Craigie. *Abers* 4J 73
Craigie. *D'dee* 4H 67
Craigie. *Per*
nr. Blairgowrie 3E 66
nr. Perth 5E 66
Craigie. *S Ayr* 6C 58
Craigielaw. *E Lot* 2B 60
Craiglemine. *Dum* 8K 51
Craig-llwyn. *Shrp* 8M 33
Craiglockhart. *Edin* 2L 59
Craig Lodge. *Arg* 2K 57
Craigmalloch. *E Ayr* 2K 51
Craigmaud. *Abers* 8H 81
Craigmill. *Stir* 8B 66
Craigmillar. *Edin* 2L 59
Craigmore. *Arg* 3L 57
Craigmuie. *Dum* 3B 52
Craignair. *Dum* 5C 52
Craignant. *Shrp* 6A 34
Craigneuk. *N Lan*
nr. Airdrie 3F 58
nr. Motherwell 4F 58
Craignure. *Arg* 4B 64
Craigo. *Ang* 1K 67
Craigrory. *High* 1G 71
Craigrothie. *Fife* 6G 67
Craigs. *Dum* 4G 53
The Craigs. *High* 4E 78
Craigshill. *W Lot* 3J 59
Craigton. *Aber* 5H 73
Craigton. *Abers* 5G 73
Craigton. *Ang*
nr. Carnoustie 4J 67
nr. Kirriemuir 2G 67
Craigton. *High* 1G 71
Craigtown. *High* 6L 85
Craig-y-Duke. *Neat* 4G 17
Craig-y-nos. *Powy* 3H 17
Craik. *Bord* 1H 53
Crail. *Fife* 7K 67
Crailing. *Bord* 7D 60
Crailinghall. *Bord* 7D 60
Crakehill. *N Yor* 8B 48
Crakemarsh. *Staf* 6J 35
Crambe. *N Yor* 1E 42
Crambeck. *N Yor* 1E 42
**Cramlington**. *Nmbd* 4F 54
Cramond. *Edin* 2K 59
Cramond Bridge. *Edin* 2K 59
Cranage. *Ches E* 3F 34
Cranagh. *Derr* 4D 92
Cranberry. *Staf* 6G 35
Cranborne. *Dors* 4J 9
Cranbourne. *Brac* 6G 21
Cranbrook. *Devn* 6K 7
Cranbrook. *Kent* 2D 12
Cranbrook Common. *Kent* 2D 12
Crane Moor. *S Yor* 7M 41
Crane's Corner. *Norf* 8F 38
Cranfield. *C Beds* 7G 29
Cranford. *G Lon* 6J 21
Cranford St Andrew. *Nptn* 4G 29
Cranford St John. *Nptn* 4G 29
Cranham. *Glos* 2G 19
Cranham. *G Lon* 5B 22
Crank. *Mers* 8D 40
**Cranleigh**. *Surr* 2H 11
Cranley. *Suff* 4H 31
Cranloch. *Mor* 8B 80
Cranmer Green. *Suff* 4G 31
Cranmore. *IOW* 6B 10
Cranmore. *Linc* 1J 29
Crannich. *Arg* 3L 63
Crannoch. *Mor* 8D 80
Cranoe. *Leics* 2E 28
Cransford. *Suff* 5K 31
Cranshaws. *Bord* 3D 60
Cranstal. *IOM* 4D 44
Crantock. *Corn* 2L 3
Cranwell. *Linc* 5H 37
Cranwich. *Norf* 2D 30
Cranworth. *Norf* 1F 30
Craobh Haven. *Arg* 7B 64
Craobhnaclag. *High* 1E 70
Crapstone. *Devn* 5H 5
Crarae. *Arg* 8D 64
Crask. *High*
nr. Bettyhill 5K 85
nr. Lairg 1F 78
Crask of Aigas. *High* 1E 70
Craster. *Nmbd* 7K 61
Craswall. *Here* 8A 26
Cratfield. *Suff* 4K 31
Crathes. *Abers* 6G 73
Crathie. *Abers* 6B 72
Crathie. *High* 6F 70
Crathorne. *N Yor* 5B 48
Craven Arms. *Shrp* 3C 26
Crawcrook. *Tyne* 5E 54
Crawford. *Lanc* 7C 40
Crawford. *S Lan* 7H 59
Crawforddyke. *S Lan* 4G 59
Crawfordjohn. *S Lan* 7G 59
Crawfordsburn. *Ards* 4J 93
Crawick. *Dum* 8F 58
Crawley. *Devn* 5A 8
Crawley. *Hants* 2B 10
Crawley. *Oxon* 2M 19
**Crawley**. *W Sus* 2K 11
Crawley Down. *W Sus* 2L 11
Crawley End. *Essx* 7M 29
Crawley Side. *Dur* 7C 54
Crawshawbooth. *Lanc* 5G 41
Crawton. *Abers* 7H 73
Cray. *N Yor* 8H 47
Cray. *Per* 1E 66
Crayford. *G Lon* 6B 22
Crayke. *N Yor* 8C 48
Craymere Beck. *Norf* 6G 39
Crays Hill. *Essx* 4D 22
Cray's Pond. *Oxon* 5D 20
Crazies Hill. *Wok* 5E 20
Creacombe. *Devn* 4H 7
Creagan. *Arg* 3D 64
Creag Aoil. *High* 8B 70
Creag Ghoraidh. *W Isl* 1D 74
Creaguaineach Lodge. *High* 1H 65
Creamore Bank. *Shrp* 6D 34
Creaton. *Nptn* 4E 28
Creca. *Dum* 4G 53
Credenhill. *Here* 7C 26
Crediton. *Devn* 5H 7
Creebridge. *Dum* 5K 51
Creech. *Dors* 7H 9
Creech Heathfield. *Som* 3A 8
Creech St Michael. *Som* 3A 8
Creed. *Corn* 7B 4
Creekmoor. *Pool* 6H 9
Creekmouth. *G Lon* 5A 22
Creeting St Mary. *Suff* 6G 31
Creeting St Peter. *Suff* 6G 31
Creeton. *Linc* 7H 37
Creetown. *Dum* 6K 51
Creggan. *Ferm* 5E 92
Creggan. *New M* 7F 93
Creggans. *Arg* 7E 64
Cregneash. *IOM* 8A 44
Cregrina. *Powy* 7L 25
Creich. *Arg* 5J 63
Creich. *Fife* 5G 67
Creighton. *Staf* 6J 35
Creigiau. *Card* 6K 17
Cremyll. *Corn* 6G 5
Crendell. *Dors* 4J 9
Crepkill. *High* 1F 68
Cressage. *Shrp* 1D 26
Cressbrook. *Derbs* 2K 35
Cresselly. *Pemb* 6G 15
Cressing. *Essx* 1D 22
Cresswell. *Nmbd* 2F 54
Cresswell. *Staf* 6H 35
Cresswell Quay. *Pemb* 6G 15
Creswell. *Derbs* 2C 36
Creswell Green. *Staf* 8J 35
Cretingham. *Suff* 5J 31
**Crewe**. *Ches E* 4F 34
Crewe-by-Farndon. *Ches W* 4C 34
Crewgreen. *Powy* 8B 34
Crewkerne. *Som* 5C 8
Crews Hill. *G Lon* 3L 21
Crewton. *Derb* 6A 36
Crianlarich. *Stir* 5H 65
Cribbs Causeway. *S Glo* 5D 18
Cribyn. *Cdgn* 1M 15
Criccieth. *Gwyn* 7D 32
Crich. *Derbs* 4A 36
Crichton. *Midl* 3A 60
Crick. *Mon* 4C 18
Crick. *Nptn* 4C 28
Crickadarn. *Powy* 8K 25
Cricket Hill. *Hants* 7F 20
Cricket Malherbie. *Som* 4B 8
Cricket St Thomas. *Som* 5B 8
Crickham. *Som* 1C 8
Crickheath. *Shrp* 7A 34
Crickhowell. *Powy* 3M 17
Cricklade. *Wilts* 4K 19
Cricklewood. *G Lon* 5K 21
Cridling Stubbs. *N Yor* 5C 42
Crieff. *Per* 5B 66
Criftins. *Shrp* 6B 34
Criggion. *Powy* 8A 34
Crigglestone. *W Yor* 6M 41
Crimchard. *Som* 5B 8
Crimdon Park. *Dur* 8H 55
Crimond. *Abers* 8K 81
Crimonmogate. *Abers* 8K 81
Crimplesham. *Norf* 1C 30
Crimscote. *Warw* 7L 27
Crinan. *Arg* 8B 64
Cringleford. *Norf* 1H 31
Crinow. *Pemb* 5H 15
Cripplesease. *Corn* 5J 3
Cripplestyle. *Dors* 4J 9
Cripp's Corner. *E Sus* 3D 12
Croanford. *Corn* 4C 4
Crockenhill. *Kent* 7B 22
Crocker End. *Oxon* 5E 20
Crockerhill. *Hants* 5C 10
Crockernwell. *Devn* 6G 7
Crocker's Ash. *Here* 2D 18
Crockerton. *Wilts* 1G 9
Crocketford. *Dum* 4C 52
Crockey Hill. *York* 3D 42
Crockham Hill. *Kent* 8M 21
Crockhurst Street. *Kent* 1C 12
Crockleford Heath. *Essx* 1G 23
Croeserw. *Neat* 5H 17
Croes-Goch. *Pemb* 3E 14
Croes Hywel. *Mon* 2B 18
Croes-lan. *Cdgn* 2K 15
Croesor. *Gwyn* 6F 32
**Croesoswallt**. *Shrp* 7A 34
Croesyceiliog. *Carm* 5L 15
Croesyceiliog. *Torf* 4B 18
Croes-y-mwyalch. *Torf* 4B 18
Croesywaun. *Gwyn* 5E 32
Croford. *Som* 3L 7
Croft. *Leics* 2C 28
Croft. *Linc* 3B 38
Croft. *Warr* 8E 40
Croftamie. *Stir* 1C 58
Croftfoot. *Glas* 3D 58
Croftmill. *Per* 4B 66
Crofton. *Cumb* 6H 53
Crofton. *W Yor* 6A 42
Crofton. *Wilts* 7L 19
Croft-on-Tees. *N Yor* 5L 47
Crofts. *Dum* 4B 52
Crofts of Benachielt. *High* 8C 86
Crofts of Dipple. *Mor* 8C 80
Crofty. *Swan* 7M 15
Croggan. *Arg* 5B 64
Croglin. *Cumb* 7K 53
Croich. *High* 4E 78
Croick. *High* 6L 85
Croig. *Arg* 2J 63
Cromarty. *High* 7H 79
Crombie. *Fife* 1J 59
Cromdale. *High* 3L 71
Cromer. *Herts* 1K 21
Cromer. *Norf* 5J 39
Cromford. *Derbs* 4L 35
Cromhall. *S Glo* 4E 18
Cromor. *W Isl* 1F 76
Cromra. *High* 7F 70
Cromwell. *Notts* 3E 36
Cronberry. *E Ayr* 7E 58
Crondall. *Hants* 1E 10
The Cronk. *IOM* 5C 44
Cronk-y-Voddy. *IOM* 6C 44
Cronton. *Mers* 1C 34
Crook. *Cumb* 6C 46
Crook. *Dur* 8E 54
Crookdake. *Cumb* 7F 52
Crooke. *G Man* 7D 40
Crookedholm. *E Ayr* 6C 58
Crooked Soley. *Wilts* 6M 19
Crookes. *S Yor* 1M 35
Crookgate Bank. *Dur* 6E 54
Crookhall. *Dur* 6E 54
Crookham. *Nmbd* 6G 61
Crookham. *W Ber* 7C 20
Crookham Village. *Hants* 8E 20
Crooklands. *Cumb* 7D 46
Crook of Devon. *Per* 7D 66
Crookston. *Glas* 3D 58
Cropredy. *Oxon* 7B 28
Cropston. *Leics* 8C 36
Cropthorne. *Worc* 7H 27
Cropton. *N Yor* 7E 48
Cropwell Bishop. *Notts* 6D 36
Cropwell Butler. *Notts* 6D 36
Cros. *W Isl* 5J 83
Crosbie. *N Ayr* 4M 57
Crosbost. *W Isl* 1E 76
Crosby. *Cumb* 8E 52
Crosby. *IOM* 7C 44
**Crosby**. *Mers* 8B 40
Crosby. *N Lin* 6F 42
Crosby Court. *N Yor* 6A 48
Crosby Garrett. *Cumb* 5F 46
Crosby Ravensworth. *Cumb* 4E 46
Crosby Villa. *Cumb* 8E 52
Croscombe. *Som* 1D 8
Crosland Moor. *W Yor* 6K 41
Cross. *Som* 8C 18
Crossaig. *Arg* 4H 57
Crossapol. *Arg* 3E 62
Cross Ash. *Mon* 2C 18
Cross-at-Hand. *Kent* 1D 12
Crossbush. *W Sus* 5H 11
Crosscanonby. *Cumb* 8E 52
Crossdale Street. *Norf* 6J 39
Cross End. *Essx* 8E 30
Crossens. *Mers* 5B 40
Crossford. *Fife* 1J 59
Crossford. *S Lan* 5G 59
Cross Foxes. *Gwyn* 1G 25
Crossgar. *New M* 6J 93
Crossgate. *Orkn* 8D 88
Crossgate. *Staf* 6H 35
Crossgatehall. *E Lot* 3A 60
Cross Gates. *W Yor* 4A 42
Crossgates. *Fife* 1K 59
Crossgates. *N Yor* 7H 49
Crossgates. *Powy* 6K 25
Crossgill. *Lanc* 1D 40
Cross Green. *Devn* 7C 6
Cross Green. *Staf* 1H 27
Cross Green. *Suff*
nr. Cockfield 6E 30
nr. Hitcham 6F 30
Cross Hands. *Carm* 3E 16
Crosshands. *Carm* 4H 15
Crosshands. *E Ayr* 6C 58
Cross Hill. *Derbs* 5B 36
Cross Hill. *Glos* 4D 18
Crosshill. *E Ayr* 7C 58
Crosshill. *Fife* 8E 66
Crosshill. *S Ayr* 1J 51
Cross Hills. *N Yor* 3J 41
Crosshills. *High* 6G 79
Cross Holme. *N Yor* 6C 48
Crosshouse. *E Ayr* 6B 58
Cross Houses. *Shrp* 1D 26
Crossings. *Cumb* 4K 53
Cross in Hand. *E Sus* 3B 12
Cross Inn. *Cdgn*
nr. Aberaeron 6E 24
nr. New Quay 1K 15
Cross Inn. *Rhon* 6K 17
Crosskeys. *Cphy* 5M 17
Crosskirk. *High* 5B 86
Crosslands. *Cumb* 7B 46
Cross Lane Head. *Shrp* 2F 26
Cross Lanes. *Corn* 6K 3
Cross Lanes. *Dur* 4J 47
Cross Lanes. *N Yor* 1C 42
Cross Lanes. *Wrex* 5B 34
Crosslanes. *Shrp* 8B 34
Crosslee. *Ren* 3C 58
Crossmaglen. *New M* 7F 93
Crossmichael. *Dum* 5B 52
Crossmoor. *Lanc* 4C 40
Crossnacreevy. *Lis* 5H 93
Cross Oak. *Powy* 2L 17
Cross of Jackston. *Abers* 2G 73
Cross o' th' Hands. *Derbs* 5L 35
Crossroads. *Abers*
nr. Aberdeen 5J 73
nr. Banchory 6G 73
Crossroads. *E Ayr* 6C 58
Cross Side. *Devn* 3H 7
Cross Street. *Suff* 4H 31
Crosston. *Ang* 2J 67
Cross Town. *Ches E* 2F 34
Crossway. *Mon* 2C 18
Crossway. *Powy* 7K 25
Crossway Green. *Mon* 4D 18
Crossway Green. *Worc* 5G 27
Crossways. *Dors* 7F 8
Crosswell. *Pemb* 3H 15
Crosswood. *Cdgn* 5F 24
Crosthwaite. *Cumb* 6C 46
Croston. *Lanc* 6C 40
Crostwick. *Norf* 8J 39
Crostwight. *Norf* 7K 39
Crothair. *W Isl* 8E 82
Crouch. *Kent* 8C 22
Croucheston. *Wilts* 3J 9
Crouch Hill. *Dors* 4F 8
Croughton. *Nptn* 8C 28
Crovie. *Abers* 7H 81
Crow. *Hants* 5K 9
Crowan. *Corn* 5K 3
**Crowborough**. *E Sus* 2B 12
Crowcombe. *Som* 2L 7
Crowcroft. *Worc* 6F 26
Crowdecote. *Derbs* 3K 35
Crowden. *Derbs* 8J 41
Crowden. *Devn* 6D 6
Crowdhill. *Hants* 4B 10
Crowdon. *N Yor* 6G 49
Crow Edge. *S Yor* 7K 41
Crow End. *Cambs* 6L 29
Crowfield. *Nptn* 7D 28
Crowfield. *Suff* 6H 31
Crow Green. *Essx* 4B 22
Crow Hill. *Here* 1E 18
Crowhurst. *E Sus* 4D 12
Crowhurst. *Surr* 1L 11
Crowhurst Lane End. *Surr* 1L 11
Crowland. *Linc* 8K 37
Crowland. *Suff* 4G 31
Crowlas. *Corn* 5J 3
Crowle. *N Lin* 6E 42
Crowle. *Worc* 6H 27
Crowle Green. *Worc* 6H 27
Crowmarsh Gifford. *Oxon* 5D 20
Crown Corner. *Suff* 4J 31
Crownthorpe. *Norf* 1G 31
Crowntown. *Corn* 5K 3
Crows-an-wra. *Corn* 6G 3
Crowshill. *Norf* 1F 30
**Crowthorne**. *Brac* 7F 20
Crowton. *Ches W* 2D 34
Croxall. *Staf* 8K 35
Croxby. *Linc* 8J 43
Croxdale. *Dur* 8F 54
Croxden. *Staf* 6J 35
Croxley Green. *Herts* 4H 21
Croxton. *Cambs* 5K 29
Croxton. *Norf*
nr. Fakenham 6F 38
nr. Thetford 3E 30
Croxton. *N Lin* 6H 43
Croxton. *Staf* 6F 34
Croxtonbank. *Staf* 6F 34
Croxton Green. *Ches E* 4D 34
Croxton Kerrial. *Leics* 7F 36
Croy. *High* 1H 71
Croy. *N Lan* 2F 58
Croyde. *Devn* 2D 6
Croydon. *Cambs* 7L 29
**Croydon**. *G Lon* 7L 21
Crubenbeg. *High* 6G 71
Crubenmore Lodge. *High* 6G 71
Cruckmeole. *Shrp* 1C 26
Cruckton. *Shrp* 8C 34
Cruden Bay. *Abers* 2K 73
Crudgington. *Telf* 8E 34
Crudie. *Abers* 8G 81
Crudwell. *Wilts* 4H 19
Cruft. *Devn* 6E 6
Crug. *Powy* 5L 25
Crughywel. *Powy* 3M 17
Crugmeer. *Corn* 4B 4
Crugybar. *Carm* 1F 16
Crug-y-byddar. *Powy* 4L 25
Crulabhig. *W Isl* 8E 82
Crumlin. *Ant* 5G 93
Crumlin. *Cphy* 5M 17
Crumpsall. *G Man* 7G 41
Crumpsbrook. *Shrp* 4E 26
Crundale. *Kent* 1G 13
Crundale. *Pemb* 5F 14
Cruwys Morchard. *Devn* 4H 7
Crux Easton. *Hants* 8B 20
Cruxton. *Dors* 6E 8
Crwbin. *Carm* 5L 15
Cryers Hill. *Buck* 4F 20
Crymych. *Pemb* 3H 15
Crynant. *Neat* 4G 17
Crystal Palace. *G Lon* 6L 21
Cuaich. *High* 7G 71
Cuaig. *High* 8J 77
Cuan. *Arg* 6B 64
Cubbington. *Warw* 5M 27
Cubert. *Corn* 3L 3
Cubley. *S Yor* 7L 41
Cubley Common. *Derbs* 6K 35
Cublington. *Buck* 1F 20
Cublington. *Here* 8B 26
Cuckfield. *W Sus* 3L 11
Cucklington. *Som* 3F 8
Cuckney. *Notts* 2C 36
Cuckron. *Shet* 2E 90
Cuddesdon. *Oxon* 3D 20
Cuddington. *Buck* 2E 20
Cuddington. *Ches W* 2E 34
Cuddington Heath. *Ches W* 5C 34
Cuddy Hill. *Lanc* 4C 40
Cudham. *G Lon* 8M 21
Cudlipptown. *Devn* 8E 6
Cudworth. *Som* 4B 8
**Cudworth**. *S Yor* 7A 42
Cudworth. *Surr* 1K 11
Cuerdley Cross. *Warr* 1D 34
Cuffley. *Herts* 3L 21
Cuidhir. *W Isl* 5C 74
Cuidhsiadar. *W Isl* 6J 83
Cuidhtinis. *W Isl* 5B 76
Culbo. *High* 7G 79
Culbokie. *High* 8G 79
Culburnie. *High* 1E 70
Culcabock. *High* 1G 71
Culcavy. *Lis* 5H 93
Culcharry. *High* 8J 79
Culcheth. *Warr* 8E 40
Culduie. *High* 1J 69
Culeave. *High* 4F 78
Culford. *Suff* 4E 30
Culgaith. *Cumb* 3E 46
Culham. *Oxon* 4C 20
Culkein. *High* 8C 84
Culkein Drumbeg. *High* 8D 84
Culkerton. *Glos* 4H 19
Cullaville. *New M* 7F 93
Cullen. *Mor* 7E 80
Cullercoats. *Tyne* 4G 55
Cullicudden. *High* 7G 79
Cullingworth. *W Yor* 4J 41
Cullipool. *Arg* 6B 64
Cullivoe. *Shet* 3K 91
Culloch. *Per* 6A 66
Culloden. *High* 1H 71
Cullompton. *Devn* 5K 7
Cullybackey. *ME Ant* 3G 93
Cullycapple. *Caus* 2F 93
Cullyhanna. *New M* 7F 93
Culm Davy. *Devn* 4L 7
Culmington. *Shrp* 3C 26
Culmore. *Derr* 2D 92
Culmstock. *Devn* 4L 7
Cul na Caepaich. *High* 7H 69
Culnacnoc. *High* 7G 77
Culnacraig. *High* 3A 78
Culnady. *M Ulst* 3F 93
Culrain. *High* 4F 78
Culross. *Fife* 1H 59
Culroy. *S Ayr* 8B 58
Culswick. *Shet* 3C 90
Cults. *Aber* 5H 73
Cults. *Abers* 2E 72
Cults. *Fife* 7G 67
Cultybraggan Camp. *Per* 5A 66
Culver. *Devn* 6H 7
Culverlane. *Devn* 5K 5
Culverstone Green. *Kent* 7C 22
Culverthorpe. *Linc* 5H 37
Culworth. *Nptn* 7C 28
Culzie Lodge. *High* 6F 78
Cumberlow Green. *Herts* 8L 29
**Cumbernauld**. *N Lan* 2F 58
Cumbernauld Village. *N Lan* 2F 58
Cumberworth. *Linc* 2B 38
Cumdivock. *Cumb* 7H 53
Cuminestown. *Abers* 8H 81
Cumledge Mill. *Bord* 4E 60
Cumlewick. *Shet* 5E 90
Cummersdale. *Cumb* 6H 53
Cummertrees. *Dum* 5F 52
Cummingstown. *Mor* 7M 79
Cumnock. *E Ayr* 7D 58
Cumnor. *Oxon* 3B 20
Cumrew. *Cumb* 6K 53
Cumwhinton. *Cumb* 6J 53
Cumwhitton. *Cumb* 6K 53
Cundall. *N Yor* 8B 48
Cunninghamhead. *N Ayr* 5B 58
Cunning Park. *S Ayr* 8B 58
Cunningsburgh. *Shet* 5E 90
Cunnister. *Shet* 4K 91
Cupar. *Fife* 6G 67
Cupar Muir. *Fife* 6G 67
Cupernham. *Hants* 3A 10
Curbar. *Derbs* 2L 35
Curborough. *Staf* 8K 35
Curbridge. *Hants* 4C 10
Curbridge. *Oxon* 3M 19
Curdridge. *Hants* 4C 10
Curdworth. *Warw* 2K 27
Curland. *Som* 4A 8
Curland Common. *Som* 4A 8
Curran. *M Ulst* 4F 93
Curridge. *W Ber* 6B 20
Currie. *Edin* 3K 59
Curry Mallet. *Som* 3B 8
Curry Rivel. *Som* 3B 8
Curtisden Green. *Kent* 1D 12
Curtisknowle. *Devn* 6K 5
Cury. *Corn* 6K 3
Cusgarne. *Corn* 4L 3
Cushendall. *Caus* 2H 93
Cushendun. *Caus* 2H 93
Cusop. *Here* 8M 25
Cusworth. *S Yor* 7C 42
Cutcombe. *Som* 2J 7
Cuthill. *E Lot* 2A 60
Cutiau. *Gwyn* 1F 24
Cutlers Green. *Essx* 8B 30
Cutmadoc. *Corn* 5C 4
Cutnall Green. *Worc* 5G 27
Cutsdean. *Glos* 8J 27
Cutthorpe. *Derbs* 2M 35
Cuttiford's Door. *Som* 4B 8
Cuttivett. *Corn* 5F 4
Cutts. *Shet* 4D 90
Cuttybridge. *Pemb* 5F 14
Cuttyhill. *Abers* 8K 81
Cuxham. *Oxon* 4D 20
Cuxton. *Medw* 7D 22
Cuxwold. *Linc* 7J 43
Cwm. *Blae* 4L 17
Cwm. *Den* 3K 33
Cwm. *Powy* 2A 26
Cwmafan. *Neat* 5G 17
Cwmaman. *Rhon* 5J 17
Cwmann. *Carm* 8E 24
Cwmbach. *Carm* 4J 15
Cwmbach. *Powy* 1L 17
Cwmbach. *Rhon* 4K 17
Cwmbach Llechrhyd. *Powy* 7K 25
Cwmbelan. *Powy* 4J 25
**Cwmbran**. *Torf* 4A 18
Cwmbrwyno. *Cdgn* 4G 25
Cwm Capel. *Carm* 6L 15
Cwmcarn. *Cphy* 5M 17
Cwmcarvan. *Mon* 3C 18
Cwm-celyn. *Blae* 4M 17
Cwmcerdinen. *Swan* 4F 16
Cwm-Cewydd. *Gwyn* 1H 25
Cwm-cou. *Cdgn* 2J 15
Cwmcych. *Pemb* 3J 15
Cwmdare. *Rhon* 4J 17
Cwmdu. *Carm* 1F 16
Cwmdu. *Powy* 2L 17
Cwmduad. *Carm* 3K 15
Cwm Dulais. *Swan* 4F 16
Cwmerfyn. *Cdgn* 4F 24
Cwmfelin. *B'end* 6H 17
Cwmfelin Boeth. *Carm* 5H 15
Cwmfelinfach. *Cphy* 5L 17
Cwmfelin Mynach. *Carm* 4J 15
Cwmffrwd. *Carm* 5L 15
Cwmgiedd. *Powy* 3G 17
Cwmgors. *Neat* 3G 17
Cwmgwili. *Carm* 3E 16
Cwmgwrach. *Neat* 4H 17
Cwmhiraeth. *Carm* 3K 15
Cwmifor. *Carm* 2F 16
Cwmisfael. *Carm* 5L 15
Cwm-Llinau. *Powy* 2H 25
Cwmllynfell. *Neat* 3G 17
Cwm-mawr. *Carm* 5M 15
Cwm-miles. *Carm* 4H 15
Cwmorgan. *Carm* 3J 15
Cwmparc. *Rhon* 5J 17
Cwm Penmachno. *Cnwy* 6G 33
Cwmpennar. *Rhon* 4K 17
Cwm Plysgog. *Pemb* 2H 15
Cwmrhos. *Powy* 2L 17
Cwmsychpant. *Cdgn* 2L 15
Cwmsyfiog. *Cphy* 4L 17
Cwmsymlog. *Cdgn* 4F 24
Cwmtillery. *Blae* 4M 17
Cwm-twrch Isaf. *Powy* 4G 17
Cwm-twrch Uchaf. *Powy* 3G 17
Cwmwysg. *Powy* 2H 17
Cwm-y-glo. *Gwyn* 4E 32
Cwmyoy. *Mon* 1B 18
Cwmystwyth. *Cdgn* 5G 25
Cwrt. *Gwyn* 2F 24
Cwrtnewydd. *Cdgn* 2L 15
Cwrt-y-Cadno. *Carm* 8F 24
Cydweli. *Carm* 6L 15
Cyffylliog. *Den* 5K 33
Cymau. *Flin* 4A 34
Cymer. *Neat* 5H 17
Cymmer. *Neat* 5H 17
Cymmer. *Rhon* 5K 17
Cyncoed. *Card* 6L 17
Cynghordy. *Carm* 1H 17
Cynheidre. *Carm* 6L 15
Cynonville. *Neat* 5H 17
Cynwyd. *Den* 6K 33
Cynwyl Elfed. *Carm* 4K 15
Cywarch. *Gwyn* 1H 25

## D

Dacre. *Cumb* 3C 46
Dacre. *N Yor* 1K 41
Dacre Banks. *N Yor* 1K 41
Daddry Shield. *Dur* 8B 54
Dadford. *Buck* 8D 28
Dadlington. *Leics* 2B 28
Dafen. *Carm* 6M 15
Daffy Green. *Norf* 1F 30
Dagdale. *Staf* 6J 35
**Dagenham**. *G Lon* 5A 22
Daggons. *Dors* 4K 9
Daglingworth. *Glos* 3H 19
Dagnall. *Buck* 2G 21
Dagtail End. *Worc* 5J 27
Dail. *Arg* 4E 64
Dail Beag. *W Isl* 7F 82
Dail bho Dheas. *W Isl* 5H 83
Dailly. *S Ayr* 1H 51
Dail Mor. *W Isl* 7F 82
Dairsie. *Fife* 6H 67
Daisy Bank. *W Mid* 2J 27
Daisy Hill. *G Man* 7E 40
Daisy Hill. *W Yor* 4K 41
Dalabrog. *W Isl* 3D 74
Dalavich. *Arg* 6D 64
Dalbeattie. *Dum* 5C 52
Dalblair. *E Ayr* 8E 58
Dalbury. *Derbs* 6L 35
Dalby. *IOM* 7B 44
Dalby Wolds. *Leics* 7D 36
Dalchalm. *High* 3K 79
Dalcharn. *High* 6J 85
Dalchork. *High* 2F 78
Dalchreichart. *High* 4C 70
Dalchruin. *Per* 6M 65
Dalcross. *High* 1H 71
Dalderby. *Linc* 3K 37
Dale. *Cumb* 7K 53
Dale. *Pemb* 6E 14
Dale Abbey. *Derbs* 6B 36
Dalebank. *Derbs* 3A 36
Dale Bottom. *Cumb* 3A 46
Dale Head. *Cumb* 4C 46
Dalehouse. *N Yor* 4E 48
Dalelia. *High* 1B 64
Dale of Walls. *Shet* 2B 90
Dalgarven. *N Ayr* 5A 58
**Dalgety Bay**. *Fife* 1K 59
Dalginross. *Per* 5A 66
Dalguise. *Per* 3C 66
Dalhalvaig. *High* 6L 85
Dalham. *Suff* 5D 30
Dalintart. *Arg* 5C 64
**Dalkeith**. *Midl* 3M 59
Dallas. *Mor* 8M 79
Dalleagles. *E Ayr* 8D 58
Dall House. *Per* 2K 65
Dallinghoo. *Suff* 6J 31
Dallington. *E Sus* 4C 12
Dallow. *N Yor* 8K 47
Dalmally. *Arg* 5F 64
Dalmarnock. *Glas* 3E 58
Dalmellington. *E Ayr* 1K 51
Dalmeny. *Edin* 2K 59
Dalmigavie. *High* 4H 71
Dalmilling. *S Ayr* 7B 58
Dalmore. *High*
nr. Alness 7G 79
nr. Rogart 3H 79
Dalmuir. *W Dun* 2C 58
Dalmunach. *Mor* 1B 72
Dalnabreck. *High* 1B 64
Dalnacardoch Lodge. *Per* 8H 71
Dalnamein Lodge. *Per* 1A 66
Dalnaspidal Lodge. *Per* 8G 71
Dalnatrat. *High* 2D 64
Dalnavie. *High* 6G 79
Dalnawillan Lodge. *High* 7B 86
Dalness. *High* 2F 64
Dalnessie. *High* 2G 79
Dalqueich. *Per* 7D 66
Dalquhairn. *S Ayr* 2J 51
Dalreavoch. *High* 3H 79
Dalreoch. *Per* 6D 66
Dalry. *Edin* 2L 59
Dalry. *N Ayr* 5A 58
Dalrymple. *E Ayr* 8B 58
Dalscote. *Nptn* 6D 28
Dalserf. *S Lan* 4G 59
Dalsmirren. *Arg* 8F 56
Dalston. *Cumb* 6H 53
Dalswinton. *Dum* 3D 52
Dalton. *Dum* 4F 52
Dalton. *Lanc* 7C 40
Dalton. *Nmbd*
nr. Hexham 6C 54
nr. Ponteland 4E 54
Dalton. *N Yor*
nr. Richmond 5K 47
nr. Thirsk 8B 48
Dalton. *S Lan* 4E 58
Dalton. *S Yor* 8B 42
Dalton-in-Furness. *Cumb* 7M 45
Dalton-le-Dale. *Dur* 7H 55
Dalton Magna. *S Yor* 8B 42
Dalton-on-Tees. *N Yor* 5L 47
Dalton Piercy. *Hart* 8H 55
Daltot. *Arg* 1G 57
Dalvey. *High* 2M 71
Dalwhinnie. *High* 7G 71
Dalwood. *Devn* 5A 8
Damerham. *Hants* 4K 9
Damgate. *Norf*
nr. Acle 1L 31
nr. Martham 8L 39
Dam Green. *Norf* 3G 31
Damhead. *Mor* 8L 79
Danaway. *Kent* 7E 22
Danbury. *Essx* 3D 22
Danby. *N Yor* 5E 48
Danby Botton. *N Yor* 5D 48
Danby Wiske. *N Yor* 6M 47
Danderhall. *Midl* 3M 59
Danebank. *Ches E* 1H 35
Danebridge. *Ches E* 3H 35
Dane End. *Herts* 1L 21
Danehill. *E Sus* 3M 11
Danesford. *Shrp* 2F 26
Daneshill. *Hants* 8D 20
Danesmoor. *Derbs* 3B 36
Danestone. *Aber* 4J 73
Dangerous Corner. *Lanc* 6D 40
Daniel's Water. *Kent* 1F 12
Dan's Castle. *Dur* 8E 54
Danzey Green. *Warw* 5K 27
Dapple Heath. *Staf* 7J 35
Daren. *Powy* 3M 17
Darenth. *Kent* 6B 22
Daresbury. *Hal* 1D 34
Darfield. *S Yor* 7B 42
Dargate. *Kent* 7G 23
Dargill. *Per* 6B 66
Darite. *Corn* 5E 4
Darkley. *Arm* 7F 93
Darlaston. *W Mid* 2H 27
Darley. *N Yor* 2L 41
Darley Abbey. *Derb* 6M 35
Darley Bridge. *Derbs* 3L 35
Darley Dale. *Derbs* 3L 35
Darley Head. *N Yor* 2K 41
Darlingscott. *Warw* 7L 27
**Darlington**. *Darl* 4L 47
Darliston. *Shrp* 6D 34
Darlton. *Notts* 2E 36
Darmsden. *Suff* 6G 31
Darnall. *S Yor* 1A 36
Darnford. *Abers* 6G 73
Darnford. *Staf* 1K 27
Darnhall. *Ches W* 3E 34
Darnick. *Bord* 6C 60
Darowen. *Powy* 2H 25
Darra. *Abers* 1G 73
Darracott. *Devn* 2D 6
Darragh Cross. *New M* 6J 93
Darras Hall. *Nmbd* 4E 54
Darrington. *W Yor* 5B 42
Darrow Green. *Norf* 3J 31
Darsham. *Suff* 5L 31
Dartfield. *Abers* 8K 81
**Dartford**. *Kent* 6B 22
**Dartford-Thurrock River Crossing**.
*Kent* 6B 22
Dartington. *Devn* 5K 5
Dartmeet. *Devn* 8F 6
Dartmouth. *Devn* 6L 5
**Darton**. *S Yor* 6M 41
Darvel. *E Ayr* 6D 58
**Darwen**. *Bkbn* 5E 40
Dassels. *Herts* 1L 21
Datchet. *Wind* 6G 21
Datchworth. *Herts* 2K 21
Datchworth Green. *Herts* 2K 21
Daubhill. *G Man* 7F 40
Dauntsey. *Wilts* 5H 19
Dauntsey Green. *Wilts* 5H 19
Dauntsey Lock. *Wilts* 5H 19
Dava. *Mor* 2L 71
Davenham. *Ches W* 2E 34
**Daventry**. *Nptn* 5C 28
Davidson's Mains. *Edin* 2L 59
Davidston. *High* 7H 79
Davidstow. *Corn* 7A 6
David's Well. *Powy* 5K 25
Davington. *Dum* 1G 53
Daviot. *Abers* 3G 73
Daviot. *High* 2H 71
Davyhulme. *G Man* 8F 40
Daw Cross. *N Yor* 2L 41
Dawdon. *Dur* 7H 55
Dawesgreen. *Surr* 1K 11
Dawley. *Telf* 1E 26
**Dawlish**. *Devn* 8J 7
Dawlish Warren. *Devn* 8J 7
Dawn. *Cnwy* 3H 33
Daws Heath. *Essx* 5E 22
Dawshill. *Worc* 6G 27
Daw's House. *Corn* 7C 6
Dawsmere. *Linc* 6M 37
Dayhills. *Staf* 6H 35
Dayhouse Bank. *Worc* 4H 27
Daylesford. *Glos* 1L 19
Daywall. *Shrp* 6A 34
Ddol. *Flin* 3L 33
Ddol Cownwy. *Powy* 1K 25
Deadman's Cross. *C Beds* 7J 29
Deadwater. *Nmbd* 2L 53
Deaf Hill. *Dur* 8G 55
**Deal**. *Kent* 8K 23
Dean. *Cumb* 2K 45
Dean. *Devn*
nr. Combe Martin 1F 6
nr. Lynton 1G 7
Dean. *Dors* 4H 9
Dean. *Hants*
nr. Bishop's Waltham 4C 10
nr. Winchester 2B 10
Dean. *Oxon* 1M 19
Dean. *Som* 1E 8
Dean Bank. *Dur* 8F 54
Deanburnhaugh. *Bord* 8A 60
Dean Cross. *Devn* 1E 6
Deane. *Hants* 8C 20
Deanich Lodge. *High* 5D 78
Deanland. *Dors* 4H 9
Deanlane End. *W Sus* 4E 10
Dean Park. *Shrp* 5E 26
Dean Prior. *Devn* 5K 5
Dean Row. *Ches E* 1G 35
Deans. *W Lot* 3J 59
Deanscales. *Cumb* 2K 45
Deanshanger. *Nptn* 7E 28
Deanston. *Stir* 7M 65
Dearham. *Cumb* 8E 52
**Dearne Valley**. *S Yor* 7A 42
Debach. *Suff* 6J 31
Debden. *Essx* 8B 30
Debden Green. *Essx*
nr. Loughton 4M 21
nr. Saffron Walden 8B 30
Debenham. *Suff* 5H 31
Dechmont. *W Lot* 2J 59
Deddington. *Oxon* 8B 28
Dedham. *Essx* 8G 31
Dedham Heath. *Essx* 8G 31
Deebank. *Abers* 6F 72
Deene. *Nptn* 2G 29
Deenethorpe. *Nptn* 2G 29
Deepcar. *S Yor* 8L 41
Deepcut. *Surr* 8G 21
Deepdale. *Cumb* 7F 46
Deepdale. *N Lin* 6H 43
Deepdale. *N Yor* 8G 47
Deeping Gate. *Pet* 1J 29
Deeping St James. *Linc* 8J 37
Deeping St Nicholas. *Linc* 8K 37
Deerhill. *Mor* 8D 80

Effirth—Fylingthorpe


n. Shet 2D 90
ch. Staf 8K 35
d. Devn 5H 7
arth. Shet 4J 91
ry. Hants 8B 20
n. Worc 6H 27
on. G Man 6F 40
on. Kent 1F 12
on Forstal. Kent 1E 12
orough. N Yor 5C 42
uckland. Plym 6G 5
sford. Devn 4F 6
ngton. C Beds 1G 21
nton. Derbs 7L 35
scliffe. Stoc T 4B 48
eston. Dur 3H 47
m. Surr 6H 21
n Hythe. Surr 6H 21
on. Rut 1F 28
gham. Nmbd 8J 61
on. Derr 2D 92
n. M Ulst 6E 92
hayle. Corn 4C 4
kerry. Corn 7B 6
sbach. Cnwy 3H 33
s-Brewis. V Glam 8K 17
s Fach. Cdgn 3F 24
swrw. Pemb 3H 15
inton. Notts 3E 36
re. Norf 6F 38
nont. Cumb 3K 45
nont. Mers 8B 40
. N Yor 5F 48
Bridge. N Yor 5F 48
. Buck 5G 21
. Hants 1B 10
Ash Green. Essx 1F 22
Mile Burn. Midl 4K 59
ig. High 3B 64
each. High 4K 69
n. Bord 6C 60
nach Lodge. High 7F 78
Fhlodaigh. W Isl 8K 75
Iarmain. High 4J 69
leit. W Isl 1C 76
in. W Isl 2E 76
grug. Gwyn 7F 32
Village. Powy 1C 26
ton. S Glo 5E 18
ge. W Sus 5G 11
ton. Plym 6H 5
. Per 5E 66
ibe. Swin 5K 19
W Ber 7A 20
ell. Cambs 2L 29
sfield. Worc 8G 27
slie. Ren 3C 58
Street. Essx 8B 30
. Dur 3L 47
h. N Yor 1F 40
ck. W Yor 3K 41
we. Cumb 6C 46
. Nmbd 6J 61
. Staf 8K 35
Closes. Cambs 4A 30
. Dur 7B 80
High 4G 69
n. Kent 1H 13
Fife 7H 67
Hants 4A 10
W Ber 6C 20
w. Nmbd 2B 54
eld. Dum 4E 52
ey. Notts 2D 36
ton. Nptn 4D 28
Green. Essx 3C 22
ne. Glos 2H 19
High 3J 71
d. W Yor 5K 41
Arg 2G 57
one. Staf 5K 35
dge. Corn 5G 5
Lanc 2C 40
ford. Bord 3E 60
beich. Arg 6B 64
borough. Cumb 8E 52
rook. Herts 3K 21
all. Staf 7G 35
s Green. Surr 2H 11
eck. N Yor 6B 48
urn. N Yor 7F 48
y. N Yor 4E 48
ne. Telf 7E 34
ne Heath. Telf 7E 34
ayes. Devn 5J 7
. Arg 3E 64
er. E Yor 5G 43
n. E Yor 4E 42
on. Shrp 7F 34
on-on-Swale. N Yor 6L 47
orough. Buck 3F 20
here. Shrp 6C 34
mere Port. Ches W 2C 34
ham. Hants 5K 9
ham. Norf 2K 31
ham. Nmbd 7J 61
string. N Yor 7K 47
ton. Cambs 4J 29
ton. Nmbd 2F 54
ton Thorpe. Cambs 4J 29
Ang 4K 67
eld. Hants 1H 10
adder. High 7G 77
wn. Leics 2B 28
Abers 2J 73
y. Cumb 8J 53
h. Suff 3L 31
hton. E Yor 5G 43
od. Glos 3D 18
Cambs 1A 30
ham. W Mid 3H 27
ridge. Glos 2G 19
ridge. Worc 5H 27
n. Essx 8A 30
n. W Mid 3K 27
n Heath. W Mid 3K 27
thorpe. Leics 2B 28
ld. IOW 6D 10
ill. Dors 3G 9
rst. Staf 8K 35
y Castle. Worc 7H 27
y Lovett. Worc 5G 27
e. Glos 2F 18
e Back. Glos 2F 18
ark. G Lon 5B 22
ott. Devn 3B 6
tt. Suff 7G 31
ead. Essx 1G 23
ead Heath. Essx 1G 23
ead Market. Essx 1G 23
ed. Kent 1H 13
one. Kent 7J 23
one Hardwicke. Glos 1H 19
ville. E Yor 2G 43
vell. Suff 5F 30
n. Derbs 3E 36
. High 2C 78
stone. E Lot 2A 60
Abers 5H 73
Mor 3D 72
Dum 7J 51
n. Nmbd 2C 54
t. S Yor 8A 42
am. Essx 1B 22
d. Oxon 2C 20
n. W Isl 6H 43
. Norf 8G 39
. N Yor 3H 41
de. S Lan 5J 59
d. Surr 1G 11
. W Sus 4F 10
Marsh. W Sus 3F 10
rpe. Linc 7H 37
. Dur 3M 47
. Devn 5G 7
. Lanc 4E 40
. Notts 5E 36
. Wilts 1J 9
e. Devn 4F 6
. Bed 7H 29
e. Herts 4J 21
e. E Yor 4K 43
k. Lanc 4C 40
k. Tyne 5F 54
rth. Cambs 5L 29
ater. Cumb 5B 46
n. G Lon 6M 21
y. Cambs 6K 29
Cambs 2H 29
Ches W 2C 34

Elton. Derbs 3L 35
Elton. Glos 2F 18
Elton. G Man 6F 40
Elton. Here 4C 26
Elton. Notts 6E 36
Elton. Stoc T 4B 48
Elton Green. Ches W 2C 34
Eltringham. Nmbd 5D 54
Elvanfoot. S Lan 8H 59
Elvaston. Derbs 6B 36
Elveden. Suff 3E 30
Elvetham Heath. Hants 8E 20
Elvingston. E Lot 2B 60
Elvington. Kent 8J 23
Elvington. York 3E 42
Elwick. Hart 8H 55
Elwick. Nmbd 6J 61
Elworth. Ches E 3F 34
Elworth. Dors 7D 8
Elworthy. Som 2K 7
**Ely**. Cambs 3B 30
Ely. Card 7L 17
Emberton. Mil 7F 28
Embleton. Cumb 8F 52
Embleton. Hart 3B 48
Embleton. Nmbd 7K 61
Embo. High 4J 79
Emborough. Som 8E 18
Embo Street. High 4J 79
Embsay. N Yor 2J 41
Emery Down. Hants 5L 9
Emley. W Yor 6L 41
Emmbrook. Wok 7E 20
Emmer Green. Read 6E 20
Emmington. Oxon 3E 20
Emneth. Norf 1A 30
Emneth Hungate. Norf 1B 30
Empingham. Rut 1G 29
Empshott. Hants 2E 10
**Emsworth**. Hants 5E 10
Enborne. W Ber 7B 20
Enborne Row. W Ber 7B 20
Enchmarsh. Shrp 2D 26
Enderby. Leics 2C 28
Endmoor. Cumb 7D 46
Endon. Staf 4H 35
Endon Bank. Staf 4H 35
**Enfield**. G Lon 4L 21
Enfield Wash. G Lon 4L 21
Enford. Wilts 8K 19
Engine Common. S Glo 5E 18
Englefield. W Ber 6D 20
Englefield Green. Surr 6G 21
Englesea-brook. Ches E 4F 34
English Bicknor. Glos 2D 18
Englishcombe. Bath 7F 18
English Frankton. Shrp 7C 34
Enham Alamein. Hants 1A 10
Enmore. Som 2M 7
Ennerdale Bridge. Cumb 3K 45
Enniscaven. Corn 6B 4
**Enniskillen**. Ferm 6C 92
Enoch. Dum 1C 52
Enochdhu. Per 1D 66
Ensay. Arg 3J 63
Ensbury. Bour 6J 9
Ensdon. Shrp 8C 34
Ensis. Devn 3E 6
Enson. Staf 7H 35
Enstone. Oxon 1A 20
Enterkinfoot. Dum 1C 52
Enville. Staf 3G 27
Eolaigearraidh. W Isl 5D 74
Eorabus. Arg 5J 63
Eoropaidh. W Isl 5J 83
Epney. Glos 2F 18
Epperstone. Notts 5D 36
**Epping**. Essx 3A 22
Epping Green. Essx 3M 21
Epping Green. Herts 3K 21
Epping Upland. Essx 3M 21
Eppleby. N Yor 4K 47
Eppleworth. E Yor 4H 43
**Epsom**. Surr 7K 21
Epwell. Oxon 7A 28
Epworth. N Lin 7E 42
Epworth Turbary. N Lin 7E 42
Erbistock. Wrex 5B 34
Erbusaig. High 3J 69
Erchless Castle. High 1E 70
Erdington. W Mid 2K 27
Eredine. Arg 7D 64
Eriboll. High 6G 85
Ericstane. Dum 8J 59
Eridge Green. E Sus 2B 12
Erines. Arg 2H 57
Eriswell. Suff 4D 30
**Erith**. G Lon 6B 22
Erlestoke. Wilts 8H 19
Ermine. Linc 2G 37
Ermington. Devn 6J 5
Ernesettle. Plym 6G 5
Erpingham. Norf 6H 39
Erriottwood. Kent 8F 22
Errogie. High 3F 70
Errol. Per 5F 66
Errol Station. Per 5F 66
**Erskine**. Ren 2C 58
**Erskine Bridge**. Ren 2C 58
Ervie. Dum 5F 50
Erwarton. Suff 8J 31
Erwood. Powy 8K 25
Eryholme. N Yor 5M 47
Eryrys. Den 4M 33
Escalls. Corn 6G 3
Escomb. Dur 8E 54
Escrick. N Yor 3D 42
Esgair. Carm
nr. Carmarthen 4K 15
nr. St Clears 5J 15
Esgairgeiliog. Powy 2G 25
Esh. Dur 7E 54
**Esher**. Surr 7J 21
Esholt. W Yor 3K 41
Eshott. Nmbd 2F 54
Eshton. N Yor 2H 41
Esh Winning. Dur 7E 54
Eskadale. High 2E 70
Eskbank. Midl 3M 59
Eskdale Green. Cumb 4L 45
Eskdalemuir. Dum 2G 53
Eskham. Linc 8L 43
Esknish. Arg 3C 56
Esk Valley. N Yor 5F 48
Eslington Hall. Nmbd 8H 61
Esprick. Lanc 4C 40
Essendine. Rut 8H 37
Essendon. Herts 3K 21
Essich. High 2G 71
Essington. Staf 1H 27
**Eston**. Red C 4C 48
Estover. Plym 6H 5
Eswick. Shet 2E 90
Etal. Nmbd 6G 61
Etchilhampton. Wilts 7J 19
Etchingham. E Sus 3D 12
Etchinghill. Kent 2H 13
Etchinghill. Staf 8J 35
Etherley Dene. Dur 3K 47
Ethie Haven. Ang 3K 67
Etling Green. Norf 8G 39
Etloe. Glos 3E 18
**Eton**. Wind 6G 21
Eton Wick. Wind 6G 21
Etteridge. High 6G 71
Ettersgill. Dur 3G 47
Ettiley Heath. Ches E 3F 34
Ettington. Warw 7L 27
Etton. E Yor 3G 43
Etton. Pet 1J 29
Ettrick. Bord 8L 59
Ettrickbridge. Bord 7A 60
Etwall. Derbs 6L 35
Eudon Burnell. Shrp 3F 26
Eudon George. Shrp 3E 26
Euston. Suff 4F 30
Euxton. Lanc 6D 40
Evanstown. B'end 6J 17
Evanton. High 7G 79
Evedon. Linc 5H 37
Evelix. High 4H 79
Evendine. Here 7F 26
Evenjobb. Powy 5A 26
Evenley. Nptn 8C 28
Evenlode. Glos 1L 19
Even Swindon. Swin 5K 19
Evenwood. Dur 3K 47
Evenwood Gate. Dur 3K 47

Everbay. Orkn 7F 88
Evercreech. Som 2E 8
Everdon. Nptn 6C 28
Everingham. E Yor 3F 42
Everleigh. Wilts 8L 19
Everley. N Yor 7G 49
Eversholt. C Beds 8G 29
Evershot. Dors 5D 8
Eversley. Hants 7E 20
Eversley Centre. Hants 7E 20
Eversley Cross. Hants 7E 20
Everthorpe. E Yor 4G 43
Everton. C Beds 6K 29
Everton. Hants 6L 9
Everton. Mers 8B 40
Everton. Notts 8D 42
Evertown. Dum 4H 53
Evesbatch. Here 7E 26
**Evesham**. Worc 7J 27
Evington. Leic 1D 28
Ewden Village. S Yor 8L 41
Ewdness. Shrp 2F 26
**Ewell**. Surr 7K 21
Ewell Minnis. Kent 1J 13
Ewelme. Oxon 4D 20
Ewen. Glos 4J 19
Ewenny. V Glam 7J 17
Ewerby. Linc 5J 37
Ewes. Dum 2H 53
Ewesley. Nmbd 2D 54
Ewhurst. Surr 1H 11
Ewhurst Green. E Sus 3D 12
Ewhurst Green. Surr 2H 11
Ewlo. Flin 3A 34
Ewloe. Flin 3A 34
Ewood Bridge. Lanc 5F 40
Eworthy. Devn 6D 6
Ewshot. Hants 8F 20
Ewyas Harold. Here 1B 18
Exbourne. Devn 5F 6
Exbury. Hants 6B 10
Exceat. E Sus 6B 12
Exebridge. Som 3J 7
Exelby. N Yor 7L 47
**Exeter**. Devn 6J 7
Exeter Airport. Devn 6K 7
Exford. Som 2H 7
Exfords Green. Shrp 1C 26
Exhall. Warw 6K 27
Exlade Street. Oxon 5D 20
Exminster. Devn 7J 7
**Exmouth**. Devn 7K 7
Exnaboe. Shet 6D 90
Exning. Suff 5C 30
Exton. Devn 7J 7
Exton. Hants 3D 10
Exton. Rut 8G 37
Exton. Som 2J 7
Exwick. Devn 6J 7
Eyam. Derbs 2L 35
Eydon. Nptn 6C 28
Eye. Here 5C 26
Eye. Pet 1K 29
Eye. Suff 4H 31
Eye Green. Pet 1K 29
Eyemouth. Bord 3G 61
Eyeworth. C Beds 7K 29
Eyhorne Street. Kent 8E 22
Eyke. Suff 6K 31
Eynesbury. Cambs 6J 29
Eynort. High 2E 68
Eynsford. Kent 7B 22
Eynsham. Oxon 3B 20
Eyre. High
on Isle of Skye 8F 76
on Raasay 2G 69
Eythorne. Kent 1J 13
Eyton. Here 5C 26
Eyton. Shrp
nr. Bishop's Castle 3B 26
nr. Shrewsbury 8B 34
Eyton. Wrex 5B 34
Eyton on Severn. Shrp 1D 26
Eyton upon the Weald Moors. Telf 8E 34


## F


Faccombe. Hants 8A 20
Faceby. N Yor 5B 48
Faddiley. Ches E 4D 34
Fadmoor. N Yor 7D 48
Fagwyr. Swan 4F 16
Faichem. High 5C 70
Faifley. W Dun 2D 58
Fail. S Ayr 7C 58
Failand. N Som 6D 18
Failford. S Ayr 7C 58
**Failsworth**. G Man 7H 41
Fairbourne. Gwyn 1F 24
Fairbourne Heath. Kent 8E 22
Fairburn. N Yor 5B 42
Fairfield. Derbs 2J 35
Fairfield. Kent 3F 12
Fairfield. Worc
nr. Bromsgrove 4H 27
nr. Evesham 7J 27
Fairford. Glos 3K 19
Fair Green. Norf 8C 38
Fair Hill. Cumb 8K 53
Fairhill. S Lan 4F 58
Fair Isle Airport. Shet 2M 89
Fairlands. Surr 8G 21
Fairlie. N Ayr 4M 57
Fairlight. E Sus 4E 12
Fairlight Cove. E Sus 4E 12
Fairmile. Devn 6K 7
Fairmile. Surr 7J 21
Fairmilehead. Edin 3L 59
Fair Oak. Devn 4K 7
Fair Oak. Hants
nr. Eastleigh 4B 10
nr. Kingsclere 7C 20
Fairoak. Staf 6F 34
Fair Oak Green. Hants 7D 20
Fairseat. Kent 7C 22
Fairstead. Essx 2D 22
Fairstead. Norf 8C 38
Fairwarp. E Sus 3A 12
Fairwater. Card 7L 17
Fairy Cross. Devn 3D 6
Fakenham. Norf 6F 38
Fakenham Magna. Suff 4F 30
Fala. Midl 3B 60
Fala Dam. Midl 3B 60
Falcon. Here 8E 26
Faldingworth. Linc 1H 37
Falfield. S Glo 4E 18
Falkenham. Suff 8J 31
**Falkirk**. Falk 1G 59
Falkland. Fife 7F 66
Fallin. Stir 8B 66
Fallowfield. G Man 8G 41
Falmer. E Sus 5L 11
**Falmouth**. Corn 5M 3
Falsgrave. N Yor 7H 49
Falstone. Nmbd 3M 53
Fanagmore. High 7D 84
Fancott. C Beds 1H 21
Fanellan. High 1E 70
Fangdale Beck. N Yor 6C 48
Fangfoss. E Yor 2E 42
Fankerton. Falk 1F 58
Fanmore. Arg 3K 63
Fanner's Green. Essx 2C 22
Fannich Lodge. High 7C 78
Fans. Bord 5D 60
Farcet. Cambs 2K 29
Far Cotton. Nptn 6E 28
**Fareham**. Hants 5C 10
Farewell. Staf 8J 35
Far Forest. Worc 4F 26
Farforth. Linc 2L 37
Far Green. Glos 3F 18
Far Hoarcross. Staf 7K 35
Faringdon. Oxon 4L 19
Farington. Lanc 5D 40
Farlam. Cumb 6K 53
Farleigh. N Som 7C 18
Farleigh. Surr 7L 21
Farleigh Hungerford. Som 8G 19
Farleigh Wallop. Hants 1D 10
Farleigh Wick. Wilts 7G 19
Farlesthorpe. Linc 2A 38
Farleton. Cumb 7D 46
Farleton. Lanc 1D 40

Farley. High 1E 70
Farley. Shrp
nr. Shrewsbury 1B 26
nr. Telford 1E 26
Farley. Staf 5J 35
Farley. Wilts 3L 9
Farley Green. Suff 6D 30
Farley Green. Surr 1H 11
Farley Hill. Wok 7E 20
Farley's End. Glos 2F 18
Farlington. N Yor 1D 42
Farlington. Port 5D 10
Farlow. Shrp 3E 26
Farmborough. Bath 7E 18
Farmcote. Glos 1J 19
Farmcote. Shrp 2F 26
Farmington. Glos 2K 19
Far Moor. G Man 7D 40
Farmoor. Oxon 3B 20
Farmtown. Mor 8E 80
Farnah Green. Derbs 5M 35
Farnborough. G Lon 7M 21
**Farnborough**. Hants 8F 20
Farnborough. Warw 7B 28
Farnborough. W Ber 5B 20
Farncombe. Surr 1G 11
Farndish. Bed 5G 29
Farndon. Ches W 4C 34
Farndon. Notts 4E 36
Farnell. Ang 2K 67
Farnham. Dors 4H 9
Farnham. Essx 1A 22
Farnham. N Yor 1A 42
Farnham. Suff 5K 31
**Farnham**. Surr 1F 10
Farnham Common. Buck 5G 21
Farnham Green. Essx 1A 22
Farnham Royal. Buck 5G 21
Farnhill. N Yor 3J 41
Farningham. Kent 7B 22
Farnley. N Yor 3L 41
Farnley Tyas. W Yor 6K 41
Farnsfield. Notts 4D 36
**Farnworth**. G Man 7F 40
Farnworth. Hal 1D 34
Far Oakridge. Glos 3H 19
Farr. High
nr. Bettyhill 5K 85
nr. Inverness 2G 71
nr. Kingussie 5J 71
Farraline. High 3F 70
Farringdon. Devn 6K 7
Farrington. Dors 4G 9
Farrington Gurney. Bath 8E 18
Far Sawrey. Cumb 6B 46
Farsley. W Yor 4L 41
Farthinghoe. Nptn 8C 28
Farthingstone. Nptn 6D 28
Farthorpe. Linc 2K 37
Fartown. W Yor 6K 41
Farway. Devn 6L 7
Fasag. High 8K 77
Fascadale. High 8G 69
Fasnacloich. Arg 3E 64
Fassfern. High 8M 69
Fatfield. Tyne 6G 55
Faugh. Cumb 6K 53
Fauld. Staf 7K 35
Fauldhouse. W Lot 3H 59
Faulkbourne. Essx 2D 22
Faulkland. Som 8F 18
Fauls. Shrp 6D 34
Faverdale. Darl 4L 47
**Faversham**. Kent 7G 23
Fawdington. N Yor 8B 48
Fawfieldhead. Staf 3J 35
Fawkham Green. Kent 7B 22
Fawler. Oxon 2A 20
Fawley. Buck 5E 20
**Fawley**. Hants 5B 10
Fawley. W Ber 5A 20
Fawley Chapel. Here 1D 18
Fawton. Corn 5D 4
Faxfleet. E Yor 5F 42
Faygate. W Sus 2K 11
Fazakerley. Mers 8B 40
Fazeley. Staf 1K 27
Feagour. High 6F 70
Fearann Dhomhnaill. High 5H 69
Fearby. N Yor 7K 47
Fearn. High 6J 79
Fearnan. Per 3M 65
Fearnbeg. High 8J 77
Fearnhead. Warr 8E 40
Fearnmore. High 7J 77
Featherstone. Staf 1H 27
**Featherstone**. W Yor 5B 42
Featherstone Castle. Nmbd 5L 53
Feckenham. Worc 5J 27
Feering. Essx 1E 22
Feetham. N Yor 6H 47
Feizor. N Yor 1F 40
Felbridge. Surr 2L 11
Felbrigg. Norf 6J 39
Felcourt. Surr 1L 11
Felden. Herts 3H 21
Felhampton. Shrp 3C 26
Felindre. Carm
nr. Llandeilo 2E 16
nr. Llandovery 1F 16
nr. Newcastle Emlyn 3K 15
Felindre. Powy 4L 25
Felindre. Swan 4F 16
Felindre Farchog. Pemb 3H 15
Felinfach. Cdgn 1M 15
Felinfach. Powy 1K 17
Felinfoel. Carm 6M 15
Felingwmisaf. Carm 4M 15
Felingwmuchaf. Carm 4M 15
Y Felinheli. Gwyn 4E 32
Felin Newydd. Powy
nr. Newtown 2K 25
nr. Oswestry 8M 33
Felin Wnda. Cdgn 2K 15
Felinwynt. Cdgn 1J 15
Felixkirk. N Yor 7B 48
**Felixstowe**. Suff 8J 31
Felixstowe Ferry. Suff 8K 31
Felkington. Nmbd 5G 61
Fell End. Cumb 6F 46
**Felling**. Tyne 5F 54
Fell Side. Cumb 8H 53
Felmersham. Bed 6G 29
Felmingham. Norf 7J 39
Felpham. W Sus 6G 11
Felsham. Suff 6F 30
Felsted. Essx 1C 22
**Feltham**. G Lon 6J 21
Felthamhill. Surr 6H 21
Felthorpe. Norf 8H 39
Felton. Here 7D 26
Felton. N Som 7D 18
Felton. Nmbd 1E 54
Felton Butler. Shrp 8B 34
Feltwell. Norf 2D 30
Fenay Bridge. W Yor 6K 41
Fence. Lanc 4G 41
Fence Houses. Tyne 6G 55
Fencott. Oxon 2C 20
Fen Ditton. Cambs 5A 30
Fen Drayton. Cambs 5L 29
Fen End. Linc 7K 37
Fen End. W Mid 4L 27
Fenham. Nmbd 5H 61
Fenham. Tyne 5F 54
Fenhouses. Linc 5K 37
Feniscowles. Bkbn 5E 40
Feniton. Devn 6L 7
Fenn Green. Shrp 3F 26
**Y Fenni**. Mon 2B 18
Fenn's Bank. Wrex 6D 34
Fenn Street. Medw 6D 22
Fenny Bentley. Derbs 4K 35
Fenny Bridges. Devn 6L 7
Fenny Compton. Warw 6B 28
Fenny Drayton. Leics 2M 27
Fenny Stratford. Mil 8F 28
Fenrother. Nmbd 2E 54
Fenstanton. Cambs 5L 29
Fen Street. Norf 2G 31
Fenton. Cambs 4L 29
Fenton. Cumb 6K 53
Fenton. Linc
nr. Caythorpe 4F 36
nr. Saxilby 2F 36
Fenton. Nmbd 6G 61

Fenton. Notts 1E 36
Fenton. Stoke 5G 35
Fentonadle. Corn 4C 4
Fenton Barns. E Lot 1C 60
Fenwick. E Ayr 5C 58
Fenwick. Nmbd
nr. Berwick-upon-Tweed 5H 61
nr. Hexham 4D 54
Fenwick. S Yor 6C 42
Feochaig. Arg 8G 57
Feock. Corn 5M 3
Feolin Ferry. Arg 3D 56
Feorlan. Arg 1B 50
Ferindonald. High 5H 69
Feriniquarrie. High 8C 76
Fern. Ang 1H 67
**Ferndale**. Rhon 5J 17
**Ferndown**. Dors 5J 9
Ferness. High 1K 71
Fernham. Oxon 4L 19
Fernhill. W Sus 1L 11
Fernhill Heath. Worc 6G 27
Fernhurst. W Sus 3F 10
Fernieflatt. Abers 8H 73
Ferniegair. S Lan 4F 58
Fernilea. High 2E 68
Fernilee. Derbs 2J 35
Ferrensby. N Yor 1A 42
Ferriby Sluice. N Lin 5G 43
Ferring. W Sus 5H 11
Ferrybridge. W Yor 5B 42
Ferryden. Ang 2L 67
Ferry Hill. Cambs 3L 29
Ferryhill. Aber 5J 73
**Ferryhill**. Dur 8F 54
Ferryhill Station. Dur 8G 55
Ferryside. Carm 5K 15
Ferryton. High 7G 79
Fersfield. Norf 3G 31
Fersit. High 8D 70
Y Ferwig. Cdgn 2H 15
Feshiebridge. High 5J 71
Fetcham. Surr 8J 21
Fetterangus. Abers 8J 81
Fettercairn. Abers 8F 72
Fewcott. Oxon 1C 20
Fewston. N Yor 2K 41
Ffairfach. Carm 3F 16
Ffair Rhos. Cdgn 6G 25
Ffaldybrenin. Carm 8F 24
Ffarmers. Carm 8F 24
Ffawyddog. Powy 3M 17
**Y Fflint**. Flin 3M 33
Ffodun. Powy 2M 25
Ffont-y-gari. V Glam 8K 17
Y Ffor. Gwyn 7C 32
Fforest. Carm 4E 16
Fforest-fach. Swan 5F 16
Fforest Goch. Neat 4G 17
Ffostrasol. Cdgn 2K 15
Ffos-y-ffin. Cdgn 6D 24
Ffrith. Flin 4A 34
Ffwl-y-mwn. V Glam 8K 17
Ffynnon-ddrain. Carm 4L 15
Ffynnongroyw. Flin 2L 33
Ffynnon Gynydd. Powy 8L 25
Ffynnon-oer. Cdgn 1M 15
Fiag Lodge. High 1E 78
Fidden. Arg 5J 63
Fiddington. Glos 8H 27
Fiddington. Som 1M 7
Fiddleford. Dors 4G 9
Fiddlers Hamlet. Essx 3A 22
Field. Staf 6J 35
Field Assarts. Oxon 2M 19
Field Broughton. Cumb 7B 46
Field Dalling. Norf 6G 39
Field Head. Leics 1B 28
Fieldhead. Cumb 8J 53
Fifehead Magdalen. Dors 3F 8
Fifehead Neville. Dors 4F 8
Fifehead St Quintin. Dors 4F 8
Fife Keith. Mor 8D 80
Fifield. Oxon 2L 19
Fifield. Wilts 8K 19
Fifield. Wind 6G 21
Fifield Bavant. Wilts 3J 9
Figheldean. Wilts 1K 9
Filby. Norf 8L 39
Filey. N Yor 7J 49
Filford. Dors 6C 8
Filgrave. Mil 7F 28
Filkins. Oxon 3L 19
Filleigh. Devn
nr. Crediton 4G 7
nr. South Molton 3F 6
Fillingham. Linc 1G 37
Fillongley. Warw 3L 27
Filton. S Glo 6E 18
Fimber. E Yor 1F 42
Finavon. Ang 2H 67
Fincham. Norf 1C 30
Finchampstead. Wok 7E 20
Fincharn. Arg 7D 64
Finchdean. Hants 4E 10
Finchingfield. Essx 8C 30
**Finchley**. G Lon 4K 21
Findern. Derbs 6M 35
Findhorn. Mor 7L 79
Findhorn Bridge. High 3J 71
Findochty. Mor 7D 80
Findo Gask. Per 5D 66
Findon. Abers 6J 73
Findon. W Sus 5J 11
Findon Mains. High 7G 79
Findon Valley. W Sus 5J 11
Finedon. Nptn 4G 29
Fingal Street. Suff 4J 31
Fingest. Buck 4E 20
Finghall. N Yor 7K 47
Fingland. Cumb 6G 53
Fingland. Dum 8F 58
Finglesham. Kent 8K 23
Fingringhoe. Essx 1G 23
Finiskaig. High 6K 69
Finmere. Oxon 8D 28
Finnart. Per 2K 65
Finningham. Suff 5G 31
Finningley. S Yor 8D 42
Finnygaud. Abers 8F 80
**Finsbury**. G Lon 5L 21
Finstall. Worc 5H 27
Finsthwaite. Cumb 7B 46
Finstock. Oxon 2A 20
Finstown. Orkn 8C 88
Fintona. Ferm 5D 92
Fintry. Abers 8G 81
Fintry. D'dee 4H 67
Fintry. Stir 1E 58
Finvoy. Caus 3F 93
Finwood. Warw 5K 27
Finzean. Abers 6F 72
Fionnphort. Arg 5J 63
Fionnsabhagh. W Isl 5B 76
Firbeck. S Yor 1C 36
Firby. N Yor
nr. Bedale 7L 47
nr. Malton 1E 42
Firgrove. G Man 6H 41
Firle. E Sus 5A 12
Firsby. Linc 3A 38
Firsdown. Wilts 2L 9
First Coast. High 4L 77
Firth. Shet 6J 91
Fir Tree. Dur 8E 54
Fishbourne. IOW 6C 10
Fishbourne. W Sus 5F 10
Fishburn. Dur 8G 55
Fishcross. Clac 8B 66
Fisherford. Abers 2F 72
Fisherrow. E Lot 2M 59
Fisher's Pond. Hants 3B 10
Fisher's Row. Lanc 3C 40
Fisherstreet. W Sus 2G 11
Fisherton. High 8H 79
Fisherton. S Ayr 8A 58
Fisherton de la Mere. Wilts 2H 9
Fishguard. Pemb 3F 14
Fishlake. S Yor 6D 42
Fishley. Norf 8L 39
Fishnish. Arg 3A 64
Fishpond Bottom. Dors 6B 8
Fishponds. Bris 6E 18
Fishpool. Glos 1E 18
Fishpool. G Man 6G 41
Fishpools. Powy 6L 25
Fishtoft. Linc 5L 37

Fishtoft Drove. Linc 5L 37
Fishwick. Bord 4G 61
Fiskavaig. High 2E 68
Fiskerton. Linc 2H 37
Fiskerton. Notts 4E 36
Fitch. Shet 3D 90
Fitling. E Yor 4K 43
Fittleton. Wilts 1K 9
Fittleworth. W Sus 4H 11
Fitton End. Cambs 8M 37
Fitz. Shrp 8C 34
Fitzhead. Som 3L 7
Fitzwilliam. W Yor 6B 42
Fiunary. High 3M 63
Five Ash Down. E Sus 3A 12
Five Ashes. E Sus 3B 12
Five Bells. Som 1K 7
Five Bridges. Here 7E 26
Fivehead. Som 3B 8
Fivelanes. Corn 7B 6
Fivemiletown. M Ulst 6D 92
Five Oak Green. Kent 1C 12
Five Oaks. W Sus 3H 11
Five Roads. Carm 6L 15
Five Ways. Warw 4L 27
Flack's Green. Essx 2D 22
Flackwell Heath. Buck 5F 20
Fladbury. Worc 7H 27
Fladda. Shet 5H 91
Fladdabister. Shet 4E 90
Flagg. Derbs 3K 35
Flamborough. E Yor 8K 49
Flamstead. Herts 2H 21
Flansham. W Sus 5G 11
Flasby. N Yor 2H 41
Flash. Staf 3J 35
Flashader. High 8E 76
The Flatt. Cumb 4K 53
Flaunden. Herts 3H 21
Flawborough. Notts 5E 36
Flawith. N Yor 1B 42
Flax Bourton. N Som 7D 18
Flaxby. N Yor 2A 42
Flaxholme. Derbs 5M 35
Flaxley. Glos 2E 18
Flaxley Green. Staf 8J 35
Flaxpool. Som 2L 7
Flaxton. N Yor 1D 42
Fleck. Shet 6D 90
Fleckney. Leics 2D 28
Flecknoe. Warw 5C 28
Fledborough. Notts 2F 36
Fleet. Dors 7E 8
**Fleet**. Hants
nr. Farnborough 8F 20
nr. South Hayling 5E 10
Fleet. Linc 7L 37
Fleet Hargate. Linc 7L 37
Fleetville. Herts 3J 21
**Fleetwood**. Lanc 3B 40
Fleggburgh. Norf 8L 39
Fleisirin. W Isl 8J 83
Flemingston. V Glam 8K 17
Flemington. S Lan
nr. Glasgow 3E 58
nr. Strathaven 5F 58
Flempton. Suff 5E 30
Fleoideabhagh. W Isl 5B 76
Fletcher's Green. Kent 1B 12
Fletchertown. Cumb 7G 53
Fletching. E Sus 3M 11
Fleuchary. High 4H 79
Flexbury. Corn 5B 6
Flexford. Surr 1G 11
Flimby. Cumb 8E 52
Flimwell. E Sus 2D 12
**Flint**. Flin 3M 33
Flintham. Notts 5E 36
Flint Mountain. Flin 3M 33
Flinton. E Yor 4K 43
Flintsham. Here 6B 26
Flishinghurst. Kent 2D 12
Flitcham. Norf 7D 38
Flitton. C Beds 8H 29
**Flitwick**. C Beds 8H 29
Flixborough. N Lin 6F 42
Flixton. G Man 8F 40
Flixton. N Yor 8H 49
Flixton. Suff 3K 31
Flockton. W Yor 6L 41
Flodden. Nmbd 6G 61
Flodigarry. High 6F 76
Flood's Ferry. Cambs 2L 29
Flookburgh. Cumb 8B 46
Flordon. Norf 2H 31
Flore. Nptn 5D 28
Flotterton. Nmbd 1C 54
Flowton. Suff 7G 31
Flushing. Abers 1K 73
Flushing. Corn 5M 3
Fluxton. Devn 6K 7
Flyford Flavell. Worc 6H 27
Fobbing. Thur 5D 22
Fochabers. Mor 8C 80
Fochriw. Cphy 4L 17
Fockerby. N Lin 6F 42
Fodderty. High 8F 78
Foddington. Som 3D 8
Foel. Powy 1J 25
Foffarty. Ang 3H 67
Foggathorpe. E Yor 4E 42
Fogo. Bord 5E 60
Fogorig. Bord 5E 60
Foindle. High 7D 84
Folda. Ang 1E 66
Fole. Staf 6J 35
Foleshill. W Mid 3A 28
Foley Park. Worc 4G 27
Folke. Dors 4E 8
**Folkestone**. Kent 2J 13
Folkingham. Linc 6H 37
Folkington. E Sus 5B 12
Folksworth. Cambs 3J 29
Folkton. N Yor 8H 49
Folla Rule. Abers 2G 73
Follifoot. N Yor 2M 41
The Folly. Herts 2J 21
Folly Cross. Devn 5D 6
Folly Gate. Devn 6E 6
Fonmon. V Glam 8K 17
Fonthill Bishop. Wilts 2H 9
Fonthill Gifford. Wilts 2H 9
Fontmell Magna. Dors 4G 9
Fontwell. W Sus 5G 11
Font-y-gary. V Glam 8K 17
Foodieash. Fife 6G 67
Foolow. Derbs 2K 35
Footdee. Aber 5J 73
Footherley. Staf 1K 27
Foots Cray. G Lon 6A 22
Forbestown. Abers 4C 72
Force Forge. Cumb 6B 46
Force Mills. Cumb 6B 46
Forcett. N Yor 4K 47
Ford. Arg 7C 64
Ford. Buck 3E 20
Ford. Derbs 1B 36
Ford. Devn
nr. Bideford 3D 6
nr. Holbeton 6J 5
nr. Salcombe 7K 5
Ford. Glos 1J 19
Ford. Nmbd 6G 61
Ford. Plym 6G 5
Ford. Shrp 8C 34
Ford. Som
nr. Wells 8D 18
nr. Wiveliscombe 3K 7
Ford. Staf 4J 35
Ford. W Sus 5H 11
Ford. Wilts
nr. Chippenham 6G 19
nr. Salisbury 2K 9
Forda. Devn 2D 6
Ford Barton. Devn 4J 7
Fordcombe. Kent 1B 12
Fordell. Fife 1K 59
Forden. Powy 2M 25
Ford End. Essx 2C 22
Forder Green. Devn 5K 5
Ford Green. Lanc 3C 40
Fordham. Cambs 4C 30
Fordham. Essx 1F 22
Fordham. Norf 2C 30
Fordham Heath. Essx 1F 22
Ford Heath. Shrp 8C 34
Fordhouses. W Mid 1H 27
Fordie. Per 5A 66

Fordingbridge. Hants 4K 9
Fordington. Linc 2M 37
Fordon. E Yor 8H 49
Fordoun. Abers 8G 73
Ford Street. Essx 1F 22
Ford Street. Som 4L 7
Fordton. Devn 6H 7
Fordwells. Oxon 2M 19
Fordwich. Kent 8H 23
Fordyce. Abers 7E 80
Forebridge. Staf 7H 35
Foreglen. Caus 3E 92
Foremark. Derbs 7M 35
Forest. N Yor 5L 47
Forestburn Gate. Nmbd 2D 54
Foresterseat. Mor 8A 80
Forest Green. Glos 4G 19
Forest Green. Surr 1J 11
Forest Hall. Cumb 5D 46
Forest Head. Cumb 6K 53
Forest Hill. Oxon 3C 20
Forest-in-Teesdale. Dur 3G 47
Forest Lodge. Per 8K 71
Forest Mill. Clac 8C 66
Forest Row. E Sus 2M 11
Forestside. W Sus 4E 10
Forest Town. Notts 3C 36
**Forfar**. Ang 2H 67
Forgandenny. Per 6D 66
Forge. Powy 3G 25
The Forge. Here 6B 26
Forge Side. Torf 4M 17
Forgewood. N Lan 4F 58
Forgie. Mor 8C 80
Forgue. Abers 1F 72
Forkill. New M 7G 93
**Formby**. Mers 7B 40
Forncett End. Norf 2H 31
Forncett St Mary. Norf 2H 31
Forncett St Peter. Norf 2H 31
Forneth. Per 3D 66
Fornham All Saints. Suff 5E 30
Fornham St Martin. Suff 5E 30
Forres. Mor 8L 79
Forrestfield. N Lan 3G 59
Forrest Lodge. Dum 3L 51
Forsbrook. Staf 5H 35
Forse. High 8D 86
Forsinard. High 7L 85
Forss. High 5B 86
The Forstal. Kent 2G 13
Forston. Dors 6E 8
Fort Augustus. High 5D 70
Forteviot. Per 6D 66
Fort George. High 8H 79
Forth. S Lan 4H 59
Forthampton. Glos 8G 27
Forthay. Glos 4F 18
Fortingall. Per 3M 65
Fort Matilda. Inv 2A 58
Forton. Hants 1B 10
Forton. Lanc 2C 40
Forton. Shrp 8C 34
Forton. Som 5B 8
Forton. Staf 7F 34
Forton Heath. Shrp 8C 34
Fortrie. Abers 1F 72
Fortrose. High 8H 79
Fortuneswell. Dors 8E 8
**Fort William**. High 8B 70
Forty Green. Buck 4G 21
Forty Hill. G Lon 4L 21
Forward Green. Suff 6G 31
Fosbury. Wilts 8M 19
Foscot. Oxon 1L 19
Fosdyke. Linc 6L 37
Foss. Per 2A 66
Fossebridge. Glos 2J 19
Foster Street. Essx 3A 22
Foston. Derbs 6K 35
Foston. Leics 2D 28
Foston. Linc 5F 36
Foston. N Yor 1D 42
Foston on the Wolds. E Yor 2J 43
Fotherby. Linc 8L 43
Fothergill. Cumb 8E 52
Fotheringhay. Nptn 2H 29
Foubister. Orkn 1G 87
Foula Airport. Shet 4B 90
Foul Anchor. Cambs 8A 38
Foulbridge. Cumb 7J 53
Foulden. Norf 2D 30
Foulden. Bord 4G 61
Foul Mile. E Sus 4C 12
Foulridge. Lanc 3G 41
Foulsham. Norf 7G 39
Fountainhall. Bord 5B 60
The Four Alls. Shrp 6E 34
Four Ashes. Staf
nr. Cannock 1H 27
nr. Kinver 3G 27
Four Ashes. Suff 4G 31
Four Crosses. Powy
nr. Llanerfyl 2K 25
nr. Llanymynech 8A 34
Four Crosses. Staf 1H 27
Four Elms. Kent 1A 12
Four Forks. Som 2M 7
Four Gotes. Cambs 8A 38
Four Lane End. S Yor 7L 41
Four Lane Ends. Lanc 2D 40
Four Lanes. Corn 5K 3
Fourlanes End. Ches E 4G 35
Four Marks. Hants 2D 10
Four Mile Bridge. IOA 3B 32
Four Oaks. E Sus 3E 12
Four Oaks. Glos 1E 18
Four Oaks. W Mid 3L 27
Four Roads. Carm 6L 15
Four Roads. IOM 8B 44
Fourstones. Nmbd 5B 54
Four Throws. Kent 3D 12
Fovant. Wilts 3J 9
Foveran. Abers 3J 73
Fowey. Corn 6D 4
Fowlershill. Aber 4J 73
Fowley Common. Warr 8E 40
Fowlis. Ang 4G 67
Fowlis Wester. Per 5C 66
Fowlmere. Cambs 7M 29
Fownhope. Here 8D 26
Fox Corner. Surr 8G 21
Foxcote. Glos 1J 19
Foxcote. Som 8F 18
Foxdale. IOM 7B 44
Foxearth. Essx 7E 30
Foxfield. Cumb 7M 45
Foxham. Wilts 6H 19
Fox Hatch. Essx 4B 22
Foxhole. Corn 6B 4
Foxholes. N Yor 8H 49
Foxhunt Green. E Sus 4B 12
Fox Lane. Hants 8F 20
Foxley. Norf 7G 39
Foxley. Nptn 6D 28
Foxley. Wilts 5G 19
Foxlydiate. Worc 5J 27
Fox Street. Essx 1G 23
Foxt. Staf 5J 35
Foxton. Cambs 7M 29
Foxton. Dur 3A 48
Foxton. Leics 3E 28
Foxton. N Yor 6B 48
Foxup. N Yor 8G 47
Foxwist Green. Ches W 3E 34
Foxwood. Shrp 4E 26
Foy. Here 1D 18
Foyers. High 3E 70
Foynesfield. High 8J 79
Fraddam. Corn 5J 3
Fraddon. Corn 6B 4
Fradley. Staf 8K 35
Fradley South. Staf 8K 35
Fradswell. Staf 6H 35
Fraisthorpe. E Yor 1J 43
Framfield. E Sus 3A 12
Framingham Earl. Norf 1J 31
Framingham Pigot. Norf 1J 31
Framlingham. Suff 5J 31
Frampton. Dors 6D 8
Frampton. Linc 6L 37
Frampton Cotterell. S Glo 5E 18
Frampton Mansell. Glos 3H 19
Frampton on Severn. Glos 3F 18
Frampton West End. Linc 5K 37
Framsden. Suff 6H 31
Framwellgate Moor. Dur 7F 54
Franche. Worc 4G 27

Frandley. Ches W 2E 34
Frankby. Mers 2M 33
Frankfort. Norf 7K 39
Frankley. Worc 3H 27
Frank's Bridge. Powy 7L 25
Frankton. Warw 4B 28
Frankwell. Shrp 8C 34
Frant. E Sus 2B 12
**Fraserburgh**. Abers 7J 81
Frating Green. Essx 1G 23
Fratton. Port 5D 10
Freathy. Corn 6G 5
Freckenham. Suff 4C 30
Freckleton. Lanc 5C 40
Freeby. Leics 7F 36
Freefolk Priors. Hants 1B 10
Freehay. Staf 5J 35
Freeland. Oxon 2B 20
Freester. Shet 2E 90
Freethorpe. Norf 1L 31
Freiston. Linc 5L 37
Freiston Shore. Linc 5L 37
Fremington. Devn 2E 6
Fremington. N Yor 6J 47
Frenchay. S Glo 6E 18
Frenchbeer. Devn 7F 6
Frenich. Stir 7J 65
Frensham. Surr 1F 10
Frenze. Norf 3H 31
Fresgoe. High 5A 86
Freshfield. Mers 7A 40
Freshford. Bath 7F 18
Freshwater. IOW 7M 9
Freshwater Bay. IOW 7M 9
Freshwater East. Pemb 7G 15
Fressingfield. Suff 4J 31
Freston. Suff 8H 31
Freswick. High 5E 86
Fretherne. Glos 3F 18
Frettenham. Norf 8J 39
Freuchie. Fife 7F 66
Freystrop. Pemb 5F 14
Friar's Gate. E Sus 2A 12
Friar Waddon. Dors 7E 8
Friday Bridge. Cambs 1A 30
Friday Street. E Sus 5C 12
Friday Street. Surr 1J 11
Fridaythorpe. E Yor 2F 42
Friden. Derbs 3K 35
Friern Barnet. G Lon 4K 21
Friesthorpe. Linc 1H 37
Frieston. Linc 5G 37
Frieth. Buck 4E 20
Friezeland. Notts 4B 36
Frilford. Oxon 4B 20
Frilsham. W Ber 6C 20
**Frimley**. Surr 8F 20
Frimley Green. Surr 8F 20
Frindsbury. Medw 7D 22
Fring. Norf 6D 38
Fringford. Oxon 1D 20
Frinsted. Kent 8E 22
**Frinton-on-Sea**. Essx 2J 23
Friockheim. Ang 3J 67
Friog. Gwyn 1F 24
Frisby. Leics 1E 28
Frisby on the Wreake. Leics 8D 36
Friskney. Linc 4A 38
Friskney Eaudyke. Linc 4A 38
Friston. E Sus 6B 12
Friston. Suff 5L 31
Fritchley. Derbs 4A 36
Fritham. Hants 4L 9
Frith Bank. Linc 5L 37
Frith Common. Worc 5E 26
Frithelstock. Devn 4D 6
Frithelstock Stone. Devn 4D 6
Frithsden. Herts 3H 21
Frithville. Linc 4L 37
Frittenden. Kent 1E 12
Frittiscombe. Devn 7L 5
Fritton. Norf
nr. Great Yarmouth 1L 31
nr. Long Stratton 2J 31
Fritwell. Oxon 1C 20
Frizinghall. W Yor 4K 41
Frizington. Cumb 3K 45
Frobost. W Isl 3D 74
Frocester. Glos 3F 18
Frochas. Powy 2L 25
Frodesley. Shrp 1D 26
Frodingham. N Lin 6G 43
Frodsham. Ches W 2D 34
Froggatt. Derbs 2L 35
Froghall. Staf 5J 35
Frogham. Hants 4K 9
Frogham. Kent 8J 23
Frogmore. Devn 7K 5
**Frogmore**. Hants 7F 20
Frogmore. Herts 3J 21
Frognall. Linc 8J 37
Frogshall. Norf 6J 39
Frogwell. Corn 5F 4
Frolesworth. Leics 2C 28
**Frome**. Som 1F 8
Fromefield. Som 1F 8
Frome St Quintin. Dors 5D 8
Fromes Hill. Here 7E 26
Fron. Gwyn 7C 32
Fron. Powy
nr. Llandrindod Wells 6K 25
nr. Newtown 3L 25
nr. Welshpool 2M 25
Y Fron. Gwyn 5E 32
Froncysyllte. Wrex 5A 34
Frongoch. Gwyn 7J 33
Fron Isaf. Wrex 5A 34
Froneleu. Gwyn 7G 33
Frosterley. Dur 8D 54
Frotoft. Orkn 7D 88
Froxfield. C Beds 8G 29
Froxfield. Wilts 7L 19
Froxfield Green. Hants 3E 10
Fryern Hill. Hants 3B 10
Fryerning. Essx 3C 22
Fryton. N Yor 8D 48
Fugglestone St Peter. Wilts 2K 9
Fulbeck. Linc 4G 37
Fulbourn. Cambs 6B 30
Fulbrook. Oxon 2L 19
Fulflood. Hants 2B 10
Fulford. Som 3M 7
Fulford. Staf 6H 35
Fulford. York 3D 42
**Fulham**. G Lon 6K 21
Fulking. W Sus 4K 11
Fuller's Moor. Ches W 4C 34
Fuller Street. Essx 2D 22
Fullerton. Hants 2A 10
Fulletby. Linc 2K 37
Full Sutton. E Yor 2E 42
Fullwood. E Ayr 4C 58
Fulmer. Buck 5G 21
Fulmodestone. Norf 6F 38
Fulnetby. Linc 2H 37
Fulney. Linc 7K 37
Fulstow. Linc 8L 43
Fulthorpe. Stoc T 3B 48
Fulwell. Tyne 6G 55
Fulwood. Lanc 4D 40
Fulwood. Notts 4B 36
Fulwood. Som 4M 7
Fulwood. S Yor 1L 35
Fundenhall. Norf 2H 31
Funtington. W Sus 5E 10
Funtley. Hants 5C 10
Funzie. Shet 4L 91
Furley. Devn 5A 8
Furnace. Arg 7E 64
Furnace. Carm 6M 15
Furnace. Cdgn 3F 24
Furner's Green. E Sus 3M 11
Furness Vale. Derbs 1J 35
Furneux Pelham. Herts 1M 21
Furzebrook. Dors 7H 9
Furzehill. Devn 1G 7
Furzehill. Dors 5J 9
Furzeley Corner. Hants 4D 10
Furzey Lodge. Hants 5A 10
Furzley. Hants 4L 9
Fyfield. Essx 3B 22
Fyfield. Glos 3L 19
Fyfield. Hants 1L 9
Fyfield. Oxon 4B 20
Fyfield. Wilts 7K 19
**The Fylde**. Lanc 4B 40
Fylingthorpe. N Yor 5G 49

Fyning—Gwynfryn


Fyning. W Sus 3F 10
Fyvie. Abers 2G 73

## G

Gabhsann bho Dheas. W Isl 6H 83
Gabhsann bho Thuath.
W Isl 6H 83
Gabroc Hill. E Ayr 4C 58
Gadbrook. Surr 1K 11
Gaddesby. Leics 8D 36
Gadfa. IOA 2D 32
Gadgirth. S Ayr 7C 58
Gaer. Powy 2L 17
Gaerwen. IOA 3D 32
Gagingwell. Oxon 1B 20
Gaick Lodge. High 7H 71
Gailey. Staf 8H 35
Gainford. Dur 4K 47
**Gainsborough**. Linc 8F 42
Gainsborough. Suff 7H 31
Gainsford End. Essx 8D 30
Gairletter. Arg 1L 57
Gairloch. Abers 5G 73
Gairloch. High 6K 77
Gairlochy. High 7B 70
Gairney Bank. Per 8E 66
Gairnshiel Lodge. Abers 5B 72
Gaisgill. Cumb 5E 46
Gaitsgill. Cumb 7H 53
**Galashiels**. Bord 6B 60
Galgate. Lanc 2C 40
Galgorm. ME Ant 3G 93
Galhampton. Som 3E 8
Gallatown. Fife 8F 66
Galley Common. Warw 2M 27
Galleyend. Essx 3D 22
Galleywood. Essx 3D 22
Gallin. Per 3K 65
Gallowfauld. Ang 3H 67
Gallowhill. Per 4E 66
Gallowhill. Ren 3C 58
Gallowhills. Abers 8K 81
Gallows Green. Staf 5J 35
Gallows Green. Worc 5H 27
Gallowstree Common.
Oxon 5D 20
Galltair. High 3K 69
Gallt Melyd. Den 2K 33
Galmington. Som 3M 7
Galmisdale. High 7F 68
Galmpton. Devn 7J 5
Galmpton. Torb 6L 5
Galmpton Warborough.
Torb 6L 5
Galphay. N Yor 8L 47
Galston. E Ayr 6C 58
Galton. Dors 7F 8
Galtrigill. High 8C 76
Gamblesby. Cumb 8L 53
Gamblestown. Arm 6G 93
Gamelsby. Cumb 6G 53
Gamesley. Derbs 8J 41
Gamlingay. Cambs 6K 29
Gamlingay Cinques. Cambs 6K 29
Gamlingay Great Heath.
Cambs 6K 29
Gammaton. Devn 3D 6
Gammersgill. N Yor 7J 47
Gamston. Notts
nr. Nottingham 6D 36
nr. Retford 2E 36
Ganarew. Here 2D 18
Ganavan. Arg 4C 64
Ganborough. Glos 1K 19
Gang. Corn 5F 4
Ganllwyd. Gwyn 8G 33
Gannochy. Ang 8E 72
Gannochy. Per 5E 66
Gansclet. High 7E 86
Ganstead. E Yor 4J 43
Ganthorpe. N Yor 8D 48
Ganton. N Yor 8G 49
Gants Hill. G Lon 5M 21
Gappah. Devn 8H 7
Garafad. High 7F 76
Garboldisham. Norf 3G 31
Garden City. Flin 3B 34
Gardeners Green. Wok 7F 20
Gardenstown. Abers 7H 81
Garden Village. S Yor 8L 41
Garden Village. Swan 5E 16
Garderhouse. Shet 3D 90
Gardham. E Yor 3G 43
Gardie. Shet
on Papa Stour 1B 90
on Unst 2L 91
Gardie Ho. Shet 3E 90
Gare Hill. Wilts 1F 8
Garelochhead. Arg 8G 65
Garford. Oxon 4B 20
**Garforth**. W Yor 4B 42
Gargrave. N Yor 2H 41
Gargunnock. Stir 8M 65
Garleffin. S Ayr 3F 50
Garlieston. Dum 7K 51
Garlinge Green. Kent 8H 23
Garlogie. Abers 5G 73
Garmelow. Staf 7F 34
Garmond. Abers 8H 81
Garmondsway. Dur 8G 55
Garmony. Arg 3A 64
Garmouth. Mor 7C 80
Garmston. Shrp 1E 26
Garnant. Carm 3F 16
Garndiffaith. Torf 3A 18
Garndolbenmaen. Gwyn 6D 32
Garnett Bridge. Cumb 6D 46
Garnfadryn. Gwyn 7B 32
Garnkirk. N Lan 3E 58
Garnlydan. Blae 3L 17
Garnsgate. Linc 7M 37
Garnswllt. Swan 4F 16
Garn yr Erw. Torf 3M 17
Garrabost. W Isl 8J 83
Garrallan. E Ayr 8D 58
Garras. Corn 6L 3
Garreg. Gwyn 6F 32
Garrigill. Cumb 7M 53
Garrison. Ferm 6A 92
Garriston. N Yor 6K 47
Garrogie Lodge. High 4F 70
Garros. High 7F 76
Garrow. Per 3B 66
Garsdale. Cumb 7F 46
Garsdale Head. Cumb 6F 46
Garsdon. Wilts 5H 19
Garshall Green. Staf 6H 35
Garsington. Oxon 3C 20
Garstang. Lanc 3C 40
Garston. Mers 1C 34
Garswood. Mers 8D 40
Gartcosh. N Lan 3E 58
Garth. B'end 5H 17
Garth. Cdgn 4F 24
Garth. Gwyn 7E 32
Garth. IOM 7C 44
Garth. Powy
nr. Builth Wells 8J 25
nr. Knighton 4A 26
Garth. Shet
nr. Sandness 2C 90
nr. Skellister 2E 90
Garth. Wrex 5A 34
Garthamlock. Glas 3E 58
Garthbrengy. Powy 1K 17
Gartheli. Cdgn 7E 24
Garthmyl. Powy 3L 25
Garthorpe. Leics 7F 36
Garthorpe. N Lin 6F 42
Garth Owen. Powy 3L 25
Garth Place. Cphy 6L 17
Garth Row. Cumb 6D 46
Gartly. Abers 2E 72
Gartmore. Stir 8K 65
Gartness. N Lan 3F 58
Gartness. Stir 1D 58
Gartocharn. W Dun 1C 58
Garton. E Yor 4K 43
Garton-on-the-Wolds. E Yor 2G 43
Gartsherrie. N Lan 3F 58
Gartymore. High 2L 79
Garvagh. Caus 3F 93
Garvaghy. Ferm 5D 92
Garvald. E Lot 2C 60
Garvamore. High 6F 70
Garvard. Arg 8J 63
Garvault. High 8K 85
Garve. High 7D 78
Garvestone. Norf 1G 31
Garvetagh. Derr 4C 92
Garvie. Arg 8E 64
Garvock. Abers 8G 73
Garvock. Inv 2A 58
Garway. Here 1C 18
Garway Common. Here 1C 18
Garway Hill. Here 1C 18
Garwick. Linc 5J 37
Gaskan. High 8K 69
Gasper. Wilts 2F 8
Gastard. Wilts 7G 19
Gasthorpe. Norf 3F 30
Gatcombe. IOW 7B 10
Gateacre. Mers 1C 34
Gatebeck. Cumb 7D 46
Gate Burton. Linc 1F 36
Gateforth. N Yor 5C 42
Gatehead. E Ayr 6B 58
Gate Helmsley. N Yor 2D 42
Gatehouse. Nmbd 3A 54
Gatehouse of Fleet. Dum 6M 51
Gatelawbridge. Dum 2D 52
Gateley. Norf 7F 38
Gatenby. N Yor 7M 47
Gatesgarth. Cumb 3L 45
**Gateshead**. Tyne 5F 54
Gatesheath. Ches W 3C 34
Gateside. Ang
nr. Forfar 3H 67
nr. Kirriemuir 3G 67
Gateside. Fife 7E 66
Gateside. N Ayr 4B 58
Gathurst. G Man 7D 40
**Gatley**. G Man 1G 35
Gatton. Surr 8K 21
Gattonside. Bord 6C 60
Gatwick Airport. W Sus 1K 11
Gaufron. Powy 6J 25
Gaulby. Leics 1D 28
Gauldry. Fife 5G 67
Gaultree. Norf 1A 30
Gaunt's Common. Dors 5J 9
Gaunt's Earthcott. S Glo 5E 18
Gautby. Linc 2J 37
Gavinton. Bord 4E 60
Gawber. S Yor 7M 41
Gawcott. Buck 8D 28
Gawsworth. Ches E 3G 35
Gawthorpe. W Yor 5L 41
Gawthrop. Cumb 7E 46
Gawthwaite. Cumb 7A 46
Gay Bowers. Essx 3D 22
Gaydon. Warw 6A 28
Gayfield. Orkn 4D 88
Gayhurst. Mil 7F 28
Gayle. N Yor 7G 47
Gayles. N Yor 5K 47
Gay Street. W Sus 3H 11
Gayton. Mers 1A 34
Gayton. Norf 8D 38
Gayton. Nptn 6E 28
Gayton. Staf 7H 35
Gayton le Marsh. Linc 1M 37
Gayton le Wold. Linc 1K 37
Gayton Thorpe. Norf 8D 38
Gaywood. Norf 7C 38
Gazeley. Suff 5D 30
Geanies. High 6J 79
Gearraidh Bhailteas. W Isl 3D 74
Gearraidh Bhaird. W Isl 2E 76
Gearraidh ma Monadh.
W Isl 4D 74
Gearraidh na h-Aibhne.
W Isl 8F 82
Geary. High 7D 76
Geddes. High 8J 79
Gedding. Suff 6F 30
Geddington. Nptn 3F 28
Gedintailor. High 2G 69
Gedling. Notts 5D 36
Gedney. Linc 7M 37
Gedney Broadgate. Linc 7M 37
Gedney Drove End. Linc 7A 38
Gedney Dyke. Linc 7M 37
Gedney Hill. Linc 8L 37
Gee Cross. G Man 8H 41
Geeston. Rut 1G 29
Geilston. Arg 2B 58
Geirinis. W Isl 1D 74
Geise. High 5C 86
Geisiadar. W Isl 8E 82
Gelder Shiel. Abers 7B 72
Geldeston. Norf 2K 31
Gell. Cnwy 4H 33
Gelli. Pemb 5G 15
Gelli. Rhon 5J 17
Gellifor. Den 4L 33
**Gelligaer**. Cphy 5L 17
Y Gelli Gandryll. Powy 8M 25
Gellilydan. Gwyn 7F 32
Gellinudd. Neat 4G 17
Gellyburn. Per 4D 66
Gellywen. Carm 4J 15
Gelston. Dum 6B 52
Gelston. Linc 5G 37
Gembling. E Yor 2J 43
Geneva. Cdgn 1L 15
Gentleshaw. Staf 8J 35
Geocrab. W Isl 4C 76
George Best Belfast City Airport.
Bel 5H 93
George Green. Buck 5G 21
Georgeham. Devn 2D 6
George Nympton. Devn 3G 7
Georgetown. Blae 4L 17
Georgetown. Ren 3C 58
Georth. Orkn 7C 88
Gerlan. Gwyn 4F 32
Germansweek. Devn 6D 6
Germoe. Corn 6J 3
Gerrans. Corn 8A 4
Gerrard's Bromley. Staf 6F 34
**Gerrards Cross**. Buck 5G 21
Gerston. High 6C 86
Gestingthorpe. Essx 8E 30
Gethsemane. Pemb 2G 15
Geuffordd. Powy 1M 25
Gibraltar. Buck 2E 20
Gibraltar. Linc 4B 38
Gibraltar. Suff 6H 31
Gibsmere. Notts 5E 36
Giddeahall. Wilts 6G 19
Gidea Park. G Lon 5B 22
Gidleigh. Devn 7F 6
**Giffnock**. E Ren 4D 58
Gifford. E Lot 3C 60
Giffordtown. Fife 6F 66
Giggetty. Staf 2G 27
Giggleswick. N Yor 1G 41
Gignog. Pemb 4E 14
Gilberdyke. E Yor 5F 42
Gilbert's End. Worc 7G 27
Gilbert's Green. Warw 4K 27
Gilchriston. E Lot 3B 60
Gilcrux. Cumb 8F 52
Gildersome. W Yor 5L 41
Gildingwells. S Yor 1C 36
Gilesgate Moor. Dur 7F 54
Gileston. V Glam 8K 17
Gilfach. Cphy 5L 17
Gilfach Goch. Rhon 6J 17
Gilfachreda. Cdgn 1L 15
Gilford. Arm 6G 93
Gilgarran. Cumb 2K 45
Gillamoor. N Yor 6D 48
Gillan. Corn 6L 3
Gillar's Green. Mers 8C 40
Gillen. High 8D 76
Gilling East. N Yor 8D 48
Gillingham. Dors 3G 9
**Gillingham**. Medw 7D 22
Gillingham. Norf 2L 31
Gilling West. N Yor 5K 47
Gillock. High 6D 86
Gillow Heath. Staf 4G 35
Gills. High 4E 86
Gill's Green. Kent 2D 12
Gilmanscleuch. Bord 7M 59
Gilmerton. Edin 3L 59
Gilmerton. Per 5B 66
Gilmonby. Dur 4H 47
Gilmorton. Leics 3C 28
Gilsland. Nmbd 5L 53
Gilsland Spa. Cumb 5L 53
Gilston. Bord 4B 60
Giltbrook. Notts 5B 36
Gilwern. Mon 3M 17
Gimingham. Norf 6J 39
Giosla. W Isl 1C 76
Gipping. Suff 5G 31
Gipsey Bridge. Linc 5K 37
Gipton. W Yor 4M 41
Girdle Toll. N Ayr 5B 58
Girlsta. Shet 2E 90
Girsby. N Yor 5A 48
Girthon. Dum 6M 51
Girton. Cambs 5M 29
Girton. Notts 3F 36
Girvan. S Ayr 2G 51
Gisburn. Lanc 3G 41
Gisleham. Suff 3M 31
Gislingham. Suff 4G 31
Gissing. Norf 3H 31
Gittisham. Devn 6L 7
Gladestry. Powy 7M 25
Gladsmuir. E Lot 2B 60
Glaichbea. High 2F 70
Glais. Swan 4G 17
Glaisdale. N Yor 5E 48
Glame. High 1G 69
Glamis. Ang 3G 67
Glanaman. Carm 3F 16
Glan-Conwy. Cnwy 5H 33
Glandford. Norf 5G 39
Glan Duar. Carm 2M 15
Glandwr. Blae 4M 17
Glandwr. Pemb 4H 15
Glan-Dwyfach. Gwyn 6D 32
Glandy Cross. Carm 4H 15
Glandyfi. Cdgn 3F 24
Glangrwyney. Powy 3M 17
Glanmule. Powy 3L 25
Glan-rhyd. Pemb 3H 15
Glan-rhyd. Powy 4G 17
Glanrhyd. Gwyn 7B 32
Glanrhyd. Pemb 2H 15
Glanton. Nmbd 8H 61
Glanton Pyke. Nmbd 8H 61
Glanvilles Wootton. Dors 5E 8
Glan-y-don. Flin 3L 33
Glan-y-nant. Powy 4J 25
Glan-yr-afon. Gwyn 6K 33
Glan-yr-afon. IOA 2F 32
Glan-yr-afon. Powy 2K 25
Glan-y-wern. Gwyn 7F 32
Glapthorn. Nptn 2H 29
Glapwell. Derbs 3B 36
Glarryford. ME Ant 3G 93
Glas Aird. Arg 8J 63
Glas-allt Shiel. Abers 7B 72
Glasbury. Powy 1L 17
Glaschoil. High 2L 71
Glascoed. Den 3J 33
Glascoed. Mon 3B 18
Glascote. Staf 1L 27
Glascwm. Powy 7L 25
Glasfryn. Cnwy 5J 33
**Glasgow**. Glas 3D 58
Glasgow Airport. Ren 3C 58
Glasgow Prestwick Airport.
S Ayr 7B 58
Glashvin. High 7F 76
Glasinfryn. Gwyn 4E 32
Glas na Cardaich. High 6H 69
Glasnacardoch. High 6H 69
Glasnakille. High 4G 69
Glaspwll. Cdgn 3G 25
Glassburn. High 2D 70
Glassenbury. Kent 2D 12
Glasserton. Dum 8K 51
Glassford. S Lan 5F 58
Glassgreen. Mor 7B 80
Glasshouse. Glos 1F 18
Glasshouses. N Yor 1K 41
Glasson. Cumb 5G 53
Glasson. Lanc 2C 40
Glassonby. Cumb 8K 53
Glasswater. New M 6J 93
Glasterlaw. Ang 2J 67
Glaston. Rut 1F 28
Glastonbury. Som 2C 8
Glatton. Cambs 3J 29
Glazebrook. Warr 8E 40
Glazebury. Warr 8E 40
Glazeley. Shrp 3F 26
Gleadless. S Yor 1A 36
Gleadsmoss. Ches E 3G 35
Gleann Dail bho Dheas.
W Isl 4D 74
Gleann Tholastaidh. W Isl 7J 83
Gleann Uige. High 8H 69
Gleaston. Cumb 8A 46
Glebe. Derr 4C 92
Glecknabae. Arg 3K 57
Gledrid. Shrp 6A 34
Gleiniant. Powy 3J 25
Glemsford. Suff 7E 30
Glen. Dum 6L 51
Glenancross. High 6H 69
Glenanne. Arm 7F 93
Glenariff. Caus 2H 93
Glenarm. ME Ant 3H 93
Glen Auldyn. IOM 5D 44
Glenavy. Lis 5G 93
Glenbarr. Arg 6F 56
Glenbeg. High 1L 63
Glen Bernisdale. High 1F 68
Glenbervie. Abers 7G 73
Glenboig. N Lan 3F 58
Glenborrodale. High 1M 63
Glenbranter. Arg 8F 64
Glenbreck. Bord 7J 59
Glenbrein Lodge. High 4E 70
Glenbrittle. High 3F 68
Glenbuchat Lodge. Abers 4C 72
Glenbuck. E Ayr 7F 58
Glenburn. Ren 3C 58
Glencalvie Lodge. High 5E 78
Glencaple. Dum 5D 52
Glencarron Lodge. High 8A 78
Glencarse. Per 5E 66
Glencassley Castle. High 3E 78
Glencat. Abers 6E 72
Glencoe. High 2F 64
Glen Cottage. High 7H 69
Glencraig. Fife 8E 66
Glendale. High 1C 68
Glendevon. Per 7C 66
Glendoebeg. High 5E 70
Glendoick. Per 5F 66
Glendoune. S Ayr 2G 51
Glenduckie. Fife 6F 66
Gleneagles. Per 7C 66
Glenegedale. Arg 4C 56
Glenegedale Lots. Arg 4C 56
Glenelg. High 4K 69
Glenernie. Mor 1L 71
Glenesslin. Dum 3C 52
Glenfarg. Per 6E 66
Glenfarquhar Lodge. Abers 7G 73
Glenferness Mains. High 1K 71
Glenfeshie Lodge. High 6J 71
Glenfiddich Lodge. Mor 2C 72
Glenfield. Leics 1C 28
Glenfinnan. High 7L 69
Glenfintaig Lodge. High 7C 70
Glenfoot. Per 6E 66
Glenfyne Lodge. Arg 6G 65
Glengap. Dum 6A 52
Glengarnock. N Ayr 4B 58
Glengolly. High 5C 86
Glengorm Castle. Arg 2K 63
Glengormley. Ant 4H 93
Glengrasco. High 1F 68
Glenhead Farm. Ang 1F 66
Glenholm. Bord 6K 59
Glen House. Bord 6L 59
Glenhurich. High 1C 64
Glenkerry. Bord 8L 59
Glenkiln. Dum 4C 52
Glenkindie. Abers 4D 72
Glenkinglass Lodge. Arg 4F 64
Glenkirk. Bord 7J 59
Glenlean. Arg 1K 57
Glenlee. Dum 3M 51
Glenleraig. High 8D 84
Glenlichorn. Per 6A 66
Glenlivet. Mor 3A 72
Glenlochar. Dum 5B 52
Glenlochsie Lodge. Per 8L 71
Glenluce. Dum 6G 51
Glenmarksie. High 8D 78
Glenmassan. Arg 1L 57
Glenmavis. N Lan 3F 58
Glen Maye. IOM 7B 44
Glenmazeran Lodge. High 3H 71
Glenmidge. Dum 3C 52
Glen Mona. IOM 6D 44
Glenmore. High
nr. Glenborrodale 1L 63
nr. Kingussie 5K 71
on Isle of Skye 1F 68
Glenmoy. Ang 1H 67
Glennoe. Arg 4E 64
Glen of Coachford. Abers 1D 72
Glenogil. Ang 1H 67
Glen Parva. Leics 2C 28
Glenprosen Village. Ang 1G 67
Glenree. N Ayr 7J 57
Glenridding. Cumb 4B 46
Glenrosa. N Ayr 6K 57
**Glenrothes**. Fife 7F 66
Glensanda. High 3C 64
Glensaugh. Abers 8F 72
Glenshero Lodge. High 6F 70
Glensluain. Arg 8E 64
Glenstockadale. Dum 5F 50
Glenstriven. Arg 2K 57
Glen Tanar House. Abers 6D 72
Glentham. Linc 8H 43
Glenton. Abers 3F 72
Glentress. Bord 6L 59
Glentromie Lodge. High 6H 71
Glentrool Lodge. Dum 3K 51
Glentrool Village. Dum 4J 51
Glentruim House. High 6G 71
Glentworth. Linc 1G 37
Glenuig. High 8H 69
Glen View. New M 7G 93
Glen Village. Falk 2G 59
Glen Vine. IOM 7C 44
Glenwhilly. Dum 4G 51
Glenzierfoot. Dum 4H 53
Glespin. S Lan 7G 59
Gletness. Shet 2E 90
Glewstone. Here 1D 18
Glib Cheois. W Isl 1E 76
Glinton. Pet 1J 29
Glooston. Leics 2E 28
**Glossop**. Derbs 8J 41
Gloster Hill. Nmbd 1F 54
**Gloucester**. Glos 2G 19
Gloucestershire Airport.
Glos 1G 19
Gloup. Shet 3K 91
Glusburn. N Yor 3J 41
Glutt Lodge. High 8A 86
Glutton Bridge. Derbs 3J 35
Gluvian. Corn 5B 4
Glympton. Oxon 1B 20
Glyn. Cnwy 3H 33
Glynarthen. Cdgn 2K 15
Glynbrochan. Powy 4J 25
Glyn Ceiriog. Wrex 7M 33
Glyncoch. Rhon 5K 17
Glyncorrwg. Neat 5H 17
Glynde. E Sus 5A 12
Glyndebourne. E Sus 5A 12
Glyndyfrdwy. Den 6L 33
**Glyn Ebwy**. Blae 4L 17
Glynllan. B'end 6J 17
Glynn. ME Ant 4J 93
Glyn-neath. Neat 4H 17
Glynogwr. B'end 6J 17
Glyntaff. Rhon 6K 17
Glyntawe. Powy 3H 17
Glynteg. Carm 3K 15
Gnosall. Staf 7G 35
Gnosall Heath. Staf 7G 35
Goadby. Leics 2E 28
Goadby Marwood. Leics 7E 36
Goatacre. Wilts 6J 19
Goathill. Dors 4E 8
Goathland. N Yor 5F 48
Goathurst. Som 2A 8
Goathurst Common. Kent 8A 22
Goat Lees. Kent 1G 13
Gobernuisgach Lodge.
High 7G 85
Gobernuisgeach. High 8A 86
Gobhaig. W Isl 3B 76
Gobowen. Shrp 6B 34
**Godalming**. Surr 1G 11
Goddard's Corner. Suff 5J 31
Goddard's Green. Kent
nr. Benenden 2E 12
nr. Cranbrook 2D 12
Goddards' Green. W Sus 3K 11
Godford Cross. Devn 5L 7
Godleybrook. Staf 5H 35
Godmanchester. Cambs 4K 29
Godmanstone. Dors 6E 8
Godmersham. Kent 8G 23
Godolphin Cross. Corn 5K 3
Godre'r-graig. Neat 4G 17
Godshill. Hants 4K 9
Godshill. IOW 7C 10
Godstone. Staf 6J 35
Godstone. Surr 8L 21
Goetre. Mon 3B 18
Goff's Oak. Herts 3L 21
Gogar. Edin 2K 59
Goginan. Cdgn 4F 24
Golan. Gwyn 6E 32
Golant. Corn 6D 4
Golberdon. Corn 8C 6
**Golborne**. G Man 8E 40
Golcar. W Yor 6J 41
Goldcliff. Newp 5B 18
Golden Cross. E Sus 4B 12
Golden Green. Kent 1C 12
Golden Grove. Carm 3E 16
Golden Grove. N Yor 5F 48
Golden Hill. Pemb 4F 14
Goldenhill. Stoke 4G 35
Golden Pot. Hants 1E 10
Golden Valley. Glos 1H 19
Golders Green. G Lon 5K 21
Goldhanger. Essx 3F 22
Gold Hill. Norf 2B 30
Golding. Shrp 1D 26
Goldington. Bed 6H 29
Goldsborough. N Yor
nr. Harrogate 2A 42
nr. Whitby 4F 48
Goldsithney. Corn 5J 3
Goldstone. Kent 7J 23
Goldstone. Shrp 7F 34
Goldthorpe. S Yor 7B 42
Goldworthy. Devn 3C 6
Golfa. Powy 8L 33
Gollanfield. High 8J 79
Gollinglith Foot. N Yor 7K 47
Golsoncott. Som 2K 7
Golspie. High 4J 79
Gomeldon. Wilts 2K 9
Gomersal. W Yor 5L 41
Gometra House. Arg 3J 63
Gomshall. Surr 1H 11
Gonalston. Notts 5D 36
Gonerby Hill Foot. Linc 6G 37
Gonfirth. Shet 1D 90
Good Easter. Essx 2C 22
Gooderstone. Norf 1D 30
Goodleigh. Devn 2F 6
Goodmanham. E Yor 3F 42
Goodmayes. G Lon 5A 22
Goodnestone. Kent
nr. Aylesham 8J 23
nr. Faversham 7G 23
Goodrich. Here 2D 18
Goodrington. Torb 6L 5
Goodshaw. Lanc 5G 41
Goodshaw Fold. Lanc 5G 41
Goodstone. Devn 8G 7
Goodwick. Pemb 3F 14
Goodworth Clatford. Hants 1A 10
**Goole**. E Yor 5E 42
Goom's Hill. Worc 6J 27
Goonabarn. Corn 6B 4
Goonbell. Corn 4L 3
Goonhavern. Corn 3L 3
Goonlaze. Corn 5L 3
Goonvrea. Corn 4L 3
Goose Green. Cumb 7D 46
Goose Green. S Glo 5F 18
Gooseham. Corn 4B 6
Goosewell. Plym 6H 5
Goosey. Oxon 4A 20
Goosnargh. Lanc 4D 40
Goostrey. Ches E 2F 34
Gorcott Hill. Warw 5J 27
Gord. Shet 5E 90
Gordon. Bord 5D 60
Gordonbush. High 3J 79
Gordonstown. Abers
nr. Cornhill 8E 80
nr. Fyvie 2G 73
Gorebridge. Midl 3M 59
Gorefield. Cambs 8M 37
Gores. Wilts 8K 19
Gorgie. Edin 2L 59
Goring. Oxon 5D 20
Goring-by-Sea. W Sus 5J 11
Goring Heath. Oxon 6D 20
Gorleston-on-Sea. Norf 1M 31
Gornalwood. W Mid 2H 27
Gorran Churchtown. Corn 7B 4
Gorran Haven. Corn 7C 4
Gorran High Lanes. Corn 7B 4
Gors. Cdgn 5F 24
Gorsedd. Flin 3L 33
**Gorseinon**. Swan 5E 16
Gorseness. Orkn 8D 88
Gorseybank. Derbs 4L 35
Gorsgoch. Cdgn 1L 15
Gorslas. Carm 3E 16
Gorsley. Glos 1E 18
Gorsley Common. Here 1E 18
Gorstan. High 7D 78
Gorstella. Ches W 3B 34
Gorsty Common. Here 8C 26
Gorsty Hill. Staf 7K 35
Gortantaoid. Arg 2C 56
Gorteneorn. High 1M 63
Gortenfern. High 1M 63
Gortin. Ferm 4D 92
Gortnahey. Caus 3E 92
Gorton. G Man 8G 41
Gosbeck. Suff 6H 31
Gosberton. Linc 6K 37
Gosberton Cheal. Linc 7K 37
Gosberton Clough. Linc 7J 37
Goseley Dale. Derbs 7M 35
Gosfield. Essx 1D 22
Gosford. Oxon 2C 20
Gosforth. Cumb 4K 45
**Gosforth**. Tyne 5F 54
Gosmore. Herts 1J 21
Gospel End. Staf 2G 27
**Gosport**. Hants 6D 10
Gossabrough. Shet 5K 91
Gossington. Glos 3F 18
Gossops Green. W Sus 2K 11
Goswick. Nmbd 5H 61
Gotham. Notts 6C 36
Gotherington. Glos 1H 19
Gott. Arg 3F 62
Gott. Shet 3E 90
Goudhurst. Kent 2D 12
Goulceby. Linc 2K 37
Gourdon. Abers 8H 73
Gourock. Inv 2M 57
Govan. Glas 3D 58
Govanhill. Glas 3D 58
Goverton. Notts 5E 36
Goveton. Devn 7K 5
Govilon. Mon 2A 18
Gowanhill. Abers 7K 81
Gowdall. E Yor 5D 42
Gowdystown. Arm 6G 93
Gowerton. Swan 5E 16
Gowkhall. Fife 1J 59
Gowthorpe. E Yor 2E 42
Goxhill. E Yor 3J 43
Goxhill. N Lin 5J 43
Goxhill Haven. N Lin 5J 43
Goytre. Neat 6G 17
Grabhair. W Isl 2E 76
Graby. Linc 7H 37
Gracehill. ME Ant 3G 93
Graffham. W Sus 4G 11
Grafham. Cambs 5J 29
Grafham. Surr 1H 11
Grafton. Here 8C 26
Grafton. N Yor 1B 42
Grafton. Oxon 3L 19
Grafton. Shrp 8C 34
Grafton. Worc
nr. Evesham 8H 27
nr. Leominster 5D 26
Grafton Flyford. Worc 6H 27
Grafton Regis. Nptn 7E 28
Grafton Underwood. Nptn 3G 29
Grafty Green. Kent 1E 12
Graianrhyd. Den 5M 33
Graig. Carm 6L 15
Graig. Cnwy 3H 33
Graig. Den 3K 33
Graig-fechan. Den 5L 33
Graig Penllyn. V Glam 7J 17
Grain. Medw 6E 22
Grainsby. Linc 8K 43
Grainthorpe. Linc 8L 43
Grainthorpe Fen. Linc 8L 43
Graiselound. N Lin 8E 42
Gramasdail. W Isl 8K 75
Grampound. Corn 7B 4
Grampound Road. Corn 6B 4
Granborough. Buck 1E 20
Granby. Notts 6E 36
Grandborough. Warw 5B 28
Grandpont. Oxon 3C 20
Grandtully. Per 2C 66
Grange. Cumb 4A 46
Grange. E Ayr 6C 58
Grange. Here 4C 26
Grange. Mers 2M 33
Grange. Per 5F 66
The Grange. N Yor 6C 48
Grange Corner. ME Ant 4G 93
Grange Crossroads. Mor 8D 80
Grange Hill. Essx 4M 21
Grangemill. Derbs 4L 35
Grange Moor. W Yor 6L 41
**Grangemouth**. Falk 1H 59
Grange of Lindores. Fife 6F 66
Grange-over-Sands. Cumb 8C 46
Grangepans. Falk 1J 59
Grange Park. New M 6J 93
Grangetown. Card 7L 17
Grangetown. Red C 3C 48
Grange Villa. Dur 6F 54
Granish. High 4J 71
Gransmoor. E Yor 2J 43
Granston. Pemb 3E 14
Grantchester. Cambs 6M 29
**Grantham**. Linc 6G 37
Grantley. N Yor 1L 41
Grantlodge. Abers 4G 73
Granton. Edin 2L 59
Grantown-on-Spey. High 3L 71
Grantshouse. Bord 3F 60
Grappenhall. Warr 1E 34
Grasby. Linc 7H 43
Grasmere. Cumb 5B 46
Grasscroft. G Man 7H 41
Grassendale. Mers 1B 34
Grassgarth. Cumb 7H 53
Grassholme. Dur 3H 47
Grassington. N Yor 1J 41
Grassmoor. Derbs 3B 36
Grassthorpe. Notts 3E 36
Grateley. Hants 1L 9
Gratton. Devn 4C 6
Gratton. Staf 4H 35
Gratwich. Staf 6J 35
Graveley. Cambs 5K 29
Graveley. Herts 1K 21
Gravelhill. Shrp 8C 34
Gravel Hole. G Man 7H 41
Gravelly Hill. W Mid 2K 27
Graven. Shet 6J 91
Graveney. Kent 7G 23
**Gravesend**. Kent 6C 22
Grayingham. Linc 8G 43
Grayrigg. Cumb 6D 46
**Grays**. Thur 6C 22
Grayshott. Hants 2F 10
Grayson Green. Cumb 2J 45
Grayswood. Surr 2G 11
Graythorp. Hart 3C 48
Grazeley. Wok 7D 20
Grealin. High 7G 77
Greasbrough. S Yor 8B 42
**Greasby**. Mers 1A 34
Great Abington. Cambs 7B 30
Great Addington. Nptn 4G 29
Great Alne. Warw 6K 27
Great Altcar. Lanc 7B 40
Great Amwell. Herts 2L 21
Great Asby. Cumb 4E 46
Great Ashfield. Suff 5F 30
Great Ayton. N Yor 4C 48
Great Baddow. Essx 3D 22
Great Bardfield. Essx 8C 30
Great Barford. Bed 6J 29
Great Barr. W Mid 2J 27
Great Barrington. Glos 2L 19
Great Barrow. Ches W 3C 34
Great Barton. Suff 5E 30
Great Barugh. N Yor 8E 48
Great Bavington. Nmbd 3C 54
Great Bealings. Suff 7J 31
Great Bedwyn. Wilts 7L 19
Great Bentley. Essx 1H 23
Great Billing. Nptn 5F 28
Great Bircham. Norf 6D 38
Great Blakenham. Suff 6H 31
Great Blencow. Cumb 8J 53
Great Bolas. Telf 7E 34
Great Bookham. Surr 8J 21
Great Bosullow. Corn 5H 3
Great Bourton. Oxon 7B 28
Great Bowden. Leics 3E 28
Great Bradley. Suff 6C 30
Great Braxted. Essx 2E 22
Great Bricett. Suff 6G 31
Great Brickhill. Buck 8G 29
Great Bridgeford. Staf 7G 35
Great Brington. Nptn 5D 28
Great Bromley. Essx 1G 23
Great Broughton. Cumb 8E 52
Great Broughton. N Yor 5C 48
Great Budworth. Ches W 2E 34
Great Burdon. Darl 4M 47
Great Burstead. Essx 4C 22
Great Busby. N Yor 5C 48
Great Canfield. Essx 2B 22
Great Carlton. Linc 1M 37
Great Casterton. Rut 1G 29
Great Chalfield. Wilts 7G 19
Great Chart. Kent 1F 12
Great Chatwell. Staf 8F 34
Great Chesterford. Essx 7B 30
Great Cheverell. Wilts 8H 19
Great Chilton. Dur 8F 54
Great Chishill. Cambs 8M 29
Great Clacton. Essx 2H 23
Great Cliff. W Yor 6M 41
Great Clifton. Cumb 2K 45
Great Coates. NE Lin 6K 43
Great Comberton. Worc 7H 27
Great Corby. Cumb 6J 53
Great Cornard. Suff 7E 30
Great Cowden. E Yor 3K 43
Great Coxwell. Oxon 4L 19
Great Crakehall. N Yor 6L 47
Great Cransley. Nptn 4F 28
Great Cressingham. Norf 1E 30
Great Crosby. Mers 7B 40
Great Cubley. Derbs 6K 35
Great Dalby. Leics 8E 36
Great Doddington. Nptn 5F 28
Great Doward. Here 2D 18
Great Dunham. Norf 8E 38
Great Dunmow. Essx 1C 22
Great Durnford. Wilts 2K 9
Great Easton. Essx 1C 22
Great Easton. Leics 2F 28
Great Eccleston. Lanc 3C 40
Great Edstone. N Yor 7E 48
Great Ellingham. Norf 2G 31
Great Elm. Som 1F 8
Great Eppleton. Tyne 7G 55
Great Eversden. Cambs 6L 29
Great Fencote. N Yor 6L 47
Great Finborough. Suff 6G 31
Greatford. Linc 8H 37
Great Fransham. Norf 8E 38
Great Gaddesden. Herts 2H 21
Great Gate. Staf 5J 35
Great Gidding. Cambs 3J 29
Great Givendale. E Yor 2F 42
Great Glemham. Suff 5K 31
Great Glen. Leics 2D 28
Great Gonerby. Linc 6F 36
Great Gransden. Cambs 6K 29
Great Green. Norf 3J 31
Great Green. Suff
nr. Lavenham 6F 30
nr. Palgrave 4H 31
Great Habton. N Yor 8E 48
Great Hale. Linc 5J 37
Great Hallingbury. Essx 2B 22
Greatham. Hants 2E 10
Greatham. Hart 3B 48
Greatham. W Sus 4H 11
Great Hampden. Buck 3F 20
Great Harrowden. Nptn 4F 28
**Great Harwood**. Lanc 4F 40
Great Haseley. Oxon 3D 20
Great Hatfield. E Yor 3J 43
Great Haywood. Staf 7H 35
Great Heath. W Mid 3M 27
Great Heck. N Yor 5C 42
Great Henny. Essx 8E 30
Great Hinton. Wilts 8H 19
Great Hockham. Norf 2F 30
Great Holland. Essx 2J 23
Great Horkesley. Essx 8F 30
Great Hormead. Herts 8M 29
Great Horton. W Yor 4K 41
Great Horwood. Buck 8E 28
Great Houghton. Nptn 6E 28
Great Houghton. S Yor 7B 42
Great Hucklow. Derbs 2K 35
Great Kelk. E Yor 2J 43
Great Kendale. E Yor 1H 43
Great Kimble. Buck 3F 20
Great Kingshill. Buck 4F 20
Great Langdale. Cumb 5A 46
Great Langton. N Yor 6L 47
Great Leighs. Essx 2D 22
Great Limber. Linc 7J 43
Great Linford. Mil 7F 28
Great Livermere. Suff 4E 30
Great Longstone. Derbs 2L 35
Great Lumley. Dur 7F 54
Great Lyth. Shrp 1C 26
**Great Malvern**. Worc 7F 26
Great Maplestead. Essx 8E 30
Great Marton. Bkpl 4B 40
Great Massingham. Norf 7D 38
Great Melton. Norf 1H 31
Great Milton. Oxon 3D 20
Great Missenden. Buck 3F 20
Great Mitton. Lanc 4F 40
Great Mongeham. Kent 8K 23
Great Moulton. Norf 2H 31
Great Munden. Herts 1L 21
Great Musgrave. Cumb 4F 46
Great Ness. Shrp 8B 34
Great Notley. Essx 1D 22
Great Oak. Mon 3B 18
Great Oakley. Essx 1H 23
Great Oakley. Nptn 3F 28
Great Offley. Herts 1J 21
Great Ormside. Cumb 4F 46
Great Orton. Cumb 6H 53
Great Ouseburn. N Yor 1B 42
Great Oxendon. Nptn 3E 28
Great Oxney Green. Essx 3C 22
Great Parndon. Essx 3M 21
Great Paxton. Cambs 5K 29
Great Plumpton. Lanc 4B 40
Great Plumstead. Norf 8K 39
Great Ponton. Linc 6G 37
Great Potheridge. Devn 4E 6
Great Preston. W Yor 5B 42
Great Raveley. Cambs 3K 29
Great Rissington. Glos 2K 19
Great Rollright. Oxon 8M 27
Great Ryburgh. Norf 7F 38
Great Ryle. Nmbd 8H 61
Great Ryton. Shrp 1C 26
Great Saling. Essx 1D 22
Great Salkeld. Cumb 8K 53
Great Sampford. Essx 8C 30
**Great Sankey**. Warr 1D 34
Great Saredon. Staf 1H 27
Great Saxham. Suff 5D 30
Great Shefford. W Ber 6A 20
Great Shelford. Cambs 6A 30
Great Shoddesden. Hants 1L 9
Great Smeaton. N Yor 5M 47
Great Snoring. Norf 6F 38
Great Somerford. Wilts 5H 19
Great Stainton. Darl 3M 47
Great Stambridge. Essx 4E 22
Great Staughton. Cambs 5J 29
Great Steeping. Linc 3M 37
Great Stonar. Kent 8K 23
Greatstone-on-Sea. Kent 3G 13
Great Strickland. Cumb 3D 46
Great Stukeley. Cambs 4K 29
Great Sturton. Linc 2K 37
Great Sutton. Ches W 2B 34
Great Sutton. Shrp 3D 26
Great Swinburne. Nmbd 4C 54
Great Tew. Oxon 1A 20
Great Tey. Essx 1E 22
Great Thirkleby. N Yor 8B 48
Great Thorness. IOW 6B 10
Great Thurlow. Suff 6C 30
Great Torr. Devn 7J 5
Great Torrington. Devn 4D 6
Great Tosson. Nmbd 1D 54
Great Totham North. Essx 2E 22
Great Totham South. Essx 2E 22
Great Tows. Linc 8K 43
Great Urswick. Cumb 8A 46
Great Wakering. Essx 5F 22
Great Waldingfield. Suff 7F 30
Great Walsingham. Norf 6F 38
Great Waltham. Essx 2C 22
Great Warley. Essx 4B 22
Great Washbourne. Glos 8H 27
Great Wenham. Suff 8G 31
Great Whelnetham. Suff 6E 30
Great Whittington. Nmbd 4D 54
Great Wigborough. Essx 2F 22
Great Wilbraham. Cambs 6B 30
Great Wilne. Derbs 6B 36
Great Wishford. Wilts 2J 9
Great Witchingham. Norf 7H 39
Great Witcombe. Glos 2H 19
Great Witley. Worc 5F 26
Great Wolford. Warw 8L 27
Greatworth. Nptn 7C 28
Great Wratting. Suff 7C 30
Great Wymondley. Herts 1K 21
**Great Wyrley**. Staf 1H 27
Great Wytheford. Shrp 8D 34
**Great Yarmouth**. Norf 1M 31
Great Yeldham. Essx 8D 30
Grebby. Linc 3M 37
Greeba Castle. IOM 6C 44
The Green. Cumb 6L 45
The Green. Wilts 2G 9
Greenbank. Shet 3K 91
Greenbottom. Corn 4L 3
Greenburn. W Lot 3H 59
Greencastle. Ferm 4D 92
Greencroft. Dur 6E 54
Greendown. Som 8D 18
Greendykes. Nmbd 7H 61
Green End. Bed
nr. Bedford 7H 29
nr. Little Staughton 5J 29
Green End. Herts
nr. Buntingford 8L 29
nr. Stevenage 1L 21
Green End. N Yor 5F 48
Green End. Warw 3L 27
Greenfield. Arg 8G 65
Greenfield. C Beds 8H 29
Greenfield. Flin 3L 33
Greenfield. G Man 7H 41
Greenfield. Oxon 4E 20
Greenfoot. N Lan 3F 58
**Greenford**. G Lon 5J 21
Greengairs. N Lan 2F 58
Greengate. Norf 8G 39
Greengill. Cumb 8F 52
Greenhalgh. Lanc 4C 40
Greenham. Dors 5C 8
Greenham. Som 3K 7
Greenham. W Ber 7B 20
Green Hammerton. N Yor 2B 42
Greenhaugh. Nmbd 3A 54
Greenhead. Nmbd 5L 53
Green Heath. Staf 8H 35
Greenhill. Dum 4F 52
Greenhill. Falk 2G 59
Greenhill. Kent 7H 23
Greenhill. S Yor 1M 35
Greenhill. Worc 4G 27
Greenhills. N Ayr 4B 58
Greenhithe. Kent 6B 22
Greenholm. E Ayr 6D 58
Greenhow Hill. N Yor 1K 41
Greenigoe. Orkn 1F 86
Greenisland. ME Ant 4H 93
Greenland. High 5D 86
Greenland Mains. High 5D 86
Greenlands. Worc 5J 27
Green Lane. Shrp 7E 34
Green Lane. Worc 5J 27
Greenlaw. Bord 5E 60
Greenlea. Dum 4E 52
Greenloaning. Per 7B 66
Greenmount. G Man 6F 40
Greenmow. Shet 5E 90
**Greenock**. Inv 2A 58
Greenock Mains. E Ayr 7E 58
Greenodd. Cumb 7B 46
Green Ore. Som 8D 18
Greenrow. Cumb 6F 52
Greens. Abers 1H 73
Greensgate. Norf 8H 39
Greenside. Tyne 5E 54
Greensidehill. Nmbd 8G 61
Greens Norton. Nptn 7D 28
Greenstead Green. Essx 1E 22
Greensted Green. Essx 3B 22
Green Street. Herts 4J 21
Green Street. Suff 4H 31
Green Street Green. G Lon 7A 22
Green Street Green. Kent 6B 22
Greenstreet Green. Suff 7G 31
Green Tye. Herts 2M 21
Greenwall. Orkn 1G 87
Greenway. Pemb 3G 15
Greenway. V Glam 7K 17
Greenwell. Cumb 6K 53
**Greenwich**. G Lon 6L 21
Greet. Glos 8J 27
Greete. Shrp 4D 26
Greetham. Linc 2L 37
Greetham. Rut 8G 37
Greetland. W Yor 5J 41
Gregson Lane. Lanc 5D 40
Grein. W Isl 5C 74
Greinetobht. W Isl 6K 75
Greinton. Som 2C 8
Gremista. Shet 3E 90
Grenaby. IOM 7B 44
Grendon. Nptn 5F 28
Grendon. Warw 1L 27
Grendon Common. Warw 2L 27
Grendon Green. Here 6D 26
Grendon Underwood.
Buck 1D 20
Grenofen. Devn 8D 6
Grenoside. S Yor 8M 41
Greosabhagh. W Isl 4C 76
Gresford. Wrex 4B 34
Gresham. Norf 6H 39
Greshornish. High 8E 76
Gressenhall. Norf 8F 38
Gressingham. Lanc 1D 40
Greta Bridge. Dur 4J 47
Gretna. Dum 5H 53
Gretna Green. Dum 5H 53
Gretton. Glos 8J 27
Gretton. Nptn 2G 29
Gretton. Shrp 2D 26
Grewelthorpe. N Yor 8L 47
Greyabbey. Ards 5J 93
Greygarth. N Yor 8K 47
Grey Green. N Lin 7E 42
Greylake. Som 2B 8
Greysouthen. Cumb 2K 45
Greysteel. Caus 2D 92
Greystoke. Cumb 8J 53
Greystoke Gill. Cumb 3C 46
Greystone. Ang 3J 67
Greystones. S Yor 1M 35
Greywell. Hants 8E 20
Griais. W Isl 7H 83
Grianan. W Isl 8H 83
Gribthorpe. E Yor 4E 42
Gribun. Arg 4K 63
Griff. Warw 3A 28
Griffithstown. Torf 4A 18
Griffydam. Leics 8B 36
Griggs Green. Hants 2F 10
Grimbister. Orkn 8C 88
Grimeford Village. Lanc 6E 40
Grimeston. Orkn 8C 88
Grimethorpe. S Yor 7B 42
Griminis. W Isl
on Benbecula
on North Uist
Grimister. Shet
Grimley. Worc
Grimness. Orkn
Grimoldby. Linc
Grimpo. Shrp
Grimsargh. Lanc
Grimsbury. Oxon
**Grimsby**. NE Lin
Grimscote. Nptn
Grimscott. Corn
Grimshaw. Bkbn
Grimshaw Green. Lanc
Grimsthorpe. Linc
Grimston. E Yor
Grimston. Leics
Grimston. Norf
Grimston. York
Grimstone. Dors
Grimstone End. Suff
Grinacombe Moor. Devn
Grindale. E Yor
Grindhill. Devn
Grindiscol. Shet
Grindle. Shrp
Grindleford. Derbs
Grindleton. Lanc
Grindley. Staf
Grindley Brook. Shrp
Grindlow. Derbs
Grindon. Nmbd
Grindon. Staf
Gringley on the Hill. Notts
Grinsdale. Cumb
Grinshill. Shrp
Grinton. N Yor
Griomsidar. W Isl
Grishipoll. Arg
Grisling Common. E Sus
Gristhorpe. N Yor
Griston. Norf
Gritley. Orkn
Grittenham. Wilts
Grittleton. Wilts
Grizebeck. Cumb
Grizedale. Cumb
Grobister. Orkn
Grobsness. Shet
Groby. Leics
Groes. Cnwy
Groes. Neat
Groes-faen. Rhon
Groesffordd. Gwyn
Groesffordd. Powy
Groeslon. Gwyn
Groes-lwyd. Powy
Groes-wen. Cphy
Grogport. Arg
Groigearraidh. W Isl
Gromford. Suff
Gronant. Flin
Groombridge. E Sus
Groomsport. Ards
Grosmont. Mon
Grosmont. N Yor
Groton. Suff
Grove. Dors
Grove. Kent
Grove. Notts
Grove. Oxon
The Grove. Dum
The Grove. Worc
Grovehill. E Yor
Grove Park. G Lon
Grovesend. Swan
Grub Street. Staf
Grudie. High
Gruids. High
Gruinard House. High
Gruinart. Arg
Grulinbeg. Arg
Gruline. Arg
Grummore. High
Grundisburgh. Suff
Gruting. Shet
Grutness. Shet
Gualachulain. High
Gualin House. High
Guardbridge. Fife
Guarlford. Worc
Guay. Per
Gubblecote. Herts
Guestling Green. E Sus
Guestling Thorn. E Sus
Guestwick. Norf
Guestwick Green. Norf
Guide. Bkbn
Guide Post. Nmbd
Guilden Down. Shrp
Guilden Morden. Cambs
Guilden Sutton. Ches W
**Guildford**. Surr
Guildtown. Per
Guilsborough. Nptn
Guilsfield. Powy
Guineaford. Devn
**Guisborough**. Red C
Guiseley. W Yor
Guist. Norf
Guiting Power. Glos
Gulberwick. Shet
Gullane. E Lot
Gulling Green. Suff
Gulval. Corn
Gulworthy. Devn
Gumfreston. Pemb
Gumley. Leics
Gunby. E Yor
Gunby. Linc
Gundleton. Hants
Gun Green. Kent
Gun Hill. E Sus
Gunn. Devn
Gunnerside. N Yor
Gunnerton. Nmbd
Gunness. N Lin
Gunnislake. Corn
Gunnista. Shet
Gunsgreenhill. Bord
Gunstone. Staf
Gunthorpe. Norf
Gunthorpe. N Lin
Gunthorpe. Notts
Gunthorpe. Pet
Gunville. IOW
Gupworthy. Som
Gurnard. IOW
Gurney Slade. Som
Gurnos. Powy
Gussage All Saints. Dors
Gussage St Andrew. Dors
Gussage St Michael. Dors
Guston. Kent
Gutcher. Shet
Guthram Gowt. Linc
Guthrie. Ang
Guyhirn. Cambs
Guyhirn Gull. Cambs
Guy's Head. Linc
Guy's Marsh. Dors
Guyzance. Nmbd
Gwaelod-y-garth. Card
Gwaenynog Bach. Den
Gwaenysgor. Flin
Gwalchmai. IOA
Gwastad. Pemb
Gwaun-Cae-Gurwen. Neat
Gwbert. Cdgn
Gweek. Corn
Gwehelog. Mon
Gwenddwr. Powy
Gwennap. Corn
Gwenter. Corn
Gwernaffield. Flin
Gwernesney. Mon
Gwernogle. Carm
Gwern-y-go. Powy
Gwernymynydd. Flin
Gwersyllt. Wrex
Gwespyr. Flin
Gwinear. Corn
Gwithian. Corn
Gwredog. IOA
Gwyddelwern. Den
Gwyddgrug. Carm
Gwynfryn. Wrex

Gwystre—Hincaster


tre. Powy 6K 25
ierin. Cnwy 4H 33
a. Wrex 5B 34
ı. Cnwy 3G 33

## H

f Houlland. Shet 3K 91
erley. Shrp 1C 26
lesthorpe. Notts 1E 36
ˈgham. Lanc 4G 41
. W Sus 3F 10
ɔugh. NE Lin 6J 43
oy. Linc 6H 37
eston. Suff 6K 31
enthorpe. S Yor 1B 36
ford. Norf 1G 31
forth. N Yor 6L 47
and. Orkn 7C 88
eton. Nptn 6F 28
man's Gate. Worc 4G 27
ness. N Yor 6G 49
ness. Orkn 2E 86
**ney**. G Lon 5L 21
thorn. Linc 1G 37
thorpe. Cumb 3D 46
it. W Isl 1E 74
nby. Linc 7J 37
en. Bord 6E 60
enham. Buck 3E 20
enham. Cambs 4A 30
enham End Field.
Cambs 4A 30
ngton. E Lot 2C 60
ngton. Linc 3G 37
scoe. Norf 2L 31
o. Abers 2H 73
on. Cambs 2J 29
more. Staf 1K 27
eld. Derbs 8J 41
am Cross. Herts 2M 21
am Ford. Herts 1M 21
igh. Essx 5E 22
igh. Suff 7G 31
igh Heath. Suff 7F 30
y. Telf 8E 34
y. Worc 5G 27
y End. Staf 7K 35
y Wood. G Lon 4K 21
w. Kent 1C 12
w Down. E Sus 3B 12
ill. Shrp 7D 34
ock. Essx 7B 30
on. Nmbd 1F 54
Derbs 2A 36
ir. Worc 5H 27
nden Quarter. Kent 1E 12
ate. Lanc 4G 41
oeck. Cumb 4J 53
ersta. Shet 3D 90
erston. Nmbd 5H 61
ister. Shet 6H 91
y. Here 7D 26
y. Worc 3H 27
aby. Linc 3L 37
orthingham. Linc 3L 37
. G Man 7E 40
Moor. W Yor 5L 41
ton Green. Lanc 4D 40
Cumb 4K 45
. Glos 8J 27
. Herts 2L 21
. Oxon 2A 20
**ham**. E Sus 5B 12
Weston. Cambs 5J 29
ult. G Lon 4A 22
ord. Norf 8J 39
on. Linc 1J 37
orth. W Yor 4J 41
orpe. E Yor 1J 43
Pemb 6E 14
. Notts 4D 36
ath. Fife 1K 59
rton. Devn 4K 7
. High 5D 86
Cumb 8D 46
G Man 1F 34
Hal 1C 34
Hants 4K 9
Surr 1F 10
ank. Hal 1C 34
arns. G Man 1F 34
Norf 2K 31
Staf 6F 34
gate. Linc 7L 37
Green. Derbs 5K 35
**owen**. W Mid 3H 27
street. Kent 1C 12
worth. Suff 4K 31
ood. Mers 1C 34
d. Shrp 3C 26
d. Warw 7L 27
enny. Cumb 7D 46
enny Furze. Carm 5J 15
enny Green. Staf 2G 27
ay. Carm
nr. Llandeilo 1F 16
nr. Llandovery 1H 17
ay. S Yor 1B 36
ay. W Ber 7B 20
ay House. Shrp 8B 34
ay Houses. Kent 6F 22
oron. Corn 3C 4
**x**. W Yor 5J 41
a. High 8D 76
. E Ayr 4C 58
k. High 6C 86
ı. Flin 3M 33
Ren 4C 58
n Fields. Derbs 5B 36
d. E Sus 4B 12
allands. N Lin 5H 43
on. Leics 2E 28
row. Bath 8E 18
nk. Cumb 6E 46
nkgate. Cumb 6K 53
unnerdale. Cumb 5M 45
. S Glo 5D 18
nd. Bed 7H 29
rth. Dur 7G 55
reen. Ches E 4G 35
reen. Norf 3H 31
reen. W Mid 3K 27
reen. W Yor 6M 41
reen. Wrex 5C 34
urton. Bord 5D 60
High 8D 76
ı. Medw 7D 22
gton. Linc 1L 37
gton. Nmbd 4C 54
ghton. Notts 4D 36
. Worc 6G 27
Heath. Worc 6G 27
sgate. Ches W 3D 34
nds. Devn 8L 5
Green. Herts 1K 21
ill. Devn 3D 6
waites. Cumb 6L 45
aberthwaite. Cumb 5L 45
ood Green. Glos 8E 26
orthy. Corn 7A 6
e. Bord 5K 59
r End. Staf 5G 35
nd's Frome. Here 7E 26
re. Glos 3E 18
ker. W Sus 5G 11
. Lanc 6B 40
Nptn 7C 28
Som 3L 7
own. Corn 5J 3
am. E Yor 5K 43
ger. Devn 2E 6
**ad**. Essx 8E 30
ad. Kent 7A 22
ad. Leics 1E 28
ck. Dors 5D 8
ay. Som 2L 7
ff Bridge. Cumb 8H 53
m. Linc 3K 37
End. Linc 5L 37
. Buck 3F 20
. Hal 1D 34
. Lanc 1D 40
. Nmbd 5C 54
. W Yor 4A 42
. Wrex 6B 34
East. N Yor 2J 41
Fenside. Linc 3M 37

Halton Gill. N Yor 8G 47
Halton Holegate. Linc 3M 37
Halton Lea Gate. Nmbd 6L 53
Halton Moor. W Yor 4M 41
Halton Shields. Nmbd 5D 54
Halton West. N Yor 2G 41
Haltwhistle. Nmbd 5M 53
Halvergate. Norf 1L 31
Halwell. Devn 6K 5
Halwill. Devn 6D 6
Halwill Junction. Devn 6D 6
Ham. Devn 5M 7
Ham. Glos 4E 18
Ham. G Lon 6J 21
Ham. High 4D 86
Ham. Kent 8K 23
Ham. Plym 6G 5
Ham. Shet 4B 90
Ham. Som
nr. Ilminster 4A 8
nr. Taunton 3A 8
nr. Wellington 3L 7
Ham. Wilts 7M 19
Hambleden. Buck 5E 20
Hambledon. Hants 4D 10
Hambledon. Surr 2G 11
Hamble-le-Rice. Hants 5B 10
Hambleton. Lanc 3B 40
Hambleton. N Yor 4C 42
Hambridge. Som 3B 8
Hambrook. S Glo 6E 18
Hambrook. W Sus 5E 10
Ham Common. Dors 3G 9
Hameringham. Linc 3L 37
Hamerton. Cambs 4J 29
Ham Green. Here 7F 26
Ham Green. Kent 7E 22
Ham Green. N Som 6D 18
Ham Green. Worc 5J 27
Ham Hill. Kent 7C 22
Hamilton. Leic 1D 28
**Hamilton**. S Lan 4F 58
Hamiltonsbawn. Arm 6F 93
Hamister. Shet 1F 90
Hammer. W Sus 2F 10
**Hammersmith**. G Lon 6K 21
Hammerwich. Staf 1J 27
Hammerwood. E Sus 2M 11
Hammill. Kent 8J 23
Hammond Street. Herts 3L 21
Hammoon. Dors 4G 9
Hamnavoe. Shet
nr. Braehoulland 5G 91
nr. Burland 4D 90
nr. Lunna 6J 91
on Yell 5J 91
Hamp. Som 2B 8
Hampden Park. E Sus 5B 12
Hampen. Glos 2J 19
Hamperden End. Essx 8B 30
Hamperley. Shrp 3C 26
Hampnett. Glos 2J 19
Hampole. S Yor 6C 42
Hampreston. Dors 6J 9
**Hampstead**. G Lon 5K 21
Hampstead Norreys. W Ber 6C 20
Hampsthwaite. N Yor 2L 41
Hampton. Devn 6A 8
Hampton. G Lon 6J 21
Hampton. Kent 7H 23
Hampton. Shrp 3F 26
Hampton. Swin 4K 19
Hampton. Worc 7J 27
Hampton Bishop. Here 8D 26
Hampton Fields. Glos 4G 19
Hampton Hargate. Pet 2J 29
Hampton Heath. Ches W 5D 34
Hampton in Arden. W Mid 3L 27
Hampton Loade. Shrp 3F 26
Hampton Lovett. Worc 5G 27
Hampton Lucy. Warw 6L 27
Hampton Magna. Warw 5L 27
Hampton on the Hill. Warw 5L 27
Hampton Poyle. Oxon 2C 20
Hampton Wick. G Lon 7J 21
Hamptworth. Wilts 4L 9
Hamrow. Norf 7F 38
Hamsey. E Sus 4M 11
Hamsey Green. Surr 8L 21
Hamstall Ridware. Staf 8K 35
Hamstead. IOW 6B 10
Hamstead. W Mid 2J 27
Hamstead Marshall. W Ber 7B 20
Hamsterley. Dur
nr. Consett 6E 54
nr. Wolsingham 8E 54
Hamsterley Mill. Dur 6E 54
Ham Street. Som 2D 8
Hamstreet. Kent 2G 13
Hamworthy. Pool 6H 9
Hanbury. Staf 7K 35
Hanbury. Worc 5H 27
Hanbury Woodend. Staf 7K 35
Hanby. Linc 6H 37
Hanchurch. Staf 5G 35
Hand and Pen. Devn 6K 7
Handbridge. Ches W 3C 34
Handcross. W Sus 2K 11
Handforth. Ches E 1G 35
Handley. Ches W 4C 34
Handley. Derbs 3A 36
Handsacre. Staf 8J 35
Handsworth. S Yor 1B 36
Handsworth. W Mid 2J 27
Handy Cross. Buck 4F 20
Hanford. Dors 4G 9
Hanford. Stoke 5G 35
Hangersley. Hants 5K 9
Hanging Houghton. Nptn 4E 28
Hanging Langford. Wilts 2J 9
Hangleton. Brig 5K 11
Hangleton. W Sus 5H 11
Hanham. S Glo 6E 18
Hanham Green. S Glo 6E 18
Hankelow. Ches E 5E 34
Hankerton. Wilts 4H 19
Hankham. E Sus 5C 12
**Hanley**. Stoke 5G 35
Hanley Castle. Worc 7G 27
Hanley Childe. Worc 5E 26
Hanley Swan. Worc 7G 27
Hanley William. Worc 5E 26
Hanlith. N Yor 1H 41
Hanmer. Wrex 6C 34
Hannaborough. Devn 5E 6
Hannaford. Devn 3F 6
Hannah. Linc 2B 38
Hannington. Hants 8C 20
Hannington. Nptn 4F 28
Hannington. Swin 4K 19
Hannington Wick. Swin 4K 19
Hanscombe End. C Beds 8J 29
Hanslope. Mil 7F 28
Hanthorpe. Linc 7H 37
Hanwell. G Lon 5J 21
Hanwell. Oxon 7B 28
Hanwood. Shrp 1C 26
Hanworth. G Lon 6J 21
Hanworth. Norf 6H 39
Happas. Ang 3H 67
Happendon. S Lan 6G 59
Happisburgh. Norf 6K 39
Happisburgh Common. Norf 7K 39
Hapsford. Ches W 2C 34
Hapton. Lanc 4F 40
Hapton. Norf 2H 31
Harberton. Devn 6K 5
Harbertonford. Devn 6K 5
Harbledown. Kent 8H 23
Harborne. W Mid 3J 27
Harborough Magna. Warw 4B 28
Harbottle. Nmbd 1C 54
Harbourneford. Devn 5K 5
Harbours Hill. Worc 5H 27
Harbridge. Hants 4K 9
Harbury. Warw 5A 28
Harby. Leics 6E 36
Harby. Notts 2F 36
Harcombe. Devn 6L 7
Harcombe Bottom. Devn 6B 8
Harcourt. Corn 5M 3
Harden. W Yor 4J 41
Hardenhuish. Wilts 6H 19
Hardgate. Abers 5G 73
Hardgate. Dum 5C 52
Hardham. W Sus 4H 11
Hardingham. Norf 1G 31
Hardingstone. Nptn 6E 28
Hardings Wood. Staf 4G 35

Hardington. Som 8F 18
Hardington Mandeville. Som 4D 8
Hardington Marsh. Som 5D 8
Hardington Moor. Som 4D 8
Hardley. Hants 5B 10
Hardley Street. Norf 1K 31
Hardmead. Mil 7G 29
Hardraw. N Yor 6G 47
Hardstoft. Derbs 3B 36
Hardway. Hants 5D 10
Hardway. Som 2F 8
Hardwick. Buck 2F 20
Hardwick. Cambs 6L 29
Hardwick. Norf 3J 31
Hardwick. Nptn 5F 28
Hardwick. Oxon
nr. Bicester 1C 20
nr. Witney 3A 20
Hardwick. Shrp 2B 26
Hardwick. S Yor 1B 36
Hardwick. Stoc T 3B 48
Hardwick. W Mid 2J 27
Hardwicke. Glos
nr. Cheltenham 1H 19
nr. Gloucester 2F 18
Hardwicke. Here 7A 26
Hardwick Village. Notts 2D 36
Hardy's Green. Essx 1F 22
Hare. Som 4A 8
Hareby. Linc 3L 37
Hareden. Lanc 2E 40
Harefield. G Lon 4H 21
Hare Green. Essx 1G 23
Hare Hatch. Wok 6F 20
Harehill. Derbs 6K 35
Harehills. W Yor 4M 41
Harehope. Nmbd 7H 61
Harelaw. Dum 4J 53
Harelaw. Dur 6E 54
Hareplain. Kent 2E 12
Haresceugh. Cumb 7L 53
Harescombe. Glos 2G 19
Haresfield. Glos 2G 19
Haresfinch. Mers 8D 40
Hareshaw. N Lan 3G 59
Hare Street. Essx 3M 21
Hare Street. Herts 1L 21
Harewood. W Yor 3M 41
Harewood End. Here 1D 18
Harford. Devn 6J 5
Hargate. Norf 2H 31
Hargatewall. Derbs 2K 35
Hargrave. Ches W 3C 34
Hargrave. Nptn 4H 29
Hargrave. Suff 6D 30
Harker. Cumb 5H 53
Harkland. Shet 5J 91
Harkstead. Suff 8H 31
Harlaston. Staf 8L 35
Harlaxton. Linc 6F 36
Harlech. Gwyn 7E 32
Harlequin. Notts 6D 36
Harlescott. Shrp 8D 34
Harleston. Devn 7K 5
Harleston. Norf 3J 31
Harleston. Suff 5G 31
Harlestone. Nptn 5E 28
Harley. Shrp 1D 26
Harley. S Yor 8A 42
Harling Road. Norf 3F 30
Harlington. C Beds 8H 29
Harlington. G Lon 6H 21
Harlington. S Yor 7B 42
Harlosh. High 1D 68
**Harlow**. Essx 2M 21
Harlow Hill. Nmbd 5D 54
Harlsey Castle. N Yor 6B 48
Harlthorpe. E Yor 4E 42
Harlton. Cambs 6L 29
Harlyn Bay. Corn 4A 4
Harman's Cross. Dors 7H 9
Harmby. N Yor 7K 47
Harmer Green. Herts 2K 21
Harmer Hill. Shrp 7C 34
Harmondsworth. G Lon 6H 21
Harmston. Linc 3G 37
Harnage. Shrp 1D 26
Harnham. Nmbd 3D 54
Harnham. Wilts 3K 9
Harnhill. Glos 3J 19
Harold Hill. G Lon 4B 22
Haroldston West. Pemb 5E 14
Haroldswick. Shet 2L 91
Harold Wood. G Lon 4B 22
Harome. N Yor 7D 48
**Harpenden**. Herts 2J 21
Harpford. Devn 6K 7
Harpham. E Yor 1H 43
Harpley. Norf 7D 38
Harpley. Worc 5E 26
Harpole. Nptn 5D 28
Harpsdale. High 6C 86
Harpsden. Oxon 5E 20
Harpswell. Linc 1G 37
Harpurhey. G Man 7G 41
Harpur Hill. Derbs 2J 35
Harraby. Cumb 6J 53
Harracott. Devn 3E 6
Harrapool. High 3H 69
Harrapul. High 3H 69
Harrietfield. Per 5C 66
Harrietsham. Kent 8E 22
Harrington. Cumb 2J 45
Harrington. Linc 2L 37
Harrington. Nptn 3E 28
Harringworth. Nptn 2G 29
Harriseahead. Staf 4G 35
Harriston. Cumb 7F 52
**Harrogate**. N Yor 2M 41
Harrold. Bed 6G 29
Harrop Dale. G Man 7J 41
**Harrow**. G Lon 5J 21
Harrowbarrow. Corn 5F 4
Harrowden. Bed 7H 29
Harrowgate Hill. Darl 4L 47
Harrow on the Hill. G Lon 5J 21
Harrow Weald. G Lon 4J 21
Harry Stoke. S Glo 6E 18
Harston. Cambs 6M 29
Harston. Leics 6F 36
Harswell. E Yor 3F 42
Hart. Hart 8H 55
Hartburn. Nmbd 3D 54
Hartburn. Stoc T 4B 48
Hartest. Suff 6E 30
Hartfield. E Sus 2A 12
Hartford. Cambs 4K 29
Hartford. Ches W 2E 34
Hartford. Som 3J 7
Hartford Bridge. Hants 8E 20
Hartford End. Essx 2C 22
Harthill. Ches W 4D 34
Harthill. N Lan 3H 59
Harthill. S Yor 1B 36
Hartington. Derbs 3K 35
Hartland. Devn 3B 6
Hartland Quay. Devn 3B 6
Hartle. Worc 4H 27
Hartlebury. Worc 4G 27
**Hartlepool**. Hart 8J 55
Hartley. Cumb 5F 46
Hartley. Kent
nr. Cranbrook 2D 12
nr. Dartford 7C 22
Hartley. Nmbd 4G 55
Hartley Green. Staf 7H 35
Hartley Mauditt. Hants 2E 10
Hartley Wespall. Hants 8D 20
Hartley Wintney. Hants 8E 20
Hartlip. Kent 7E 22
Hartmount Holdings. High 6H 79
Hartoft End. N Yor 6E 48
Harton. N Yor 1E 42
Harton. Shrp 3C 26
Harton. Tyne 5G 55
Hartpury. Glos 1G 19
Hartshead. W Yor 5K 41
**Hartshill**. Warw 2M 27
Hartshorne. Derbs 7M 35
Hartsop. Cumb 4C 46
Hart Station. Hart 8H 55
Hartswell. Som 3K 7
Hartwell. Nptn 6E 28
Hartwood. Lanc 6D 40
Hartwood. N Lan 4G 59
Harvel. Kent 7C 22
Harvington. Worc
nr. Evesham 7J 27
nr. Kidderminster 4G 27

Harwell. Oxon 5B 20
**Harwich**. Essx 8J 31
Harwood. Dur 8B 54
Harwood. G Man 6F 40
Harwood Dale. N Yor 6G 49
Harworth. Notts 8D 42
Hascombe. Surr 2G 11
Haselbech. Nptn 4E 28
Haselbury Plucknett. Som 4C 8
Haseley. Warw 5L 27
Hasfield. Glos 1G 19
Hasguard. Pemb 6E 14
Haskayne. Lanc 7B 40
Hasketon. Suff 6J 31
Hasland. Derbs 3A 36
**Haslemere**. Surr 2G 11
**Haslingden**. Lanc 5F 40
Haslingfield. Cambs 6M 29
Haslington. Ches E 4F 34
Hassall. Ches E 4F 34
Hassall Green. Ches E 4F 34
Hassell Street. Kent 1G 13
Hassendean. Bord 7C 60
Hassingham. Norf 1K 31
Hassness. Cumb 3L 45
Hassocks. W Sus 4L 11
Hassop. Derbs 2L 35
Haster. High 6E 86
Hasthorpe. Linc 3A 38
Hastigrow. High 5D 86
Hastingleigh. Kent 1G 13
**Hastings**. E Sus 5E 12
Hastingwood. Essx 3A 22
Hastoe. Herts 3G 21
Haston. Shrp 7D 34
Haswell. Dur 7G 55
Haswell Plough. Dur 7G 55
Hatch. C Beds 7J 29
Hatch Beauchamp. Som 3B 8
Hatch End. G Lon 4J 21
Hatch Green. Som 4B 8
Hatching Green. Herts 2J 21
Hatchmere. Ches W 2D 34
Hatch Warren. Hants 1D 10
Hatcliffe. NE Lin 7K 43
Hatfield. Here 6D 26
**Hatfield**. Herts 3K 21
**Hatfield**. S Yor 7D 42
Hatfield. Worc 6G 27
Hatfield Broad Oak. Essx 2B 22
Hatfield Garden Village.
Herts 3K 21
Hatfield Heath. Essx 2B 22
Hatfield Hyde. Herts 2K 21
Hatfield Peverel. Essx 2D 22
Hatfield Woodhouse. S Yor 7D 42
Hatford. Oxon 4M 19
Hatherden. Hants 8M 19
Hatherleigh. Devn 5E 6
Hathern. Leics 7B 36
Hatherop. Glos 3K 19
Hathersage. Derbs 1L 35
Hathersage Booths. Derbs 1L 35
Hatherton. Ches E 5E 34
Hatherton. Staf 8H 35
Hatley St George. Cambs 6K 29
Hatt. Corn 5F 4
Hattersley. G Man 8H 41
Hattingley. Hants 2D 10
Hatton. Abers 2K 73
Hatton. Derbs 6L 35
Hatton. G Lon 6H 21
Hatton. Linc 2J 37
Hatton. Shrp 2C 26
Hatton. Warr 1E 34
Hatton. Warw 5L 27
Hattoncrook. Abers 3H 73
Hatton Heath. Ches W 3C 34
Hatton of Fintray. Abers 4H 73
Haugh. E Ayr 7C 58
Haugh. Linc 2M 37
Haugham. Linc 1L 37
Haugh Head. Nmbd 7H 61
Haughley. Suff 5G 31
Haughley Green. Suff 5G 31
Haugh of Ballechin. Per 2C 66
Haugh of Glass. Mor 2D 72
Haugh of Urr. Dum 5C 52
Haughton. Ches E 4D 34
Haughton. Notts 2D 36
Haughton. Shrp
nr. Bridgnorth 2E 26
nr. Oswestry 7B 34
nr. Shifnal 1F 26
nr. Shrewsbury 8D 34
Haughton. Staf 7G 35
Haughton Green. G Man 8H 41
Haughton le Skerne. Darl 4M 47
Haultwick. Herts 1L 21
Haunn. Arg 3J 63
Haunn. W Isl 4D 74
Haunton. Staf 8L 35
Hauxton. Cambs 6M 29
Havannah. Ches E 3G 35
**Havant**. Hants 5E 10
Haven. Here 6C 26
The Haven. W Sus 2H 11
Haven Bank. Linc 4K 37
Havenstreet. IOW 6C 10
Havercroft. W Yor 6A 42
**Haverfordwest**. Pemb 5F 14
**Haverhill**. Suff 7C 30
Haverigg. Cumb 7L 45
Havering-Atte-Bower. G Lon 4B 22
Havering's Grove. Essx 4C 22
Haversham. Mil 7F 28
Haverthwaite. Cumb 7B 46
Haverton Hill. Stoc T 3B 48
Havyatt. Som 2D 8
**Hawarden**. Flin 3B 34
Hawbridge. Worc 7H 27
Hawcoat. Cumb 7M 45
Hawcross. Glos 8F 26
Hawen. Cdgn 2K 15
Hawes. N Yor 7G 47
Hawes Green. Norf 2J 31
**Hawick**. Bord 8C 60
Hawkchurch. Devn 5B 8
Hawkedon. Suff 6D 30
Hawkenbury. Kent 1E 12
Hawkeridge. Wilts 8G 19
Hawkerland. Devn 7K 7
Hawkesbury. S Glo 5F 18
Hawkesbury. Warw 3A 28
Hawkesbury Upton. S Glo 5F 18
Hawkes End. W Mid 3L 27
Hawk Green. G Man 1H 35
Hawkhurst. Kent 2D 12
Hawkhurst Common. E Sus 4B 12
Hawkinge. Kent 1J 13
Hawkley. Hants 3E 10
Hawkridge. Som 2H 7
Hawksdale. Cumb 7H 53
Hawkshaw. G Man 6F 40
Hawkshead. Cumb 6B 46
Hawkshead Hill. Cumb 6B 46
Hawkswick. N Yor 8H 47
Hawksworth. Notts 5E 36
Hawksworth. W Yor 3K 41
Hawkwell. Essx 4E 22
Hawley. Hants 8F 20
Hawley. Kent 6B 22
Hawling. Glos 1J 19
Hawnby. N Yor 7C 48
Haworth. W Yor 4J 41
Hawstead. Suff 6E 30
Hawthorn. Dur 7H 55
Hawthorn Hill. Brac 6F 20
Hawthorn Hill. Linc 4K 37
Hawthorpe. Linc 7H 37
Hawton. Notts 4E 36
**Haxby**. York 2D 42
Haxey. N Lin 8E 42
Haybridge. Shrp 4E 26
Haybridge. Som 1D 8
**Haydock**. Mers 8D 40
Haydon. Bath 8E 18
Haydon. Dors 4E 8
Haydon. Som 3A 8
Haydon Bridge. Nmbd 5B 54
Haydon Wick. Swin 5K 19
Haye. Corn 5F 4
Hayes. G Lon
nr. Bromley 7M 21
**Hayes**. G Lon
nr. Uxbridge 5H 21
Hayfield. Derbs 1J 35
Hay Green. Norf 8B 38
Hayhill. E Ayr 8C 58

Haylands. IOW 6C 10
Hayle. Corn 5J 3
Hayley Green. W Mid 3H 27
**Hayling Island**. Hants 6E 10
Hayne. Devn 5H 7
Haynes. C Beds 7H 29
Haynes West End. C Beds 7H 29
Hay-on-Wye. Powy 8M 25
Hayscastle. Pemb 4E 14
Hayscastle Cross. Pemb 4F 14
Hayshead. Ang 3K 67
Hay Street. Herts 1L 21
Hayton. Aber 5J 73
Hayton. Cumb
nr. Aspatria 7F 52
nr. Brampton 6K 53
Hayton. E Yor 3F 42
Hayton. Notts 1E 36
Hayton's Bent. Shrp 3D 26
Haytor Vale. Devn 8G 7
Haytown. Devn 4C 6
**Haywards Heath**. W Sus 3L 11
Haywood. S Lan 4H 59
Hazelbank. S Lan 5G 59
Hazelbury Bryan. Dors 5F 8
Hazeleigh. Essx 3E 22
Hazeley. Hants 8E 20
**Hazel Grove**. G Man 1H 35
Hazelhead. S Yor 7K 41
Hazelslade. Staf 8J 35
Hazel Street. Kent 2C 12
Hazelton Walls. Fife 5G 67
Hazelwood. Derbs 5M 35
Hazlemere. Buck 4F 20
Hazler. Shrp 2C 26
Hazlerigg. Tyne 4F 54
Hazles. Staf 5J 35
Hazleton. Glos 2J 19
Hazon. Nmbd 1E 54
Heacham. Norf 6C 38
Headbourne Worthy. Hants 2B 10
Headcorn. Kent 1E 12
Headingley. W Yor 4L 41
Headington. Oxon 3C 20
Headlam. Dur 4K 47
Headless Cross. Worc 5J 27
Headley. Hants
nr. Haslemere 2F 10
nr. Kingsclere 7C 20
Headley. Surr 8K 21
Headley Down. Hants 2F 10
Headley Heath. Worc 4J 27
Headley Park. Bris 7D 18
Head of Muir. Falk 1G 59
Headon. Notts 2E 36
Heads Nook. Cumb 6J 53
Heage. Derbs 4A 36
Healaugh. N Yor
nr. Grinton 6J 47
nr. York 3C 42
Heald Green. G Man 1G 35
Heale. Devn 1F 6
Healey. G Man 6G 41
Healey. Nmbd 6D 54
Healey. N Yor 7K 47
Healeyfield. Dur 7D 54
Healing. NE Lin 6K 43
Heamoor. Corn 5H 3
Heanish. Arg 3F 62
**Heanor**. Derbs 5B 36
Heanton Punchardon. Devn 2E 6
Heapham. Linc 1F 36
Heartsease. Powy 6L 25
Heasley Mill. Devn 2G 7
Heaste. High 4H 69
Heath. Derbs 3B 36
The Heath. Norf
nr. Buxton 7J 39
nr. Fakenham 7F 38
nr. Hevingham 7H 39
The Heath. Staf 6J 35
The Heath. Suff 8H 31
Heath and Reach. C Beds 1G 21
Heath Common. W Sus 4J 11
Heathcote. Derbs 3K 35
Heath Cross. Devn 6G 7
Heathencote. Nptn 7E 28
Heath End. Hants 7C 20
Heath End. Leics 7A 36
Heath End. W Mid 1J 27
Heather. Leics 8A 36
Heatherfield. High 1F 68
Heatherton. Derb 6M 35
Heathfield. Cambs 7A 30
Heathfield. Cumb 7F 52
Heathfield. Devn 8H 7
Heathfield. E Sus 3B 12
Heathfield. Ren 3B 58
Heathfield. Som
nr. Lydeard St Lawrence 2L 7
nr. Norton Fitzwarren 3L 7
Heath Green. Worc 4J 27
Heathhall. Dum 4D 52
Heath Hayes. Staf 8J 35
Heath Hill. Shrp 8F 34
Heath House. Som 1C 8
Heathrow Airport. G Lon 6H 21
Heathstock. Devn 5M 7
Heathton. Shrp 2G 27
Heathtop. Derbs 6L 35
Heath Town. W Mid 2H 27
Heatley. Staf 7J 35
Heatley. Warr 1F 34
Heaton. Lanc 1C 40
Heaton. Staf 3H 35
Heaton. Tyne 5F 54
Heaton. W Yor 4K 41
Heaton Moor. G Man 8G 41
Heaton's Bridge. Lanc 6C 40
Heaverham. Kent 8B 22
Heavitree. Devn 6J 7
**Hebburn**. Tyne 5G 55
Hebden. N Yor 1J 41
Hebden Bridge. W Yor 5H 41
Hebden Green. Ches W 3E 34
Hebing End. Herts 1L 21
Hebron. Carm 4H 15
Hebron. Nmbd 3E 54
Heck. Dum 3E 52
Heckdyke. Notts 8E 42
Heckfield. Hants 7E 20
Heckfield Green. Suff 4H 31
Heckfordbridge. Essx 1F 22
Heckington. Linc 5J 37
**Heckmondwike**. W Yor 5L 41
Heddington. Wilts 7H 19
Heddle. Orkn 8C 88
Heddon. Devn 3F 6
Heddon-on-the-Wall. Nmbd 5E 54
Hedenham. Norf 2K 31
**Hedge End**. Hants 4B 10
Hedgerley. Buck 5G 21
Hedging. Som 3B 8
Hedley on the Hill. Nmbd 6D 54
Hednesford. Staf 8J 35
Hedon. E Yor 5J 43
Hegdon Hill. Here 6D 26
Heglibister. Shet 2D 90
Heighington. Darl 3L 47
Heighington. Linc 3H 37
Heightington. Worc 4F 26
Heights of Brae. High 7F 78
Heights of Fodderty. High 7F 78
Heights of Kinlochewe. High 7A 78
Heiton. Bord 6E 60
Hele. Devn
nr. Exeter 5J 7
nr. Holsworthy 6C 6
nr. Ilfracombe 1E 6
Hele. Torb 5M 5
Helen's Bay. Ards 4J 93
**Helensburgh**. Arg 1A 58
Helford. Corn 6L 3
Helhoughton. Norf 7E 38
Helions Bumpstead. Essx 7C 30
Helland. Corn 4C 4
Helland. Som 3B 8
Hellandbridge. Corn 4C 4
Hellesdon. Norf 8J 39
Hellesveor. Corn 4J 3
Hellidon. Nptn 6C 28
Hellifield. N Yor 2G 41
Hellingly. E Sus 4B 12
Hellington. Norf 1K 31
Hellister. Shet 3D 90
Helmdon. Nptn 7C 28
Helmingham. Suff 6H 31
Helmington Row. Dur 8E 54
Helmsdale. High 2L 79

Helmshore. Lanc 5F 40
Helmsley. N Yor 7D 48
Helperby. N Yor 1B 42
Helperthorpe. N Yor 8G 49
Helpringham. Linc 5J 37
Helpston. Pet 1J 29
Helsby. Ches W 2C 34
Helsey. Linc 2B 38
Helston. Corn 6K 3
Helstone. Corn 3C 4
Helton. Cumb 3D 46
Helwith. N Yor 5J 47
Helwith Bridge. N Yor 1G 41
Helygain. Flin 3M 33
The Hem. Shrp 1F 26
Hemblington. Norf 8K 39
**Hemel Hempstead**. Herts 3H 21
Hemerdon. Devn 6H 5
Hemingbrough. N Yor 4D 42
Hemingby. Linc 2K 37
Hemingfield. S Yor 7A 42
Hemingford Abbots. Cambs 4K 29
Hemingford Grey. Cambs 4K 29
Hemingstone. Suff 6H 31
Hemington. Leics 7B 36
Hemington. Nptn 3H 29
Hemington. Som 8F 18
Hemley. Suff 7J 31
Hemlington. Midd 4B 48
Hempholme. E Yor 2H 43
Hempnall. Norf 2J 31
Hempnall Green. Norf 2J 31
Hempriggs. High 7E 86
Hemp's Green. Essx 1F 22
Hempstead. Essx 8C 30
Hempstead. Medw 7D 22
Hempstead. Norf
nr. Holt 6H 39
nr. Stalham 7L 39
Hempsted. Glos 2G 19
Hempton. Norf 7F 38
Hempton. Oxon 8B 28
Hemsby. Norf 8L 39
Hemswell. Linc 8G 43
Hemswell Cliff. Linc 1G 37
Hemsworth. Dors 5H 9
**Hemsworth**. W Yor 6B 42
Hemyock. Devn 4L 7
Henallt. Carm 4L 15
Henbury. Bris 6D 18
Henbury. Ches E 2G 35
Hendomen. Powy 3M 25
**Hendon**. G Lon 5K 21
Hendon. Tyne 6H 55
Hendra. Corn 6B 4
Hendre. B'end 6J 17
Hendreforgan. Rhon 6J 17
Hendy. Carm 4E 16
Heneglwys. IOA 3D 32
Henfeddau Fawr. Pemb 3J 15
Henfield. S Glo 6E 18
Henfield. W Sus 4K 11
Henford. Devn 6C 6
Hengoed. Cphy 5L 17
Hengoed. Shrp 6A 34
Hengrave. Suff 5E 30
Henham. Essx 1B 22
Heniarth. Powy 2L 25
Henlade. Som 3A 8
Henley. Dors 5E 8
Henley. Shrp
nr. Church Stretton 3C 26
nr. Ludlow 4D 26
Henley. Som 2C 8
Henley. Suff 6H 31
Henley. W Sus 3F 10
Henley Down. E Sus 4D 12
Henley-in-Arden. Warw 5K 27
**Henley-on-Thames**. Oxon 5E 20
Henley Street. Kent 7C 22
Henllan. Cdgn 2K 15
Henllan. Den 4K 33
Henllan. Mon 1A 18
Henllan Amgoed. Carm 5H 15
Henllys. Torf 4A 18
Henlow. C Beds 8J 29
Hennock. Devn 7H 7
Henny Street. Essx 8E 30
Henryd. Cnwy 3G 33
Henry's Moat. Pemb 4G 15
Hensall. N Yor 5C 42
Henshaw. Nmbd 5A 54
Hensingham. Cumb 3J 45
Henstead. Suff 3L 31
Hensting. Hants 3B 10
Henstridge. Som 4F 8
Henstridge Ash. Som 3F 8
Henstridge Bowden. Som 3E 8
Henstridge Marsh. Som 3F 8
Henton. Oxon 3E 20
Henton. Som 1C 8
Henwood. Corn 8B 6
Heogan. Shet 3E 90
Heolgerrig. Mer T 4K 17
Heol Senni. Powy 2J 17
Heol-y-Cyw. B'end 6J 17
Hepburn. Nmbd 7H 61
Hepple. Nmbd 1C 54
Hepscott. Nmbd 3F 54
Heptonstall. W Yor 5H 41
Hepworth. Suff 4F 30
Hepworth. W Yor 7K 41
Herbrandston. Pemb 6E 14
**Hereford**. Here 8D 26
Heribusta. High 6F 76
Heriot. Bord 4B 60
Hermiston. Edin 2K 59
Hermitage. Dors 5E 8
Hermitage. Bord 2K 53
Hermitage. W Ber 6C 20
Hermitage. W Sus 5E 10
Hermon. Carm
nr. Llandeilo 2F 16
nr. Newcastle Emlyn 3K 15
Hermon. IOA 4C 32
Hermon. Pemb 3J 15
Herne. Kent 7H 23
**Herne Bay**. Kent 7H 23
Herne Common. Kent 7H 23
Herne Pound. Kent 8C 22
Herner. Devn 3E 6
Hernhill. Kent 7G 23
Herodsfoot. Corn 5E 4
Heronden. Kent 8J 23
Herongate. Essx 4C 22
Heronsford. S Ayr 3G 51
Heronsgate. Herts 4H 21
Heron's Ghyll. E Sus 3A 12
Herra. Shet 4L 91
Herriard. Hants 1D 10
Herringfleet. Suff 2L 31
Herringswell. Suff 5D 30
Herrington. Tyne 6G 55
Hersden. Kent 7J 23
Hersham. Corn 5B 6
Hersham. Surr 7J 21
Herstmonceux. E Sus 4C 12
Herston. Dors 8J 9
Herston. Orkn 2F 86
**Hertford**. Herts 2L 21
Hertford Heath. Herts 2L 21
Hertingfordbury. Herts 2L 21
Hesketh. Lanc 5C 40
Hesketh Bank. Lanc 5C 40
Hesketh Lane. Lanc 3E 40
Hesket Newmarket. Cumb 8H 53
Heskin Green. Lanc 6D 40
Hesleden. Dur 8H 55
Hesleyside. Nmbd 3B 54
Heslington. York 2D 42
Hessay. York 2C 42
Hessenford. Corn 6F 4
Hessett. Suff 5F 30
Hessilhead. N Ayr 4B 58
Hessle. E Yor 5H 43
Hestaford. Shet 2C 90
Hest Bank. Lanc 1C 40
Hester's Way. Glos 1H 19
Hestinsetter. Shet 3C 90
Heston. G Lon 6J 21
Hestwall. Orkn 8B 88
**Heswall**. Mers 1A 34
Hethe. Oxon 1C 20
Hethelpit Cross. Glos 1F 18
Hethersett. Norf 1H 31
Hethersgill. Cumb 5J 53
Hetherside. Cumb 5J 53
Hethpool. Nmbd 7F 60
Hett. Dur 8F 54

Hetton. N Yor 2H 41
**Hetton-le-Hole**. Tyne 7G 55
Hetton Steads. Nmbd 6H 61
Heugh. Nmbd 4D 54
Heugh-head. Abers 4C 72
Heveningham. Suff 4K 31
Hever. Kent 1A 12
Heversham. Cumb 7C 46
Hevingham. Norf 7H 39
Hewas Water. Corn 7B 4
Hewelsfield. Glos 3D 18
Hewish. N Som 7C 18
Hewish. Som 5C 8
Hewood. Dors 5B 8
Heworth. York 2D 42
**Hexham**. Nmbd 5C 54
Hextable. Kent 6B 22
Hexton. Herts 8J 29
Hexworthy. Devn 8F 6
Heybridge. Essx
nr. Brentwood 4C 22
nr. Maldon 3E 22
Heybridge Basin. Essx 3E 22
Heybrook Bay. Devn 7G 5
Heydon. Cambs 7M 29
Heydon. Norf 7H 39
Heydour. Linc 6H 37
Heylipol. Arg 3E 62
Heyop. Powy 5M 25
Heysham. Lanc 1C 40
Heyshott. W Sus 4F 10
Heytesbury. Wilts 1H 9
Heythrop. Oxon 1A 20
**Heywood**. G Man 6G 41
Heywood. Wilts 8G 19
Hibaldstow. N Lin 7G 43
Hickleton. S Yor 7B 42
Hickling. Norf 7L 39
Hickling. Notts 7D 36
Hickling Green. Norf 7L 39
Hickling Heath. Norf 7L 39
Hickstead. W Sus 3K 11
Hidcote Bartrim. Glos 7K 27
Hidcote Boyce. Glos 7K 27
Higford. Shrp 1F 26
High Ackworth. W Yor 6B 42
Higham. Derbs 4A 36
Higham. Kent 6D 22
Higham. Lanc 4G 41
Higham. S Yor 7M 41
Higham. Suff
nr. Ipswich 8G 31
nr. Newmarket 5D 30
Higham Dykes. Nmbd 4E 54
Higham Ferrers. Nptn 5G 29
Higham Gobion. C Beds 8J 29
Higham on the Hill. Leics 2A 28
Highampton. Devn 5D 6
Higham Wood. Kent 1C 12
High Angerton. Nmbd 3D 54
High Auldgirth. Dum 3D 52
High Bankhill. Cumb 7K 53
High Banton. N Lan 1F 58
High Barnet. G Lon 4K 21
High Beech. Essx 4M 21
High Bentham. N Yor 1E 40
High Bickington. Devn 3F 6
High Biggins. Cumb 8D 46
High Birkwith. N Yor 8F 46
High Blantyre. S Lan 4E 58
High Bonnybridge. Falk 2G 59
High Borrans. Cumb 5C 46
High Bradfield. S Yor 8L 41
High Bray. Devn 2F 6
Highbridge. Cumb 7H 53
Highbridge. High 7C 70
Highbridge. Som 1B 8
Highbrook. W Sus 2L 11
High Brooms. Kent 1B 12
High Bullen. Devn 3E 6
Highburton. W Yor 6K 41
Highbury. Som 1E 8
High Buston. Nmbd 1F 54
High Callerton. Nmbd 4E 54
High Carlingill. Cumb 5E 46
High Catton. E Yor 2E 42
High Church. Nmbd 3E 54
Highclere. Hants 7B 20
Highcliffe. Dors 6L 9
High Cogges. Oxon 3A 20
High Common. Norf 1F 30
High Coniscliffe. Darl 4L 47
High Crosby. Cumb 6J 53
High Cross. Hants 3E 10
High Cross. Herts 2L 21
High Easter. Essx 2C 22
High Eggborough. N Yor 5C 42
High Ellington. N Yor 7K 47
Higher Alham. Som 1E 8
Higher Ansty. Dors 5F 8
Higher Ashton. Devn 7H 7
Higher Ballam. Lanc 4B 40
Higher Bartle. Lanc 4D 40
Higher Bockhampton. Dors 6F 8
Higher Bojewyan. Corn 5G 3
High Ercall. Telf 8D 34
Higher Cheriton. Devn 5L 7
Higher Clovelly. Devn 3C 6
Higher Compton. Plym 6G 5
Higher Dean. Devn 5K 5
Higher Dinting. Derbs 8J 41
Higher Dunstone. Devn 8G 7
Higher End. G Man 7D 40
Higherford. Lanc 3G 41
Higher Gabwell. Devn 5M 5
Higher Halstock Leigh. Dors 5D 8
Higher Heysham. Lanc 1C 40
Higher Hurdsfield. Ches E 2H 35
Higher Kingcombe. Dors 6D 8
Higher Kinnerton. Flin 3B 34
Higher Melcombe. Dors 5F 8
Higher Penwortham. Lanc 5D 40
Higher Porthpean. Corn 6C 4
Higher Poynton. Ches E 1H 35
Higher Shotton. Flin 3B 34
Higher Shurlach. Ches W 2E 34
Higher Slade. Devn 1E 6
Higher Tale. Devn 5K 7
Higher Town. IOS 1H 3
Higher Town. Som 1J 7
Highertown. Corn 4M 3
Higher Vexford. Som 2L 7
Higher Walton. Lanc 5D 40
Higher Walton. Warr 1D 34
Higher Whatcombe. Dors 5G 9
Higher Wheelton. Lanc 5E 40
Higher Whiteleigh. Corn 6B 6
Higher Whitley. Ches W 1E 34
Higher Wincham. Ches W 2E 34
Higher Wraxall. Dors 5D 8
Higher Wych. Ches W 5C 34
Higher Yalberton. Torb 6L 5
High Etherley. Dur 3K 47
High Ferry. Linc 5L 37
Highfield. E Yor 4E 42
Highfield. N Ayr 4B 58
Highfield. Tyne 6E 54
Highfields Caldecote.
Cambs 6L 29
High Gallowhill. E Dun 2E 58
High Garrett. Essx 1D 22
Highgate. G Lon 5K 21
Highgate. N Ayr 4B 58
Highgate. Powy 3L 25
High Grange. Dur 8E 54
High Green. Cumb 5C 46
High Green. Norf 1H 31
High Green. Shrp 3F 26
High Green. S Yor 8M 41
High Green. W Yor 6K 41
High Green. Worc 7G 27
Highgreen Manor. Nmbd 2B 54
High Halden. Kent 2E 12
High Halstow. Medw 6D 22
High Ham. Som 2C 8
High Harrington. Cumb 2K 45
High Haswell. Dur 7G 55
High Hatton. Shrp 7E 34
High Hawsker. N Yor 5G 49
High Hesket. Cumb 7J 53
High Hesleden. Dur 8H 55
High Hoyland. S Yor 6L 41
High Hunsley. E Yor 4G 43
High Hurstwood. E Sus 3A 12
High Hutton. N Yor 1E 42
High Ireby. Cumb 8G 53
High Keil. Arg 1B 50
High Kelling. Norf 6H 39
High Kilburn. N Yor 8C 48

High Knipe. Cumb 4D 46
High Lands. Dur 3K 47
The Highlands. Shrp 3E 26
High Lane. G Man 1H 35
High Lane. Worc 5E 26
Highlane. Ches E 3G 35
Highlane. Derbs 1B 36
High Laver. Essx 3B 22
Highlaws. Cumb 7F 52
Highleadon. Glos 1F 18
High Legh. Ches E 1F 34
Highleigh. W Sus 6F 10
High Leven. Stoc T 4B 48
Highley. Shrp 3F 26
High Littleton. Bath 8E 18
High Longthwaite. Cumb 7G 53
High Lorton. Cumb 2L 45
High Marishes. N Yor 8F 48
High Marnham. Notts 2F 36
High Melton. S Yor 7C 42
High Mickley. Nmbd 5D 54
High Moor. Lanc 6D 40
Highmoor. Cumb 7G 53
Highmoor. Oxon 5E 20
Highmoor Cross. Oxon 5E 20
Highmoor Hill. Mon 5C 18
Highnam. Glos 2F 18
High Newport. Tyne 6G 55
High Newton. Cumb 7C 46
High Newton-by-the-Sea.
Nmbd 7K 61
High Nibthwaite. Cumb 7A 46
High Offley. Staf 7F 34
High Ongar. Essx 3B 22
High Onn. Staf 8G 35
High Orchard. Glos 2G 19
High Park. Mers 6B 40
High Roding. Essx 2C 22
High Row. Cumb 8H 53
High Salvington. W Sus 5J 11
High Scales. Cumb 7F 52
High Shaw. N Yor 6G 47
High Shincliffe. Dur 7F 54
High Side. Cumb 8G 53
High Spen. Tyne 5E 54
Highsted. Kent 7F 22
High Stoop. Dur 7E 54
High Street. Corn 6B 4
High Street. Suff
nr. Aldeburgh 6L 31
nr. Bungay 3K 31
nr. Yoxford 4L 31
High Street Green. Suff 6G 31
Highstreet Green. Essx 8D 30
Highstreet Green. Surr 2G 11
Hightae. Dum 4E 52
High Throston. Hart 8H 55
High Town. Staf 8H 35
Hightown. Ches E 3G 35
Hightown. Mers 7A 40
Hightown Green. Suff 6F 30
High Toynton. Linc 3K 37
High Trewhitt. Nmbd 1D 54
High Valleyfield. Fife 1J 59
Highway. Here 7C 26
Highweek. Devn 8H 7
High Westwood. Dur 6E 54
Highwood. Staf 6J 35
Highwood. Worc 5E 26
High Worsall. N Yor 5A 48
Highworth. Swin 4L 19
High Wray. Cumb 6B 46
High Wych. Herts 2A 22
**High Wycombe**. Buck 4F 20
Hilborough. Norf 1E 30
Hilcott. Wilts 8K 19
Hildenborough. Kent 1B 12
Hildersham. Cambs 7B 30
Hilderstone. Staf 6H 35
Hilderthorpe. E Yor 1J 43
Hilfield. Dors 5E 8
Hilgay. Norf 2C 30
Hill. S Glo 4E 18
Hill. Warw 5B 28
Hill. Worc 7H 27
The Hill. Cumb 6L 45
Hillam. N Yor 5C 42
Hillbeck. Cumb 4F 46
Hillberry. IOM 7C 44
Hillborough. Kent 7J 23
Hillbourne. Pool 6J 9
Hillbrae. Abers
nr. Aberchirder 1F 72
nr. Inverurie 3G 73
nr. Methlick 2H 73
Hill Brow. Hants 3E 10
Hillbutts. Dors 5H 9
Hillclifflane. Derbs 5L 35
Hillcommon. Som 3L 7
Hill Deverill. Wilts 1G 9
Hilldyke. Linc 5L 37
Hill End. Dur 8D 54
Hill End. Fife 8D 66
Hill End. N Yor 2J 41
Hillend. Fife 1K 59
Hillend. N Lan 3G 59
Hillend. Shrp 2G 27
Hillend. Swan 7L 15
Hillersland. Glos 2D 18
Hillerton. Devn 6G 7
Hillesden. Buck 1D 20
Hillesley. Glos 5F 18
Hillfarrance. Som 3L 7
Hill Gate. Here 1C 18
Hill Green. Essx 8A 30
Hill Green. W Ber 6B 20
Hillhall. Lis 5H 93
Hill Head. Hants 5C 10
Hillhead. Abers 2E 72
Hillhead. Devn 6M 5
Hillhead. S Ayr 8C 58
Hillhead of Auchentumb.
Abers 8J 81
Hilliard's Cross. Staf 8K 35
Hilliclay. High 5C 86
Hillingdon. G Lon 5H 21
Hillington. Glas 3D 58
Hillington. Norf 7D 38
Hillmorton. Warw 4C 28
Hill of Beath. Fife 8E 66
Hill of Fearn. High 6J 79
Hill of Fiddes. Abers 3J 73
Hill of Keillor. Ang 3F 66
Hill of Overbrae. Abers 7H 81
Hill Ridware. Staf 8J 35
Hillsborough. Lis 6H 93
Hillsborough. S Yor 8M 41
Hill Side. W Yor 6K 41
Hillside. Abers 6J 73
Hillside. Ang 1L 67
Hillside. Devn 5K 5
Hillside. Mers 6B 40
Hillside. Orkn 7C 88
Hillside. Shet 1E 90
Hillside. Shrp 3E 26
Hillside. Worc 5F 26
Hillside of Prieston. Ang 4G 67
Hill Somersal. Derbs 6K 35
Hillstown. Derbs 3B 36
Hillstreet. Hants 4M 9
Hillswick. Shet 6G 91
Hill Top. Dur
nr. Barnard Castle 3H 47
nr. Durham 7F 54
nr. Stanley 6E 54
Hilltown. New M 7H 93
Hill View. Dors 6H 9
Hillwell. Shet 6D 90
Hill Wootton. Warw 5M 27
Hillyland. Per 5D 66
Hilmarton. Wilts 6J 19
Hilperton. Wilts 8G 19
Hilperton Marsh. Wilts 8G 19
Hilsea. Port 5D 10
Hilston. E Yor 4K 43
Hiltingbury. Hants 3B 10
Hilton. Cambs 5K 29
Hilton. Cumb 3F 46
Hilton. Derbs 6L 35
Hilton. Dors 5F 8
Hilton. Dur 3K 47
Hilton. High 5H 79
Hilton. Shrp 2F 26
Hilton. Staf 1J 27
Hilton. Stoc T 4B 48
Hilton of Cadboll. High 6J 79
Himbleton. Worc 6H 27
Himley. Staf 2G 27
Hincaster. Cumb 7D 46

Hinchwick—Kidsgrove


Hinchwick. Glos 1K 19
**Hinckley**. Leics 2B 28
Hinderclay. Suff 4G 31
Hinderwell. N Yor 4E 48
Hindford. Shrp 6B 34
Hindhead. Surr 2F 10
**Hindley**. G Man 7E 40
Hindley. Nmbd 6D 54
Hindley Green. G Man 7E 40
Hindlip. Worc 6G 27
Hindolveston. Norf 7G 39
Hindon. Wilts 2H 9
Hindringham. Norf 6F 38
Hingham. Norf 1G 31
Hinksford. Staf 3G 27
Hinstock. Shrp 7E 34
Hintlesham. Suff 7G 31
Hinton. Hants 6L 9
Hinton. Here 8B 26
Hinton. Nptn 6C 28
Hinton. Shrp 1C 26
Hinton. S Glo 6F 18
Hinton Ampner. Hants 3C 10
Hinton Blewett. Bath 8D 18
Hinton Charterhouse. Bath 8F 18
Hinton-in-the-Hedges. Nptn 8C 28
Hinton Martell. Dors 5J 9
Hinton on the Green. Worc 7J 27
Hinton Parva. Swin 5L 19
Hinton St George. Som 4C 8
Hinton St Mary. Dors 4F 8
Hinton Waldrist. Oxon 4A 20
Hints. Shrp 4E 26
Hints. Staf 1K 27
Hinwick. Bed 5G 29
Hinxhill. Kent 1G 13
Hinxton. Cambs 7A 30
Hinxworth. Herts 7K 29
Hipley. Hants 4D 10
Hipperholme. W Yor 5K 41
Hipsburn. Nmbd 8K 61
Hipswell. N Yor 6K 47
Hiraeth. Carm 4H 15
Hirn. Abers 5G 73
Hirnant. Powy 8K 33
Hirst. N Lan 3G 59
Hirst. Nmbd 3F 54
Hirst Courtney. N Yor 5D 42
Hirwaen. Den 4L 33
Hirwaun. Rhon 4J 17
Hiscott. Devn 3E 6
Histon. Cambs 5M 29
Hitcham. Suff 6F 30
**Hitchin**. Herts 1J 21
Hittisleigh. Devn 6G 7
Hittisleigh Barton. Devn 6G 7
Hive. E Yor 4F 42
Hixon. Staf 7J 35
Hoaden. Kent 8J 23
Hoar Cross. Staf 7K 35
Hoarwithy. Here 1D 18
Hoath. Kent 7J 23
Yr Hôb. Flin 4B 34
Hobarris. Shrp 4B 26
Hobbister. Orkn 1E 86
Hobbles Green. Suff 6D 30
Hobbs Cross. Essx 4A 22
Hobkirk. Bord 8C 60
Hobson. Dur 6E 54
Hoby. Leics 8D 36
Hockering. Norf 8G 39
Hockering Heath. Norf 8G 39
Hockerton. Notts 4E 36
**Hockley**. Essx 4E 22
Hockley. Staf 1L 27
Hockley. W Mid 4L 27
Hockley Heath. W Mid 4K 27
Hockliffe. C Beds 1G 21
Hockwold cum Wilton. Norf 3D 30
Hockworthy. Devn 4K 7
**Hoddesdon**. Herts 3L 21
Hoddlesden. Bkbn 5F 40
Hoddomcross. Dum 4F 52
Hodgeston. Pemb 7G 15
Hodley. Powy 3L 25
Hodnet. Shrp 7E 34
Hodsoll Street. Kent 7C 22
Hodson. Swin 5K 19
Hodthorpe. Derbs 2C 36
Hoe. Norf 8F 38
The Hoe. Plym 6G 5
Hoe Gate. Hants 4D 10
Hoff. Cumb 4E 46
Hoffleet Stow. Linc 6K 37
Hogaland. Shet 6H 91
Hogben's Hill. Kent 8G 23
Hoggard's Green. Suff 6E 30
Hoggeston. Buck 1F 20
Hoggrill's End. Warw 2L 27
Hogha Gearraidh. W Isl 6J 75
Hoghton. Lanc 5E 40
Hoghton Bottoms. Lanc 5E 40
Hognaston. Derbs 4L 35
Hogsthorpe. Linc 2B 38
Hogstock. Dors 5H 9
Holbeach. Linc 7L 37
Holbeach Bank. Linc 7L 37
Holbeach Clough. Linc 7L 37
Holbeach Drove. Linc 8L 37
Holbeach Hurn. Linc 7L 37
Holbeach St Johns. Linc 8L 37
Holbeach St Marks. Linc 6L 37
Holbeach St Matthew. Linc 6M 37
Holbeck. Notts 2C 36
Holbeck. W Yor 4L 41
Holbeck Woodhouse. Notts 2C 36
Holberrow Green. Worc 6J 27
Holbeton. Devn 6J 5
Holborn. G Lon 5L 21
Holbrook. Derbs 5A 36
Holbrook. S Yor 1B 36
Holbrook. Suff 8H 31
Holburn. Nmbd 6H 61
Holbury. Hants 5B 10
Holcombe. Devn 8J 7
Holcombe. G Man 6F 40
Holcombe. Som 1E 8
Holcombe Brook. G Man 6F 40
Holcombe Rogus. Devn 4K 7
Holcot. Nptn 5E 28
Holden. Lanc 3F 40
Holdenby. Nptn 5D 28
Holder's Green. Essx 1C 22
Holdgate. Shrp 3D 26
Holdingham. Linc 5H 37
Holditch. Dors 5B 8
Holemoor. Devn 5D 6
Hole Street. W Sus 4J 11
Holford. Som 1L 7
Holker. Cumb 8B 46
Holkham. Norf 5E 38
Hollacombe. Devn 5C 6
Holland. Orkn
  on Papa Westray 4D 88
  on Stronsay 7F 88
Holland Fen. Linc 5K 37
Holland Lees. Lanc 7D 40
Holland-on-Sea. Essx 2J 23
Holland Park. W Mid 1J 27
Hollandstoun. Orkn 4G 89
Hollesley. Suff 7K 31
Hollinfare. Warr 8E 40
Hollingbourne. Kent 8E 22
Hollingbury. Brig 5L 11
Hollingdon. Buck 1F 20
Hollingrove. E Sus 3C 12
Hollington. Derbs 6L 35
Hollington. E Sus 4D 12
Hollington. Staf 6J 35
Hollington Grove. Derbs 6L 35
Hollingworth. G Man 8J 41
Hollins. Derbs 2M 35
Hollins. G Man
  nr. Bury 7G 41
  nr. Middleton 7G 41
Hollinsclough. Staf 3J 35
Hollinswood. Telf 1F 26
Hollinthorpe. W Yor 4A 42
Hollinwood. G Man 7H 41
Hollinwood. Shrp 6D 34
Hollocombe. Devn 4F 6
Holloway. Derbs 4M 35
Hollowell. Nptn 4D 28
Hollow Meadows. S Yor 1L 35
Hollows. Dum 4H 53
Hollybush. Cphy 4L 17
Hollybush. E Ayr 8B 58
Hollybush. Worc 8F 26
Holly End. Norf 1A 30
Holly Hill. N Yor 5K 47
Hollyhurst. Shrp 5D 34
Hollym. E Yor 5L 43
Hollywood. Worc 4J 27
Holmacott. Devn 3E 6
Holmbridge. W Yor 7K 41
Holmbury St Mary. Surr 1J 11
Holmbush. Corn 6C 4
Holmcroft. Staf 7H 35
Holme. Cambs 3J 29
Holme. Cumb 8D 46
Holme. N Lin 7G 43
Holme. N Yor 7A 48
Holme. Notts 4F 36
Holme. W Yor 7K 41
Holmebridge. Dors 7G 9
Holme Chapel. Lanc 5G 41
Holme Hale. Norf 1E 30
Holme Lacy. Here 8D 26
Holme Marsh. Here 6B 26
Holmend. Dum 1E 52
Holme next the Sea. Norf 5D 38
Holme-on-Spalding-Moor. E Yor 4F 42
Holme on the Wolds. E Yor 3G 43
Holme Pierrepont. Notts 6D 36
Holmer. Here 7D 26
Holmer Green. Buck 4G 21
Holmes. Lanc 6C 40
Holme St Cuthbert. Cumb 7F 52
Holmes Chapel. Ches E 3F 34
Holmesfield. Derbs 2M 35
Holmeswood. Lanc 6C 40
Holmewood. Derbs 3B 36
**Holmfirth**. W Yor 7K 41
Holmhead. E Ayr 7D 58
Holmisdale. High 1C 68
Holm of Drumlanrig. Dum 2C 52
Holmpton. E Yor 5L 43
Holmrook. Cumb 5K 45
Holmsgarth. Shet 3E 90
Holmside. Dur 7F 54
Holmwrangle. Cumb 7K 53
Holne. Devn 5K 5
Holsworthy. Devn 5C 6
Holsworthy Beacon. Devn 5C 6
Holt. Dors 5J 9
Holt. Norf 6G 39
Holt. Wilts 7G 19
Holt. Worc 5G 27
Holt. Wrex 4C 34
Holtby. York 2D 42
Holt End. Hants 2D 10
Holt End. Worc 5J 27
Holt Fleet. Worc 5G 27
Holt Green. Lanc 7B 40
Holt Heath. Dors 5J 9
Holt Heath. Worc 5G 27
Holton. Oxon 3C 20
Holton. Som 3E 8
Holton. Suff 4K 31
Holton cum Beckering. Linc 1J 37
Holton Heath. Dors 6H 9
Holton le Clay. Linc 7K 43
Holton le Moor. Linc 8H 43
Holton St Mary. Suff 8G 31
Holt Pound. Hants 1F 10
Holtsmere End. Herts 2H 21
Holtye. E Sus 2A 12
Holwell. Dors 4F 8
Holwell. Herts 8J 29
Holwell. Leics 7E 36
Holwell. Oxon 3L 19
Holwell. Som 1F 8
Holwick. Dur 3H 47
Holworth. Dors 7F 8
Holybourne. Hants 1E 10
Holy City. Devn 5B 8
Holy Cross. Worc 4H 27
Holyfield. Essx 3L 21
**Holyhead**. IOA 2B 32
Holy Island. Nmbd 5J 61
Holymoorside. Derbs 3M 35
Holyport. Wind 6F 20
Holystone. Nmbd 1C 54
Holytown. N Lan 3F 58
Holywell. Cambs 4L 29
Holywell. Corn 3L 3
Holywell. Dors 5D 8
Holywell. Flin 3L 33
Holywell. Glos 4F 18
Holywell. Nmbd 4G 55
Holywell. Warw 5K 27
Holywell Green. W Yor 6J 41
Holywell Lake. Som 3L 7
Holywell Row. Suff 4D 30
**Holywood**. Ards 5J 93
Holywood. Dum 3D 52
Homer. Shrp 1E 26
Homer Green. Mers 7B 40
Homersfield. Suff 3J 31
Hom Green. Here 1D 18
Homington. Wilts 3K 9
Honeyborough. Pemb 6F 14
Honeybourne. Worc 7K 27
Honeychurch. Devn 5F 6
Honeydon. Bed 6J 29
Honey Hill. Kent 7H 23
Honey Street. Wilts 7K 19
Honey Tye. Suff 8F 30
Honeywick. C Beds 1G 21
Honiley. Warw 4L 27
Honing. Norf 7K 39
Honingham. Norf 8H 39
Honington. Linc 5G 37
Honington. Suff 4F 30
Honington. Warw 7L 27
Honiton. Devn 5L 7
Honley. W Yor 6K 41
Honnington. Telf 8F 34
Hoo. Suff 6J 31
Hoobrook. Worc 4G 27
Hood Green. S Yor 7M 41
Hooe. E Sus 5C 12
Hooe. Plym 6H 5
Hooe Common. E Sus 4C 12
Hoo Green. Ches E 1F 34
Hoohill. Bkpl 4B 40
Hook. Cambs 2M 29
Hook. E Yor 5E 42
Hook. G Lon 7J 21
Hook. Hants
  nr. Basingstoke 8E 20
  nr. Fareham 5C 10
Hook. Pemb 5F 14
Hook. Wilts 5J 19
Hook-a-Gate. Shrp 1C 26
Hook Bank. Worc 7G 27
Hooke. Dors 5D 8
Hooker Gate. Tyne 6E 54
Hookgate. Staf 6F 34
Hook Green. Kent
  nr. Lamberhurst 2C 12
  nr. Meopham 7C 22
  nr. Southfleet 6C 22
Hook Norton. Oxon 8A 28
Hook's Cross. Herts 1K 21
Hook Street. Glos 4E 18
Hookway. Devn 6H 7
Hookwood. Surr 1K 11
Hoole. Ches W 3C 34
Hooley. Surr 8K 21
Hooley Bridge. G Man 6G 41
Hooley Brow. G Man 6G 41
Hoo St Werburgh. Medw 6D 22
Hooton. Ches W 2B 34
Hooton Levitt. S Yor 8C 42
Hooton Pagnell. S Yor 7B 42
Hooton Roberts. S Yor 8B 42
Hoove. Shet 3D 90
Hope. Derbs 1K 35
Hope. Flin 4B 34
Hope. High 5G 85
Hope. Powy 1A 26
Hope. Shrp 1B 26
Hope. Staf 4K 35
Hope Bagot. Shrp 4D 26
Hope Bowdler. Shrp 2C 26
Hopedale. Staf 4K 35
Hope Green. Ches E 1H 35
Hopeman. Mor 7M 79
Hope Mansell. Here 2E 18
Hopesay. Shrp 3B 26
Hope's Green. Essx 5D 22
Hopetown. W Yor 5A 42
Hope under Dinmore. Here 6D 26
Hopley's Green. Here 6B 26
Hopperton. N Yor 2B 42
Hop Pole. Linc 8J 37
Hopstone. Shrp 2F 26
Hopton. Derbs 4L 35
Hopton. Powy 3M 25
Hopton. Shrp
  nr. Oswestry 7B 34
  nr. Wem 7D 34
Hopton. Staf 7H 35
Hopton. Suff 4F 30
Hopton Cangeford. Shrp 3D 26
Hopton Castle. Shrp 4B 26
Hopton Heath. Staf 7H 35
Hoptonheath. Shrp 4B 26
Hopton on Sea. Norf 1M 31
Hopton Wafers. Shrp 4E 26
Hopwas. Staf 1K 27
Hopwood. Worc 4J 27
Horam. E Sus 4B 12
Horbling. Linc 6J 37
Horbury. W Yor 6L 41
Horcott. Glos 3K 19
Horden. Dur 7H 55
Horderley. Shrp 3C 26
Hordle. Hants 6L 9
Hordley. Shrp 6B 34
Horeb. Carm
  nr. Brechfa 4M 15
  nr. Llanelli 6L 15
Horeb. Cdgn 2K 15
Horfield. Bris 6D 18
Horgabost. W Isl 4B 76
Horham. Suff 4J 31
Horkstow. N Lin 6G 43
Horley. Oxon 7B 28
**Horley**. Surr 1K 11
Horn Ash. Dors 5B 8
Hornblotton Green. Som 2D 8
Hornby. Lanc 1D 40
Hornby. N Yor
  nr. Appleton Wiske 5A 48
  nr. Catterick Garrison 6L 47
Horncastle. Linc 3K 37
**Hornchurch**. G Lon 5B 22
Horncliffe. Nmbd 5G 61
Horndean. Hants 4E 10
Horndean. Bord 5F 60
Horndon. Devn 7E 6
Horndon on the Hill. Thur 5C 22
Horne. Surr 1L 11
Horner. Som 1J 7
Horning. Norf 8K 39
Horninghold. Leics 2F 28
Horninglow. Staf 7L 35
Horningsea. Cambs 5A 30
Horningsham. Wilts 1G 9
Horningtoft. Norf 7F 38
Hornsbury. Som 4B 8
Hornsby. Cumb 6K 53
Hornsbygate. Cumb 6K 53
Horns Corner. Kent 3D 12
Horns Cross. Devn 3C 6
Hornsea. E Yor 3K 43
Hornsea Burton. E Yor 3K 43
**Hornsey**. G Lon 5L 21
Hornton. Oxon 7A 28
Horpit. Swin 5L 19
Horrabridge. Devn 5H 5
Horringer. Suff 5E 30
Horringford. IOW 7C 10
Horrocks Fold. G Man 6F 40
Horrocksford. Lanc 3F 40
Horsbrugh Ford. Bord 6L 59
Horsebridge. Devn 8D 6
Horsebridge. Hants 2M 9
Horsebrook. Staf 8G 35
Horsecastle. N Som 7C 18
Horsehay. Telf 1E 26
Horseheath. Cambs 7C 30
Horsehouse. N Yor 7J 47
Horsell. Surr 8G 21
Horseman's Green. Wrex 5C 34
Horsenden. Buck 3E 20
Horseway. Cambs 3M 29
Horsey. Norf 7L 39
Horsey. Som 2B 8
Horsford. Norf 8H 39
**Horsforth**. W Yor 4L 41
**Horsham**. W Sus 2J 11
Horsham. Worc 6F 26
Horsham St Faith. Norf 8J 39
Horsington. Linc 3J 37
Horsington. Som 3F 8
Horsley. Derbs 5A 36
Horsley. Glos 4G 19
Horsley. Nmbd
  nr. Prudhoe 5D 54
  nr. Rochester 2B 54
Horsley Cross. Essx 1H 23
Horsleycross Street. Essx 1H 23
Horsleyhill. Bord 8C 60
Horsleyhope. Dur 7D 54
Horsley Woodhouse. Derbs 5A 36
Horsmonden. Kent 1C 12
Horspath. Oxon 3C 20
Horstead. Norf 8J 39
Horsted Keynes. W Sus 3L 11
Horton. Buck 2G 21
Horton. Dors 5J 9
Horton. Lanc 2G 41
Horton. Nptn 6F 28
Horton. Shrp 6C 34
Horton. Som 4B 8
Horton. S Glo 5F 18
Horton. Staf 4H 35
Horton. Swan 8L 15
Horton. Wilts 7J 19
Horton. Wind 6H 21
Horton Cross. Som 4B 8
Horton-cum-Studley. Oxon 2C 20
Horton Grange. Nmbd 4F 54
Horton Green. Ches W 5C 34
Horton Heath. Hants 4B 10
Horton in Ribblesdale. N Yor 8G 47
Horton Kirby. Kent 7B 22
Hortonwood. Telf 8E 34
**Horwich**. G Man 6E 40
Horwich End. Derbs 1J 35
Horwood. Devn 3E 6
Hoscar. Lanc 6C 40
Hose. Leics 7E 36
Hosh. Per 5B 66
Hosta. W Isl 6J 75
Hoswick. Shet 5E 90
Hotham. E Yor 4F 42
Hothfield. Kent 1F 12
Hoton. Leics 7C 36
Houbie. Shet 4L 91
Hough. Arg 3E 62
Hough. Ches E
  nr. Crewe 4F 34
  nr. Wilmslow 2G 35
Hougham. Linc 5F 36
Hough Green. Hal 1C 34
Hough-on-the-Hill. Linc 5G 37
Houghton. Cambs 4K 29
Houghton. Cumb 6J 53
Houghton. Hants 2M 9
Houghton. Nmbd 5E 54
Houghton. Pemb 6F 14
Houghton. W Sus 4H 11
Houghton Bank. Darl 3L 47
Houghton Conquest. C Beds 7H 29
Houghton Green. E Sus 3F 12
Houghton-le-Side. Darl 3L 47
**Houghton-le-Spring**. Tyne 6G 55
Houghton on the Hill. Leics 1D 28
Houghton Regis. C Beds 1H 21
Houghton St Giles. Norf 6F 38
Houlland. Shet
  on Mainland 2D 90
  on Yell 6K 91
Houlsyke. N Yor 5E 48
Houlton. Warw 4C 28
Hound. Hants 5B 10
Hound Green. Hants 8E 20
Houndslow. Bord 5D 60
Houndsmoor. Som 3L 7
Houndwood. Bord 3F 60
Hounsdown. Hants 4M 9
**Hounslow**. G Lon 6J 21
Housabister. Shet 2E 90
Housay. Shet 6L 91
Househill. High 8J 79
Housetter. Shet 5H 91
Houss. Shet 4D 90
Houston. Ren 3C 58
Housty. High 8C 86
Houton. Orkn 1E 86
**Hove**. Brig 5K 11
Hoveringham. Notts 5D 36
Hoveton. Norf 8K 39
Hovingham. N Yor 8D 48
How. Cumb 6K 53
How Caple. Here 8E 26
Howden. E Yor 5E 42
Howden-le-Wear. Dur 8E 54
Howe. High 5E 86
Howe. Norf 1J 31
Howe. N Yor 7A 48
The Howe. Cumb 7C 46
The Howe. IOM 8A 44
Howe Green. Essx 3D 22
Howe Green. Warw 3M 27
Howegreen. Essx 3E 22
Howell. Linc 5J 37
How End. C Beds 7H 29
Howe of Teuchar. Abers 1G 73
Howes. Dum 5F 52
Howe Street. Essx
  nr. Chelmsford 2C 22
  nr. Finchingfield 8C 30
Howey. Powy 7K 25
Howgate. Midl 4L 59
Howgill. Lanc 3G 41
Howgill. N Yor 2J 41
How Green. Kent 1A 12
How Hill. Norf 8K 39
Howick. Nmbd 8K 61
Howle. Telf 7E 34
Howle Hill. Here 1E 18
Howleigh. Som 4M 7
Howlett End. Essx 8B 30
Howley. Som 5A 8
Howley. Warr 1E 34
Hownam. Bord 8E 60
Howsham. N Lin 7H 43
Howsham. N Yor 1E 42
Howtel. Nmbd 6F 60
Howt Green. Kent 7E 22
Howton. Here 1C 18
Howwood. Ren 3B 58
Hoxne. Suff 4H 31
**Hoylake**. Mers 2M 33
**Hoyland**. S Yor 7A 42
Hoylandswaine. S Yor 7L 41
Hoyle. W Sus 4G 11
Hubberholme. N Yor 8H 47
Hubberston. Pemb 6E 14
Hubbert's Bridge. Linc 5K 37
Huby. N Yor
  nr. Harrogate 3L 41
  nr. York 1C 42
Hucclecote. Glos 2G 19
Hucking. Kent 8E 22
**Hucknall**. Notts 5C 36
**Huddersfield**. W Yor 6K 41
Huddington. Worc 6H 27
Huddlesford. Staf 1K 27
Hudswell. N Yor 5K 47
Huggate. E Yor 2F 42
Hugglescote. Leics 8B 36
Hughenden Valley. Buck 4F 20
Hughley. Shrp 2D 26
Hughton. High 1E 70
Hugh Town. IOS 1H 3
Hugus. Corn 4L 3
Huish. Devn 4E 6
Huish. Wilts 7K 19
Huish Champflower. Som 3K 7
Huish Episcopi. Som 3C 8
Huisinis. W Isl 2A 76
Hulcote. Nptn 7E 28
Hulcott. Buck 2F 20
Hulham. Devn 7K 7
**Hull**. Hull 5J 43
Hulland. Derbs 5L 35
Hulland Moss. Derbs 5L 35
Hulland Ward. Derbs 5L 35
Hullavington. Wilts 5G 19
Hullbridge. Essx 4E 22
Hulme. G Man 8G 41
Hulme. Staf 5H 35
Hulme End. Staf 4K 35
Hulme Walfield. Ches E 3G 35
Hulverstone. IOW 7A 10
Hulver Street. Suff 3L 31
Humber. Devn 8J 7
Humber. Here 6D 26
**Humber Bridge**. N Lin 5H 43
Humberside Airport. N Lin 6H 43
Humberston. NE Lin 7L 43
Humberstone. Leic 1D 28
Humbie. E Lot 3B 60
Humbleton. E Yor 4K 43
Humbleton. Nmbd 7G 61
Humby. Linc 6H 37
Hume. Bord 5E 60
Humshaugh. Nmbd 4C 54
Huna. High 4E 86
Huncoat. Lanc 4F 40
Huncote. Leics 2C 28
Hundall. Derbs 2A 36
Hunderthwaite. Dur 3H 47
Hundleby. Linc 3L 37
Hundle Houses. Linc 4K 37
Hundleton. Pemb 6F 14
Hundon. Suff 7D 30
The Hundred. Here 5D 26
Hundred Acres. Hants 4C 10
Hundred House. Powy 7L 25
Hungarton. Leics 1D 28
Hungerford. Hants 4K 9
Hungerford. Shrp 3D 26
Hungerford. Som 1K 7
Hungerford. W Ber 7M 19
Hungerford Newtown. W Ber 6A 20
Hunger Hill. G Man 7E 40
Hungerton. Linc 6F 36
Hungladder. High 6E 76
Hungryhatton. Shrp 7E 34
Hunmanby. N Yor 8H 49
Hunmanby Sands. N Yor 8J 49
Hunningham. Warw 5A 28
Hunnington. Worc 3H 27
Hunny Hill. IOW 7B 10
Hunsdon. Herts 2M 21
Hunsdonbury. Herts 2M 21
Hunsingore. N Yor 2B 42
Hunslet. W Yor 4M 41
Hunslet Carr. W Yor 4M 41
Hunsonby. Cumb 8K 53
Hunspow. High 4D 86
Hunstanton. Norf 5C 38
Hunstanworth. Dur 7C 54
Hunston. Suff 5F 30
Hunston. W Sus 5F 10
Hunstrete. Bath 7E 18
Hunt End. Worc 5J 27
Hunterfield. Midl 3M 59
Hunters Forstal. Kent 7H 23
Hunter's Quay. Arg 2L 57
Huntham. Som 3B 8
Hunthill Lodge. Ang 8D 72
**Huntingdon**. Cambs 4K 29
Huntingfield. Suff 4K 31
Huntingford. Wilts 3G 9
Huntington. Ches W 3C 34
Huntington. E Lot 2B 60
Huntington. Here 6A 26
Huntington. Staf 8H 35
Huntington. Telf 1E 26
Huntington. York 2D 42
Huntingtower. Per 5D 66
Huntley. Glos 2F 18
Huntley. Staf 5J 35
Huntly. Abers 2E 72
Huntlywood. Bord 5D 60
Hunton. Hants 2B 10
Hunton. Kent 1D 12
Hunton. N Yor 6K 47
Hunton Bridge. Herts 4H 21
Hunt's Corner. Norf 3G 31
Huntscott. Som 1J 7
Hunt's Cross. Mers 1C 34
Hunts Green. Warw 2K 27
Huntsham. Devn 3K 7
Huntshaw. Devn 3E 6
Huntspill. Som 1B 8
Huntstile. Som 2A 8
Huntworth. Som 2B 8
Hunwick. Dur 8E 54
Hunworth. Norf 6G 39
Hurcott. Som
  nr. Ilminster 4B 8
  nr. Somerton 3D 8
Hurdcott. Wilts 2K 9
Hurdley. Powy 2A 26
Hurdsfield. Ches E 2H 35
Hurlet. Glas 3D 58
Hurley. Warw 2L 27
Hurley. Wind 5F 20
Hurlford. E Ayr 6C 58
Hurliness. Orkn 3D 86
Hurlston Green. Lanc 6C 40
Hurn. Dors 6K 9
Hursey. Dors 5C 8
Hursley. Hants 3B 10
Hurst. G Man 7H 41
Hurst. N Yor 5J 47
Hurst. Som 4C 8
Hurst. Wok 6E 20
Hurstbourne Priors. Hants 1B 10
Hurstbourne Tarrant. Hants 8A 20
Hurst Green. Ches E 5D 34
Hurst Green. E Sus 3D 12
Hurst Green. Essx 2G 23
Hurst Green. Lanc 4E 40
Hurst Green. Surr 8L 21
Hurstley. Here 7B 26
Hurstpierpoint. W Sus 4K 11
Hurstway Common. Here 7B 26
Hurst Wickham. W Sus 4K 11
Hurstwood. Lanc 4G 41
Hurtmore. Surr 1G 11
Hurworth-on-Tees. Darl 4M 47
Hurworth Place. Darl 5L 47
Hury. Dur 4H 47
Husbands Bosworth. Leics 3D 28
Husborne Crawley. C Beds 8G 29
Husthwaite. N Yor 8C 48
Hutcherleigh. Devn 6K 5
Hut Green. N Yor 5C 42
Huthwaite. Notts 4B 36
Huttoft. Linc 2B 38
Hutton. Cumb 3C 46
Hutton. E Yor 2H 43
Hutton. Essx 4C 22
Hutton. Lanc 5C 40
Hutton. N Som 8B 18
Hutton. Bord 4G 61
Hutton Bonville. N Yor 5M 47
Hutton Buscel. N Yor 7G 49
Hutton Conyers. N Yor 8M 47
Hutton Cranswick. E Yor 2H 43
Hutton End. Cumb 8J 53
Hutton Gate. Red C 4C 48
Hutton Henry. Dur 8H 55
Hutton-le-Hole. N Yor 7E 48
Hutton Magna. Dur 4K 47
Hutton Mulgrave. N Yor 5F 48
Hutton Roof. Cumb
  nr. Kirkby Lonsdale 8D 46
  nr. Penrith 8H 53
Hutton Rudby. N Yor 5B 48
Huttons Ambo. N Yor 1E 42
Hutton Sessay. N Yor 8B 48
Hutton Village. Red C 4D 48
Hutton Wandesley. N Yor 2C 42
Huxham. Devn 6J 7
Huxham Green. Som 2D 8
Huxley. Ches W 3D 34
Huxter. Shet
  on Mainland 2B 90
  on Whalsay 1F 90
**Huyton**. Mers 8C 40
**Hwlffordd**. Pemb 5F 14
Hycemoor. Cumb 6K 45
Hyde. Glos
  nr. Stroud 3G 19
  nr. Winchcombe 1J 19
**Hyde**. G Man 8H 41
Hyde Heath. Buck 3G 21
Hyde Lea. Staf 8H 35
Hyde Park. S Yor 7C 42
Hydestile. Surr 1G 11
Hyndford Bridge. S Lan 5H 59
Hynish. Arg 4E 62
Hyssington. Powy 2B 26
**Hythe**. Hants 5B 10
**Hythe**. Kent 2H 13
Hythe End. Wind 6H 21
Hythie. Abers 8K 81
Hyton. Cumb 6K 45


## I


Ianstown. Mor 7D 80
Iarsiadar. W Isl 8E 82
Ibberton. Dors 5F 8
Ible. Derbs 4L 35
Ibrox. Glas 3D 58
Ibsley. Hants 5K 9
Ibstock. Leics 8B 36
Ibstone. Buck 4E 20
Ibthorpe. Hants 8A 20
Iburndale. N Yor 5F 48
Ibworth. Hants 8C 20
Icelton. N Som 7B 18
Ichrachan. Arg 4E 64
Ickburgh. Norf 2E 30
Ickenham. G Lon 5H 21
Ickenthwaite. Cumb 7B 46
Ickford. Buck 3D 20
Ickham. Kent 8J 23
Ickleford. Herts 8J 29
Icklesham. E Sus 4E 12
Ickleton. Cambs 7A 30
Icklingham. Suff 4D 30
Ickwell. C Beds 7J 29
Icomb. Glos 1L 19
Idbury. Oxon 2L 19
Iddesleigh. Devn 5E 6
Ide. Devn 6H 7
Ideford. Devn 8H 7
Ide Hill. Kent 8A 22
Iden. E Sus 3F 12
Iden Green. Kent
  nr. Benenden 2E 12
  nr. Goudhurst 2D 12
Idle. W Yor 4K 41
Idless. Corn 4M 3
Idlicote. Warw 7L 27
Idmiston. Wilts 2K 9
Idole. Carm 5L 15
Idridgehay. Derbs 5L 35
Idrigill. High 7E 76
Idstone. Oxon 5L 19
Iffley. Oxon 3C 20
Ifield. W Sus 2K 11
Ifieldwood. W Sus 2K 11
Ifold. W Sus 2H 11
Iford. E Sus 5M 11
Ifton Heath. Shrp 6B 34
Ightfield. Shrp 6D 34
Ightham. Kent 8B 22
Iken. Suff 6L 31
Ilam. Staf 4K 35
Ilchester. Som 3D 8
Ilderton. Nmbd 7H 61
**Ilford**. G Lon 5M 21
Ilford. Som 4B 8
**Ilfracombe**. Devn 1E 6
**Ilkeston**. Derbs 5B 36
Ilketshall St Andrew. Suff 3K 31
Ilketshall St Lawrence. Suff 3K 31
Ilketshall St Margaret. Suff 3K 31
**Ilkley**. W Yor 3K 41
Illand. Corn 8B 6
Illey. W Mid 3H 27
Illidge Green. Ches E 3F 34
Illington. Norf 3F 30
Illingworth. W Yor 5J 41
Illogan. Corn 4K 3
Illogan Highway. Corn 4K 3
Illston on the Hill. Leics 2E 28
Ilmer. Buck 3E 20
Ilmington. Warw 7L 27
Ilminster. Som 4B 8
Ilsington. Devn 8G 7
Ilsington. Dors 6F 8
Ilston. Swan 5E 16
Ilton. N Yor 8K 47
Ilton. Som 4B 8
Imachar. N Ayr 5H 57
Imber. Wilts 1H 9
**Immingham**. NE Lin 6J 43
Immingham Dock. NE Lin 6K 43
Impington. Cambs 5M 29
Ince. Ches W 2C 34
Ince Blundell. Mers 7B 40
**Ince-in-Makerfield**. G Man 7D 40
Inchbae Lodge. High 7E 78
Inchbare. Ang 1K 67
Inchberry. Mor 8C 80
Inchbraoch. Ang 2L 67
Inchbrook. Glos 3G 19
Incheril. High 7M 77
Inchinnan. Ren 3C 58
Inchlaggan. High 5B 70
Inchmichael. Per 5F 66
Inchnadamph. High 1C 78
Inchree. High 1E 64
Inchture. Per 5F 66
Inchyra. Per 5E 66
Indian Queens. Corn 6B 4
Ingatestone. Essx 4C 22
Ingbirchworth. S Yor 7L 41
Ingestre. Staf 7H 35
Ingham. Linc 1G 37
Ingham. Norf 7K 39
Ingham. Suff 4E 30
Ingham Corner. Norf 7K 39
Ingleborough. Norf 8A 38
Ingleby. Derbs 7M 35
Ingleby Arncliffe. N Yor 5B 48
Ingleby Barwick. Stoc T 4B 48
Ingleby Greenhow. N Yor 5C 48
Ingleigh Green. Devn 5F 6
Inglemire. Hull 4H 43
Inglesbatch. Bath 7F 18
Ingleton. Dur 3K 47
Ingleton. N Yor 8E 46
Inglewhite. Lanc 3D 40
Ingoe. Nmbd 4D 54
Ingol. Lanc 4D 40
Ingoldisthorpe. Norf 6C 38
Ingoldmells. Linc 3B 38
Ingoldsby. Linc 6H 37
Ingon. Warw 6L 27
Ingram. Nmbd 8H 61
Ingrave. Essx 4C 22
Ingrow. W Yor 4J 41
Ings. Cumb 6C 46
Ingst. S Glo 5D 18
Ingthorpe. Rut 1G 29
Ingworth. Norf 7H 39
Inishrush. M Ulst 3F 93
Inkberrow. Worc 6J 27
Inkford. Worc 4J 27
Inkpen. W Ber 7A 20
Inkstack. High 4D 86
Innellan. Arg 3L 57
Inner Hope. Devn 8J 5
Innerleith. Fife 6F 66
Innerleithen. Bord 6M 59
Innerleven. Fife 7G 67
Innermessan. Dum 5F 50
Innerwick. E Lot 2E 60
Innerwick. Per 3K 65
Innsworth. Glos 1G 19
Insch. Abers 3F 72
Insh. High 5J 71
Inshegra. High 6E 84
Inshore. High 4F 84
Inskip. Lanc 4C 40
Instow. Devn 2D 6
Intwood. Norf 1H 31
Inver. Abers 6B 72
Inver. High 5J 79
Inver. Per 3D 66
Inverailort. High 7J 69
Inveralligin. High 8K 77
Inverallochy. Abers 7K 81
Inveramsay. Abers 3G 73
Inveran. High 4F 78
Inveraray. Arg 7E 64
Inverarish. High 2G 69
Inverarity. Ang 3H 67
Inverarnan. Stir 6H 65
Inverarnie. High 2G 71
Inverbeg. Arg 8H 65
Inverbervie. Abers 8H 73
Inverboyndie. Abers 7F 80
Invercassley. High 3E 78
Invercharnan. High 3F 64
Inverchoran. High 8C 78
Invercreran. Arg 3E 64
Inverdruie. High 4K 71
Inverebrie. Abers 2J 73
Invereck. Arg 1L 57
Inveresk. E Lot 2M 59
Inveresragan. Arg 4D 64
Inverey. Abers 7L 71
Inverfarigaig. High 3F 70
Invergarry. High 5D 70
Invergeldie. Per 5M 65
Invergordon. High 7H 79
Invergowrie. Per 4G 67
Inverguseran. High 5J 69
Inverharroch. Mor 2C 72
Inverie. High 5J 69
Inverinan. Arg 6D 64
Inverinate. High 3L 69
Inverkeilor. Ang 3K 67
**Inverkeithing**. Fife 1K 59
Inverkeithny. Abers 1F 72
Inverkip. Inv 2M 57
Inverkirkaig. High 2A 78
Inverlael. High 5B 78
Inverliever Lodge. Arg 7C 64
Inverliver. Arg 4E 64
Inverlochlarig. Stir 6J 65
Inverlochy. High 8B 70
Inverlussa. Arg 1F 56
Inver Mallie. High 7B 70
Invermarkie. Abers 2D 72
Invermoriston. High 4E 70
Invernaver. High 5K 85
Inverneil House. Arg 1H 57
**Inverness**. High 1G 71
Inverness Airport. High 8H 79
Invernettie. Abers 1L 73
Inverpolly Lodge. High 2A 78
Inverquhomery. Abers 1K 73
Inverroy. High 7C 70
Inversanda. High 2D 64
Invershiel. High 4L 69
Invershin. High 4F 78
Invershore. High 8D 86
Inversnaid. Stir 7H 65
Inverugie. Abers 1L 73
Inveruglas. Arg 7H 65
**Inverurie**. Abers 3G 73
Invervar. Per 3L 65
Inverythan. Abers 1G 73
Inwardleigh. Devn 6E 6
Inworth. Essx 2E 22
Iochdar. W Isl 1D 74
Iping. W Sus 3F 10
Ipplepen. Devn 5L 5
Ipsden. Oxon 5D 20
Ipstones. Staf 5J 35
**Ipswich**. Suff 7H 31
Irby. Mers 1A 34
Irby in the Marsh. Linc 3A 38
Irby upon Humber. NE Lin 7J 43
Irchester. Nptn 5G 29
Ireby. Cumb 8G 53
Ireby. Lanc 8E 46
Ireland. Shet 5D 90
Ireleth. Cumb 7M 45
Ireshopeburn. Dur 8B 54
Ireton Wood. Derbs 5L 35
**Irlam**. G Man 8F 40
Irnham. Linc 7H 37
Iron Acton. S Glo 5E 18
Iron Bridge. Cambs 2A 30
Ironbridge. Telf 1E 26
Iron Cross. Warw 6J 27
Ironville. Derbs 4B 36
Irstead. Norf 7K 39
Irthington. Cumb 5J 53
Irthlingborough. Nptn 4G 29
Irton. N Yor 7H 49
**Irvine**. N Ayr 6B 58
Irvine Mains. N Ayr 6B 58
Irvinestown. Ferm 6C 92
Isabella Pit. Nmbd 3G 55
Isauld. High 5A 86
Isbister. Orkn 8C 88
Isbister. Shet
  on Mainland 4H 91
  on Whalsay 1F 90
Isfield. E Sus 4A 12
Isham. Nptn 4F 28
Island Carr. N Lin 7G 43
Islay Airport. Arg 4C 56
Isle Abbotts. Som 3B 8
Isle Brewers. Som 3B 8
Isleham. Cambs 4C 30
Isle of Man Airport. IOM 8B 44
**Isle of Thanet**. Kent 7K 23
Isle of Whithorn. Dum 8K 51
**Isle of Wight**. IOW 7B 10
Isleornsay. High 4J 69
Islesburgh. Shet 1D 90
Isles of Scilly Airport. IOS 1H 3
Islesteps. Dum 4D 52
**Isleworth**. G Lon 6J 21
Isley Walton. Leics 7B 36
Islibhig. W Isl 1A 76
**Islington**. G Lon 5L 21
Islington. Telf 7F 34
Islip. Nptn 4G 29
Islip. Oxon 2C 20
Isombridge. Telf 8E 34
Istead Rise. Kent 7C 22
Itchen. Sotn 4B 10
Itchen Abbas. Hants 2C 10
Itchenor. W Sus 5E 10
Itchen Stoke. Hants 2C 10
Itchingfield. W Sus 3J 11
Itchington. S Glo 5E 18
Itlaw. Abers 8F 80
Itteringham. Norf 6H 39
Itteringham Common. Norf 7H 39
Itton. Devn 6F 6
Itton Common. Mon 4C 18
Ivegill. Cumb 7J 53
Ivelet. N Yor 6H 47
Iverchaolain. Arg 2K 57
Iver Heath. Buck 5H 21
Iveston. Dur 6E 54
Ivetsey Bank. Staf 8G 35
Ivinghoe. Buck 2G 21
Ivinghoe Aston. Buck 2G 21
Ivington. Here 6C 26
Ivington Green. Here 6C 26
Ivybridge. Devn 6J 5
Ivychurch. Kent 3G 13
Ivy Hatch. Kent 8B 22
Ivy Todd. Norf 1E 30
Iwade. Kent 7F 22
Iwerne Courtney. Dors 4G 9
Iwerne Minster. Dors 4G 9
Ixworth. Suff 4F 30
Ixworth Thorpe. Suff 4F 30


## J


Jackfield. Shrp 1E 26
Jack Hill. N Yor 2K 41
Jacksdale. Notts 4B 36
Jackton. S Lan 4D 58
Jacobstow. Corn 6A 6
Jacobstowe. Devn 5E 6
Jacobs Well. Surr 8G 21
Jameston. Pemb 7G 15
Jamestown. Dum 2H 53
Jamestown. Fife 1K 59
Jamestown. High 8E 78
Jamestown. W Dun 1B 58
Janetstown. High
  nr. Thurso 5B 86
  nr. Wick 6E 86
**Jarrow**. Tyne 5G 55
Jarvis Brook. E Sus 3B 12
Jasper's Green. Essx 1D 22
Jaywick. Essx 2H 23
Jedburgh. Bord 7D 60
Jeffreyston. Pemb 6G 15
Jemimaville. High 7H 79
Jenkins Park. High 5D 70
Jersey Marine. Neat 5G 17
Jesmond. Tyne 5F 54
Jevington. E Sus 5B 12
Jingle Street. Mon 2C 18
Jockey End. Herts 2H 21
Jodrell Bank. Ches E 2F 34
Johnby. Cumb 8J 53
John O'Gaunts. W Yor 5M 41
John o' Groats. High 4E 86
John's Cross. E Sus 3D 12
Johnshaven. Abers 1L 67
Johnson Street. Norf 8K 39
Johnston. Pemb 5F 14
**Johnstone**. Ren 3C 58
Johnstonebridge. Dum 2E 52
Johnstown. Carm 5L 15
Johnstown. Wrex 5B 34
Jonesborough. New M 7G 93
Joppa. Edin 2M 59
Joppa. S Ayr 8C 58
Jordan Green. Norf 7G 39
Jordans. Buck 4G 21
Jordanston. Pemb 3F 14
Jump. S Yor 7A 42
Jumpers Common. Dors 6K 9
Juniper. Nmbd 6C 54
Juniper Green. Edin 3K 59
Jurby East. IOM 5C 44
Jurby West. IOM 5C 44
Jury's Gap. E Sus 4F 12


## K


Kaber. Cumb 4F 46
Kaimend. S Lan 5H 59
Kaimes. Edin 3L 59
Kaimrig End. Bord 5J 59
Kames. Arg 2J 57
Kames. E Ayr 7E 58
Katesbridge. Arm 6H 93
Kea. Corn 4M 3
Keadby. N Lin 6F 42
Keady. Arm 7F 93
Keal Cotes. Linc 3L 37
Kearsley. G Man 7F 40
Kearsney. Kent 1J 13
Kearstwick. Cumb 7E 46
Kearton. N Yor 6H 47
Kearvaig. High 4E 84
Keasden. N Yor 1F 40
Keason. Corn 5F 4
Keckwick. Hal 1D 34
Keddington. Linc 1L 37
Keddington Corner. Linc 1L 37
Kedington. Suff 7D 30
Kedleston. Derbs 5M 35
Kedlock Feus. Fife 6G 67
Keekle. Cumb 3K 45
Keelby. Linc 6J 43
Keele. Staf 5G 35
Keeley Green. Bed 7H 29
Keeston. Pemb 5F 14
Keevil. Wilts 8H 19
Kegworth. Leics 7B 36
Kehelland. Corn 4K 3
Keig. Abers 4F 72
**Keighley**. W Yor 3J 41
Keilarsbrae. Clac 8B 66
Keillmore. Arg 1F 56
Keillor. Per 3F 66
Keillour. Per 5C 66
Keills. Arg 3D 56
Keiloch. Abers 6A 72
Keils. Arg 3E 56
Keinton Mandeville. Som 2D 8
Keir Mill. Dum 2C 52
Keirsleywell Row. Nmbd 6A 54
Keisby. Linc 7H 37
Keisley. Cumb 3F 46
Keiss. High 5E 86
Keith. Mor 8D 80
Keith Inch. Abers 1L 73
Kelbrook. Lanc 3H 41
Kelby. Linc 5H 37
Keld. Cumb 4D 46
Keld. N Yor 5G 47
Keldholme. N Yor 7E 48
Kelfield. N Lin 7F 42
Kelfield. N Yor 4C 42
Kelham. Notts 4E 36
Kellacott. Devn 7D 6
Kellan. Arg 3L 63
Kellas. Ang 4H 67
Kellas. Mor 8A 80
Kellaton. Devn 8L 5
Kelleth. Cumb 5E 46
Kelling. Norf 5G 39
Kellingley. N Yor 5C 42
Kellington. N Yor 5C 42
Kelloe. Dur 8G 55
Kelloholm. Dum 8F 58
Kells. Cumb 3J 45
Kells. ME Ant 4G 93
Kelly. Devn 7C 6
Kelly Bray. Corn 8C 6
Kelmarsh. Nptn 4E 28
Kelmscott. Oxon 4L 19
Kelsale. Suff
Kelsall. Ches W
Kelshall. Herts
Kelsick. Cumb
Kelso. Bord
Kelstedge. Derbs
Kelstern. Linc
Kelsterton. Flin
Kelston. Bath
Keltneyburn. Per
Kelton. Dum
Kelton Hill. Dum
Kelty. Fife
Kelvedon. Essx
Kelvedon Hatch. Essx
Kelvinside. Glas
Kelynack. Corn
Kemback. Fife
Kemberton. Shrp
Kemble. Glos
Kemerton. Worc
Kemeys Commander. Mon
Kemnay. Abers
Kempe's Corner. Kent
Kempley. Glos
Kempley Green. Glos
Kempsey. Worc
Kempsford. Glos
Kemps Green. Warw
Kempshott. Hants
**Kempston**. Bed
Kempston Hardwick. Bed
Kempton. Shrp
Kemp Town. Brig
Kemsing. Kent
Kemsley. Kent
Kenardington. Kent
Kenchester. Here
Kencot. Oxon
**Kendal**. Cumb
Kendleshire. S Glo
Kendray. S Yor
Kenfig. B'end
Kenfig Hill. B'end
Kengharair. Arg
**Kenilworth**. Warw
Kenknock. Stir
Kenley. G Lon
Kenley. Shrp
Kenmore. High
Kenmore. Per
Kenn. Devn
Kenn. N Som
Kennacraig. Arg
Kenneggy Downs. Corn
Kennerleigh. Devn
Kennet. Clac
Kennethmont. Abers
Kennett. Cambs
Kennford. Devn
Kenninghall. Norf
Kennington. Kent
Kennington. Oxon
Kennoway. Fife
Kennyhill. Suff
Kennythorpe. N Yor
Kenovay. Arg
Kensaleyre. High
**Kensington**. G Lon
Kenstone. Shrp
Kensworth. C Beds
Kensworth Common. C Beds
Kentallen. High
Kentchurch. Here
Kentford. Suff
Kentisbeare. Devn
Kentisbury. Devn
Kentisbury Ford. Devn
Kentmere. Cumb
Kenton. Devn
Kenton. G Lon
Kenton. Suff
Kenton Bankfoot. Tyne
Kentra. High
Kentrigg. Cumb
Kents Bank. Cumb
Kent's Green. Glos
Kent's Oak. Hants
Kent Street. E Sus
Kent Street. Kent
Kent Street. W Sus
Kenwick. Shrp
Kenwyn. Corn
Kenyon. Warr
Keoldale. High
Keppoch. High
Kepwick. N Yor
Keresley. W Mid
Keresley Newland. Warw
Keristal. IOM
Kerne Bridge. Here
Kerridge. Ches E
Kerris. Corn
Kerrow. High
Kerry. Powy
Kerrycroy. Arg
Kerry's Gate. Here
Kersall. Notts
Kersbrook. Devn
Kerse. Ren
Kersey. Suff
Kershopefoot. Cumb
Kersoe. Worc
Kerswell. Devn
Kerswell Green. Worc
Kesgrave. Suff
Kesh. Ferm
Kessingland. Suff
Kessingland Beach. Suff
Kestle. Corn
Kestle Mill. Corn
Keston. G Lon
Keswick. Cumb
Keswick. Norf
  nr. North Walsham
  nr. Norwich
Ketsby. Linc
**Kettering**. Nptn
Ketteringham. Norf
Kettins. Per
Kettlebaston. Suff
Kettlebridge. Fife
Kettlebrook. Staf
Kettleburgh. Suff
Kettleholm. Dum
Kettleness. N Yor
Kettleshulme. Ches E
Kettlesing. N Yor
Kettlesing Bottom. N Yor
Kettlestone. Norf
Kettlethorpe. Linc
Kettletoft. Orkn
Kettlewell. N Yor
Ketton. Rut
Kew. G Lon
Kewaigue. IOM
Kewstoke. N Som
Kexbrough. S Yor
Kexby. Linc
Kexby. York
Keyford. Som
Key Green. Ches E
Key Green. N Yor
Keyham. Leics
Keyhaven. Hants
Keyhead. Abers
Keyingham. E Yor
Keymer. W Sus
**Keynsham**. Bath
Keysoe. Bed
Keysoe Row. Bed
Key's Toft. Linc
Keyston. Cambs
Key Street. Kent
Keyworth. Notts
Kibblesworth. Tyne
Kibworth Beauchamp. Leics
Kibworth Harcourt. Leics
Kidbrooke. G Lon
Kidburngill. Cumb
Kiddemore Green. Staf
**Kidderminster**. Worc
Kiddington. Oxon
Kidd's Moor. Norf
**Kidlington**. Oxon
Kidmore End. Oxon
Kidnal. Ches W
**Kidsgrove**. Staf

Kidstones—Limerigg


nes. N Yor 7H 47
lly. Carm 6L 15
rofts. Arg 4D 64
r. Nmbd 2L 53
ie. Fife 8C 66
chan. Ren 3C 58
. High 5H 69
ry. Arg 3G 57
ie. N Ayr 4B 58
e. Arg 5C 64
e. High 3G 69
ho Place. Bord 6J 59
. Derbs 5A 36
. G Lon 5K 21
. N Yor 8C 48
Leics 2D 28
ttan. Arg 8J 63
ttan Bay. Arg 4L 57
nzie. Arg 7F 56
ran. Arg 4C 64
aran. Arg 3B 56
an. High
r. Inverie 6J 69
r. Tobermory 1K 63
man. Arg 3B 56
enan. Arg 5E 64
. New M 6J 93
quhar. Fife 7H 67
. New M 7H 93
Glos 1E 18
. High 8F 78
ggan. Arg 1M 57
. N Yor 5D 48
y. High 6H 79
morie Lodge. High 6F 78
an. Dum 6F 50
an. High
r. Helmsdale 1K 79
n Isle of Skye 8E 76
an. N Ayr 7K 57
nan. High 7F 68
mmy. Abers 4D 72
ck. N Yor 3J 41
n. Dum 6H 51
n. Arg 2J 57
an. High 6C 70
y. Pemb 6H 15
r. Fife 7F 66
mmie. S Ayr 1H 51
. E Yor 1H 43
. Nmbd 6F 60
. New M 7H 93
neth. Arg 3E 62
mpton. Corn 4B 6
as. Ferm 6C 92
arsh. Derbs 1B 36
rist. Arg 3C 64
Swan 5F 16
. Arg 5F 56
. Stir 1D 58
. M Ulst 5F 93
n. Arg 8F 56
Derr 4C 92
High 8G 79
y. Darl 4K 47
. Derr 4C 92
onan. Per 2K 65
ronan. Arg 3L 63
rankie. Per 1C 66
. High 2L 69
ster. High 6E 86
Stir 4K 65
ny. Ards 5J 93
hall. N Yor 2L 41
ton. Cumb 7E 46
**rworth**. Tyne 4F 54
Lodge. High 5F 70
chonoch. Arg 8C 64
ryett. Bord 5B 60
gh. New M 7J 93
en. New M 7G 93
dine. High 3L 63
a. Arm 6E 92
agh. New M 6J 93
mmer. Caus 2F 93
colm. Inv 3B 58
nog. Stir 7L 65
numaig. Arg 8B 64
eu. High 2C 64
uag. High 6F 76
ny. Fife 5G 67
ie. High 4G 69
**rnock**. E Ayr 6C 58
on. Fife 6G 67
tin. Arg 8C 64
urs. E Ayr 5C 58
ford. Arg 6C 64
ny. Arg 3C 56
sdon. Som 8E 18
ston. Hants 3C 10
hael Glassary. Arg 8C 64
hael of Inverlussa.
rg 1G 57
gton. Devn 6A 8
gton. Wilts 2F 8
uaig. Arg 3E 62
rack. High 1E 70
e. Arg 5C 64
e. Arm 6F 93
e. High 5H 69
e. New M 6J 93
y. Arg 2G 57
y. High
r. Kilchoan 8G 69
n Rùm 5E 68
y. N Ayr 7J 57
y Lodge. Arg 7B 64
e. High 2K 79
r. High
r. Dunvegan 1D 68
r. Invergordon 6H 79
r. Inverness 1G 71
r. Uig 6E 76
. Arg 1L 57
e. Arg 2B 56
dzow. S Lan 5G 59
wn. Kent 2D 12
reen. Here 2E 18
reen. Wok 6F 20
. Cumb 8G 53
rst. S Yor 8B 42
an. Arg 3J 63
ver. Arg 5C 64
t Hill. Nmbd 6D 54
a. E Yor 6M 43
y. N Yor 1H 41
ck. E Yor 3G 43
. Arg 8J 63
ick. N Ayr 7J 57
. Here 8C 26
E Yor 5E 42
Pike. E Yor 5E 42
Caus 3F 93
ny. Fife 7J 67
Nptn 4C 28
die. Per 5F 66
. N Lan 2F 58
ty. High 1F 70
Som 1L 7
Thorpe. Red C 4D 48
er. High 7E 76
Som 1L 7
ton. Notts 5F 36
**ning**. N Ayr 5A 58
rley. Norf 1G 31
**rley**. Notts 5B 36
esworth. Dur 7F 54
Wick. Buck 3F 20
lton. Cambs 5H 29
lton. Here 5D 26
te. Leics 3C 28
eridge. Dors 8H 9
erston. Nmbd 6G 61
on. Hants 1L 9
on. Herts 2J 21
n. Arm 6H 93
ey. Ferm 7C 92
chie. High 7G 79
ce. High 8L 85
ck. Stir 7A 66
le. Fife 6H 67
dine. Fife 1H 59
dine. High 5G 79
**dine Bridge**. Falk 1H 59
dine O'Neil. Abers 6E 72
ackine. Arg 5F 64
th. Aber 5J 73
g. High 5J 71
gie. Per 3C 66

Kindallachan. Per 2C 66
Kineton. Glos 1J 19
Kineton. Warw 6M 27
Kinfauns. Per 5E 66
Kingairloch. High 2C 64
Kingarth. Arg 4K 57
Kingcoed. Mon 3C 18
King Edward. Abers 8G 81
Kingerby. Linc 8H 43
Kingham. Oxon 1L 19
Kingholm Quay. Dum 4D 52
Kinghorn. Fife 1L 59
Kingie. High 5B 70
Kinglassie. Fife 8F 66
Kingledores. Bord 7K 59
King o' Muirs. Clac 8B 66
Kingoodie. Per 5G 67
King's Acre. Here 7C 26
Kingsand. Corn 6G 5
Kingsash. Buck 3F 20
Kingsbarns. Fife 6J 67
Kingsbridge. Devn 7K 5
Kingsbridge. Som 2J 7
King's Bromley. Staf 8K 35
Kingsburgh. High 8E 76
Kingsbury. G Lon 5J 21
Kingsbury. Warw 2L 27
Kingsbury Episcopi. Som 3C 8
Kings Caple. Here 1D 18
Kingscavil. W Lot 2J 59
Kingsclere. Hants 8C 20
King's Cliffe. Nptn 2H 29
Kings Clipstone. Notts 3D 36
Kingscote. Glos 4G 19
Kingscott. Devn 4E 6
Kings Coughton. Warw 6J 27
Kingscross. N Ayr 7K 57
Kingsdon. Som 3D 8
Kingsdown. Kent 1K 13
Kingsdown. Swin 5K 19
Kingsdown. Wilts 7G 19
Kingseat. Fife 8E 66
Kingsey. Buck 3E 20
Kingsfold. Lanc 5D 40
Kingsfold. W Sus 2J 11
Kingsford. E Ayr 5C 58
Kingsford. Worc 3G 27
Kingsforth. N Lin 6H 43
Kingsgate. Kent 6K 23
King's Green. Glos 8F 26
Kingshall Street. Suff 5F 30
Kingsheanton. Devn 2E 6
King's Heath. W Mid 3J 27
Kings Hill. Kent 8C 22
Kingsholm. Glos 2G 19
Kingshouse. High 2G 65
Kingshouse. Stir 5K 65
Kingshurst. W Mid 3K 27
Kingskerswell. Devn 5L 5
Kingskettle. Fife 7G 67
Kingsland. Here 5C 26
Kingsland. IOA 2B 32
Kings Langley. Herts 3H 21
Kingsley. Ches W 2D 34
Kingsley. Hants 2E 10
Kingsley. Staf 5J 35
Kingsley Green. W Sus 2F 10
Kingsley Holt. Staf 5J 35
**King's Lynn**. Norf 7C 38
King's Meaburn. Cumb 3E 46
Kings Moss. Mers 7D 40
Kings Muir. Bord 6L 59
Kingsmuir. Ang 3H 67
Kingsmuir. Fife 7J 67
King's Newnham. Warw 4B 28
King's Newton. Derbs 7A 36
Kingsnorth. Kent 2G 13
Kingsnorth. Medw 6E 22
King's Norton. Leics 1D 28
Kings Norton. W Mid 4J 27
King's Nympton. Devn 4F 6
King's Pyon. Here 6C 26
Kings Ripton. Cambs 4K 29
King's Somborne. Hants 2A 10
King's Stag. Dors 4F 8
King's Stanley. Glos 3G 19
King's Sutton. Nptn 8B 28
Kingstanding. W Mid 2J 27
Kingsteignton. Devn 8H 7
Kingsteps. High 8K 79
King Sterndale. Derbs 2J 35
King's Thorn. Here 8D 26
Kingsthorpe. Nptn 5E 28
Kingston. Cambs 6L 29
Kingston. Devn 7J 5
Kingston. Dors
nr. Sturminster Newton 5F 8
nr. Swanage 8H 9
Kingston. E Lot 1C 60
Kingston. Hants 5K 9
Kingston. IOW 7B 10
Kingston. Kent 8H 23
Kingston. Mor 7C 80
Kingston. W Sus 5H 11
Kingston Bagpuize. Oxon 4B 20
Kingston Blount. Oxon 4E 20
Kingston by Sea. W Sus 5K 11
Kingston Deverill. Wilts 2G 9
Kingstone. Here 8C 26
Kingstone. Som 4B 8
Kingstone. Staf 7J 35
Kingston Lisle. Oxon 5M 19
Kingston Maurward. Dors 6F 8
Kingston near Lewes. E Sus 5L 11
Kingston on Soar. Notts 7C 36
Kingston Russell. Dors 6D 8
Kingston St Mary. Som 3M 7
Kingston Seymour. N Som 7C 18
Kingston Stert. Oxon 3E 20
**Kingston upon Hull**. Hull 5J 43
**Kingston upon Thames**.
G Lon 7J 21
King's Walden. Herts 1J 21
Kingswear. Devn 6L 5
Kingswells. Aber 5H 73
Kingswinford. W Mid 3G 27
Kingswood. Buck 2D 20
Kingswood. Glos 4F 18
Kingswood. Here 6A 26
Kingswood. Kent 8E 22
Kingswood. Per 4D 66
Kingswood. Powy 2M 25
Kingswood. Som 2L 7
**Kingswood**. S Glo 6E 18
Kingswood. Surr 8K 21
Kingswood. Warw 4K 27
Kingswood Common. Staf 1G 27
Kings Worthy. Hants 2B 10
Kingthorpe. Linc 2J 37
Kington. Here 6A 26
Kington. S Glo 4E 18
Kington. Worc 6H 27
Kington Langley. Wilts 6H 19
Kington Magna. Dors 3F 8
Kington St Michael. Wilts 6H 19
Kingussie. High 5H 71
Kingweston. Som 2D 8
Kinharrachie. Abers 2J 73
Kinhrive. High 6G 79
Kinkell Bridge. Per 6C 66
Kinknockie. Abers 1K 73
Kinkry Hill. Cumb 4K 53
Kinlet. Shrp 3F 26
Kinloch. High
nr. Lochaline 2A 64
nr. Loch More 8F 84
on Rùm 6E 68
Kinloch. Per 3E 66
Kinlochard. Stir 7J 65
Kinlochbervie. High 6E 84
Kinlocheil. High 8L 69
Kinlochewe. High 7M 77
Kinloch Hourn. High 5L 69
Kinloch Laggan. High 7F 70
Kinlochleven. High 1F 64
Kinloch Lodge. High 6H 85
Kinlochmoidart. High 8J 69
Kinlochmore. High 1F 64
Kinloch Rannoch. Per 2L 65
Kinlochspelve. Arg 5A 64
Kinloid. High 7H 69
Kinloss. Mor 7L 79
Kinmel Bay. Cnwy 2J 33
Kinmuck. Abers 4H 73
Kinnadie. Abers 1J 73
Kinnaird. Per 5F 66
Kinneff. Abers 8H 73
Kinnelhead. Dum 1E 52
Kinnell. Ang 2K 67

Kinnerley. Shrp 7B 34
Kinnernie. Abers 5G 73
Kinnersley. Here 7B 26
Kinnersley. Worc 7G 27
Kinnerton. Powy 6M 25
Kinnerton. Shrp 2B 26
Kinnesswood. Per 7E 66
Kinninvie. Dur 3J 47
Kinnordy. Ang 2G 67
Kinoulton. Notts 6D 36
Kinross. Per 7E 66
Kinrossie. Per 4E 66
Kinsbourne Green. Herts 2J 21
Kinsey Heath. Ches E 5E 34
Kinsham. Here 5B 26
Kinsham. Worc 8H 27
Kinsley. W Yor 6B 42
Kinson. Bour 6J 9
Kintbury. W Ber 7A 20
Kintessack. Mor 7L 79
Kintillo. Per 6E 66
Kinton. Here 4C 26
Kinton. Shrp 8B 34
Kintore. Abers 4G 73
Kintour. Arg 4D 56
Kintra. Arg 5J 63
Kintraw. Arg 7C 64
Kinveachy. High 4K 71
Kinver. Staf 3G 27
Kinwarton. Warw 6K 27
Kiplingcotes. E Yor 3G 43
Kippax. W Yor 4B 42
Kippen. Stir 8L 65
Kippford. Dum 6C 52
Kipping's Cross. Kent 1C 12
Kirbister. Orkn
nr. Hobbister 1E 86
nr. Quholm 8B 88
Kirbuster. Orkn 7F 88
Kirby Bedon. Norf 1J 31
Kirby Bellars. Leics 8E 36
Kirby Cane. Norf 2K 31
Kirby Cross. Essx 1J 23
Kirby Fields. Leics 1C 28
Kirby Green. Norf 2K 31
Kirby Grindalythe. N Yor 1G 43
Kirby Hill. N Yor
nr. Richmond 5K 47
nr. Ripon 1A 42
Kirby Knowle. N Yor 7B 48
Kirby-le-Soken. Essx 1J 23
Kirby Misperton. N Yor 8E 48
Kirby Muxloe. Leics 1C 28
Kirby Sigston. N Yor 6B 48
Kirby Underdale. E Yor 2F 42
Kirby Wiske. N Yor 7A 48
Kircubbin. Ards 5K 93
Kirdford. W Sus 3H 11
Kirk. High 6D 86
Kirkabister. Shet
on Bressay 4E 90
on Mainland 2E 90
Kirkandrews. Dum 7M 51
Kirkandrews-on-Eden.
Cumb 6H 53
Kirkapol. Arg 3F 62
Kirkbampton. Cumb 6H 53
Kirkbean. Dum 6D 52
Kirk Bramwith. S Yor 6D 42
Kirkbride. Cumb 6G 53
Kirkbridge. N Yor 6L 47
Kirkbuddo. Ang 3J 67
Kirkburn. E Yor 2G 43
Kirkburton. W Yor 6K 41
Kirkby. Linc 8H 43
**Kirkby**. Mers 8C 40
Kirkby. N Yor 5C 48
Kirkby Fenside. Linc 3L 37
Kirkby Fleetham. N Yor 6L 47
Kirkby Green. Linc 4H 37
**Kirkby-in-Ashfield**. Notts 4C 36
Kirkby-in-Furness. Cumb 6M 45
Kirkby la Thorpe. Linc 5J 37
Kirkby Lonsdale. Cumb 8E 46
Kirkby Malham. N Yor 1G 41
Kirkby Mallory. Leics 1B 28
Kirkby Malzeard. N Yor 8L 47
Kirkby Mills. N Yor 7E 48
Kirkbymoorside. N Yor 7D 48
Kirkby on Bain. Linc 3K 37
Kirkby Overblow. N Yor 3M 41
Kirkby Stephen. Cumb 5F 46
Kirkby Thore. Cumb 3E 46
Kirkby Underwood. Linc 7H 37
Kirkby Wharfe. N Yor 3C 42
**Kirkcaldy**. Fife 8F 66
Kirkcambeck. Cumb 5K 53
Kirkcolm. Dum 5F 50
Kirkconnel. Dum 8F 58
Kirkconnell. Dum 5D 52
Kirkcowan. Dum 5J 51
Kirkcudbright. Dum 6A 52
Kirkdale. Mers 8B 40
Kirk Deighton. N Yor 2A 42
Kirk Ella. E Yor 5H 43
Kirkfieldbank. S Lan 5G 59
Kirkforthar Feus. Fife 7F 66
Kirkgunzeon. Dum 5C 52
Kirk Hallam. Derbs 5B 36
Kirkham. Lanc 4C 40
Kirkham. N Yor 1E 42
Kirkhamgate. W Yor 5L 41
Kirk Hammerton. N Yor 2B 42
Kirkharle. Nmbd 3D 54
Kirkheaton. Nmbd 4D 54
Kirkheaton. W Yor 6K 41
Kirkhill. Ang 1K 67
Kirkhill. High 1F 70
Kirkhope. S Lan 1D 52
Kirkhouse. Bord 6M 59
Kirkibost. High 4G 69
Kirkinch. Ang 3G 67
Kirkinner. Dum 6K 51
**Kirkintilloch**. E Dun 2E 58
Kirk Ireton. Derbs 4L 35
Kirkland. Cumb
nr. Cleator Moor 3K 45
nr. Penrith 8L 53
nr. Wigton 7G 53
Kirkland. Dum
nr. Kirkconnel 8F 58
nr. Moniaive 2C 52
Kirkland Guards. Cumb 7F 52
Kirk Langley. Derbs 6L 35
Kirklauchline. Dum 6F 50
Kirkleatham. Red C 3C 48
Kirklevington. Stoc T 5B 48
Kirkley. Suff 2M 31
Kirklington. N Yor 7M 47
Kirklington. Notts 4D 36
Kirklinton. Cumb 5J 53
Kirkliston. Edin 2K 59
Kirkmabreck. Dum 6K 51
Kirkmaiden. Dum 8G 51
Kirk Merrington. Dur 8F 54
Kirk Michael. IOM 5C 44
Kirkmichael. Per 1D 66
Kirkmichael. S Ayr 1J 51
Kirkmuirhill. S Lan 5F 58
Kirknewton. Nmbd 6G 61
Kirknewton. W Lot 3K 59
Kirkney. Abers 2E 72
Kirk of Shotts. N Lan 3G 59
Kirkoswald. Cumb 7K 53
Kirkoswald. S Ayr 1H 51
Kirkpatrick. Dum 2D 52
Kirkpatrick Durham. Dum 4B 52
Kirkpatrick-Fleming. Dum 4G 53
**Kirk Sandall**. S Yor 7D 42
Kirksanton. Cumb 6L 45
Kirk Smeaton. N Yor 6C 42
Kirkstall. W Yor 4L 41
Kirkstile. Dum 2H 53
Kirkstyle. High 4E 86
Kirkthorpe. W Yor 5A 42
Kirkton. Abers
nr. Alford 4F 72
nr. Insch 3F 72
nr. Turriff 1H 73
Kirkton. Ang
nr. Dundee 4H 67
nr. Forfar 3H 67
nr. Tarfside 7D 72
Kirkton. Dum 3D 52
Kirkton. Fife 5G 67
Kirkton. High
nr. Golspie 4H 79
nr. Kyle of Lochalsh 3K 69
nr. Lochcarron 1L 69

Kirkton. Bord 8C 60
Kirkton. S Lan 7H 59
Kirktonhill. W Dun 2B 58
Kirkton Manor. Bord 6L 59
Kirkton of Airlie. Ang 2G 67
Kirkton of Auchterhouse.
Ang 4G 67
Kirkton of Bourtie. Abers 3H 73
Kirkton of Collace. Per 4E 66
Kirkton of Craig. Ang 2L 67
Kirkton of Culsalmond.
Abers 2F 72
Kirkton of Durris. Abers 6G 73
Kirkton of Glenbuchat.
Abers 4C 72
Kirkton of Glenisla. Ang 1F 66
Kirkton of Kingoldrum. Ang 2G 67
Kirkton of Largo. Fife 7H 67
Kirkton of Lethendy. Per 3E 66
Kirkton of Logie Buchan.
Abers 3J 73
Kirkton of Maryculter.
Abers 6H 73
Kirkton of Menmuir. Ang 1J 67
Kirkton of Monikie. Ang 4J 67
Kirkton of Oyne. Abers 3F 72
Kirkton of Rayne. Abers 2F 72
Kirkton of Skene. Abers 5H 73
Kirktown. Abers
nr. Fraserburgh 7J 81
nr. Peterhead 8K 81
Kirktown of Alvah. Abers 7F 80
Kirktown of Auchterless.
Abers 1G 73
Kirktown of Deskford. Mor 7E 80
Kirktown of Fetteresso.
Abers 7H 73
Kirktown of Mortlach. Mor 2C 72
Kirktown of Slains. Abers 3K 73
Kirkurd. Bord 5K 59
Kirkwall. Orkn 8D 88
Kirkwall Airport. Orkn 1F 86
Kirkwhelpington. Nmbd 3C 54
Kirk Yetholm. Bord 7F 60
Kirmington. N Lin 6J 43
Kirmond le Mire. Linc 8J 43
Kirn. Arg 2L 57
Kirriemuir. Ang 2G 67
Kirstead Green. Norf 2J 31
Kirtlebridge. Dum 4G 53
Kirtleton. Dum 4G 53
Kirtling. Cambs 6C 30
Kirtling Green. Cambs 6C 30
Kirtlington. Oxon 2C 20
Kirtomy. High 5K 85
Kirton. Linc 6L 37
Kirton. Notts 3D 36
Kirton. Suff 8J 31
Kirton End. Linc 5K 37
Kirton Holme. Linc 5K 37
Kirton in Lindsey. N Lin 8G 43
Kishorn. High 1K 69
Kislingbury. Nptn 6D 28
Kites Hardwick. Warw 5B 28
Kittisford. Som 3K 7
Kittle. Swan 6E 16
Kittybrewster. Aber 5J 73
Kitwood. Hants 2D 10
Kivernoll. Here 8C 26
Kiveton Park. S Yor 1B 36
Knaith. Linc 1F 36
Knaith Park. Linc 1F 36
Knaphill. Surr 8G 21
Knapp. Hants 3B 10
Knapp. Per 4F 66
Knapp. Som 3B 8
Knapperfield. High 6D 86
Knapton. Norf 6K 39
Knapton. York 2C 42
Knapton Green. Here 6C 26
Knapwell. Cambs 5L 29
**Knaresborough**. N Yor 2A 42
Knarsdale. Nmbd 6L 53
Knatts Valley. Kent 7B 22
Knaven. Abers 1H 73
Knayton. N Yor 7B 48
Knebworth. Herts 1K 21
Knedlington. E Yor 5E 42
Kneesall. Notts 3E 36
Kneesworth. Cambs 7L 29
Kneeton. Notts 5E 36
Knelston. Swan 8L 15
Knenhall. Staf 6H 35
Knightacott. Devn 2F 6
Knightcote. Warw 6B 28
Knightcott. N Som 8B 18
Knightley. Staf 7G 35
Knightley Dale. Staf 7G 35
Knightlow Hill. Warw 4B 28
Knighton. Devn 7H 5
Knighton. Dors 4E 8
Knighton. Leic 1C 28
Knighton. Powy 4A 26
Knighton. Som 1L 7
Knighton. Staf
nr. Eccleshall 7F 34
nr. Woore 5F 34
Knighton. Wilts 6L 19
Knighton. Worc 6J 27
Knighton Common. Worc 4E 26
Knight's End. Cambs 2M 29
Knightswood. Glas 3D 58
Knightwick. Worc 6F 26
Knill. Here 5A 26
Knipton. Leics 6F 36
Knitsley. Dur 7E 54
Kniveton. Derbs 4L 35
Knock. Arg 4L 63
Knock. Cumb 3E 46
Knock. Mor 8E 80
Knockally. High 1M 79
Knockan. Arg 5K 63
Knockan. High 2C 78
Knockandhu. Mor 3B 72
Knockando. Mor 1A 72
Knockarthur. High 3H 79
Knockbain. High 8G 79
Knockbreck. High 7D 76
Knockcloghrim. M Ulst 4F 93
Knockdee. High 5C 86
Knockdolian. S Ayr 3G 51
Knockdon. S Ayr 8B 58
Knockdown. Glos 5G 19
Knockenbaird. Abers 3F 72
Knockenkelly. N Ayr 7K 57
Knockentiber. E Ayr 6B 58
Knockfarrel. High 8F 78
Knockglass. High 5B 86
Knockholt. Kent 8A 22
Knockholt Pound. Kent 8A 22
Knockie Lodge. High 4E 70
Knockin. Shrp 7B 34
Knockinlaw. E Ayr 6C 58
Knockinnon. High 8C 86
Knocknacarry. Caus 2H 93
Knockrome. Arg 2E 56
Knocksharry. IOM 6B 44
Knockshinnoch. E Ayr 8C 58
Knockvennie. Dum 4B 52
Knockvologan. Arg 6J 63
Knodishall. Suff 5L 31
Knole. Som 3C 8
Knollbury. Mon 5C 18
Knolls Green. Ches E 2G 35
Knolton. Wrex 6B 34
Knook. Wilts 1H 9
Knossington. Leics 1F 28
Knott. High 8E 76
Knott End-on-Sea. Lanc 3B 40
Knotting. Bed 5H 29
Knotting Green. Bed 5H 29
**Knottingley**. W Yor 5B 42
Knotts. Cumb 3C 46
Knotty Ash. Mers 8C 40
Knotty Green. Buck 4G 21
Knowbury. Shrp 4D 26
Knowe. Dum 4J 51
Knowefield. Cumb 6J 53
Knowehead. Dum 2M 51
Knowes. E Lot 2D 60
Knowesgate. Nmbd 3C 54
Knoweside. S Ayr 8A 58
Knowes of Elrick. Abers 8F 80
Knowle. Bris 6E 18
Knowle. Devn
nr. Braunton 2D 6
nr. Budleigh Salterton 7K 7
nr. Crediton 5G 7
Knowle. Shrp 4D 26

**Knowle**. W Mid 4K 27
Knowle Green. Lanc 4E 40
Knowle St Giles. Som 4B 8
Knowlesands. Shrp 2F 26
Knowle Village. Hants 5C 10
Knowl Hill. Wind 6F 20
Knowlton. Kent 8J 23
Knowsley. Mers 8C 40
Knowstone. Devn 3H 7
Knucklas. Powy 4A 26
Knuston. Nptn 5G 29
**Knutsford**. Ches E 2F 34
Knypersley. Staf 4G 35
Krumlin. W Yor 6J 41
Kuggar. Corn 7L 3
Kyleakin. High 3J 69
Kyle of Lochalsh. High 3J 69
Kylerhea. High 3J 69
Kylesku. High 8E 84
Kyles Lodge. W Isl 5A 76
Kylesmorar. High 6K 69
Kylestrome. High 8E 84
Kymin. Mon 2D 18
Kynaston. Here 8E 26
Kynaston. Shrp 7B 34
Kynnersley. Telf 8E 34
Kyre Green. Worc 5E 26
Kyre Park. Worc 5E 26
Kyrewood. Worc 5E 26


## L


Labost. W Isl 7F 82
Lacasaidh. W Isl 1E 76
Lacasdail. W Isl 8H 83
Laceby. NE Lin 7K 43
Lacey Green. Buck 3F 20
Lach Dennis. Ches W 2F 34
Lache. Ches W 3B 34
Lack. Ferm 5C 92
Lackagh. Caus 3E 92
Lackford. Suff 4D 30
Lacock. Wilts 7H 19
Ladbroke. Warw 6B 28
Laddingford. Kent 1C 12
Lade Bank. Linc 4L 37
Ladock. Corn 6A 4
Lady. Orkn 5F 88
Ladybank. Fife 6G 67
Ladycross. Corn 7C 6
Lady Green. Mers 7B 40
Lady Hall. Cumb 6L 45
Ladykirk. Bord 5F 60
Ladysford. Abers 7J 81
Ladywood. W Mid 3J 27
Ladywood. Worc 5G 27
Laga. High 1M 63
Lagavulin. Arg 5D 56
Lagg. Arg 2E 56
Lagg. N Ayr 7J 57
Laggan. Arg 4B 56
Laggan. High
nr. Fort Augustus 6C 70
nr. Newtonmore 6G 71
Laggan. Mor 2C 72
Lagganlia. High 5J 71
Lagganulva. Arg 3K 63
Laghey Corner. M Ulst 5F 93
Laglingarten. Arg 7F 64
Lagness. W Sus 5F 10
Laid. High 6G 85
Laide. High 4K 77
Laigh Fenwick. E Ayr 5C 58
Laindon. Essx 5C 22
Lairg. High 3F 78
Lairg Muir. High 3F 78
Laithes. Cumb 8J 53
Laithkirk. Dur 3H 47
Lake. Devn 2E 6
Lake. IOW 7C 10
Lake. Wilts 2K 9
Lakenham. Norf 1J 31
Lakenheath. Suff 3D 30
Lakesend. Norf 2B 30
Lakeside. Cumb 7B 46
Laleham. Surr 7H 21
Laleston. B'end 6H 17
Lamancha. Bord 4L 59
Lamarsh. Essx 8E 30
Lamas. Norf 7J 39
Lamb Corner. Essx 8G 31
Lambden. Bord 5E 60
Lamberhead Green. G Man 7D 40
Lamberhurst. Kent 2C 12
Lamberhurst Quarter. Kent 2C 12
Lamberton. Bord 4G 61
**Lambeth**. G Lon 6L 21
Lambfell Moar. IOM 6B 44
Lambhill. Glas 3D 58
Lambley. Nmbd 6L 53
Lambley. Notts 5D 36
Lambourn. W Ber 6M 19
Lambourne End. Essx 4A 22
Lambourn Woodlands.
W Ber 6M 19
Lambs Green. Dors 6H 9
Lambs Green. W Sus 2K 11
Lambston. Pemb 5F 14
Lamellion. Corn 5E 4
Lamerton. Devn 8D 6
Lamesley. Tyne 6F 54
Laminess. Orkn 6F 88
Lamington. High 6H 79
Lamington. S Lan 6H 59
Lamlash. N Ayr 6K 57
Lamonby. Cumb 8J 53
Lamorick. Corn 5C 4
Lamorna. Corn 6H 3
Lamorran. Corn 7A 4
Lampeter. Cdgn 8E 24
Lampeter Velfrey. Pemb 5H 15
Lamphey. Pemb 6G 15
Lamplugh. Cumb 2K 45
Lamport. Nptn 4E 28
Lamyatt. Som 2E 8
Lana. Devn
nr. Ashwater 6C 6
nr. Holsworthy 5C 6
Lanark. S Lan 5G 59
Lanarth. Corn 6L 3
**Lancaster**. Lanc 1C 40
Lanchester. Dur 7E 54
**Lancing**. W Sus 5J 11
Landbeach. Cambs 5A 30
Landcross. Devn 3D 6
Landerberry. Abers 5G 73
Landford. Wilts 4L 9
Land Gate. G Man 7D 40
Landhallow. High 8C 86
Landimore. Swan 7L 15
Landkey. Devn 2E 6
Landkey Newland. Devn 2E 6
Landore. Swan 5F 16
Landport. Port 5D 10
Landrake. Corn 5F 4
Landscove. Devn 5K 5
Land's End Airport. Corn 6G 3
Landshipping. Pemb 5G 15
Landulph. Corn 5G 5
Landywood. Staf 1H 27
Lane. Corn 2M 3
Laneast. Corn 7B 6
Lane Bottom. Lanc 4G 41
Lane End. Buck 4F 20
Lane End. Hants 3C 10
Lane End. IOW 7D 10
Lane End. Wilts 1G 9
Lane Ends. Derbs 6L 35
Lane Ends. Dur 8E 54
Lane Ends. Lanc 2F 40
Laneham. Notts 2F 36
Lane Head. Dur
nr. Hutton Magna 4K 47
nr. Woodland 3J 47
Lane Head. G Man 8E 40
Lane Head. W Yor 7K 41
Lanehead. Dur 7B 54
Lanehead. Nmbd 3A 54
Lane Heads. Lanc 4C 40
Lanercost. Cumb 5K 53
Laneshaw Bridge. Lanc 3H 41
Laney Green. Staf 1H 27
Langais. W Isl 7K 75
Langal. High 1B 64
Langar. Notts 6E 36
Langbank. Ren 2B 58
Langbar. N Yor 2J 41
Langburnshiels. Bord 1K 53

Langcliffe. N Yor 1G 41
Langdale End. N Yor 6G 49
Langdon. Corn 6B 6
Langdon Beck. Dur 8B 54
Langdon Cross. Corn 7C 6
Langdon Hills. Essx 5C 22
Langdown. Hants 5B 10
Langdyke. Fife 7G 67
Langenhoe. Essx 2G 23
Langford. C Beds 7J 29
Langford. Devn 5K 7
Langford. Essx 3E 22
Langford. Notts 4F 36
Langford. Oxon 3L 19
Langford. Som 3M 7
Langford Budville. Som 3L 7
Langham. Dors 3F 8
Langham. Essx 8G 31
Langham. Norf 5G 39
Langham. Rut 8F 36
Langham. Suff 5F 30
Langho. Lanc 4F 40
Langholm. Dum 3H 53
Langland. Swan 6F 16
Langleeford. Nmbd 7G 61
Langley. Ches E 2H 35
Langley. Derbs 5B 36
Langley. Essx 8M 29
Langley. Glos 1J 19
Langley. Hants 5B 10
Langley. Herts 1K 21
Langley. Kent 8E 22
Langley. Nmbd 5B 54
Langley. Slo 6H 21
Langley. Som 3K 7
Langley. Warw 5K 27
Langley. W Sus 3F 10
Langley Burrell. Wilts 6H 19
Langleybury. Herts 3H 21
Langley Common. Derbs 6L 35
Langley Green. Derbs 6L 35
Langley Green. Norf 1K 31
Langley Green. Warw 5K 27
Langley Green. W Sus 2K 11
Langley Heath. Kent 8E 22
Langley Marsh. Som 3K 7
Langley Moor. Dur 7F 54
Langley Park. Dur 7F 54
Langley Street. Norf 1K 31
Langney. E Sus 5C 12
Langold. Notts 1C 36
Langore. Corn 7B 6
Langport. Som 3C 8
Langrick. Linc 5K 37
Langridge. Bath 7F 18
Langridgeford. Devn 3E 6
Langrigg. Cumb 7F 52
Langrish. Hants 3E 10
Langsett. S Yor 7L 41
Langshaw. Bord 6C 60
Langstone. Hants 5E 10
Langthorne. N Yor 6L 47
Langthorpe. N Yor 1A 42
Langthwaite. N Yor 5J 47
Langtoft. E Yor 1H 43
Langtoft. Linc 8J 37
Langton. Dur 4K 47
Langton. Linc
nr. Horncastle 3K 37
nr. Spilsby 2L 37
Langton. N Yor 1E 42
Langton by Wragby. Linc 2J 37
Langton Green. Kent 2B 12
Langton Herring. Dors 7E 8
Langton Long Blandford.
Dors 5G 9
Langton Matravers. Dors 8H 9
Langtree. Devn 4D 6
Langwathby. Cumb 8K 53
Langwith. Derbs 2C 36
Langworth. Linc 2H 37
Lanivet. Corn 5C 4
Lanjeth. Corn 6B 4
Lank. Corn 4C 4
Lanlivery. Corn 6C 4
Lanner. Corn 5L 3
Lanreath. Corn 6D 4
Lansallos. Corn 6D 4
Lansdown. Bath 7F 18
Lansdown. Glos 1H 19
Lanteglos Highway. Corn 6D 4
Lanton. Nmbd 6G 61
Lanton. Bord 7D 60
Lapford. Devn 5G 7
Lapford Cross. Devn 5G 7
Laphroaig. Arg 5C 56
Lapley. Staf 8G 35
Lapworth. Warw 4K 27
Larachbeg. High 3A 64
Larbert. Falk 1G 59
Larden Green. Ches E 4D 34
Larel. High 6C 86
Largie. Abers 2F 72
Largiemore. Arg 1J 57
Largoward. Fife 7H 67
**Largs**. N Ayr 4M 57
Largue. Abers 1F 72
Largybeg. N Ayr 7K 57
Largymeanoch. N Ayr 7K 57
Largymore. N Ayr 7K 57
Larkfield. Inv 2M 57
Larkfield. Kent 8D 22
Larkhall. Bath 7F 18
**Larkhall**. S Lan 4F 58
Larkhill. Wilts 1K 9
Larling. Norf 3F 30
**Larne**. ME Ant 3J 93
Larport. Here 8D 26
Lartington. Dur 4J 47
Lary. Abers 5C 72
Lasham. Hants 1D 10
Lashenden. Kent 1E 12
Lasswade. Midl 3M 59
Lastingham. N Yor 6E 48
Latchford. Herts 1L 21
Latchford. Oxon 3D 20
Latchingdon. Essx 3E 22
Latchley. Corn 8D 6
Latchmere Green. Hants 8D 20
Lathbury. Mil 7F 28
Latheron. High 8C 86
Latheronwheel. High 8C 86
Lathom. Lanc 7C 40
Lathones. Fife 7H 67
Latimer. Buck 4H 21
Latteridge. S Glo 5E 18
Lattiford. Som 3E 8
Latton. Wilts 4J 19
Laudale House. High 2B 64
Lauder. Bord 5C 60
Laugharne. Carm 5K 15
Laughterton. Linc 2F 36
Laughton. E Sus 4B 12
Laughton. Leics 3D 28
Laughton. Linc
nr. Gainsborough 8F 42
nr. Grantham 6H 37
Laughton Common. S Yor 1C 36
Laughton en le Morthen.
S Yor 1C 36
Launcells. Corn 5B 6
Launceston. Corn 7C 6
Launcherley. Som 1D 8
Launton. Oxon 1D 20
Laurelvale. Arm 6G 93
Laurencekirk. Abers 8G 73
Laurieston. Dum 5A 52
Laurieston. Falk 2H 59
Lavendon. Mil 6G 29
Lavenham. Suff 7F 30
Laverhay. Dum 2F 52
Laversdale. Cumb 5J 53
Laverstock. Wilts 2K 9
Laverstoke. Hants 1B 10
Laverton. Glos 8J 27
Laverton. N Yor 8L 47
Laverton. Som 8F 18
Lavister. Wrex 4B 34
Law. S Lan 4G 59
Lawers. Per 4L 65
Lawford. Essx 8G 31
Lawhitton. Corn 7C 6
Lawkland. N Yor 1F 40
Lawley. Telf 1E 26
Lawnhead. Staf 7G 35
Lawrencetown. Arm 6G 93
Lawrenny. Pemb 6G 15
Lawshall. Suff 6E 30
Lawton. Here 6C 26

Laxey. IOM 6D 44
Laxfield. Suff 4J 31
Laxfirth. Shet 2E 90
Laxo. Shet 1E 90
Laxton. E Yor 5E 42
Laxton. Nptn 2G 29
Laxton. Notts 3E 36
Laycock. W Yor 3J 41
Layer Breton. Essx 2F 22
Layer-de-la-Haye. Essx 1F 22
Layer Marney. Essx 2F 22
Laymore. Dors 5B 8
Laysters Pole. Here 5D 26
Layter's Green. Buck 4G 21
Laytham. E Yor 4E 42
Lazenby. Red C 4C 48
Lazonby. Cumb 8K 53
Lea. Derbs 4M 35
Lea. Here 1E 18
Lea. Linc 1F 36
Lea. Shrp
nr. Bishop's Castle 3B 26
nr. Shrewsbury 1C 26
Lea. Wilts 5H 19
Leabrooks. Derbs 4B 36
Leac a Li. W Isl 4C 76
Leachd. Arg 8E 64
Leachkin. High 1G 71
Leachpool. Pemb 5F 14
Leadburn. Midl 4L 59
Leadenham. Linc 4G 37
Leaden Roding. Essx 2B 22
Leaderfoot. Bord 6C 60
Leadgate. Cumb 7M 53
Leadgate. Dur 6E 54
Leadgate. Nmbd 6E 54
Leadhills. S Lan 8G 59
Leadingcross Green. Kent 8E 22
Lea End. Worc 4J 27
Leafield. Oxon 2M 19
Leagrave. Lutn 1H 21
Lea Hall. W Mid 3K 27
Lea Heath. Staf 7J 35
Leake. N Yor 6B 48
Leake Common Side. Linc 4L 37
Leake Fold Hill. Linc 4M 37
Leake Hurn's End. Linc 5M 37
Lealholm. N Yor 5E 48
Lealt. Arg 8A 64
Lealt. High 7G 77
Leam. Derbs 2L 35
Lea Marston. Warw 2L 27
Leamington Hastings. Warw 5B 28
**Leamington Spa, Royal**.
Warw 5M 27
Leamonsley. Staf 1K 27
Leamside. Dur 7G 55
Leargybreck. Arg 2E 56
Lease Rigg. N Yor 5F 48
Leasgill. Cumb 7C 46
Leasingham. Linc 5H 37
Leasingthorne. Dur 8F 54
Leasowe. Mers 8A 40
**Leatherhead**. Surr 8J 21
Leathley. N Yor 3L 41
Leaths. Dum 5B 52
Leaton. Shrp 8C 34
Leaton. Telf 8E 34
Lea Town. Lanc 4C 40
Leaveland. Kent 8G 23
Leavenheath. Suff 8F 30
Leavening. N Yor 1E 42
Leaves Green. G Lon 7M 21
Lea Yeat. Cumb 7F 46
Leazes. Dur 6E 54
Lebberston. N Yor 7H 49
Lechlade on Thames. Glos 4L 19
Leck. Lanc 8E 46
Leckford. Hants 2A 10
Leckfurin. High 6K 85
Leckgruinart. Arg 3B 56
Leckhampstead. Buck 8E 28
Leckhampstead. W Ber 6B 20
Leckhampton. Glos 2H 19
Leckmelm. High 4B 78
Leckwith. V Glam 7L 17
Leconfield. E Yor 3H 43
Ledaig. Arg 4D 64
Ledburn. Buck 1G 21
Ledbury. Here 8F 26
Ledgemoor. Here 6C 26
Ledgowan. High 8B 78
Ledicot. Here 5C 26
Ledmore. High 2C 78
Lednabirichen. High 4H 79
Lednagullin. High 5L 85
Ledsham. Ches W 2B 34
Ledsham. W Yor 5B 42
Ledston. W Yor 5B 42
Ledstone. Devn 7K 5
Ledwell. Oxon 1B 20
Lee. Devn
nr. Ilfracombe 1D 6
nr. South Molton 3H 7
Lee. G Lon 6L 21
Lee. Hants 4A 10
Lee. Lanc 2D 40
Lee. Shrp 6C 34
The Lee. Buck 3G 21
Leeans. Shet 3D 90
Leebotten. Shet 5E 90
Leebotwood. Shrp 2C 26
Lee Brockhurst. Shrp 7D 34
Leece. Cumb 8M 45
Leechpool. Mon 5D 18
Lee Clump. Buck 3G 21
Leeds. Kent 8E 22
**Leeds**. W Yor 4L 41
Leeds Bradford Airport.
W Yor 3L 41
Leedstown. Corn 5K 3
Leegomery. Telf 8E 34
Lee Head. Derbs 8J 41
**Leek**. Staf 4H 35
Leekbrook. Staf 4H 35
Leek Wootton. Warw 5L 27
Lee Mill. Devn 6H 5
Leeming. N Yor 7L 47
Leeming Bar. N Yor 6L 47
Lee Moor. Devn 5H 5
Lee Moor. W Yor 5M 41
Lee-on-the-Solent. Hants 5C 10
Lees. Derbs 6L 35
Lees. G Man 7H 41
Lees. W Yor 4J 41
The Lees. Kent 8G 23
Leeswood. Flin 3A 34
Leetown. Per 5F 66
Leftwich. Ches W 2E 34
Legbourne. Linc 1L 37
Legburthwaite. Cumb 4B 46
Legerwood. Bord 5C 60
Legsby. Linc 1J 37
**Leicester**. Leic 1C 28
Leicester Forest East. Leics 1C 28
Leigh. Dors 5E 8
**Leigh**. G Man 7E 40
Leigh. Kent 1B 12
Leigh. Shrp 1B 26
Leigh. Surr 1K 11
Leigh. Wilts 4J 19
Leigh. Worc 6F 26
The Leigh. Glos 1G 19
Leigham. Plym 6H 5
Leigh Beck. Essx 5E 22
Leigh Common. Som 3F 8
Leigh Delamere. Wilts 6G 19
Leigh Green. Kent 2F 12
Leighland Chapel. Som 2K 7
Leigh-on-Sea. S'end 5E 22
Leigh Park. Hants 5E 10
Leigh Sinton. Worc 6F 26
Leighterton. Glos 4G 19
Leighton. N Yor 8K 47
Leighton. Powy 2M 25
Leighton. Shrp 1E 26
Leighton. Som 1F 8
Leighton Bromswold.
Cambs 4J 29
**Leighton Buzzard**. C Beds 1G 21
Leigh-upon-Mendip. Som 1E 8
Leinthall Earls. Here 5C 26
Leinthall Starkes. Here 5C 26
Leintwardine. Here 4C 26
Leire. Leics 2C 28
Leirinmore. High 5G 85
Leishmore. High 1E 70
Leiston. Suff 5L 31
Leitfie. Per 3F 66

Leith. Edin 2L 59
Leitholm. Bord 5E 60
Leitrim. New M 7H 93
Lelant. Corn 5J 3
Lelant Downs. Corn 5J 3
Lelley. E Yor 4K 43
Lem Hill. Shrp 4F 26
Lemington. Tyne 5E 54
Lempitlaw. Bord 6E 60
Lemsford. Herts 2K 21
Lenacre. Cumb 7E 46
Lenchie. Abers 2E 72
Lenchwick. Worc 7J 27
Lendalfoot. S Ayr 3G 51
Lendrick. Stir 7K 65
Lenham. Kent 8E 22
Lenham Heath. Kent 1F 12
Lenimore. N Ayr 5H 57
Lennel. Bord 5F 60
Lennoxtown. E Dun 2E 58
Lenton. Linc 6H 37
Lentran. High 1F 70
Lenwade. Norf 8G 39
**Lenzie**. E Dun 2E 58
Leochel Cushnie. Abers 4E 72
Leogh. Shet 2M 89
**Leominster**. Here 6C 26
Leonard Stanley. Glos 3G 19
Lepe. Hants 6B 10
Lephenstrath. Arg 1B 50
Lephin. High 1C 68
Lephinchapel. Arg 8D 64
Lephinmore. Arg 8D 64
Leppington. N Yor 1E 42
Lepton. W Yor 6L 41
Lerryn. Corn 6D 4
Lerwick. Shet 3E 90
Lerwick (Tingwall) Airport.
Shet 3E 90
Lesbury. Nmbd 8K 61
Leslie. Abers 3E 72
Leslie. Fife 7F 66
Lesmahagow. S Lan 6G 59
Lesnewth. Corn 2D 4
Lessingham. Norf 7K 39
Lessonhall. Cumb 6G 53
Leswalt. Dum 5F 50
Letchmore Heath. Herts 4J 21
**Letchworth Garden City**.
Herts 8K 29
Letcombe Bassett. Oxon 5A 20
Letcombe Regis. Oxon 5A 20
Letham. Ang 3J 67
Letham. Falk 1G 59
Letham. Fife 6G 67
Lethanhill. E Ayr 8C 58
Lethenty. Abers 1H 73
Letheringham. Suff 6J 31
Letheringsett. Norf 6G 39
Lettaford. Devn 7G 7
Lettan. Orkn 5G 89
Letter. Abers 4G 73
Letterewe. High 6L 77
Letterfearn. High 3K 69
Lettermore. Arg 3K 63
Letters. High 5B 78
Lettershendoney. Derr 3D 92
Letterston. Pemb 4F 14
Letton. Here
nr. Kington 7B 26
nr. Leintwardine 4B 26
Letty Green. Herts 2K 21
Letwell. S Yor 1C 36
Leuchars. Fife 5H 67
Leumrabhagh. W Isl 2E 76
Leusdon. Devn 8G 7
Levaneap. Shet 1E 90
Levedale. Staf 8G 35
Leven. E Yor 3J 43
Leven. Fife 7G 67
Levencorroch. N Ayr 7K 57
Levenhall. E Lot 2A 60
Levens. Cumb 7C 46
Levens Green. Herts 1L 21
Levenshulme. G Man 8G 41
Levenwick. Shet 5E 90
Leverburgh. W Isl 5B 76
Leverington. Cambs 8M 37
Leverton. Linc 5L 37
Leverton. W Ber 6M 19
Leverton Lucasgate. Linc 5M 37
Leverton Outgate. Linc 5M 37
Levington. Suff 8J 31
Levisham. N Yor 6F 48
Levishie. High 4E 70
Lew. Oxon 3M 19
Lewaigue. IOM 5D 44
Lewannick. Corn 7B 6
Lewdown. Devn 7D 6
**Lewes**. E Sus 4M 11
Leweston. Pemb 4F 14
**Lewisham**. G Lon 6L 21
Lewiston. High 3F 70
Lewistown. B'end 6J 17
Lewknor. Oxon 4E 20
Leworthy. Devn
nr. Barnstaple 2F 6
nr. Holsworthy 5C 6
Lewson Street. Kent 7F 22
Lewthorn Cross. Devn 8G 7
Lewtrenchard. Devn 7D 6
Ley. Corn 5D 4
Leybourne. Kent 8C 22
Leyburn. N Yor 6K 47
Leycett. Staf 5F 34
Leyfields. Staf 1L 27
Ley Green. Herts 1J 21
Ley Hill. Buck 3G 21
**Leyland**. Lanc 5D 40
Leylodge. Abers 4G 73
Leymoor. W Yor 6K 41
Leys. Per 4F 66
Leysdown-on-Sea. Kent 6G 23
Leysmill. Ang 3K 67
**Leyton**. G Lon 5L 21
Leytonstone. G Lon 5M 21
Lezant. Corn 8C 6
Leziate. Norf 8C 38
Lhanbryde. Mor 7B 80
The Lhen. IOM 4C 44
Liatrie. High 2C 70
Libanus. Powy 2J 17
Libberton. S Lan 5H 59
Libbery. Worc 6H 27
Liberton. Edin 3L 59
Liceasto. W Isl 4C 76
**Lichfield**. Staf 1K 27
Lickey. Worc 4H 27
Lickey End. Worc 4H 27
Lickfold. W Sus 3G 11
Liddaton. Devn 7D 6
Liddington. Swin 5L 19
Liddle. Orkn 3F 86
Lidgate. Suff 6D 30
Lidgett. Notts 3D 36
Lidham Hill. E Sus 4E 12
Lidlington. C Beds 8G 29
Lidsey. W Sus 5G 11
Lidstone. Oxon 1A 20
Lienassie. High 3L 69
Liff. Ang 4G 67
Lifford. W Mid 3J 27
Lifton. Devn 7C 6
Liftondown. Devn 7C 6
Lighthorne. Warw 6M 27
Light Oaks. Stoke 4H 35
Lightwater. Surr 7G 21
Lightwood. Staf 5J 35
Lightwood. Stoke 5H 35
Lightwood Green. Ches E 5E 34
Lightwood Green. Wrex 5B 34
Lilbourne. Nptn 4C 28
Lilburn Tower. Nmbd 7H 61
Lillesdon. Som 3B 8
Lilleshall. Telf 8F 34
Lilley. Herts 1J 21
Lilliesleaf. Bord 7C 60
Lillingstone Dayrell. Buck 8E 28
Lillingstone Lovell. Buck 7E 28
Lillington. Dors 4E 8
Lilstock. Som 1L 7
Lilybank. Inv 2B 58
Lilyhurst. Shrp 8F 34
**Limavady**. Caus 2E 92
Limbrick. Lanc 6E 40
Limbury. Lutn 1H 21
Limekilnburn. S Lan 4F 58
Limekilns. Fife 1J 59
Limerigg. Falk 2G 59

Limestone Brae—Low Hesket

Limestone Brae. Nmbd 7A 54
Lime Street. Worc 8G 27
Limington. Som 3D 8
Limpenhoe. Norf 1K 31
Limpley Stoke. Wilts 7F 18
Limpsfield. Surr 8M 21
Limpsfield Chart. Surr 8M 21
Linburn. W Lot 3K 59
Linby. Notts 4C 36
Linchmere. W Sus 2F 10
Lincluden. Dum 4D 52
**Lincoln**. Linc 2G 37
Lincomb. Worc 5G 27
Lindale. Cumb 7C 46
Lindal in Furness. Cumb 8A 46
Lindean. Bord 6B 60
Linden. Glos 2G 19
Lindfield. W Sus 3L 11
Lindford. Hants 2F 10
Lindores. Fife 6F 66
Lindridge. Worc 5E 26
Lindsell. Essx 1C 22
Lindsey. Suff 7F 30
Lindsey Tye. Suff 7F 30
Linford. Hants 5K 9
Linford. Thur 6C 22
Lingague. IOM 7B 44
Lingdale. Red C 4D 48
Lingen. Here 5B 26
Lingfield. Surr 1L 11
Lingreabhagh. W Isl 5B 76
Lingwood. Norf 1K 31
Lingy Close. Cumb 6H 53
Linicro. High 7E 76
Linkend. Worc 8G 27
Linkenholt. Hants 8A 20
Linkinhorne. Corn 8C 6
Linklater. Orkn 3F 86
Linksness. Orkn 8E 88
Linktown. Fife 8F 66
Linkwood. Mor 7B 80
Linley. Shrp
nr. Bishop's Castle 2B 26
nr. Bridgnorth 2E 26
Linley Green. Here 6E 26
**Linlithgow**. W Lot 2H 59
Linlithgow Bridge. Falk 2H 59
Linneraineach. High 3B 78
Linshiels. Nmbd 1B 54
Linsiadar. W Isl 8F 82
Linsidemore. High 4F 78
Linslade. C Beds 1G 21
Linstead Parva. Suff 4K 31
Linstock. Cumb 6J 53
Linthwaite. W Yor 6K 41
Lintlaw. Bord 4F 60
Lintmill. Mor 7E 80
Linton. Cambs 7B 30
Linton. Derbs 8L 35
Linton. Here 1E 18
Linton. Kent 1D 12
Linton. N Yor 1H 41
Linton. Bord 7E 60
Linton. W Yor 3A 42
Linton Colliery. Nmbd 2F 54
Linton Hill. Here 1E 18
Linton-on-Ouse. N Yor 1B 42
Lintzford. Dur 6E 54
Lintzgarth. Dur 7C 54
Linwood. Hants 5K 9
Linwood. Linc 1J 37
**Linwood**. Ren 3C 58
Lionacleit. W Isl 1D 74
Lionacro. High 7E 76
Lionacuidhe. W Isl 1D 74
Lional. W Isl 5J 83
Liphook. Hants 2F 10
Lipley. Shrp 6F 34
Lipyeate. Som 8E 18
Liquo. N Lan 4G 59
Lisbane. Ards 5J 93
Lisbellaw. Ferm 6C 92
**Lisburn**. Lis 5H 93
Liscard. Mers 8B 40
Liscolman. Caus 2F 93
Liscombe. Som 2H 7
Lishahawley. Derr 2D 92
Liskeard. Corn 5E 4
Lislea. New M 7G 93
Lisle Court. Hants 6M 9
Lisnarick. Ferm 6B 92
Lisnaskea. Ferm 7C 92
Liss. Hants 3E 10
Lissett. E Yor 2J 43
Liss Forest. Hants 3E 10
Lissington. Linc 1J 37
Liston. Essx 7E 30
Listooder. New M 6J 93
Lisvane. Card 6L 17
Liswerry. Newp 5B 18
Litcham. Norf 8E 38
Litchard. B'end 6J 17
Litchborough. Nptn 6D 28
Litchfield. Hants 8B 20
**Litherland**. Mers 8B 40
Litlington. Cambs 7L 29
Litlington. E Sus 5B 12
Littemill. Nmbd 8K 61
Litterty. Abers 8G 81
Little Abington. Cambs 7B 30
Little Addington. Nptn 4G 29
Little Airmyn. N Yor 5E 42
Little Alne. Warw 5K 27
Little Ardo. Abers 2H 73
Little Asby. Cumb 5E 46
Little Aston. Staf 1J 27
Little Atherfield. IOW 7B 10
Little Ayton. N Yor 4C 48
Little Baddow. Essx 3D 22
Little Badminton. S Glo 5G 19
Little Ballinluig. Per 2C 66
Little Bampton. Cumb 6G 53
Little Bardfield. Essx 8C 30
Little Barford. Bed 6J 29
Little Barningham. Norf 6H 39
Little Barrington. Glos 2L 19
Little Barrow. Ches W 3C 34
Little Barugh. N Yor 8E 48
Little Bavington. Nmbd 4C 54
Little Bealings. Suff 7J 31
Littlebeck. Cumb 4E 46
Little Bedwyn. Wilts 7L 19
Little Bentley. Essx 1H 23
Little Berkhamsted. Herts 3K 21
Little Billing. Nptn 5F 28
Little Billington. C Beds 1G 21
Little Birch. Here 8D 26
Little Bispham. Bkpl 3B 40
Little Blakenham. Suff 7H 31
Little Blencow. Cumb 8J 53
Little Bognor. W Sus 3H 11
Little Bolas. Shrp 7E 34
Little Bollington. Ches E 1F 34
Little Bookham. Surr 8J 21
Littleborough. Devn 4H 7
**Littleborough**. G Man 6H 41
Littleborough. Notts 1F 36
Littlebourne. Kent 8J 23
Little Bourton. Oxon 7B 28
Little Bowden. Leics 3E 28
Little Bradley. Suff 6C 30
Little Brampton. Shrp 3B 26
Little Brechin. Ang 1J 67
Littlebredy. Dors 7D 8
Little Brickhill. Mil 8G 29
Little Bridgeford. Staf 7G 35
Little Brington. Nptn 5D 28
Little Bromley. Essx 1G 23
Little Broughton. Cumb 8E 52
Little Budworth. Ches W 3D 34
Little Burstead. Essx 4C 22
Little Burton. E Yor 3J 43
Littlebury. Essx 8B 30
Littlebury Green. Essx 8A 30
Little Bytham. Linc 8H 37
Little Canfield. Essx 1B 22
Little Canford. Dors 6J 9
Little Carlton. Linc 1L 37
Little Carlton. Notts 4E 36
Little Casterton. Rut 1H 29
Little Catwick. E Yor 3J 43
Little Catworth. Cambs 4J 29
Little Cawthorpe. Linc 1L 37
Little Chalfont. Buck 4G 21
Little Chart. Kent 1F 12
Little Chesterford. Essx 7B 30
Little Cheverell. Wilts 8H 19
Little Chishill. Cambs 8M 29
Little Clacton. Essx 2H 23
Little Clanfield. Oxon 3L 19
Little Clifton. Cumb 2K 45
Little Coates. NE Lin 7K 43
Little Comberton. Worc 7H 27
Little Common. E Sus 5D 12
Little Compton. Warw 8L 27
Little Cornard. Suff 8E 30
Littlecote. Buck 1F 20
Littlecott. Wilts 8K 19
Little Cowarne. Here 6E 26
Little Coxwell. Oxon 4L 19
Little Crakehall. N Yor 6L 47
Little Crawley. Mil 7G 29
Little Creich. High 5G 79
Little Cressingham. Norf 1E 30
Little Crosby. Mers 7B 40
Little Crosthwaite. Cumb 2M 45
Little Cubley. Derbs 6K 35
Little Dalby. Leics 8E 36
Little Dawley. Telf 1E 26
Littledean. Glos 2E 18
Little Dens. Abers 1K 73
Little Dewchurch. Here 8D 26
Little Ditton. Cambs 6C 30
Little Down. Hants 8A 20
Little Downham. Cambs 3B 30
Little Drayton. Shrp 6E 34
Little Driffield. E Yor 2H 43
Little Dunham. Norf 8E 38
Little Dunkeld. Per 3D 66
Little Dunmow. Essx 1C 22
Little Easton. Essx 1C 22
Little Eaton. Derbs 5A 36
Little Eccleston. Lanc 3C 40
Little Ellingham. Norf 2G 31
Little Elm. Som 1F 8
Little End. Essx 3B 22
Little Everdon. Nptn 6C 28
Little Eversden. Cambs 6L 29
Little Faringdon. Oxon 3L 19
Little Fencote. N Yor 6L 47
Little Fenton. N Yor 4C 42
Littleferry. High 4J 79
Little Fransham. Norf 8F 38
Little Gaddesden. Herts 2G 21
Little Garway. Here 1C 18
Little Gidding. Cambs 3J 29
Little Glemham. Suff 6K 31
Little Glenshee. Per 4C 66
Little Gransden. Cambs 6K 29
Little Green. Suff 4G 31
Little Green. Wrex 5C 34
Little Grimsby. Linc 8L 43
Little Habton. N Yor 8E 48
Little Hadham. Herts 1M 21
Little Hale. Linc 5J 37
Little Hallingbury. Essx 2A 22
Littleham. Devn
nr. Bideford 3D 6
nr. Exmouth 7K 7
Little Hampden. Buck 3F 20
**Littlehampton**. W Sus 5H 11
Little Haresfield. Glos 3G 19
Little Harrowden. Nptn 4F 28
Little Haseley. Oxon 3D 20
Little Hatfield. E Yor 3J 43
Little Hautbois. Norf 7J 39
Little Haven. Pemb 5E 14
Little Hay. Staf 1K 27
Little Hayfield. Derbs 1J 35
Little Haywood. Staf 7J 35
Little Heath. W Mid 3M 27
Little Heck. N Yor 5C 42
Littlehempston. Devn 5L 5
Little Herbert's. Glos 2H 19
Little Hereford. Here 5D 26
Little Horkesley. Essx 8F 30
Little Hormead. Herts 1L 21
Little Horsted. E Sus 4A 12
Little Horton. W Yor 4K 41
Little Horwood. Buck 8E 28
Little Houghton. Nptn 6F 28
Little Houghton. S Yor 7B 42
Littlehoughton. Nmbd 8K 61
Little Hucklow. Derbs 2K 35
Little Hulton. G Man 7F 40
Little Irchester. Nptn 5G 29
Little Kelk. E Yor 1H 43
Little Kimble. Buck 3F 20
Little Kineton. Warw 6M 27
Little Kingshill. Buck 4F 20
Little Langdale. Cumb 5B 46
Little Langford. Wilts 2J 9
Little Laver. Essx 3B 22
Little Lawford. Warw 4B 28
Little Leigh. Ches W 2E 34
Little Leighs. Essx 2D 22
Little Leven. E Yor 3H 43
**Little Lever**. G Man 7F 40
Little Linford. Mil 7F 28
Little London. Buck 2D 20
Little London. E Sus 4B 12
Little London. Hants
nr. Andover 1A 10
nr. Basingstoke 8D 20
Little London. Linc
nr. Long Sutton 7M 37
nr. Spalding 7K 37
Little London. Norf
nr. North Walsham 6J 39
nr. Northwold 2D 30
nr. Saxthorpe 6H 39
nr. Southery 2C 30
Little London. Powy 4K 25
Little Longstone. Derbs 2K 35
Little Malvern. Worc 7F 26
Little Maplestead. Essx 8E 30
Little Marcle. Here 8E 26
Little Marlow. Buck 5F 20
Little Massingham. Norf 7D 38
Little Melton. Norf 1H 31
Little Mill. Mon 3B 18
Littlemill. Abers 6C 72
Littlemill. E Ayr 8C 58
Littlemill. High 1K 71
Little Milton. Oxon 3D 20
Little Missenden. Buck 4G 21
Littlemoor. Derbs 3A 36
Littlemoor. Dors 7E 8
Littlemore. Oxon 3C 20
Little Mountain. Flin 3A 34
Little Musgrave. Cumb 4F 46
Little Ness. Shrp 8C 34
Little Neston. Ches W 2A 34
Little Newcastle. Pemb 4F 14
Little Newsham. Dur 4K 47
Little Oakley. Essx 1J 23
Little Oakley. Nptn 3F 28
Little Onn. Staf 8G 35
Little Ormside. Cumb 4F 46
Little Orton. Cumb 6H 53
Little Orton. Leics 1M 27
Little Ouse. Cambs 3C 30
Little Ouseburn. N Yor 1B 42
Littleover. Derb 6M 35
Little Packington. Warw 3L 27
Little Paxton. Cambs 5J 29
Little Petherick. Corn 4B 4
Little Plumpton. Lanc 4B 40
Little Plumstead. Norf 8K 39
Little Ponton. Linc 6G 37
Littleport. Cambs 3B 30
Little Posbrook. Hants 5C 10
Little Potheridge. Devn 4E 6
Little Preston. Nptn 6C 28
Little Raveley. Cambs 4K 29
Little Reynoldston. Swan 8L 15
Little Ribston. N Yor 2A 42
Little Rissington. Glos 2K 19
Little Rogart. High 3H 79
Little Rollright. Oxon 8L 27
Little Ryburgh. Norf 7F 38
Little Ryle. Nmbd 8H 61
Little Ryton. Shrp 1C 26
Little Salkeld. Cumb 8K 53
Little Sampford. Essx 8C 30
Little Sandhurst. Brac 7F 20
Little Saredon. Staf 1H 27
Little Saxham. Suff 5D 30
Little Scatwell. High 8D 78
Little Shelford. Cambs 6A 30
Little Shoddesden. Hants 1L 9
Little Singleton. Lanc 4B 40
Little Smeaton. N Yor 6C 42
Little Snoring. Norf 6F 38
Little Sodbury. S Glo 5F 18
Little Somborne. Hants 2A 10
Little Somerford. Wilts 5H 19
Little Soudley. Shrp 7F 34
Little Stainforth. N Yor 1G 41
Little Stainton. Darl 4M 47
Little Stanney. Ches W 2C 34
Little Staughton. Bed 5J 29
Little Steeping. Linc 3M 37
Littlester. Shet 5K 91
Little Stoke. Staf 6H 35
Littlestone-on-Sea. Kent 3G 13
Little Stonham. Suff 5H 31
Little Stretton. Leics 1D 28
Little Stretton. Shrp 2C 26
Little Strickland. Cumb 4D 46
Little Stukeley. Cambs 4K 29
Little Sugnall. Staf 6G 35
Little Sutton. Ches W 2B 34
Little Sutton. Linc 7A 38
Little Swinburne. Nmbd 4C 54
Little Tew. Oxon 1A 20
Little Tey. Essx 1E 22
Little Thetford. Cambs 4B 30
Little Thirkleby. N Yor 8B 48
Little Thornage. Norf 6G 39
Little Thornton. Lanc 3B 40
Little Thorpe. W Yor 5K 41
Littlethorpe. Leics 2C 28
Littlethorpe. N Yor 1M 41
Little Thurlow. Suff 6C 30
Little Thurrock. Thur 6C 22
Littleton. Ches W 3C 34
Littleton. Hants 2B 10
Littleton. Som 2C 8
Littleton. Surr
nr. Guildford 1G 11
nr. Staines 7H 21
Littleton Drew. Wilts 5G 19
Littleton Pannell. Wilts 8J 19
Littleton-upon-Severn. S Glo 5D 18
Little Torboll. High 4H 79
Little Torrington. Devn 4D 6
Little Totham. Essx 2E 22
Little Town. Cumb 3M 45
Little Town. Lanc 4E 40
Littletown. Dur 7G 55
Littletown. High 5H 79
Little Twycross. Leics 1M 27
Little Urswick. Cumb 8A 46
Little Wakering. Essx 5F 22
Little Walden. Essx 7B 30
Little Waldingfield. Suff 7F 30
Little Walsingham. Norf 6F 38
Little Waltham. Essx 2D 22
Little Warley. Essx 4C 22
Little Weighton. E Yor 4G 43
Little Wenham. Suff 8G 31
Little Wenlock. Telf 1E 26
Little Whelnetham. Suff 5E 30
Little Whittingham Green. Suff 4J 31
Littlewick Green. Wind 6F 20
Little Wilbraham. Cambs 6B 30
Littlewindsor. Dors 5C 8
Little Wisbeach. Linc 6J 37
Little Witcombe. Glos 2H 19
Little Witley. Worc 5F 26
Little Wittenham. Oxon 4C 20
Little Wolford. Warw 8L 27
Littleworth. Bed 7H 29
Littleworth. Glos 8K 27
Littleworth. Oxon 4M 19
Littleworth. Staf
nr. Cannock 8J 35
nr. Eccleshall 7F 34
nr. Stafford 7H 35
Littleworth. W Sus 3J 11
Littleworth. Worc
nr. Redditch 5H 27
nr. Worcester 6G 27
Little Wratting. Suff 7C 30
Little Wymondley. Herts 1K 21
Little Wyrley. Staf 1J 27
Little Yeldham. Essx 8D 30
Littley Green. Essx 2C 22
Litton. Derbs 2K 35
Litton. N Yor 8H 47
Litton. Som 8D 18
Litton Cheney. Dors 6D 8
Liurbost. W Isl 1E 76
**Liverpool**. Mers 8B 40
Liverpool John Lennon Airport. Mers 1C 34
**Liversedge**. W Yor 5K 41
Liverton. Devn 8H 7
Liverton. Red C 4E 48
Liverton Mines. Red C 4E 48
**Livingston**. W Lot 3J 59
Livingston Village. W Lot 3J 59
Lixwm. Flin 3L 33
Lizard. Corn 7L 3
Llaingoch. IOA 2B 32
Llaithddu. Powy 4K 25
Llampha. V Glam 7J 17
Llan. Powy 2H 25
Llanaber. Gwyn 1F 24
Llanaelhaearn. Gwyn 6C 32
Llanaeron. Cdgn 6D 24
Llanafan. Cdgn 5F 24
Llanafan-fawr. Powy 7J 25
Llanafan-fechan. Powy 7J 25
Llanallgo. IOA 2D 32
Llanandras. Powy 5B 26
Llananno. Powy 5K 25
Llanarmon. Gwyn 7D 32
Llanarmon Dyffryn Ceiriog. Wrex 7L 33
Llanarmon-yn-Ial. Den 5L 33
Llanarth. Cdgn 1L 15
Llanarth. Mon 2B 18
Llanarthne. Carm 4M 15
Llanasa. Flin 2L 33
Llanbabo. IOA 2C 32
Llanbadarn Fawr. Cdgn 4F 24
Llanbadarn Fynydd. Powy 5L 25
Llanbadarn-y-garreg. Powy 8L 25
Llanbadoc. Mon 3B 18
Llanbadrig. IOA 1C 32
Llanbeder. Newp 4B 18
Llanbedr. Gwyn 8E 32
Llanbedr. Powy
nr. Crickhowell 2M 17
nr. Hay-on-Wye 8L 25
Llanbedr-Dyffryn-Clwyd. Den 5L 33
Llanbedrgoch. IOA 2E 32
Llanbedrog. Gwyn 7C 32
Llanbedr Pont Steffan. Cdgn 8E 24
Llanbedr-y-cennin. Cnwy 4G 33
Llanberis. Gwyn 4E 32
Llanbethery. V Glam 8K 17
Llanbister. Powy 5L 25
Llanblethian. V Glam 7J 17
Llanboidy. Carm 4J 15
Llanbradach. Cphy 5L 17
Llanbrynmair. Powy 2H 25
Llanbydderi. V Glam 8K 17
Llancadle. V Glam 8K 17
Llancarfan. V Glam 7K 17
Llancatal. V Glam 8K 17
Llancayo. Mon 3B 18
Llancloudy. Here 1C 18
Llancoch. Powy 5M 25
Llancynfelyn. Cdgn 3F 24
Llandaff. Card 7L 17
Llandanwg. Gwyn 8E 32
Llandarcy. Neat 5G 17
Llandawke. Carm 5J 15
Llanddaniel Fab. IOA 3D 32
Llanddarog. Carm 5M 15
Llanddeiniol. Cdgn 5E 24
Llanddeiniolen. Gwyn 4E 32
Llandderfel. Gwyn 7J 33
Llanddeusant. Carm 2G 17
Llanddeusant. IOA 2C 32
Llanddew. Powy 1K 17
Llanddewi. Swan 8L 15
Llanddewi Brefi. Cdgn 7F 24
Llanddewi'r Cwm. Powy 8K 25
Llanddewi Rhydderch. Mon 2B 18
Llanddewi Velfrey. Pemb 5H 15
Llanddewi Ystradenni. Powy 6L 25
Llanddoged. Cnwy 4H 33
Llanddona. IOA 3E 32
Llanddowror. Carm 5J 15
Llanddulas. Cnwy 3J 33
Llanddwywe. Gwyn 8E 32
Llanddyfnan. IOA 3E 32
Llandecwyn. Gwyn 7F 32
Llandefaelog Fach. Powy 1K 17
Llandefaelog-tre'r-graig. Powy 1L 17
Llandefalle. Powy 1L 17
Llandegfan. IOA 3E 32
Llandegla. Den 5L 33
Llandegley. Powy 6L 25
Llandegveth. Mon 4B 18
Llandeilo. Carm 2F 16
Llandeilo Graban. Powy 8K 25
Llandeilo'r Fan. Powy 1H 17
Llandeloy. Pemb 4E 14
Llandenny. Mon 3C 18
Llandevaud. Newp 4C 18
Llandevenny. Mon 5C 18
Llandilo. Pemb 4H 15
Llandinabo. Here 1D 18
Llandinam. Powy 4K 25
Llandissilio. Pemb 4H 15
Llandogo. Mon 3D 18
Llandough. V Glam
nr. Cowbridge 7J 17
nr. Penarth 7L 17
Llandovery. Carm 1G 17
Llandow. V Glam 7J 17
Llandre. Cdgn 4F 24
Llandrillo. Den 7K 33
Llandrillo-yn-Rhos. Cnwy 2H 33
Llandrindod. Powy 6K 25
Llandrindod Wells. Powy 6K 25
Llandrinio. Powy 8A 34
**Llandudno**. Cnwy 2G 33
Llandudno Junction. Cnwy 3G 33
Llandudoch. Pemb 2H 15
Llandw. V Glam 7J 17
Llandwrog. Gwyn 5D 32
Llandybie. Carm 3F 16
Llandyfaelog. Carm 5L 15
Llandyfan. Carm 3F 16
Llandyfriog. Cdgn 2K 15
Llandyfrydog. IOA 2D 32
Llandygai. Gwyn 3F 32
Llandygwydd. Cdgn 2J 15
Llandynan. Den 6L 33
Llandyrnog. Den 4L 33
Llandysilio. Powy 8A 34
Llandyssil. Powy 3L 25
Llandysul. Cdgn 2L 15
Llanedeyrn. Card 6M 17
Llaneglwys. Powy 1K 17
Llanegryn. Gwyn 2F 24
Llanegwad. Carm 4M 15
Llaneilian. IOA 1D 32
Llanelian-yn-Rhos. Cnwy 3H 33
Llanelidan. Den 5L 33
Llanelieu. Powy 1L 17
Llanellen. Mon 2B 18
**Llanelli**. Carm 7M 15
Llanelltyd. Gwyn 1G 25
Llanelly. Mon 3M 17
Llanelly Hill. Mon 3M 17
Llanelwedd. Powy 7K 25
**Llan-Elwy**. Den 3K 33
Llanenddwyn. Gwyn 8E 32
Llanengan. Gwyn 8B 32
Llanerch. Powy 2B 26
Llanerchymedd. IOA 2D 32
Llanerfyl. Powy 2K 25
Llaneuddog. IOA 2D 32
Llanfachraeth. IOA 2C 32
Llanfachreth. Gwyn 8G 33
Llanfaelog. IOA 3C 32
Llanfaelrhys. Gwyn 8B 32
Llanfaenor. Mon 2C 18
Llanfaes. IOA 3F 32
Llanfaes. Powy 2K 17
Llanfaethlu. IOA 2C 32
Llanfaglan. Gwyn 4D 32
Llanfair. Gwyn 8E 32
Llanfair. Here 7A 26
Llanfair Caereinion. Powy 2L 25
Llanfair Clydogau. Cdgn 7F 24
Llanfair Dyffryn Clwyd. Den 5L 33
Llanfairfechan. Cnwy 3F 32
Llanfair-Nant-Gwyn. Pemb 3H 15
Llanfair Pwllgwyngyll. IOA 3E 32
Llanfair Talhaiarn. Cnwy 3J 33
Llanfair Waterdine. Shrp 5M 25
Llanfair-ym-Muallt. Powy 7K 25
Llanfairyneubwll. IOA 3C 32
Llanfairynghornwy. IOA 1C 32
Llanfallteg. Carm 5H 15
Llanfallteg West. Carm 5H 15
Llanfaredd. Powy 7K 25
Llanfarian. Cdgn 5E 24
Llanfechain. Powy 8L 33
Llanfechell. IOA 1C 32
Llanfendigaid. Gwyn 2E 24
Llanferres. Den 4L 33
Llan Ffestiniog. Gwyn 6G 33
Llanfflewyn. IOA 2C 32
Llanfihangel-ar-Arth. Carm 3L 15
Llanfihangel Glyn Myfyr. Cnwy 6J 33
Llanfihangel Nant Bran. Powy 1J 17
Llanfihangel-Nant-Melan. Powy 7L 25
Llanfihangel near Rogiet. Mon 5C 18
Llanfihangel Rhydithon. Powy 6L 25
Llanfihangel Tal-y-llyn. Powy 2L 17
Llanfihangel-uwch-Gwili. Carm 4L 15
Llanfihangel-y-Creuddyn. Cdgn 5F 24
Llanfihangel-yng-Ngwynfa. Powy 1K 25
Llanfihangel yn Nhowyn. IOA 3C 32
Llanfihangel-y-pennant. Gwyn
nr. Golan 6E 32
nr. Tywyn 2F 24
Llanfihangel-y-traethau. Gwyn 7E 32
Llanfilo. Powy 1L 17
Llanfleiddan. V Glam 7J 17
Llanfoist. Mon 2A 18
Llanfor. Gwyn 7J 33
Llanfrechfa. Torf 4B 18
Llanfrothen. Gwyn 6F 32
Llanfrynach. Powy 2K 17
Llanfwrog. Den 5L 33
Llanfwrog. IOA 2C 32
Llanfyllin. Powy 1L 25
Llanfynydd. Carm 2E 16
Llanfynydd. Flin 4A 34
Llanfyrnach. Pemb 3J 15
Llangadfan. Powy 1K 25
Llangadog. Carm
nr. Llandovery 2G 17
nr. Llanelli 6L 15
Llangadwaladr. IOA 4C 32
Llangadwaladr. Powy 7L 33
Llangaffo. IOA 4D 32
Llangain. Carm 5K 15
Llangammarch Wells. Powy 8J 25
Llangan. V Glam 7J 17
Llangarron. Here 1D 18
Llangasty-Talyllyn. Powy 2L 17
Llangathen. Carm 2E 16
Llangattock. Powy 3M 17
Llangattock Lingoed. Mon 1B 18
Llangattock-Vibon-Avel. Mon 2C 18
Llangedwyn. Powy 8L 33
Llangefni. IOA 3D 32
Llangeinor. B'end 6J 17
Llangeitho. Cdgn 7F 24
Llangeler. Carm 3K 15
Llangelynin. Gwyn 2E 24
Llangendeirne. Carm 5L 15
Llangennech. Carm 4E 16
Llangennith. Swan 7L 15
Llangenny. Powy 3M 17
Llangernyw. Cnwy 4H 33
Llangian. Gwyn 8B 32
Llangiwg. Neat 4G 17
Llangloffan. Pemb 3F 14
Llanglydwen. Carm 4H 15
Llangoed. IOA 3F 32
Llangoedmor. Cdgn 2H 15
Llangollen. Den 6M 33
Llangolman. Pemb 4H 15
Llangorse. Powy 2L 17
Llangorwen. Cdgn 4F 24
Llangovan. Mon 3C 18
Llangower. Gwyn 7J 33
Llangranog. Cdgn 1K 15
Llangristiolus. IOA 3D 32
Llangrove. Here 2D 18
Llangua. Mon 1B 18
Llangunllo. Powy 5M 25
Llangunnor. Carm 4L 15
Llangurig. Powy 5J 25
Llangwm. Cnwy 6J 33
Llangwm. Mon 3C 18
Llangwm. Pemb 6F 14
Llangwm-isaf. Mon 3C 18
Llangwnnadl. Gwyn 7B 32
Llangwyfan. Den 4L 33
Llangwyfan-isaf. IOA 4C 32
Llangwyllog. IOA 3D 32
Llangwyryfon. Cdgn 5F 24
Llangybi. Cdgn 7F 24
Llangybi. Gwyn 6D 32
Llangybi. Mon 4B 18
Llangyfelach. Swan 5F 16
Llangynhafal. Den 4L 33
Llangynidr. Powy 3L 17
Llangynin. Carm 5J 15
Llangynog. Carm 5K 15
Llangynog. Powy 8K 33
Llangynwyd. B'end 6H 17
Llanhamlach. Powy 2K 17
Llanharan. Rhon 6K 17
Llanharry. Rhon 6K 17
Llanhennock. Mon 4B 18
Llanhilleth. Blae 4M 17
Llanidloes. Powy 4J 25
Llaniestyn. Gwyn 7B 32
Llanigon. Powy 8M 25
Llanilar. Cdgn 5F 24
Llanilid. Rhon 6J 17
**Llanilltud Fawr**. V Glam 8J 17
Llanishen. Card 6L 17
Llanishen. Mon 3C 18
Llanllawddog. Carm 4L 15
Llanllechid. Gwyn 4F 32
Llanllowell. Mon 4B 18
Llanllugan. Powy 2K 25
Llanllwch. Carm 5K 15
Llanllwchaiarn. Powy 3L 25
Llanllwni. Carm 3L 15
Llanllyfni. Gwyn 5D 32
Llanmadoc. Swan 7L 15
Llanmaes. V Glam 8J 17
Llanmartin. Newp 5B 18
Llanmerwig. Powy 3L 25
Llanmihangel. V Glam 7J 17
Llan-mill. Pemb 5H 15
Llanmiloe. Carm 6J 15
Llanmorlais. Swan 7M 15
Llannefydd. Cnwy 3J 33
Llan-non. Cdgn 6E 24
Llannon. Carm 6M 15
Llannor. Gwyn 7C 32
Llanover. Mon 3B 18
Llanpumsaint. Carm 4L 15
Llanrhaeadr. Den 4K 33
Llanrhaeadr-ym-Mochnant. Powy 8L 33
Llanrhian. Pemb 3E 14
Llanrhidian. Swan 7L 15
Llanrhos. Cnwy 2G 33
Llanrhyddlad. IOA 2C 32
Llanrhystud. Cdgn 6E 24
Llanrothal. Here 2C 18
Llanrug. Gwyn 4E 32
Llanrumney. Card 6M 17
Llanrwst. Cnwy 4G 33
Llansadurnen. Carm 5J 15
Llansadwrn. Carm 1F 16
Llansadwrn. IOA 3E 32
Llansaint. Carm 6K 15
Llansamlet. Swan 5F 16
Llansanffraid Glan Conwy. Cnwy 3H 33
Llansannan. Cnwy 4J 33
Llansannor. V Glam 7J 17
Llansantffraed. Cdgn 6E 24
Llansantffraed. Powy 2L 17
Llansantffraed Cwmdeuddwr. Powy 6J 25
Llansantffraed-in-Elwel. Powy 7K 25
Llansantffraid-ym-Mechain. Powy 8M 33
Llansawel. Carm 1F 16
Llansawel. Neat 5G 17
Llansilin. Powy 8M 33
Llansoy. Mon 3C 18
Llanspyddid. Powy 2K 17
Llanstadwell. Pemb 6F 14
Llansteffan. Carm 5K 15
Llanstephan. Powy 8L 25
Llantarnam. Torf 4B 18
Llanteg. Pemb 5H 15
Llanthony. Mon 1A 18
Llantilio Crossenny. Mon 2B 18
Llantilio Pertholey. Mon 2B 18
Llantood. Pemb 2H 15
Llantrisant. Mon 4B 18
Llantrisant. Rhon 6K 17
Llantrithyd. V Glam 7K 17
Llantwit Fardre. Rhon 6K 17
**Llantwit Major**. V Glam 8J 17
Llanuwchllyn. Gwyn 7H 33
Llanvaches. Newp 4C 18
Llanvair Discoed. Mon 4C 18
Llanvapley. Mon 2B 18
Llanvetherine. Mon 2B 18
Llanveynoe. Here 8B 26
Llanvihangel Crucorney. Mon 1B 18
Llanvihangel Gobion. Mon 3B 18
Llanvihangel Ystern-Llewern. Mon 2C 18
Llanwarne. Here 1D 18
Llanwddyn. Powy 1K 25
Llanwenarth. Mon 2A 18
Llanwenog. Cdgn 2L 15
Llanwern. Newp 5B 18
Llanwinio. Carm 4J 15
Llanwnda. Gwyn 5D 32
Llanwnda. Pemb 3F 14
Llanwnnen. Cdgn 2M 15
Llanwnog. Powy 3K 25
Llanwrda. Carm 1G 17
Llanwrin. Powy 2G 25
Llanwrthwl. Powy 6J 25
Llanwrtud. Powy 8H 25
Llanwrtyd. Powy 8H 25
Llanwrtyd Wells. Powy 8H 25
Llanwyddelan. Powy 2K 25
Llanyblodwel. Shrp 8M 33
Llanybri. Carm 5K 15
Llanybydder. Carm 2M 15
Llanycefn. Pemb 4G 15
Llanychaer. Pemb 3F 14
Llanycil. Gwyn 7J 33
Llanymawddwy. Gwyn 1J 25
Llanymddyfri. Carm 1G 17
Llanymynech. Powy 7A 34
Llanynghenedl. IOA 2C 32
Llanynys. Den 4L 33
Llan-y-pwll. Wrex 4B 34
Llanyrafon. Torf 4B 18
Llanyre. Powy 6K 25
Llanystumdwy. Gwyn 7D 32
Llanywern. Powy 2L 17
Llawhaden. Pemb 5G 15
Llawndy. Flin 2L 33
Llawnt. Shrp 6A 34
Llawr Dref. Gwyn 8B 32
Llawryglyn. Powy 3J 25
Llay. Wrex 4B 34
Llechfaen. Powy 2K 17
Llechryd. Cphy 4L 17
Llechryd. Cdgn 2J 15
Llechrydau. Wrex 7M 33
Lledrod. Cdgn 5F 24
Llethrid. Swan 7M 15
Llidiad-Nenog. Carm 3M 15
Llidiardau. Gwyn 7H 33
Llidiart y Parc. Den 6L 33
Llithfaen. Gwyn 6C 32
Lloc. Flin 3L 33
Llong. Flin 3A 34
Llowes. Powy 8L 25
Lloyney. Powy 5M 25
Llundain-fach. Cdgn 7E 24
Llwydcoed. Rhon 4J 17
Llwyncelyn. Cdgn 1L 15
Llwyncelyn. Swan 4F 16
Llwyndafydd. Cdgn 1K 15
Llwynderw. Powy 2M 25
Llwyn-du. Mon 2A 18
Llwyngwril. Gwyn 2E 24
Llwynhendy. Carm 7M 15
Llwynmawr. Wrex 7M 33
Llwyn-on Village. Mer T 3K 17
Llwyn-têg. Carm 4E 16
Llwyn-y-brain. Carm 5H 15
Llwynygog. Powy 3H 25
Llwyn-y-groes. Cdgn 7E 24
Llwynypia. Rhon 5J 17
Llynclys. Shrp 7A 34
Llynfaes. IOA 3D 32
Llysfaen. Cnwy 3H 33
Llyswen. Powy 1L 17
Llysworney. V Glam 7J 17
Llys-y-fran. Pemb 4G 15
Llywel. Powy 1H 17
Llywernog. Cdgn 4G 25
Loan. Falk 2H 59
Loanend. Nmbd 4G 61
Loanhead. Midl 3L 59
Loaningfoot. Dum 6D 52
Loanreoch. High 6G 79
Loans. S Ayr 6B 58
Loansdean. Nmbd 3E 54
Lobb. Devn 2D 6
Lobhillcross. Devn 7D 6
Lochaber. Mor 8L 79
Loch a Charnain. W Isl 1E 74
Loch a Ghainmhich. W Isl 1D 76
Lochailort. High 7J 69
Lochaline. High 3A 64
Lochans. Dum 6F 50
Locharbriggs. Dum 3D 52
Lochardil. High 1G 71
Lochassynt Lodge. High 1B 78
Lochavich. Arg 6D 64
Lochawe. Arg 5F 64
Loch Baghasdail. W Isl 4D 74
Lochboisdale. W Isl 4D 74
Lochbuie. Arg 5M 63
Lochcarron. High 2K 69
Loch Choire Lodge. High 8J 85
Lochdochart House. Stir 5J 65
Lochdon. Arg 4B 64
Lochearnhead. Stir 5K 65
Lochee. D'dee 4G 67
Lochend. High
nr. Inverness 2F 70
nr. Thurso 5D 86
Locherben. Dum 2D 52
Loch Euphort. W Isl 7K 75
Lochfoot. Dum 4C 52
Lochgair. Arg 8D 64
Lochgarthside. High 4F 70
Lochgelly. Fife 8E 66
Lochgilphead. Arg 1H 57
Lochgoilhead. Arg 7F 64
Loch Head. Dum 7J 51
Lochhill. Mor 7B 80
Lochindorb Lodge. High 2K 71
Lochinver. High 1A 78
Lochlane. Per 5B 66
**Loch Lomond**. Arg 7H 65
Loch Loyal Lodge. High 7J 85
Lochluichart. High 7D 78
Lochmaben. Dum 3E 52
Lochmaddy. W Isl 7L 75
Loch nam Madadh. W Isl 7L 75
Lochore. Fife 8E 66
Lochportain. W Isl 6L 75
Lochranza. N Ayr 4J 57
Loch Sgioport. W Isl 2E 74
Lochside. Abers 1L 67
Lochside. High
nr. Achentoul 8L 85
nr. Nairn 8J 79
Lochslin. High 5J 79
Lochstack Lodge. High 7E 84
Lochton. Abers 6G 73
Lochty. Fife 7J 67
Lochuisge. High 2B 64
Lochussie. High 8E 78
Lochwinnoch. Ren 4B 58
Lochyside. High 8B 70
Lockengate. Corn 5C 4
Lockerbie. Dum 3F 52
Lockeridge. Wilts 7K 19
Lockerley. Hants 3L 9
Lockhills. Cumb 7K 53
Locking. N Som 8B 18
Lockington. E Yor 3G 43
Lockington. Leics 7B 36
Lockleywood. Shrp 7E 34
Locksgreen. IOW 6B 10
**Locks Heath**. Hants 5C 10
Lockton. N Yor 6F 48
Loddington. Leics 1E 28
Loddington. Nptn 4F 28
Loddiswell. Devn 7K 5
Loddon. Norf 2K 31
Lode. Cambs 5B 30
Loders. Dors 6C 8
Lodsworth. W Sus 3G 11
Lofthouse. N Yor 8K 47
Lofthouse. W Yor 5M 41
Lofthouse Gate. W Yor 5M 41
Loftus. Red C 4E 48
Logan. E Ayr 7D 58
Loganlea. W Lot 3H 59
Logaston. Here 6B 26
Loggerheads. Den 4L 33
Loggerheads. Staf 6F 34
Loggie. High 4B 78
Logie. Ang 1K 67
Logie. Fife 5H 67
Logie. Mor 8L 79
Logie Coldstone. Abers 5D 72
Logie Pert. Ang 1K 67
Logierait. Per 2C 66
Login. Carm 4H 15
Lolworth. Cambs 5L 29
Lonbain. High 8H 77
Londesborough. E Yor 3F 42
**London**. G Lon 5L 21
London Apprentice. Corn 6C 4
London Ashford Airport. Kent 3G 13
London City Airport. G Lon 5M 21
London Colney. Herts 3J 21
**Londonderry**. Derr 3D 92
Londonderry. N Yor 7M 47
London Gatwick Airport. W Sus 1K 11
London Heathrow Airport. G Lon 6H 21
London Luton Airport. Lutn 1J 21
London Southend Airport. Essx 5E 22
London Stansted Airport. Essx 1B 22
Londonthorpe. Linc 6G 37
Londubh. High 5K 77
Lone. High 7F 84
Lonemore. High
nr. Dornoch 5H 79
nr. Gairloch 6J 77
Long Ashton. N Som 6D 18
Long Bank. Worc 4F 26
Longbar. N Ayr 4B 58
Long Bennington. Linc 5F 36
**Longbenton**. Tyne 5F 54
Longborough. Glos 1K 19
Long Bredy. Dors 6D 8
Longbridge. Warw 5L 27
Longbridge. W Mid 4J 27
Longbridge Deverill. Wilts 1G 9
Long Buckby. Nptn 5D 28
Long Buckby Wharf. Nptn 5D 28
Longburgh. Cumb 6H 53
Longburton. Dors 4E 8
Long Clawson. Leics 7E 36
Longcliffe. Derbs 4L 35
Long Common. Hants 4C 10
Long Compton. Staf 7G 35
Long Compton. Warw 8L 27
Longcot. Oxon 4L 19
Long Crendon. Buck 3D 20
Long Crichel. Dors 4H 9
Longcroft. Cumb 6G 53
Longcroft. Falk 2F 58
Longcross. Surr 7G 21
Longdale. Cumb 5E 46
Longdales. Cumb 7K 53
Longden. Shrp 1C 26
Longden Common. Shrp 1C 26
Long Ditton. Surr 7J 21
Longdon. Staf 8J 35
Longdon. Worc 8G 27
Longdon Green. Staf 8J 35
Longdon on Tern. Telf 8E 34
Longdown. Devn 6H 7
Longdowns. Corn 5L 3
Long Drax. N Yor 5D 42
Long Duckmanton. Derbs 2B 36
**Long Eaton**. Derbs 6B 36
Longfield. Kent 7C 22
Longfield. Shet 6D 90
Longfield Hill. Kent 7C 22
Longford. Derbs 6L 35
Longford. Glos 1G 19
Longford. G Lon 6H 21
Longford. Shrp 6E 34
Longford. Telf 8F 34
Longford. W Mid 3A 28
Longforgan. Per 4G 67
Longformacus. Bord 4D 60
Longframlington. Nmbd 1E 54
Long Gardens. Essx 8E 30
Long Green. Ches W 2C 34
Long Green. Worc 8G 27
Longham. Dors 6J 9
Longham. Norf 8F 38
Long Hanborough. Oxon 2B 20
Longhedge. Wilts 1G 9
Longhill. Abers 8K 81
Longhirst. Nmbd 3F 54
Longhope. Glos 2E 18
Longhope. Orkn 2E 86
Longhorsley. Nmbd 2E 54
Longhoughton. Nmbd 8K 61
Long Itchington. Warw 5B 28
Longlands. Cumb 8G 53
Long Lane. Telf 8E 34
Longlane. Derbs 6L 35
Longlane. W Ber 6B 20
Long Lawford. Warw 4B 28
Long Lease. N Yor 5G 49
Longley Green. Worc 6F 26
Long Load. Som 3C 8
Longmanhill. Abers 7G 81
Long Marston. Herts 2F 20
Long Marston. N Yor 2C 42
Long Marston. Warw 7K 27
Long Marton. Cumb 3E 46
Long Meadow. Cambs 5B 30
Long Meadowend. Shrp 3C 26
Long Melford. Suff 7E 30
Longmoor Camp. Hants 2E 10
Longmorn. Mor 8B 80
Longmoss. Ches E 2G 35
Long Newnton. Glos 4H 19
Long Newton. Stoc T 4A 48
Longnewton. Bord 7C 60
Longney. Glos 2F 18
Longniddry. E Lot 2B 60
Longnor. Shrp 1C 26
Longnor. Staf
nr. Leek 3J 35
nr. Stafford 8G 35
Longparish. Hants 1B 10
Longpark. Cumb 5J 53
Long Preston. N Yor 2G 41
Longridge. Lanc 4E 40
Longridge. Staf 8H 35
Longridge. W Lot 3H 59
Longriggend. N Lan 2G 59
Long Riston. E Yor 3J 43
Longrock. Corn 5J 3
Longsdon. Staf 4H 35
Longshaw. G Man 7D 40
Longshaw. Staf 5J 35
Longside. Abers 1K 73
Longslow. Shrp 6E 34
Longstanton. Cambs 5L 29
Longstock. Hants 2A 10
Longstowe. Cambs 6L 29
Long Stratton. Norf 2H 31
Long Street. Mil 7E 28
Longstreet. Wilts 8K 19
Long Sutton. Hants 1E 10
Long Sutton. Linc 7M 37
Long Sutton. Som 3C 8
Longthorpe. Pet 2J 29
Long Thurlow. Suff 5G 31
Longthwaite. Cumb 3C 46
**Longton**. Lanc 5C 40
Longton. Stoke 5H 35
Longtown. Cumb 5H 53
Longtown. Here 1B 18
Longville in the Dale. Shrp 2D 26
Long Whatton. Leics 7B 36
Longwick. Buck 3E 20
Long Wittenham. Oxon 4C 20
Longwitton. Nmbd 3D 54
Longworth. Oxon 4A 20
Longyester. E Lot 3C 60
Lonmore. High 1D 68
Looe. Corn 6E 4
Loose. Kent 8D 22
Loosegate. Linc 7L 37
Loosley Row. Buck 3F 20
Lopcombe Corner. Wilts 2L 9
Lopen. Som 4C 8
Loppington. Shrp 7C 34
Lorbottle. Nmbd 1D 54
Lordington. W Sus 5E 10
Loscoe. Derbs 5B 36
Loscombe. Dors 6D 8
Losgaintir. W Isl 4B 76
Lossiemouth. Mor 7B 80
Lossit. Arg 4A 56
Lostock Gralam. Ches W 2E 34
Lostock Green. Ches W 2E 34
Lostock Hall. Lanc 5D 40
Lostock Junction. G Man 7E 40
Lostwithiel. Corn 6D 4
Lothbeg. High 2K 79
Lothersdale. N Yor 3H 41
Lothianbridge. Midl 3M 59
Lothianburn. Midl 3L 59
Lothmore. High 2K 79
Lottisham. Som 2D 8
Loudwater. Buck 4G 21
**Loughborough**. Leics 8C 36
Loughbrickland. Arm 6G 93
Loughgall. Arm 6F 93
Loughguile. Caus 2G 93
Loughinisland. New M 6J 93
Loughmacrory. Ferm 5D 92
Loughor. Swan 5E 16
Loughries. Ards 5J 93
**Loughton**. Essx 4M 21
Loughton. Mil 8F 28
Loughton. Shrp 3E 26
Lound. Linc 8H 37
Lound. Notts 1D 36
Lound. Suff 2M 31
Lount. Leics 8A 36
The Loup. M Ulst 4F 93
**Louth**. Linc 1L 37
Love Clough. Lanc 5G 41
Lovedean. Hants 4D 10
Lover. Wilts 3L 9
Loversall. S Yor 8C 42
Loves Green. Essx 3C 22
Loveston. Pemb 6G 15
Lovington. Som 2D 8
Low Ackworth. W Yor 6B 42
Low Angerton. Nmbd 3D 54
Low Ardwell. Dum 7F 50
Low Ballochdowan. S Ayr 4F 50
Lowbands. Glos 8F 26
Low Barlings. Linc 2H 37
Low Bell End. N Yor 6E 48
Low Bentham. N Yor 1E 40
Low Borrowbridge. Cumb 5E 46
Low Bradfield. S Yor 8L 41
Low Bradley. N Yor 3J 41
Low Braithwaite. Cumb 7J 53
Low Brunton. Nmbd 4C 54
Low Burnham. N Lin 7E 42
Lowca. Cumb 2J 45
Low Catton. E Yor 2E 42
Low Coniscliffe. Darl 4L 47
Low Coylton. S Ayr 8C 58
Low Crosby. Cumb 6J 53
Low Dalby. N Yor 7F 48
Lowdham. Notts 5D 36
Low Dinsdale. Darl 4M 47
Lowe. Shrp 6D 34
Low Ellington. N Yor 7L 47
Lower Amble. Corn 4B 4
Lower Ansty. Dors 5F 8
Lower Arboll. High 5J 79
Lower Arncott. Oxon 2D 20
Lower Ashton. Devn 7H 7
Lower Assendon. Oxon 5E 20
Lower Auchenreath. Mor
Lower Badcall. High
Lower Ballam. Lanc
Lower Ballinderry. Lis
Lower Basildon. W Ber
Lower Beeding. W Sus
Lower Benefield. Nptn
Lower Bentley. Worc
Lower Beobridge. Shrp
Lower Bockhampton. Dors
Lower Boddington. Nptn
Lower Bordean. Hants
Lower Brailes. Warw
Lower Breakish. High
Lower Broadheath. Worc
Lower Brynamman. Neat
Lower Bullingham. Here
Lower Bullington. Hants
Lower Burgate. Hants
Lower Cam. Glos
Lower Catesby. Nptn
Lower Chapel. Powy
Lower Cheriton. Devn
Lower Chicksgrove. Wilts
Lower Chute. Wilts
Lower Clopton. Warw
Lower Common. Hants
Lower Crossings. Derbs
Lower Cumberworth. W Yor
Lower Darwen. Bkbn
Lower Dean. Bed
Lower Dean. Devn
Lower Diabaig. High
Lower Dicker. E Sus
Lower Dounreay. High
Lower Down. Shrp
Lower Dunsforth. N Yor
Lower East Carleton. Norf
Lower Egleton. Here
Lower Ellastone. Staf
Lower End. Nptn
Lower Everleigh. Wilts
Lower Eype. Dors
Lower Failand. N Som
Lower Faintree. Shrp
Lower Farringdon. Hants
Lower Foxdale. IOM
Lower Frankton. Shrp
Lower Froyle. Hants
Lower Gabwell. Devn
Lower Gledfield. High
Lower Godney. Som
Lower Gravenhurst. C Beds
Lower Green. Essx
Lower Green. Norf
Lower Green. W Ber
Lower Halstow. Kent
Lower Hardres. Kent
Lower Hardwick. Here
Lower Hartshay. Derbs
Lower Hawthwaite. Cumb
Lower Haysden. Kent
Lower Hayton. Shrp
Lower Hergest. Here
Lower Heyford. Oxon
Lower Heysham. Lanc
Lower Higham. Kent
Lower Holbrook. Suff
Lower Holditch. Dors
Lower Hordley. Shrp
Lower Horncroft. W Sus
Lower Horsebridge. E Sus
Lower Kilcott. Glos
Lower Killeyan. Arg
Lower Kingcombe. Dors
Lower Kingswood. Surr
Lower Kinnerton. Ches W
Lower Langford. N Som
Lower Largo. Fife
Lower Layham. Suff
Lower Ledwyche. Shrp
Lower Leigh. Staf
Lower Lemington. Glos
Lower Lenie. High
Lower Ley. Glos
Lower Llanfadog. Powy
Lower Lode. Glos
Lower Lovacott. Devn
Lower Loxhore. Devn
Lower Loxley. Staf
Lower Lydbrook. Glos
Lower Lye. Here
Lower Machen. Newp
Lower Maes-coed. Here
Lower Meend. Glos
Lower Midway. Derbs
Lower Milovaig. High
Lower Moor. Worc
Lower Morton. S Glo
Lower Mountain. Flin
Lower Nazeing. Essx
Lower Netchwood. Shrp
Lower Nyland. Dors
Lower Oakfield. Fife
Lower Oddington. Glos
Lower Ollach. High
Lower Penarth. V Glam
Lower Penn. Staf
Lower Pennington. Hants
Lower Peover. Ches W
Lower Pilsley. Derbs
Lower Pitkerrie. High
Lower Place. G Man
Lower Quinton. Warw
Lower Rainham. Medw
Lower Raydon. Suff
Lower Seagry. Wilts
Lower Shelton. C Beds
Lower Shiplake. Oxon
Lower Shuckburgh. Warw
Lower Sketty. Swan
Lower Slade. Devn
Lower Slaughter. Glos
Lower Soudley. Glos
Lower Stanton St Quintin. Wilts
Lower Stoke. Medw
Lower Stondon. C Beds
Lower Stonnall. Staf
Lower Stow Bedon. Norf
Lower Street. Norf
Lower Strensham. Worc
Lower Sundon. C Beds
Lower Swanwick. Hants
Lower Swell. Glos
Lower Tale. Devn
Lower Tean. Staf
Lower Thurlton. Norf
Lower Thurnham. Lanc
Lower Thurvaston. Derbs
Lower Town. Here
Lower Town. IOS
Lower Town. Pemb
Lowertown. Corn
Lowertown. Orkn
Lower Tysoe. Warw
Lower Upham. Hants
Lower Upnor. Medw
Lower Vexford. Som
Lower Walton. Warr
Lower Wear. Devn
Lower Weare. Som
Lower Welson. Here
Lower Whatcombe. Dors
Lower Whitley. Ches W
Lower Wield. Hants
Lower Withington. Ches E
Lower Woodend. Buck
Lower Woodford. Wilts
Lower Wraxall. Dors
Lower Wych. Ches W
Lower Wyche. Worc
Lowesby. Leics
**Lowestoft**. Suff
Loweswater. Cumb
Low Etherley. Dur
Lowfield Heath. W Sus
Lowford. Hants
Low Fulney. Linc
Low Gate. Nmbd
Lowgill. Cumb
Lowgill. Lanc
Low Grantley. N Yor
Low Green. N Yor
Low Habberley. Worc
Low Ham. Som
Low Hameringham. Linc
Low Hawsker. N Yor
Low Hesket. Cumb

Low Hesleyhurst—Monea


esleyhurst. Nmbd 2D 54
k. Cumb 7A 46
k. Nptn 3G 29
k. Nmbd 6H 61
k Bridge. Cumb 7A 46
k Green. Cumb 7A 46
nipe. Cumb 3D 46
eighton. Derbs 1J 35
orton. Cumb 2L 45
Marishes. N Yor 8F 48
Marnham. Notts 3F 36
Mill. N Yor 6D 48
Moor. Lanc 3F 40
Moor. W Yor 5K 41
Moorsley. Tyne 7G 55
Newton-by-the-Sea.
Nmbd 7K 61
e Moor. Ang 3H 67
od. Bord 6C 60
ow. Cumb
r. Brampton 5K 53
r. Wigton 7F 52
ow. N Yor 6H 47
onford. Warw 5K 27
treet. Norf 1G 31
er. Cumb 3D 46
orpe. E Yor 1H 43
n. Devn 5F 6
n. G Man 8E 40
n. Som 4L 7
n Common. G Man 8E 40
orry. Fife 1J 59
oynton. Linc 2K 37
alleyfield. Fife 1H 59
Westwood. Dur 6E 54
Whinnow. Cumb 6H 53
Wood. Cumb 7B 46
Worsall. N Yor 5A 48
Wray. Cumb 5B 46
are. Devn 4J 7
. Surr 2H 11
re. Devn 2F 6
S Yor 1M 35
Warw 6L 27
Green. Staf 6J 35
. N Som 8B 18
od. W Sus 2H 11
y. High 3D 78
ham. Leics 3E 28
ullin. High 5H 85
mbe. Som 1J 7
mbe Village. IOW 7C 10
. Nmbd 6J 61
t. Corn 8C 6
gton. Wilts 5G 19
whill. Fife 5H 67
ell Bridge. Som 2J 7
. Here 5C 26
W Isl 4D 74
rough. Linc 8K 43
urch. Pemb 5H 15
nden. W Yor 5J 41
nden Foot. W Yor 5J 41
nham. Kent 7F 22
burn. Cumb 6C 46
sdown. Kent 7C 22
gton. N Lin 6F 42
gton. Warw 6K 27
gton in the Brook.
ptn 3J 29
d. Linc 1J 37
d. Shrp 4D 26
shall. Buck 2D 20
shall. Wilts 8L 19
n. Corn 5J 3
n. Norf 8K 39
. Shrp 4D 26
ne. Shrp 2G 27
l. Wilts 3H 9
rth. Dur 7G 55
nall. Herts 1K 21
ott. Devn 6C 6
E Ayr 7D 58
e Burn. E Lot 2D 60
reen. Here 5C 26
bank. N Lan 2F 58
. E Ayr 4C 58
rdine. Here 7D 26
High 3G 69
Stir 5J 65
. Here 7C 26
ton. Derbs 8L 35
ton. E Sus 5B 12
ton. Som 8F 18
e Bottom. N Som 7D 18
. Worc 6F 26
th Camp. Dors 7G 9
Lanc 5G 41
N Yor 4B 42
anan. Abers 5E 72
innans. Fife 8E 66
aine. Bord 3F 60
en. Abers 3D 72
Ang 2K 67
ead. Ang 2H 67
ty. Per 5D 66
Yor 3G 43
N Yor 4D 42
. Ang 4F 66
Links. Fife 7H 67
Green. Norf 2J 31
Shet 1E 90
g. Shet 1F 90
. Swan 8M 15
rd. Kent 8C 22
rd's Cross. E Sus 4D 12
Mers 7B 40
. Devn 5L 7
e. Devn 6K 5
W Yor 6M 41
. Cumb 7D 46
. Arm 6G 93
are. New M 7G 93
hall. W Sus 3G 11
Devn 4J 7
Linc 3L 37
mbe. Devn 6K 5
Devn 7J 5
Arg 8H 65
iven. Arg 1F 56
High 8D 76
gh. Devn 7G 7
. Here 5C 26
muir. Abers 1K 67
. Fife 6G 67
Staf 3G 27
Devn
. Honiton 5K 7
. Teignmouth 8J 7
Lutn 1H 21
Airport. Lutn 1J 21
worth. Leics 3C 28
Devn
Ivybridge 6H 5
South Brent 5J 5
Linc 7M 37
Nptn 3J 29
Gowts. Linc 7M 37
thy. Devn 4G 7
ough. Som 2J 7
Glos 1E 18
n. Corn 6C 4
. High 8D 86
North. Shrp 3B 26
. Devn 2F 6
Kent 3G 13
rport. Kent 3G 13
. Kent
Dover 1J 13
Margate 7K 23
ton. Rut 2F 28
n-Sea. Kent 3G 13
St Lawrence. Som 2L 7
reen. Hants 8E 20
. Devn 7E 6
Fair Place. Som 2D 8
. G Man 7H 41
. W Yor 5H 41
. Shrp 2B 26
Millicent. Wilts 5J 19
Mers 7B 40
Ash. Worc 4H 27
n. Dors 4F 8
sh. Som 5B 8
Glos 3E 18
. Pemb 7G 15
Mid 3H 27
. Shrp 2E 26
en. Buck 3G 21
Lye Green. E Sus 2B 12
Lye Head. Worc 4F 26
Lyford. Oxon 4A 20
Lyham. Nmbd 6H 61
Lylestone. N Ayr 5B 58
Lymbridge Green. Kent 1H 13
Lyme Regis. Dors 6B 8
Lyminge. Kent 1H 13
**Lymington**. Hants 6M 9
Lyminster. W Sus 5H 11
**Lymm**. Warr 1E 34
Lymore. Hants 6L 9
Lympne. Kent 2H 13
Lympsham. Som 8B 18
Lympstone. Devn 7J 7
Lynaberack Lodge. High 6H 71
Lynbridge. Devn 1G 7
Lynch. Som 1J 7
Lynchat. High 5H 71
Lynch Green. Norf 1H 31
Lyndhurst. Hants 5M 9
Lyndon. Rut 1G 29
Lyne. Bord 5L 59
Lyne. Surr 7H 21
Lyneal. Shrp 6C 34
Lyne Down. Here 8E 26
Lyneham. Oxon 1L 19
Lyneham. Wilts 6J 19
Lyneholmeford. Cumb 4K 53
Lynemouth. Nmbd 2F 54
Lyne of Gorthleck. High 3F 70
Lyne of Skene. Abers 4G 73
Lynesack. Dur 3J 47
Lyness. Orkn 2E 86
Lyng. Norf 8G 39
Lyngate. Norf
nr. North Walsham 6J 39
nr. Worstead 7K 39
Lynmouth. Devn 1G 7
Lynn. Staf 1J 27
Lynn. Telf 8F 34
Lynsted. Kent 7F 22
Lynstone. Corn 5B 6
Lynton. Devn 1G 7
Lynwilg. High 4J 71
Lyon's Gate. Dors 5E 8
Lyonshall. Here 6B 26
Lytchett Matravers. Dors 6H 9
Lytchett Minster. Dors 6H 9
Lyth. High 5D 86
Lytham. Lanc 5B 40
**Lytham St Anne's**. Lanc 5B 40
Lythe. N Yor 4F 48
Lythes. Orkn 3F 86
Lythmore. High 5B 86


## M


Mabe Burnthouse. Corn 5L 3
Mabie. Dum 4D 52
Mablethorpe. Linc 1B 38
Macbiehill. Bord 4K 59
**Macclesfield**. Ches E 2H 35
Macclesfield Forest. Ches E 2H 35
Macduff. Abers 7G 81
Machan. S Lan 4F 58
Macharioch. Arg 1C 50
Machen. Cphy 6M 17
Machrie. N Ayr 6H 57
Machrihanish. Arg 7F 56
Machroes. Gwyn 8C 32
Machynlleth. Powy 2G 25
Mackerye End. Herts 2J 21
Mackworth. Derb 6M 35
Macmerry. E Lot 2B 60
Macosquin. Caus 2F 93
Madderty. Per 5C 66
Maddington. Wilts 1J 9
Maddiston. Falk 2H 59
Madehurst. W Sus 4G 11
Madeley. Staf 5F 34
Madeley. Telf 1E 26
Madeley Heath. Staf 5F 34
Madeley Heath. Worc 4H 27
Madford. Devn 4L 7
Madingley. Cambs 5L 29
Madley. Here 8C 26
Madresfield. Worc 7G 27
Madron. Corn 5H 3
Maenaddwyn. IOA 2D 32
Maenclochog. Pemb 4G 15
Maendy. V Glam 7K 17
Maenporth. Corn 6L 3
Maentwrog. Gwyn 6F 32
Maen-y-groes. Cdgn 1K 15
Maer. Staf 6F 34
Maerdy. Carm 2F 16
Maerdy. Cnwy 6K 33
Maerdy. Rhon 5J 17
Maesbrook. Shrp 7B 34
Maesbury. Shrp 7B 34
Maesbury Marsh. Shrp 7B 34
Maes-glas. Flin 3L 33
Maesgwyn-Isaf. Powy 1L 25
Maeshafn. Den 4M 33
Maes Llyn. Cdgn 2K 15
Maesmynis. Powy 8K 25
**Maesteg**. B'end 5H 17
Maestir. Cdgn 8E 24
Maesybont. Carm 3E 16
Maesycrugiau. Carm 2L 15
Maesycwmmer. Cphy 5L 17
Maesyrhandir. Powy 3K 25
Magdalen Laver. Essx 3B 22
Maggieknockater. Mor 1C 72
Maghaberry. Lis 5G 93
Magham Down. E Sus 4C 12
Maghera. M Ulst 3F 93
Maghera. New M 7H 93
Magherafelt. M Ulst 4F 93
Magheralin. Arm 6G 93
Magheramason. Derr 3C 92
Magheraveely. Ferm 7D 92
Maghery. Arm 5F 93
**Maghull**. Mers 7B 40
Magna Park. Leics 3C 28
Magor. Mon 5C 18
Magpie Green. Suff 4G 31
Maguiresbridge. Ferm 7C 92
Magwyr. Mon 5C 18
Maidenbower. W Sus 2K 11
Maiden Bradley. Wilts 2G 9
Maidencombe. Torb 5M 5
Maidenhayne. Devn 6A 8
**Maidenhead**. Wind 5F 20
Maiden Law. Dur 7E 54
Maiden Newton. Dors 6D 8
Maidens. S Ayr 1H 51
Maiden's Green. Brac 6F 20
Maidensgrove. Oxon 5E 20
Maidenwell. Corn 4D 4
Maidenwell. Linc 2L 37
Maiden Wells. Pemb 7F 14
Maidford. Nptn 6D 28
Maids Moreton. Buck 8E 28
**Maidstone**. Kent 8D 22
Maidwell. Nptn 4E 28
Mail. Shet 5E 90
Maindee. Newp 5B 18
Mainsforth. Dur 8G 55
Mains of Auchindachy. Mor 1D 72
Mains of Auchnagatt. Abers 1J 73
Mains of Drum. Abers 6H 73
Mains of Edingight. Mor 8E 80
Mainsriddle. Dum 6D 52
Mainstone. Shrp 3A 26
Maisemore. Glos 1G 19
Major's Green. Worc 4K 27
Makeney. Derbs 5A 36
Makerstoun. Bord 6D 60
Malacleit. W Isl 6J 75
Malaig. High 6H 69
Malaig Bheag. High 6H 69
Malborough. Devn 8K 5
Malcoff. Derbs 1J 35
Malcolmburn. Mor 8C 80
Malden Rushett. G Lon 7J 21
**Maldon**. Essx 3E 22
Malham. N Yor 1H 41
Maligar. High 7F 76
Malinslee. Telf 1E 26
Mallaig. High 6H 69
Malleny Mills. Edin 3K 59
Mallows Green. Essx 1A 22
Malltraeth. IOA 4D 32
Mallusk. Ant 4H 93
Mallwyd. Gwyn 1H 25
Malmesbury. Wilts 5H 19
Malmsmead. Devn 1G 7
Malpas. Ches W 5C 34
Malpas. Corn 4M 3
Malpas. Newp 4B 18
Malswick. Glos 1F 18
**Maltby**. S Yor 8C 42
Maltby. Stoc T 4B 48
Maltby le Marsh. Linc 1A 38
Malt Lane. Arg 7E 64
Maltman's Hill. Kent 1F 12
Malton. N Yor 8E 48
Malvern Link. Worc 7F 26
Malvern Wells. Worc 7F 26
Mamble. Worc 4E 26
Mamhilad. Mon 3B 18
Manaccan. Corn 6L 3
Manafon. Powy 2L 25
Manais. W Isl 5C 76
Manaton. Devn 7G 7
Manby. Linc 1L 37
Mancetter. Warw 2M 27
**Manchester**. G Man 8G 41
Manchester Airport. G Man 1G 35
Mancot. Flin 3B 34
Manea. Cambs 3A 30
Maney. W Mid 2K 27
Manfield. N Yor 4L 47
**Mangotsfield**. S Glo 6E 18
Mangurstadh. W Isl 8D 82
Mankinholes. W Yor 5H 41
Manley. Ches W 2D 34
Manmoel. Cphy 4L 17
Mannal. Arg 3E 62
Mannerston. Falk 2J 59
Manningford Bohune. Wilts 8K 19
Manningford Bruce. Wilts 8K 19
Manningham. W Yor 4K 41
Mannings Heath. W Sus 3K 11
Mannington. Dors 5J 9
Manningtree. Essx 8H 31
Mannofield. Aber 5J 73
Manorbier. Pemb 7G 15
Manorbier Newton. Pemb 7G 15
Manordeilo. Carm 2F 16
Manorowen. Pemb 3F 14
Manor Park. G Lon 5M 21
Mansell Gamage. Here 7B 26
Mansell Lacy. Here 7C 26
Mansergh. Cumb 7E 46
Mansewood. Glas 3D 58
Mansfield. E Ayr 8E 58
**Mansfield**. Notts 3C 36
**Mansfield Woodhouse**.
Notts 3C 36
Mansriggs. Cumb 7A 46
Manston. Dors 4G 9
Manston. Kent 7K 23
Manston. W Yor 4A 42
Manswood. Dors 5H 9
Manthorpe. Linc
nr. Bourne 8H 37
nr. Grantham 6G 37
Manton. N Lin 7G 43
Manton. Notts 2C 36
Manton. Rut 1F 28
Manton. Wilts 7K 19
Manuden. Essx 1A 22
Maperton. Som 3E 8
Maplebeck. Notts 3E 36
Maple Cross. Herts 4H 21
Mapledurham. Oxon 6D 20
Mapledurwell. Hants 8D 20
Maplehurst. W Sus 3J 11
Maplescombe. Kent 7B 22
Mapleton. Derbs 5K 35
Mapperley. Derbs 5B 36
Mapperley. Nott 5C 36
Mapperley Park. Nott 5C 36
Mapperton. Dors
nr. Beaminster 6D 8
nr. Poole 6H 9
Mappleborough Green.
Warw 5J 27
Mappleton. E Yor 3K 43
Mapplewell. S Yor 7M 41
Mappowder. Dors 5F 8
Maraig. W Isl 3D 76
Marazion. Corn 5J 3
Marbhig. W Isl 2F 76
Marbury. Ches E 5D 34
**March**. Cambs 2M 29
Marcham. Oxon 4B 20
Marchamley. Shrp 7D 34
Marchington. Staf 6K 35
Marchington Woodlands.
Staf 7K 35
Marchwiel. Wrex 5B 34
Marchwood. Hants 4A 10
Marcross. V Glam 8J 17
Marden. Here 7D 26
Marden. Kent 1D 12
Marden. Wilts 8J 19
Marden Beech. Kent 1D 12
Marden Thorn. Kent 1D 12
Mardu. Shrp 3A 26
Mardy. Mon 2B 18
Marefield. Leics 1E 28
Mareham le Fen. Linc 3K 37
Mareham on the Hill. Linc 3K 37
Marehay. Derbs 5B 36
Marehill. W Sus 4H 11
Maresfield. E Sus 3A 12
Marfleet. Hull 5J 43
Marford. Wrex 4B 34
Margam. Neat 6G 17
Margaret Marsh. Dors 4G 9
Margaret Roding. Essx 2B 22
Margaretting. Essx 3C 22
Margaretting Tye. Essx 3C 22
**Margate**. Kent 6K 23
Margery. Surr 8K 21
Margnaheglish. N Ayr 6K 57
Marham. Norf 1D 30
Marhamchurch. Corn 5B 6
Marholm. Pet 1J 29
Marian Cwm. Den 3K 33
Mariandyrys. IOA 2F 32
Marian-glas. IOA 2E 32
Mariansleigh. Devn 3G 7
Marian-y-de. Gwyn 7C 32
Marian-y-mor. Gwyn 7C 32
Marine Town. Kent 6F 22
Marishader. High 7F 76
Marjoriebanks. Dum 3E 52
Mark. Dum 6G 51
Mark. Som 1B 8
Markbeech. Kent 1A 12
Markby. Linc 2A 38
Mark Causeway. Som 1B 8
Mark Cross. E Sus 2B 12
Markeaton. Derb 6M 35
Market Bosworth. Leics 1B 28
**Market Deeping**. Linc 8J 37
Market Drayton. Shrp 6E 34
Market End. Warw 3M 27
**Market Harborough**. Leics 3E 28
Markethill. Arm 7F 93
Markethill. Per 4F 66
Market Lavington. Wilts 8J 19
Market Overton. Rut 8F 36
Market Rasen. Linc 1J 37
Market Stainton. Linc 1K 37
Market Weighton. E Yor 3F 42
Market Weston. Suff 4F 30
Markfield. Leics 8B 36
Markham. Cphy 4L 17
Markinch. Fife 7F 66
Markington. N Yor 1L 41
Marksbury. Bath 7E 18
Mark's Corner. IOW 6B 10
Marks Tey. Essx 1F 22
Markwell. Corn 6F 4
Markyate. Herts 2H 21
Marlborough. Wilts 7K 19
Marlcliff. Warw 6J 27
Marldon. Devn 5L 5
Marle Green. E Sus 4B 12
Marlesford. Suff 6K 31
Marley Green. Ches E 5D 34
Marley Hill. Tyne 6F 54
Marlingford. Norf 1H 31
Mar Lodge. Abers 7L 71
Marloes. Pemb 6D 14
**Marlow**. Buck 5F 20
Marlow. Here 4B 26
Marlow Bottom. Buck 5F 20
Marlow Common. Buck 5F 20
Marlpit Hill. Kent 1M 11
Marlpits. E Sus 3M 11
Marlpool. Derbs 5B 36
Marnhull. Dors 4F 8
Marnoch. Abers 8E 80
Marnock. N Lan 3F 58
**Marple**. G Man 1H 35
Marr. S Yor 7C 42
Marrel. High 2L 79
Marrick. N Yor 6J 47
Marrister. Shet 1F 90
Marros. Carm 6J 15
Marsden. Tyne 5G 55
Marsden. W Yor 6J 41
Marsett. N Yor 7H 47
Marsh. Buck 3F 20
Marsh. Devn 4A 8
The Marsh. Powy 2B 26
The Marsh. Shrp 7E 34
Marshall Meadows. Nmbd 4G 61
Marshalsea. Dors 5B 8
Marshalswick. Herts 3J 21
Marsham. Norf 7H 39
Marshaw. Lanc 2D 40
Marsh Baldon. Oxon 4C 20
Marsh Benham. W Ber 7B 20
Marshborough. Kent 8K 23
Marshbrook. Shrp 3C 26
Marshchapel. Linc 8L 43
Marshfield. Newp 5A 18
Marshfield. S Glo 6F 18
Marshgate. Corn 6A 6
Marsh Gibbon. Buck 1D 20
Marsh Green. Devn 6K 7
Marsh Green. Kent 1M 11
Marsh Green. Staf 4G 35
Marsh Green. Telf 8E 34
Marsh Lane. Derbs 2B 36
Marsh Side. Norf 5D 38
Marshside. Kent 7J 23
Marshside. Mers 6B 40
Marsh Street. Som 1J 7
Marshwood. Dors 6B 8
Marske. N Yor 5K 47
Marske-by-the-Sea. Red C 3D 48
Marston. Ches W 2E 34
Marston. Here 6B 26
Marston. Linc 5F 36
Marston. Oxon 3C 20
Marston. Staf
nr. Stafford 7H 35
nr. Wheaton Aston 8G 35
Marston. Warw 2L 27
Marston. Wilts 8H 19
Marston Doles. Warw 6B 28
Marston Green. W Mid 3K 27
Marston Hill. Glos 4K 19
Marston Jabbett. Warw 3A 28
Marston Magna. Som 3D 8
Marston Meysey. Wilts 4K 19
Marston Montgomery.
Derbs 6K 35
Marston Moretaine. C Beds 7G 29
Marston on Dove. Derbs 7L 35
Marston St Lawrence. Nptn 7C 28
Marston Stannett. Here 6D 26
Marston Trussell. Nptn 3D 28
Marstow. Here 2D 18
Marsworth. Buck 2G 21
Marten. Wilts 8L 19
Marthall. Ches E 2G 35
Martham. Norf 8L 39
Marthwaite. Cumb 6E 46
Martin. Hants 4J 9
Martin. Kent 1K 13
Martin. Linc
nr. Horncastle 3K 37
nr. Metheringham 4J 37
Martindale. Cumb 4C 46
Martin Dales. Linc 3J 37
Martin Drove End. Hants 3J 9
Martinhoe. Devn 1F 6
Martinhoe Cross. Devn 1F 6
Martin Hussingtree. Worc 5G 27
Martin Mill. Kent 1K 13
Martinscroft. Warr 1E 34
Martin's Moss. Ches E 3G 35
Martinstown. Dors 7E 8
Martinstown. ME Ant 3G 93
Martlesham. Suff 7J 31
Martlesham Heath. Suff 7J 31
Martletwy. Pemb 5G 15
Martley. Worc 5F 26
Martock. Som 4C 8
Marton. Ches E 3G 35
Marton. Cumb 7M 45
Marton. E Yor
nr. Bridlington 1K 43
nr. Hull 4J 43
Marton. Linc 1F 36
Marton. Midd 4C 48
Marton. N Yor
nr. Boroughbridge 1B 42
nr. Pickering 7E 48
Marton. Shrp
nr. Myddle 7C 34
nr. Worthen 1A 26
Marton. Warw 5B 28
Marton Abbey. N Yor 1C 42
Marton-le-Moor. N Yor 8A 48
Martyr's Green. Surr 8H 21
Martyr Worthy. Hants 2C 10
Marwick. Orkn 7B 88
Marwood. Devn 2E 6
Marybank. High
nr. Dingwall 8E 78
nr. Invergordon 6H 79
Maryburgh. High 8F 78
Maryfield. Corn 6G 5
Maryhill. Glas 3D 58
Marykirk. Abers 1K 67
**Marylebone**. G Lon 5K 21
Marylebone. G Man 7D 40
Marypark. Mor 2A 72
**Maryport**. Cumb 8E 52
Maryport. Dum 8G 51
Marystow. Devn 7D 6
Mary Tavy. Devn 8E 6
Maryton. Ang
nr. Kirriemuir 2G 67
nr. Montrose 2K 67
Marywell. Abers 6E 72
Marywell. Ang 3K 67
Masham. N Yor 7L 47
Mashbury. Essx 2C 22
Masongill. N Yor 8E 46
Masons Lodge. Abers 5H 73
Mastin Moor. Derbs 2B 36
Mastrick. Aber 5J 73
Matching. Essx 2B 22
Matching Green. Essx 2B 22
Matching Tye. Essx 2B 22
Matfen. Nmbd 4D 54
Matfield. Kent 1C 12
Mathern. Mon 4D 18
Mathon. Here 7F 26
Mathry. Pemb 3E 14
Matlaske. Norf 6H 39
**Matlock**. Derbs 4L 35
Matlock Bath. Derbs 4L 35
Matterdale End. Cumb 3B 46
Mattersey. Notts 1D 36
Mattersey Thorpe. Notts 1D 36
Mattingley. Hants 8E 20
Mattishall. Norf 8G 39
Mattishall Burgh. Norf 8G 39
Mauchline. E Ayr 7C 58
Maud. Abers 1J 73
Maudlin. Corn 5C 4
Maugersbury. Glos 1K 19
Maughold. IOM 5D 44
Maulden. C Beds 8H 29
Maulds Meaburn. Cumb 4E 46
Maunby. N Yor 7A 48
Maund Bryan. Here 6D 26
Mautby. Norf 8L 39
Mavesyn Ridware. Staf 8J 35
Mavis Enderby. Linc 3L 37
Mawbray. Cumb 7E 52
Mawdesley. Lanc 6C 40
Mawdlam. B'end 6H 17
Mawgan. Corn 6L 3
Mawgan Porth. Corn 2M 3
Maw Green. Ches E 4F 34
Mawla. Corn 4L 3
Mawnan. Corn 6L 3
Mawnan Smith. Corn 6L 3
Mawsley Village. Nptn 4E 28
Mawthorpe. Linc 2A 38
Maxey. Pet 1J 29
Maxstoke. Warw 3L 27
Maxted Street. Kent 1H 13
Maxton. Kent 1J 13
Maxton. Bord 6D 60
Maxwellheugh. Bord 6E 60
Maxwelltown. Dum 4D 52
Maxworthy. Corn 6B 6
Mayals. Swan 6F 16
Maybole. S Ayr 8B 58
Maybush. Sotn 4A 10
Maydown. Derr 3D 92
Mayes Green. Surr 2J 11
Mayfield. E Sus 3B 12
**Mayfield**. Midl 3A 60
Mayfield. Per 5D 66
Mayfield. Staf 5K 35
Mayford. Surr 8G 21
Mayhill. Swan 5F 16
Mayland. Essx 3F 22
Maylandsea. Essx 3F 22
Maynard's Green. E Sus 4B 12
Mayobridge. New M 7G 93
Maypole. IOS 1H 3
Maypole. Kent 7J 23
Maypole. Mon 2C 18
Maypole Green. Norf 2L 31
Maypole Green. Suff 6F 30
Maywick. Shet 5D 90
Mazetown. Lis 5H 93
Mead. Devn 4B 6
Meadgate. Bath 8E 18
Meadle. Buck 3F 20
Meadowbank. Ches W 3E 34
Meadowfield. Dur 8F 54
Meadow Green. Here 6F 26
Meadowmill. E Lot 2B 60
Meadows. Nott 6C 36
Meadowtown. Shrp 1B 26
Meadwell. Devn 7D 6
Meaford. Staf 6G 35
Mealabost. W Isl
nr. Borgh 6H 83
nr. Stornoway 8H 83
Mealasta. W Isl 1A 76
Meal Bank. Cumb 6D 46
Mealrigg. Cumb 7F 52
Mealsgate. Cumb 7G 53
Meanwood. W Yor 4L 41
Mearbeck. N Yor 1G 41
Meare. Som 1C 8
Meare Green. Som
nr. Curry Mallet 3A 8
nr. Stoke St Gregory 3B 8
Mears Ashby. Nptn 5F 28
Measham. Leics 8M 35
Meath Green. Surr 1K 11
Meathop. Cumb 7C 46
Meaux. E Yor 4H 43
Meavy. Devn 5H 5
Medbourne. Leics 2E 28
Medburn. Nmbd 4E 54
Meddon. Devn 4B 6
Meden Vale. Notts 3C 36
Medlam. Linc 4L 37
Medlicott. Shrp 2C 26
Medmenham. Buck 5F 20
Medomsley. Dur 6E 54
Medstead. Hants 2D 10
**Medway Towns**. Medw 7D 22
Meerbrook. Staf 3H 35
Meer End. W Mid 4L 27
Meers Bridge. Linc 1A 38
Meesden. Herts 8M 29
Meeson. Telf 7E 34
Meeth. Devn 5E 6
Meeting Green. Suff 6D 30
Meeting House Hill. Norf 7K 39
Meidrim. Carm 4J 15
Meifod. Powy 1L 25
Meigh. New M 7G 93
Meigle. Per 3F 66
Meikle Earnock. S Lan 4F 58
Meikle Kilchattan Butts. Arg 4K 57
Meikleour. Per 4E 66
Meikle Tarty. Abers 3J 73
Meikle Wartle. Abers 2G 73
Meinciau. Carm 5L 15
Meir. Stoke 5H 35
Meir Heath. Staf 5H 35
Melbourn. Cambs 7L 29
Melbourne. Derbs 7A 36
Melbourne. E Yor 3E 42
Melbury Abbas. Dors 3G 9
Melbury Bubb. Dors 5D 8
Melbury Osmond. Dors 5D 8
Melbury Sampford. Dors 5D 8
Melby. Shet 2B 90
Melchbourne. Bed 5H 29
Melcombe Bingham. Dors 5F 8
Melcombe Regis. Dors 7E 8
Meldon. Devn 6E 6
Meldon. Nmbd 3E 54
Meldreth. Cambs 7L 29
Melfort. Arg 6C 64
Melgarve. High 6E 70
Meliden. Den 2K 33
Melinbyrhedyn. Powy 3H 25
Melincourt. Neat 4H 17
Melin-y-coed. Cnwy 4H 33
Melin-y-ddol. Powy 2K 25
Melin-y-wig. Den 6K 33
Melkington. Nmbd 5F 60
Melkinthorpe. Cumb 3D 46
Melkridge. Nmbd 5M 53
**Melksham**. Wilts 7H 19
Mellangaun. High 5K 77
Melldalloch. Arg 2J 57
Mellguards. Cumb 7J 53
Melling. Lanc 8D 46
Melling. Mers 7B 40
Melling Mount. Mers 7C 40
Mellis. Suff 4G 31
Mellon Charles. High 4K 77
Mellon Udrigle. High 4K 77
Mellor. G Man 1H 35
Mellor. Lanc 4E 40
Mellor Brook. Lanc 4E 40
Mells. Som 1F 8
Melmerby. Cumb 8L 53
Melmerby. N Yor
nr. Middleham 7J 47
nr. Ripon 8M 47
Melplash. Dors 6C 8
Melrose. Bord 6C 60
Melsetter. Orkn 3D 86
Melsonby. N Yor 5K 47
Meltham. W Yor 6K 41
Meltham Mills. W Yor 6K 41
Melton. E Yor 5G 43
Melton. Suff 6J 31
Meltonby. E Yor 2E 42
Melton Constable. Norf 6G 39
**Melton Mowbray**. Leics 8E 36
Melton Ross. N Lin 6H 43
Melvaig. High 5J 77
Melverley. Shrp 8B 34
Melverley Green. Shrp 8B 34
Melvich. High 5L 85
Membury. Devn 5A 8
Memsie. Abers 7J 81
Memus. Ang 2H 67
Menabilly. Corn 6C 4
Menai Bridge. IOA 3E 32
Mendham. Suff 3J 31
Mendlesham. Suff 5H 31
Mendlesham Green. Suff 5G 31
Menethorpe. N Yor 1E 42
Menheniot. Corn 5E 4
Menithwood. Worc 5F 26
Menna. Corn 6B 4
Mennock. Dum 1C 52
Menston. W Yor 3K 41
Menstrie. Clac 8B 66
Menthorpe. N Yor 4E 42
Mentmore. Buck 2G 21
Meole Brace. Shrp 8C 34
Meols. Mers 1M 33
Meon. Hants 5C 10
Meonstoke. Hants 3D 10
Meopham. Kent 7C 22
Meopham Green. Kent 7C 22
Meopham Station. Kent 7C 22
Mepal. Cambs 3M 29
Meppershall. C Beds 8J 29
Merbach. Here 7B 26
Mercaston. Derbs 5L 35
Merchiston. Edin 2L 59
Mere. Ches E 1F 34
Mere. Wilts 2G 9
Mere Brow. Lanc 6C 40
Mereclough. Lanc 4G 41
Mere Green. W Mid 2K 27
Mere Green. Worc 5H 27
Mere Heath. Ches W 2E 34
Mereside. Bkpl 4B 40
Meretown. Staf 7F 34
Mereworth. Kent 8C 22
Meriden. W Mid 3L 27
Merkadale. High 2E 68
Merkland. S Ayr 2H 51
Merkland Lodge. High 1D 78
Merley. Pool 6J 9
Merlin's Bridge. Pemb 5F 14
Merridge. Som 2M 7
Merrington. Shrp 7C 34
Merrion. Pemb 7F 14
Merriott. Som 4C 8
Merrivale. Devn 8E 6
Merrow. Surr 8H 21
Merrybent. Darl 4L 47
Merry Lees. Leics 1B 28
Merrymeet. Corn 5E 4
Mersham. Kent 2G 13
Merstham. Surr 8K 21
Merston. W Sus 5F 10
Merstone. IOW 7C 10
Merther. Corn 7A 4
Merthyr. Carm 4K 15
Merthyr Cynog. Powy 1J 17
Merthyr Dyfan. V Glam 7L 17
Merthyr Mawr. B'end 7H 17
**Merthyr Tudful**. Mer T 4K 17
**Merthyr Tydfil**. Mer T 4K 17
Merthyr Vale. Mer T 5K 17
Merton. Devn 4E 6
**Merton**. G Lon 7K 21
Merton. Norf 2F 30
Merton. Oxon 2C 20
Meshaw. Devn 4G 7
Messing. Essx 2E 22
Messingham. N Lin 7F 42
Metcombe. Devn 6K 7
Metfield. Suff 3J 31
Metherell. Corn 5G 5
Metheringham. Linc 3H 37
Methil. Fife 8G 67
Methilhill. Fife 8G 67
Methley. W Yor 5A 42
Methley Junction. W Yor 5A 42
Methlick. Abers 2H 73
Methven. Per 5D 66
Methwold. Norf 2D 30
Methwold Hythe. Norf 2D 30
Mettingham. Suff 3K 31
Metton. Norf 6H 39
Mevagissey. Corn 7C 4
**Mexborough**. S Yor 7B 42
Mey. High 4D 86
Meysey Hampton. Glos 4K 19
Miabhag. W Isl 4C 76
Miabhaig. W Isl
nr. Cliasmol 3B 76
nr. Timsgearraidh 8D 82
Mial. High 6J 77
Michaelchurch. Here 1D 18
Michaelchurch Escley. Here 8B 26
Michaelchurch-on-Arrow.
Powy 7M 25
Michaelston-le-Pit. V Glam 7L 17
Michaelston-y-Fedw. Newp 6M 17
Michaelstow. Corn 4C 4
Michelcombe. Devn 5J 5
Micheldever. Hants 2C 10
Micheldever Station. Hants 1C 10
Michelmersh. Hants 3M 9
Mickfield. Suff 5H 31
Micklebring. S Yor 8C 42
Mickleby. N Yor 4F 48
Micklefield. W Yor 4B 42
Micklefield Green. Herts 4H 21
Mickleham. Surr 8J 21
Mickleover. Derb 6M 35
Micklethwaite. Cumb 6G 53
Micklethwaite. W Yor 3K 41
Mickleton. Dur 3H 47
Mickleton. Glos 7K 27
Mickletown. W Yor 5A 42
Mickle Trafford. Ches W 3C 34
Mickley. N Yor 8L 47
Mickley Green. Suff 6E 30
Mickley Square. Nmbd 5D 54
Mid Ardlaw. Abers 7J 81
Midbea. Orkn 5D 88
Mid Beltie. Abers 5F 72
Mid Calder. W Lot 3J 59
Mid Clyth. High 8D 86
Middle Assendon. Oxon 5E 20
Middle Aston. Oxon 1B 20
Middle Barton. Oxon 1B 20
Middlebie. Dum 4G 53
Middle Chinnock. Som 4C 8
Middle Claydon. Buck 1E 20
Middlecliffe. S Yor 7B 42
Middlecott. Devn 7G 7
Middle Drums. Ang 2J 67
Middle Duntisbourne. Glos 3H 19
Middle Essie. Abers 8K 81
Middleforth Green. Lanc 5D 40
Middleham. N Yor 7K 47
Middle Handley. Derbs 2B 36
Middle Harling. Norf 3F 30
Middlehope. Shrp 3C 26
Middle Littleton. Worc 7J 27
Middle Maes-coed. Here 8B 26
Middlemarsh. Dors 5E 8
Middle Marwood. Devn 2E 6
Middle Mayfield. Staf 5K 35
Middlemoor. Devn 8D 6
Middlemuir. Abers
nr. New Deer 1H 73
nr. Strichen 8J 81
Middle Rainton. Tyne 7G 55
Middle Rasen. Linc 1H 37
The Middles. Dur 6F 54
**Middlesbrough**. Midd 4B 48
Middlesceugh. Cumb 7H 53
Middleshaw. Cumb 7D 46
Middlesmoor. N Yor 8J 47
Middlestone. Dur 8F 54
Middlestone Moor. Dur 8F 54
Middle Stoughton. Som 1C 8
Middlestown. W Yor 6L 41
Middle Street. Glos 3F 18
Middle Taphouse. Corn 5D 4
Middleton. Ang 3J 67
Middleton. Arg 3E 62
Middleton. Cumb 7E 46
Middleton. Derbs
nr. Bakewell 3K 35
nr. Wirksworth 4L 35
Middleton. Essx 8E 30
**Middleton**. G Man 7G 41
Middleton. Hants 1B 10
Middleton. Hart 8J 55
Middleton. Here 5D 26
Middleton. IOW 7M 9
Middleton. Lanc 2C 40
Middleton. Midl 4A 60
Middleton. Norf 8C 38
Middleton. Nptn 3F 28
Middleton. Nmbd
nr. Belford 6J 61
nr. Morpeth 3D 54
Middleton. N Yor
nr. Ilkley 3K 41
nr. Pickering 7E 48
Middleton. Per 7E 66
Middleton. Shrp
nr. Ludlow 4D 26
nr. Oswestry 7B 34
Middleton. Suff 5L 31
Middleton. Swan 8L 15
Middleton. Warw 2K 27
Middleton. W Yor 5L 41
Middleton Cheney. Nptn 7C 28
Middleton Green. Staf 6H 35
Middleton-in-Teesdale. Dur 3H 47
Middleton One Row. Darl 4A 48
Middleton-on-Leven. N Yor 5B 48
Middleton-on-Sea. W Sus 5G 11
Middleton on the Hill. Here 5D 26
Middleton-on-the-Wolds.
E Yor 3G 43
Middleton Priors. Shrp 2E 26
Middleton Quernhow. N Yor 8M 47
Middleton St George. Darl 4M 47
Middleton Scriven. Shrp 3E 26
Middleton Stoney. Oxon 1C 20
Middleton Tyas. N Yor 5L 47
Middle Town. IOS 1H 3
Middletown. Arm 7E 92
Middletown. Cumb 4J 45
Middletown. Powy 8B 34
Middle Tysoe. Warw 7M 27
Middle Wallop. Hants 2L 9
**Middlewich**. Ches E 3F 34
Middle Winterslow. Wilts 2L 9
Middlewood. Corn 8B 6
Middlewood. S Yor 8M 41
Middle Woodford. Wilts 2K 9
Middlewood Green. Suff 5G 31
Middleyard. Glos 3G 19
Middlezoy. Som 2B 8
Middridge. Dur 3L 47
Midelney. Som 3C 8
Midfield. High 5H 85
Midford. Bath 7F 18
Mid Garrary. Dum 4L 51
Midge Hall. Lanc 5D 40
Midgeholme. Cumb 6L 53
Midgham. W Ber 7C 20
Midgley. W Yor
nr. Halifax 5J 41
nr. Horbury 6L 41
Mid Ho. Shet 4K 91
Midhopestones. S Yor 8L 41
Midhurst. W Sus 3F 10
Mid Kirkton. N Ayr 4L 57
Mid Lambrook. Som 4C 8
Midland. Orkn 1E 86
Mid Lavant. W Sus 5F 10
Midlem. Bord 7C 60
Midney. Som 3D 8
**Midsomer Norton**. Bath 8E 18
Midton. Inv 2M 57
Midtown. High
nr. Poolewe 5K 77
nr. Tongue 5H 85
Midville. Linc 4L 37
Mid Walls. Shet 3B 90
Mid Yell. Shet 4K 91
Migdale. High 4G 79
Migvie. Abers 5D 72
Milborne Port. Som 4E 8
Milborne St Andrew. Dors 6G 9
Milborne Wick. Som 3E 8
Milbourne. Nmbd 4E 54
Milbourne. Wilts 5H 19
Milburn. Cumb 3E 46
Milbury Heath. S Glo 4E 18
Milby. N Yor 1B 42
Milcombe. Oxon 8B 28
Milden. Suff 7F 30
**Mildenhall**. Suff 4D 30
Mildenhall. Wilts 7L 19
Milebrook. Powy 4B 26
Milebush. Kent 1D 12
Mile End. Cambs 3C 30
Mile End. Essx 1F 22
Mileham. Norf 8F 38
Mile Oak. Brig 5K 11
Miles Green. Staf 4G 35
Miles Hope. Here 5D 26
Milesmark. Fife 1J 59
Mile Town. Kent 6F 22
Milfield. Nmbd 6G 61
Milford. Arm 6F 93
Milford. Derbs 5A 36
Milford. Devn 3B 6
Milford. Powy 3K 25
Milford. Staf 7H 35
Milford. Surr 1G 11
**Milford Haven**. Pemb 6F 14
Milford on Sea. Hants 6L 9
Milkwall. Glos 3D 18
Milkwell. Wilts 3H 9
Milland. W Sus 3F 10
Mill Bank. W Yor 5J 41
Millbank. Ant 4H 93
Millbank. High 5C 86
Millbay. ME Ant 4J 93
Millbeck. Cumb 3A 46
Millbounds. Orkn 6E 88
Millbreck. Abers 1K 73
Millbridge. Surr 1F 10
Millbrook. C Beds 8H 29
Millbrook. Corn 6G 5
Millbrook. G Man 8H 41
Millbrook. ME Ant 3H 93
Millbrook. Sotn 4A 10
Mill Common. Suff 3L 31
Mill Corner. E Sus 3E 12
Milldale. Staf 4K 35
Millden Lodge. Ang 8E 72
Milldens. Ang 2J 67
Millearn. Per 6C 66
Mill End. Buck 5E 20
Mill End. Cambs 6C 30
Mill End. Glos 2K 19
Mill End. Herts 8L 29
Millend. Glos 4F 18
Millerhill. Midl 3M 59
Miller's Dale. Derbs 2K 35
Millers Green. Derbs 4L 35
Millerston. Glas 3E 58
Millfield. Abers 6D 72
Millfield. Pet 1J 29
Millgate. Lanc 6G 41
Mill Green. Essx 3C 22
Mill Green. Norf 3H 31
Mill Green. Shrp 7E 34
Mill Green. Staf 7J 35
Mill Green. Suff 7F 30
Millhalf. Here 7A 26
Millhall. E Ren 4D 58
Millhayes. Devn
nr. Honiton 5M 7
nr. Wellington 4L 7
Millhead. Lanc 8C 46
Millheugh. S Lan 4F 58
Mill Hill. Bkbn 5E 40
Mill Hill. G Lon 4K 21
Millholme. Cumb 6D 46
Millhouse. Arg 2J 57
Millhouse. Cumb 8H 53
Millhousebridge. Dum 3F 52
Millhouses. S Yor 1M 35
Millikenpark. Ren 3C 58
Millington. E Yor 2F 42
Millington Green. Derbs 5L 35
Millisle. Ards 5J 93
Mill Knowe. Arg 7G 57
Mill Lane. Hants 8E 20
Millmeece. Staf 6G 35
Mill of Craigievar. Abers 4E 72
Mill of Fintray. Abers 4H 73
Mill of Haldane. W Dun 1C 58
Millom. Cumb 6L 45
Millow. C Beds 7K 29
Millpool. Corn 4D 4
Millport. N Ayr 4L 57
Mill Side. Cumb 7C 46
Mill Street. Norf
nr. Lyng 8G 39
nr. Swanton Morley 8G 39
Millthorpe. Derbs 2M 35
Millthorpe. Linc 6J 37
Millthrop. Cumb 6E 46
Milltimber. Aber 5H 73
Mill Town. Ant 4G 93
Milltown. Abers
nr. Corgarff 5B 72
nr. Lumsden 4D 72
Milltown. Ant 4G 93
Milltown. Arm
nr. Banbridge 6G 93
nr. Coalisland 5F 93
nr. Richhill 6F 93
Milltown. Corn 6D 4
Milltown. Derbs 3A 36
Milltown. Devn 2E 6
Milltown. Dum 4H 53
Milltown of Aberdalgie. Per 5D 66
Milltown of Auchindoun.
Mor 1C 72
Milltown of Campfield.
Abers 5F 72
Milltown of Edinvillie. Mor 1B 72
Milltown of Rothiemay. Mor 1E 72
Milltown of Towie. Abers 4D 72
Milnacraig. Ang 2F 66
Milnathort. Per 7E 66
**Milngavie**. E Dun 2D 58
Milnholm. Stir 1F 58
**Milnrow**. G Man 6H 41
Milnthorpe. Cumb 7C 46
Milnthorpe. W Yor 6M 41
Milson. Shrp 4E 26
Milstead. Kent 8F 22
Milston. Wilts 1K 9
Milthorpe. Nptn 7C 28
Milton. Ang 3G 67
Milton. Cambs 5A 30
Milton. Cumb
nr. Brampton 5K 53
nr. Crooklands 7D 46
Milton. Derbs 7M 35
Milton. Dum
nr. Crocketford 4C 52
nr. Glenluce 6H 51
Milton. Glas 3D 58
Milton. High
nr. Achnasheen 8D 78
nr. Applecross 1J 69
nr. Drumnadrochit 2E 70
nr. Invergordon 6H 79
nr. Inverness 1F 70
nr. Wick 6E 86
Milton. Mor
nr. Cullen 7E 80
nr. Tomintoul 4A 72
Milton. N Som 7B 18
Milton. Notts 2E 36
Milton. Oxon
nr. Bloxham 8B 28
nr. Didcot 4B 20
Milton. Pemb 6G 15
Milton. Port 6D 10
Milton. Som 3C 8
Milton. S Ayr 7C 58
Milton. Stir
nr. Aberfoyle 7K 65
nr. Drymen 8J 65
Milton. Stoke 4H 35
Milton. W Dun 2C 58
Milton Abbas. Dors 5G 9
Milton Abbot. Devn 8D 6
Milton Auchlossan. Abers 5E 72
Milton Bridge. Midl 3L 59
Milton Bryan. C Beds 8G 29
Milton Clevedon. Som 2E 8
Milton Coldwells. Abers 2J 73
Milton Combe. Devn 5G 5
Milton Common. Oxon 3D 20
Milton Damerel. Devn 4C 6
Miltonduff. Mor 7A 80
Milton End. Glos 3K 19
Milton Ernest. Bed 6H 29
Milton Green. Ches W 4C 34
Milton Hill. Devn 8J 7
Milton Hill. Oxon 4B 20
**Milton Keynes**. Mil 8F 28
Milton Keynes Village. Mil 8F 28
Milton Lilbourne. Wilts 7K 19
Milton Malsor. Nptn 6E 28
Milton Morenish. Per 4L 65
Milton of Auchinhove. Abers 5E 72
Milton of Balgonie. Fife 7G 67
Milton of Barras. Abers 8H 73
Milton of Campsie. E Dun 2E 58
Milton of Cultoquhey. Per 5B 66
Milton of Cushnie. Abers 4E 72
Milton of Finavon. Ang 2H 67
Milton of Gollanfield. High 8H 79
Milton of Lesmore. Abers 3D 72
Milton of Leys. High 1G 71
Milton of Tullich. Abers 6C 72
Milton on Stour. Dors 3F 8
Milton Regis. Kent 7E 22
Milton Street. E Sus 5B 12
Milton-under-Wychwood.
Oxon 2L 19
Milverton. Som 3L 7
Milverton. Warw 5M 27
Milwich. Staf 6H 35
Mimbridge. Surr 7G 21
Minard. Arg 8D 64
Minchington. Dors 4H 9
Minchinhampton. Glos 3G 19
Mindrum. Nmbd 6F 60
Minehead. Som 1J 7
Minera. Wrex 4A 34
Minerstown. New M 7J 93
Minety. Wilts 4J 19
Minffordd. Gwyn 7E 32
Mingarrypark. High 1A 64
Mingary. High 1L 63
Mingearraidh. W Isl 3D 74
Miningsby. Linc 3L 37
Minions. Corn 8B 6
Minishant. S Ayr 8B 58
Minllyn. Gwyn 1H 25
Minnigaff. Dum 5K 51
Minorca. IOM 6D 44
Minskip. N Yor 1A 42
Minstead. Hants 4L 9
Minsted. W Sus 3F 10
Minster. Kent
nr. Ramsgate 7K 23
**Minster**. Kent
nr. Sheerness 6F 22
Minsteracres. Nmbd 6D 54
Minsterley. Shrp 1B 26
Minster Lovell. Oxon 2M 19
Minsterworth. Glos 2F 18
Minterne Magna. Dors 5E 8
Minterne Parva. Dors 5E 8
Minting. Linc 2J 37
Mintlaw. Abers 1K 73
Minto. Bord 7C 60
Minton. Shrp 2C 26
Minwear. Pemb 5G 15
Minworth. W Mid 2K 27
Miodar. Arg 3F 62
Mirbister. Orkn 7C 88
Mirehouse. Cumb 3J 45
Mireland. High 5E 86
**Mirfield**. W Yor 6L 41
Miserden. Glos 3H 19
Miskin. Rhon 6K 17
Misson. Notts 8D 42
Misterton. Leics 3C 28
Misterton. Notts 8E 42
Misterton. Som 5C 8
Mistley. Essx 8H 31
Mistley Heath. Essx 8H 31
**Mitcham**. G Lon 7K 21
Mitcheldean. Glos 2E 18
Mitchell. Corn 6A 4
Mitchel Troy. Mon 2C 18
Mitcheltroy Common. Mon 3C 18
Mitford. Nmbd 3E 54
Mithian. Corn 3L 3
Mitton. Staf 8G 35
Mixbury. Oxon 8D 28
Mixenden. W Yor 5J 41
Mixon. Staf 4J 35
Moaness. Orkn 1D 86
Moarfield. Shet 3K 91
Moat. Cumb 4J 53
Moats Tye. Suff 6G 31
Mobberley. Ches E 2F 34
Mobberley. Staf 5J 35
Moccas. Here 7B 26
Mochdre. Cnwy 3H 33
Mochdre. Powy 4K 25
Mochrum. Dum 7J 51
Mockbeggar. Hants 5K 9
Mockerkin. Cumb 2K 45
Modbury. Devn 6J 5
Moddershall. Staf 6H 35
Modsarie. High 5J 85
Moelfre. Cnwy 3J 33
Moelfre. IOA 2E 32
Moelfre. Powy 8L 33
Moffat. Dum 1E 52
Moggerhanger. C Beds 7J 29
Mogworthy. Devn 4H 7
Moira. Leics 8M 35
Moira. Lis 5G 93
Molash. Kent 8G 23
Mol-chlach. High 4F 68
Mold. Flin 4M 33
Molehill Green. Essx 1B 22
Molescroft. E Yor 3H 43
Molesden. Nmbd 3E 54
Molesworth. Cambs 4H 29
Moll. High 3G 69
Molland. Devn 3H 7
Mollington. Ches W 2B 34
Mollington. Oxon 7B 28
Mollinsburn. N Lan 2F 58
Monachty. Cdgn 6E 24
Monachyle. Stir 6J 65
Monar Lodge. High 1C 70
Monaughty. Powy 6M 25
Monea. Ferm 6B 92

Monewden—North Kilvington


Monewden. Suff 6J 31
Moneydie. Per 5D 66
Moneyglass. Ant 4G 93
Moneymore. M Ulst 4F 93
Moneyneany. M Ulst 4E 92
Moneyreagh. Lis 5J 93
Moneyrow Green. Wind 6F 20
Moneyslane. Arm 7H 93
Moniaive. Dum 2B 52
Monifieth. Ang 4J 67
Monikie. Ang 4J 67
Monimail. Fife 6F 66
Monington. Pemb 2H 15
Monk Bretton. S Yor 7A 42
Monken Hadley. G Lon 4K 21
Monk Fryston. N Yor 5C 42
Monk Hesleden. Dur 8H 55
Monkhide. Here 7E 26
Monkhill. Cumb 6H 53
Monkhopton. Shrp 2E 26
Monkland. Here 6C 26
Monkleigh. Devn 3D 6
Monknash. V Glam 7J 17
Monkokehampton. Devn 5E 6
Monkseaton. Tyne 4G 55
Monks Eleigh. Suff 7F 30
Monk's Gate. W Sus 3K 11
Monk's Heath. Ches E 2G 35
Monk Sherborne. Hants 8D 20
Monkshill. Abers 1G 73
Monksilver. Som 2K 7
Monks Kirby. Warw 3B 28
Monk Soham. Suff 5J 31
Monk Soham Green. Suff 5J 31
Monkspath. W Mid 4K 27
Monks Risborough. Buck 3F 20
Monksthorpe. Linc 3M 37
Monkstown. Ant 4H 93
Monk Street. Essx 1C 22
Monkswood. Mon 3B 18
Monkton. Devn 5L 7
Monkton. Kent 7J 23
Monkton. Pemb 6F 14
Monkton. S Ayr 7B 58
Monkton Combe. Bath 7F 18
Monkton Deverill. Wilts 2G 9
Monkton Farleigh. Wilts 7G 19
Monkton Heathfield. Som 3A 8
Monktonhill. S Ayr 7B 58
Monkton Up Wimborne. Dors 4J 9
Monkton Wyld. Dors 6B 8
Monkwearmouth. Tyne 6G 55
Monkwood. Dors 6C 8
Monkwood. Hants 2D 10
Monmarsh. Here 7D 26
Monmouth. Mon 2D 18
Monnington on Wye. Here 7B 26
Monreith. Dum 7J 51
Montacute. Som 4C 8
Monteith. Arm 6G 93
Montford. Arg 3L 57
Montford. Shrp 8C 34
Montford Bridge. Shrp 8C 34
Montgarrie. Abers 4E 72
Montgarswood. E Ayr 7D 58
Montgomery. Powy 3M 25
Montgreenan. N Ayr 5B 58
Montrave. Fife 7G 67
**Montrose**. Ang 2L 67
Monxton. Hants 1M 9
Monyash. Derbs 3K 35
Monymusk. Abers 4F 72
Monzie. Per 5B 66
Moodiesburn. N Lan 2E 58
Moon's Green. Kent 3E 12
Moonzie. Fife 6G 67
Moor. Som 4C 8
The Moor. Kent 3D 12
Moor Allerton. W Yor 4L 41
Moorbath. Dors 6C 8
Moorbrae. Shet 5J 91
Moorby. Linc 3K 37
Moorcot. Here 6B 26
Moor Crichel. Dors 5H 9
Moor Cross. Devn 6J 5
Moordown. Bour 6J 9
Moore. Hal 1D 34
Moor End. E Yor 4F 42
Moorend. Dum 4G 53
Moorend. Glos
nr. Dursley 3F 18
nr. Gloucester 2G 19
Moorends. S Yor 6D 42
Moorfields. ME Ant 4G 93
Moorgate. S Yor 8B 42
Moor Green. Wilts 7G 19
Moorgreen. Hants 4B 10
Moorgreen. Notts 5B 36
Moorhaigh. Notts 3C 36
Moorhall. Derbs 2M 35
Moorhampton. Here 7B 26
Moorhouse. Cumb
nr. Carlisle 6H 53
nr. Wigton 6G 53
Moorhouse. Notts 3E 36
Moorhouse. Surr 8M 21
Moorhouses. Linc 4K 37
Moorland. Som 2B 8
Moorlinch. Som 2C 8
Moor Monkton. N Yor 2C 42
Moor of Granary. Mor 8L 79
Moor Row. Cumb
nr. Whitehaven 3K 45
nr. Wigton 7G 53
Moorsholm. Red C 4D 48
Moorside. Dors 4F 8
Moorside. G Man 7H 41
Moortown. Devn 6C 6
Moortown. Hants 5K 9
Moortown. IOW 7B 10
Moortown. Linc 8H 43
Moortown. M Ulst 5F 93
Moortown. Telf 8E 34
Moortown. W Yor 4M 41
Morangie. High 5H 79
Morar. High 6H 69
Morborne. Cambs 2J 29
Morchard Bishop. Devn 5G 7
Morcombelake. Dors 6C 8
Morcott. Rut 1G 29
Morda. Shrp 7A 34
**Morden**. G Lon 7K 21
Mordiford. Here 8D 26
Mordon. Dur 3M 47
More. Shrp 2B 26
Morebath. Devn 3J 7
Morebattle. Bord 7E 60
**Morecambe**. Lanc 1C 40
Morefield. High 4B 78
Moreleigh. Devn 6K 5
Morenish. Per 4K 65
Moresby Parks. Cumb 3J 45
Morestead. Hants 3C 10
Moreton. Dors 7G 9
Moreton. Essx 3B 22
Moreton. Here 5D 26
**Moreton**. Mers 8A 40
Moreton. Oxon 3D 20
Moreton. Staf 8F 34
Moreton Corbet. Shrp 7D 34
Moretonhampstead. Devn 7G 7
Moreton-in-Marsh. Glos 8L 27
Moreton Jeffries. Here 7E 26
Moreton Morrell. Warw 6M 27
Moreton on Lugg. Here 7D 26
Moreton Pinkney. Nptn 7C 28
Moreton Say. Shrp 6E 34
Moreton Valence. Glos 3F 18
Morfa. Cdgn 1K 15
Morfa Bach. Carm 5K 15
Morfa Bychan. Gwyn 7E 32
Morfa Glas. Neat 4H 17
Morfa Nefyn. Gwyn 6B 32
Morganstown. Card 6L 17
Morgan's Vale. Wilts 3K 9
Morham. E Lot 2C 60
Moriah. Cdgn 5F 24
Morland. Cumb 3D 46
Morley. Ches E 1G 35
Morley. Derbs 5A 36
Morley. Dur 3K 47
**Morley**. W Yor 5L 41
Morley St Botolph. Norf 2G 31
Morningside. Edin 2L 59
Morningside. N Lan 4G 59
Morningthorpe. Norf 2J 31
**Morpeth**. Nmbd 3F 54
Morrey. Staf 8K 35
Morridge Side. Staf 4J 35
Morridge Top. Staf 3J 35
Morrington. Dum 3C 52
Morris Green. Essx 8D 30
Morriston. Swan 5F 16
Morston. Norf 5G 39
Mortehoe. Devn 1D 6
Morthen. S Yor 1B 36
Mortimer. W Ber 7D 20
Mortimer's Cross. Here 5C 26
Mortimer West End. Hants 7D 20
Mortomley. S Yor 8M 41
Morton. Cumb
nr. Calthwaite 8J 53
nr. Carlisle 6H 53
Morton. Derbs 3B 36
Morton. Linc
nr. Bourne 7H 37
nr. Gainsborough 8F 42
nr. Lincoln 3F 36
Morton. Norf 8H 39
Morton. Notts 4E 36
Morton. Shrp 7A 34
Morton. S Glo 4E 18
Morton Bagot. Warw 5K 27
Morton Mill. Shrp 7D 34
Morton-on-Swale. N Yor 6M 47
Morton Tinmouth. Dur 3K 47
Morvah. Corn 5H 3
Morval. Corn 6E 4
Morvich. High
nr. Golspie 3H 79
nr. Shiel Bridge 3L 69
Morvil. Pemb 3G 15
Morville. Shrp 2E 26
Morwenstow. Corn 4B 6
Morwick. Nmbd 1F 54
**Mosborough**. S Yor 1B 36
Moscow. E Ayr 5C 58
Mose. Shrp 2F 26
Mosedale. Cumb 8H 53
Moseley. W Mid
nr. Birmingham 3J 27
nr. Wolverhampton 1H 27
Moseley. Worc 6G 27
Moss. Arg 3E 62
Moss. High 1A 64
Moss. S Yor 6C 42
Moss. Wrex 4B 34
Mossatt. Abers 4D 72
Moss Bank. Mers 8D 40
Mossbank. Shet 6J 91
Mossblown. S Ayr 7C 58
Mossbrow. G Man 1F 34
Mossburnford. Bord 8D 60
Mossdale. Dum 4A 52
Mossedge. Cumb 5J 53
Mossend. N Lan 3F 58
Mossgate. Staf 6H 35
Moss Lane. Ches E 2H 35
Mossley. Ant 4H 93
Mossley. Ches E 3G 35
**Mossley**. G Man 7H 41
Mossley Hill. Mers 1B 34
Moss of Barmuckity. Mor 7B 80
Mosspark. Glas 3D 58
Mosspaul. Bord 2J 53
Moss Side. Cumb 6F 52
Moss Side. G Man 8G 41
Moss Side. Lanc
nr. Blackpool 4B 40
nr. Preston 5D 40
Moss Side. Mers 7B 40
Moss-Side. Caus 2G 93
Moss-side. High 8J 79
Moss-side of Cairness.
Abers 7K 81
Mosstodloch. Mor 7C 80
Mosswood. Nmbd 6D 54
Mossy Lea. Lanc 6D 40
Mosterton. Dors 5C 8
Moston. Shrp 7D 34
Moston Green. Ches E 3F 34
Mostyn. Flin 2L 33
Mostyn Quay. Flin 2L 33
Motcombe. Dors 3G 9
Mothecombe. Devn 7J 5
Motherby. Cumb 3C 46
**Motherwell**. N Lan 4F 58
Mottingham. G Lon 6M 21
Mottisfont. Hants 3M 9
Mottistone. IOW 7B 10
**Mottram in Longdendale**.
G Man 8H 41
Mottram St Andrew. Ches E 2G 35
Mott's Mill. E Sus 2B 12
Mouldsworth. Ches W 2D 34
Moulin. Per 2C 66
Moulsecoomb. Brig 5L 11
Moulsford. Oxon 5C 20
Moulsoe. Mil 7G 29
Moulton. Ches W 3E 34
Moulton. Linc 7L 37
Moulton. Nptn 5E 28
Moulton. N Yor 5L 47
Moulton. Suff 5C 30
Moulton. V Glam 7K 17
Moulton Chapel. Linc 8K 37
Moulton Eaugate. Linc 8L 37
Moulton St Mary. Norf 1K 31
Moulton Seas End. Linc 7L 37
Mount. Corn
nr. Bodmin 5D 4
nr. Newquay 3L 3
**Mountain Ash**. Rhon 5K 17
Mountain Cross. Bord 5K 59
Mountain Street. Kent 8G 23
Mountain Water. Pemb 4F 14
Mount Ambrose. Corn 4L 3
Mountbenger. Bord 7M 59
Mountblow. W Dun 2C 58
Mount Bures. Essx 8F 30
Mountfield. E Sus 3D 12
Mountfield. Ferm 5D 92
Mountgerald. High 7F 78
Mount Hawke. Corn 4L 3
Mount High. High 7G 79
Mountjoy. Corn 5A 4
Mountjoy. Ferm 5D 92
Mount Lothian. Midl 4L 59
Mountnessing. Essx 4C 22
Mountnorris. Arm 7F 93
Mounton. Mon 4D 18
Mount Pleasant. Buck 8D 28
Mount Pleasant. Ches E 4G 35
Mount Pleasant. Derbs
nr. Derby 5M 35
nr. Swadlincote 8L 35
Mount Pleasant. E Sus 4M 11
Mount Pleasant. Hants 6L 9
Mount Pleasant. Norf 2F 30
Mount Skippett. Oxon 2A 20
Mountsorrel. Leics 8C 36
Mount Stuart. Arg 4L 57
Mousehole. Corn 6H 3
Mouswald. Dum 4E 52
Mow Cop. Ches E 4G 35
Mowden. Darl 4L 47
Mowhaugh. Bord 7F 60
Mowmacre Hill. Leic 1C 28
Mowsley. Leics 3D 28
Moy. High 2H 71
Moy. M Ulst 6F 93
Moygashel. M Ulst 5F 93
Moylgrove. Pemb 2H 15
Moy Lodge. High 7E 70
Muasdale. Arg 5F 56
Muchalls. Abers 6J 73
Much Birch. Here 8D 26
Much Cowarne. Here 7E 26
Much Dewchurch. Here 8C 26
Muchelney. Som 3C 8
Muchelney Ham. Som 3C 8
Much Hadham. Herts 2M 21
Much Hoole. Lanc 5C 40
Muchlarnick. Corn 6E 4
Much Marcle. Here 8E 26
Muchrachd. High 2C 70
Much Wenlock. Shrp 1E 26
Mucking. Thur 5C 22
Muckle Breck. Shet 1F 90
Muckleford. Dors 6E 8
Mucklestone. Staf 6F 34
Muckleton. Norf 6E 38
Muckleton. Shrp 7D 34
Muckley. Shrp 2E 26
Muckley Corner. Staf 1J 27
Muckton. Linc 1L 37
Mudale. High 8H 85
Muddiford. Devn 2E 6
Mudeford. Dors 6K 9
Mudford. Som 4D 8
Mudgley. Som 1C 8
Mugdock. Stir 2D 58
Mugeary. High 2F 68
Muggington. Derbs 5L 35
Muggintonlane End. Derbs 5L 35
Muggleswick. Dur 6D 54
Mugswell. Surr 8K 21
Muie. High 3G 79
Muirden. Abers 8G 81
Muirdrum. Ang 4J 67
Muiredge. Per 5F 66
Muirend. Glas 3D 58
Muirhead. Ang 4G 67
Muirhead. Fife 7F 66
Muirhead. N Lan 3E 58
Muirhouses. Falk 1J 59
Muirkirk. E Ayr 7E 58
Muir of Alford. Abers 4E 72
Muir of Fairburn. High 8E 78
Muir of Fowlis. Abers 4E 72
Muir of Miltonduff. Mor 8A 80
Muir of Ord. High 8F 78
Muir of Tarradale. High 8F 78
Muirshearlich. High 7B 70
Muirtack. Abers 2J 73
Muirton. High 7H 79
Muirton. Per 5E 66
Muirton of Ardblair. Per 3E 66
Muirtown. Per 6C 66
Muiryfold. Abers 8G 81
Muker. N Yor 6H 47
Mulbarton. Norf 1H 31
Mulben. Mor 8C 80
Mulindry. Arg 4C 56
Mulla. Shet 1E 90
Mullach Charlabhaigh. W Isl 7F 82
Mullacott. Devn 1E 6
Mullaghbane. New M 7F 93
Mullaghboy. ME Ant 3J 93
Mullaghglass. New M 7G 93
Mullion. Corn 7K 3
Mullion Cove. Corn 7K 3
Mumbles. Swan 6F 16
Mumby. Linc 2B 38
Munderfield Row. Here 6E 26
Munderfield Stocks. Here 6E 26
Mundesley. Norf 6K 39
Mundford. Norf 2E 30
Mundham. Norf 2K 31
Mundon. Essx 3E 22
Munerigie. High 5C 70
Muness. Shet 3L 91
Mungasdale. High 4L 77
Mungrisdale. Cumb 8H 53
Munlochy. High 8G 79
Munsley. Here 7E 26
Munslow. Shrp 3D 26
Murchington. Devn 7F 6
Murcot. Worc 7J 27
Murcott. Oxon 2C 20
Murdishaw. Hal 1D 34
Murieston. W Lot 3J 59
Murkle. High 5C 86
Murlaggan. High 6M 69
Murra. Orkn 1D 86
The Murray. S Lan 4E 58
Murrayfield. Edin 2L 59
Murrell Green. Hants 8E 20
Murroes. Ang 4H 67
Murrow. Cambs 1L 29
Mursley. Buck 1F 20
Murthly. Per 4D 66
Murton. Cumb 3F 46
Murton. Dur 7G 55
Murton. Nmbd 5G 61
Murton. Swan 6E 16
Murton. York 2D 42
Musbury. Devn 6A 8
Muscoates. N Yor 7D 48
Muscott. Nptn 5D 28
**Musselburgh**. E Lot 2M 59
Muston. Leics 6F 36
Muston. N Yor 8H 49
Mustow Green. Worc 4G 27
Muswell Hill. G Lon 5K 21
Mutehill. Dum 7A 52
Mutford. Suff 3L 31
Muthill. Per 6B 66
Mutterton. Devn 5K 7
Muxton. Telf 8F 34
Mwmbwls. Swan 6F 16
Mybster. High 6C 86
Myddfai. Carm 1G 17
Myddle. Shrp 7C 34
Mydroilyn. Cdgn 1L 15
Myerscough. Lanc 4C 40
Mylor Bridge. Corn 5M 3
Mylor Churchtown. Corn 5M 3
Mynachlog-ddu. Pemb 3H 15
Mynydd-bach. Mon 4C 18
Mynydd Isa. Flin 3A 34
Mynyddislwyn. Cphy 5L 17
Mynydd Llandegai. Gwyn 4F 32
Mynydd Mechell. IOA 1C 32
Mynydd-y-briw. Powy 8L 33
Mynyddygarreg. Carm 6L 15
Mynytho. Gwyn 7C 32
Myrebird. Abers 6G 73
Myrelandhorn. High 6D 86
Mytchett. Surr 8F 20
The Mythe. Glos 8G 27
Mytholmroyd. W Yor 5J 41
Myton-on-Swale. N Yor 1B 42
Mytton. Shrp 8C 34


## N


Naast. High 5K 77
Na Buirgh. W Isl 4B 76
Naburn. York 3C 42
Nab Wood. W Yor 4K 41
Nackington. Kent 8H 23
Nacton. Suff 7J 31
Nafferton. E Yor 2H 43
Na Gearrannan. W Isl 7E 82
Nailbridge. Glos 2E 18
Nailsbourne. Som 3M 7
**Nailsea**. N Som 6C 18
Nailstone. Leics 1B 28
Nailsworth. Glos 4G 19
Nairn. High 8J 79
Nalderswood. Surr 1K 11
Nancegollan. Corn 5K 3
Nancledra. Corn 5H 3
Nangreaves. G Man 6G 41
Nanhyfer. Pemb 3G 15
Nannerch. Flin 4L 33
Nanpantan. Leics 8C 36
Nanpean. Corn 6B 4
Nanstallon. Corn 5C 4
Nant-ddu. Powy 3K 17
Nanternis. Cdgn 1K 15
Nantgaredig. Carm 4L 15
Nantgarw. Rhon 6L 17
Nant Glas. Powy 6J 25
Nantglyn. Den 4K 33
Nantgwyn. Powy 5J 25
Nantlle. Gwyn 5E 32
Nantmawr. Shrp 7A 34
Nantmel. Powy 6K 25
Nantmor. Gwyn 6F 32
Nant Peris. Gwyn 5F 32
**Nantwich**. Ches E 4E 34
Nant-y-bai. Carm 8G 25
Nant-y-bwch. Blae 3L 17
Nant-y-Derry. Mon 3B 18
Nant-y-dugoed. Powy 1J 25
Nant-y-felin. Cnwy 3F 32
Nantyffyllon. B'end 5H 17
Nantyglo. Blae 3L 17
Nant-y-meichiaid. Powy 1L 25
Nant-y-moel. B'end 5J 17
Nant-y-pandy. Cnwy 3F 32
Naphill. Buck 4F 20
Nappa. N Yor 2G 41
Napton on the Hill. Warw 5B 28
Narberth. Pemb 5H 15
Narberth Bridge. Pemb 5H 15
Narborough. Leics 2C 28
Narborough. Norf 8D 38
Narkurs. Corn 6F 4
The Narth. Mon 3D 18
Narthwaite. Cumb 6F 46
Nasareth. Gwyn 5D 32
Naseby. Nptn 4D 28
Nash. Buck 8E 28
Nash. Here 5B 26
Nash. Kent 8J 23
Nash. Newp 5B 18
Nash. Shrp 4E 26
Nash Lee. Buck 3F 20
Nassington. Nptn 2H 29
Nasty. Herts 1L 21
Natcott. Devn 3B 6
Nateby. Cumb 5F 46
Nateby. Lanc 3C 40
Nately Scures. Hants 8E 20
Natland. Cumb 7D 46
Naughton. Suff 7G 31
Naunton. Glos 1K 19
Naunton. Worc 8G 27
Naunton Beauchamp. Worc 6H 27
Navenby. Linc 4G 37
Navestock. Essx 4B 22
Navestock Side. Essx 4B 22
Navidale. High 2L 79
Nawton. N Yor 7D 48
Nayland. Suff 8F 30
Nazeing. Essx 3M 21
Neacroft. Hants 6K 9
Nealhouse. Cumb 6H 53
Neal's Green. Warw 3M 27
Near Sawrey. Cumb 6B 46
Neasden. G Lon 5K 21
Neasham. Darl 4M 47
**Neath**. Neat 5G 17
Neath Abbey. Neat 5G 17
Neatishead. Norf 7K 39
Neaton. Norf 1F 30
Nebo. Cdgn 6E 24
Nebo. Cnwy 5H 33
Nebo. Gwyn 5D 32
Nebo. IOA 1D 32
Necton. Norf 1E 30
Nedd. High 8D 84
Nedderton. Nmbd 3F 54
Nedging. Suff 7G 31
Nedging Tye. Suff 7G 31
Needham. Norf 3J 31
Needham Market. Suff 6G 31
Needham Street. Suff 5D 30
Needingworth. Cambs 4L 29
Needwood. Staf 7K 35
Neen Savage. Shrp 4E 26
Neen Sollars. Shrp 4E 26
Neenton. Shrp 3E 26
Nefyn. Gwyn 6C 32
Neilston. E Ren 4C 58
Neithrop. Oxon 7B 28
Nelly Andrews Green. Powy 1A 26
Nelson. Cphy 5L 17
**Nelson**. Lanc 4G 41
Nelson Village. Nmbd 4F 54
Nemphlar. S Lan 5G 59
Nempnett Thrubwell. Bath 7D 18
Nene Terrace. Linc 1K 29
Nenthall. Cumb 7A 54
Nenthead. Cumb 7A 54
Nenthorn. Bord 6D 60
Nercwys. Flin 4M 33
Neribus. Arg 4B 56
Nerston. S Lan 4E 58
Nesbit. Nmbd 6G 61
Nesfield. N Yor 3J 41
Ness. Ches W 2B 34
Nesscliffe. Shrp 8B 34
Ness of Tenston. Orkn 8B 88
**Neston**. Ches W 2A 34
Neston. Wilts 7G 19
Nethanfoot. S Lan 5G 59
Nether Alderley. Ches E 2G 35
Netheravon. Wilts 1K 9
Nether Blainslie. Bord 5C 60
Netherbrae. Abers 8G 81
Netherbrough. Orkn 8C 88
Nether Broughton. Leics 7D 36
Netherburn. S Lan 5G 59
Nether Burrow. Lanc 8E 46
Netherbury. Dors 6C 8
Netherby. Cumb 4H 53
Nether Careston. Ang 2J 67
Nether Cerne. Dors 6E 8
Nether Compton. Dors 4D 8
Nethercote. Glos 1K 19
Nethercote. Warw 5C 28
Nethercott. Devn 2D 6
Nethercott. Oxon 1B 20
Nether Dallachy. Mor 7C 80
Nether Durdie. Per 5F 66
Nether End. Derbs 2L 35
Netherend. Glos 3D 18
Nether Exe. Devn 5J 7
Netherfield. E Sus 4D 12
Netherfield. Notts 5D 36
Nethergate. Norf 7G 39
Netherhampton. Wilts 3K 9
Nether Handley. Derbs 2B 36
Nether Haugh. S Yor 8B 42
Nether Heage. Derbs 4A 36
Nether Heyford. Nptn 6D 28
Netherhouses. Cumb 7A 46
Nether Howcleugh. S Lan 8J 59
Nether Kellet. Lanc 1D 40
Nether Kinmundy. Abers 1K 73
Netherland Green. Staf 6K 35
Nether Langwith. Notts 2C 36
Netherlaw. Dum 7B 52
Netherley. Abers 6H 73
Nethermill. Dum 3E 52
Nethermills. Mor 8E 80
Nether Moor. Derbs 3A 36
Nether Padley. Derbs 2L 35
Netherplace. E Ren 4D 58
Nether Poppleton. York 2C 42
Netherseal. Derbs 8L 35
Nether Silton. N Yor 6B 48
Nether Stowey. Som 2L 7
Nether Street. Essx 2B 22
Netherstreet. Wilts 7H 19
Netherthird. E Ayr 8D 58
Netherthong. W Yor 7K 41
Netherton. Ang 2J 67
Netherton. Cumb 8E 52
Netherton. Devn 8H 7
Netherton. Hants 8A 20
Netherton. Here 1D 18
Netherton. Mers 8B 40
Netherton. N Lan 4F 58
Netherton. Nmbd 1C 54
Netherton. Per 2E 66
Netherton. Shrp 3F 26
Netherton. Stir 2D 58
Netherton. W Mid 3H 27
Netherton. W Yor
nr. Armitage Bridge 6K 41
nr. Horbury 6L 41
Netherton. Worc 7H 27
Nethertown. Cumb 4J 45
Nethertown. High 4E 86
Nethertown. Staf 8K 35
Nether Urquhart. Fife 7E 66
Nether Wallop. Hants 2M 9
Nether Wasdale. Cumb 4L 45
Nether Welton. Cumb 7H 53
Nether Westcote. Glos 1L 19
Nether Whitacre. Warw 2L 27
Nether Winchendon. Buck 2E 20
Netherwitton. Nmbd 2E 54
Nether Worton. Oxon 8B 28
Nethy Bridge. High 3L 71
Netley. Shrp 1C 26
Netley Abbey. Hants 5B 10
Netley Marsh. Hants 4M 9
Nettlebed. Oxon 5E 20
Nettlebridge. Som 1E 8
Nettlecombe. Dors 6D 8
Nettlecombe. IOW 8C 10
Nettleden. Herts 2H 21
Nettleham. Linc 2H 37
Nettlestead. Kent 8C 22
Nettlestead Green. Kent 8C 22
Nettlestone. IOW 6D 10
Nettlesworth. Dur 7F 54
Nettleton. Linc 7J 43
Nettleton. Wilts 6G 19
Netton. Devn 7H 5
Netton. Wilts 2K 9
Neuadd. Powy 2K 25
The Neuk. Abers 6G 73
Nevendon. Essx 4D 22
Nevern. Pemb 3G 15
New Abbey. Dum 5D 52
New Aberdour. Abers 7H 81
**New Addington**. G Lon 7L 21
Newall. W Yor 3L 41
New Alresford. Hants 2C 10
New Alyth. Per 3F 66
Newark. Orkn 5G 89
Newark. Pet 1K 29
**Newark-on-Trent**. Notts 4E 36
New Arley. Warw 3L 27
Newarthill. N Lan 4F 58
New Ash Green. Kent 7C 22
New Balderton. Notts 4F 36
New Barn. Kent 7C 22
New Barnetby. N Lin 6H 43
Newbattle. Midl 3M 59
New Bewick. Nmbd 7H 61
Newbie. Dum 5F 52
Newbiggin. Cumb
nr. Appleby 3E 46
nr. Barrow-in-Furness 8M 45
nr. Cumrew 7K 53
nr. Penrith 3C 46
nr. Seascale 5K 45
Newbiggin. Dur
nr. Consett 7E 54
nr. Holwick 3H 47
Newbiggin. Nmbd 7C 54
Newbiggin. N Yor
nr. Askrigg 6H 47
nr. Filey 7J 49
nr. Thoralby 7H 47
Newbiggin-by-the-Sea.
Nmbd 3G 55
Newbigging. Ang
nr. Monikie 4H 67
nr. Newtyle 3F 66
nr. Tealing 4H 67
Newbigging. Edin 2K 59
Newbigging. S Lan 5J 59
Newbiggin-on-Lune. Cumb 5F 46
Newbold. Derbs 2A 36
Newbold. Leics 8B 36
Newbold on Avon. Warw 4B 28
Newbold on Stour. Warw 7L 27
Newbold Pacey. Warw 6L 27
Newbold Verdon. Leics 1B 28
New Bolingbroke. Linc 4L 37
Newborough. IOA 4D 32
Newborough. Pet 1K 29
Newborough. Staf 7K 35
Newbottle. Nptn 8C 28
Newbottle. Tyne 6G 55
New Boultham. Linc 2G 37
Newbourne. Suff 7J 31
New Brancepeth. Dur 7F 54
New Bridge. Dum 4D 52
Newbridge. Cphy 5M 17
Newbridge. Cdgn 1M 15
Newbridge. Corn 5H 3
Newbridge. Edin 2K 59
Newbridge. Hants 4L 9
Newbridge. IOW 7B 10
Newbridge. N Yor 7F 48
Newbridge. Pemb 3F 14
Newbridge. Wrex 5A 34
Newbridge Green. Worc 8G 27
Newbridge-on-Usk. Mon 4B 18
Newbridge on Wye. Powy 7K 25
New Brighton. Flin 3A 34
New Brighton. Hants 5E 10
New Brighton. Mers 8B 40
New Brinsley. Notts 4B 36
Newbrough. Nmbd 5B 54
New Broughton. Wrex 4B 34
New Buckenham. Norf 2G 31
New Buildings. Derr 3D 92
Newbuildings. Devn 5G 7
Newburgh. Abers 3J 73
Newburgh. Fife 6F 66
Newburgh. Lanc 6C 40
**Newburn**. Tyne 5E 54
**Newbury**. W Ber 7B 20
Newbury. Wilts 1G 9
Newby. Cumb 3D 46
Newby. N Yor
nr. Ingleton 8F 46
nr. Scarborough 7H 49
nr. Stokesley 4C 48
Newby Bridge. Cumb 7B 46
Newby Cote. N Yor 8F 46
Newby East. Cumb 6J 53
Newby Head. Cumb 3D 46
New Byth. Abers 8H 81
Newby West. Cumb 6H 53
Newby Wiske. N Yor 7A 48
Newcastle. Ards 6K 93
Newcastle. B'end 6H 17
Newcastle. Mon 2C 18
Newcastle. New M 7H 93
Newcastle. Shrp 4M 25
Newcastle Emlyn. Carm 2K 15
Newcastle International Airport.
Tyne 4E 54
Newcastleton. Bord 3J 53
**Newcastle-under-Lyme**.
Staf 5G 35
**Newcastle upon Tyne**.
Tyne 5F 54
Newchapel. Pemb 3J 15
Newchapel. Powy 4J 25
Newchapel. Staf 4G 35
Newchapel. Surr 1L 11
New Cheriton. Hants 3C 10
Newchurch. Carm 4K 15
Newchurch. Here 6B 26
Newchurch. IOW 7C 10
Newchurch. Kent 2G 13
Newchurch. Lanc 5G 41
Newchurch. Mon 4C 18
Newchurch. Powy 7M 25
Newchurch. Staf 7K 35
Newchurch in Pendle. Lanc 4G 41
New Costessey. Norf 8H 39
Newcott. Devn 5M 7
New Cowper. Cumb 7F 52
Newcraighall. Edin 2M 59
New Crofton. W Yor 6A 42
New Cross. Cdgn 5F 24
New Cross. Som 4C 8
New Cumnock. E Ayr 8E 58
New Deer. Abers 1H 73
New Denham. Buck 5H 21
Newdigate. Surr 1J 11
New Duston. Nptn 5E 28
New Earswick. York 2D 42
New Edlington. S Yor 8C 42
New Elgin. Mor 7B 80
New Ellerby. E Yor 4J 43
Newell Green. Brac 6F 20
New Eltham. G Lon 6M 21
New End. Warw 5K 27
New End. Worc 6J 27
Newenden. Kent 3E 12
New England. Essx 7D 30
New England. Pet 1J 29
Newent. Glos 1F 18
New Ferry. Mers 1B 34
Newfield. Dur
nr. Chester-le-Street 6F 54
nr. Willington 8F 54
Newfound. Hants 8C 20
New Fryston. W Yor 5B 42
Newgale. Pemb 4E 14
New Galloway. Dum 4M 51
Newgate. Norf 5G 39
Newgate Street. Herts 3L 21
New Greens. Herts 3J 21
New Grimsby. IOS 1G 3
New Hainford. Norf 8J 39
Newhall. Ches E 5E 34
Newhall. Derbs 7L 35
Newham. Nmbd 7J 61
New Hartley. Nmbd 4G 55
Newhaven. Derbs 3K 35
**Newhaven**. E Sus 5M 11
Newhaven. Edin 2L 59
New Haw. Surr 7H 21
New Hedges. Pemb 6H 15
New Herrington. Tyne 6G 55
Newhey. G Man 6H 41
New Holkham. Norf 6E 38
New Holland. N Lin 5H 43
Newholm. N Yor 4F 48
New Houghton. Derbs 3C 36
New Houghton. Norf 7D 38
Newhouse. N Lan 3F 58
New Houses. N Yor 8G 47
New Hutton. Cumb 6D 46
New Hythe. Kent 8D 22
Newick. E Sus 3M 11
Newingreen. Kent 2H 13
Newington. Edin 2L 59
Newington. Kent
nr. Folkestone 2H 13
nr. Sittingbourne 7E 22
Newington. Notts 8D 42
Newington. Oxon 4D 20
Newington Bagpath. Glos 4G 19
New Inn. Carm 3L 15
New Inn. Mon 3C 18
New Inn. N Yor 8G 47
New Inn. Torf 4B 18
New Invention. Shrp 4A 26
New Kelso. High 1L 69
New Lanark. S Lan 5G 59
Newland. Glos 3D 18
Newland. Hull 4H 43
Newland. N Yor 5D 42
Newland. Som 2H 7
Newland. Worc 7F 26
Newlandrig. Midl 3A 60
Newlands. Cumb 8H 53
Newlands. High 1H 71
Newlands. Nmbd 6D 54
Newlands. Staf 7J 35
Newlands of Geise. High 5B 86
Newlands of Tynet. Mor 7C 80
Newlands Park. IOA 2B 32
New Lane. Lanc 6C 40
New Lane End. Warr 8E 40
New Langholm. Dum 3H 53
New Leake. Linc 4M 37
New Leeds. Abers 8J 81
New Lenton. Nott 6C 36
New Longton. Lanc 5D 40
Newlot. Orkn 8E 88
New Luce. Dum 5G 51
Newlyn. Corn 6H 3
Newmachar. Abers 4H 73
Newmains. N Lan 4G 59
New Mains of Ury. Abers 7H 73
**New Malden**. G Lon 7K 21
Newman's Green. Suff 7E 30
**Newmarket**. Suff 5C 30
Newmarket. W Isl 8H 83
New Marske. Red C 3D 48
New Marton. Shrp 6B 34
New Micklefield. W Yor 4B 42
New Mill. Abers 1G 73
New Mill. Corn 5H 3
New Mill. Herts 2G 21
New Mill. W Yor 7K 41
New Mill. Wilts 7K 19
Newmill. Ant 4H 93
Newmill. Mor 8D 80
Newmill. Bord 8B 60
Newmillerdam. W Yor 6M 41
New Mills. Corn 6A 4
New Mills. Derbs 1J 35
New Mills. Mon 3D 18
New Mills. Powy 2K 25
Newmills. Arm 6G 93
Newmills. Fife 1J 59
Newmills. High 7G 79
Newmills. M Ulst 5F 93
Newmiln. Per 4E 66
Newmilns. E Ayr 6D 58
**New Milton**. Hants 6L 9
New Mistley. Essx 8H 31
New Moat. Pemb 4G 15
Newmore. High
nr. Dingwall 8F 78
nr. Invergordon 6G 79
Newnham. Cambs 6M 29
Newnham. Glos 2E 18
Newnham. Hants 8E 20
Newnham. Herts 8K 29
Newnham. Kent 8F 22
Newnham. Nptn 6C 28
Newnham. Warw 5K 27
Newnham Bridge. Worc 5E 26
New Ollerton. Notts 3D 36
New Oscott. W Mid 2J 27
New Park. N Yor 2L 41
Newpark. Fife 6H 67
New Pitsligo. Abers 8H 81
New Polzeath. Corn 4B 4
Newport. Corn 7C 6
Newport. Devn 2E 6
Newport. E Yor 4F 42
Newport. Essx 8B 30
Newport. Glos 4E 18
Newport. High 1M 79
**Newport**. IOW 7C 10
**Newport**. Newp 5B 18
Newport. Norf 8M 39
Newport. Pemb 3G 15
Newport. Som 3B 8
**Newport**. Telf 8F 34
Newport-on-Tay. Fife 5H 67
**Newport Pagnell**. Mil 7F 28
Newpound Common.
W Sus 3H 11
New Prestwick. S Ayr 7B 58
New Quay. Cdgn 1K 15
**Newquay**. Corn 2M 3
Newquay Cornwall Airport.
Corn 5A 4
New Rackheath. Norf 8J 39
New Radnor. Powy 6M 25
New Rent. Cumb 8J 53
New Ridley. Nmbd 6D 54
New Romney. Kent 3G 13
**New Rossington**. S Yor 8D 42
New Row. Cdgn 5G 25
**Newry**. New M 7G 93
New Sauchie. Clac 8B 66
Newsbank. Ches E 3G 35
Newseat. Abers 2G 73
Newsham. Lanc 4D 40
Newsham. Nmbd 4G 55
Newsham. N Yor
nr. Richmond 4K 47
nr. Thirsk 7A 48
New Sharlston. W Yor 5A 42
Newsholme. E Yor 5E 42
Newsholme. Lanc 2G 41
New Shoreston. Nmbd 6J 61
New Springs. G Man 7D 40
Newstead. Notts 4C 36
Newstead. Bord 6C 60
New Stevenston. N Lan 4F 58
New Street. Here 6B 26
Newstreet Lane. Shrp 6E 34
New Swanage. Dors 7J 9
New Swannington. Leics 8B 36
Newthorpe. N Yor 4B 42
Newthorpe. Notts 5B 36
Newton. Arg 8E 64
Newton. B'end 7H 17
Newton. Cambs
nr. Cambridge 7M 29
nr. Wisbech 8M 37
Newton. Ches W
nr. Chester 3C 34
nr. Tattenhall 4D 34
Newton. Cumb 7M 45
Newton. Derbs 4B 36
Newton. Dors 4F 8
Newton. Dum
nr. Annan 4G 53
nr. Moffat 2F 52
Newton. G Man 8H 41
Newton. Here
nr. Ewyas Harold 8B 26
nr. Leominster 6D 26
Newton. High
nr. Cromarty 7H 79
nr. Inverness 1H 71
nr. Kylestrome 8E 84
nr. Wick 7E 86
Newton. Lanc
nr. Blackpool 4B 40
nr. Carnforth 8D 46
nr. Clitheroe 2E 40
Newton. Linc 6H 37
Newton. Mers 2M 33
Newton. Mor 7A 80
Newton. Norf 8E 38
Newton. Nptn 3F 28
Newton. Nmbd 5D 54
Newton. Notts 5D 36
Newton. Bord 7D 60
Newton. Shet 4D 90
Newton. Shrp
nr. Bridgnorth 2F 26
nr. Wem 6C 34
Newton. Som 2L 7
Newton. S Lan
nr. Glasgow 3E 58
nr. Lanark 6H 59
Newton. Staf 7J 35
Newton. Suff 7F 30
Newton. Swan 6F 16
Newton. Warw 4C 28
Newton. W Lot 2J 59
Newton. Wilts 3L 9
**Newton Abbot**. Devn 8H 7
Newtonairds. Dum 3C 52
Newton Arlosh. Cumb 6G 53
**Newton Aycliffe**. Dur 3L 47
Newton Bewley. Hart 3B 48
Newton Blossomville. Mil 6G 29
Newton Bromswold. Nptn 5G 29
Newton Burgoland. Leics 1A 28
Newton by Toft. Linc 1H 37
Newton Ferrers. Devn 7H 5
Newton Flotman. Norf 2J 31
Newtongrange. Midl 3M 59
Newton Green. Mon 4D 18
Newton Hall. Dur 7F 54
Newton Hall. Nmbd 5D 54
Newton Harcourt. Leics 2D 28
Newton Heath. G Man 7G 41
Newton Hill. W Yor 5M 41
Newtonhill. Abers 6J 73
Newtonhill. High 1F 70
Newton Ketton. Darl 3M 47
Newton Kyme. N Yor 3B 42
**Newton-le-Willows**. Mers 8D 40
Newton-le-Willows. N Yor 7L 47
Newton Longville. Buck 8F 28
**Newton Mearns**. E Ren 4D 58
Newtonmore. High 6H 71
Newton Morrell. N Yor 5L 47
Newton Mulgrave. N Yor 4E 48
Newton of Ardtoe. High 8H 69
Newton of Balcanquhal. Per 6E 66
Newton of Beltrees. Ren 4B 58
Newton of Falkland. Fife 7F 66
Newton of Mountblairy.
Abers 8F 80
Newton of Pitcairns. Per 6D 66
Newton-on-Ouse. N Yor 2C 42
Newton-on-Rawcliffe. N Yor 6F 48
Newton on the Hill. Shrp 7C 34
Newton-on-the-Moor. Nmbd 1E 54
Newton on Trent. Linc 2F 36
Newton Poppleford. Devn 7K 7
Newton Purcell. Oxon 8D 28
Newton Regis. Warw 1L 27
Newton Reigny. Cumb 8J 53
Newton Rigg. Cumb 8J 53
Newton St Cyres. Devn 6H 7
Newton St Faith. Norf 8J 39
Newton St Loe. Bath 7F 18
Newton St Petrock. Devn 4D 6
Newton Solney. Derbs 7L 35
Newton Stacey. Hants 1B 10
Newton Stewart. Dum 5K 51
Newton Toney. Wilts 1L 9
Newton Tony. Wilts 1L 9
Newton Tracey. Devn 3E 6
Newton under Roseberry.
Red C 4C 48
Newton upon Ayr. S Ayr 7B 58
Newton upon Derwent.
E Yor 3E 42
Newton Valence. Hants 2E 10
Newton-with-Scales. Lanc 4C 40
New Town. Dors 4H 9
New Town. E Lot 2B 60
New Town. Lutn 1H 21
New Town. W Yor 5B 42
Newtown. Abers 7G 81
Newtown. Cambs 5H 29
Newtown. Corn 8B 6
Newtown. Cumb
nr. Aspatria 7E 52
nr. Brampton 5K 53
nr. Penrith 3D 46
Newtown. Derbs 1H 35
Newtown. Devn 3G 7
Newtown. Dors 5C 8
Newtown. Falk 1H 59
Newtown. Glos
nr. Lydney 3E 18
nr. Tewkesbury 8H 27
Newtown. Hants
nr. Bishop's Waltham 4C 10
nr. Liphook 2F 10
nr. Lyndhurst 4L 9
nr. Newbury 7B 20
nr. Romsey 3M 9
nr. Warsash 5B 10
nr. Wickham 4D 10
Newtown. Here
nr. Little Dewchurch 8D 26
nr. Stretton Grandison 7E 26
Newtown. High 5D 70
Newtown. IOM 7C 44
Newtown. IOW 6B 10
Newtown. Lanc 6D 40
Newtown. Nmbd
nr. Rothbury 1D 54
nr. Wooler 7H 61
Newtown. Pool 6J 9
**Newtown**. Powy 3L 25
Newtown. Rhon 5K 17
Newtown. Shet 5J 91
Newtown. Shrp 6C 34
Newtown. Som 4A 8
Newtown. Staf
nr. Biddulph 3H 35
nr. Cannock 1H 27
nr. Longnor 3J 35
Newtown. Wilts 3H 9
**Newtownabbey**. Ant 4H 93
**Newtownards**. Ards 5J 93
Newtownbutler. Ferm 7D 92
Newtown-Crommelin.
ME Ant 3G 93
Newtownhamilton. New M 7F 93
Newtown-in-St Martin. Corn 6L 3
Newtown Linford. Leics 1C 28
Newtown St Boswells. Bord 6C 60
Newtownstewart. Derr 4D 92
Newtown Unthank. Leics 1B 28
New Tredegar. Cphy 4L 17
Newtyle. Ang 3F 66
New Village. E Yor 4H 43
New Village. S Yor 7C 42
New Walsoken. Cambs 1A 30
New Waltham. NE Lin 7K 43
New Winton. E Lot 2B 60
New World. Cambs 2L 29
New Yatt. Oxon 2A 20
Newyears Green. G Lon 5H 21
New York. Linc 4K 37
New York. Tyne 4G 55
Nextend. Here 6B 26
Neyland. Pemb 6F 14
Nib Heath. Shrp 8C 34
Nicholashayne. Devn 4L 7
Nicholaston. Swan 8M 15
Nidd. N Yor 1M 41
Niddrie. Edin 2M 59
Niddry. W Lot 2J 59
Nigg. Aber 5J 73
Nigg. High 6J 79
Nigg Ferry. High 7H 79
Nightcott. Som 3H 7
Nimmer. Som 4B 8
Nine Ashes. Essx 3B 22
Ninebanks. Nmbd 6A 54
Nine Elms. Swin 5K 19
Ninemile Bar. Dum 4C 52
Nine Mile Burn. Midl 4K 59
Ninfield. E Sus 4D 12
Ningwood. IOW 7B 10
Nisbet. Bord 7D 60
Nisbet Hill. Bord 4E 60
Niton. IOW 8C 10
Nitshill. Glas 3D 58
Niwbwrch. IOA 4D 32
Nixon's Corner. Derr 3D 92
Noak Hill. G Lon 4B 22
Nobold. Shrp 8C 34
Nobottle. Nptn 5D 28
Nocton. Linc 3H 37
Nogdam End. Norf 1K 31
Noke. Oxon 2C 20
Nolton. Pemb 5E 14
Nolton Haven. Pemb 5E 14
No Man's Heath. Ches W 5D 34
No Man's Heath. Warw 1L 27
Nomansland. Devn 4H 7
Nomansland. Wilts 4L 9
Noneley. Shrp 7C 34
Noness. Shet 5E 90
Nonikiln. High
Nonington. Kent
Nook. Cumb
nr. Longtown
nr. Milnthorpe
Noranside. Ang
Norbreck. Bkpl
Norbridge. Here
Norbury. Ches E
Norbury. Derbs
Norbury. Shrp
Norbury. Staf
Norby. N Yor
Norby. Shet
Norcross. Lanc
Nordelph. Norf
Norden. G Man
Nordley. Shrp
Norham. Nmbd
Norland Town. W Yor
Norley. Ches W
Norleywood. Hants
Normanby. N Lin
Normanby. N Yor
Normanby. Red C
Normanby-by-Spital. Linc
Normanby le Wold. Linc
Norman Cross. Cambs
Normandy. Surr
Norman's Bay. E Sus
Norman's Green. Devn
Normanton. Derb
Normanton. Leics
Normanton. Notts
**Normanton**. W Yor
Normanton le Heath. Leics
Normanton-on-Cliffe. Linc
Normanton on Soar. Notts
Normanton-on-the-Wolds.
Notts
Normanton on Trent. Notts
Normoss. Lanc
Norrington Common. Wilts
Norris Green. Mers
Norris Hill. Leics
Norristhorpe. W Yor
Northacre. Norf
Northall. Buck
**Northallerton**. N Yor
Northam. Devn
Northam. Sotn
**Northampton**. Nptn
North Anston. S Yor
North Ascot. Brac
North Aston. Oxon
Northaw. Herts
Northay. Som
North Baddesley. Hants
North Balfern. Dum
North Ballachulish. High
North Barrow. Som
North Barsham. Norf
Northbeck. Linc
North Benfleet. Essx
North Bersted. W Sus
North Berwick. E Lot
North Bitchburn. Dur
North Blyth. Nmbd
North Boarhunt. Hants
North Bockhampton. Dors
Northborough. Pet
Northbourne. Kent
Northbourne. Oxon
North Bovey. Devn
North Bowood. Dors
North Bradley. Wilts
North Brentor. Devn
North Brewham. Som
Northbrook. Oxon
North Brook End. Cambs
North Broomhill. Nmbd
North Buckland. Devn
North Burlingham. Norf
North Cadbury. Som
North Carlton. Linc
North Cave. E Yor
North Cerney. Glos
North Chailey. E Sus
Northchapel. W Sus
North Charford. Hants
North Charlton. Nmbd
North Cheriton. Som
North Chideock. Dors
Northchurch. Herts
North Cliffe. E Yor
North Clifton. Notts
North Close. Dur
North Cockerington. Linc
North Coker. Som
North Collafirth. Shet
North Common. E Sus
North Commonty. Abers
North Coombe. Devn
North Cornelly. B'end
North Cotes. Linc
Northcott. Devn
nr. Boyton
nr. Culmstock
Northcourt. Oxon
North Cove. Suff
North Cowton. N Yor
North Craigo. Ang
North Crawley. Mil
North Cray. G Lon
North Creake. Norf
North Curry. Som
North Dalton. E Yor
North Deighton. N Yor
North Dronley. Ang
North Duffield. N Yor
Northdyke. Orkn
Northedge. Derbs
North Elkington. Linc
North Elmham. Norf
North Elmsall. W Yor
North End. E Yor
North End. Essx
nr. Great Dunmow
nr. Great Yeldham
North End. Hants
North End. Leics
North End. Linc
North End. Norf
North End. N Som
North End. Port
North End. W Sus
North End. Wilts
Northend. Buck
Northend. Warw
North Erradale. High
North Evington. Leic
North Fambridge. Essx
North Fearns. High
North Featherstone. W Yor
North Feorline. N Ayr
North Ferriby. E Yor
Northfield. Aber
Northfield. E Yor
Northfield. Som
Northfield. W Mid
**Northfleet**. Kent
North Frodingham. E Yor
Northgate. Linc
North Gluss. Shet
North Gorley. Hants
North Green. Norf
North Green. Suff
nr. Framlingham
nr. Halesworth
nr. Saxmundham
North Greetwell. Linc
North Grimston. N Yor
North Halling. Medw
North Hayling. Hants
North Hazelrigg. Nmbd
North Heasley. Devn
North Heath. W Sus
North Hill. Corn
North Holmwood. Surr
North Huish. Devn
North Hykeham. Linc
Northiam. E Sus
Northill. C Beds
Northington. Hants
North Kelsey. Linc
North Kelsey Moor. Linc
North Kessock. High
North Killingholme. N Lin
North Kilvington. N Yor

North Kilworth—Pettinain

Kilworth. *Leics* 3D 28
Kyme. *Linc* 4J 37
Lancing. *W Sus* 5J 11
ands. *Linc* 4L 37
each. *Glos* 2K 19
Lee. *Buck* 3F 20
Lees. *N Yor* 8L 47
Leigh. *Kent* 1H 13
Leigh. *Oxon* 2A 20
eigh. *Devn*
r. Barnstaple 2F 6
r. Honiton 6L 7
Leverton. *Notts* 1E 36
ew. *Devn* 6E 6
Littleton. *Worc* 7J 27
Lopham. *Norf* 3G 31
Luffenham. *Rut* 1G 29
Marden. *W Sus* 4F 10
Marston. *Buck* 1E 20
Middleton. *Midl* 4A 60
Middleton. *Nmbd* 7H 61
Molton. *Devn* 3G 7
Moor. *N Yor* 7G 49
moor. *Oxon* 3B 20
moor Green. *Som* 2B 8
Moreton. *Oxon* 5C 20
uir. *Ang* 2G 67
Mundham. *W Sus* 5F 10
Murie. *Per* 5F 66
Muskham. *Notts* 4E 36
Ness. *Orkn* 2E 86
Newbald. *E Yor* 4G 43
Newington. *Oxon* 8B 28
Newnton. *Wilts* 8K 19
Newton. *Som* 2A 8
ey. *Hants* 5E 10
Nibley. *Glos* 4F 18
Oakley. *Hants* 8C 20
Ockendon. *G Lon* 5B 22
**lt**. *G Lon* 5J 21
p. *Flin* 4M 33
p Hall. *Flin* 3A 34
Ormesby. *Midd* 4C 48
Ormsby. *Linc* 8K 43
rpe. *Linc*
r. Bourne 8H 37
r. Donington 6K 37
r. Gainsborough 8F 42
Otterington. *N Yor* 7A 48
ver. *Som*
r. Glastonbury 2C 8
r. Yeovil 3D 8
Owersby. *Linc* 8H 43
wram. *W Yor* 5K 41
Perrott. *Som* 5C 8
Petherton. *Som* 2A 8
Petherwin. *Corn* 7B 6
Pickenham. *Norf* 1E 30
Piddle. *Worc* 6H 27
Poorton. *Dors* 6D 8
Port. *Arg* 5E 64
ort. *Dors* 7H 9
Queensferry. *Fife* 1K 59
Radworthy. *Devn* 2G 7
Rauceby. *Linc* 5H 37
epps. *Norf* 6J 39
Rigton. *N Yor* 3L 41
Rode. *Ches E* 3G 35
Roe. *Shet* 5H 91
Ronaldsay Airport.
rkn 4G 89
Row. *Cumb* 8G 53
Runcton. *Norf* 8C 38
Sannox. *N Ayr* 5K 57
Scale. *Cumb* 7L 45
Scarle. *Linc* 3F 36
Seaton. *Nmbd* 3F 54
Seaton Colliery.
mbd 3F 54
Sheen. *G Lon* 6J 21
Shian. *Arg* 3D 64
**Shields**. *Tyne* 5G 55
Shoebury. *S'end* 5F 22
Shore. *Bkpl* 4B 40
Side. *Cumb* 2K 45
Skelton. *Red C* 4D 48
Somercotes. *Linc* 8M 43
Stainley. *N Yor* 8L 47
Stainmore. *Cumb* 4G 47
Stifford. *Thur* 5C 22
Stoke. *Bath* 7F 18
Stoke. *Oxon* 5D 20
Stoke. *W Sus* 4H 11
towe. *Cambs* 5M 29
Street. *Hants* 2D 10
Street. *Kent* 8G 23
Street. *Medw* 6E 22
Street. *W Ber* 6D 20
Sunderland. *Nmbd* 6K 61
Tamerton. *Corn* 6C 6
Tawton. *Devn* 5F 6
Thoresby. *Linc* 8K 43
Tidworth. *Wilts* 1L 9
Town. *Devn* 5E 6
Town. *Shet* 6D 90
own. *Orkn* 2F 86
Tuddenham. *Norf* 8G 39
Walbottle. *Tyne* 5E 54
all. *Orkn* 5G 89
Walney. *Cumb* 8L 45
**Walsham**. *Norf* 6J 39
Waltham. *Hants* 1C 10
Warnborough. *Hants* 8E 20
Water Bridge. *Ang* 1K 67
Watten. *High* 6D 86
ay. *Glos* 8H 27
ay. *Swan* 6E 16
Weald Bassett. *Essx* 3B 22
Weston. *N Som* 6C 18
Weston. *Oxon* 3D 20
Wheatley. *Notts* 1E 36
Whilborough. *Devn* 5L 5
**ich**. *Ches W* 2E 34
Wick. *Bath* 7D 18
ick. *Som* 1B 8
ick. *S Glo* 5D 18
Widcombe. *Bath* 8D 18
Willingham. *Linc* 1J 37
**Wingfield**. *Derbs* 3B 36
Witham. *Linc* 7G 37
old. *Norf* 2D 30
ood. *Derbs* 3L 35
**ood**. *G Lon* 4H 21
ood. *IOW* 6B 10
ood. *Kent* 7K 23
ood. *Shrp* 6C 34
ood. *Stoke* 5G 35
ood Green. *Glos* 2F 18
Wootton. *Dors* 4E 8
Wootton. *Norf* 7C 38
Wootton. *Som* 1D 8
Wraxall. *Wilts* 6G 19
Wroughton. *Swin* 5K 19
Yardhope. *Nmbd* 1C 54
. *Devn* 6L 5
. *Glos* 1G 19
. *Hal* 1D 34
. *Herts* 8K 29
. *IOW* 7M 9
. *Mon* 1C 18
. *Nptn* 5D 28
. *Notts* 2C 36
. *Powy* 5B 26
. *Shrp*
. Ludlow 3C 26
. Madeley 1F 26
. Shrewsbury 1D 26
. *S Yor*
. Askern 6C 42
. Sheffield 1A 36
. *Stoc T* 3B 48
. *Suff* 5F 30
. *Swan* 6F 16
. *W Sus*
. Selsey 6F 10
. Westergate 5G 11
. *Wilts* 5G 19
. *Worc*
. Evesham 7J 27
. Worcester 6G 27
Bavant. *Wilts* 1H 9
Bridge. *Staf* 6G 35
Canes. *Staf* 1J 27
Canon. *Here* 7B 26
Corner. *Norf* 7G 39
Disney. *Linc* 4F 36
East. *Staf* 1J 27
Ferris. *Wilts* 2F 8
Fitzwarren. *Som* 3M 7
Norton Green. *IOW* 7M 9
Norton Green. *Stoke* 4H 35
Norton Hawkfield. *Bath* 7D 18
Norton Heath. *Essx* 3B 22
Norton in Hales. *Shrp* 6F 34
Norton in the Moors. *Stoke* 4G 35
Norton-Juxta-Twycross.
*Leics* 1M 27
Norton-le-Clay. *N Yor* 8B 48
Norton Lindsey. *Warw* 5L 27
Norton Little Green. *Suff* 5F 30
Norton Malreward. *Bath* 7E 18
Norton Mandeville. *Essx* 3B 22
Norton-on-Derwent. *N Yor* 8E 48
Norton St Philip. *Som* 8F 18
Norton Subcourse. *Norf* 2L 31
Norton sub Hamdon. *Som* 4C 8
Norton Woodseats. *S Yor* 1A 36
Norwell. *Notts* 3E 36
Norwell Woodhouse. *Notts* 3E 36
**Norwich**. *Norf* 1J 31
Norwich Airport. *Norf* 8J 39
Norwick. *Shet* 2L 91
Norwood. *Derbs* 1B 36
Norwood Green. *W Yor* 5K 41
Norwood Hill. *Surr* 1K 11
Norwood Park. *Som* 2D 8
Norwoodside. *Cambs* 2M 29
Noseley. *Leics* 2E 28
Noss. *Shet* 6D 90
Noss Mayo. *Devn* 7H 5
Nosterfield. *N Yor* 7L 47
Nostie. *High* 3K 69
Notgrove. *Glos* 1K 19
Nottage. *B'end* 7H 17
**Nottingham**. *Nott* 5C 36
Nottington. *Dors* 7E 8
Notton. *Dors* 6E 8
Notton. *W Yor* 6M 41
Notton. *Wilts* 7H 19
Nounsley. *Essx* 2D 22
Noutard's Green. *Worc* 5F 26
Nox. *Shrp* 8C 34
Noyadd Trefawr. *Cdgn* 2J 15
Nuffield. *Oxon* 5D 20
Nunburnholme. *E Yor* 3F 42
Nuncargate. *Notts* 4C 36
Nunclose. *Cumb* 7J 53
**Nuneaton**. *Warw* 2A 28
Nuneham Courtenay. *Oxon* 4C 20
Nun Monkton. *N Yor* 2C 42
Nunnerie. *S Lan* 8H 59
Nunney. *Som* 1F 8
Nunnington. *N Yor* 8D 48
Nunnykirk. *Nmbd* 2D 54
Nunsthorpe. *NE Lin* 7K 43
Nunthorpe. *Midd* 4C 48
Nunthorpe. *York* 2C 42
Nunton. *Wilts* 3K 9
Nunwick. *Nmbd* 4B 54
Nunwick. *N Yor* 8M 47
Nupend. *Glos* 3F 18
Nursling. *Hants* 4A 10
Nursted. *Hants* 3E 10
Nursteed. *Wilts* 7J 19
Nurston. *V Glam* 8K 17
Nutbourne. *W Sus*
nr. Chichester 5E 10
nr. Pulborough 4H 11
Nutfield. *Surr* 8L 21
Nuthall. *Notts* 5C 36
Nuthampstead. *Herts* 8M 29
Nuthurst. *Warw* 4K 27
Nuthurst. *W Sus* 3J 11
Nutley. *E Sus* 3M 11
Nuttall. *G Man* 6F 40
Nutwell. *S Yor* 7D 42
Nybster. *High* 5E 86
Nyetimber. *W Sus* 6F 10
Nyewood. *W Sus* 3F 10
Nymet Rowland. *Devn* 5G 7
Nymet Tracey. *Devn* 5G 7
Nympsfield. *Glos* 3G 19
Nynehead. *Som* 3L 7
Nyton. *W Sus* 5G 11

## O

**Oadby**. *Leics* 1D 28
Oad Street. *Kent* 7E 22
Oakamoor. *Staf* 5J 35
Oakbank. *Arg* 4B 64
Oakbank. *W Lot* 3J 59
Oakdale. *Cphy* 5L 17
Oakdale. *Pool* 6J 9
Oake. *Som* 3L 7
Oaken. *Staf* 1G 27
Oakenclough. *Lanc* 3D 40
Oakengates. *Telf* 8E 34
Oakenholt. *Flin* 2A 34
Oakenshaw. *Dur* 8F 54
Oakenshaw. *W Yor* 5K 41
Oakerthorpe. *Derbs* 4A 36
Oakford. *Cdgn* 1L 15
Oakford. *Devn* 3J 7
Oakfordbridge. *Devn* 3J 7
Oakgrove. *Ches E* 3H 35
Oakham. *Rut* 1F 28
Oakhanger. *Ches E* 4F 34
Oakhanger. *Hants* 2E 10
Oakhill. *Som* 1E 8
Oakington. *Cambs* 5M 29
Oaklands. *Powy* 7K 25
Oakle Street. *Glos* 2F 18
Oakley. *Bed* 6H 29
Oakley. *Buck* 2D 20
Oakley. *Fife* 1J 59
Oakley. *Hants* 8C 20
Oakley. *Suff* 4H 31
Oakley Green. *Wind* 6G 21
Oakley Park. *Powy* 4J 25
Oakmere. *Ches W* 3D 34
Oakridge Lynch. *Glos* 3H 19
Oaks. *Shrp* 1C 26
Oaksey. *Wilts* 4H 19
Oaks Green. *Derbs* 6K 35
Oakshaw Ford. *Cumb* 4K 53
Oakshott. *Hants* 3E 10
Oakthorpe. *Leics* 8M 35
Oak Tree. *Darl* 4A 48
Oakwood. *Derb* 6A 36
Oakwood. *W Yor* 4M 41
Oakwoodhill. *Surr* 2J 11
Oakworth. *W Yor* 4J 41
Oape. *High* 3E 78
Oare. *Kent* 7G 23
Oare. *Som* 1H 7
Oare. *W Ber* 6C 20
Oare. *Wilts* 7K 19
Oareford. *Som* 1H 7
Oasby. *Linc* 6H 37
Oath. *Som* 3B 8
Oathlaw. *Ang* 2H 67
Oatlands. *N Yor* 2M 41
**Oban**. *Arg* 5C 64
Oban. *W Isl* 3C 76
Oborne. *Dors* 4E 8
Obsdale. *High* 7G 79
Obthorpe. *Linc* 8H 37
Occlestone Green. *Ches W* 3E 34
Occold. *Suff* 4H 31
Ochiltree. *E Ayr* 7D 58
Ochtermuthill. *Per* 6B 66
Ochtertyre. *Per* 5B 66
Ockbrook. *Derbs* 6B 36
Ockeridge. *Worc* 5F 26
Ockham. *Surr* 8H 21
Ockle. *High* 8G 69
Ockley. *Surr* 1J 11
Ocle Pychard. *Here* 7D 26
Octofad. *Arg* 4B 56
Octomore. *Arg* 4B 56
Octon. *E Yor* 1H 43
Odcombe. *Som* 4D 8
Odd Down. *Bath* 7F 18
Oddingley. *Worc* 6H 27
Oddington. *Oxon* 2C 20
Oddsta. *Shet* 4K 91
Odell. *Bed* 6G 29
Odie. *Orkn* 7F 88
Odiham. *Hants* 8E 20
Odsey. *Cambs* 8K 29
Odstock. *Wilts* 3K 9
Odstone. *Leics* 1A 28
Offchurch. *Warw* 5A 28
Offenham. *Worc* 7J 27
Offenham Cross. *Worc* 7J 27
Offerton. *G Man* 1H 35
Offerton. *Tyne* 6G 55
Offham. *E Sus* 4L 11
Offham. *Kent* 8C 22
Offham. *W Sus* 5H 11
Offleyhay. *Staf* 7G 35
Offley Hoo. *Herts* 1J 21
Offleymarsh. *Staf* 7F 34
Offord Cluny. *Cambs* 5K 29
Offord D'Arcy. *Cambs* 5K 29
Offton. *Suff* 7G 31
Offwell. *Devn* 6L 7
Ogbourne Maizey. *Wilts* 6K 19
Ogbourne St Andrew. *Wilts* 6K 19
Ogbourne St George. *Wilts* 6L 19
Ogden. *G Man* 6H 41
Ogle. *Nmbd* 4E 54
Ogmore. *V Glam* 7H 17
Ogmore-by-Sea. *V Glam* 7H 17
Ogmore Vale. *B'end* 5J 17
Okeford Fitzpaine. *Dors* 4G 9
Okehampton. *Devn* 6E 6
Okehampton Camp. *Devn* 6E 6
Okraquoy. *Shet* 4E 90
Okus. *Swin* 5K 19
Old. *Nptn* 4E 28
Old Aberdeen. *Aber* 5J 73
Old Alresford. *Hants* 2C 10
Oldany. *High* 8D 84
Old Arley. *Warw* 2L 27
Old Basford. *Nott* 5C 36
Old Basing. *Hants* 8D 20
Oldberrow. *Warw* 5K 27
Old Bewick. *Nmbd* 7H 61
Old Bexley. *G Lon* 6A 22
Old Blair. *Per* 1B 66
Old Bolingbroke. *Linc* 3L 37
Oldborough. *Devn* 5G 7
Old Brampton. *Derbs* 2M 35
Old Bridge of Tilt. *Per* 1B 66
Old Bridge of Urr. *Dum* 5B 52
Old Brumby. *N Lin* 7F 42
Old Buckenham. *Norf* 2G 31
Old Burghclere. *Hants* 8B 20
Oldbury. *Shrp* 2F 26
Oldbury. *Warw* 2M 27
**Oldbury**. *W Mid* 3H 27
Oldbury-on-Severn. *S Glo* 4E 18
Oldbury on the Hill. *Glos* 5G 19
Old Byland. *N Yor* 7C 48
Old Cassop. *Dur* 8G 55
Oldcastle. *Mon* 1B 18
Oldcastle Heath. *Ches W* 5C 34
Old Catton. *Norf* 8J 39
Old Clee. *NE Lin* 7K 43
Old Cleeve. *Som* 1K 7
Old Colwyn. *Cnwy* 3H 33
Oldcotes. *Notts* 1C 36
Old Coulsdon. *G Lon* 8L 21
Old Dailly. *S Ayr* 2H 51
Old Dalby. *Leics* 7D 36
Old Dam. *Derbs* 2K 35
Old Deer. *Abers* 1J 73
Old Dilton. *Wilts* 1G 9
Old Down. *S Glo* 5E 18
Oldeamere. *Cambs* 2L 29
Old Edlington. *S Yor* 8C 42
Old Eldon. *Dur* 3L 47
Old Ellerby. *E Yor* 4J 43
Old Fallings. *W Mid* 1H 27
Oldfallow. *Staf* 8H 35
Old Felixstowe. *Suff* 8K 31
Oldfield. *Shrp* 3E 26
Oldfield. *Worc* 5G 27
Old Fletton. *Pet* 2J 29
Oldford. *Som* 8F 18
Old Forge. *Here* 2D 18
Old Glossop. *Derbs* 8J 41
Old Goole. *E Yor* 5E 42
Old Gore. *Here* 1E 18
Old Graitney. *Dum* 5H 53
Old Grimsby. *IOS* 1G 3
Oldhall. *High* 6D 86
Old Hall Street. *Norf* 6K 39
**Oldham**. *G Man* 7H 41
Oldhamstocks. *E Lot* 2E 60
Old Heathfield. *E Sus* 3B 12
Old Hill. *W Mid* 3H 27
Old Hunstanton. *Norf* 5C 38
Oldhurst. *Cambs* 4K 29
Old Hutton. *Cumb* 7D 46
Old Kea. *Corn* 4M 3
Old Kilpatrick. *W Dun* 2C 58
Old Kinnernie. *Abers* 5G 73
Old Knebworth. *Herts* 1K 21
Oldland. *S Glo* 6E 18
Old Laxey. *IOM* 6D 44
Old Leake. *Linc* 4M 37
Old Lenton. *Nott* 6C 36
Old Llanberis. *Gwyn* 5F 32
Old Malton. *N Yor* 8E 48
Oldmeldrum. *Abers* 3H 73
Old Micklefield. *W Yor* 4B 42
Old Mill. *Corn* 8C 6
Oldmixon. *N Som* 8B 18
Old Monkland. *N Lan* 3F 58
Old Newton. *Suff* 5G 31
Old Park. *Telf* 1E 26
Old Pentland. *Midl* 3L 59
Old Philpstoun. *W Lot* 2J 59
Old Quarrington. *Dur* 8G 55
Old Radnor. *Powy* 6A 26
Old Rayne. *Abers* 3F 72
Oldridge. *Devn* 6H 7
Old Romney. *Kent* 3G 13
Old Scone. *Per* 5E 66
Oldshore Beg. *High* 6D 84
Oldshoremore. *High* 6E 84
Old Snydale. *W Yor* 5B 42
Old Sodbury. *S Glo* 5F 18
Old Somerby. *Linc* 6G 37
Old Spital. *Dur* 4H 47
Oldstead. *N Yor* 7C 48
Old Stratford. *Nptn* 7E 28
Old Swan. *Mers* 8B 40
Old Swarland. *Nmbd* 1E 54
Old Tebay. *Cumb* 5E 46
Old Town. *Cumb* 7J 53
Old Town. *E Sus* 6B 12
Old Town. *IOS* 1H 3
Old Town. *Nmbd* 2B 54
Oldtown. *High* 5F 78
Old Trafford. *G Man* 8G 41
Old Tupton. *Derbs* 3A 36
Oldwall. *Cumb* 5J 53
Oldwalls. *Swan* 7L 15
Old Warden. *C Beds* 7J 29
Oldways End. *Som* 3H 7
Old Westhall. *Abers* 3F 72
Old Weston. *Cambs* 4H 29
Oldwhat. *Abers* 8H 81
Old Windsor. *Wind* 6G 21
Old Wives Lees. *Kent* 8G 23
Old Woking. *Surr* 8H 21
Oldwood Common. *Worc* 5D 26
Old Woodstock. *Oxon* 2B 20
Olgrinmore. *High* 6B 86
Oliver's Battery. *Hants* 3B 10
Ollaberry. *Shet* 5H 91
Ollerton. *Ches E* 2F 34
Ollerton. *Notts* 3D 36
Ollerton. *Shrp* 7E 34
Olmarch. *Cdgn* 7F 24
Olmstead Green. *Cambs* 7C 30
Olney. *Mil* 6F 28
Olrig. *High* 5C 86
Olton. *W Mid* 3K 27
Olveston. *S Glo* 5E 18
**Omagh**. *Ferm* 5D 92
Ombersley. *Worc* 5G 27
Ompton. *Notts* 3D 36
Omunsgarth. *Shet* 3D 90
Onchan. *IOM* 7D 44
Onecote. *Staf* 4J 35
Onehouse. *Suff* 6G 31
Onen. *Mon* 2C 18
Ongar Hill. *Norf* 7B 38
Ongar Street. *Here* 5B 26
Onibury. *Shrp* 4C 26
Onich. *High* 1E 64
Onllwyn. *Neat* 3H 17
Onneley. *Staf* 5F 34
Onslow Green. *Essx* 2C 22
Onslow Village. *Surr* 1G 11
Onthank. *E Ayr* 6C 58
Openwoodgate. *Derbs* 5A 36
Opinan. *High*
nr. Gairloch 6J 77
nr. Laide 4K 77
Orasaigh. *W Isl* 2E 76
Orbost. *High* 1D 68
Orby. *Linc* 3A 38
Orchard Hill. *Devn* 3D 6
Orchard Portman. *Som* 3M 7
Orcheston. *Wilts* 1J 9
Orcop. *Here* 1C 18
Orcop Hill. *Here* 1C 18
Ord. *High* 4H 69
Ordale. *Shet* 3L 91
Ordhead. *Abers* 4F 72
Ordie. *Abers* 5D 72
Ordiquish. *Mor* 8C 80
Ordley. *Nmbd* 6C 54
Ordsall. *Notts* 2E 36
Ore. *E Sus* 4E 12
Oreton. *Shrp* 3E 26
Orford. *Suff* 7L 31
Orford. *Warr* 8E 40
Organford. *Dors* 6H 9
Orgil. *Orkn* 1D 86
Orgreave. *Staf* 8K 35
Oridge Street. *Glos* 1F 18
Orlestone. *Kent* 2F 12
Orleton. *Here* 5C 26
Orleton. *Worc* 5E 26
Orleton Common. *Here* 5C 26
Orlingbury. *Nptn* 4F 28
Ormacleit. *W Isl* 2D 74
Ormathwaite. *Cumb* 3A 46
Ormesby. *Red C* 4C 48
Ormesby St Margaret. *Norf* 8L 39
Ormesby St Michael. *Norf* 8L 39
Ormiscaig. *High* 4K 77
Ormiston. *E Lot* 3B 60
Ormsaigbeg. *High* 1K 63
Ormsaigmore. *High* 1K 63
Ormsary. *Arg* 2G 57
Ormsgill. *Cumb* 7L 45
**Ormskirk**. *Lanc* 7C 40
Orphir. *Orkn* 1E 86
**Orpington**. *G Lon* 7A 22
**Orrell**. *G Man* 7D 40
Orrell. *Mers* 8B 40
Orrisdale. *IOM* 5C 44
Orsett. *Thur* 5C 22
Orslow. *Staf* 8G 35
Orston. *Notts* 5E 36
Orthwaite. *Cumb* 8G 53
Orton. *Cumb* 5E 46
Orton. *Mor* 8C 80
Orton. *Nptn* 4F 28
Orton. *Staf* 2G 27
Orton Longueville. *Pet* 2J 29
Orton-on-the-Hill. *Leics* 1M 27
Orton Waterville. *Pet* 2J 29
Orton Wistow. *Pet* 2J 29
Orwell. *Cambs* 6L 29
Osbaldeston. *Lanc* 4E 40
Osbaldwick. *York* 2D 42
Osbaston. *Leics* 1B 28
Osbaston. *Shrp* 7B 34
Osbournby. *Linc* 6H 37
Osclay. *High* 8D 86
Oscroft. *Ches W* 3D 34
Ose. *High* 1E 68
Osgathorpe. *Leics* 8B 36
Osgodby. *Linc* 8H 43
Osgodby. *N Yor*
nr. Scarborough 7H 49
nr. Selby 4D 42
Oskaig. *High* 2G 69
Oskamull. *Arg* 4K 63
Osleston. *Derbs* 6L 35
Osmaston. *Derb* 6A 36
Osmaston. *Derbs* 5L 35
Osmington. *Dors* 7F 8
Osmington Mills. *Dors* 7F 8
Osmondthorpe. *W Yor* 4M 41
Osmondwall. *Orkn* 3E 86
Osmotherley. *N Yor* 6B 48
Osnaburgh. *Fife* 6H 67
Ospisdale. *High* 5H 79
Ospringe. *Kent* 7G 23
**Ossett**. *W Yor* 5L 41
Ossington. *Notts* 3E 36
Ostend. *Essx* 4F 22
Ostend. *Norf* 6K 39
Osterley. *G Lon* 6J 21
Oswaldkirk. *N Yor* 8D 48
**Oswaldtwistle**. *Lanc* 5F 40
**Oswestry**. *Shrp* 7A 34
Otby. *Linc* 8J 43
Otford. *Kent* 8B 22
Otham. *Kent* 8D 22
Otherton. *Staf* 8H 35
Othery. *Som* 2B 8
Otley. *Suff* 6J 31
**Otley**. *W Yor* 3L 41
Otterbourne. *Hants* 3B 10
Otterburn. *Nmbd* 2B 54
Otterburn. *N Yor* 2G 41
Otterburn Camp. *Nmbd* 2B 54
Otterburn Hall. *Nmbd* 2B 54
Otter Ferry. *Arg* 1J 57
Otterford. *Som* 4M 7
Otterham. *Corn* 6A 6
Otterhampton. *Som* 1M 7
Otterham Quay. *Medw* 7E 22
Ottershaw. *Surr* 7H 21
Otterspool. *Mers* 1B 34
Otterswick. *Shet* 5K 91
Otterton. *Devn* 7K 7
Otterwood. *Hants* 5B 10
Ottery St Mary. *Devn* 6K 7
Ottinge. *Kent* 1H 13
Ottringham. *E Yor* 5K 43
Oughterby. *Cumb* 6G 53
Oughtershaw. *N Yor* 7G 47
Oughterside. *Cumb* 7F 52
Oughtibridge. *S Yor* 8M 41
Oughtrington. *Warr* 1E 34
Oulston. *N Yor* 8C 48
Oulton. *Cumb* 6G 53
Oulton. *Norf* 7H 39
Oulton. *Staf*
nr. Gnosall Heath 7F 34
nr. Stone 6H 35
Oulton. *Suff* 2M 31
Oulton. *W Yor* 5A 42
Oulton Broad. *Suff* 2M 31
Oulton Street. *Norf* 7H 39
Oundle. *Nptn* 3H 29
Ousby. *Cumb* 8L 53
Ousdale. *High* 2L 79
Ousden. *Suff* 6D 30
Ousefleet. *E Yor* 5F 42
Ouston. *Dur* 6F 54
Ouston. *Nmbd*
nr. Bearsbridge 6A 54
nr. Stamfordham 4D 54
Outer Hope. *Devn* 7J 5
Outertown. *Orkn* 8B 88
Outgate. *Cumb* 6B 46
Outhgill. *Cumb* 5F 46
Outlands. *Staf* 6F 34
Outlane. *W Yor* 6J 41
Out Newton. *E Yor* 5L 43
Out Rawcliffe. *Lanc* 3C 40
Outwell. *Norf* 1B 30
Outwick. *Hants* 4K 9
Outwood. *Surr* 1L 11
Outwood. *W Yor* 5M 41
Outwood. *Worc* 4H 27
Outwoods. *Leics* 8B 36
Outwoods. *Staf* 8F 34
Ouzlewell Green. *W Yor* 5M 41
Ovenden. *W Yor* 5J 41
Over. *Cambs* 4L 29
Over. *Ches W* 3E 34
Over. *Glos* 2G 19
Over. *S Glo* 5D 18
Overbister. *Orkn* 5F 88
Over Burrows. *Derbs* 6L 35
Overbury. *Worc* 8H 27
Overcombe. *Dors* 7E 8
Over Compton. *Dors* 4D 8
Over End. *Cambs* 2H 29
Over Finlarg. *Ang* 3H 67
Over Green. *Warw* 2K 27
Overgreen. *Derbs* 2M 35
Over Haddon. *Derbs* 3L 35
Over Hulton. *G Man* 7E 40
Over Kellet. *Lanc* 8D 46
Over Kiddington. *Oxon* 1B 20
Overleigh. *Som* 2C 8
Overley. *Staf* 8K 35
Over Monnow. *Mon* 2D 18
Over Norton. *Oxon* 1M 19
Over Peover. *Ches E* 2F 34
Overpool. *Ches W* 2B 34
Overscaig. *High* 1E 78
Overseal. *Derbs* 8L 35
Over Silton. *N Yor* 6B 48
Oversland. *Kent* 8G 23
Overstone. *Nptn* 5F 28
Over Stowey. *Som* 2L 7
Overstrand. *Norf* 5J 39
Over Stratton. *Som* 4C 8
Over Street. *Wilts* 2J 9
Overthorpe. *Nptn* 7B 28
Overton. *Aber* 4H 73
Overton. *Ches W* 2D 34
Overton. *Hants* 1C 10
Overton. *High* 8D 86
Overton. *Lanc* 2C 40
Overton. *N Yor* 2C 42
Overton. *Shrp*
nr. Bridgnorth 3E 26
nr. Ludlow 4D 26
Overton. *Swan* 8L 15
Overton. *W Yor* 6L 41
Overton. *Wrex* 5B 34
Overtown. *Lanc* 8E 46
Overtown. *N Lan* 4G 59
Overtown. *Swin* 6K 19
Over Wallop. *Hants* 2L 9
Over Whitacre. *Warw* 2L 27
Over Worton. *Oxon* 1B 20
Oving. *Buck* 1E 20
Oving. *W Sus* 5G 11
Ovingdean. *Brig* 5L 11
Ovingham. *Nmbd* 5D 54
Ovington. *Dur* 4K 47
Ovington. *Essx* 7D 30
Ovington. *Hants* 2C 10
Ovington. *Norf* 1F 30
Ovington. *Nmbd* 5D 54
Owen's Bank. *Staf* 7L 35
Ower. *Hants*
nr. Holbury 5B 10
nr. Totton 4M 9
Owermoigne. *Dors* 7F 8
Owlbury. *Shrp* 2B 26
Owler Bar. *Derbs* 2L 35
Owlerton. *S Yor* 8M 41
Owlsmoor. *Brac* 7F 20
Owlswick. *Buck* 3E 20
Owmby. *Linc* 7H 43
Owmby-by-Spital. *Linc* 1H 37
Ownham. *W Ber* 6B 20
Owrytn. *Wrex* 5B 34
Owslebury. *Hants* 3C 10
Owston. *Leics* 1E 28
Owston. *S Yor* 6C 42
Owston Ferry. *N Lin* 7F 42
Owstwick. *E Yor* 4K 43
Owthorne. *E Yor* 5L 43
Owthorpe. *Notts* 6D 36
Owton Manor. *Hart* 3B 48
Oxborough. *Norf* 1D 30
Oxbridge. *Dors* 6C 8
Oxcombe. *Linc* 2L 37
Oxen End. *Essx* 1C 22
Oxenhall. *Glos* 1F 18
Oxenholme. *Cumb* 6D 46
Oxenhope. *W Yor* 4J 41
Oxen Park. *Cumb* 7B 46
Oxenpill. *Som* 1C 8
Oxenton. *Glos* 8H 27
Oxenwood. *Wilts* 8M 19
**Oxford**. *Oxon* 3C 20
Oxgangs. *Edin* 3L 59
Oxhey. *Herts* 4J 21
Oxhill. *Warw* 7M 27
Oxley. *W Mid* 1H 27
Oxley Green. *Essx* 2F 22
Oxley's Green. *E Sus* 3C 12
Oxlode. *Cambs* 3A 30
Oxnam. *Bord* 8E 60
Oxshott. *Surr* 7J 21
Oxspring. *S Yor* 7L 41
**Oxted**. *Surr* 8L 21
Oxton. *Mers* 1B 34
Oxton. *N Yor* 3C 42
Oxton. *Notts* 4D 36
Oxton. *Bord* 4B 60
Oxwich. *Swan* 8L 15
Oxwich Green. *Swan* 8L 15
Oxwick. *Norf* 7F 38
Oykel Bridge. *High* 3D 78
Oyne. *Abers* 3F 72
Oystermouth. *Swan* 6F 16
Ozleworth. *Glos* 4F 18

## P

Pabail Iarach. *W Isl* 8J 83
Pabail Uarach. *W Isl* 8J 83
Pachesham Park. *Surr* 8J 21
Packers Hill. *Dors* 4F 8
Packington. *Leics* 8A 36
Packmoor. *Stoke* 4G 35
Packmores. *Warw* 5L 27
Packwood. *W Mid* 4K 27
Packwood Gullet. *W Mid* 4K 27
Padanaram. *Ang* 2H 67
Padbury. *Buck* 8E 28
**Paddington**. *G Lon* 5K 21
Paddington. *Warr* 1E 34
Paddlesworth. *Kent* 2H 13
Paddock. *Kent* 8F 22
Paddockhole. *Dum* 3G 53
Paddock Wood. *Kent* 1C 12
Paddolgreen. *Shrp* 6D 34
Padeswood. *Flin* 3A 34
**Padiham**. *Lanc* 4F 40
Padside. *N Yor* 2K 41
Padson. *Devn* 6E 6
Padstow. *Corn* 4B 4
Padworth. *W Ber* 7D 20
Page Bank. *Dur* 8F 54
Pagham. *W Sus* 6F 10
Paglesham Churchend. *Essx* 4F 22
Paglesham Eastend. *Essx* 4F 22
Paibeil. *W Isl*
on North Uist 7J 75
on Taransay 4B 76
Paiblesgearraidh. *W Isl* 7J 75
**Paignton**. *Torb* 5L 5
Pailton. *Warw* 3B 28
Paine's Corner. *E Sus* 3C 12
Painleyhill. *Staf* 6J 35
Painscastle. *Powy* 8L 25
Painshawfield. *Nmbd* 5D 54
Painsthorpe. *E Yor* 2F 42
Painswick. *Glos* 3G 19
Painter's Forstal. *Kent* 8F 22
Painthorpe. *W Yor* 6M 41
Pairc Shiaboist. *W Isl* 7F 82
**Paisley**. *Ren* 3C 58
Pakefield. *Suff* 2M 31
Pakenham. *Suff* 5F 30
Pale. *Gwyn* 7J 33
Palehouse Common. *E Sus* 4A 12
Palestine. *Hants* 1L 9
Paley Street. *Wind* 6F 20
Palgowan. *Dum* 3J 51
Palgrave. *Suff* 4H 31
Pallington. *Dors* 6F 8
Palmarsh. *Kent* 2H 13
Palmer Moor. *Derbs* 6K 35
Palmers Cross. *W Mid* 1G 27
Palmerstown. *V Glam* 8L 17
Palnackie. *Dum* 6C 52
Palnure. *Dum* 5K 51
Palterton. *Derbs* 3B 36
Pamber End. *Hants* 8D 20
Pamber Green. *Hants* 8D 20
Pamber Heath. *Hants* 7D 20
Pamington. *Glos* 8H 27
Pamphill. *Dors* 5H 9
Pampisford. *Cambs* 7A 30
Panborough. *Som* 1C 8
Panbride. *Ang* 4J 67
Pancrasweek. *Devn* 5B 6
Pandy. *Gwyn*
nr. Bala 7H 33
nr. Tywyn 2F 24
Pandy. *Mon* 1B 18
Pandy. *Powy* 2J 25
Pandy. *Wrex* 7L 33
Pandy Tudur. *Cnwy* 4H 33
Panfield. *Essx* 1D 22
Pangbourne. *W Ber* 6D 20
Pannal. *N Yor* 2M 41
Pannal Ash. *N Yor* 2L 41
Pannanich. *Abers* 6C 72
Pant. *Shrp* 7A 34
Pant. *Wrex* 5A 34
Pantasaph. *Flin* 3L 33
Pant Glas. *Gwyn* 6D 32
Pant-glas. *Shrp* 6A 34
Pantgwyn. *Carm* 2E 16
Pantgwyn. *Cdgn* 2J 15
Pant-lasau. *Swan* 4F 16
Panton. *Linc* 2J 37
Pant-pastynog. *Den* 4K 33
Pantperthog. *Gwyn* 2G 25
Pant-teg. *Carm* 4L 15
Pant-y-Caws. *Carm* 4H 15
Pant-y-dwr. *Powy* 5J 25
Pant-y-ffridd. *Powy* 2L 25
Pantyffynnon. *Carm* 3F 16
Pantygasseg. *Torf* 3A 18
Pant-y-llyn. *Carm* 3F 16
Pant-yr-awel. *B'end* 6J 17
Pant y Wacco. *Flin* 3L 33
Panxworth. *Norf* 8K 39
Papa Stour Airport. *Shet* 2B 90
Papa Westray Airport. *Orkn* 4D 88
Papcastle. *Cumb* 8F 52
Papigoe. *High* 6E 86
Papil. *Shet* 4D 90
Papple. *E Lot* 2C 60
Papplewick. *Notts* 4C 36
Papworth Everard. *Cambs* 5K 29
Papworth St Agnes. *Cambs* 5K 29
Par. *Corn* 6C 4
Paramour Street. *Kent* 7J 23
Parbold. *Lanc* 6C 40
Parbrook. *Som* 2D 8
Parbrook. *W Sus* 3H 11
Parc. *Gwyn* 7H 33
Parcllyn. *Cdgn* 1J 15
Parc-Seymour. *Newp* 4C 18
Pardown. *Hants* 1C 10
Pardshaw. *Cumb* 2K 45
Parham. *Suff* 5K 31
Park. *Abers* 6G 73
Park. *Arg* 3D 64
Park. *Derr* 3D 92
Park. *Dum* 2D 52
Park Bottom. *Corn* 4K 3
Parkburn. *Abers* 2G 73
Park Corner. *E Sus* 2B 12
Park Corner. *Oxon* 5D 20
Park End. *Nmbd* 4B 54
Parkend. *Glos* 3E 18
Parkeston. *Essx* 8J 31
Parkfield. *Corn* 5F 4
Park Gate. *Hants* 5C 10
Park Gate. *Worc* 4H 27
Parkgate. *Ant* 4H 93
Parkgate. *Ches W* 2A 34
Parkgate. *Cumb* 7G 53
Parkgate. *Dum* 3E 52
Parkgate. *Surr* 1K 11
Parkhall. *W Dun* 2C 58
Parkham. *Devn* 3C 6
Parkham Ash. *Devn* 3C 6
Parkhead. *Cumb* 7H 53
Parkhead. *Glas* 3E 58
Park Hill. *Mers* 7C 40
Parkhouse. *Mon* 3D 18
Parkhurst. *IOW* 6B 10
Park Lane. *G Man* 7F 40
Park Lane. *Staf* 1G 27
Park Mill. *W Yor* 6L 41
Parkmill. *Swan* 8M 15
Parkneuk. *Abers* 8G 73
Parkside. *N Lan* 4G 59
Parkstone. *Pool* 6J 9
Park Street. *Herts* 3J 21
Park Street. *W Sus* 2J 11
Park Town. *Oxon* 3C 20
Park Village. *Nmbd* 5L 53
Parkway. *Here* 8F 26
Parley Cross. *Dors* 6J 9
Parmoor. *Buck* 5E 20
Parr. *Mers* 8D 40
Parracombe. *Devn* 1F 6
Parrog. *Pemb* 3G 15
Parsonage Green. *Essx* 2D 22
Parsonby. *Cumb* 8F 52
Parson Cross. *S Yor* 8M 41
Parson Drove. *Cambs* 1L 29
Partick. *Glas* 3D 58
Partington. *G Man* 8F 40
Partney. *Linc* 3M 37
Parton. *Cumb*
nr. Whitehaven 2J 45
nr. Wigton 6G 53
Parton. *Dum* 4A 52
Partridge Green. *W Sus* 4J 11
Parwich. *Derbs* 4K 35
Passenham. *Nptn* 8E 28
Passfield. *Hants* 2F 10
Passingford Bridge. *Essx* 4B 22
Paston. *Norf* 6K 39
Pasturefields. *Staf* 7H 35
Patchacott. *Devn* 6D 6
Patcham. *Brig* 5L 11
Patchetts Green. *Herts* 4J 21
Patching. *W Sus* 5H 11
Patchole. *Devn* 1F 6
Patchway. *S Glo* 5E 18
Pateley Bridge. *N Yor* 1K 41
Pathe. *Som* 2B 8
Pathfinder Village. *Devn* 6H 7
Pathhead. *Abers* 1L 67
Pathhead. *E Ayr* 8E 58
Pathhead. *Fife* 8F 66
Pathhead. *Midl* 3A 60
Pathlow. *Warw* 6K 27
Path of Condie. *Per* 6D 66
Pathstruie. *Per* 6D 66
Patmore Heath. *Herts* 1M 21
Patna. *E Ayr* 8C 58
Patney. *Wilts* 8J 19
Patrick. *IOM* 6B 44
Patrick Brompton. *N Yor* 6L 47
Patrington. *E Yor* 5L 43
Patrington Haven. *E Yor* 5L 43
Patrixbourne. *Kent* 8H 23
Patterdale. *Cumb* 4B 46
Pattiesmuir. *Fife* 1J 59
Pattingham. *Staf* 2G 27
Pattishall. *Nptn* 6D 28
Pattiswick. *Essx* 1E 22
Patton Bridge. *Cumb* 6D 46
Paul. *Corn* 6H 3
Paulerspury. *Nptn* 7E 28
Paull. *E Yor* 5J 43
Paulton. *Bath* 8E 18
Pauperhaugh. *Nmbd* 2E 54
Pave Lane. *Telf* 8F 34
Pavenham. *Bed* 6G 29
Pawlett. *Som* 1A 8
Pawston. *Nmbd* 6F 60
Paxford. *Glos* 8K 27
Paxton. *Bord* 4G 61
Payhembury. *Devn* 5K 7
Paythorne. *Lanc* 2G 41
Payton. *Som* 3L 7
**Peacehaven**. *E Sus* 5M 11
Peak Dale. *Derbs* 2J 35
Peak Forest. *Derbs* 2K 35
Peak Hill. *Linc* 8K 37
Peakirk. *Pet* 1J 29
Pearsie. *Ang* 2G 67
Peasedown St John. *Bath* 8F 18
Peaseland Green. *Norf* 8G 39
Peasemore. *W Ber* 6B 20
Peasenhall. *Suff* 5K 31
Pease Pottage. *W Sus* 2K 11
Peaslake. *Surr* 1H 11
Peasley Cross. *Mers* 8D 40
Peasmarsh. *E Sus* 3E 12
Peasmarsh. *Som* 4B 8
Peasmarsh. *Surr* 1G 11
Peaston. *E Lot* 3B 60
Peastonbank. *E Lot* 3B 60
Peathill. *Abers* 7J 81
Peat Inn. *Fife* 7H 67
Peatling Magna. *Leics* 2C 28
Peatling Parva. *Leics* 3C 28
Peaton. *Arg* 1M 57
Peaton. *Shrp* 3D 26
Peats Corner. *Suff* 5H 31
Pebmarsh. *Essx* 8E 30
Pebworth. *Worc* 7K 27
Pecket Well. *W Yor* 5H 41
Peckforton. *Ches E* 4D 34
Peckham Bush. *Kent* 8C 22
Peckleton. *Leics* 1B 28
Pedair-ffordd. *Powy* 8L 33
Pedham. *Norf* 8K 39
Pedlinge. *Kent* 2H 13
Pedmore. *W Mid* 3H 27
Pedwell. *Som* 2C 8
Peebles. *Bord* 5L 59
Peel. *IOM* 6B 44
Peel. *Bord* 6B 60
Peel Common. *Hants* 5C 10
Peening Quarter. *Kent* 3E 12
Peggs Green. *Leics* 8B 36
Pegsdon. *C Beds* 8J 29
Pegswood. *Nmbd* 3F 54
Peinchorran. *High* 2G 69
Peinlich. *High* 8F 76
Pelaw. *Tyne* 5F 54
Pelcomb Bridge. *Pemb* 5F 14
Pelcomb Cross. *Pemb* 5F 14
Peldon. *Essx* 2F 22
**Pelsall**. *W Mid* 1J 27
Pelton. *Dur* 6F 54
Pelutho. *Cumb* 7F 52
Pelynt. *Corn* 6E 4
Pemberton. *Carm* 6M 15
Pembrey. *Carm* 6L 15
Pembridge. *Here* 6B 26
Pembroke. *Pemb* 6F 14
Pembroke Dock. *Pemb* 6F 14
Pembroke Ferry. *Pemb* 6F 14
Pembury. *Kent* 1C 12
Penallt. *Mon* 2D 18
Penally. *Pemb* 7H 15
Penalt. *Here* 1D 18
Penalum. *Pemb* 7H 15
Penare. *Corn* 7B 4
**Penarth**. *V Glam* 7L 17
Penbeagle. *Corn* 5J 3
Penberth. *Corn* 6H 3
Pen-bont Rhydybeddau.
*Cdgn* 4F 24
Penbryn. *Cdgn* 1J 15
Pencader. *Carm* 3L 15
Pen-cae. *Cdgn* 1L 15
Pencaenewydd. *Gwyn* 6D 32
Pencaerau. *Neat* 5G 17
Pencaitland. *E Lot* 3B 60
Pencarnisiog. *IOA* 3C 32
Pencarreg. *Carm* 2M 15
Pencarrow. *Corn* 3D 4
Pencelli. *Powy* 2K 17
Pen-clawdd. *Swan* 7M 15
Pencoed. *B'end* 6J 17
Pencombe. *Here* 6D 26
Pencraig. *Here* 1D 18
Pencraig. *Powy* 8K 33
Pendeen. *Corn* 5G 3
Pendeford. *W Mid* 1G 27
Penderyn. *Rhon* 4J 17
Pendine. *Carm* 6J 15
**Pendlebury**. *G Man* 7F 40
Pendleton. *G Man* 8G 41
Pendleton. *Lanc* 4F 40
Pendock. *Worc* 8F 26
Pendoggett. *Corn* 4C 4
Pendomer. *Som* 4D 8
Pendoylan. *V Glam* 7K 17
Pendre. *B'end* 6J 17
Penegoes. *Powy* 2G 25
Penelewey. *Corn* 4M 3
Penffordd. *Pemb* 4G 15
Penffordd-Lâs. *Powy* 3H 25
Penfro. *Pemb* 6F 14
Pengam. *Cphy* 5L 17
Pengam. *Card* 7M 17
**Penge**. *G Lon* 7L 21
Pengelly. *Corn* 3C 4
Pengenffordd. *Powy* 1L 17
Pengersick. *Corn* 6J 3
Pengorffwysfa. *IOA* 1D 32
Pengover Green. *Corn* 5E 4
Pengwern. *Den* 3K 33
Penhale. *Corn*
nr. Mullion 7K 3
nr. St Austell 6B 4
Penhale Camp. *Corn* 3L 3
Penhallow. *Corn* 3L 3
Penhalvean. *Corn* 5L 3
Penhelig. *Gwyn* 3F 24
Penhill. *Swin* 5K 19
Penhow. *Newp* 4C 18
Penhurst. *E Sus* 4C 12
Peniarth. *Gwyn* 2F 24
**Penicuik**. *Midl* 3L 59
Peniel. *Carm* 4L 15
Penifiler. *High* 1F 68
Peninver. *Arg* 7G 57
Penisa'r Waun. *Gwyn* 4E 32
Penistone. *S Yor* 7L 41
Penketh. *Warr* 1D 34
Penkill. *S Ayr* 2H 51
Penkridge. *Staf* 8H 35
Penley. *Wrex* 6C 34
Penllech. *Gwyn* 7B 32
Penllergaer. *Swan* 5F 16
Pen-llyn. *IOA* 2C 32
Penmachno. *Cnwy* 5G 33
Penmaen. *Swan* 8M 15
Penmaenmawr. *Cnwy* 3G 33
Penmaenpool. *Gwyn* 1F 24
Penmaen Rhos. *Cnwy* 3H 33
Pen-marc. *V Glam* 8K 17
Penmark. *V Glam* 8K 17
Penmarth. *Corn* 5L 3
Penmon. *IOA* 2F 32
Penmorfa. *Gwyn* 6E 32
Penmynydd. *IOA* 3E 32
Penn. *Buck* 4G 21
Penn. *Dors* 6B 8
Penn. *W Mid* 2G 27
Pennal. *Gwyn* 2G 25
Pennan. *Abers* 7H 81
Pennant. *Cdgn* 6E 24
Pennant. *Den* 7K 33
Pennant. *Gwyn* 8J 33
Pennant. *Powy* 3H 25
Pennant Melangell. *Powy* 8K 33
Pennar. *Pemb* 6F 14
Pennard. *Swan* 6E 16
Pennerley. *Shrp* 2B 26
Pennington. *Cumb* 8A 46
Pennington. *G Man* 8E 40
Pennington. *Hants* 6M 9
Pennorth. *Powy* 2L 17
Penn Street. *Buck* 4G 21
Pennsylvania. *Devn* 6J 7
Pennsylvania. *S Glo* 6F 18
Penny Bridge. *Cumb* 7B 46
Pennycross. *Plym* 6G 5
Pennygate. *Norf* 7K 39
Pennyghael. *Arg* 5L 63
Penny Hill. *Linc* 7L 37
Pennylands. *Lanc* 7C 40
Pennymoor. *Devn* 4H 7
Pennyvenie. *E Ayr* 1K 51
Pennywell. *Tyne* 6G 55
Penparc. *Cdgn* 2J 15
Penparcau. *Cdgn* 4E 24
Pen-pedair-heol. *Cphy* 5L 17
Penperlleni. *Mon* 3B 18
Penpillick. *Corn* 6C 4
Penpol. *Corn* 5M 3
Penpoll. *Corn* 6D 4
Penponds. *Corn* 5K 3
Penpont. *Corn* 4C 4
Penpont. *Dum* 2C 52
Penpont. *Powy* 2J 17
Penprysg. *B'end* 6J 17
Penquit. *Devn* 6J 5
Penrherber. *Carm* 3J 15
Penrhiw. *Pemb* 2J 15
Penrhiwceiber. *Rhon* 5K 17
Pen-Rhiw-fawr. *Neat* 3G 17
Penrhiw-llan. *Cdgn* 2K 15
Penrhiw-pal. *Cdgn* 2K 15
Penrhos. *Gwyn* 7C 32
Penrhos. *Here* 6B 26
Penrhos. *IOA* 2B 32
Penrhos. *Mon* 2C 18
Penrhos. *Powy* 3H 17
Penrhos Garnedd. *Gwyn* 3E 32
Penrhyn. *IOA* 1C 32
Penrhyn Bay. *Cnwy* 2H 33
Penrhyn-coch. *Cdgn* 4F 24
Penrhyndeudraeth. *Gwyn* 7F 32
Penrhyn-side. *Cnwy* 2H 33
Penrice. *Swan* 8L 15
**Penrith**. *Cumb* 3D 46
Penrose. *Corn* 4A 4
Penruddock. *Cumb* 3C 46
Penryn. *Corn* 5L 3
Pen-sarn. *Carm* 5L 15
Pen-sarn. *Gwyn* 8E 32
Pensax. *Worc* 5F 26
Pensby. *Mers* 1A 34
Penselwood. *Som* 2F 8
Pensford. *Bath* 7E 18
Pensham. *Worc* 7H 27
Penshaw. *Tyne* 6G 55
Penshurst. *Kent* 1B 12
Pensilva. *Corn* 5E 4
Pensnett. *W Mid* 3H 27
Penston. *E Lot* 2B 60
Penstone. *Devn* 5G 7
Pentewan. *Corn* 7C 4
Pentir. *Gwyn* 4E 32
Pentire. *Corn* 2L 3
Pentlepoir. *Pemb* 6H 15
Pentlow. *Essx* 7E 30
Pentney. *Norf* 8D 38
Penton Mewsey. *Hants* 1M 9
Pentraeth. *IOA* 3E 32
Pentre. *Powy*
nr. Church Stoke 2A 26
nr. Kerry 4L 25
nr. Mochdre 4K 25
Pentre. *Rhon* 5J 17
Pentre. *Shrp* 8B 34
Pentre. *Wrex*
nr. Chirk 5A 34
nr. Llanarmon Dyffryn Ceiriog 7L 33
Pentre-bach. *Cdgn* 2M 15
Pentre-bach. *Powy* 1J 17
Pentrebach. *Carm* 1H 17
Pentrebach. *Mer T* 4K 17
Pentrebach. *Swan* 4F 16
Pentre Berw. *IOA* 3D 32
Pentre-bont. *Cnwy* 5G 33
Pentrecagal. *Carm* 2K 15
Pentre-celyn. *Den* 5L 33
Pentre-clawdd. *Shrp* 6A 34
Pentreclwydau. *Neat* 4H 17
Pentre-cwrt. *Carm* 3K 15
Pentre Dolau Honddu. *Powy* 8J 25
Pentre-dwr. *Swan* 5F 16
Pentrefelin. *Carm* 2E 16
Pentrefelin. *Cdgn* 8F 24
Pentrefelin. *Cnwy* 3H 33
Pentrefelin. *Gwyn* 7E 32
Pentrefoelas. *Cnwy* 5H 33
Pentre Galar. *Pemb* 3H 15
Pentregat. *Cdgn* 1K 15
Pentre Gwenlais. *Carm* 3F 16
Pentre Gwynfryn. *Gwyn* 8E 32
Pentre Halkyn. *Flin* 3M 33
Pentre Hodre. *Shrp* 4B 26
Pentre-Llanrhaeadr. *Den* 4K 33
Pentre Llifior. *Powy* 3L 25
Pentrellwyn. *IOA* 2E 32
Pentre-llwyn-llwyd. *Powy* 7J 25
Pentre-llyn-cymmer. *Cnwy* 5J 33
Pentre Meyrick. *V Glam* 7J 17
Pentre-piod. *Gwyn* 7H 33
Pentre-poeth. *Newp* 5A 18
Pentre'r beirdd. *Powy* 1L 25
Pentre'r-felin. *Powy* 1J 17
Pentre-tafarn-y-fedw. *Cnwy* 4H 33
Pentre-ty-gwyn. *Carm* 1H 17
Pentre-uchaf. *Gwyn* 7C 32
Pentrich. *Derbs* 4A 36
Pentridge. *Dors* 4J 9
Pen-twyn. *Cphy* 4M 17
Pentwyn. *Cphy* 4L 17
Pentwyn. *Card* 6M 17
Pentyrch. *Card* 6L 17
Pentywyn. *Carm* 6J 15
Penuwch. *Cdgn* 6E 24
Penwithick. *Corn* 6C 4
Penwyllt. *Powy* 3H 17
Pen-y-banc. *Carm* 2F 16
Penybanc. *Carm* 3F 16
Pen-y-bont. *Carm* 4K 15
Pen-y-bont. *Powy* 8M 33
Penybont. *Powy* 6L 25
**Pen-y-Bont Ar Ogwr**. *B'end* 6J 17
Penybontfawr. *Powy* 8K 33
Pen-y-bryn. *Pemb* 2H 15
Pen-y-bryn. *Wrex* 5A 34
Penybryn. *Cphy* 5L 17
Pen-y-cae. *Powy* 3H 17
Penycae. *Wrex* 5A 34
Pen-y-cae mawr. *Mon* 4C 18
Penycaerau. *Gwyn* 8A 32
Pen-y-cefn. *Flin* 3L 33
Pen-y-clawdd. *Mon* 3C 18
Pen-y-coedcae. *Rhon* 6K 17
Penycwm. *Pemb* 4E 14
Pen-y-Darren. *Mer T* 4K 17
Pen-y-fai. *B'end* 6H 17
Pen-y-ffordd. *Flin* 2L 33
Penyffordd. *Flin* 3B 34
Penyffridd. *Gwyn* 5E 32
Pen-y-garn. *Cdgn* 4F 24
Pen-y-garnedd. *IOA* 3E 32
Penygarnedd. *Powy* 8L 33
Pen-y-graig. *Gwyn* 7B 32
Penygraig. *Rhon* 5J 17
Penygraigwen. *IOA* 2D 32
Pen-y-groes. *Carm* 3E 16
Penygroes. *Gwyn* 5D 32
Penygroes. *Pemb* 3H 15
Pen-y-Mynydd. *Carm* 6L 15
Penymynydd. *Flin* 3B 34
Pen-yr-heol. *Mon* 2C 18
Penyrheol. *Cphy* 6L 17
Penyrheol. *Swan* 5E 16
Penysarn. *IOA* 1D 32
Pen-y-stryt. *Den* 5L 33
Penywaun. *Rhon* 4J 17
**Penzance**. *Corn* 5H 3
Peopleton. *Worc* 6H 27
Peover Heath. *Ches E* 2F 34
Peper Harow. *Surr* 1G 11
Peplow. *Shrp* 7E 34
Pepper Arden. *N Yor* 5L 47
Perceton. *N Ayr* 5B 58
Percyhorner. *Abers* 7J 81
Perham Down. *Wilts* 1L 9
Periton. *Som* 1J 7
Perkinsville. *Dur* 6F 54
Perlethorpe. *Notts* 2D 36
Perranarworthal. *Corn* 5L 3
Perranporth. *Corn* 3L 3
Perranuthnoe. *Corn* 6J 3
Perranwell. *Corn* 5L 3
Perranzabuloe. *Corn* 3L 3
Perrott's Brook. *Glos* 3J 19
Perry. *W Mid* 2J 27
Perry Barr. *W Mid* 2J 27
Perry Crofts. *Staf* 1L 27
Perry Green. *Essx* 1E 22
Perry Green. *Herts* 2M 21
Perry Green. *Wilts* 5H 19
Perry Street. *Kent* 6C 22
Perry Street. *Som* 5B 8
Perrywood. *Kent* 8G 23
Pershall. *Staf* 7G 35
Pershore. *Worc* 7H 27
Pertenhall. *Bed* 5H 29
**Perth**. *Per* 5E 66
Perthy. *Shrp* 6B 34
Perton. *Staf* 2G 27
Pertwood. *Wilts* 2G 9
**Peterborough**. *Pet* 2J 29
Peterburn. *High* 5J 77
Peterchurch. *Here* 8B 26
Peterculter. *Aber* 5H 73
**Peterhead**. *Abers* 1L 73
**Peterlee**. *Dur* 7H 55
**Petersfield**. *Hants* 3E 10
Petersfinger. *Wilts* 3K 9
Peters Green. *Herts* 2J 21
Peters Marland. *Devn* 4D 6
Peterstone Wentlooge.
*Newp* 5A 18
Peterston-super-Ely. *V Glam* 7K 17
Peterstow. *Here* 1D 18
Peters Village. *Kent* 7D 22
Peter Tavy. *Devn* 8E 6
Petertown. *Orkn* 1E 86
Petham. *Kent* 8H 23
Petherwin Gate. *Corn* 7B 6
Petrockstowe. *Devn* 5E 6
Petsoe End. *Mil* 7F 28
Pett. *E Sus* 4E 12
Pettaugh. *Suff* 6H 31
Pett Bottom. *Kent* 8H 23
Petteridge. *Kent* 1C 12
Pettinain. *S Lan* 5H 59

**Column entries (selected, left to right):**

Royston. *Herts* .......7L 29
**Royston.** *S Yor* .......6A 42
Royston Water. *Som* .....4M 7
**Royton.** *G Man* .......7H 41

**Rossendale.** *Lanc* ....5F 40
**Rotherham.** *S Yor* ....8B 42
**Rothwell.** *W Yor* .....5M 41
St Asaph. *Den* ...........3K 33
**Rugby.** *Warw* .........4C 28
**Rugeley.** *Staf* ........8J 35
**Runcorn.** *Hal* ........5F 10
**Ruislip.** *G Lon* ......5L 21
**Rushden.** *Nptn* .......5G 29
**Rutherglen.** *S Lan* ...3E 58
**Ruthin.** *Den* .........5L 33
**Ryde.** *IOW* ...........6C 10

**Royal Leamington Spa.** *Warw* ...5M 27
**Royal Sutton Coldfield.** *W Mid* ...2K 27
**Royal Tunbridge Wells.** *Kent* ...2B 12
**Royal Wootton Bassett.** *Wilts* ...5J 19

# S

**Saddleworth.** *G Man* ...7H 41
**Saffron Walden.** *Essx* ...8B 30
**St Albans.** *Herts* .....3J 21
**St Andrews.** *Fife* .....6J 67
St Andrews Major. *V Glam* ...7L 17

**St Austell.** *Corn* .....6B 4
St Davids. *Pemb* .........4D 14
**St Helens.** *Mers* ......8D 40
**St Ives.** *Cambs* .......4L 29
**St Ives.** *Corn* ........5K 9
**St Neots.** *Cambs* ......5H 29

**Salford.** *G Man* .......8G 41
**Salisbury.** *Wilts* .....2K 9
**Saltash.** *Corn* ........6G 5
**Saltburn-by-the-Sea.** *Red C* ...3D 48
**Saltcoats.** *N Ayr* .....5K 57
**Sandbach.** *Ches E* .....3F 34
**Sandhurst.** *Brac* ......1G 19
**Sandown.** *IOW* .........7C 10
**Sandwich.** *Kent* .......8K 23

**Sawbridgeworth.** *Herts* ...2A 22

**Scarborough.** *N Yor* ...7H 49
**Scotch Corner.** *N Yor* ...5L 47
**Scunthorpe.** *N Lin* ....6F 42

**Seaford.** *E Sus* .......6A 12
**Seaham.** *Dur* ..........7H 55
**Sevenoaks.** *Kent* ......8B 22
**Selby.** *N Yor* .........4D 42
**Shanklin.** *IOW* ........7C 10
**Sheerness.** *Kent* ......7H 23
**Sheffield.** *S Yor* .....1A 36

Shelton—Stocksbridge


Shelton. *Bed* 5H **29**
Shelton. *Norf* 2J **31**
Shelton. *Notts* 5E **36**
Shelton. *Shrp* 8C **34**
Shelton Green. *Norf* 2J **31**
Shelton Lock. *Derb* 6A **36**
Shelve. *Shrp* 2B **26**
Shelwick. *Here* 7D **26**
Shelwick Green. *Here* 7D **26**
Shenfield. *Essx* 4C **22**
Shenington. *Oxon* 7A **28**
Shenley. *Herts* 3J **21**
Shenley Brook End. *Mil* 8F **28**
Shenleybury. *Herts* 3J **21**
Shenley Church End. *Mil* 8F **28**
Shenmore. *Here* 8B **26**
Shennanton. *Dum* 5J **51**
Shenstone. *Staf* 1K **27**
Shenstone. *Worc* 4G **27**
Shenstone Woodend. *Staf* 1K **27**
Shenton. *Leics* 1A **28**
Shenval. *Mor* 3B **72**
Shepeau Stow. *Linc* 8L **37**
Shephall. *Herts* 1K **21**
Shepherd's Bush. *G Lon* 5K **21**
Shepherd's Gate. *Norf* 8B **38**
Shepherd's Green. *Oxon* 5E **20**
Shepherd's Port. *Norf* 6C **38**
Shepherdswell. *Kent* 1J **13**
Shepley. *W Yor* 7K **41**
Sheppardstown. *High* 7C **86**
Shepperdine. *S Glo* 4E **18**
Shepperton. *Surr* 7H **21**
Shepreth. *Cambs* 7L **29**
**Shepshed**. *Leics* 8B **36**
Shepton Beauchamp. *Som* 4C **8**
Shepton Mallet. *Som* 1E **8**
Shepton Montague. *Som* 2E **8**
Shepway. *Kent* 8D **22**
Sheraton. *Dur* 8H **55**
Sherborne. *Dors* 4E **8**
Sherborne. *Glos* 2K **19**
Sherborne. *Som* 8D **18**
Sherborne Causeway. *Dors* 3G **9**
Sherborne St John. *Hants* 8D **20**
Sherbourne. *Warw* 5L **27**
Sherburn. *Dur* 7G **55**
Sherburn. *N Yor* 8G **49**
Sherburn Hill. *Dur* 7G **55**
Sherburn in Elmet. *N Yor* 4B **42**
Shere. *Surr* 1H **11**
Shereford. *Norf* 7E **38**
Sherfield English. *Hants* 3L **9**
Sherfield on Loddon.
  *Hants* 8D **20**
Sherford. *Devn* 7K **5**
Sherford. *Dors* 6H **9**
Sheriffhales. *Shrp* 8F **34**
Sheriff Hutton. *N Yor* 1D **42**
Sheriffston. *Mor* 7B **80**
Sheringham. *Norf* 5H **39**
Sherington. *Mil* 7F **28**
Shermanbury. *W Sus* 4K **11**
Shernal Green. *Worc* 5H **27**
Shernborne. *Norf* 6D **38**
Sherrington. *Wilts* 2H **9**
Sherston. *Wilts* 5G **19**
Sherwood. *Nott* 5C **36**
Sherwood Green. *Devn* 3E **6**
Shettleston. *Glas* 3E **58**
Shevington. *G Man* 7D **40**
Shevington Moor. *G Man* 6D **40**
Shevington Vale. *G Man* 7D **40**
Sheviock. *Corn* 6F **4**
Shide. *IOW* 7B **10**
Shiel Bridge. *High* 4L **69**
Shieldaig. *High*
  nr. Charlestown 6K **77**
  nr. Torridon 8K **77**
Shieldhill. *Dum* 3E **52**
Shieldhill. *Falk* 2G **59**
Shieldhill. *S Lan* 5J **59**
Shieldmuir. *N Lan* 4F **58**
Shielfoot. *High* 8H **69**
Shielhill. *Abers* 8K **81**
Shielhill. *Ang* 2H **67**
Shifnal. *Shrp* 1F **26**
Shilbottle. *Nmbd* 1E **54**
Shilbottle Grange. *Nmbd* 1F **54**
**Shildon**. *Dur* 3L **47**
Shillford. *E Ren* 4C **58**
Shillingford. *Devn* 3J **7**
Shillingford. *Oxon* 4C **20**
Shillingford St George. *Devn* 7J **7**
Shillingstone. *Dors* 4G **9**
Shillington. *C Beds* 8J **29**
Shillmoor. *Nmbd* 1B **54**
Shilton. *Oxon* 3L **19**
Shilton. *Warw* 3B **28**
Shilvinghampton. *Dors* 7E **8**
Shilvington. *Nmbd* 3E **54**
Shimpling. *Norf* 3H **31**
Shimpling. *Suff* 6E **30**
Shimpling Street. *Suff* 6E **30**
Shincliffe. *Dur* 7F **54**
Shiney Row. *Tyne* 6G **55**
Shinfield. *Wok* 7E **20**
Shingay. *Cambs* 7L **29**
Shingham. *Norf* 1D **30**
Shingle Street. *Suff* 7K **31**
Shinner's Bridge. *Devn* 5K **5**
Shinness. *High* 2F **78**
Shipbourne. *Kent* 8B **22**
Shipdham. *Norf* 1F **30**
Shipham. *Som* 8C **18**
Shiphay. *Torb* 5L **5**
Shiplake. *Oxon* 6E **20**
Shipley. *Derbs* 5B **36**
Shipley. *Nmbd* 8J **61**
Shipley. *Shrp* 2G **27**
Shipley. *W Sus* 3J **11**
**Shipley**. *W Yor* 4K **41**
Shipley Bridge. *Surr* 1L **11**
Shipmeadow. *Suff* 3K **31**
Shippon. *Oxon* 4B **20**
Shipston-on-Stour. *Warw* 7L **27**
Shipton. *Buck* 1E **20**
Shipton. *Glos* 2J **19**
Shipton. *N Yor* 2C **42**
Shipton. *Shrp* 2D **26**
Shipton Bellinger. *Hants* 1L **9**
Shipton Gorge. *Dors* 6C **8**
Shipton Green. *W Sus* 6F **10**
Shipton Moyne. *Glos* 5G **19**
Shipton-on-Cherwell. *Oxon* 2B **20**
Shiptonthorpe. *E Yor* 3F **42**
Shipton-under-Wychwood.
  *Oxon* 2L **19**
Shirburn. *Oxon* 4D **20**
Shirdley Hill. *Lanc* 6B **40**
Shire. *Cumb* 8L **53**
**Shirebrook**. *Derbs* 3C **36**
Shiregreen. *S Yor* 8A **42**
Shirehampton. *Bris* 6D **18**
Shiremoor. *Tyne* 4G **55**
Shirenewton. *Mon* 4C **18**
Shireoaks. *Notts* 1C **36**
Shires Mill. *Fife* 1J **59**
Shirkoak. *Kent* 2F **12**
Shirland. *Derbs* 4A **36**
Shirley. *Derbs* 5L **35**
Shirley. *Sotn* 4A **10**
Shirley. *W Mid* 4K **27**
Shirleywich. *Staf* 7H **35**
Shirl Heath. *Here* 6C **26**
Shirrell Heath. *Hants* 4C **10**
Shirwell. *Devn* 2E **6**
Shiskine. *N Ayr* 7J **57**
Shobdon. *Here* 5B **26**
Shobnall. *Staf* 7L **35**
Shobrooke. *Devn* 5H **7**
Shoby. *Leics* 7D **36**
Shocklach. *Ches W* 5C **34**
Shoeburyness. *S'end* 5F **22**
Sholden. *Kent* 8K **23**
Sholing. *Sotn* 4B **10**
Sholver. *G Man* 7H **41**
Shoot Hill. *Shrp* 8C **34**
Shop. *Corn*
  nr. Bude 4B **6**
  nr. Padstow 4A **4**
Shop. *Devn* 4C **6**
Shopford. *Cumb* 4K **53**
**Shoreditch**. *G Lon* 5L **21**
Shoreditch. *Som* 3M **7**
Shoregill. *Cumb* 5F **46**
Shoreham. *Kent* 7B **22**
**Shoreham-by-Sea**. *W Sus* 5K **11**
Shoresdean. *Nmbd* 5G **61**
Shoreswood. *Nmbd* 5G **61**
Shorncote. *Glos* 4J **19**
Shorne. *Kent* 6C **22**
Shorne Ridgeway. *Kent* 6C **22**
Shortacombe. *Devn* 7E **6**
Shortbridge. *E Sus* 3A **12**
Shortgate. *E Sus* 4A **12**
Short Green. *Norf* 3G **31**
Shorthampton. *Oxon* 1M **19**
Short Heath. *Derbs* 8M **35**
Short Heath. *W Mid*
  nr. Erdington 2J **27**
  nr. Wednesfield 1H **27**
Shortlanesend. *Corn* 4M **3**
Shorton. *Torb* 5L **5**
Shortstown. *Bed* 7H **29**
Shortwood. *S Glo* 6E **18**
Shorwell. *IOW* 7B **10**
Shoscombe. *Bath* 8F **18**
Shotesham. *Norf* 2J **31**
Shotgate. *Essx* 4D **22**
Shotley. *Suff* 8J **31**
Shotley Bridge. *Dur* 6D **54**
Shotleyfield. *Nmbd* 6D **54**
Shotley Gate. *Suff* 8J **31**
Shottenden. *Kent* 8G **23**
Shottermill. *Surr* 2F **10**
Shottery. *Warw* 6K **27**
Shotteswell. *Warw* 7B **28**
Shottisham. *Suff* 7K **31**
Shottle. *Derbs* 5M **35**
Shotton. *Dur*
  nr. Peterlee 8H **55**
  nr. Sedgefield 3A **48**
**Shotton**. *Flin* 3B **34**
Shotton. *Nmbd*
  nr. Morpeth 4F **54**
  nr. Town Yetholm 6F **60**
Shotton Colliery. *Dur* 7G **55**
Shotts. *N Lan* 3G **59**
Shotwick. *Ches W* 2B **34**
Shouldham. *Norf* 1C **30**
Shouldham Thorpe. *Norf* 1C **30**
Shoulton. *Worc* 6G **27**
Shrawardine. *Shrp* 8C **34**
Shrawley. *Worc* 5G **27**
Shreding Green. *Buck* 5H **21**
Shrewley. *Warw* 5L **27**
**Shrewsbury**. *Shrp* 8C **34**
Shrewton. *Wilts* 1J **9**
Shrigley. *New M* 6J **93**
Shripney. *W Sus* 5G **11**
Shrivenham. *Oxon* 5L **19**
Shropham. *Norf* 2F **30**
Shroton. *Dors* 4G **9**
Shrub End. *Essx* 1F **22**
Shucknall. *Here* 7D **26**
Shudy Camps. *Cambs* 7C **30**
Shulishadermor. *High* 1F **68**
Shulista. *High* 6F **76**
Shurdington. *Glos* 2H **19**
Shurlock Row. *Wind* 6F **20**
Shurrery. *High* 6B **86**
Shurton. *Som* 1M **7**
Shustoke. *Warw* 2L **27**
Shute. *Devn*
  nr. Axminster 6A **8**
  nr. Crediton 5H **7**
Shutford. *Oxon* 7A **28**
Shut Heath. *Staf* 7G **35**
Shuthonger. *Glos* 8G **27**
Shutlanehead. *Staf* 5G **35**
Shutlanger. *Nptn* 7E **28**
Shutt Green. *Staf* 1G **27**
Shuttington. *Warw* 1L **27**
Shuttlewood. *Derbs* 2B **36**
Shuttleworth. *G Man* 6G **41**
Siabost. *W Isl* 7F **82**
Siabost bho Dheas. *W Isl* 7F **82**
Siabost bho Thuath. *W Isl* 7F **82**
Siadar. *W Isl* 6G **83**
Siadar Uarach. *W Isl* 6G **83**
Sibbaldbie. *Dum* 3F **52**
Sibbertoft. *Nptn* 3D **28**
Sibdon Carwood. *Shrp* 3C **26**
Sibertswold. *Kent* 1J **13**
Sibford Ferris. *Oxon* 8A **28**
Sibford Gower. *Oxon* 8A **28**
Sible Hedingham. *Essx* 8D **30**
Sibsey. *Linc* 4L **37**
Sibsey Fen Side. *Linc* 4L **37**
Sibson. *Cambs* 2H **29**
Sibson. *Leics* 1A **28**
Sibster. *High* 6E **86**
Sibthorpe. *Notts* 5E **36**
Sibton. *Suff* 5K **31**
Sicklesmere. *Suff* 5E **30**
Sicklinghall. *N Yor* 3A **42**
Sid. *Devn* 7L **7**
Sidbury. *Devn* 6L **7**
Sidbury. *Shrp* 3E **26**
Sidcot. *N Som* 8C **18**
**Sidcup**. *G Lon* 6A **22**
Siddick. *Cumb* 8E **52**
Siddington. *Ches E* 2G **35**
Siddington. *Glos* 4J **19**
Side of the Moor. *G Man* 6F **40**
Sidestrand. *Norf* 6J **39**
Sidford. *Devn* 6L **7**
Sidlesham. *W Sus* 6F **10**
Sidley. *E Sus* 5D **12**
Sidlow. *Surr* 1K **11**
**Sidmouth**. *Devn* 7L **7**
Sigford. *Devn* 8G **7**
Sigglesthorne. *E Yor* 3J **43**
Sighthill. *Edin* 2K **59**
Sigingstone. *V Glam* 7J **17**
Signet. *Oxon* 2L **19**
Silchester. *Hants* 7D **20**
Sildinis. *W Isl* 2D **76**
Sileby. *Leics* 8D **36**
Silecroft. *Cumb* 6L **45**
Silfield. *Norf* 2H **31**
Silian. *Cdgn* 7E **24**
Silkstone. *S Yor* 7L **41**
Silkstone Common. *S Yor* 7L **41**
Silksworth. *Tyne* 6G **55**
Silk Willoughby. *Linc* 5H **37**
Silloth. *Cumb* 6F **52**
Sills. *Nmbd* 1B **54**
Sillyearn. *Mor* 8E **80**
Silpho. *N Yor* 6G **49**
Silsden. *W Yor* 3J **41**
Silsoe. *C Beds* 8H **29**
Silverbank. *Abers* 6G **73**
Silverbridge. *New M* 7F **93**
Silverburn. *Midl* 3L **59**
Silverdale. *Lanc* 8C **46**
Silverdale. *Staf* 5G **35**
Silverdale Green. *Lanc* 8C **46**
Silver End. *Essx* 2E **22**
Silver End. *W Mid* 3H **27**
Silvergate. *Norf* 7H **39**
Silver Green. *Norf* 2J **31**
Silverhillocks. *Abers* 7G **81**
Silverley's Green. *Suff* 4J **31**
Silverstone. *Nptn* 7D **28**
Silverton. *Devn* 5J **7**
Silverton. *W Dun* 2C **58**
Silvington. *Shrp* 4E **26**
Simm's Cross. *Hal* 1D **34**
Simm's Lane End. *Mers* 7D **40**
Simonburn. *Nmbd* 4B **54**
Simonsbath. *Som* 2G **7**
Simonstone. *Lanc* 4F **40**
Simprim. *Bord* 5F **60**
Simpson. *Pemb* 5E **14**
Simpson Cross. *Pemb* 5E **14**
Sinclairston. *E Ayr* 8C **58**
Sinclairtown. *Fife* 8F **66**
Sinderby. *N Yor* 7M **47**
Sinderhope. *Nmbd* 6B **54**
Sindlesham. *Wok* 7E **20**
Sinfin. *Derb* 6M **35**
Singleborough. *Buck* 8E **28**
Singleton. *Kent* 1F **12**
Singleton. *Lanc* 4B **40**
Singleton. *W Sus* 4F **10**
Singlewell. *Kent* 6C **22**
Sinkhurst Green. *Kent* 1E **12**
Sinnahard. *Abers* 4D **72**
Sinnington. *N Yor* 7E **48**
Sinton Green. *Worc* 5G **27**
Sion Mills. *Derr* 4C **92**
Sipson. *G Lon* 6H **21**
Sirhowy. *Blae* 3L **17**
Sisland. *Norf* 2K **31**
Sissinghurst. *Kent* 2D **12**
Siston. *S Glo* 6E **18**
Sithney. *Corn* 6K **3**
**Sittingbourne**. *Kent* 7F **22**
Six Ashes. *Staf* 3F **26**
Six Bells. *Blae* 4M **17**
Six Hills. *Leics* 7D **36**
Sixhills. *Linc* 1J **37**
Six Mile Bottom. *Cambs* 6B **30**
Sixmilecross. *Ferm* 5D **92**
Sixpenny Handley. *Dors* 4H **9**
Sizewell. *Suff* 5L **31**
Skail. *High* 7K **85**
Skaill. *Orkn* 8B **88**
Skaills. *Orkn* 1G **87**
Skares. *E Ayr* 8D **58**
Skateraw. *E Lot* 2E **60**
Skaw. *Shet* 1F **90**
Skeabost. *High* 1F **68**
Skeabrae. *Orkn* 7B **88**
Skeeby. *N Yor* 5K **47**
Skeffington. *Leics* 1E **28**
Skeffling. *E Yor* 6L **43**
Skegby. *Notts*
  nr. Mansfield 3B **36**
  nr. Tuxford 2E **36**
**Skegness**. *Linc* 3B **38**
Skelberry. *Shet*
  nr. Boddam 6D **90**
  nr. Housetter 5H **91**
Skelbo. *High* 4H **79**
Skelbo Street. *High* 4H **79**
Skelbrooke. *S Yor* 6C **42**
Skeldyke. *Linc* 6L **37**
Skelfhill. *Bord* 1J **53**
Skellingthorpe. *Linc* 2G **37**
Skellister. *Shet* 2E **90**
Skellorn Green. *Ches E* 1H **35**
Skellow. *S Yor* 6C **42**
Skelmanthorpe. *W Yor* 6L **41**
**Skelmersdale**. *Lanc* 7C **40**
Skelmorlie. *N Ayr* 3L **57**
Skelpick. *High* 6K **85**
Skelton. *Cumb* 8J **53**
Skelton. *E Yor* 5E **42**
Skelton. *N Yor*
  nr. Richmond 5J **47**
  nr. Ripon 1A **42**
Skelton. *Red C* 4D **48**
Skelton. *York* 2C **42**
Skelton Green. *Red C* 4D **48**
Skelwick. *Orkn* 5D **88**
Skelwith Bridge. *Cumb* 5B **46**
Skendleby. *Linc* 3M **37**
Skendleby Psalter. *Linc* 2M **37**
Skenfrith. *Mon* 1C **18**
Skerne. *E Yor* 2H **43**
Skeroblingarry. *Arg* 7G **57**
Skerray. *High* 5J **85**
Skerricha. *High* 6E **84**
Skerries Airport. *Shet* 6L **91**
Skerton. *Lanc* 1C **40**
Sketchley. *Leics* 2B **28**
Sketty. *Swan* 5F **16**
Skewen. *Neat* 5G **17**
Skewsby. *N Yor* 8D **48**
Skeyton. *Norf* 7J **39**
Skeyton Corner. *Norf* 7J **39**
Skiall. *High* 5B **86**
Skidbrooke. *Linc* 8M **43**
Skidbrooke North End.
  *Linc* 8M **43**
Skidby. *E Yor* 4H **43**
Skilgate. *Som* 3J **7**
Skillington. *Linc* 7F **36**
Skinburness. *Cumb* 6F **52**
Skinflats. *Falk* 1H **59**
Skinidin. *High* 1D **68**
Skinnet. *High* 5H **85**
Skinningrove. *Red C* 4E **48**
Skipness. *Arg* 4H **57**
Skippool. *Lanc* 3B **40**
Skiprigg. *Cumb* 7H **53**
Skipsea. *E Yor* 2J **43**
Skipsea Brough. *E Yor* 2J **43**
**Skipton**. *N Yor* 2H **41**
Skipton-on-Swale. *N Yor* 8A **48**
Skipwith. *N Yor* 4D **42**
Skirbeck. *Linc* 5L **37**
Skirbeck Quarter. *Linc* 5L **37**
Skirlaugh. *E Yor* 4J **43**
Skirling. *Bord* 6J **59**
Skirmett. *Buck* 4E **20**
Skirpenbeck. *E Yor* 2E **42**
Skirwith. *Cumb* 8L **53**
Skirwith. *N Yor* 8F **46**
Skirza. *High* 5E **86**
Skitby. *Cumb* 5J **53**
Skitham. *Lanc* 3C **40**
Skittle Green. *Buck* 3E **20**
Skroo. *Shet* 2M **89**
Skulamus. *High* 3H **69**
Skullomie. *High* 5J **85**
Skyborry Green. *Shrp* 4A **26**
Skye Green. *Essx* 1E **22**
Skye of Curr. *High* 3K **71**
Slack. *W Yor* 5H **41**
The Slack. *Dur* 3K **47**
Slackhall. *Derbs* 1J **35**
Slack Head. *Cumb* 8C **46**
Slackhead. *Mor* 7D **80**
Slackholme End. *Linc* 2B **38**
Slacks of Cairnbanno.
  *Abers* 1H **73**
Slad. *Glos* 3G **19**
Slade. *Swan* 8L **15**
The Slade. *W Ber* 7C **20**
Slade End. *Oxon* 4C **20**
Slade Field. *Cambs* 3L **29**
Slade Green. *G Lon* 6B **22**
Slade Heath. *Staf* 1H **27**
Slade Hooton. *S Yor* 1C **36**
Sladesbridge. *Corn* 4C **4**
Slaggyford. *Nmbd* 6L **53**
Slaidburn. *Lanc* 2F **40**
Slaid Hill. *W Yor* 3M **41**
Slaithwaite. *W Yor* 6J **41**
Slaley. *Derbs* 4L **35**
Slaley. *Nmbd* 6C **54**
Slamannan. *Falk* 2G **59**
Slapton. *Buck* 1G **21**
Slapton. *Devn* 7L **5**
Slapton. *Nptn* 7D **28**
Slattocks. *G Man* 7G **41**
Slaugham. *W Sus* 3K **11**
Slaughterbridge. *Corn* 3D **4**
Slaughterford. *Wilts* 6G **19**
Slawston. *Leics* 2E **28**
Sleaford. *Hants* 2F **10**
**Sleaford**. *Linc* 5H **37**
Sleagill. *Cumb* 4D **46**
Sleap. *Shrp* 7C **34**
Sledmere. *E Yor* 1G **43**
Sleightholme. *Dur* 4H **47**
Sleights. *N Yor* 5F **48**
Slepe. *Dors* 6H **9**
Slickly. *High* 5D **86**
Sliddery. *N Ayr* 7J **57**
Sligachan. *High* 3F **68**
Slimbridge. *Glos* 3F **18**
Slindon. *Staf* 6G **35**
Slindon. *W Sus* 5G **11**
Slinfold. *W Sus* 2J **11**
Slingsby. *N Yor* 8D **48**
Slip End. *C Beds* 2H **21**
Slipton. *Nptn* 4G **29**
Slitting Mill. *Staf* 8J **35**
Slochd. *High* 3J **71**
Slockavullin. *Arg* 8C **64**
Sloley. *Norf* 7J **39**
Sloncombe. *Devn* 7G **7**
Sloothby. *Linc* 2A **38**
**Slough**. *Slo* 6G **21**
Slough Green. *Som* 3A **8**
Slough Green. *W Sus* 3K **11**
Sluggan. *High* 3J **71**
Slyne. *Lanc* 1C **40**
Smailholm. *Bord* 6D **60**
Smallbridge. *G Man* 6H **41**
Smallbrook. *Devn* 6H **7**
Smallburgh. *Norf* 7K **39**
Smallburn. *E Ayr* 7E **58**
Smalldale. *Derbs* 2J **35**
Small Dole. *W Sus* 4K **11**
Smalley. *Derbs* 5B **36**
Smallfield. *Surr* 1L **11**
Small Heath. *W Mid* 3J **27**
Smallholm. *Dum* 4F **52**
Small Hythe. *Kent* 2E **12**
Smallrice. *Staf* 6H **35**
Smallridge. *Devn* 5B **8**
Smallwood Hey. *Lanc* 3B **40**
Smallworth. *Norf* 3G **31**
Smannell. *Hants* 1A **10**
Smardale. *Cumb* 5F **46**
Smarden. *Kent* 1E **12**
Smarden Bell. *Kent* 1E **12**
Smart's Hill. *Kent* 1B **12**
Smeatharpe. *Devn* 4M **7**
Smeeth. *Kent* 2G **13**
The Smeeth. *Norf* 8B **38**
Smeeton Westerby. *Leics* 2D **28**
Smeircleit. *W Isl* 4D **74**
Smerral. *High* 8C **86**
Smestow. *Staf* 2G **27**
**Smethwick**. *W Mid* 3J **27**
Smirisary. *High* 8H **69**
Smisby. *Derbs* 8M **35**
Smitham Hill. *Bath* 8D **18**
Smith End Green. *Worc* 6F **26**
Smithfield. *Cumb* 5J **53**
Smith Green. *Lanc* 2C **40**
The Smithies. *Shrp* 2E **26**
Smithincott. *Devn* 4K **7**
Smith's Green. *Essx* 1B **22**
Smithstown. *High* 6J **77**
Smithton. *High* 1H **71**
Smithwood Green. *Suff* 6F **30**
Smithy Bridge. *G Man* 6H **41**
Smithy Green. *Ches E* 2F **34**
Smithy Lane Ends. *Lanc* 6C **40**
Smockington. *Leics* 3B **28**
Smoogro. *Orkn* 1E **86**
Smythe's Green. *Essx* 2F **22**
Snaigow House. *Per* 3D **66**
Snailbeach. *Shrp* 1B **26**
Snailwell. *Cambs* 5C **30**
Snainton. *N Yor* 7G **49**
Snaith. *E Yor* 5D **42**
Snape. *N Yor* 7L **47**
Snape. *Suff* 6K **31**
Snape Green. *Lanc* 6B **40**
Snapper. *Devn* 2E **6**
Snarestone. *Leics* 1M **27**
Snarford. *Linc* 1H **37**
Snargate. *Kent* 3F **12**
Snave. *Kent* 3G **13**
Sneachill. *Worc* 6H **27**
Snead. *Powy* 2B **26**
Snead Common. *Worc* 5F **26**
Sneaton. *N Yor* 5F **48**
Sneatonthorpe. *N Yor* 5G **49**
Snelland. *Linc* 1H **37**
Snelston. *Derbs* 5K **35**
Snetterton. *Norf* 2F **30**
Snettisham. *Norf* 6C **38**
Snibston. *Leics* 8B **36**
Sniseabhal. *W Isl* 2D **74**
Snitter. *Nmbd* 1D **54**
Snitterby. *Linc* 8G **43**
Snitterfield. *Warw* 6L **27**
Snitton. *Shrp* 4D **26**
Snodhill. *Here* 7B **26**
Snodland. *Kent* 7D **22**
Snods Edge. *Nmbd* 6D **54**
Snowshill. *Glos* 8J **27**
Snow Street. *Norf* 3G **31**
Snydale. *W Yor* 5B **42**
Soake. *Hants* 4D **10**
Soar. *Carm* 2F **16**
Soar. *Gwyn* 7F **32**
Soar. *IOA* 3C **32**
Soar. *Powy* 1J **17**
Soberton. *Hants* 4D **10**
Soberton Heath. *Hants* 4D **10**
Sockbridge. *Cumb* 3D **46**
Sockburn. *Darl* 5M **47**
Sodom. *Den* 3K **33**
Sodom. *Shet* 1F **90**
Soham. *Cambs* 4B **30**
Soham Cotes. *Cambs* 4B **30**
Solas. *W Isl* 6K **75**
Soldon Cross. *Devn* 4C **6**
Soldridge. *Hants* 2D **10**
Solent Breezes. *Hants* 5C **10**
Sole Street. *Kent*
  nr. Meopham 7C **22**
  nr. Waltham 1G **13**
**Solihull**. *W Mid* 3K **27**
Sollers Dilwyn. *Here* 6C **26**
Sollers Hope. *Here* 8E **26**
Sollom. *Lanc* 6C **40**
Solva. *Pemb* 4D **14**
Somerby. *Leics* 8E **36**
Somerby. *Linc* 7H **43**
Somercotes. *Derbs* 4B **36**
Somerford. *Dors* 6K **9**
Somerford. *Staf* 1G **27**
Somerford Keynes. *Glos* 4J **19**
Somerley. *W Sus* 6F **10**
Somerleyton. *Suff* 2L **31**
Somersal Herbert. *Derbs* 6K **35**
Somersby. *Linc* 2L **37**
Somersham. *Cambs* 4L **29**
Somersham. *Suff* 7G **31**
Somerton. *Oxon* 1B **20**
Somerton. *Som* 3C **8**
Somerton. *Suff* 6E **30**
**Sompting**. *W Sus* 5J **11**
Sonning. *Wok* 6E **20**
Sonning Common. *Oxon* 5E **20**
Sonning Eye. *Oxon* 6E **20**
Sookholme. *Notts* 3C **36**
Sopley. *Hants* 6K **9**
Sopworth. *Wilts* 5G **19**
Sorbie. *Dum* 7K **51**
Sordale. *High* 5C **86**
Sorisdale. *Arg* 1H **63**
Sorn. *E Ayr* 7D **58**
Sornhill. *E Ayr* 6D **58**
Sortat. *High* 5D **86**
Sotby. *Linc* 2K **37**
Sots Hole. *Linc* 3J **37**
Sotterley. *Suff* 3L **31**
Soudley. *Shrp*
  nr. Church Stretton 2C **26**
  nr. Market Drayton 7F **34**
Soughton. *Flin* 4M **33**
Soulbury. *Buck* 1F **20**
Soulby. *Cumb*
  nr. Appleby 4F **46**
  nr. Penrith 3C **46**
Souldern. *Oxon* 8C **28**
Souldrop. *Bed* 5G **29**
Sound. *Ches E* 5E **34**
Sound. *Shet*
  nr. Lerwick 3E **90**
  nr. Tresta 2D **90**
Soundwell. *S Glo* 6E **18**
Sourhope. *Bord* 7F **60**
Sourin. *Orkn* 6D **88**
Sour Nook. *Cumb* 7H **53**
Sourton. *Devn* 6E **6**
Soutergate. *Cumb* 6M **45**
South Acre. *Norf* 8E **38**
**Southall**. *G Lon* 6J **21**
South Allington. *Devn* 8K **5**
South Alloa. *Falk* 8B **66**
Southam. *Glos* 1H **19**
Southam. *Warw* 5B **28**
South Ambersham. *W Sus* 3G **11**
**Southampton**. *Sotn* 4B **10**
Southampton Airport.
  *Hants* 4B **10**
Southannan. *N Ayr* 4M **57**
South Anston. *S Yor* 1C **36**
South Ascot. *Wind* 7G **21**
South Baddesley. *Hants* 6A **10**
South Balfern. *Dum* 6K **51**
South Ballachulish. *High* 2E **64**
**South Bank**. *Red C* 3C **48**
South Barrow. *Som* 3E **8**
**South Benfleet**. *Essx* 5D **22**
South Bents. *Tyne* 5H **55**
South Bersted. *W Sus* 5G **11**
Southborough. *Kent* 1B **12**
Southbourne. *Bour* 6K **9**
Southbourne. *W Sus* 5E **10**
South Bowood. *Dors* 6C **8**
South Brent. *Devn* 6J **5**
South Brewham. *Som* 2F **8**
South Broomage. *Falk* 1G **59**
South Broomhill. *Nmbd* 2F **54**
Southburgh. *Norf* 1F **30**
South Burlingham. *Norf* 1K **31**
Southburn. *E Yor* 2G **43**
South Cadbury. *Som* 3E **8**
South Carlton. *Linc* 2G **37**
South Cave. *E Yor* 4G **43**
South Cerney. *Glos* 4J **19**
South Chailey. *E Sus* 4L **11**
South Chard. *Som* 5B **8**
South Charlton. *Nmbd* 7J **61**
South Cheriton. *Som* 3E **8**
South Church. *Dur* 3L **47**
Southchurch. *S'end* 5F **22**
South Cleatlam. *Dur* 4K **47**
South Cliffe. *E Yor* 4F **42**
South Clifton. *Notts* 2F **36**
South Clunes. *High* 1F **70**
South Cockerington. *Linc* 1L **37**
South Common. *Devn* 5B **8**
South Cornelly. *B'end* 6H **17**
Southcott. *Devn*
  nr. Great Torrington 4D **6**
  nr. Okehampton 6E **6**
Southcott. *Wilts* 8K **19**
Southcourt. *Buck* 2F **20**
South Cove. *Suff* 3L **31**
South Creagan. *Arg* 3D **64**
South Creake. *Norf* 6E **38**
South Crosland. *W Yor* 6K **41**
South Croxton. *Leics* 8D **36**
South Dalton. *E Yor* 3G **43**
South Darenth. *Kent* 7B **22**
Southdean. *Bord* 1L **53**
Southdown. *Bath* 7F **18**
South Duffield. *N Yor* 4D **42**
Southease. *E Sus* 5M **11**
South Elkington. *Linc* 1K **37**
South Elmsall. *W Yor* 6B **42**
South End. *Cumb* 8M **45**
South End. *N Lin* 5J **43**
Southend. *Arg* 1B **50**
Southend. *Glos* 4F **18**
Southend. *W Ber* 6C **20**
Southend Airport. *Essx* 5E **22**
**Southend-on-Sea**. *S'end* 5E **22**
Southerfield. *Cumb* 7F **52**
Southerhouse. *Shet* 4D **90**
Southerly. *Devn* 7E **6**
Southernden. *Kent* 1E **12**
Southerndown. *V Glam* 7H **17**
Southerness. *Dum* 6D **52**
South Erradale. *High* 6J **77**
Southerton. *Devn* 6K **7**
Southery. *Norf* 2C **30**
Southey Green. *Essx* 8D **30**
South Fambridge. *Essx* 4E **22**
South Fawley. *W Ber* 5A **20**
South Feorline. *N Ayr* 7J **57**
South Ferriby. *N Lin* 5G **43**
South Field. *E Yor* 5H **43**
Southfleet. *Kent* 6C **22**
South Garvan. *High* 8L **69**
Southgate. *Cdgn* 4E **24**
**Southgate**. *G Lon* 4L **21**
Southgate. *Norf*
  nr. Aylsham 7H **39**
  nr. Fakenham 6E **38**
Southgate. *Swan* 6E **16**
South Gluss. *Shet* 6H **91**
South Godstone. *Surr* 1L **11**
South Gorley. *Hants* 4K **9**
South Green. *Essx*
  nr. Billericay 4C **22**
  nr. Colchester 2G **23**
South Green. *Kent* 7E **22**
South Hanningfield. *Essx* 4D **22**
South Harting. *W Sus* 4E **10**
South Hayling. *Hants* 6E **10**
South Hazelrigg. *Nmbd* 6H **61**
South Heath. *Buck* 3G **21**
South Heath. *Essx* 2H **23**
South Heighton. *E Sus* 5M **11**
South Hetton. *Dur* 7G **55**
South Hiendley. *W Yor* 6A **42**
South Hill. *Corn* 8C **6**
South Hill. *Som* 3C **8**
South Hinksey. *Oxon* 3C **20**
South Hole. *Devn* 3B **6**
South Holme. *N Yor* 8E **48**
South Holmwood. *Surr* 1J **11**
South Hornchurch. *G Lon* 5B **22**
South Huish. *Devn* 7J **5**
South Hykeham. *Linc* 3G **37**
South Hylton. *Tyne* 6G **55**
Southill. *C Beds* 7J **29**
Southington. *Hants* 1C **10**
South Kelsey. *Linc* 8H **43**
South Kessock. *High* 1G **71**
South Killingholme. *N Lin* 6J **43**
South Kilvington. *N Yor* 7B **48**
South Kilworth. *Leics* 3D **28**
South Kirkby. *W Yor* 6B **42**
South Kirkton. *Abers* 5G **73**
South Knighton. *Devn* 8H **7**
South Kyme. *Linc* 5J **37**
South Lancing. *W Sus* 5J **11**
South Ledaig. *Arg* 4D **64**
South Leigh. *Oxon* 3A **20**
Southleigh. *Devn* 6M **7**
South Leverton. *Notts* 1E **36**
South Littleton. *Worc* 7J **27**
South Lopham. *Norf* 3G **31**
South Luffenham. *Rut* 1G **29**
South Malling. *E Sus* 4M **11**
South Marston. *Swin* 5K **19**
South Middleton. *Nmbd* 7G **61**
South Milford. *N Yor* 4B **42**
South Milton. *Devn* 7K **5**
South Mimms. *Herts* 3K **21**
Southminster. *Essx* 4F **22**
South Molton. *Devn* 3G **7**
South Moor. *Dur* 6E **54**
Southmoor. *Oxon* 4A **20**
South Moreton. *Oxon* 5C **20**
South Mundham. *W Sus* 5F **10**
South Muskham. *Notts* 4E **36**
South Newbald. *E Yor* 4G **43**
South Newington. *Oxon* 8B **28**
South Newsham. *Nmbd* 4G **55**
South Newton. *N Ayr* 4J **57**
South Newton. *Wilts* 2J **9**
South Normanton. *Derbs* 4B **36**
South Norwood. *G Lon* 7L **21**
South Nutfield. *Surr* 1L **11**
**South Ockendon**. *Thur* 5B **22**
Southoe. *Cambs* 5J **29**
Southolt. *Suff* 5H **31**
South Ormsby. *Linc* 2L **37**
Southorpe. *Pet* 1H **29**
South Otterington. *N Yor* 7A **48**
South Owersby. *Linc* 8H **43**
Southowram. *W Yor* 5K **41**
**South Oxhey**. *Herts* 4J **21**
South Perrott. *Dors* 5C **8**
South Petherton. *Som* 4C **8**
South Petherwin. *Corn* 7C **6**
South Pickenham. *Norf* 1E **30**
South Pool. *Devn* 7K **5**
South Poorton. *Dors* 6D **8**
South Port. *Arg* 5E **64**
**Southport**. *Mers* 6B **40**
Southpunds. *Shet* 6E **90**
South Queensferry. *Edin* 2K **59**
South Radworthy. *Devn* 2G **7**
South Rauceby. *Linc* 5H **37**
South Raynham. *Norf* 7E **38**
Southrepps. *Norf* 6J **39**
South Reston. *Linc* 1M **37**
Southrey. *Linc* 3J **37**
Southrop. *Glos* 3K **19**
Southrope. *Hants* 1D **10**
South Runcton. *Norf* 1C **30**
South Scarle. *Notts* 3F **36**
Southsea. *Port* 6D **10**
**South Shields**. *Tyne* 5G **55**
South Shore. *Bkpl* 4B **40**
Southside. *Orkn* 7E **88**
South Somercotes. *Linc* 8M **43**
South Stainley. *N Yor* 1M **41**
South Stainmore. *Cumb* 4G **47**
South Stifford. *Thur* 6B **22**
South Stoke. *Bath* 7F **18**
South Stoke. *Oxon* 5C **20**
South Stoke. *W Sus* 5H **11**
South Street. *E Sus* 4L **11**
South Street. *Kent*
  nr. Faversham 8G **23**
  nr. Whitstable 7H **23**
South Tawton. *Devn* 6F **6**
South Thoresby. *Linc* 2M **37**
South Tidworth. *Wilts* 1L **9**
South Town. *Devn* 7J **7**
South Town. *Hants* 2D **10**
Southtown. *Norf* 1M **31**
Southtown. *Orkn* 2F **86**
South View. *Shet* 3D **90**
Southwaite. *Cumb* 7J **53**
South Walsham. *Norf* 8K **39**
South Warnborough. *Hants* 1E **10**
Southwater. *W Sus* 3J **11**
Southwater Street. *W Sus* 3J **11**
Southway. *Som* 1D **8**
South Weald. *Essx* 4B **22**
South Weirs. *Hants* 5L **9**
Southwell. *Dors* 8E **8**
Southwell. *Notts* 4E **36**
South Weston. *Oxon* 4E **20**
South Wheatley. *Corn* 6B **6**
South Wheatley. *Notts* 1E **36**
Southwick. *Hants* 5D **10**
Southwick. *Nptn* 2H **29**
Southwick. *Tyne* 6G **55**
**Southwick**. *W Sus* 5K **11**
Southwick. *Wilts* 8G **19**
South Widcombe. *Bath* 8D **18**
South Wigston. *Leics* 2C **28**
South Willingham. *Linc* 1J **37**
South Wingfield. *Derbs* 4A **36**
South Witham. *Linc* 8G **37**
Southwold. *Suff* 4M **31**
South Wonston. *Hants* 2B **10**
Southwood. *Norf* 1K **31**
Southwood. *Som* 2D **8**
**South Woodham Ferrers**.
  *Essx* 4E **22**
South Wootton. *Norf* 7C **38**
South Wraxall. *Wilts* 7G **19**
South Zeal. *Devn* 6F **6**
Soval Lodge. *W Isl* 1E **76**
Sowerby. *N Yor* 7B **48**
Sowerby. *W Yor* 5J **41**
Sowerby Bridge. *W Yor* 5J **41**
Sowerby Row. *Cumb* 7H **53**
Sower Carr. *Lanc* 3B **40**
Sowley Green. *Suff* 6D **30**
Sowood. *W Yor* 6J **41**
Sowton. *Devn* 6J **7**
Soyal. *High* 4F **78**
Soyland Town. *W Yor* 5J **41**
The Spa. *New M* 6H **93**
Spacey Houses. *N Yor* 2M **41**
Spa Common. *Norf* 6J **39**
**Spalding**. *Linc* 7K **37**
Spaldington. *E Yor* 4E **42**
Spaldwick. *Cambs* 4J **29**
Spalford. *Notts* 3F **36**
Spamount. *Derr* 4C **92**
Spanby. *Linc* 6H **37**
Sparham. *Norf* 8G **39**
Sparhamhill. *Norf* 8G **39**
Spark Bridge. *Cumb* 7B **46**
Sparket. *Cumb* 3C **46**
Sparkford. *Som* 3E **8**
Sparkwell. *Devn* 6H **5**
Sparrow Green. *Norf* 8F **38**
Sparrowpit. *Derbs* 1J **35**
Sparrow's Green. *E Sus* 2C **12**
Sparsholt. *Hants* 2B **10**
Sparsholt. *Oxon* 5M **19**
Spartylea. *Nmbd* 7B **54**
Spath. *Staf* 6J **35**
Spaunton. *N Yor* 7E **48**
Spaxton. *Som* 2M **7**
Spean Bridge. *High* 7C **70**
Spear Hill. *W Sus* 4J **11**
Speen. *Buck* 4F **20**
Speen. *W Ber* 7B **20**
Speeton. *N Yor* 8J **49**
Speke. *Mers* 1C **34**
Speldhurst. *Kent* 1B **12**
Spellbrook. *Herts* 2A **22**
Spelsbury. *Oxon* 1A **20**
Spencers Wood. *Wok* 7E **20**
Spennithorne. *N Yor* 7K **47**
**Spennymoor**. *Dur* 8F **54**
Spernall. *Warw* 5J **27**
Sperrin. *Derr* 4E **92**
Spetchley. *Worc* 6G **27**
Spetisbury. *Dors* 5H **9**
Spexhall. *Suff* 3K **31**
Speybank. *High* 5J **71**
Spey Bay. *Mor* 7C **80**
Speybridge. *High* 3L **71**
Speyview. *Mor* 1B **72**
Spilsby. *Linc* 3M **37**
Spindlestone. *Nmbd* 6J **61**
Spinkhill. *Derbs* 2B **36**
Spinney Hills. *Leic* 1D **28**
Spinningdale. *High* 5G **79**
Spital. *Mers* 1B **34**
Spitalhill. *Derbs* 5K **35**
Spital in the Street. *Linc* 8G **43**
Spithurst. *E Sus* 4M **11**
Spittal. *Dum* 6J **51**
Spittal. *E Lot* 2B **60**
Spittal. *High* 6C **86**
Spittal. *Nmbd* 4H **61**
Spittal. *Pemb* 4F **14**
Spittalfield. *Per* 3E **66**
Spittal of Glenmuick.
  *Abers* 7C **72**
Spittal of Glenshee. *Per* 8M **71**
Spittal-on-Rule. *Bord* 7C **60**
Spixworth. *Norf* 8J **39**
Splatt. *Corn* 7B **6**
Spofforth. *N Yor* 2A **42**
Spondon. *Derb* 6B **36**
Spon End. *W Mid* 4M **27**
Spooner Row. *Norf* 2G **31**
Sporle. *Norf* 8E **38**
Spott. *E Lot* 2D **60**
Spratton. *Nptn* 4E **28**
Spreakley. *Surr* 1F **10**
Spreyton. *Devn* 6G **7**
Spridlington. *Linc* 1H **37**
Springburn. *Glas* 3E **58**
Springfield. *Dum* 5H **53**
Springfield. *Ferm* 6B **92**
Springfield. *Fife* 6G **67**
Springfield. *High* 7G **79**
Springfield. *W Mid* 3J **27**
Spring Hill. *W Mid* 2G **27**
Springhill. *Staf* 1H **27**
Springholm. *Dum* 5C **52**
Springside. *N Ayr* 6B **58**
Springthorpe. *Linc* 1F **36**
Spring Vale. *IOW* 6D **10**
Spring Valley. *IOM* 7C **44**
Springwell. *Tyne* 6F **54**
Sproatley. *E Yor* 4J **43**
Sproston Green. *Ches W* 3F **34**
Sprotbrough. *S Yor* 7C **42**
Sproughton. *Suff* 7H **31**
Sprouston. *Bord* 6E **60**
Sprowston. *Norf* 8J **39**
Sproxton. *Leics* 7F **36**
Sproxton. *N Yor* 7D **48**
Sprunston. *Cumb* 7J **53**
Spurstow. *Ches E* 4D **34**
Squires Gate. *Bkpl* 4B **40**
Sraid Ruadh. *Arg* 3E **62**
Srannda. *W Isl* 5B **76**
Sron an t-Sithein. *High* 1C **64**
Sronphadruig Lodge. *Per* 8H **71**
Sruth Mor. *W Isl* 7L **75**
Stableford. *Shrp* 2F **26**
Stackhouse. *N Yor* 1G **41**
Stackpole. *Pemb* 7F **14**
Stackpole Elidor. *Pemb* 7F **14**
Stacksford. *Norf* 2G **31**
Stacksteads. *Lanc* 5G **41**
Staddiscombe. *Plym* 6H **5**
Staddlethorpe. *E Yor* 5F **42**
Staddon. *Devn* 5C **6**
Stadhampton. *Oxon* 4D **20**
Stadhlaigearraidh. *W Isl* 2D **74**
Stafainn. *High* 7F **76**
Staffield. *Cumb* 7K **53**
Staffin. *High* 7F **76**
**Stafford**. *Staf* 7H **35**
Stafford Park. *Telf* 1F **26**
Stagden Cross. *Essx* 2C **22**
Stagsden. *Bed* 7G **29**
Stag's Head. *Devn* 3F **6**
Stainburn. *Cumb* 2K **45**
Stainburn. *N Yor* 3L **41**
Stainby. *Linc* 7G **37**
Staincliffe. *W Yor* 5L **41**
Staincross. *S Yor* 6M **41**
Staindrop. *Dur* 3K **47**
**Staines-upon-Thames**.
  *Surr* 6H **21**
Stainfield. *Linc*
  nr. Bourne 7H **37**
  nr. Lincoln 2J **37**
Stainforth. *N Yor* 1G **41**
Stainforth. *S Yor* 6D **42**
Staining. *Lanc* 4B **40**
Stainland. *W Yor* 6J **41**
Stainsacre. *N Yor* 5G **49**
Stainton. *Cumb*
  nr. Carlisle 6H **53**
  nr. Kendal 7D **46**
  nr. Penrith 3C **46**
Stainton. *Dur* 4J **47**
Stainton. *Midd* 4B **48**
Stainton. *N Yor* 6K **47**
Stainton. *S Yor* 8C **42**
Stainton by Langworth.
  *Linc* 2H **37**
Staintondale. *N Yor* 6G **49**
Stainton le Vale. *Linc* 8J **43**
Stainton with Adgarley.
  *Cumb* 8A **46**
Stair. *Cumb* 2M **45**
Stair. *E Ayr* 7C **58**
Stairhaven. *Dum* 6H **51**
Staithes. *N Yor* 4E **48**
Stakeford. *Nmbd* 3F **54**
Stake Pool. *Lanc* 3C **40**
Stakes. *Hants* 5D **10**
Stalbridge. *Dors* 4F **8**
Stalbridge Weston. *Dors* 4F **8**
Stalham. *Norf* 7K **39**
Stalham Green. *Norf* 7K **39**
Stalisfield Green. *Kent* 8F **22**
Stallen. *Dors* 4E **8**
Stallingborough. *NE Lin* 6K **43**
Stalling Busk. *N Yor* 7H **47**
Stallington. *Staf* 6H **35**
Stalmine. *Lanc* 3B **40**
**Stalybridge**. *G Man* 8H **41**
Stambourne. *Essx* 8D **30**
**Stamford**. *Linc* 1H **29**
Stamford. *Nmbd* 8K **61**
Stamford Bridge. *Ches W* 3C **34**
Stamford Bridge. *E Yor* 2E **42**
Stamfordham. *Nmbd* 4D **54**
Stamperland. *E Ren* 4D **58**
Stanah. *Lanc* 3B **40**
Stanborough. *Herts* 2K **21**
Stanbridge. *C Beds* 1G **21**
Stanbridge. *Dors* 5J **9**
Stanbury. *W Yor* 4J **41**
Stand. *N Lan* 3F **58**
Standburn. *Falk* 2H **59**
Standeford. *Staf* 1H **27**
Standen. *Kent* 1E **12**
Standen Street. *Kent* 2E **12**
Standerwick. *Som* 8G **19**
Standford. *Hants* 2F **10**
Standford Bridge. *Telf* 7F **34**
Standingstone. *Cumb* 7G **53**
Standish. *Glos* 3G **19**
**Standish**. *G Man* 6D **40**
Standish Lower Ground.
  *G Man* 7D **40**
Standlake. *Oxon* 3A **20**
Standon. *Hants* 3B **10**
Standon. *Herts* 1L **21**
Standon. *Staf* 6G **35**
Standon Green End. *Herts* 2L **21**
Stane. *N Lan* 4G **59**
Stanecastle. *N Ayr* 6B **58**
Stanfield. *Norf* 7F **38**
Stanfield. *Suff* 6D **30**
Stanford. *C Beds* 7J **29**
Stanford. *Kent* 2H **13**
Stanford Bishop. *Here* 6E **26**
Stanford Bridge. *Worc* 5F **26**
Stanford Dingley. *W Ber* 6C **20**
Stanford in the Vale. *Oxon* 4M **19**
**Stanford-le-Hope**. *Thur* 5C **22**
Stanford on Avon. *Nptn* 4C **28**
Stanford on Soar. *Notts* 7C **36**
Stanford on Teme. *Worc* 5F **26**
Stanford Rivers. *Essx* 3B **22**
Stanfree. *Derbs* 2B **36**
Stanghow. *Red C* 4D **48**
Stanground. *Pet* 2K **29**
Stanhoe. *Norf* 6E **38**
Stanhope. *Dur* 8C **54**
Stanhope. *Bord* 7K **59**
Stanion. *Nptn* 3G **29**
Stanley. *Derbs* 5B **36**
**Stanley**. *Dur* 6E **54**
Stanley. *Per* 4E **66**
Stanley. *Shrp* 3F **26**
Stanley. *Staf* 4H **35**
**Stanley**. *W Yor* 5M **41**
Stanley Common. *Derbs* 5B **36**
Stanley Crook. *Dur* 8E **54**
Stanley Hill. *Here* 7E **26**
Stanlow. *Ches W* 2C **34**
Stanmer. *Brig* 5L **11**
**Stanmore**. *G Lon* 4J **21**
Stanmore. *Hants* 3B **10**
Stanmore. *W Ber* 6B **20**
Stannersburn. *Nmbd* 3M **53**
Stanningfield. *Suff* 6E **30**
Stannington. *Nmbd* 4F **54**
Stannington. *S Yor* 1M **35**
Stansbatch. *Here* 5B **26**
Stanshope. *Staf* 4K **35**
Stanstead. *Suff* 7E **30**
Stanstead Abbotts. *Herts* 2L **21**
Stansted. *Kent* 7C **22**
Stansted Airport. *Essx* 1B **22**
Stansted Mountfitchet. *Essx* 1B **22**
Stanthorne. *Ches W* 3E **34**
Stanton. *Derbs* 8L **35**
Stanton. *Glos* 8J **27**
Stanton. *Nmbd* 2E **54**
Stanton. *Staf* 5K **35**
Stanton. *Suff* 4F **30**
Stanton by Bridge. *Derbs* 7A **36**
Stanton-by-Dale. *Derbs* 6B **36**
Stanton Chare. *Suff* 4F **30**
Stanton Drew. *Bath* 7D **18**
Stanton Fitzwarren. *Swin* 4K **19**
Stanton Harcourt. *Oxon* 3B **20**
Stanton Hill. *Notts* 3B **36**
Stanton in Peak. *Derbs* 3L **35**
Stanton Lacy. *Shrp* 4C **26**
Stanton Long. *Shrp* 2D **26**
Stanton-on-the-Wolds.
  *Notts* 6D **36**
Stanton Prior. *Bath* 7E **18**
Stanton St Bernard. *Wilts* 7J **19**
Stanton St John. *Oxon* 3C **20**
Stanton St Quintin. *Wilts* 6H **19**
Stanton Street. *Suff* 5F **30**
Stanton under Bardon.
  *Leics* 8B **36**
Stanton upon Hine Heath.
  *Shrp* 7D **34**
Stanton Wick. *Bath* 7E **18**
Stanwardine in the Fields.
  *Shrp* 7C **34**
Stanwardine in the Wood.
  *Shrp* 7C **34**
Stanway. *Essx* 1F **22**
Stanway. *Glos* 8J **27**
Stanwell. *Surr* 6H **21**
Stanwell Green. *Suff* 4H **31**
Stanwell Moor. *Surr* 6H **21**
Stanwick. *Nptn* 4G **29**
Stanydale. *Shet* 2C **90**
Staoinebrig. *W Isl* 2D **74**
Stape. *N Yor* 6E **48**
Stapehill. *Dors* 5J **9**
Stapeley. *Ches E* 5E **34**
Stapenhill. *Staf* 7L **35**
Staple. *Kent* 8J **23**
Staple Cross. *Devn* 3K **7**
Staplecross. *E Sus* 3D **12**
Staplefield. *W Sus* 3K **11**
Staple Fitzpaine. *Som* 4A **8**
Stapleford. *Cambs* 6A **30**
Stapleford. *Herts* 2L **21**
Stapleford. *Leics* 8F **36**
Stapleford. *Linc* 4F **36**
**Stapleford**. *Notts* 6B **36**
Stapleford. *Wilts* 2J **9**
Stapleford Abbotts. *Essx* 4B **22**
Stapleford Tawney. *Essx* 4B **22**
Staplegrove. *Som* 3M **7**
Staplehay. *Som* 3M **7**
Staple Hill. *S Glo* 6E **18**
Staplehurst. *Kent* 1D **12**
Staplers. *IOW* 7C **10**
Stapleton. *Bris* 6E **18**
Stapleton. *Cumb* 4K **53**
Stapleton. *Here* 5B **26**
Stapleton. *Leics*
Stapleton. *N Yor*
Stapleton. *Shrp*
Stapleton. *Som*
Stapley. *Som*
Staploe. *Bed*
Staplow. *Here*
Star. *Fife*
Star. *Pemb*
Starbeck. *N Yor*
Starbotton. *N Yor*
Starcross. *Devn*
Stareton. *Warw*
Starkholmes. *Derbs*
Starling. *G Man*
Starling's Green. *Essx*
Starston. *Norf*
Start. *Devn*
Startforth. *Dur*
Start Hill. *Essx*
Startley. *Wilts*
Stathe. *Som*
Stathern. *Leics*
Station Town. *Dur*
Staughton Green. *Cambs*
Staughton Highway. *Cambs*
Staunton. *Glos*
  nr. Cheltenham
  nr. Monmouth
Staunton in the Vale. *Notts*
Staunton on Arrow. *Here*
Staunton on Wye. *Here*
Staveley. *Cumb*
**Staveley**. *Derbs*
Staveley. *N Yor*
Staveley-in-Cartmel. *Cumb*
Staverton. *Devn*
Staverton. *Glos*
Staverton. *Nptn*
Staverton. *Wilts*
Stawell. *Som*
Stawley. *Som*
Staxigoe. *High*
Staxton. *N Yor*
Staylittle. *Powy*
Staynall. *Lanc*
Staythorpe. *Notts*
Stean. *N Yor*
Stearsby. *N Yor*
Steart. *Som*
Stebbing. *Essx*
Stebbing Green. *Essx*
Stedham. *W Sus*
Steel. *Nmbd*
Steel Cross. *E Sus*
Steelend. *Fife*
Steele Road. *Bord*
Steel Heath. *Shrp*
Steen's Bridge. *Here*
Steep. *Hants*
Steep Lane. *W Yor*
Steeple. *Dors*
Steeple. *Essx*
Steeple Ashton. *Wilts*
Steeple Aston. *Oxon*
Steeple Barton. *Oxon*
Steeple Bumpstead. *Essx*
Steeple Claydon. *Buck*
Steeple Gidding. *Cambs*
Steeple Langford. *Wilts*
Steeple Morden. *Cambs*
Steeton. *W Yor*
Stein. *High*
Steinmanhill. *Abers*
Stelling Minnis. *Kent*
Stembridge. *Som*
Stemster. *High*
  nr. Halkirk
  nr. Westfield
Stenalees. *Corn*
Stenhill. *Devn*
Stenhouse. *Edin*
**Stenhousemuir**. *Falk*
Stenigot. *Linc*
Stenscholl. *High*
Stenso. *Orkn*
Stenson. *Derbs*
Stenson Fields. *Derbs*
Stenton. *E Lot*
Stenwith. *Linc*
Steòrnabhagh. *W Isl*
Stepaside. *Pemb*
Stepford. *Dum*
**Stepney**. *G Lon*
Steppingley. *C Beds*
Stepps. *N Lan*
Sterndale Moor. *Derbs*
Sternfield. *Suff*
Stert. *Wilts*
Stetchworth. *Cambs*
**Stevenage**. *Herts*
**Stevenston**. *N Ayr*
Stevenstone. *Devn*
Steventon. *Hants*
Steventon. *Oxon*
Steventon End. *Essx*
Stevington. *Bed*
Stewartby. *Bed*
Stewarton. *Arg*
Stewarton. *E Ayr*
Stewartstown. *M Ulst*
Stewkley. *Buck*
Stewkley Dean. *Buck*
Stewley. *Som*
Stewton. *Linc*
Steyning. *W Sus*
Steynton. *Pemb*
Stibb. *Corn*
Stibbard. *Norf*
Stibb Cross. *Devn*
Stibb Green. *Wilts*
Stibbington. *Cambs*
Stichill. *Bord*
Sticker. *Corn*
Stickford. *Linc*
Sticklepath. *Devn*
Sticklinch. *Som*
Stickling Green. *Essx*
Stickney. *Linc*
Stiffkey. *Norf*
Stifford's Bridge. *Here*
Stileway. *Som*
Stillingfleet. *N Yor*
Stillington. *N Yor*
Stillington. *Stoc T*
Stilton. *Cambs*
Stinchcombe. *Glos*
Stinsford. *Dors*
Stiperstones. *Shrp*
Stirchley. *Telf*
Stirchley. *W Mid*
Stirling. *Abers*
**Stirling**. *Stir*
Stirton. *N Yor*
Stisted. *Essx*
Stitchcombe. *Wilts*
Stithians. *Corn*
Stittenham. *High*
Stivichall. *W Mid*
Stixwould. *Linc*
Stoak. *Ches W*
Stobo. *Bord*
Stobo Castle. *Bord*
Stoborough. *Dors*
Stoborough Green. *Dors*
Stobs Castle. *Bord*
Stobswood. *Nmbd*
Stock. *Essx*
Stockbridge. *Hants*
Stockbridge. *W Yor*
Stockbury. *Kent*
Stockcross. *W Ber*
Stockdalewath. *Cumb*
Stocker's Head. *Kent*
Stockerston. *Leics*
Stock Green. *Worc*
Stocking. *Here*
Stockingford. *Warw*
Stocking Green. *Essx*
Stocking Pelham. *Herts*
Stockland. *Devn*
Stockland Bristol. *Som*
Stockleigh English. *Devn*
Stockleigh Pomeroy. *Devn*
Stockley. *Wilts*
Stocklinch. *Som*
**Stockport**. *G Man*
The Stocks. *Kent*
**Stocksbridge**. *S Yor*

sfield. *Nmbd* 5D **54**
street. *Essx* 1E **22**
ton. *Here* 5D **26**
ton. *Norf* 2K **31**
ton. *Shrp*
r. Bridgnorth 2F **26**
r. Chirbury 1A **26**
ton. *Telf* 8F **34**
ton. *Warw* 5B **28**
ton. *Wilts* 2H **9**
ton Brook. *Staf* 4H **35**
ton Cross. *Here* 5D **26**
ton Heath. *Warr* 1E **34**
**on-on-Tees**. *Stoc T* 4B **48**
ton on Teme. *Worc* 5F **26**
ton-on-the-Forest.
*York* 2D **42**
well Heath. *Staf* 7J **35**
Wood. *Worc* 6J **27**
wood. *Bris* 7E **18**
arsh. *Kent* 7J **23**
*Norf* 6G **39**
*High* 1M **77**
d. *Som* 4D **8**
d. *Wilts* 2J **9**
mber. *Som* 2K **7**
rsey. *Som* 1M **7**
*Devn* 3B **6**
*Hants*
r. Andover 8B **20**
r. South Hayling 5E **10**
*Medw* 6E **22**
*W Mid* 4A **28**
Abbott. *Dors* 5C **8**
Albany. *Nptn* 3F **28**
Ash. *Suff* 4H **31**
Bardolph. *Notts* 5D **36**
Bliss. *Worc* 5E **26**
Bruerne. *Nptn* 7E **28**
by Clare. *Suff* 7D **30**
by-Nayland. *Suff* 8F **30**
Canon. *Devn* 6J **7**
Charity. *Hants* 2B **10**
Climsland. *Corn* 8C **6**
Cross. *Here* 6E **26**
D'Abernon. *Surr* 8J **21**
Doyle. *Nptn* 3H **29**
Dry. *Rut* 2F **28**
Edith. *Here* 7E **26**
Farthing. *Wilts* 3J **9**
Ferry. *Norf* 1D **30**
Fleming. *Devn* 7L **5**
ord. *Dors* 7G **9**
Gabriel. *Devn* 6L **5**
Gifford. *S Glo* 6E **18**
Golding. *Leics* 2A **28**
Goldington. *Mil* 7F **28**
am. *Notts* 2E **36**
Hammond. *Buck* 1F **20**
Heath. *Shrp* 7E **34**
Holy Cross. *Norf* 1J **31**
nteignhead. *Devn* 8J **7**
Lacy. *Here* 7E **26**
Lyne. *Oxon* 1C **20**
Mandeville. *Buck* 2F **20**
church. *Buck* 4E **20**
**Newington**. *G Lon* 5L **21**
ham. *Devn* 7L **5**
on Tern. *Shrp* 7E **34**
**on-Trent**. *Stoke* 5G **35**
Orchard. *Glos* 1H **19**
Pero. *Som* 1H **7**
Poges. *Buck* 5G **21**
Prior. *Here* 6D **26**
Prior. *Worc* 5H **27**
Rivers. *Devn* 2F **6**
Rochford. *Linc* 7G **37**
Row. *Oxon* 5D **20**
St Gregory. *Som* 3B **8**
St Mary. *Som* 3A **8**
St Michael. *Som* 1E **8**
St Milborough. *Shrp* 3D **26**
ay. *Shrp* 3C **26**
by. *Norf* 8L **39**
ley. *N Yor* 5C **48**
sub Hamdon. *Som* 4C **8**
Talmage. *Oxon* 4D **20**
Town. *Stoke* 5G **35**
Trister. *Som* 3F **8**
Wake. *Dors* 5F **8**
d. *Som* 1M **7**
on Massey. *Essx* 3B **22**
*Buck* 2E **20**
*Glos* 4E **18**
*Kent* 6B **22**
*Som* 2D **8**
*Staf* 6H **35**
*Worc* 4G **27**
. *Cambs* 2A **30**
cton. *Shrp* 2D **26**
Allerton. *Som* 8C **18**
aston. *Som* 8E **18**
ridge. *N Som* 8B **18**
ridge. *Surr* 1J **11**
Bridge Corner. *Pet* 1K **29**
room. *Derbs* 4B **36**
yres Holdings.
*Lan* 5G **59**
Chair. *W Yor* 5K **41**
Cross. *E Sus* 5C **12**
Cross. *Kent* 2B **12**
edge Batch. *N Som* 6C **18**
erry. *Hull* 4H **43**
eld. *Arg* 4D **64**
eld. *S Lan* 4E **58**
ate. *E Sus* 3C **12**
ate. *N Yor* 5E **48**
rave. *N Yor* 8D **48**
all. *Worc* 7G **27**
augh. *Nmbd* 4A **54**
**aven**. *Abers* 7H **73**
Heath. *Staf* 6H **35**
Hill. *Kent* 2G **13**
House. *Cumb* 7F **46**
ouse. *Glos* 3G **19**
ouse. *Nmbd* 6L **53**
ouse. *S Lan* 5F **58**
n Oxney. *Kent* 3F **12**
eigh. *Warw* 4M **27**
ey Green. *Ches E* 4E **34**
. *Cambs* 5J **29**
its. *Worc* 6J **27**
Hill. *Hants* 3E **10**
by. *Leics* 7F **36**
field. *Oxon* 2A **20**
Green. *Essx* 1H **23**
Street. *Kent* 8B **22**
Street. *Suff*
. Boxford 8F **30**
. Halesworth 3K **31**
nwaite. *Cumb* 4A **46**
burn. *W Lot* 3H **59**
Cross. *Hants* 4L **9**
ford. *Devn* 5K **7**
gate. *Leic* 1D **28**
hills. *Essx* 4F **22**
kirk. *Dum* 6F **50**
Middleton. *Derbs* 2L **35**
Stanton. *Leics* 2B **28**
Stoke. *Som* 2F **8**
Stratton. *Som* 2E **8**
Stretton. *Shrp* 1B **26**
wood. *Aber* 4H **73**
m Aspal. *Suff* 6H **31**
ll. *Staf* 1J **27**
. *Oxon* 5E **20**
n Wyville. *Leics* 2E **28**
reck. *Shet* 2M **89**
Cross. *Devn* 3E **6**
Cross. *Here*
. Great Malvern 7F **26**
. Leominster 5D **26**
ord. *Lis* 5H **93**
Houghton. *Derbs* 3B **36**
Stratford. *Mil* 7E **28**
eigh. *Devn*
. Barnstaple 2F **6**
. Tiverton 4J **7**
m. *W Sus* 4H **11**
ey. *Lutn* 1J **21**
e. *Corn* 4B **4**
on. *Mers* 1B **34**
ontfield. *Per* 5E **66**
way. *W Isl* 8H **83**
way Airport. *W Isl* 8H **83**
ge. *Here* 7F **26**
gton. *W Sus* 4H **11**
*Cumb* 6B **46**
*Cumb* 7C **46**

Storwood. *E Yor* 3E **42**
Stotfield. *Mor* 6B **80**
Stotfold. *C Beds* 8K **29**
Stottesdon. *Shrp* 3E **26**
Stoughton. *Leics* 1D **28**
Stoughton. *Surr* 8G **21**
Stoughton. *W Sus* 4F **10**
Stoul. *High* 6J **69**
Stoulton. *Worc* 7H **27**
**Stourbridge**. *W Mid* 3G **27**
Stourpaine. *Dors* 5G **9**
**Stourport-on-Severn**.
*Worc* 4G **27**
Stour Provost. *Dors* 3F **8**
Stour Row. *Dors* 3G **9**
Stourton. *Staf* 3G **27**
Stourton. *Warw* 8L **27**
Stourton. *W Yor* 4M **41**
Stourton. *Wilts* 2F **8**
Stourton Caundle. *Dors* 4F **8**
Stove. *Orkn* 6F **88**
Stove. *Shet* 5E **90**
Stoven. *Suff* 3L **31**
Stow. *Linc*
nr. Billingborough 6H **37**
nr. Gainsborough 1F **36**
Stow. *Bord* 5B **60**
Stow Bardolph. *Norf* 1C **30**
Stow Bedon. *Norf* 2F **30**
Stowbridge. *Norf* 1C **30**
Stow cum Quy. *Cambs* 5B **30**
Stowe. *Glos* 3D **18**
Stowe. *Shrp* 4B **26**
Stowe. *Staf* 8K **35**
Stowe-by-Chartley. *Staf* 7J **35**
Stowell. *Som* 3E **8**
Stowey. *Bath* 8D **18**
Stowford. *Devn*
nr. Colaton Raleigh 7K **7**
nr. Combe Martin 1F **6**
nr. Tavistock 7D **6**
Stowlangtoft. *Suff* 5F **30**
Stow Longa. *Cambs* 4J **29**
Stow Maries. *Essx* 4E **22**
**Stowmarket**. *Suff* 6G **31**
Stow-on-the-Wold. *Glos* 1K **19**
Stowting. *Kent* 1H **13**
Stowupland. *Suff* 6G **31**
Straad. *Arg* 3K **57**
**Strabane**. *Derr* 4C **92**
Strachan. *Abers* 6F **72**
Stradbroke. *Suff* 4J **31**
Stradishall. *Suff* 6D **30**
Stradsett. *Norf* 1C **30**
Stragglethorpe. *Linc* 4G **37**
Stragglethorpe. *Notts* 6D **36**
Straid. *Ant* 4H **93**
Straid. *ME Ant* 4G **93**
Straid. *S Ayr* 2G **51**
Straight Soley. *Wilts* 6M **19**
Straiton. *Midl* 3L **59**
Straiton. *S Ayr* 1J **51**
Straloch. *Per* 1D **66**
Stramshall. *Staf* 6J **35**
Strang. *IOM* 7C **44**
Strangford. *Here* 1D **18**
Strangford. *New M* 6J **93**
Stranocum. *Caus* 2G **93**
**Stranraer**. *Dum* 5F **50**
Strata Florida. *Cdgn* 6G **25**
Stratfield Mortimer. *W Ber* 7D **20**
Stratfield Saye. *Hants* 7D **20**
Stratfield Turgis. *Hants* 8D **20**
**Stratford**. *G Lon* 5L **21**
Stratford. *Worc* 8G **27**
Stratford St Andrew. *Suff* 5K **31**
Stratford St Mary. *Suff* 8G **31**
Stratford sub Castle. *Wilts* 2K **9**
Stratford Tony. *Wilts* 3J **9**
**Stratford-upon-Avon**.
*Warw* 6L **27**
Strath. *High*
nr. Gairloch 6J **77**
nr. Wick 6D **86**
Strathan. *High*
nr. Fort William 6L **69**
nr. Lochinver 1A **78**
nr. Tongue 5H **85**
Strathan Skerray. *High* 5J **85**
Strathaven. *S Lan* 5F **58**
Strathblane. *Stir* 2D **58**
Strathcanaird. *High* 3B **78**
Strathcarron. *High* 1L **69**
Strathcoil. *Arg* 4A **64**
Strathdon. *Abers* 4C **72**
Strathkinness. *Fife* 6H **67**
Strathmashie House.
*High* 6F **70**
Strathmiglo. *Fife* 6F **66**
Strathmore Lodge. *High* 7C **86**
Strathpeffer. *High* 8E **78**
Strathrannoch. *High* 6D **78**
Strathtay. *Per* 2C **66**
Strathvaich Lodge. *High* 6D **78**
Strathwhillan. *N Ayr* 6K **57**
Strathy. *High*
nr. Invergordon 6G **79**
nr. Melvich 5L **85**
Strathyre. *Stir* 6K **65**
Stratton. *Corn* 5B **6**
Stratton. *Dors* 6E **8**
Stratton. *Glos* 3J **19**
Stratton Audley. *Oxon* 1D **20**
Stratton-on-the-Fosse.
*Som* 8E **18**
Stratton St Margaret. *Swin* 5K **19**
Stratton St Michael. *Norf* 2J **31**
Stratton Strawless. *Norf* 7J **39**
Stravithie. *Fife* 6J **67**
Straw. *M Ulst* 4E **92**
Stream. *Som* 2K **7**
Streat. *E Sus* 4L **11**
**Streatham**. *G Lon* 6L **21**
Streatley. *C Beds* 1H **21**
Streatley. *W Ber* 5C **20**
Street. *Corn* 6B **6**
Street. *Lanc* 2D **40**
Street. *N Yor* 5E **48**
Street. *Som*
nr. Chard 5B **8**
**Street**. *Som*
nr. Glastonbury 2C **8**
Street Ash. *Som* 4A **8**
Street Dinas. *Shrp* 6B **34**
Street End. *Kent* 8H **23**
Street End. *W Sus* 6F **10**
Streetgate. *Tyne* 6F **54**
Streethay. *Staf* 8K **35**
Streethouse. *W Yor* 5A **42**
Streetlam. *N Yor* 6M **47**
Street Lane. *Derbs* 5A **36**
Streetly. *W Mid* 2J **27**
Streetly End. *Cambs* 7C **30**
Street on the Fosse. *Som* 2E **8**
Strefford. *Shrp* 3C **26**
Strelley. *Notts* 5C **36**
Strensall. *York* 1D **42**
Strensall Camp. *York* 2D **42**
Stretcholt. *Som* 1A **8**
Strete. *Devn* 7L **5**
**Stretford**. *G Man* 8G **41**
Stretford. *Here* 6D **26**
Strethall. *Essx* 8A **30**
Stretham. *Cambs* 4B **30**
Stretton. *Ches W* 4C **34**
Stretton. *Derbs* 3A **36**
Stretton. *Rut* 8G **37**
Stretton. *Staf*
nr. Brewood 8G **35**
nr. Burton upon Trent 7L **35**
Stretton. *Warr* 1E **34**
Stretton en le Field. *Leics* 8M **35**
Stretton Grandison. *Here* 7E **26**
Stretton Heath. *Shrp* 8B **34**
Stretton-on-Dunsmore.
*Warw* 4B **28**
Stretton-on-Fosse. *Warw* 8L **27**
Stretton Sugwas. *Here* 7C **26**
Stretton under Fosse.
*Warw* 3B **28**
Stretton Westwood. *Shrp* 2D **26**
Strichen. *Abers* 8J **81**
Strines. *G Man* 1H **35**
Stringston. *Som* 1L **7**
Strixton. *Nptn* 5G **29**
Stroanfreggan. *Dum* 2M **51**
Stroat. *Glos* 4D **18**
Stromeferry. *High* 2K **69**
Stromemore. *High* 2K **69**

Stromness. *Orkn* 1D **86**
Stronachie. *Per* 7D **66**
Stronachlachar. *Stir* 6J **65**
Stronchreggan. *High* 8A **70**
Strone. *Arg* 1L **57**
Strone. *High*
nr. Drumnadrochit 3F **70**
nr. Kingussie 5H **71**
Stronenaba. *High* 7C **70**
Stronganess. *Shet* 3K **91**
Stronmilchan. *Arg* 5F **64**
Stronsay Airport. *Orkn* 7F **88**
Strontian. *High* 1C **64**
Strood. *Kent* 2E **12**
**Strood**. *Medw* 7D **22**
Strood Green. *Surr* 1K **11**
Strood Green. *W Sus*
nr. Billingshurst 3H **11**
nr. Horsham 2J **11**
Strothers Dale. *Nmbd* 6C **54**
**Stroud**. *Glos* 3G **19**
Stroud. *Hants* 3E **10**
Stroud Green. *Essx* 4E **22**
Stroxton. *Linc* 6G **37**
Struan. *High* 2E **68**
Struan. *Per* 1B **66**
Struanmore. *High* 2E **68**
Strubby. *Linc* 1A **38**
Strugg's Hill. *Linc* 6K **37**
Strumpshaw. *Norf* 1K **31**
Strutherhill. *S Lan* 4F **58**
Struy. *High* 2E **70**
Stryd. *IOA* 2B **32**
Stryt-issa. *Wrex* 5A **34**
Stuartfield. *Abers* 1J **73**
**Stubbington**. *Hants* 5C **10**
Stubbins. *Lanc* 6F **40**
Stubble Green. *Cumb* 5K **45**
Stubb's Cross. *Kent* 2F **12**
Stubbs Green. *Norf* 2K **31**
Stubhampton. *Dors* 4H **9**
Stubton. *Linc* 5F **36**
Stubwood. *Staf* 6J **35**
Stuckton. *Hants* 4K **9**
Studham. *C Beds* 2H **21**
Studland. *Dors* 7J **9**
Studley. *Warw* 5J **27**
Studley. *Wilts* 6H **19**
Studley Roger. *N Yor* 8L **47**
Stuntney. *Cambs* 4B **30**
Stunts Green. *E Sus* 4C **12**
Sturbridge. *Staf* 6G **35**
Sturgate. *Linc* 1F **36**
Sturmer. *Essx* 7C **30**
Sturminster Marshall. *Dors* 5H **9**
Sturminster Newton. *Dors* 4F **8**
Sturry. *Kent* 7H **23**
Sturton. *N Lin* 7G **43**
Sturton by Stow. *Linc* 1F **36**
Sturton le Steeple. *Notts* 1E **36**
Stuston. *Suff* 4H **31**
Stutton. *N Yor* 3B **42**
Stutton. *Suff* 8H **31**
Styal. *Ches E* 1G **35**
Stydd. *Lanc* 4E **40**
Styrrup. *Notts* 8D **42**
Suainebost. *W Isl* 5J **83**
Suardail. *W Isl* 8H **83**
Succoth. *Abers* 2D **72**
Succoth. *Arg* 7G **65**
Suckley. *Worc* 6F **26**
Suckley Knowl. *Worc* 6F **26**
Sudborough. *Nptn* 3G **29**
Sudbourne. *Suff* 6L **31**
Sudbrook. *Linc* 5G **37**
Sudbrook. *Mon* 5D **18**
Sudbrooke. *Linc* 2H **37**
Sudbury. *Derbs* 6K **35**
**Sudbury**. *Suff* 7E **30**
Sudgrove. *Glos* 3H **19**
Suffield. *Norf* 6J **39**
Suffield. *N Yor* 6G **49**
Sugnall. *Staf* 6F **34**
Sugwas Pool. *Here* 7C **26**
Suisnish. *High* 2G **69**
Sulaisiadar. *W Isl* 8J **83**
Sùlaisiadar Mòr. *High* 1F **68**
Sulby. *IOM* 5C **44**
Sulgrave. *Nptn* 7C **28**
Sulham. *W Ber* 6D **20**
Sulhamstead. *W Ber* 7D **20**
Sullington. *W Sus* 4H **11**
Sullom. *Shet* 6H **91**
Sully. *V Glam* 8L **17**
Sumburgh. *Shet* 7E **90**
Sumburgh Airport. *Shet* 6D **90**
Summer Bridge. *N Yor* 1L **41**
Summercourt. *Corn* 6A **4**
Summergangs. *Hull* 4J **43**
Summer Hill. *W Mid* 2H **27**
Summerhill. *Aber* 5J **73**
Summerhill. *Pemb* 6H **15**
Summerhouse. *Darl* 4L **47**
Summersdale. *W Sus* 5F **10**
Summerseat. *G Man* 6F **40**
Summit. *G Man* 6H **41**
**Sunbury**. *Surr* 7J **21**
Sunderland. *Cumb* 8F **52**
Sunderland. *Lanc* 2C **40**
**Sunderland**. *Tyne* 6G **55**
Sunderland Bridge. *Dur* 8F **54**
Sundon Park. *Lutn* 1H **21**
Sundridge. *Kent* 8A **22**
Sunk Island. *E Yor* 6K **43**
Sunningdale. *Wind* 7G **21**
Sunninghill. *Wind* 7G **21**
Sunningwell. *Oxon* 3B **20**
Sunniside. *Dur* 8E **54**
Sunniside. *Tyne* 6F **54**
Sunny Bank. *Cumb* 6A **46**
Sunny Hill. *Derb* 6M **35**
Sunnyhurst. *Bkbn* 5E **40**
Sunnylaw. *Stir* 8A **66**
Sunnymead. *Oxon* 3C **20**
Sunnyside. *S Yor* 8B **42**
Sunnyside. *W Sus* 2L **11**
Sunton. *Wilts* 8L **19**
**Surbiton**. *G Lon* 7J **21**
Surby. *IOM* 7B **44**
Surfleet. *Linc* 7K **37**
Surfleet Seas End. *Linc* 7K **37**
Surlingham. *Norf* 1K **31**
Surrex. *Essx* 1E **22**
Sustead. *Norf* 6H **39**
Susworth. *Linc* 7F **42**
Sutcombe. *Devn* 4C **6**
Suton. *Norf* 2G **31**
Sutors of Cromarty. *High* 7J **79**
Sutterby. *Linc* 2L **37**
Sutterton. *Linc* 6K **37**
Sutterton Dowdyke. *Linc* 6K **37**
Sutton. *Buck* 6H **21**
Sutton. *Cambs* 4M **29**
Sutton. *C Beds* 7K **29**
Sutton. *E Sus* 6A **12**
**Sutton**. *G Lon* 7K **21**
Sutton. *Kent* 1K **13**
Sutton. *Norf* 7K **39**
Sutton. *Notts* 6E **36**
Sutton. *Oxon* 3B **20**
Sutton. *Pemb* 5F **14**
Sutton. *Pet* 2H **29**
Sutton. *Shrp*
nr. Bridgnorth 3F **26**
nr. Market Drayton 6E **34**
nr. Oswestry 7B **34**
nr. Shrewsbury 8D **34**
Sutton. *Som* 2E **8**
Sutton. *S Yor* 6C **42**
Sutton. *Staf* 7F **34**
Sutton. *Suff* 7K **31**
Sutton. *W Sus* 4G **11**
Sutton. *Worc* 5E **26**
Sutton Abinger. *Surr* 1J **11**
Sutton at Hone. *Kent* 6B **22**
Sutton Bassett. *Nptn* 2E **28**
Sutton Benger. *Wilts* 6H **19**
Sutton Bingham. *Som* 4D **8**
Sutton Bonington. *Notts* 7C **36**
Sutton Bridge. *Linc* 7A **38**
Sutton Cheney. *Leics* 1B **28**
**Sutton Coldfield, Royal**.
*W Mid* 2K **27**
Sutton Corner. *Linc* 7M **37**
Sutton Courtenay. *Oxon* 4C **20**
Sutton Crosses. *Linc* 7M **37**
Sutton cum Lound. *Notts* 1D **36**
Sutton Gault. *Cambs* 4M **29**
Sutton Grange. *N Yor* 8L **47**

Sutton Green. *Surr* 8H **21**
Sutton Howgrave. *N Yor* 8M **47**
**Sutton in Ashfield**. *Notts* 4B **36**
Sutton-in-Craven. *N Yor* 3J **41**
Sutton Ings. *Hull* 4J **43**
Sutton in the Elms. *Leics* 2C **28**
Sutton Lane Ends. *Ches E* 2H **35**
Sutton Leach. *Mers* 8D **40**
Sutton Maddock. *Shrp* 1F **26**
Sutton Mallet. *Som* 2B **8**
Sutton Mandeville. *Wilts* 3H **9**
Sutton Montis. *Som* 3E **8**
Sutton on Hull. *Hull* 4J **43**
Sutton on Sea. *Linc* 1B **38**
Sutton-on-the-Forest.
*N Yor* 1C **42**
Sutton on the Hill. *Derbs* 6L **35**
Sutton on Trent. *Notts* 3E **36**
Sutton Poyntz. *Dors* 7F **8**
Sutton St Edmund. *Linc* 8L **37**
Sutton St Edmund's Common.
*Linc* 1L **29**
Sutton St James. *Linc* 8L **37**
Sutton St Michael. *Here* 7D **26**
Sutton St Nicholas. *Here* 7D **26**
Sutton Scarsdale. *Derbs* 3B **36**
Sutton Scotney. *Hants* 2B **10**
Sutton-under-Brailes.
*Warw* 8M **27**
Sutton-under-Whitestonecliffe.
*N Yor* 7B **48**
Sutton upon Derwent.
*E Yor* 3E **42**
Sutton Valence. *Kent* 1E **12**
Sutton Veny. *Wilts* 1H **9**
Sutton Waldron. *Dors* 4G **9**
Sutton Weaver. *Ches W* 2D **34**
Swaby. *Linc* 2L **37**
**Swadlincote**. *Derbs* 8L **35**
Swaffham. *Norf* 1E **30**
Swaffham Bulbeck.
*Cambs* 5B **30**
Swaffham Prior. *Cambs* 5B **30**
Swafield. *Norf* 6J **39**
Swainby. *N Yor* 5B **48**
Swainshill. *Here* 7C **26**
Swainsthorpe. *Norf* 1J **31**
Swainswick. *Bath* 7F **18**
Swalcliffe. *Oxon* 8A **28**
Swalecliffe. *Kent* 7H **23**
Swallow. *Linc* 7J **43**
Swallow Beck. *Linc* 3G **37**
Swallowcliffe. *Wilts* 3H **9**
Swallowfield. *Wok* 7E **20**
Swallownest. *S Yor* 1B **36**
Swampton. *Hants* 8B **20**
**Swanage**. *Dors* 8J **9**
Swanbister. *Orkn* 1E **86**
Swanbourne. *Buck* 1F **20**
Swanbridge. *V Glam* 8L **17**
Swan Green. *Ches W* 2F **34**
Swanland. *E Yor* 5G **43**
**Swanley**. *Kent* 7B **22**
Swanmore. *Hants* 4C **10**
Swannington. *Leics* 8B **36**
Swannington. *Norf* 8H **39**
Swanpool. *Linc* 3G **37**
Swanscombe. *Kent* 6C **22**
**Swansea**. *Swan* 5F **16**
Swan Street. *Essx* 1E **22**
Swanton Abbott. *Norf* 7J **39**
Swanton Morley. *Norf* 8G **39**
Swanton Novers. *Norf* 6G **39**
Swanton Street. *Kent* 8E **22**
Swanwick. *Derbs* 4B **36**
Swanwick. *Hants* 5C **10**
Swanwick Green. *Ches E* 5D **34**
Swarby. *Linc* 5H **37**
Swardeston. *Norf* 1J **31**
Swarister. *Shet* 5K **91**
Swarkestone. *Derbs* 7A **36**
Swarland. *Nmbd* 1E **54**
Swarraton. *Hants* 2C **10**
Swartha. *W Yor* 3J **41**
Swarthmoor. *Cumb* 8A **46**
Swaton. *Linc* 6J **37**
Swatragh. *M Ulst* 3F **93**
Swavesey. *Cambs* 5L **29**
Sway. *Hants* 6L **9**
Swayfield. *Linc* 7G **37**
Swaythling. *Sotn* 4B **10**
Sweet Green. *Worc* 5E **26**
Sweetham. *Devn* 6H **7**
Sweetholme. *Cumb* 4D **46**
Sweets. *Corn* 6A **6**
Sweetshouse. *Corn* 5C **4**
Swefling. *Suff* 5K **31**
Swell. *Som* 3B **8**
Swepstone. *Leics* 8A **36**
Swerford. *Oxon* 8A **28**
Swettenham. *Ches E* 3G **35**
Swetton. *N Yor* 8K **47**
Swffryd. *Blae* 5M **17**
Swiftsden. *E Sus* 3D **12**
Swilland. *Suff* 6H **31**
Swillington. *W Yor* 4A **42**
Swimbridge. *Devn* 3F **6**
Swimbridge Newland.
*Devn* 2F **6**
Swinbrook. *Oxon* 2L **19**
Swincliffe. *N Yor* 2L **41**
Swincliffe. *W Yor* 5L **41**
Swinderby. *Linc* 3F **36**
Swindon. *Glos* 1H **19**
Swindon. *Nmbd* 2C **54**
Swindon. *Staf* 2G **27**
**Swindon**. *Swin* 5K **19**
Swine. *E Yor* 4J **43**
Swinefleet. *E Yor* 5E **42**
Swineford. *S Glo* 7E **18**
Swineshead. *Bed* 5H **29**
Swineshead. *Linc* 5K **37**
Swineshead Bridge. *Linc* 5K **37**
Swiney. *High* 8D **86**
Swinford. *Leics* 4C **28**
Swinford. *Oxon* 3B **20**
Swingate. *Notts* 5C **36**
Swingbrow. *Cambs* 3L **29**
Swingfield Minnis. *Kent* 1J **13**
Swingfield Street. *Kent* 1J **13**
Swingleton Green. *Suff* 7F **30**
Swinhill. *S Lan* 5F **58**
Swinhoe. *Nmbd* 7K **61**
Swinhope. *Linc* 8K **43**
Swinister. *Shet* 5H **91**
Swinithwaite. *N Yor* 7J **47**
Swinmore Common. *Here* 7E **26**
Swinscoe. *Staf* 5K **35**
Swinside Hall. *Bord* 8E **60**
Swinstead. *Linc* 7H **37**
**Swinton**. *G Man* 7F **40**
Swinton. *N Yor*
nr. Malton 8E **48**
nr. Masham 8L **47**
Swinton. *Bord* 5F **60**
**Swinton**. *S Yor* 8B **42**
Swithland. *Leics* 8C **36**
Swordale. *High* 7F **78**
Swordly. *High* 5K **85**
Sworton Heath. *Ches E* 1E **34**
Swyddffynnon. *Cdgn* 6F **24**
Swynnerton. *Staf* 6G **35**
Swyre. *Dors* 7D **8**
Sycharth. *Powy* 8M **33**
Sychdyn. *Flin* 4M **33**
Sychnant. *Powy* 5J **25**
Sychtyn. *Powy* 2J **25**
Syde. *Glos* 2H **19**
Sydenham. *G Lon* 6L **21**
Sydenham. *Oxon* 3E **20**
Sydenham. *Som* 2B **8**
Sydenham Damerel. *Devn* 8D **6**
Syderstone. *Norf* 6E **38**
Sydling St Nicholas. *Dors* 6E **8**
Sydmonton. *Hants* 8B **20**
Sydney. *Ches E* 4F **34**
Syerston. *Notts* 5E **36**
Syke. *G Man* 6G **41**
Sykehouse. *S Yor* 6D **42**
Sykes. *Lanc* 2E **40**
Syleham. *Suff* 4J **31**
Sylen. *Carm* 6M **15**
Sylfaen. *Powy* 2L **25**
Symbister. *Shet* 1F **90**
Symington. *S Ayr* 6B **58**
Symington. *S Lan* 6H **59**
Symondsbury. *Dors* 6C **8**
Symonds Yat. *Here* 2D **18**
Synod Inn. *Cdgn* 1L **15**

Syre. *High* 7J **85**
Syreford. *Glos* 1J **19**
Syresham. *Nptn* 7D **28**
Syston. *Leics* 8D **36**
Syston. *Linc* 5G **37**
Sytchampton. *Worc* 5G **27**
Sywell. *Nptn* 5F **28**

T

Tabost. *W Isl*
nr. Cearsiadar 2E **76**
nr. Suainebost 5J **83**
Tachbrook Mallory. *Warw* 5M **27**
Tackley. *Oxon* 1B **20**
Tacleit. *W Isl* 8E **82**
Tacolneston. *Norf* 2H **31**
Tadcaster. *N Yor* 3B **42**
Taddington. *Derbs* 2K **35**
Taddington. *Glos* 8J **27**
Taddiport. *Devn* 4D **6**
**Tadley**. *Hants* 7D **20**
Tadlow. *Cambs* 7K **29**
Tadmarton. *Oxon* 8A **28**
Tadwick. *Bath* 6F **18**
**Tadworth**. *Surr* 8K **21**
Tafarnaubach. *Blae* 3L **17**
Tafarn-y-bwlch. *Pemb* 3G **15**
Tafarn-y-Gelyn. *Den* 4L **33**
Taff's Well. *Rhon* 6L **17**
Tafolwern. *Powy* 2H **25**
Tai-bach. *Powy* 8L **33**
Taibach. *Neat* 6G **17**
Taigh a Ghearraidh. *W Isl* 6J **75**
Taigh Bhuirgh. *W Isl* 4B **76**
Tain. *High*
nr. Invergordon 5H **79**
nr. Thurso 5D **86**
Tai-Nant. *Wrex* 5A **34**
Tai'n Lon. *Gwyn* 5D **32**
Tairbeart. *W Isl* 4C **76**
Tairgwaith. *Neat* 3G **17**
Takeley. *Essx* 1B **22**
Takeley Street. *Essx* 1B **22**
Talachddu. *Powy* 1K **17**
Talacre. *Flin* 2L **33**
Talardd. *Gwyn* 8H **33**
Talaton. *Devn* 6K **7**
Talbenny. *Pemb* 5E **14**
Talbot Green. *Rhon* 6K **17**
Taleford. *Devn* 6K **7**
Talerddig. *Powy* 2J **25**
Talgarreg. *Cdgn* 1L **15**
Talgarth. *Powy* 1L **17**
Talisker. *High* 2E **68**
Talke. *Staf* 4G **35**
Talkin. *Cumb* 6K **53**
Talladale. *High* 6L **77**
Talla Linnfoots. *Bord* 7K **59**
Tallaminnock. *S Ayr* 2J **51**
Tallarn Green. *Wrex* 5C **34**
Tallentire. *Cumb* 8F **52**
Talley. *Carm* 1F **16**
Tallington. *Linc* 1H **29**
Talmine. *High* 5H **85**
Talog. *Carm* 4K **15**
Talsarn. *Carm* 2G **17**
Talsarn. *Cdgn* 1M **15**
Talsarnau. *Gwyn* 7F **32**
Talskiddy. *Corn* 5B **4**
Talwrn. *IOA* 3D **32**
Talwrn. *Wrex* 5A **34**
Tal-y-Bont. *Cnwy* 4G **33**
Tal-y-bont. *Cdgn* 4F **24**
Tal-y-bont. *Gwyn*
nr. Bangor 3F **32**
nr. Barmouth 8E **32**
Talybont-on-Usk. *Powy* 2L **17**
Tal-y-cafn. *Cnwy* 3G **33**
Tal-y-coed. *Mon* 2C **18**
Tal-y-llyn. *Gwyn* 2G **25**
Talyllyn. *Powy* 2L **17**
Talysarn. *Gwyn* 5D **32**
Tal-y-waenydd. *Gwyn* 6F **32**
Talywain. *Torf* 3A **18**
Tal-y-Wern. *Powy* 2H **25**
Tamerton Foliot. *Plym* 5G **5**
Tamlaght. *Ferm* 6C **92**
Tamlaght O'Crilly. *M Ulst* 3F **93**
Tamnamore. *M Ulst* 5F **93**
**Tamworth**. *Staf* 1L **27**
Tamworth Green. *Linc* 5L **37**
Tandlehill. *Ren* 3C **58**
Tandragee. *Arm* 6G **93**
Tandridge. *Surr* 8L **21**
Tanerdy. *Carm* 4L **15**
Tanfield. *Dur* 6E **54**
Tanfield Lea. *Dur* 6E **54**
Tangasdal. *W Isl* 5C **74**
Tang Hall. *York* 2D **42**
Tangiers. *Pemb* 5F **14**
Tangley. *Hants* 8M **19**
Tangmere. *W Sus* 5G **11**
Tangwick. *Shet* 6G **91**
Tankerness. *Orkn* 1G **87**
Tankersley. *S Yor* 8M **41**
Tankerton. *Kent* 7H **23**
Tan-lan. *Cnwy* 4G **33**
Tan-lan. *Gwyn* 6F **32**
Tannach. *High* 7E **86**
Tannadice. *Ang* 2H **67**
Tanner's Green. *Worc* 4J **27**
Tannington. *Suff* 5J **31**
Tannochside. *N Lan* 3F **58**
Tan Office Green. *Suff* 6D **30**
Tansley. *Derbs* 4M **35**
Tansley Knoll. *Derbs* 3M **35**
Tansor. *Nptn* 2H **29**
Tantobie. *Dur* 6E **54**
Tanton. *N Yor* 4C **48**
Tanvats. *Linc* 3J **37**
Tanworth-in-Arden. *Warw* 4K **27**
Tan-y-bwlch. *Gwyn* 6F **32**
Tan-y-fron. *Cnwy* 4J **33**
Tanyfron. *Wrex* 4A **34**
Tanygrisiau. *Gwyn* 6F **32**
Tan-y-groes. *Cdgn* 2J **15**
Tan-y-pistyll. *Powy* 8K **33**
Tan-yr-allt. *Den* 2K **33**
Taobh a Chaolais. *W Isl* 4D **74**
Taobh a Deas Loch Aineort.
*W Isl* 3D **74**
Taobh a Ghlinne. *W Isl* 2E **76**
Taobh a Tuath Loch Aineort.
*W Isl* 3D **74**
Taplow. *Buck* 5G **21**
Tapton. *Derbs* 2A **36**
Tarbert. *Arg*
on Jura 1F **56**
on Kintyre 3H **57**
Tarbert. *W Isl* 4C **76**
Tarbet. *Arg* 7H **65**
Tarbet. *High*
nr. Mallaig 6J **69**
nr. Scourie 7D **84**
Tarbock Green. *Mers* 1C **34**
Tarbolton. *S Ayr* 7C **58**
Tarbrax. *S Lan* 4J **59**
Tardebigge. *Worc* 5H **27**
Tarfside. *Ang* 8D **72**
Tarland. *Abers* 5D **72**
Tarleton. *Lanc* 5C **40**
Tarlogie. *High* 5H **79**
Tarlscough. *Lanc* 6C **40**
Tarlton. *Glos* 4H **19**
Tarnbrook. *Lanc* 2D **40**
Tarnock. *Som* 8B **18**
Tarns. *Cumb* 7F **52**
Tarporley. *Ches W* 3D **34**
Tarpots. *Essx* 5D **22**
Tarr. *Som* 2L **7**
Tarrant Crawford. *Dors* 5H **9**
Tarrant Gunville. *Dors* 4H **9**
Tarrant Hinton. *Dors* 4H **9**
Tarrant Keyneston. *Dors* 5H **9**
Tarrant Launceston. *Dors* 5H **9**
Tarrant Monkton. *Dors* 5H **9**
Tarrant Rawston. *Dors* 5H **9**
Tarrant Rushton. *Dors* 5H **9**
Tarrel. *High* 5J **79**
Tarring Neville. *E Sus* 5M **11**
Tarrington. *Here* 7E **26**
Tarsappie. *Per* 5E **66**
Tarscabhaig. *High* 5G **69**
Tarskavaig. *High* 5G **69**
Tarves. *Abers* 2H **73**
Tarvie. *High* 8E **78**
Tarvin. *Ches W* 3C **34**

Tasburgh. *Norf* 2J **31**
Tasley. *Shrp* 2E **26**
Tassagh. *Arm* 7F **93**
Taston. *Oxon* 1A **20**
Tatenhill. *Staf* 7L **35**
Tathall End. *Mil* 7F **28**
Tatham. *Lanc* 1E **40**
Tathwell. *Linc* 1L **37**
Tatling End. *Buck* 5H **21**
Tatsfield. *Surr* 8M **21**
Tattenhall. *Ches W* 4C **34**
Tatterford. *Norf* 7E **38**
Tattersett. *Norf* 6E **38**
Tattershall. *Linc* 4K **37**
Tattershall Bridge. *Linc* 4J **37**
Tattershall Thorpe. *Linc* 4K **37**
Tattingstone. *Suff* 8H **31**
Tattingstone White Horse.
*Suff* 8H **31**
Tattle Bank. *Warw* 5K **27**
Tatworth. *Som* 5B **8**
**Taunton**. *Som* 3M **7**
**Taverham**. *Norf* 8H **39**
Taverners Green. *Essx* 2B **22**
Tavernspite. *Pemb* 5H **15**
**Tavistock**. *Devn* 8D **6**
Tavool House. *Arg* 5K **63**
Taw Green. *Devn* 6F **6**
Tawstock. *Devn* 3E **6**
Taxal. *Derbs* 1J **35**
Tayinloan. *Arg* 5F **56**
Taynish. *Arg* 1G **57**
Taynton. *Glos* 1F **18**
Taynton. *Oxon* 2L **19**
Taynuilt. *Arg* 4E **64**
Tayport. *Fife* 5H **67**
**Tay Road Bridge**. *D'dee* 5H **67**
Tayvallich. *Arg* 1G **57**
Tealby. *Linc* 8J **43**
Tealing. *Ang* 4H **67**
Teams. *Tyne* 5F **54**
Teangue. *High* 5H **69**
Teanna Mhachair. *W Isl* 7J **75**
Tebay. *Cumb* 5E **46**
Tebworth. *C Beds* 1G **21**
Tedburn St Mary. *Devn* 6H **7**
Teddington. *Glos* 8H **27**
**Teddington**. *G Lon* 6J **21**
Tedsmore. *Shrp* 7B **34**
Tedstone Delamere. *Here* 6E **26**
Tedstone Wafer. *Here* 6E **26**
Teemore. *Ferm* 7C **92**
Teesport. *Red C* 3C **48**
**Teesside**. *Stoc T* 3C **48**
Teeton. *Nptn* 4D **28**
Teffont Evias. *Wilts* 2H **9**
Teffont Magna. *Wilts* 2H **9**
Tegryn. *Pemb* 3J **15**
Teigh. *Rut* 8F **36**
Teigncombe. *Devn* 7F **6**
Teigngrace. *Devn* 8H **7**
Teignmouth. *Devn* 8J **7**
**Telford**. *Telf* 8E **34**
Telham. *E Sus* 4D **12**
Tellisford. *Som* 8G **19**
Telscombe. *E Sus* 5M **11**
Telscombe Cliffs. *E Sus* 5L **11**
Tempar. *Per* 2L **65**
Templand. *Dum* 3E **52**
Temple. *Corn* 4D **4**
Temple. *Glas* 3D **58**
Temple. *Midl* 4M **59**
Temple Balsall. *W Mid* 4L **27**
Temple Bar. *Carm* 3E **16**
Temple Bar. *Cdgn* 1M **15**
Temple Cloud. *Bath* 8E **18**
Templecombe. *Som* 3F **8**
Temple Ewell. *Kent* 1J **13**
Temple Grafton. *Warw* 6K **27**
Temple Guiting. *Glos* 1J **19**
Templehall. *Fife* 8F **66**
Temple Hirst. *N Yor* 5D **42**
Temple Normanton. *Derbs* 3B **36**
Templepatrick. *Ant* 4H **93**
Temple Sowerby. *Cumb* 3E **46**
Templeton. *Devn* 4H **7**
Templeton. *Pemb* 5H **15**
Templeton. *W Ber* 7A **20**
Templetown. *Dur* 7E **54**
Tempo. *Ferm* 6C **92**
Tempsford. *C Beds* 6J **29**
Tenandry. *Per* 1C **66**
Tenbury Wells. *Worc* 5D **26**
Tenby. *Pemb* 6H **15**
Tendring. *Essx* 1H **23**
Tendring Green. *Essx* 1H **23**
Tenga. *Arg* 3L **63**
Ten Mile Bank. *Norf* 2C **30**
Tenterden. *Kent* 2E **12**
Terfyn. *Cnwy* 3J **33**
Terhill. *Som* 2L **7**
Terling. *Essx* 2D **22**
Termon Rock. *Ferm* 5E **92**
Ternhill. *Shrp* 6E **34**
Terregles. *Dum* 4D **52**
Terrick. *Buck* 3F **20**
Terrington. *N Yor* 8D **48**
Terrington St Clement.
*Norf* 7B **38**
Terrington St John. *Norf* 8B **38**
Terry's Green. *Warw* 4K **27**
Teston. *Kent* 8D **22**
Testwood. *Hants* 4M **9**
Tetbury. *Glos* 4G **19**
Tetbury Upton. *Glos* 4G **19**
Tetchill. *Shrp* 6B **34**
Tetcott. *Devn* 6C **6**
Tetford. *Linc* 2L **37**
Tetney. *Linc* 7L **43**
Tetney Lock. *Linc* 7L **43**
Tetsworth. *Oxon* 3D **20**
Tettenhall. *W Mid* 1G **27**
Teversal. *Notts* 3B **36**
Teversham. *Cambs* 6A **30**
Teviothead. *Bord* 1J **53**
Tewel. *Abers* 7H **73**
Tewin. *Herts* 2K **21**
**Tewkesbury**. *Glos* 8G **27**
Teynham. *Kent* 7F **22**
Teynham Street. *Kent* 7F **22**
Thackthwaite. *Cumb* 3C **46**
Thakeham. *W Sus* 4J **11**
**Thame**. *Oxon* 3E **20**
Thames Ditton. *Surr* 7J **21**
Thames Haven. *Thur* 5D **22**
Thamesmead. *G Lon* 5A **22**
**Thamesport**. *Medw* 6E **22**
Thanington Without. *Kent* 8H **23**
Thankerton. *S Lan* 6H **59**
Tharston. *Norf* 2H **31**
**Thatcham**. *W Ber* 7C **20**
Thatto Heath. *Mers* 8D **40**
Thaxted. *Essx* 8C **30**
Theakston. *N Yor* 7M **47**
Thealby. *N Lin* 6F **42**
Theale. *Som* 1C **8**
Theale. *W Ber* 6D **20**
Thearne. *E Yor* 4H **43**
Theberton. *Suff* 5L **31**
Theddingworth. *Leics* 3D **28**
Theddlethorpe All Saints.
*Linc* 1A **38**
Theddlethorpe St Helen.
*Linc* 1A **38**
Thelbridge Barton. *Devn* 4G **7**
Thelnetham. *Suff* 4G **31**
Thelveton. *Norf* 3H **31**
Thelwall. *Warr* 1E **34**
Themelthorpe. *Norf* 7G **39**
Thenford. *Nptn* 7C **28**
Therfield. *Herts* 8L **29**
Thetford. *Linc* 8J **37**
**Thetford**. *Norf* 3E **30**
Thethwaite. *Cumb* 7H **53**
Theydon Bois. *Essx* 4M **21**
Thick Hollins. *W Yor* 6K **41**
Thickwood. *Wilts* 6G **19**
Thimbleby. *Linc* 3K **37**
Thimbleby. *N Yor* 6B **48**
Thingwall. *Mers* 1A **34**
Thirlby. *N Yor* 7B **48**
Thirlestane. *Bord* 5C **60**
Thirn. *N Yor* 7L **47**
Thirsk. *N Yor* 7B **48**
Thirtleby. *E Yor* 4J **43**
Thistleton. *Lanc* 4C **40**
Thistleton. *Rut* 8G **37**
Thistley Green. *Suff* 4C **30**
Thixendale. *N Yor* 1F **42**

Thockrington. *Nmbd* 4C **54**
Tholomas Drove. *Cambs* 1M **29**
Tholthorpe. *N Yor* 1B **42**
Thomas Chapel. *Pemb* 6H **15**
Thomas Close. *Cumb* 7J **53**
Thomastown. *Abers* 1G **73**
Thomastown. *Rhon* 6K **17**
Thompson. *Norf* 2F **30**
Thomshill. *Mor* 8B **80**
Thong. *Kent* 6C **22**
Thongsbridge. *W Yor* 7K **41**
Thoralby. *N Yor* 7J **47**
Thoresby. *Notts* 2D **36**
Thoresway. *Linc* 8J **43**
Thorganby. *Linc* 8K **43**
Thorganby. *N Yor* 3D **42**
Thorgill. *N Yor* 6E **48**
Thorington. *Suff* 4L **31**
Thorington Street. *Suff* 8G **31**
Thorlby. *N Yor* 2H **41**
Thorley. *Herts* 2A **22**
Thorley Street. *Herts* 2A **22**
Thorley Street. *IOW* 7A **10**
Thormanby. *N Yor* 8B **48**
Thorn. *Powy* 5A **26**
**Thornaby-on-Tees**. *Stoc T* 4B **48**
Thornage. *Norf* 6G **39**
Thornborough. *Buck* 8E **28**
Thornborough. *N Yor* 8L **47**
Thornbury. *Devn* 5D **6**
Thornbury. *Here* 6E **26**
**Thornbury**. *S Glo* 4E **18**
Thornby. *Cumb* 6G **53**
Thornby. *Nptn* 4D **28**
Thorncliffe. *Staf* 4J **35**
Thorncombe. *Dors* 5B **8**
Thorncombe Street. *Surr* 1G **11**
Thorncote Green. *C Beds* 7J **29**
Thorndon. *Suff* 5H **31**
Thorndon Cross. *Devn* 6E **6**
**Thorne**. *S Yor* 6D **42**
Thornehillhead. *Devn* 4D **6**
Thorner. *W Yor* 3A **42**
Thorne St Margaret. *Som* 3K **7**
Thorney. *Notts* 2F **36**
Thorney. *Pet* 1K **29**
Thorney. *Som* 3C **8**
Thorney Hill. *Hants* 6K **9**
Thorney Toll. *Cambs* 1L **29**
Thornfalcon. *Som* 3A **8**
Thornford. *Dors* 4E **8**
Thorngrafton. *Nmbd* 5A **54**
Thorngrove. *Som* 2B **8**
Thorngumbald. *E Yor* 5K **43**
Thornham. *Norf* 5D **38**
Thornham Magna. *Suff* 4H **31**
Thornham Parva. *Suff* 4H **31**
Thornhaugh. *Pet* 1H **29**
Thornhill. *Cphy* 6L **17**
Thornhill. *Cumb* 4K **45**
Thornhill. *Derbs* 1K **35**
Thornhill. *Dum* 2C **52**
Thornhill. *Sotn* 4B **10**
Thornhill. *Stir* 8L **65**
Thornhill. *W Yor* 6L **41**
Thornhill Lees. *W Yor* 6L **41**
Thornhills. *W Yor* 5K **41**
Thornholme. *E Yor* 1J **43**
Thornicombe. *Dors* 5G **9**
Thornington. *Nmbd* 6F **60**
Thornley. *Dur*
nr. Durham 8G **55**
nr. Tow Law 8E **54**
Thornley Gate. *Nmbd* 6B **54**
Thornliebank. *E Ren* 3D **58**
Thornroan. *Abers* 2H **73**
Thorns. *Suff* 6D **30**
Thornsett. *Derbs* 1J **35**
Thornthwaite. *Cumb* 2M **45**
Thornthwaite. *N Yor* 2K **41**
Thornton. *Ang* 3G **67**
Thornton. *Buck* 8E **28**
Thornton. *E Yor* 3E **42**
Thornton. *Fife* 8F **66**
**Thornton**. *Lanc* 3B **40**
Thornton. *Leics* 1B **28**
Thornton. *Linc* 3K **37**
Thornton. *Mers* 7B **40**
Thornton. *Midd* 4B **48**
Thornton. *Nmbd* 5G **61**
Thornton. *Pemb* 6F **14**
Thornton. *W Yor* 4J **41**
Thornton Curtis. *N Lin* 6H **43**
Thorntonhall. *S Lan* 4D **58**
Thornton Heath. *G Lon* 7L **21**
Thornton Hough. *Mers* 1B **34**
Thornton-in-Craven. *N Yor* 3H **41**
Thornton in Lonsdale.
*N Yor* 8E **46**
Thornton-le-Beans. *N Yor* 6A **48**
Thornton-le-Clay. *N Yor* 1D **42**
Thornton-le-Dale. *N Yor* 7F **48**
Thornton le Moor. *Linc* 8H **43**
Thornton-le-Moor. *N Yor* 7A **48**
Thornton-le-Moors.
*Ches W* 2C **34**
Thornton-le-Street. *N Yor* 7B **48**
Thorntonloch. *E Lot* 2E **60**
Thornton Rust. *N Yor* 7H **47**
Thornton Steward. *N Yor* 7K **47**
Thornton Watlass. *N Yor* 7L **47**
Thornwood Common. *Essx* 3A **22**
Thornythwaite. *Cumb* 3B **46**
Thoroton. *Notts* 5E **36**
Thorp Arch. *W Yor* 3B **42**
Thorpe. *Derbs* 4K **35**
Thorpe. *E Yor* 3G **43**
Thorpe. *Linc* 1A **38**
Thorpe. *Norf* 2L **31**
Thorpe. *N Yor* 1J **41**
Thorpe. *Notts* 5E **36**
Thorpe. *Surr* 7H **21**
Thorpe Abbotts. *Norf* 4H **31**
Thorpe Acre. *Leics* 7C **36**
Thorpe Arnold. *Leics* 7E **36**
Thorpe Audlin. *W Yor* 6B **42**
Thorpe Bassett. *N Yor* 8F **48**
Thorpe Bay. *S'end* 5F **22**
Thorpe by Water. *Rut* 2F **28**
Thorpe Common. *S Yor* 8A **42**
Thorpe Common. *Suff* 8J **31**
Thorpe Constantine. *Staf* 1L **27**
Thorpe End. *Norf* 8J **39**
Thorpe Fendike. *Linc* 3A **38**
Thorpe Green. *Essx* 1H **23**
Thorpe Green. *Suff* 6F **30**
Thorpe Hall. *N Yor* 8C **48**
Thorpe Hamlet. *Norf* 1J **31**
Thorpe Hesley. *S Yor* 8A **42**
Thorpe in Balne. *S Yor* 6C **42**
Thorpe in the Fallows. *Linc* 1G **37**
Thorpe Langton. *Leics* 2E **28**
Thorpe Larches. *Dur* 3A **48**
Thorpe Latimer. *Linc* 5J **37**
Thorpe-le-Soken. *Essx* 1H **23**
Thorpe le Street. *E Yor* 3F **42**
Thorpe Malsor. *Nptn* 4F **28**
Thorpe Mandeville. *Nptn* 7C **28**
Thorpe Market. *Norf* 6J **39**
Thorpe Marriott. *Norf* 8H **39**
Thorpe Morieux. *Suff* 6F **30**
Thorpeness. *Suff* 6L **31**
Thorpe on the Hill. *Linc* 3G **37**
Thorpe on the Hill. *W Yor* 5M **41**
Thorpe St Andrew. *Norf* 1J **31**
Thorpe St Peter. *Linc* 3A **38**
Thorpe Salvin. *S Yor* 1C **36**
Thorpe Satchville. *Leics* 8E **36**
Thorpe Thewles. *Stoc T* 3A **48**
Thorpe Tilney. *Linc* 4J **37**
Thorpe Underwood. *N Yor* 2B **42**
Thorpe Waterville. *Nptn* 3H **29**
Thorpe Willoughby. *N Yor* 4C **42**
Thorpland. *Norf* 1C **30**
Thorrington. *Essx* 1G **23**
Thorverton. *Devn* 5J **7**
Thrandeston. *Suff* 4H **31**
Thrapston. *Nptn* 4G **29**
Thrashbush. *N Lan* 3F **58**
Threapland. *Cumb* 8F **52**
Threapland. *N Yor* 1H **41**
Threapwood. *Ches W* 5C **34**
Threapwood. *Staf* 5J **35**
Three Ashes. *Here* 1D **18**
Three Bridges. *Linc* 1M **37**
Three Bridges. *W Sus* 2K **11**
Three Burrows. *Corn* 4L **3**
Three Chimneys. *Kent* 2E **12**
Three Cocks. *Powy* 1L **17**

Three Crosses. *Swan* 5E **16**
Three Cups Corner. *E Sus* 3C **12**
Threehammer Common.
*Norf* 7K **39**
Three Holes. *Norf* 1B **30**
Threekingham. *Linc* 6H **37**
Three Leg Cross. *E Sus* 2C **12**
Three Legged Cross. *Dors* 5J **9**
Three Mile Cross. *Wok* 7E **20**
Threemilestone. *Corn* 4L **3**
Three Oaks. *E Sus* 4E **12**
Threlkeld. *Cumb* 3B **46**
Threshfield. *N Yor* 1H **41**
Thrigby. *Norf* 8L **39**
Thringarth. *Dur* 3H **47**
Thringstone. *Leics* 8B **36**
Thrintoft. *N Yor* 6M **47**
Thriplow. *Cambs* 7M **29**
Throckenholt. *Linc* 1L **29**
Throcking. *Herts* 8L **29**
Throckley. *Tyne* 5E **54**
Throckmorton. *Worc* 7H **27**
Throop. *Bour* 6K **9**
Throphill. *Nmbd* 3E **54**
Thropton. *Nmbd* 1D **54**
Throsk. *Stir* 8B **66**
Througham. *Glos* 3H **19**
Throughgate. *Dum* 3C **52**
Throwleigh. *Devn* 6F **6**
Throwley. *Kent* 8F **22**
Throwley Forstal. *Kent* 8F **22**
Throxenby. *N Yor* 7H **49**
Thrumpton. *Notts* 6C **36**
Thrumster. *High* 7E **86**
Thrunton. *Nmbd* 8H **61**
Thrupp. *Glos* 3G **19**
Thrupp. *Oxon* 2B **20**
Thrushelton. *Devn* 7D **6**
Thrushgill. *Lanc* 1E **40**
Thrussington. *Leics* 8D **36**
Thruxton. *Hants* 1L **9**
Thruxton. *Here* 8C **26**
Thrybergh. *S Yor* 8B **42**
Thulston. *Derbs* 6B **36**
Thundergay. *N Ayr* 5H **57**
Thundersley. *Essx* 5D **22**
Thundridge. *Herts* 2L **21**
Thurcaston. *Leics* 8C **36**
Thurcroft. *S Yor* 1B **36**
Thurdon. *Corn* 4B **6**
Thurgarton. *Norf* 6H **39**
Thurgarton. *Notts* 5D **36**
Thurgoland. *S Yor* 7L **41**
Thurlaston. *Leics* 2C **28**
Thurlaston. *Warw* 4B **28**
Thurlbear. *Som* 3A **8**
Thurlby. *Linc*
nr. Alford 2A **38**
nr. Baston 8J **37**
nr. Lincoln 3G **37**
Thurleigh. *Bed* 6H **29**
Thurlestone. *Devn* 7J **5**
Thurloxton. *Som* 2A **8**
Thurlstone. *S Yor* 7L **41**
Thurlton. *Norf* 2L **31**
Thurmaston. *Leics* 1D **28**
Thurnby. *Leics* 1D **28**
Thurne. *Norf* 8L **39**
Thurnham. *Kent* 8E **22**
Thurning. *Norf* 7G **39**
Thurning. *Nptn* 3H **29**
Thurnscoe. *S Yor* 7B **42**
Thursby. *Cumb* 6H **53**
Thursford. *Norf* 6F **38**
Thursford Green. *Norf* 6F **38**
Thursley. *Surr* 2G **11**
Thurso. *High* 5C **86**
Thurso East. *High* 5C **86**
Thurstaston. *Mers* 2M **33**
Thurston. *Suff* 5F **30**
Thurston End. *Suff* 6D **30**
Thurstonfield. *Cumb* 6H **53**
Thurstonland. *W Yor* 6K **41**
Thurton. *Norf* 1K **31**
Thurvaston. *Derbs*
nr. Ashbourne 6K **35**
nr. Derby 6L **35**
Thuxton. *Norf* 1G **31**
Thwaite. *Dur* 4J **47**
Thwaite. *N Yor* 6G **47**
Thwaite. *Suff* 5H **31**
Thwaite Head. *Cumb* 6B **46**
Thwaites. *W Yor* 3J **41**
Thwaite St Mary. *Norf* 2K **31**
Thwing. *E Yor* 8H **49**
Tibbermore. *Per* 5D **66**
Tibberton. *Glos* 1F **18**
Tibberton. *Telf* 7E **34**
Tibberton. *Worc* 6H **27**
Tibenham. *Norf* 3H **31**
Tibshelf. *Derbs* 3B **36**
Tibthorpe. *E Yor* 2G **43**
Ticehurst. *E Sus* 2C **12**
Tichborne. *Hants* 2C **10**
Tickencote. *Rut* 1G **29**
Tickenham. *N Som* 6C **18**
Tickhill. *S Yor* 8C **42**
Ticklerton. *Shrp* 2C **26**
Ticknall. *Derbs* 7A **36**
Tickton. *E Yor* 3H **43**
Tidbury Green. *W Mid* 4K **27**
Tidcombe. *Wilts* 8L **19**
Tiddington. *Oxon* 3D **20**
Tiddington. *Warw* 6L **27**
Tiddleywink. *Wilts* 6G **19**
Tidebrook. *E Sus* 3C **12**
Tideford. *Corn* 6F **4**
Tideford Cross. *Corn* 5F **4**
Tidenham. *Glos* 4D **18**
Tideswell. *Derbs* 2K **35**
Tidmarsh. *W Ber* 6D **20**
Tidmington. *Warw* 8L **27**
Tidpit. *Hants* 4J **9**
Tidworth. *Wilts* 1L **9**
Tidworth Camp. *Wilts* 1L **9**
Tiers Cross. *Pemb* 5F **14**
Tiffield. *Nptn* 6D **28**
Tifty. *Abers* 1G **73**
Tigerton. *Ang* 1J **67**
Tighnabruaich. *Arg* 2J **57**
Tigley. *Devn* 5K **5**
Tilbrook. *Cambs* 5H **29**
**Tilbury**. *Thur* 6C **22**
Tilbury Green. *Essx* 7D **30**
Tilbury Juxta Clare. *Essx* 7D **30**
Tile Hill. *W Mid* 4L **27**
Tilehurst. *Read* 6D **20**
Tilford. *Surr* 1F **10**
Tilgate Forest Row. *W Sus* 2K **11**
Tillathrowie. *Abers* 2D **72**
Tillers Green. *Glos* 8E **26**
Tillery. *Abers* 3J **73**
Tilley. *Shrp* 7D **34**
Tillicoultry. *Clac* 8C **66**
Tillingham. *Essx* 3F **22**
Tillington. *Here* 7C **26**
Tillington. *W Sus* 3G **11**
Tillington Common. *Here* 7C **26**
Tillybirloch. *Abers* 5F **72**
Tillyfourie. *Abers* 4F **72**
Tilmanstone. *Kent* 8K **23**
Tilney All Saints. *Norf* 8B **38**
Tilney Fen End. *Norf* 8B **38**
Tilney High End. *Norf* 8B **38**
Tilney St Lawrence. *Norf* 8B **38**
Tilshead. *Wilts* 1J **9**
Tilstock. *Shrp* 6D **34**
Tilston. *Ches W* 4C **34**
Tilstone Fearnall. *Ches W* 3D **34**
Tilsworth. *C Beds* 1G **21**
Tilton on the Hill. *Leics* 1E **28**
Tiltups End. *Glos* 4G **19**
Timberland. *Linc* 4J **37**
Timbersbrook. *Ches E* 3G **35**
Timberscombe. *Som* 1J **7**
Timble. *N Yor* 2K **41**
Timperley. *G Man* 1F **34**
Timsbury. *Bath* 8E **18**
Timsbury. *Hants* 3M **9**
Timsgearraidh. *W Isl* 8D **82**
Timworth Green. *Suff* 5E **30**
Tincleton. *Dors* 6F **8**
Tindale. *Cumb* 6L **53**
Tindale Crescent. *Dur* 3L **47**
Tingewick. *Buck* 8D **28**
Tingrith. *C Beds* 8H **29**
Tingwall. *Orkn* 7D **88**
Tinhay. *Devn* 7C **6**
Tinshill. *W Yor* 4L **41**

Tinsley—Walton


Tinsley. S Yor 8B 42
Tinsley Green. W Sus 2K 11
Tintagel. Corn 3C 4
Tintern. Mon 3D 18
Tintinhull. Som 4C 8
Tintwistle. Derbs 8J 41
Tinwald. Dum 3E 52
Tinwell. Rut 1H 29
Tippacott. Devn 1G 7
Tipperty. Abers 3J 73
Tipps End. Cambs 2B 30
Tiptoe. Hants 6L 9
Tipton. W Mid 2H 27
Tipton St John. Devn 6K 7
Tiptree. Essx 2E 22
Tiptree Heath. Essx 2E 22
Tirabad. Powy 8H 25
Tircoed Forest Village.
Swan 4F 16
Tiree Airport. Arg 3F 62
Tirinie. Per 1B 66
Tirley. Glos 1G 19
Tiroran. Arg 5K 63
Tir-Phil. Cphy 4L 17
Tirril. Cumb 3D 46
Tirryside. High 2F 78
Tir-y-dail. Carm 3F 16
Tisbury. Wilts 3H 9
Tisman's Common. W Sus 2H 11
Tissington. Derbs 4K 35
Titchberry. Devn 3B 6
Titchfield. Hants 5C 10
Titchmarsh. Nptn 4H 29
Titchwell. Norf 5D 38
Tithby. Notts 6D 36
Titley. Here 6B 26
Titlington. Nmbd 8H 61
Titsey. Surr 8M 21
Titson. Corn 5B 6
Tittensor. Staf 6G 35
Tittleshall. Norf 7E 38
Titton. Worc 5G 27
Tiverton. Ches W 3D 34
**Tiverton**. Devn 4J 7
Tivetshall St Margaret.
Norf 3H 31
Tivetshall St Mary. Norf 3H 31
Tivington. Som 1J 7
Tixall. Staf 7H 35
Tixover. Rut 1G 29
Toab. Orkn 1G 87
Toab. Shet 6D 90
Toadmoor. Derbs 4A 36
Tobermore. M Ulst 4F 93
Tobermory. Arg 2L 63
Toberonochy. Arg 7B 64
Tobha Beag. W Isl 2D 74
Tobha-Beag. W Isl 6A 76
Tobha Mor. W Isl 2D 74
Tobhtarol. W Isl 8E 82
Tobson. W Isl 8E 82
Tocabhaig. High 4H 69
Tocher. Abers 2F 72
Tockenham. Wilts 6J 19
Tockenham Wick. Wilts 5J 19
Tockholes. Bkbn 5E 40
Tockington. S Glo 5E 18
Tockwith. N Yor 2B 42
Todber. Dors 3G 9
Todding. Here 4C 26
Toddington. C Beds 1H 21
Toddington. Glos 8J 27
Todenham. Glos 8L 27
Todhills. Cumb 5H 53
**Todmorden**. W Yor 5H 41
Todwick. S Yor 1B 36
Toft. Cambs 6L 29
Toft. Linc 8H 37
Toft Hill. Dur 3K 47
Toft Monks. Norf 2L 31
Toft next Newton. Linc 1H 37
Toftrees. Norf 7E 38
Tofts. High 5E 86
Toftwood. Norf 8F 38
Togston. Nmbd 1F 54
Tokavaig. High 4H 69
Tokers Green. Oxon 6E 20
Tolastadh a Chaolais. W Isl 8E 82
Tolladine. Worc 6G 27
Tolland. Som 2L 7
Tollard Farnham. Dors 4H 9
Tollard Royal. Wilts 4H 9
Toll Bar. S Yor 7C 42
Toller Fratrum. Dors 6D 8
Toller Porcorum. Dors 6D 8
Tollerton. N Yor 1C 42
Tollerton. Notts 6D 36
Toller Whelme. Dors 5D 8
Tollesbury. Essx 2F 22
Tolleshunt D'Arcy. Essx 2F 22
Tolleshunt Knights. Essx 2F 22
Tolleshunt Major. Essx 2F 22
Tollie. High 8F 78
Tollie Farm. High 6K 77
Tolm. W Isl 8H 83
Tolpuddle. Dors 6F 8
Tolstadh bho Thuath. W Isl 7J 83
Tolworth. G Lon 7J 21
Tomachlaggan. Mor 3A 72
Tomaknock. Per 5B 66
Tomatin. High 3J 71
Tombuidhe. Arg 7E 64
Tomdoun. High 5B 70
Tomich. High
nr. Cannich 3D 70
nr. Invergordon 6H 79
nr. Lairg 3G 79
Tomintoul. Mor 4A 72
Tomnavoulin. Mor 3B 72
Tomsléibhe. Arg 4M 63
Ton. Mon 4B 18
**Tonbridge**. Kent 1B 12
Tondu. B'end 6H 17
Tonedale. Som 3L 7
Tonfanau. Gwyn 2E 24
Tong. Shrp 1F 26
Tonge. Leics 7B 36
Tong Forge. Shrp 1F 26
Tongham. Surr 1F 10
Tongland. Dum 6A 52
Tong Norton. Shrp 1F 26
Tongue. High 6H 85
Tongue End. Linc 8J 37
Tongwynlais. Card 6L 17
Tonmawr. Neat 5H 17
Tonna. Neat 5G 17
Tonnau. Neat 5G 17
Ton Pentre. Rhon 5J 17
Ton-Teg. Rhon 6K 17
Tonwell. Herts 2L 21
Tonypandy. Rhon 5J 17
Tonyrefail. Rhon 6K 17
Toome. Ant 4F 93
Toot Baldon. Oxon 3C 20
Toot Hill. Essx 3B 22
Toothill. Hants 4A 10
Topcliffe. N Yor 8B 48
Topcliffe. W Yor 5L 41
Topcroft. Norf 2J 31
Topcroft Street. Norf 2J 31
Toppesfield. Essx 8D 30
Toppings. G Man 6F 40
Toprow. Norf 2H 31
Topsham. Devn 7J 7
**Torbay**. Torb 5M 5
Torbeg. N Ayr 7H 57
Torbothie. N Lan 4G 59
Torbryan. Devn 5L 5
Torcross. Devn 7L 5
Tore. High 8G 79
Torgyle. High 4D 70
Torinturk. Arg 3H 57
Torksey. Linc 2F 36
Torlum. W Isl 8J 75
Torlundy. High 8B 70
Tormarton. S Glo 6F 18
Tormitchell. S Ayr 2H 51
Tormore. High 5H 69
Tormore. N Ayr 6H 57
Tornagrain. High 1H 71
Tornaveen. Abers 5F 72
Torness. High 3F 70
Toronto. Dur 8E 54
Torpenhow. Cumb 8G 53
Torphichen. W Lot 2H 59
Torphins. Abers 5F 72
Torpoint. Corn 6G 5
**Torquay**. Torb 5M 5
Torr. Devn 6H 5
Torra. Arg 4C 56
Torran. High 1G 69
Torrance. E Dun 2E 58
Torrans. Arg 5K 63
Torranyard. N Ayr 5B 58
Torre. Som 2K 7
Torre. Torb 5M 5
Torridon. High 8L 77
Torrin. High 3G 69
Torrisdale. Arg 6G 57
Torrisdale. High 5J 85
Torrish. High 2K 79
Torrisholme. Lanc 1C 40
Torroble. High 3F 78
Torroy. High 4F 78
Torry. Aber 5J 73
Torryburn. Fife 1J 59
Torthorwald. Dum 4E 52
Tortington. W Sus 5H 11
Tortworth. S Glo 4F 18
Torvaig. High 1F 68
Torver. Cumb 6A 46
Torwood. Falk 1G 59
Torworth. Notts 1D 36
Toscaig. High 2J 69
Toseland. Cambs 5K 29
Tosside. N Yor 2F 40
Tostock. Suff 5F 30
Totaig. High 8C 76
Totardor. High 2E 68
Tote. High 1F 68
Totegan. High 5L 85
Tothill. Linc 1M 37
Totland. IOW 7M 9
Totley. S Yor 2M 35
Totnell. Dors 5E 8
Totnes. Devn 5L 5
Toton. Notts 6B 36
Totronald. Arg 2G 63
Totscore. High 7E 76
**Tottenham**. G Lon 4L 21
Tottenhill. Norf 8C 38
Tottenhill Row. Norf 8C 38
Totteridge. G Lon 4K 21
Totternhoe. C Beds 1G 21
Tottington. G Man 6F 40
**Totton**. Hants 4A 10
Touchen-end. Wind 6F 20
Toulvaddie. High 5J 79
The Towans. Corn 5J 3
Toward. Arg 3L 57
Towcester. Nptn 7D 28
Towednack. Corn 5H 3
Tower End. Norf 8C 38
Tower Hill. Mers 7C 40
Tower Hill. W Sus 3J 11
Towersey. Oxon 3E 20
Towie. Abers 4D 72
Towiemore. Mor 1C 72
Tow Law. Dur 8E 54
The Town. IOS 1G 3
Town End. Cambs 2M 29
Town End. Cumb
nr. Ambleside 5C 46
nr. Kirkby Thore 3E 46
nr. Lindale 7C 46
nr. Newby Bridge 7B 46
Town End. Mers 1C 34
Townend. W Dun 2C 58
Townfield. Dur 7C 54
Towngate. Cumb 7K 53
Towngate. Linc 8J 37
Town Green. Lanc 7C 40
Town Head. Cumb
nr. Grasmere 5B 46
nr. Great Asby 4E 46
Townhead. Cumb
nr. Lazonby 8K 53
nr. Maryport 8E 52
nr. Ousby 8L 53
Townhead. Dum 7A 52
Townhead of Greenlaw.
Dum 5B 52
Townhill. Fife 1K 59
Townhill. Swan 5F 16
Townjoy. M Ulst 5F 93
Town Kelloe. Dur 8G 55
Town Littleworth. E Sus 4M 11
Town Row. E Sus 2B 12
Towns End. Hants 8C 20
Townsend. Herts 3J 21
Townshend. Corn 5J 3
Town Street. Suff 3D 30
Town Yetholm. Bord 7F 60
Towthorpe. E Yor 1G 43
Towthorpe. York 2D 42
Towton. N Yor 4B 42
Towyn. Cnwy 3J 33
Toxteth. Mers 1B 34
Toynton All Saints. Linc 3L 37
Toynton Fen Side. Linc 3L 37
Toynton St Peter. Linc 3M 37
Toy's Hill. Kent 8A 22
Trabboch. E Ayr 7C 58
Traboe. Corn 6L 3
Tradespark. High 8J 79
Tradespark. Orkn 1F 86
Trafford Park. G Man 8F 40
Trallong. Powy 2J 17
Y Trallwng. Powy 2M 25
Tranent. E Lot 2B 60
Tranmere. Mers 1B 34
Trantlebeg. High 6L 85
Trantlemore. High 6L 85
Tranwell. Nmbd 3E 54
Trapp. Carm 3F 16
Traquair. Bord 6M 59
Trash Green. W Ber 7D 20
Trawden. Lanc 4H 41
Trawscoed. Powy 1K 17
Trawsfynydd. Gwyn 7G 33
Trawsgoed. Cdgn 5F 24
Treaddow. Here 1D 18
Trealaw. Rhon 5K 17
Treales. Lanc 4C 40
Trearddur. IOA 3B 32
Treaslane. High 8E 76
Treator. Corn 4B 4
Trebanog. Rhon 5K 17
Trebanos. Neat 4G 17
Trebarber. Corn 5A 4
Trebartha. Corn 8B 6
Trebarwith. Corn 3C 4
Trebetherick. Corn 4B 4
Treborough. Som 2K 7
Trebudannon. Corn 5A 4
Trebullett. Corn 8C 6
Treburley. Corn 8C 6
Treburrick. Corn 4A 4
Trebyan. Corn 5C 4
Trecastle. Powy 2H 17
Trecenydd. Cphy 6L 17
Trecott. Devn 5F 6
Trecwn. Pemb 3F 14
Trecynon. Rhon 4J 17
Tredaule. Corn 7B 6
Tredavoe. Corn 6H 3
**Tredegar**. Blae 4L 17
Trederwen. Powy 8A 34
Tredington. Glos 1H 19
Tredington. Warw 7L 27
Tredinnick. Corn
nr. Bodmin 5D 4
nr. Looe 6E 4
nr. Padstow 4B 4
Tredogan. V Glam 8K 17
Tredomen. Powy 1L 17
Tredunnock. Mon 4B 18
Tredustan. Powy 1L 17
Treen. Corn
nr. Land's End 6G 3
nr. St Ives 5H 3
Treeton. S Yor 1B 36
Trefaldwyn. Powy 3M 25
Trefasser. Pemb 3E 14
Trefdraeth. IOA 3D 32
Trefdraeth. Pemb 3G 15
Trefecca. Powy 1L 17
Trefechan. Mer T 4K 17
Trefeglwys. Powy 3J 25
Trefenter. Cdgn 6F 24
Treffgarne. Pemb 4F 14
Treffynnon. Flin 3L 33
Treffynnon. Pemb 4E 14
Trefil. Blae 3L 17
Trefilan. Cdgn 1M 15
Trefin. Pemb 3E 14
Treflach. Shrp 7A 34
Trefnant. Den 3K 33
Trefonen. Shrp 7A 34
Trefor. Gwyn 6C 32
Trefor. IOA 2C 32
Treforest. Rhon 6K 17
Trefrew. Corn 3D 4
Trefriw. Cnwy 4G 33
Tref-y-Clawdd. Powy 4A 26
Trefynwy. Mon 2D 18
Tregada. Corn 7C 6
Tregadillett. Corn 7B 6
Tregare. Mon 2C 18
Tregarne. Corn 6L 3
Tregaron. Cdgn 7F 24
Tregarth. Gwyn 4F 32
Tregear. Corn 6A 4
Tregeare. Corn 7B 6
Tregeiriog. Wrex 7L 33
Tregele. IOA 1C 32
Tregeseal. Corn 5G 3
Tregiskey. Corn 7C 4
Tregole. Corn 6A 6
Tregolwyn. V Glam 7J 17
Tregonetha. Corn 5B 4
Tregonhawke. Corn 6G 5
Tregony. Corn 7B 4
Tregoodwell. Corn 3D 4
Tregorrick. Corn 6C 4
Tregoss. Corn 5B 4
Tregowris. Corn 6L 3
Tregoyd. Powy 1L 17
Tregrehan Mills. Corn 6C 4
Tre-groes. Cdgn 2L 15
Tregullon. Corn 5C 4
Tregurrian. Corn 5A 4
Tregynon. Powy 3K 25
Trehafod. Rhon 5K 17
Trehan. Corn 6G 5
**Treharris**. Mer T 5K 17
Treherbert. Rhon 5J 17
Trehunist. Corn 5F 4
Trekenner. Corn 8C 6
Trekenning. Corn 5B 4
Treknow. Corn 3C 4
Trelales. B'end 6H 17
Trelan. Corn 7L 3
Trelash. Corn 6A 6
Trelassick. Corn 6A 4
Trelawnyd. Flin 3K 33
Trelech. Carm 3J 15
Treleddyd-fawr. Pemb 4D 14
Trelewis. Mer T 5L 17
Treligga. Corn 3C 4
Trelights. Corn 4B 4
Trelill. Corn 4C 4
Trelissick. Corn 5M 3
Trellech. Mon 3D 18
Trelleck Grange. Mon 3C 18
Trelogan. Flin 2L 33
Trelystan. Powy 1A 26
Tremadog. Gwyn 6E 32
Tremail. Corn 7A 6
Tremain. Cdgn 2J 15
Tremaine. Corn 7B 6
Tremar. Corn 5E 4
Trematon. Corn 6F 4
Tremeirchion. Den 3K 33
Tremore. Corn 5C 4
Tremorfa. Card 7M 17
Trenance. Corn
nr. Newquay 5A 4
nr. Padstow 4B 4
Trenarren. Corn 7C 4
Trench. Telf 8E 34
Trencreek. Corn 2M 3
Trendeal. Corn 6A 4
Trenear. Corn 5K 3
Treneglos. Corn 7B 6
Trenewan. Corn 6D 4
Trengune. Corn 6A 6
Trent. Dors 4D 8
Trentham. Stoke 5G 35
Trentishoe. Devn 1F 6
Trentlock. Derbs 6B 36
Treoes. V Glam 7J 17
Treorchy. Rhon 5J 17
Treorci. Rhon 5J 17
Tre'r-ddol. Cdgn 3F 24
Tre'r llai. Powy 2M 25
Trerulefoot. Corn 6F 4
Tresaith. Cdgn 1J 15
Trescott. Staf 2G 27
Trescowe. Corn 5J 3
Tresham. Glos 4F 18
Tresigin. V Glam 7J 17
Tresillian. Corn 7A 4
Tresimwn. V Glam 7K 17
Tresinney. Corn 3D 4
Treskillard. Corn 5K 3
Treskinnick Cross. Corn 6B 6
Tresmeer. Corn 7B 6
Tresparrett. Corn 2D 4
Tresparrett Posts. Corn 6A 6
Tressady. High 3G 79
Tressait. Per 1B 66
Tresta. Shet
on Fetlar 4L 91
on Mainland 2D 90
Treswell. Notts 2E 36
Treswithian. Corn 5K 3
Tre Taliesin. Cdgn 3F 24
Trethomas. Cphy 6L 17
Trethosa. Corn 6B 4
Trethurgy. Corn 6C 4
Tretio. Pemb 4D 14
Tretire. Here 1D 18
Tretower. Powy 2L 17
Treuddyn. Flin 4A 34
Trevadlock. Corn 8B 6
Trevalga. Corn 3C 4
Trevalyn. Wrex 4B 34
Trevance. Corn 4B 4
Trevanger. Corn 4B 4
Trevanson. Corn 4B 4
Trevarrack. Corn 5H 3
Trevarren. Corn 5B 4
Trevarrian. Corn 5A 4
Trevarrick. Corn 7B 4
Trevaughan. Carm
nr. Carmarthen 4L 15
nr. Whitland 5H 15
Treveighan. Corn 4C 4
Trevellas. Corn 3L 3
Trevelmond. Corn 5E 4
Treverva. Corn 5L 3
Trevescan. Corn 6G 3
Trevethin. Torf 3A 18
Trevia. Corn 3C 4
Trevigro. Corn 5F 4
Trevilley. Corn 6G 3
Treviscoe. Corn 6B 4
Trevivian. Corn 7A 6
Trevone. Corn 4A 4
Trevor. Wrex 5A 34
Trevor Uchaf. Den 6M 33
Trew. Corn 6K 3
Trewalder. Corn 3C 4
Trewarlett. Corn 7C 6
Trewarmett. Corn 3C 4
Trewassa. Corn 3D 4
Treween. Corn 7B 6
Trewellard. Corn 5G 3
Trewen. Corn 7B 6
Trewennack. Corn 6K 3
Trewern. Powy 8A 34
Trewetha. Corn 4C 4
Trewidland. Corn 6E 4
Trewint. Corn 6A 6
Trewithian. Corn 8A 4
Trewoofe. Corn 6H 3
Trewoon. Corn 6B 4
Treworthal. Corn 8A 4
Trewyddel. Pemb 2H 15
Treyarnon. Corn 4A 4
Treyford. W Sus 4F 10
Triangle. Staf 1J 27
Triangle. W Yor 5J 41
Trickett's Cross. Dors 5J 9
Trillick. Ferm 6C 92
Trimdon. Dur 8G 55
Trimdon Colliery. Dur 8G 55
Trimdon Grange. Dur 8G 55
Trimingham. Norf 6J 39
Trimley Lower Street. Suff 8J 31
Trimley St Martin. Suff 8J 31
Trimley St Mary. Suff 8J 31
Trimpley. Worc 4F 26
Trimsaran. Carm 6L 15
Trimstone. Devn 1E 6
Trinafour. Per 1M 65
Trinant. Cphy 5M 17
**Tring**. Herts 2G 21
Trinity. Ang 1K 67
Trinity. Edin 2L 59
Trisant. Cdgn 5G 25
Triscombe. Som 2L 7
Trislaig. High 8A 70
Trispen. Corn 3M 3
Tritlington. Nmbd 2F 54
Trochry. Per 3C 66
Troedrhiwdalar. Powy 7J 25
Troedrhiwfuwch. Cphy 4L 17
Troedrhiw-gwair. Blae 4L 17
Troedyraur. Cdgn 2K 15
Troedyrhiw. Mer T 4K 17
Trondavoe. Shet 6H 91
Troon. Corn 5K 3
**Troon**. S Ayr 6B 58
Troqueer. Dum 4D 52
Troston. Suff 4E 30
Trottiscliffe. Kent 7C 22
Trotton. W Sus 3F 10
Troutbeck. Cumb
nr. Ambleside 5C 46
nr. Penrith 3B 46
Troutbeck Bridge. Cumb 5C 46
Troway. Derbs 2A 36
**Trowbridge**. Wilts 8G 19
Trowell. Notts 6B 36
Trowle Common. Wilts 8G 19
Trowley Bottom. Herts 2H 21
Trowse Newton. Norf 1J 31
Trudoxhill. Som 1F 8
Trull. Som 3M 7
Trumaisgearraidh. W Isl 6K 75
Trumpan. High 7D 76
Trumpet. Here 8E 26
Trumpington. Cambs 6M 29
Trumps Green. Surr 7G 21
Trunch. Norf 6J 39
Trunnah. Lanc 3B 40
**Truro**. Corn 4M 3
Trusham. Devn 7H 7
Trusley. Derbs 6L 35
Trusthorpe. Linc 1B 38
Tryfil. IOA 2D 32
Trysull. Staf 2G 27
Tubney. Oxon 4B 20
Tuckenhay. Devn 6L 5
Tuckhill. Shrp 3F 26
Tuckingmill. Corn 4K 3
Tuckton. Bour 6K 9
Tuddenham. Suff 4D 30
Tuddenham St Martin.
Suff 7H 31
Tudeley. Kent 1C 12
Tudhoe. Dur 8F 54
Tudhoe Grange. Dur 8F 54
Tudorville. Here 1D 18
Tudweiliog. Gwyn 7B 32
Tuesley. Surr 1G 11
Tufton. Hants 1B 10
Tufton. Pemb 4G 15
Tugby. Leics 1E 28
Tugford. Shrp 3D 26
Tughall. Nmbd 7K 61
Tulchan. Per 5C 66
Tullibardine. Per 6C 66
Tullibody. Clac 8B 66
Tullich. Arg 6E 64
Tullich. High
nr. Lochcarron 1L 69
nr. Tain 6J 79
Tullich. Mor 1C 72
Tullich Muir. High 6H 79
Tulliemet. Per 2C 66
Tulloch. Abers 2H 73
Tulloch. High
nr. Bonar Bridge 4G 79
nr. Fort William 7D 70
nr. Grantown-on-Spey 4K 71
Tulloch. Per 5D 66
Tullochgorm. Arg 8D 64
Tullybeagles Lodge. Per 4D 66
Tullyhogue. M Ulst 5F 93
Tullymurdoch. Per 2F 66
Tullynessle. Abers 4E 72
Tumble. Carm 5M 15
Tumbler's Green. Essx 1E 22
Tumby. Linc 3K 37
Tumby Woodside. Linc 4K 37
Tummel Bridge. Per 2A 66
**Tunbridge Wells, Royal**.
Kent 2B 12
Tunga. W Isl 8H 83
Tungate. Norf 7J 39
Tunley. Bath 8E 18
Tunstall. E Yor 4L 43
Tunstall. Kent 7E 22
Tunstall. Lanc 8E 46
Tunstall. Norf 1L 31
Tunstall. N Yor 6L 47
Tunstall. Staf 7F 34
Tunstall. Stoke 4G 35
Tunstall. Suff 6K 31
Tunstall. Tyne 6G 55
Tunstead. Derbs 2K 35
Tunstead. Norf 7J 39
Tunstead Milton. Derbs 1J 35
Tunworth. Hants 1D 10
Tupsley. Here 7D 26
Tupton. Derbs 3A 36
Turfholm. S Lan 6G 59
Turfmoor. Devn 5A 8
Turgis Green. Hants 8D 20
Turkdean. Glos 2K 19
Turkey Island. Hants 4C 10
Tur Langton. Leics 2E 28
Turleigh. Wilts 7G 19
Turlin Moor. Pool 6H 9
Turnastone. Here 8B 26
Turnberry. S Ayr 1H 51
Turnchapel. Plym 6G 5
Turnditch. Derbs 5L 35
Turners Hill. W Sus 2L 11
Turners Puddle. Dors 6G 9
Turnford. Herts 3L 21
Turnhouse. Edin 2K 59
Turnworth. Dors 5G 9
Turriff. Abers 1G 73
Tursdale. Dur 8G 55
Turton Bottoms. Bkbn 6F 40
Turtory. Mor 1E 72
Turves Green. W Mid 4J 27
Turvey. Bed 6G 29
Turville. Buck 4E 20
Turville Heath. Buck 4E 20
Turweston. Buck 8D 28
Tushielaw. Bord 8M 59
Tutbury. Staf 7L 35
Tutnall. Worc 4H 27
Tutshill. Glos 4D 18
Tuttington. Norf 7J 39
Tutts Clump. W Ber 6C 20
Tutwell. Corn 8C 6
Tuxford. Notts 2E 36
Twatt. Orkn 7B 88
Twatt. Shet 2D 90
Twechar. E Dun 2E 58
Tweedale. Telf 1F 26
Tweedbank. Bord 6C 60
Tweedmouth. Nmbd 4G 61
Tweedsmuir. Bord 7J 59
Twelveheads. Corn 4L 3
Twemlow Green. Ches E 3F 34
Twenty. Linc 7J 37
Twerton. Bath 7F 18
**Twickenham**. G Lon 6J 21
Twigworth. Glos 1G 19
Twineham. W Sus 4K 11
Twinhoe. Bath 8F 18
Twinstead. Essx 8E 30
Twinstead Green. Essx 8E 30
Twiss Green. Warr 8E 40
Twiston. Lanc 3G 41
Twitchen. Devn 2G 7
Twitchen. Shrp 4B 26
Two Bridges. Devn 8F 6
Two Bridges. Glos 3E 18
Two Dales. Derbs 3L 35
Two Gates. Staf 1L 27
Two Mile Oak. Devn 5L 5
Twycross. Leics 1M 27
Twyford. Buck 1D 20
Twyford. Derbs 7M 35
Twyford. Dors 4G 9
Twyford. Hants 3B 10
Twyford. Leics 8E 36
Twyford. Norf 7G 39
Twyford. Wok 6E 20
Twyford Common. Here 8D 26
Twynholm. Dum 6A 52
Twyning. Glos 8G 27
Twyning Green. Glos 8H 27
Twynllanan. Carm 2G 17
Twyn-y-Sheriff. Mon 3C 18
Twywell. Nptn 4G 29
Tyberton. Here 8B 26
Tyburn. W Mid 2K 27
Tyby. Norf 7G 39
Tycroes. Carm 3F 16
Tycrwyn. Powy 1L 25
**Tyddewi**. Pemb 4D 14
Tydd Gote. Linc 8A 38
Tydd St Giles. Cambs 8M 37
Tydd St Mary. Linc 8M 37
Tye. Hants 5E 10
Tye Green. Essx
nr. Bishop's Stortford 1B 22
nr. Braintree 1D 22
nr. Saffron Walden 8B 30
Tyersal. W Yor 4K 41
Ty Issa. Powy 7L 33
**Tyldesley**. G Man 7E 40
Tyler Hill. Kent 7H 23
Tyler's Green. Essx 3B 22
Tylers Green. Buck 4F 20
Tylorstown. Rhon 5K 17
Tylwch. Powy 4J 25
Y Tymbl. Carm 5M 15
Tynan. Arm 6E 92
Ty-nant. Cnwy 6J 33
Tyndrum. Stir 4H 65
Tyneham. Dors 7G 9
Tynehead. Midl 4A 60
**Tynemouth**. Tyne 5G 55
**Tyneside**. Tyne 5F 54
**Tyne Tunnel**. Tyne 5G 55
Tynewydd. Rhon 5J 17
Tyninghame. E Lot 2D 60
Tynron. Dum 2C 52
Ty'n-y-bryn. Rhon 6K 17
Tyn-y-celyn. Wrex 7L 33
Tyn-y-cwm. Swan 4F 16
Tyn-y-ffridd. Powy 7L 33
Tynygongl. IOA 2E 32
Tynygraig. Cdgn 6F 24
Ty'n-y-groes. Cnwy 3G 33
Ty'n-yr-eithin. Cdgn 6F 24
Tyn-y-rhyd. Powy 1K 25
Tyn-y-wern. Powy 8K 33
Tyrie. Abers 7J 81
Tyringham. Mil 7F 28
Tythecott. Devn 4D 6
Tythegston. B'end 7H 17
Tytherington. Ches E 2H 35
Tytherington. Som 1F 8
Tytherington. S Glo 5E 18
Tytherington. Wilts 1H 9
Tytherleigh. Devn 5B 8
Tywardreath. Corn 6C 4
Tywardreath Highway. Corn 6C 4
Tywyn. Cnwy 3G 33
Tywyn. Gwyn 2E 24


## U


Uachdar. W Isl 8K 75
Uags. High 2J 69
Ubbeston Green. Suff 4K 31
Ubley. Bath 8D 18
Uckerby. N Yor 5L 47
**Uckfield**. E Sus 3A 12
Uckinghall. Worc 8G 27
Uckington. Glos 1H 19
Uckington. Shrp 1D 26
Uddingston. S Lan 3E 58
Uddington. S Lan 6G 59
Udimore. E Sus 4E 12
Udny Green. Abers 3H 73
Udny Station. Abers 3J 73
Udston. S Lan 4E 58
Udstonhead. S Lan 5F 58
Uffcott. Wilts 6K 19
Uffculme. Devn 4K 7
Uffington. Linc 1H 29
Uffington. Oxon 5M 19
Uffington. Shrp 8D 34
Ufford. Pet 1H 29
Ufford. Suff 6J 31
Ufton. Warw 5A 28
Ufton Nervet. W Ber 7D 20
Ugadale. Arg 7G 57
Ugborough. Devn 6J 5
Ugford. Wilts 2J 9
Uggeshall. Suff 3L 31
Ugglebarnby. N Yor 5F 48
Ugley. Essx 1B 22
Ugley Green. Essx 1B 22
Ugthorpe. N Yor 4E 48
Uidh. W Isl 6C 74
Uig. Arg 2G 63
Uig. High
nr. Balgown 7E 76
nr. Dunvegan 8C 76
Uigshader. High 1F 68
Uisken. Arg 6J 63
Ulbster. High 7E 86
Ulcat Row. Cumb 3C 46
Ulceby. Linc 2M 37
Ulceby. N Lin 6J 43
Ulceby Skitter. N Lin 6J 43
Ulcombe. Kent 1E 12
Uldale. Cumb 8G 53
Uley. Glos 4F 18
Ulgham. Nmbd 2F 54
Ullapool. High 4B 78
Ullenhall. Warw 5K 27
Ulleskelf. N Yor 4C 42
Ullesthorpe. Leics 3C 28
Ulley. S Yor 1B 36
Ullingswick. Here 6D 26
Ullinish. High 2E 68
Ullock. Cumb 2K 45
Ulpha. Cumb 5L 45
Ulrome. E Yor 2J 43
Ulsta. Shet 5J 91
Ulting. Essx 3E 22
Ulva House. Arg 4K 63
**Ulverston**. Cumb 8A 46
Ulwell. Dors 7J 9
Umberleigh. Devn 3F 6
Unapool. High 8E 84
Underbarrow. Cumb 6C 46
Undercliffe. W Yor 4K 41
Underdale. Shrp 8D 34
Underhoull. Shet 3K 91
Underriver. Kent 8B 22
Under Tofts. S Yor 1M 35
Underton. Shrp 2E 26
Underwood. Newp 5B 18
Underwood. Notts 4B 36
Underwood. Plym 6H 5
Undley. Suff 3C 30
Undy. Mon 5C 18
Union Mills. IOM 7C 44
Union Street. E Sus 2D 12
Unstone. Derbs 2A 36
Unstone Green. Derbs 2A 36
Unthank. Cumb
nr. Carlisle 7H 53
nr. Gamblesby 7L 53
nr. Penrith 8J 53
Unthank End. Cumb 8J 53
Upavon. Wilts 8K 19
Up Cerne. Dors 5E 8
Upchurch. Kent 7E 22
Upcott. Devn 5E 6
Upcott. Here 6B 26
Upend. Cambs 6C 30
Up Exe. Devn 5J 7
Upgate. Norf 8H 39
Upgate Street. Norf 2G 31
Uphall. Dors 5D 8
Uphall. W Lot 2J 59
Uphall Station. W Lot 2J 59
Upham. Devn 5H 7
Upham. Hants 3C 10
Uphampton. Here 5B 26
Uphampton. Worc 5G 27
Up Hatherley. Glos 1H 19
Uphill. N Som 8B 18
Up Holland. Lanc 7D 40
Uplawmoor. E Ren 4C 58
Upleadon. Glos 1F 18
Upleatham. Red C 4D 48
Uplees. Kent 7F 22
Uploders. Dors 6D 8
Uplowman. Devn 4K 7
Uplyme. Devn 6B 8
Up Marden. W Sus 4E 10
**Upminster**. G Lon 5B 22
Up Nately. Hants 8D 20
Upottery. Devn 5M 7
Uppat. High 3J 79
Upper Affcot. Shrp 3C 26
Upper Arley. Worc 3F 26
Upper Armley. W Yor 4L 41
Upper Arncott. Oxon 2D 20
Upper Astrop. Nptn 8C 28
Upper Badcall. High 7D 84
Upper Ballinderry. Lis 5G 93
Upper Bangor. Gwyn 3E 32
Upper Basildon. W Ber 6C 20
Upper Batley. W Yor 5L 41
Upper Beeding. W Sus 4J 11
Upper Benefield. Nptn 3G 29
Upper Bentley. Worc 5H 27
Upper Bighouse. High 6L 85
Upper Boddam. Abers 2F 72
Upper Boddington. Nptn 6B 28
Upper Bogside. Mor 8B 80
Upper Booth. Derbs 1K 35
Upper Borth. Cdgn 4F 24
Upper Boyndlie. Abers 7J 81
Upper Brailes. Warw 7M 27
Upper Breinton. Here 7C 26
Upper Broughton. Notts 7D 36
Upper Brynamman. Carm 3G 17
Upper Bucklebury. W Ber 7C 20
Upper Bullington. Hants 1B 10
Upper Burgate. Hants 4K 9
Upper Caldecote. C Beds 7J 29
Upper Canterton. Hants 4L 9
Upper Catesby. Nptn 6C 28
Upper Chapel. Powy 8K 25
Upper Cheddon. Som 3M 7
Upper Chicksgrove. Wilts 3H 9
Upper Church Village.
Rhon 6K 17
Upper Chute. Wilts 8L 19
Upper Clatford. Hants 1A 10
Upper Coberley. Glos 2H 19
Upper Coedcae. Torf 3A 18
Upper Cound. Shrp 1D 26
Upper Cudworth. S Yor 7A 42
Upper Cumberworth. W Yor 7L 41
Upper Cuttlehill. Abers 1D 72
Upper Cwmbran. Torf 4A 18
Upper Dallachy. Mor 7C 80
Upper Dean. Bed 5H 29
Upper Denby. W Yor 7L 41
Upper Derraid. High 2L 71
Upper Diabaig. High 7K 77
Upper Dicker. E Sus 5B 12
Upper Dinchope. Shrp 3C 26
Upper Dochcarty. High 7F 78
Upper Dounreay. High 5A 86
Upper Dovercourt. Essx 8J 31
Upper Dunsforth. N Yor 1B 42
Upper Dunsley. Herts 2G 21
Upper Eastern Green.
W Mid 3L 27
Upper Elkstone. Staf 4J 35
Upper Ellastone. Staf 5K 35
Upper End. Derbs 2J 35
Upper Enham. Hants 1A 10
Upper Farmcote. Shrp 2F 26
Upper Farringdon. Hants 2E 10
Upper Framilode. Glos 2F 18
Upper Froyle. Hants 1E 10
Upper Gills. High 4E 86
Upper Glenfintaig. High 7C 70
Upper Godney. Som 1C 8
Upper Gravenhurst.
C Beds 8J 29
Upper Green. Essx 8M 29
Upper Green. W Ber 7A 20
Upper Green. W Yor 5L 41
Upper Grove Common.
Here 1D 18
Upper Hackney. Derbs 3L 35
Upper Hale. Surr 1F 10
Upper Halliford. Surr 7H 21
Upper Halling. Medw 7C 22
Upper Hambleton. Rut 1G 29
Upper Hardres Court. Kent 8H 23
Upper Hardwick. Here 6C 26
Upper Hartfield. E Sus 2A 12
Upper Haugh. S Yor 8B 42
Upper Hayton. Shrp 3D 26
Upper Heath. Shrp 3D 26
Upper Hellesdon. Norf 8J 39
Upper Helmsley. N Yor 2D 42
Upper Hengoed. Shrp 6A 34
Upper Hergest. Here 6A 26
Upper Heyford. Nptn 6D 28
Upper Heyford. Oxon 1B 20
Upper Hill. Here 6C 26
Upper Hindhope. Bord 1A 54
Upper Hopton. W Yor 6K 41
Upper Howsell. Worc 7F 26
Upper Hulme. Staf 3J 35
Upper Inglesham. Swin 4L 19
Upper Kilcott. S Glo 5F 18
Upper Killay. Swan 5E 16
Upper Kirkton. Abers 2G 73
Upper Kirkton. N Ayr 4L 57
Upper Knockando. Mor 1A 72
Upper Knockchoilum. High 4E 70
Upper Lambourn. W Ber 5M 19
Upperlands. M Ulst 3F 93
Upper Langford. N Som 8C 18
Upper Langwith. Derbs 3C 36
Upper Largo. Fife 7H 67
Upper Latheron. High 8C 86
Upper Layham. Suff 7G 31
Upper Leigh. Staf 6J 35
Upper Lenie. High 3F 70
Upper Lochton. Abers 6F 72
Upper Longdon. Staf 8J 35
Upper Longwood. Shrp 1E 26
Upper Lybster. High 8D 86
Upper Lydbrook. Glos 2E 18
Upper Lye. Here 5B 26
Upper Maes-coed. Here 8B 26
Upper Midway. Derbs 7L 35
Uppermill. G Man 7H 41
Upper Millichope. Shrp 3D 26
Upper Milovaig. High 1C 68
Upper Minety. Wilts 4J 19
Upper Mitton. Worc 4G 27
Upper Nash. Pemb 6G 15
Upper Neepaback. Shet 5K 91
Upper Netchwood. Shrp 2E 26
Upper Nobut. Staf 6J 35
Upper North Dean. Buck 4F 20
Upper Norwood. W Sus 4G 11
Upper Nyland. Dors 3F 8
Upper Oddington. Glos 1L 19
Upper Ollach. High 2G 69
Upper Outwoods. Staf 7L 35
Upper Padley. Derbs 2L 35
Upper Pennington. Hants 6M 9
Upper Poppleton. York 2C 42
Upper Quinton. Warw 7K 27
Upper Rissington. Glos 2L 19
Upper Rochford. Worc 5E 26
Upper Rusko. Dum 5L 51
Upper Sandaig. High 4J 69
Upper Sanday. Orkn 1G 87
Upper Sapey. Here 5E 26
Upper Seagry. Wilts 5H 19
Upper Shelton. C Beds 7G 29
Upper Sheringham. Norf 5H 39
Upper Skelmorlie. N Ayr 3L 57
Upper Slaughter. Glos 1K 19
Upper Sonachan. Arg 5E 64
Upper Soudley. Glos 2E 18
Upper Staploe. Bed 6J 29
Upper Stoke. Norf 1J 31
Upper Stondon. C Beds 8J 29
Upper Stowe. Nptn 6D 28
Upper Street. Hants 4K 9
Upper Street. Norf
nr. Horning 8K 39
nr. Hoveton 8K 39
Upper Street. Suff 8H 31
Upper Strensham. Worc 8H 27
Upper Studley. Wilts 8G 19
Upper Sundon. C Beds 1H 21
Upper Swell. Glos 1K 19
Upper Tankersley. S Yor 8M 41
Upper Tean. Staf 6J 35
Upperthong. W Yor 7K 41
Upperthorpe. N Lin 7E 42
Upper Thurnham. Lanc 2C 40
Upper Tillyrie. Per 7E 66
Upperton. W Sus 3G 11
Upper Tooting. G Lon 6K 21
Upper Town. Derbs
nr. Bonsall 4L 35
nr. Hognaston 4L 35
Upper Town. Here 7D 26
Upper Town. N Som 7D 18
Uppertown. Derbs 3M 35
Uppertown. High 4E 86
Uppertown. Nmbd 4B 54
Uppertown. Orkn 2F 86
Upper Tysoe. Warw 7M 27
Upper Upham. Wilts 6L 19
Upper Upnor. Medw 6D 22
Upper Urquhart. Fife 7E 66
Upper Wardington. Oxon 7B 28
Upper Weald. Mil 8E 28
Upper Weedon. Nptn 6D 28
Upper Wellingham. E Sus 4M 11
Upper Whiston. S Yor 1B 36
Upper Wield. Hants 2D 10
Upper Winchendon. Buck 2E 20
Upperwood. Derbs 4L 35
Upper Woodford. Wilts 2K 9
Upper Wootton. Hants 8C 20
Upper Wraxall. Wilts 6G 19
Upper Wyche. Worc 7F 26
Uppincott. Devn 5H 7
Uppingham. Rut 2F 28
Uppington. Shrp 1E 26
Upsall. N Yor 7B 48
Upsettlington. Bord 5F 60
Upshire. Essx 3M 21
Up Somborne. Hants 2A 10
Upstreet. Kent 7J 23
Up Sydling. Dors 5E 8
Upthorpe. Suff 4F 30
Upton. Buck 2E 20
Upton. Cambs 4J 29
Upton. Ches W 3C 34
Upton. Corn
nr. Bude 5B 6
nr. Liskeard 8B 6
Upton. Cumb 8H 53
Upton. Devn
nr. Honiton 5K 7
nr. Kingsbridge 7K 5
Upton. Dors
nr. Poole 6H 9
nr. Weymouth 7F 8
Upton. E Yor 2J 43
Upton. Hants
nr. Andover 8A 20
nr. Southampton 4A 10
Upton. IOW 6C 10
Upton. Leics 2A 28
Upton. Linc 1F 36
Upton. Mers 1A 34
Upton. Norf 8K 39
Upton. Nptn 5E 28
Upton. Notts
nr. Retford 2E 36
nr. Southwell 4E 36
Upton. Oxon 5C 20
Upton. Pemb 6G 15
Upton. Pet 1J 29
Upton. Slo 6G 21
Upton. Som
nr. Somerton 3C 8
nr. Wiveliscombe 3J 7
Upton. Warw 6K 27
Upton. W Yor 6B 42
Upton. Wilts 2G 9
Upton Bishop. Here 1E 18
Upton Cheyney. S Glo 7E 18
Upton Cressett. Shrp 2E 26
Upton Crews. Here 1E 18
Upton Cross. Corn 8B 6
Upton End. C Beds 8J 29
Upton Grey. Hants 1D 10
Upton Heath. Ches W 3C 34
Upton Hellions. Devn 5H 7
Upton Lovell. Wilts 1H 9
Upton Magna. Shrp 8D 34
Upton Noble. Som 2F 8
Upton Pyne. Devn 6J 7
Upton St Leonards. Glos 2G 19
Upton Scudamore. Wilts 1G 9
Upton Snodsbury. Worc 6H 27
Upton upon Severn. Worc 7G 27
Upton Warren. Worc 5H 27
Upwaltham. W Sus 4G 11
Upware. Cambs 4B 30
Upwell. Norf 1B 30
Upwey. Dors 7E 8
Upwick Green. Herts 1A 22
Upwood. Cambs 3K 29
Urafirth. Shet 6H 91
Uragaig. Arg 8J 63
Urchany. High 1J 71
Urchfont. Wilts 8J 19
Urdimarsh. Here 7D 26
Ure. Shet 6G 91
Ure Bank. N Yor 8M 47
Urgha. W Isl 4C 76
Urlay Nook. Stoc T 4B 48
**Urmston**. G Man 8F 40
Urquhart. Mor 7B 80
Urra. N Yor 5C 48
Urray. High 8F 78
Usan. Ang 2L 67
Ushaw Moor. Dur 7F 54
Usk. Mon 3B 18
Usselby. Linc 8H 43
Usworth. Tyne 6G 55
Utkinton. Ches W 3D 34
Uton. Devn 6H 7
Utterby. Linc 8L 43
**Uttoxeter**. Staf 6J 35
Uwchmynydd. Gwyn 8A 32
**Uxbridge**. G Lon 5H 21
Uyeasound. Shet 3K 91
Uzmaston. Pemb 5F 14


## V


Valley. IOA 3B 32
Valley End. Surr 7G 21
Valley Truckle. Corn 3D 4
Valsgarth. Shet 2L 91
Valtos. High 7G 77
Van. Powy 4J 25
Vange. Essx 5D 22
Varteg. Torf 3A 18
Vatsetter. Shet 5K 91
Vatten. High 1D 68
Vaul. Arg 3F 62
The Vauld. Here 7D 26
Vaynor. Mer T 3K 17
Veensgarth. Shet 3E 90
Velindre. Powy 1L 17
Vellow. Som 2K 7
Velly. Devn 3B 6
Veness. Orkn 7E 88
Venhay. Devn 4G 7
Venn. Devn 7K 5
Venngreen. Devn 4C 6
Vennington. Shrp 1B 26
Venn Ottery. Devn 6K 7
Venn's Green. Here 7D 26
Venny Tedburn. Devn 6H 7
Venterdon. Corn 8C 6
Ventnor. IOW 8C 10
Vernham Dean. Hants 8M 19
Vernham Street. Hants 8M 19
Vernolds Common. Shrp 3C 26
Verwood. Dors 5J 9
Veryan. Corn 8B 4
Veryan Green. Corn 8B 4
Vicarage. Devn 7M 7
Vickerstown. Cumb 8L 45
Victoria. Corn 5B 4
Victoria Bridge. Derr 4C 92
Vidlin. Shet 1E 90
**Viewpark**. N Lan 3F 58
Vigo. W Mid 1J 27
Vigo Village. Kent 7C 22
Vinehall Street. E Sus 3D 12
Vine's Cross. E Sus 4B 12
Viney Hill. Glos 3E 18
Virginia Water. Surr 7G 21
Virginstow. Devn 6C 6
Vobster. Som 1F 8
Voe. Shet
nr. Hillside 1E 90
nr. Swinister 5H 91
Vole. Som
Vowchurch. Here
Voxter. Shet
Voy. Orkn
Vulcan Village. Mers


## W


Waberthwaite. Cumb
Wackerfield. Dur
Wacton. Norf
Wadbister. Shet
Wadborough. Worc
Wadbrook. Devn
Waddesdon. Buck
Waddeton. Devn
Waddicar. Mers
Waddingham. Linc
Waddington. Lanc
Waddington. Linc
Waddon. Devn
Wadebridge. Corn
Wadeford. Som
Wadenhoe. Nptn
Wadesmill. Herts
Wadhurst. E Sus
Wadshelf. Derbs
Wadsley. S Yor
Wadsley Bridge. S Yor
Wadswick. Wilts
Wadwick. Hants
Wadworth. S Yor
Waen. Den
nr. Llandymog
nr. Nantglyn
Waen. Powy
Waen Fach. Powy
Waen Goleugoed. Den
Wag. High
Wainfleet All Saints. Linc
Wainfleet Bank. Linc
Wainfleet St Mary. Linc
Wainhouse Corner. Corn
Wainscott. Medw
Wainstalls. W Yor
Waitby. Cumb
Waithe. Linc
**Wakefield**. W Yor
Wakerley. Nptn
Wakes Colne. Essx
Walberswick. Suff
Walberton. W Sus
Walbottle. Tyne
Walby. Cumb
Walcombe. Som
Walcot. Linc
Walcot. N Lin
Walcot. Swin
Walcot. Telf
Walcot. Warw
Walcote. Leics
Walcot Green. Norf
Walcott. Linc
Walcott. Norf
Walden. N Yor
Walden Head. N Yor
Walden Stubbs. N Yor
Walderslade. Medw
Walderton. W Sus
Walditch. Dors
Waldley. Derbs
Waldridge. Dur
Waldringfield. Suff
Waldron. E Sus
Wales. S Yor
Walesby. Linc
Walesby. Notts
Walford. Here
nr. Leintwardine
nr. Ross-on-Wye
Walford. Shrp
Walford. Staf
Walford Heath. Shrp
Walgherton. Ches E
Walgrave. Nptn
Walhampton. Hants
**Walkden**. G Man
Walker. Tyne
Walkerburn. Bord
Walker Fold. Lanc
Walkeringham. Notts
Walkerith. Linc
Walkern. Herts
Walker's Green. Here
Walkerton. Fife
Walkerville. N Yor
Walkford. Dors
Walkhampton. Devn
Walkington. E Yor
Walkley. S Yor
Walk Mill. Lanc
Wall. Corn
Wall. Nmbd
Wall. Staf
Wallaceton. Dum
Wallacetown. Shet
Wallacetown. S Ayr
nr. Ayr
nr. Dailly
Wallands Park. E Sus
**Wallasey**. Mers
Wallaston Green. Pemb
Wallbrook. W Mid
Wallcrouch. E Sus
Wall End. Cumb
Wallend. Medw
Wall Heath. W Mid
Wallingford. Oxon
**Wallington**. G Lon
Wallington. Hants
Wallington. Herts
Wallis. Pemb
Wallisdown. Bour
Walliswood. Surr
Wall Nook. Dur
Walls. Shet
**Wallsend**. Tyne
Wallsworth. Glos
Wall under Heywood. Shrp
Wallyford. E Lot
Walmer. Kent
Walmer Bridge. Lanc
Walmersley. G Man
Walmley. W Mid
Walnut Grove. Per
Walpole. Suff
Walpole Cross Keys. Norf
Walpole Gate. Norf
Walpole Highway. Norf
Walpole Marsh. Norf
Walpole St Andrew. Norf
Walpole St Peter. Norf
**Walsall**. W Mid
Walsall Wood. W Mid
Walsden. W Yor
Walsgrave on Sowe.
W Mid
Walsham le Willows. Suff
Walshaw. G Man
Walshford. N Yor
Walsoken. Norf
Walston. S Lan
Walsworth. Herts
Walter's Ash. Buck
Walterston. V Glam
Walterstone. Here
Waltham. Kent
Waltham. NE Lin
**Waltham Abbey**. Essx
Waltham Chase. Hants
Waltham Cross. Herts
Waltham on the Wolds.
Leics
Waltham St Lawrence.
Wind
Waltham's Cross. Essx
**Walthamstow**. G Lon
Walton. Cumb
Walton. Derbs
Walton. Leics
Walton. Mers
Walton. Mil
Walton. Pet
Walton. Powy
Walton. Som
Walton. Staf
nr. Eccleshall
nr. Stone

Walton—Wilmcote


n. Suff 8J 31
n. Telf 8D 34
n. Warw 6L 27
n. W Yor
r. Wakefield 6A 42
r. Wetherby 3B 42
n Cardiff. Glos 8H 27
n East. Pemb 4G 15
Elm. Dors 4F 8
Highway. Norf 8A 38
n in Gordano. N Som 6C 18
-le-Dale. Lanc 5D 40
**n-on-Thames**. Surr 7J 21
on the Hill. Surr 8K 21
-on-the-Hill. Staf 7H 35
**n-on-the-Naze**. Essx 1J 23
on the Wolds.
eics 8C 36
-on-Trent. Derbs 8L 35
West. Pemb 5E 14
k. Nmbd 4C 54
rth. Darl 4L 47
rth Gate. Darl 3L 47
n's Castle. Pemb 5E 14
rook. Som 5A 8
ool. Cumb 6G 53
rough. Surr 1G 11
rough. Swin 5L 19
l. S Lan 7H 59
**worth**. G Lon 6K 21
ord. Suff
. Lakenheath 3D 30
. Southwold 4L 31
. Leics 8C 36
ckhead. Dum 8G 59
ck. E Sus 5B 12
ord. E Yor 2H 43
ord. Pet 2H 29
urst Green. Kent 1D 12
**ead**. G Lon 5M 21
ow. Som 1F 8
ell. Glos 3E 18
ge. Oxon 5B 20
. S Glo 6F 18
nbury. Warw 5A 28
nham. Nptn 7D 28
ton. E Sus 4C 12
ngton. Hants 5E 10
rough. Oxon 4C 20
ys. Cambs 3L 29
ck. Bkpl 4B 40
ow. Corn 6B 6
ton. G Man 1F 34
. Cumb 4F 46
n. Kent 6G 23
n. Nmbd 5C 54
nd. W Mid 3K 27
reen. Suff 5G 31
reen Cross. Lanc 4E 40
edges. C Beds 8H 29
ouse. Abers 2E 72
gton. Oxon 7B 28
Ches E 4E 34
G Man 6H 41
. Rut 1F 28
. W Sus 3F 10
w. Derbs 2K 35
nd. Ches E 1H 35
Hill. Cambs 3A 30
Herts 2L 21
Kent 7J 23
m. Dors 7H 9
rne. Kent 2F 12
ord. Nmbd 7J 61
Mill. Nmbd 6J 61
on. Nmbd 6J 61
de. Herts 2L 21
ey. Cambs 6K 29
ey. Worc 5G 27
d. Brac 6F 20
t. Devn 6L 5
e. Linc 6K 37
ve. Wok 6E 20
n. Norf 5F 38
sford. Arm 6H 93
stown. Arm 6G 93
Nmbd
Coldstream 6F 60
Hexham 4B 54
gh. Devn 3F 6
n. Nptn 4F 28
orth. Nptn 7B 28
orth. Nmbd 1F 54
. N Yor 6M 47
d. W Yor 5H 41
gan. Corn 5D 4
**gham**. Surr 8L 21
nbie. Dum 5F 52
eld. W Yor 5A 42
gham. Ches E 3F 34
ghurst. W Sus 4J 11
gton. Nptn 2H 29
gton. Warw 7B 28
**nster**. Wilts 1G 9
y. S Glo 6E 18
worth. S Yor 7C 42
ell. Dors 7F 8
n. Worc 6G 27
s End. Herts 3H 21
rd. Hants 3D 10
m. W Sus 2J 11
gcamp. W Sus 5H 11
glid. W Sus 3K 11
Ches E 2G 35
Pemb 7F 14
oy. Red C 3C 48
Corner. Hants
Aldershot 1F 10
Petersfield 3E 10
point. New M 7G 93
Row. Wind 5F 20
Street. Kent 8F 22
ton. Mil 6F 28
**gton**. Warr 1E 34
n. Hants 5B 10
High 4E 86
w. Staf 4J 35
. Notts 3C 36
Vale. Notts 3C 36
E Yor 2F 42
marske. N Yor 8L 47
. N Yor 2D 42
g. E Sus 5C 12
oy. Leics 7E 36
Lanc
Carnforth 8C 46
Freckleton 5C 40
Nmbd 1D 54
Warw 1L 27
**k**. Warw 5L 27
k Bridge. Cumb 6J 53
k-on-Eden. Cumb 6J 53
k Wold. Surr 8L 21
er. Orkn 6C 88
e Head. Cumb 4L 45
Derbs 1J 35
way. Corn 5C 4
urne. Devn 6K 5
ook. Suff 7H 31
ommon. W Ber 7B 20
wall. Staf 5H 35
ld. Devn 4J 7
ld. N Yor 5J 47
rd. Som 1K 7
rd Pyne. Devn 4H 7
gborough. Linc 2H 37
**gton**. Tyne 6G 55
gton. W Sus 4J 11
gton Village. Tyne 6G 55
ey. Dur 7D 54
ton. Warw 6L 27
reen. Surr 1L 11
West. Linc 3H 37
l Yor 8C 48
. Som 1K 7
eld. Oxon 4L 19
ate. Cumb 6D 46
ill. Cumb 7F 52
be. Torb 5M 5
ath. Cumb 4A 46
Devn 7G 7
Lanc 5G 41
each. Cambs 5A 30
each. W Sus 5F 10
eck. Dum 4G 53
tch. Hants 6K 9
nd. C Beds 8H 29
nd. E Yor 4E 42

Water End. Essx 7B 30
Water End. Herts
nr. Hatfield 3K 21
nr. Hemel Hempstead 2H 21
Waterfall. Staf 4J 35
Waterfoot. Caus 2H 93
Waterfoot. E Ren 4D 58
Waterfoot. Lanc 5G 41
Waterford. Herts 2L 21
Water Fryston. W Yor 5B 42
Waterhead. Cumb 5B 46
Waterhead. E Ayr 8D 58
Waterhead. S Ayr 2J 51
Waterheads. Bord 4L 59
Waterhouses. Dur 7E 54
Waterhouses. Staf 4J 35
Wateringbury. Kent 8C 22
Waterlane. Glos 3H 19
Waterlip. Som 1E 8
Waterloo. Cphy 6L 17
Waterloo. Corn 4D 4
Waterloo. Here 7B 26
Waterloo. High 3H 69
Waterloo. Mers 8B 40
Waterloo. Norf 8J 39
Waterloo. N Lan 4G 59
Waterloo. Pemb 6F 14
Waterloo. Per 4D 66
Waterloo. Pool 6J 9
Waterloo. Shrp 6C 34
**Waterlooville**. Hants 5D 10
Watermead. Buck 2F 20
Watermillock. Cumb 3C 46
Water Newton. Cambs 2J 29
Water Orton. Warw 2K 27
Waterperry. Oxon 3D 20
Waterrow. Som 3K 7
Watersfield. W Sus 4H 11
Waterside. Buck 3G 21
Waterside. Cambs 4C 30
Waterside. Cumb 7G 53
Waterside. E Ayr
nr. Ayr 1K 51
nr. Kilmarnock 5C 58
Waterside. E Dun 2E 58
Waterstein. High 1C 68
Waterstock. Oxon 3D 20
Waterston. Pemb 6F 14
Water Stratford. Buck 8D 28
Waters Upton. Telf 8E 34
Water Yeat. Cumb 7A 46
**Watford**. Herts 4J 21
Watford. Nptn 5D 28
Wath. Cumb 5E 46
Wath. N Yor
nr. Pateley Bridge 1K 41
nr. Ripon 8M 47
Wath Brow. Cumb 3K 45
**Wath upon Dearne**.
S Yor 7B 42
Watlington. Norf 8C 38
Watlington. Oxon 4D 20
Watten. High 6D 86
Wattisfield. Suff 4G 31
Wattisham. Suff 6G 31
Wattlesborough Heath.
Shrp 8B 34
Watton. Dors 6C 8
Watton. E Yor 2H 43
Watton. Norf 1F 30
Watton at Stone. Herts 2K 21
Wattston. N Lan 2F 58
Wattstown. Rhon 5K 17
Wattsville. Cphy 5M 17
Wauldby. E Yor 5G 43
Waulkmill. Abers 6F 72
Waun. Powy 1M 25
Y Waun. Wrex 6A 34
Waunarlwydd. Swan 5F 16
Waun Fawr. Cdgn 4F 24
Waunfawr. Gwyn 5E 32
Waungilwen. Carm 3K 15
Waun-Lwyd. Blae 4L 17
Waun y Clyn. Carm 6L 15
Wavendon. Mil 8G 29
Waverbridge. Cumb 7G 53
Waverley. Surr 1F 10
Waverton. Ches W 3C 34
Waverton. Cumb 7G 53
Wavertree. Mers 1B 34
Wawne. E Yor 4H 43
Waxham. Norf 7L 39
Waxholme. E Yor 5L 43
Wayford. Som 5C 8
Way Head. Cambs 3A 30
Waytown. Dors 6C 8
Way Village. Devn 4H 7
Wdig. Pemb 3F 14
Wealdstone. G Lon 5J 21
Weardley. W Yor 3L 41
Weare. Som 8C 18
Weare Giffard. Devn 3D 6
Wearhead. Dur 8B 54
Wearne. Som 3C 8
Weasdale. Cumb 5E 46
Weasenham All Saints.
Norf 7E 38
Weasenham St Peter. Norf 7E 38
Weaverham. Ches W 2E 34
Weaverthorpe. N Yor 8G 49
Webheath. Worc 5J 27
Webton. Here 8C 26
Wedderlairs. Abers 2H 73
Weddington. Warw 2A 28
Wedhampton. Wilts 8J 19
Wedmore. Som 1C 8
Wednesbury. W Mid 2H 27
Wednesfield. W Mid 1H 27
Weecar. Notts 3F 36
Weedon. Buck 2F 20
Weedon Bec. Nptn 6D 28
Weedon Lois. Nptn 7D 28
Weeford. Staf 1K 27
Week. Devn
nr. Barnstaple 3E 6
nr. Okehampton 5F 6
nr. South Molton 4G 7
nr. Totnes 5K 5
Week. Som 2J 7
Weeke. Devn 5G 7
Weeke. Hants 2B 10
Week Green. Corn 6B 6
Weekley. Nptn 3F 28
Week St Mary. Corn 6B 6
Weel. E Yor 4H 43
Weeley. Essx 1H 23
Weeley Heath. Essx 1H 23
Weem. Per 3B 66
Weeping Cross. Staf 7H 35
Weethly. Warw 6J 27
Weeting. Norf 3D 30
Weeton. E Yor 5L 43
Weeton. Lanc 4B 40
Weeton. N Yor 3L 41
Weetwood Hall. Nmbd 7H 61
Weir. Lanc 5G 41
Welborne. Norf 8G 39
Welbourn. Linc 4G 37
Welburn. N Yor
nr. Kirkbymoorside 7D 48
nr. Malton 1E 42
Welbury. N Yor 5A 48
Welby. Linc 6G 37
Welches Dam. Cambs 3A 30
Welcombe. Devn 4B 6
Weld Bank. Lanc 6D 40
Weldon. Nptn 3G 29
Weldon. Nmbd 2E 54
Welford. Nptn 3D 28
Welford. W Ber 6B 20
Welford-on-Avon. Warw 6K 27
Welham. Leics 2E 28
Welham. Notts 1E 36
Welham Green. Herts 3K 21
Well. Hants 1E 10
Well. Linc 2M 37
Well. N Yor 7L 47
Welland. Worc 7F 26
Wellbank. Ang 4H 67
Well Bottom. Dors 4H 9
Welldale. Dum 5F 52
Wellesbourne. Warw 6L 27
Well Hill. Kent 7A 22
Wellhouse. W Ber 6C 20
Welling. G Lon 6A 22
**Wellingborough**. Nptn 5F 28
Wellingham. Norf 7E 38
Wellingore. Linc 4G 37

Wellington. Cumb 4K 45
Wellington. Here 7C 26
**Wellington**. Som 3L 7
Wellington. Telf 8E 34
Wellington Heath. Here 7F 26
Wellow. Bath 8F 18
Wellow. IOW 7A 10
Wellow. Notts 3D 36
Wellpond Green. Herts 1M 21
**Wells**. Som 1D 8
Wellsborough. Leics 1A 28
Wells Green. Ches E 4E 34
Wells-next-the-Sea. Norf 5F 38
Wellswood. Torb 5M 5
Wellwood. Fife 1J 59
Welney. Norf 2B 30
Welsford. Devn 3B 6
Welshampton. Shrp 6C 34
Welsh End. Shrp 6D 34
Welsh Frankton. Shrp 6B 34
Welsh Hook. Pemb 4F 14
Welsh Newton. Here 2C 18
Welsh Newton Common.
Here 2D 18
Welshpool. Powy 2M 25
Welsh St Donats. V Glam 7K 17
Welton. Bath 8E 18
Welton. Cumb 7H 53
Welton. E Yor 5G 43
Welton. Linc 1H 37
Welton. Nptn 5C 28
Welton Hill. Linc 1H 37
Welton le Marsh. Linc 3A 38
Welton le Wold. Linc 1K 37
Welwick. E Yor 5L 43
Welwyn. Herts 2K 21
**Welwyn Garden City**.
Herts 2K 21
Wem. Shrp 7D 34
Wembdon. Som 2A 8
**Wembley**. G Lon 5J 21
Wembury. Devn 7H 5
Wembworthy. Devn 5F 6
Wemyss Bay. Inv 2L 57
Wenallt. Cdgn 5F 24
Wenallt. Gwyn 6J 33
Wendens Ambo. Essx 8B 30
Wendlebury. Oxon 2C 20
Wendling. Norf 8F 38
Wendover. Buck 3F 20
Wendron. Corn 5K 3
Wendy. Cambs 7L 29
Wenfordbridge. Corn 4C 4
Wenhaston. Suff 4L 31
Wennington. Cambs 4K 29
Wennington. G Lon 5B 22
Wennington. Lanc 8E 46
Wensley. Derbs 3L 35
Wensley. N Yor 7J 47
Wentbridge. W Yor 6B 42
Wentnor. Shrp 2B 26
Wentworth. Cambs 4A 30
Wentworth. S Yor 8A 42
Wenvoe. V Glam 7L 17
Weobley. Here 6C 26
Weobley Marsh. Here 6C 26
Wepham. W Sus 5H 11
Wereham. Norf 1C 30
Wergs. W Mid 1G 27
Wern. Gwyn 6E 32
Wern. Powy
nr. Brecon 3L 17
nr. Guilsfield 8A 34
nr. Llangadfan 1J 25
nr. Llanymynech 7A 34
Wernffrwd. Swan 7M 15
Wernyrheolydd. Mon 2B 18
Werrington. Corn 7C 6
Werrington. Pet 1J 29
Werrington. Staf 5H 35
Wervin. Ches W 2C 34
Wesham. Lanc 4C 40
Wessington. Derbs 4A 36
West Aberthaw. V Glam 8K 17
West Acre. Norf 8D 38
West Allerdean. Nmbd 5G 61
West Alvington. Devn 7K 5
West Amesbury. Wilts 1K 9
West Anstey. Devn 3H 7
West Appleton. N Yor 6L 47
West Ardsley. W Yor 5L 41
West Arthurlie. E Ren 4C 58
West Ashby. Linc 2K 37
West Ashling. W Sus 5F 10
West Ashton. Wilts 8G 19
West Auckland. Dur 3K 47
West Ayton. N Yor 7G 49
West Bagborough. Som 2L 7
West Bank. Hal 1D 34
West Barkwith. Linc 1J 37
West Barnby. N Yor 4F 48
West Barns. E Lot 2D 60
West Barsham. Norf 6F 38
West Bay. Dors 6C 8
West Beckham. Norf 6H 39
West Bennan. N Ayr 7J 57
Westbere. Kent 7H 23
West Bergholt. Essx 1F 22
West Bexington. Dors 7D 8
West Bilney. Norf 8D 38
West Blackdene. Dur 8B 54
West Blatchington. Brig 5K 11
Westborough. Linc 5F 36
Westbourne. Bour 6J 9
Westbourne. W Sus 5E 10
West Bowling. W Yor 4K 41
West Brabourne. Kent 1G 13
West Bradford. Lanc 3F 40
West Bradley. Som 2D 8
West Bretton. W Yor 6L 41
**West Bridgford**. Notts 6C 36
West Briggs. Norf 8C 38
**West Bromwich**. W Mid 2J 27
Westbrook. Here 7A 26
Westbrook. Kent 6K 23
Westbrook. Wilts 7H 19
West Buckland. Devn
nr. Barnstaple 2F 6
nr. Thurlestone 7J 5
West Buckland. Som 3L 7
West Burnside. Abers 8G 73
West Burrafirth. Shet 2C 90
West Burton. N Yor 7J 47
West Burton. W Sus 4H 11
Westbury. Buck 8D 28
Westbury. Shrp 1B 26
**Westbury**. Wilts 8G 19
Westbury Leigh. Wilts 8G 19
Westbury-on-Severn. Glos 2F 18
Westbury on Trym. Bris 6D 18
Westbury-sub-Mendip.
Som 1D 8
West Butsfield. Dur 7E 54
West Butterwick. N Lin 7F 42
Westby. Linc 7G 37
West Byfleet. Surr 7H 21
West Caister. Norf 8M 39
West Calder. W Lot 3J 59
West Camel. Som 3D 8
West Carr. N Lin 7E 42
West Chaldon. Dors 7F 8
West Challow. Oxon 5A 20
West Charleton. Devn 7K 5
West Chelborough. Dors 5D 8
West Chevington. Nmbd 2F 54
West Chiltington. W Sus 4H 11
West Chiltington Common.
W Sus 4H 11
West Chinnock. Som 4C 8
West Chisenbury. Wilts 8K 19
West Clandon. Surr 8H 21
West Cliffe. Kent 1K 13
Westcliff-on-Sea. S'end 5E 22
West Clyne. High 3J 79
West Coker. Som 4D 8
Westcombe. Som
nr. Evercreech 2E 8
nr. Somerton 3C 8
West Compton. Dors 6D 8
West Compton. Som 1D 8
West Cornforth. Dur 8G 55
Westcot. Oxon 5M 19
Westcott. Buck 2E 20
Westcott. Devn 5K 7
Westcott. Surr 1J 11
Westcott Barton. Oxon 1B 20
West Cowick. E Yor 5D 42
West Cranmore. Som 1E 8

West Croftmore. High 4K 71
West Cross. Swan 6F 16
West Cullerlie. Abers 5G 73
West Culvennan. Dum 5H 51
West Curry. Corn 6B 6
West Curthwaite. Cumb 7H 53
West Dean. W Sus 4F 10
West Dean. Wilts 3L 9
Westdean. E Sus 6B 12
West Deeping. Linc 1J 29
West Derby. Mers 8B 40
West Dereham. Norf 1C 30
West Down. Devn 1E 6
Westdowns. Corn 3C 4
**West Drayton**. G Lon 6H 21
West Drayton. Notts 2E 36
West Dunnet. High 4D 86
West Ella. E Yor 5H 43
West End. Bed 6G 29
West End. Cambs 2M 29
West End. Dors 5H 9
West End. E Yor
nr. Kilham 1H 43
nr. Preston 4J 43
nr. South Cove 4G 43
nr. Ulrome 2J 43
**West End**. G Lon 5K 21
West End. Hants 4B 10
West End. Herts 3K 21
West End. Kent 7H 23
West End. Lanc 1C 40
West End. Linc 5L 37
West End. Norf 8M 39
West End. N Som 7C 18
West End. N Yor 2K 41
West End. S Glo 5F 18
West End. S Lan 5H 59
West End. Surr 7G 21
West End. Wilts 3H 9
West End. Wind 6F 20
West End Green. Hants 7D 20
Westenhanger. Kent 2H 13
Wester Aberchalder. High 4F 70
Wester Balgedie. Per 7E 66
Wester Brae. High 7G 79
Wester Culbeuchly. Abers 7F 80
Westerdale. High 6C 86
Westerdale. N Yor 5D 48
Wester Dechmont.
W Lot 2J 59
Wester Fearn. High 5G 79
Westerfield. Suff 7H 31
Wester Galcantray. High 1J 71
Westergate. W Sus 5G 11
Wester Gruinards. High 4F 78
Westerham. Kent 8M 21
Westerleigh. S Glo 6F 18
Westerloch. High 6E 86
Wester Mandally. High 5C 70
Wester Quarff. Shet 4E 90
Wester Rarichie. High 6J 79
Wester Shian. Per 4B 66
Wester Skeld. Shet 3C 90
Westerton. Ang 2K 67
Westerton. Dur 8F 54
Westerton. W Sus 5F 10
Westerwick. Shet 3C 90
West Farleigh. Kent 8D 22
West Farndon. Nptn 6C 28
West Felton. Shrp 7B 34
Westfield. Cumb 2J 45
Westfield. E Sus 4E 12
Westfield. High 5B 86
Westfield. Norf 1F 30
Westfield. N Lan 2F 58
Westfield. W Lot 2H 59
Westfields. Dors 5F 8
Westfields of Rattray. Per 3E 66
West Fleetham. Nmbd 7J 61
Westford. Som 3L 7
West Garforth. W Yor 4A 42
Westgate. Dur 8C 54
Westgate. Norf 5F 38
Westgate. N Lin 7E 42
Westgate on Sea. Kent 6K 23
West Ginge. Oxon 5B 20
West Grafton. Wilts 7L 19
West Green. Hants 8E 20
West Grimstead. Wilts 3L 9
West Grinstead. W Sus 3J 11
West Haddlesey. N Yor 5C 42
West Haddon. Nptn 4D 28
West Hagbourne. Oxon 5C 20
West Hagley. Worc 3H 27
West Hall. Cumb 5K 53
Westhall. Suff 3L 31
West Hallam. Derbs 5B 36
Westhall Terrace. Ang 4H 67
West Halton. N Lin 5G 43
**West Ham**. G Lon 5L 21
Westham. Dors 8E 8
Westham. E Sus 5C 12
Westham. Som 1C 8
Westhampnett. W Sus 5F 10
West Handley. Derbs 2A 36
West Hanney. Oxon 4B 20
West Hanningfield. Essx 4D 22
West Hardwick. W Yor 6B 42
West Harptree. Bath 8D 18
West Harting. W Sus 3E 10
West Harton. Tyne 5G 55
West Hatch. Som 3A 8
Westhay. Som 1C 8
West Head. Norf 1B 30
Westhead. Lanc 7C 40
West Heath. Hants
nr. Basingstoke 8C 20
nr. Farnborough 8F 20
West Helmsdale. High 2L 79
West Hendred. Oxon 5B 20
West Heogaland. Shet 6G 91
West Heslerton. N Yor 8G 49
West Hewish. N Som 7B 18
Westhide. Here 7D 26
West Hill. Devn 6K 7
West Hill. E Yor 1J 43
West Hill. N Som 6C 18
West Hill. W Sus 2L 11
Westhill. Abers 5H 73
Westhill. High 1H 71
West Hoathly. W Sus 2L 11
West Holme. Dors 7G 9
Westhope. Here 6C 26
Westhope. Shrp 3C 26
West Horndon. Essx 5C 22
Westhorp. Nptn 6C 28
Westhorpe. Linc 6K 37
Westhorpe. Suff 5G 31
West Horrington. Som 1D 8
West Horsley. Surr 8H 21
West Horton. Nmbd 6H 61
West Hougham. Kent 1J 13
**Westhoughton**. G Man 7E 40
West Houlland. Shet 2C 90
Westhouse. N Yor 8E 46
Westhouses. Derbs 4B 36
West Howe. Bour 6J 9
Westhumble. Surr 8J 21
West Huntspill. Som 1B 8
West Hyde. Herts 4H 21
West Hynish. Arg 4E 62
West Hythe. Kent 2H 13
West Ilsley. W Ber 5B 20
Westing. Shet 3K 91
West Keal. Linc 3L 37
West Kennett. Wilts 7K 19
West Kilbride. N Ayr 5M 57
West Kingsdown. Kent 7B 22
West Kington. Wilts 6G 19
**West Kirby**. Mers 2M 33
West Knapton. N Yor 8F 48
West Knighton. Dors 7F 8
West Knoyle. Wilts 2G 9
West Kyloe. Nmbd 5H 61
Westlake. Devn 6J 5
West Lambrook. Som 4C 8
West Langdon. Kent 1K 13
West Langwell. High 3G 79
West Lavington. W Sus 3F 10
West Lavington. Wilts 8J 19
West Layton. N Yor 5K 47
West Leake. Notts 7C 36
West Learmouth. Nmbd 6F 60
West Leigh. Devn 5F 6
Westleigh. Devn
nr. Bideford 3D 6
nr. Tiverton 4K 7
Westleigh. G Man 7E 40

West Leith. Herts 2G 21
Westleton. Suff 5L 31
West Lexham. Norf 8E 38
Westley. Shrp 1B 26
Westley. Suff 5E 30
Westley Waterless.
Cambs 6C 30
West Lilling. N Yor 1D 42
West Lingo. Fife 7H 67
Westlington. Buck 2E 20
West Linton. Bord 4K 59
Westlinton. Cumb 5H 53
West Littleton. S Glo 6F 18
West Looe. Corn 6E 4
West Lulworth. Dors 7G 9
West Lutton. N Yor 1G 43
West Lydford. Som 2D 8
West Lyng. Som 3B 8
West Lynn. Norf 8C 38
West Mains. Per 6C 66
West Malling. Kent 8C 22
West Malvern. Worc 7F 26
Westmancote. Worc 8H 27
West Marden. W Sus 4E 10
West Markham. Notts 2E 36
West Marsh. NE Lin 7K 43
Westmarsh. Kent 7J 23
West Marton. N Yor 2G 41
West Meon. Hants 3D 10
West Mersea. Essx 2G 23
Westmeston. E Sus 4L 11
Westmill. Herts
nr. Buntingford 1L 21
nr. Hitchin 8J 29
West Milton. Dors 6D 8
**Westminster**. G Lon 6K 21
West Molesey. Surr 7J 21
West Monkton. Som 3A 8
Westmoor End. Cumb 8E 52
West Moors. Dors 5J 9
West Morden. Dors 6H 9
West Muir. Ang 1J 67
Westmuir. Ang 2G 67
West Murkle. High 5C 86
West Ness. N Yor 8D 48
Westness. Orkn 7C 88
West Newton. E Yor 4J 43
West Newton. Norf 7C 38
West Newton. Som 3A 8
Westnewton. Cumb 7F 52
Westnewton. Nmbd 6G 61
West Norwood. G Lon 6L 21
Westoe. Tyne 5G 55
West Ogwell. Devn 5L 5
Weston. Bath 7F 18
Weston. Ches E
nr. Crewe 4F 34
nr. Macclesfield 2G 35
Weston. Devn
nr. Honiton 5L 7
nr. Sidmouth 7L 7
Weston. Dors
nr. Weymouth 8E 8
nr. Yeovil 5D 8
Weston. Hal 1D 34
Weston. Hants 3E 10
Weston. Here 6B 26
Weston. Herts 8K 29
Weston. Linc 7K 37
Weston. Nptn 7C 28
Weston. Notts 3E 36
Weston. Shrp
nr. Bridgnorth 2D 26
nr. Knighton 4B 26
nr. Wem 7D 34
Weston. S Lan 5J 59
Weston. Staf 7H 35
Weston. Suff 3L 31
Weston. W Ber 6A 20
Weston Bampfylde. Som 3E 8
Weston Beggard. Here 7D 26
Westonbirt. Glos 5G 19
Weston by Welland. Nptn 2E 28
Weston Colville. Cambs 6C 30
Westoncommon. Shrp 7C 34
Weston Coyney. Stoke 5H 35
Weston Ditch. Suff 4C 30
Weston Favell. Nptn 5E 28
Weston Green. Cambs 6C 30
Weston Green. Norf 8H 39
Weston Heath. Shrp 8F 34
Weston Hills. Linc 8K 37
Weston in Arden. Warw 3A 28
Westoning. C Beds 8H 29
Weston in Gordano.
N Som 6C 18
Weston Jones. Staf 7F 34
Weston Longville. Norf 8H 39
Weston Lullingfields. Shrp 7C 34
Weston-on-Avon. Warw 6K 27
Weston-on-the-Green.
Oxon 2C 20
Weston-on-Trent. Derbs 7B 36
Weston Patrick. Hants 1D 10
Weston Rhyn. Shrp 6A 34
Weston-sub-Edge. Glos 7K 27
**Weston-super-Mare**.
N Som 7B 18
Weston Town. Som 1F 8
Weston Turville. Buck 2F 20
Weston under Lizard. Staf 8G 35
Weston under Penyard.
Here 1E 18
Weston under Wetherley.
Warw 5A 28
Weston Underwood. Derbs 5L 35
Weston Underwood. Mil 6F 28
Westonzoyland. Som 2B 8
West Orchard. Dors 4G 9
West Overton. Wilts 7K 19
Westow. N Yor 1E 42
Westown. Per 5F 66
West Panson. Devn 6C 6
West Park. Hart 8H 55
West Parley. Dors 6J 9
West Peckham. Kent 8C 22
West Pelton. Dur 6F 54
West Pennard. Som 2D 8
West Pentire. Corn 2L 3
West Perry. Cambs 5J 29
West Pitcorthie. Fife 7J 67
West Plean. Stir 1G 59
West Poringland. Norf 1J 31
West Porlock. Som 1H 7
Westport. Som 4B 8
West Putford. Devn 4C 6
West Quantoxhead. Som 1L 7
Westra. V Glam 7L 17
West Rainton. Dur 7G 55
West Rasen. Linc 1H 37
West Ravendale. NE Lin 8K 43
Westray Airport. Orkn 4D 88
West Raynham. Norf 7E 38
Westrigg. W Lot 3H 59
West Rounton. N Yor 5B 48
West Row. Suff 4C 30
West Rudham. Norf 7E 38
West Runton. Norf 5H 39
Westruther. Bord 4D 60
Westry. Cambs 2L 29
West Saltoun. E Lot 3B 60
West Sandford. Devn 5H 7
West Sandwick. Shet 5J 91
West Scrafton. N Yor 7J 47
Westside. Orkn 7C 88
West Sleekburn. Nmbd 3F 54
West Somerton. Norf 8L 39
West Stafford. Dors 7F 8
West Stockwith. Notts 8E 42
West Stoke. W Sus 5F 10
West Stonesdale. N Yor 5G 47
West Stoughton. Som 1C 8
West Stour. Dors 3F 8
West Stourmouth. Kent 7J 23
West Stow. Suff 4E 30
West Stowell. Wilts 7K 19
West Strathan. High 5H 85
West Stratton. Hants 1C 10
West Street. Kent 8F 22
West Tanfield. N Yor 8L 47
West Taphouse. Corn 5D 4
West Tarbert. Arg 3H 57
West Thirston. Nmbd 1E 54
West Thorney. W Sus 5E 10
West Thurrock. Thur 6B 22
West Tilbury. Thur 6C 22
West Tisted. Hants 3D 10
West Tofts. Norf 2E 30

West Torrington. Linc 1J 37
West Town. Bath 7D 18
West Town. Hants 6E 10
West Town. N Som 7C 18
West Tytherley. Hants 3L 9
West Tytherton. Wilts 6H 19
West View. Hart 8H 55
Westville. Notts 5C 36
West Walton. Norf 8A 38
Westward. Cumb 7G 53
Westward Ho!. Devn 3D 6
Westwell. Kent 1F 12
Westwell. Oxon 3L 19
Westwell Leacon. Kent 1F 12
West Wellow. Hants 4L 9
West Wemyss. Fife 8G 67
West Wick. N Som 7B 18
Westwick. Cambs 5M 29
Westwick. Dur 4J 47
Westwick. Norf 7J 39
West Wickham. Cambs 7C 30
West Wickham. G Lon 7L 21
West Williamston. Pemb 6G 15
West Willoughby. Linc 5G 37
West Winch. Norf 8C 38
West Winterslow. Wilts 2L 9
West Wittering. W Sus 6E 10
West Witton. N Yor 7J 47
Westwood. Devn 6K 7
Westwood. Kent 7K 23
Westwood. Pet 1J 29
Westwood. S Lan 4E 58
Westwood. Wilts 8G 19
West Woodburn. Nmbd 3B 54
West Woodhay. W Ber 7A 20
West Woodlands. Som 1F 8
West Woodside. Cumb 7H 53
Westwoodside. N Lin 8E 42
West Worldham. Hants 2E 10
West Worlington. Devn 4G 7
West Worthing. W Sus 5J 11
West Wratting. Cambs 6C 30
West Wycombe. Buck 4F 20
West Wylam. Nmbd 5E 54
West Yatton. Wilts 6G 19
West Yell. Shet 5J 91
West Youlstone. Corn 4B 6
Wetheral. Cumb 6J 53
Wetherby. W Yor 3B 42
Wetherden. Suff 5G 31
Wetheringsett. Suff 5H 31
Wethersfield. Essx 8D 30
Wethersta. Shet 1D 90
Wetherup Street. Suff 5H 31
Wetley Rocks. Staf 5H 35
Wettenhall. Ches E 3E 34
Wetton. Staf 4K 35
Wetwang. E Yor 2G 43
Wetwood. Staf 6F 34
Wexcombe. Wilts 8L 19
Wexham Street. Buck 5G 21
Weybourne. Norf 5H 39
Weybourne. Surr 1F 10
Weybread. Suff 3J 31
**Weybridge**. Surr 7H 21
Weycroft. Devn 6B 8
Weydale. High 5C 86
Weyhill. Hants 1M 9
**Weymouth**. Dors 8E 8
Weythel. Powy 7M 25
Whaddon. Buck 8F 28
Whaddon. Cambs 7L 29
Whaddon. Glos 2G 19
Whaddon. Wilts 3K 9
Whale. Cumb 3D 46
Whaley. Derbs 2C 36
Whaley Bridge. Derbs 1J 35
Whaley Thorns. Derbs 2C 36
Whalley. Lanc 4F 40
Whalton. Nmbd 3E 54
Whaplode. Linc 7L 37
Whaplode Drove. Linc 8L 37
Whaplode St Catherine.
Linc 7L 37
Wharfe. N Yor 1F 40
Wharles. Lanc 4C 40
Wharley End. C Beds 7G 29
Wharncliffe Side. S Yor 8L 41
Wharram-le-Street.
N Yor 1F 42
Wharton. Ches W 3E 34
Wharton. Here 6D 26
Whashton. N Yor 5K 47
Whasset. Cumb 7D 46
Whatcote. Warw 7M 27
Whateley. Warw 2L 27
Whatfield. Suff 7G 31
Whatley. Som
nr. Chard 5B 8
nr. Frome 1F 8
Whatlington. E Sus 4D 12
Whatmore. Shrp 4E 26
Whatstandwell. Derbs 4M 35
Whatton. Notts 6E 36
Whauphill. Dum 7K 51
Whaw. N Yor 5H 47
Wheatacre. Norf 2L 31
Wheatcroft. Derbs 4A 36
Wheathampstead. Herts 2J 21
Wheathill. Shrp 3E 26
Wheatley. Devn 6H 7
Wheatley. Hants 1E 10
Wheatley. Oxon 3D 20
Wheatley. S Yor 7C 42
Wheatley. W Yor 5J 41
Wheatley Hill. Dur 8G 55
Wheatley Lane. Lanc 4G 41
Wheatley Park. S Yor 7C 42
Wheaton Aston. Staf 8G 35
Wheatstone Park. Staf 1G 27
Wheddon Cross. Som 2J 7
Wheelerstreet. Surr 1G 11
Wheelock. Ches E 4F 34
Wheelock Heath. Ches E 4F 34
Wheelton. Lanc 5E 40
Wheldrake. York 3D 42
Whelford. Glos 4K 19
Whelpley Hill. Buck 3G 21
Whelpo. Cumb 8H 53
Whelston. Flin 3M 33
Whenby. N Yor 1D 42
Whepstead. Suff 6E 30
Wherstead. Suff 7H 31
Wherwell. Hants 1A 10
Wheston. Derbs 2K 35
Whetsted. Kent 1C 12
Whetstone. G Lon 4K 21
Whetstone. Leics 2C 28
Whicham. Cumb 6L 45
Whichford. Warw 8M 27
**Whickham**. Tyne 5F 54
Whiddon. Devn 5D 6
Whiddon Down. Devn 6F 6
Whigstreet. Ang 3H 67
Whilton. Nptn 5D 28
Whimble. Devn 5C 6
Whimple. Devn 6K 7
Whimpwell Green. Norf 7K 39
Whinburgh. Norf 1G 31
Whin Lane End. Lanc 3B 40
Whinney Hill. Stoc T 4A 48
Whinnyfold. Abers 2K 73
Whippingham. IOW 6C 10
Whipsnade. C Beds 2H 21
Whipton. Devn 6J 7
Whirlow. S Yor 1M 35
Whisby. Linc 3G 37
Whissendine. Rut 8F 36
Whissonsett. Norf 7F 38
Whisterfield. Ches E 2G 35
Whistley Green. Wok 6E 20
Whiston. Mers 8C 40
Whiston. Nptn 5F 28
Whiston. S Yor 8B 42
Whiston. Staf
nr. Cheadle 5J 35
nr. Penkridge 8G 35
Whiston Cross. Shrp 1F 26
Whiston Eaves. Staf 5J 35
Whitacre Heath. Warw 2L 27
Whitbeck. Cumb 6L 45
Whitbourne. Here 6F 26
Whitburn. Tyne 5H 55
**Whitburn**. W Lot 3H 59
Whitburn Colliery. Tyne 5H 55
Whitby. Ches W 2B 34
**Whitby**. N Yor 4F 48
Whitbyheath. Ches W 2B 34

Whitchester. Bord 4E 60
Whitchurch. Bath 7E 18
Whitchurch. Buck 1E 20
Whitchurch. Card 7L 17
Whitchurch. Devn 8D 6
Whitchurch. Hants 1B 10
Whitchurch. Here 2D 18
Whitchurch. Pemb 4D 14
Whitchurch. Shrp 5D 34
Whitchurch Canonicorum.
Dors 6B 8
Whitchurch Hill. Oxon 6D 20
Whitchurch-on-Thames.
Oxon 6D 20
Whitcombe. Dors 7F 8
Whitcot. Shrp 2B 26
Whitcott Keysett. Shrp 3A 26
Whiteabbey. Ant 4H 93
Whiteash Green. Essx 8D 30
Whitebog. High 7H 79
Whitebridge. High 4E 70
Whitebrook. Mon 3D 18
Whitecairns. Abers 4J 73
Whitechapel. Lanc 3D 40
Whitechurch. Pemb 3H 15
White Colne. Essx 1E 22
White Coppice. Lanc 6E 40
White Corries. High 2G 65
Whitecraig. E Lot 2A 60
Whitecroft. Glos 3E 18
White Cross. Corn 6K 3
Whitecross. Corn 4B 4
Whitecross. Falk 2H 59
Whitecross. New M 7F 93
White End. Worc 8F 26
Whiteface. High 5H 79
Whitefarland. N Ayr 5H 57
Whitefaulds. S Ayr 1H 51
Whitefield. Dors 6H 9
**Whitefield**. G Man 7G 41
Whitefield. Som 3K 7
Whiteford. Abers 3G 73
Whitegate. Ches W 3E 34
Whitehall. Devn 4L 7
Whitehall. Hants 8E 20
Whitehall. Orkn 7F 88
Whitehall. W Sus 3J 11
**Whitehaven**. Cumb 3J 45
Whitehaven. Shrp 7A 34
Whitehead. ME Ant 4J 93
Whitehill. Hants 2E 10
Whitehill. N Ayr 4A 58
Whitehills. Abers 7F 80
Whitehills. Ang 2H 67
White Horse Common.
Norf 7K 39
Whitehough. Derbs 1J 35
Whitehouse. Abers 4F 72
Whitehouse. Arg 3H 57
Whiteinch. Glas 3D 58
Whitekirk. E Lot 1C 60
White Kirkley. Dur 8D 54
White Lackington. Dors 6F 8
Whitelackington. Som 4B 8
White Ladies Aston. Worc 6H 27
White Lee. W Yor 5L 41
Whiteley. Hants 5C 10
Whiteley Bank. IOW 7C 10
Whiteley Village. Surr 7H 21
Whitemans Green. W Sus 3L 11
White Mill. Carm 4L 15
Whitemire. Mor 8K 79
Whitemoor. Corn 6B 4
Whitenap. Hants 3A 10
Whiteness. Shet 3E 90
White Notley. Essx 2D 22
Whiteoak Green. Oxon 2M 19
Whiteparish. Wilts 3L 9
White Pit. Linc 2L 37
Whiterashes. Abers 3H 73
Whiterock. Ards 5J 93
White Rocks. Here 1C 18
White Roding. Essx 2B 22
Whiterow. High 7E 86
Whiterow. Mor 8L 79
Whiteshill. Glos 3G 19
Whiteside. Nmbd 5M 53
Whiteside. W Lot 3H 59
Whitesmith. E Sus 4B 12
Whitestaunton. Som 4A 8
White Stone. Here 7D 26
Whitestone. Abers 6F 72
Whitestone. Devn 6H 7
Whitestones. Abers 8H 81
Whitestreet Green. Suff 8F 30
Whitewall Corner. N Yor 8E 48
White Waltham. Wind 6F 20
Whiteway. Glos 2H 19
Whitewell. Lanc 3E 40
Whitewell Bottom. Lanc 5G 41
Whiteworks. Devn 8F 6
Whitewreath. Mor 8B 80
Whitfield. D'dee 4H 67
Whitfield. Kent 1K 13
Whitfield. Nptn 8D 28
Whitfield. Nmbd 6A 54
Whitfield. S Glo 4E 18
Whitford. Devn 6A 8
Whitford. Flin 3L 33
Whitgift. E Yor 5F 42
Whitgreave. Staf 7G 35
Whithorn. Dum 7K 51
Whiting Bay. N Ayr 7K 57
Whitkirk. W Yor 4A 42
Whitland. Carm 5J 15
Whitleigh. Plym 6G 5
Whitletts. S Ayr 7B 58
Whitley. N Yor 5C 42
Whitley. Wilts 7G 19
**Whitley Bay**. Tyne 4G 55
Whitley Chapel. Nmbd 6C 54
Whitley Heath. Staf 7G 35
Whitley Lower. W Yor 6L 41
Whitley Thorpe. N Yor 5C 42
Whitlock's End. W Mid 4K 27
Whitminster. Glos 3F 18
Whitmore. Dors 5J 9
Whitmore. Staf 5G 35
Whitnage. Devn 4K 7
Whitnash. Warw 5M 27
Whitney. Here 7A 26
Whitrigg. Cumb
nr. Kirkbride 6G 53
nr. Torpenhow 8G 53
Whitsbury. Hants 4K 9
Whitsome. Bord 4F 60
Whitson. Newp 5B 18
**Whitstable**. Kent 7H 23
Whitstone. Corn 6B 6
Whittingham. Nmbd 8H 61
Whittingslow. Shrp 3C 26
Whittington. Derbs 2B 36
Whittington. Glos 1J 19
Whittington. Lanc 8E 46
Whittington. Norf 2D 30
Whittington. Shrp 6B 34
Whittington. Staf
nr. Kinver 3G 27
nr. Lichfield 1K 27
Whittington. Warw 2L 27
Whittington. Worc 6G 27
Whittington Barracks. Staf 1K 27
Whittlebury. Nptn 7D 28
Whittleford. Warw 2M 27
Whittle-le-Woods. Lanc 5D 40
**Whittlesey**. Cambs 2K 29
Whittlesford. Cambs 7A 30
Whittlestone Head. Bkbn 6F 40
Whitton. N Lin 5G 43
Whitton. Nmbd 1D 54
Whitton. Powy 5A 26
Whitton. Bord 7E 60
Whitton. Shrp 4D 26
Whitton. Stoc T 3A 48
Whittonditch. Wilts 6L 19
Whittonstall. Nmbd 6D 54
Whitway. Hants 8B 20
Whitwell. Derbs 2C 36
Whitwell. Herts 1J 21
Whitwell. IOW 8C 10
Whitwell. N Yor 6L 47
Whitwell. Rut 1G 29
Whitwell-on-the-Hill.
N Yor 1E 42
Whitwick. Leics 8B 36
Whitwood. W Yor 5B 42
Whitworth. Lanc 6G 41
Whixall. Shrp 6D 34

Whixley. N Yor 2B 42
Whoberley. W Mid 4M 27
Whorlton. Dur 4K 47
Whorlton. N Yor 5B 48
Whygate. Nmbd 4A 54
Whyle. Here 5D 26
Whyteleafe. Surr 8L 21
Wibdon. Glos 4D 18
Wibtoft. Warw 3B 28
Wichenford. Worc 5F 26
Wichling. Kent 8F 22
Wick. Bour 6K 9
Wick. Devn 5L 7
Wick. High 6E 86
Wick. Shet
on Mainland 4E 90
on Unst 3K 91
Wick. Som
nr. Bridgwater 1M 7
nr. Burnham-on-Sea 8B 18
nr. Somerton 3C 8
Wick. S Glo 6F 18
Wick. V Glam 7J 17
Wick. W Sus 5H 11
Wick. Wilts 3K 9
Wick. Worc 7H 27
Wick Airport. High 6E 86
Wicken. Cambs 4B 30
Wicken. Nptn 8E 28
Wicken Bonhunt. Essx 8A 30
Wickenby. Linc 1H 37
Wicken Green Village.
Norf 6E 38
Wickersley. S Yor 8B 42
Wicker Street Green. Suff 7F 30
**Wickford**. Essx 4D 22
Wickham. Hants 4C 10
Wickham. W Ber 6A 20
Wickham Bishops. Essx 2E 22
Wickhambreaux. Kent 8J 23
Wickhambrook. Suff 6D 30
Wickhamford. Worc 7J 27
Wickham Green. Suff 5G 31
Wickham Heath. W Ber 7B 20
Wickham Market. Suff 6K 31
Wickhampton. Norf 1L 31
Wickham St Paul. Essx 8E 30
Wickham Skeith. Suff 5G 31
Wickham Street. Suff 5G 31
Wick Hill. Wok 7E 20
Wicklewood. Norf 1G 31
Wickmere. Norf 6H 39
Wick St Lawrence. N Som 7B 18
Wickwar. S Glo 5F 18
Widdington. Essx 8B 30
Widdrington. Nmbd 2F 54
Widdrington Station.
Nmbd 2F 54
Widecombe in the Moor.
Devn 8G 7
Widegates. Corn 6E 4
Widemouth Bay. Corn 5B 6
Wide Open. Tyne 4F 54
Widewall. Orkn 2F 86
Widford. Essx 3C 22
Widford. Herts 2M 21
Widham. Wilts 5J 19
Widmer End. Buck 4F 20
Widmerpool. Notts 7D 36
**Widnes**. Hal 1D 34
Widworthy. Devn 6M 7
**Wigan**. G Man 7D 40
Wigbeth. Dors 5J 9
Wigborough. Som 4C 8
Wiggaton. Devn 6L 7
Wiggenhall St Germans.
Norf 8B 38
Wiggenhall St Mary Magdalen.
Norf 8B 38
Wiggenhall St Mary the Virgin.
Norf 8B 38
Wiggenhall St Peter. Norf 8C 38
Wiggens Green. Essx 7C 30
Wigginton. Herts 2G 21
Wigginton. Oxon 8A 28
Wigginton. Staf 1L 27
Wigginton. York 2C 42
Wigglesworth. N Yor 2G 41
Wiggonby. Cumb 6G 53
Wiggonholt. W Sus 4H 11
Wighill. N Yor 3B 42
Wighton. Norf 6F 38
Wightwick. W Mid 2G 27
Wigley. Hants 4M 9
Wigmore. Here 5C 26
Wigmore. Medw 7D 22
Wigsley. Notts 2F 36
Wigsthorpe. Nptn 3H 29
**Wigston**. Leics 2D 28
Wigtoft. Linc 6K 37
Wigton. Cumb 7G 53
Wigtown. Dum 6K 51
Wike. W Yor 3M 41
Wilbarston. Nptn 3F 28
Wilberfoss. E Yor 2E 42
Wilburton. Cambs 4A 30
Wilby. Norf 3G 31
Wilby. Nptn 5F 28
Wilby. Suff 4J 31
Wilcot. Wilts 7K 19
Wilcott. Shrp 8B 34
Wilcove. Corn 6G 5
Wildboarclough. Ches E 3H 35
Wilden. Bed 6H 29
Wilden. Worc 4G 27
Wildern. Hants 4B 10
Wilderspool. Warr 1E 34
Wilde Street. Suff 4D 30
Wildhern. Hants 8A 20
Wildmanbridge. S Lan 4G 59
Wildmoor. Worc 4H 27
Wildsworth. Linc 8F 42
Wildwood. Staf 7H 35
Wilford. Nott 6C 36
Wilkesley. Ches E 5E 34
Wilkhaven. High 5K 79
Wilkieston. W Lot 3K 59
Wilksby. Linc 3K 37
Willand. Devn 4K 7
Willaston. Ches E 4E 34
Willaston. Ches W 2B 34
Willaston. IOM 7C 44
Willen. Mil 7F 28
Willenhall. W Mid
nr. Coventry 4A 28
nr. Wolverhampton 2H 27
Willerby. E Yor 4H 43
Willerby. N Yor 8H 49
Willersey. Glos 8K 27
Willersley. Here 7B 26
Willesborough. Kent 1G 13
Willesborough Lees. Kent 1G 13
**Willesden**. G Lon 5K 21
Willesley. Wilts 5G 19
Willett. Som 2L 7
Willey. Shrp 2E 26
Willey. Warw 3B 28
Willey Green. Surr 8G 21
Williamscot. Oxon 7B 28
Williamsetter. Shet 5D 90
Willian. Herts 8K 29
Willingale. Essx 3B 22
Willingdon. E Sus 5B 12
Willingham. Cambs 4M 29
Willingham by Stow. Linc 1F 36
Willingham Green. Cambs 6C 30
Willington. Bed 7J 29
Willington. Derbs 7L 35
Willington. Dur 8E 54
Willington. Tyne 5G 55
Willington. Warw 8L 27
Willington Corner. Ches W 3D 34
Willisham Tye. Suff 6G 31
Willitoft. E Yor 4E 42
Williton. Som 1K 7
Willoughbridge. Staf 5F 34
Willoughby. Linc 2A 38
Willoughby. Warw 5C 28
Willoughby-on-the-Wolds.
Notts 7D 36
Willoughby Waterleys.
Leics 2C 28
Willoughton. Linc 8G 43
Willow Green. Worc 6F 26
Willows Green. Essx 2D 22
Willsbridge. S Glo 6E 18
Willslock. Staf 6J 35
Wilmcote. Warw 6K 27

Wilmington—Zouch


Wilmington. Bath 7E 18
Wilmington. Devn 6M 7
Wilmington. E Sus 5B 12
Wilmington. Kent 6B 22
**Wilmslow**. Ches E 1G 35
Wilnecote. Staf 1L 27
Wilney Green. Norf 3G 31
Wilpshire. Lanc 4E 40
Wilsden. W Yor 4J 41
Wilsford. Linc 5H 37
Wilsford. Wilts
nr. Amesbury 2K 9
nr. Devizes 8J 19
Wilsill. N Yor 1K 41
Wilsley Green. Kent 2D 12
Wilson. Here 1D 18
Wilson. Leics 7B 36
Wilsontown. S Lan 4H 59
Wilstead. Bed 7H 29
Wilsthorpe. E Yor 1J 43
Wilsthorpe. Linc 8H 37
Wilstone. Herts 2G 21
Wilton. Cumb 3K 45
Wilton. N Yor 7F 48
Wilton. Red C 4C 48
Wilton. Bord 8C 60
Wilton. Wilts
nr. Marlborough 7L 19
nr. Salisbury 2J 9
Wimbish. Essx 8B 30
Wimbish Green. Essx 8C 30
Wimblebury. Staf 8J 35
**Wimbledon**. G Lon 6K 21
Wimblington. Cambs 2M 29
Wimboldsley. Ches W 3E 34
**Wimborne Minster**. Dors 5J 9
Wimborne St Giles. Dors 4J 9
Wimbotsham. Norf 1C 30
Wimpole. Cambs 7L 29
Wimpstone. Warw 7L 27
Wincanton. Som 3F 8
Winceby. Linc 3L 37
Wincham. Ches W 2E 34
Winchburgh. W Lot 2J 59
Winchcombe. Glos 1J 19
Winchelsea. E Sus 4F 12
Winchelsea Beach. E Sus 4F 12
**Winchester**. Hants 3B 10
Winchet Hill. Kent 1D 12
Winchfield. Hants 8E 20
Winchmore Hill. Buck 4G 21
Winchmore Hill. G Lon 4L 21
Wincle. Ches E 3H 35
Windermere. Cumb 6C 46
Winderton. Warw 7M 27
Windhill. High 1F 70
Windle Hill. Ches W 2B 34
Windlesham. Surr 7G 21
Windley. Derbs 5M 35
Windmill. Derbs 2K 35
Windmill Hill. E Sus 4C 12
Windmill Hill. Som 4B 8
Windrush. Glos 2K 19
**Windsor**. Wind 6G 21
Windsor Green. Suff 6E 30
Windyedge. Abers 6H 73
Windygates. Fife 7G 67
Windyharbour. Ches E 2G 35
Windyknowe. W Lot 3H 59
Wineham. W Sus 3K 11
Winestead. E Yor 5L 43
Winfarthing. Norf 3H 31
Winford. IOW 7C 10
Winford. N Som 7D 18
Winforton. Here 7A 26
Winfrith Newburgh. Dors 7G 9
Wing. Buck 1F 20
Wing. Rut 1F 28
Wingate. Dur 8H 55
Wingates. G Man 7E 40
Wingates. Nmbd 2E 54
Wingerworth. Derbs 3A 36
Wingfield. C Beds 1H 21
Wingfield. Suff 4J 31
Wingfield. Wilts 8G 19
Wingfield Park. Derbs 4A 36
Wingham. Kent 8J 23
Wingmore. Kent 1H 13
Wingrave. Buck 2F 20
Winkburn. Notts 4E 36
Winkfield. Brac 6G 21
Winkfield Row. Brac 6F 20
Winkhill. Staf 4J 35
Winklebury. Hants 8D 20
Winkleigh. Devn 5F 6
Winksley. N Yor 8L 47
Winkton. Dors 6K 9
Winlaton. Tyne 5E 54
Winlaton Mill. Tyne 5E 54
Winless. High 6E 86
Winmarleigh. Lanc 3C 40
Winnal Common. Here 8C 26
Winnard's Perch. Corn 5B 4
Winnersh. Wok 6E 20
Winnington. Ches W 2E 34
Winnington. Staf 6F 34
Winnothdale. Staf 5J 35
Winscales. Cumb 2K 45
Winscombe. N Som 8C 18
**Winsford**. Ches W 3E 34
Winsford. Som 2J 7
Winsham. Devn 2D 6
Winsham. Som 5B 8
Winshill. Staf 7L 35
Winsh-wen. Swan 5F 16
Winskill. Cumb 8K 53
Winslade. Hants 1D 10
Winsley. Wilts 7G 19
Winslow. Buck 1E 20
Winson. Glos 3J 19
Winson Green. W Mid 3J 27
Winsor. Hants 4M 9
Winster. Cumb 6C 46
Winster. Derbs 3L 35
Winston. Dur 4K 47
Winston. Suff 5H 31
Winstone. Glos 3H 19
Winswell. Devn 4D 6
Winterborne Clenston. Dors 5G 9
Winterborne Herringston.
Dors 7E 8
Winterborne Houghton. Dors 5G 9
Winterborne Kingston. Dors 6G 9
Winterborne Monkton. Dors 7E 8
Winterborne St Martin. Dors 7E 8
Winterborne Stickland. Dors 5G 9
Winterborne Whitechurch.
Dors 5G 9
Winterborne Zelston. Dors 6G 9
Winterbourne. S Glo 5E 18
Winterbourne. W Ber 6B 20
Winterbourne Abbas. Dors 6E 8
Winterbourne Bassett. Wilts 6K 19
Winterbourne Dauntsey.
Wilts 2K 9
Winterbourne Earls. Wilts 2K 9
Winterbourne Gunner. Wilts 2K 9
Winterbourne Monkton.
Wilts 6K 19
Winterbourne Steepleton.
Dors 7E 8
Winterbourne Stoke. Wilts 1J 9
Winterbrook. Oxon 5D 20
Winterburn. N Yor 2H 41
Winter Gardens. Essx 5D 22
Winterhay Green. Som 4B 8
Winteringham. N Lin 5G 43
Winterley. Ches E 4F 34
Wintersett. W Yor 6A 42
Winterton. N Lin 6G 43
Winterton-on-Sea. Norf 8L 39
Winthorpe. Linc 3B 38
Winthorpe. Notts 4F 36
Winton. Bour 6J 9
Winton. Cumb 4F 46
Winton. E Sus 5B 12
Wintringham. N Yor 8F 48
Winwick. Cambs 3J 29
Winwick. Nptn 4D 28
Winwick. Warr 8E 40
Wirksworth. Derbs 4L 35
Wirswall. Ches E 5D 34
**Wisbech**. Cambs 8A 38
Wisbech St Mary. Cambs 1M 29
Wisborough Green. W Sus 3H 11
Wiseton. Notts 1E 36
**Wishaw**. N Lan 4F 58
Wishaw. Warw 2K 27
Wisley. Surr 8H 21
Wispington. Linc 2K 37
Wissenden. Kent 1F 12
Wissett. Suff 4K 31
Wistanstow. Shrp 3C 26
Wistanswick. Shrp 7E 34
Wistaston. Ches E 4E 34
Wiston. Pemb 5G 15
Wiston. S Lan 6H 59
Wiston. W Sus 4J 11
Wistow. Cambs 3K 29
Wistow. N Yor 4C 42
Wiswell. Lanc 4F 40
Witcham. Cambs 3A 30
Witchampton. Dors 5H 9
Witchford. Cambs 4B 30
**Witham**. Essx 2E 22
Witham Friary. Som 1F 8
Witham on the Hill. Linc 8H 37
Witham St Hughs. Linc 3F 36
Withcall. Linc 1K 37
Witherenden Hill. E Sus 3C 12
Withergate. Norf 7J 39
Witheridge. Devn 4H 7
Witheridge Hill. Oxon 5D 20
Witherley. Leics 2M 27
Withermarsh Green. Suff 8G 31
Withern. Linc 1M 37
Withernsea. E Yor 5L 43
Withernwick. E Yor 3J 43
Withersdale Street. Suff 3J 31
Withersfield. Suff 7C 30
Witherslack. Cumb 7C 46
Withiel. Corn 5B 4
Withiel Florey. Som 2J 7
Withington. Glos 2J 19
Withington. G Man 8G 41
Withington. Here 7D 26
Withington. Shrp 8D 34
Withington. Staf 6J 35
Withington Green. Ches E 2G 35
Withington Marsh. Here 7D 26
Withleigh. Devn 4J 7
Withnell. Lanc 5E 40
Withnell Fold. Lanc 5E 40
Withybrook. Warw 3B 28
Withycombe. Som 1K 7
Withycombe Raleigh. Devn 7K 7
Withyham. E Sus 2A 12
Withypool. Som 2H 7
Witley. Surr 1G 11
Witnesham. Suff 6H 31
**Witney**. Oxon 2A 20
Wittering. Pet 1H 29
Wittersham. Kent 3E 12
Witton. Norf 1K 31
Witton. Worc 5G 27
Witton Bridge. Norf 6K 39
Witton Gilbert. Dur 7F 54
Witton-le-Wear. Dur 8E 54
Witton Park. Dur 8E 54
Wiveliscombe. Som 3K 7
Wivelrod. Hants 2D 10
Wivelsfield. E Sus 3L 11
Wivelsfield Green. E Sus 4L 11
Wivenhoe. Essx 1G 23
Wiveton. Norf 5G 39
Wix. Essx 1H 23
Wixford. Warw 6J 27
Wixhill. Shrp 7D 34
Wixoe. Suff 7D 30
Woburn. C Beds 8G 29
Woburn Sands. Mil 8G 29
**Woking**. Surr 8H 21
**Wokingham**. Wok 7F 20
Wolborough. Devn 8H 7
Woldingham. Surr 8L 21
Wold Newton. E Yor 8H 49
Wold Newton. NE Lin 8K 43
Wolferlow. Here 5E 26
Wolferton. Norf 7C 38
Wolfhill. Per 4E 66
Wolf's Castle. Pemb 4F 14
Wolfsdale. Pemb 4F 14
Wolgarston. Staf 8H 35
Wollaston. Nptn 5G 29
Wollaston. Shrp 8B 34
Wollaston. W Mid 3G 27
Wollaton. Nott 5C 36
Wollerton. Shrp 6E 34
Wollescote. W Mid 3H 27
Wolseley Bridge. Staf 7J 35
Wolsingham. Dur 8D 54
Wolstanton. Staf 5G 35
Wolston. Warw 4B 28
Wolsty. Cumb 6F 52
Wolterton. Norf 6H 39
Wolvercote. Oxon 3B 20
**Wolverhampton**. W Mid 2H 27
Wolverley. Shrp 6C 34
Wolverley. Worc 4G 27
Wolverton. Hants 8C 20
Wolverton. Mil 7F 28
Wolverton. Warw 5L 27
Wolverton. Wilts 2F 8
Wolverton Common.
Hants 8C 20
Wolvesnewton. Mon 4C 18
Wolvey. Warw 3B 28
Wolvey Heath. Warw 3B 28
Wolviston. Stoc T 3B 48
Womaston. Powy 5A 26
Wombleton. N Yor 7D 48
**Wombourne**. Staf 2G 27
**Wombwell**. S Yor 7A 42
Womenswold. Kent 8J 23
Womersley. N Yor 6C 42
Wonersh. Surr 1H 11
Wonson. Devn 7F 6
Wonston. Dors 5F 8
Wonston. Hants 2B 10
Wooburn. Buck 5G 21
Wooburn Green. Buck 5G 21
Wood. Pemb 4E 14
Woodacott. Devn 5C 6
Woodale. N Yor 8J 47
Woodall. S Yor 1B 36
Woodbank. Ches W 2B 34
Woodbastwick. Norf 8K 39
Woodbeck. Notts 2E 36
Woodborough. Notts 5D 36
Woodborough. Wilts 8K 19
Woodbridge. Devn 6L 7
Woodbridge. Dors 4F 8
**Woodbridge**. Suff 7J 31
Wood Burcote. Nptn 7D 28
Woodbury. Devn 7K 7
Woodbury Salterton. Devn 7K 7
Woodchester. Glos 3G 19
Woodchurch. Kent 2F 12
Woodchurch. Mers 1A 34
Woodcock Heath. Staf 7J 35
Woodcombe. Som 1J 7
Woodcote. Oxon 5D 20
Woodcote Green. Worc 4H 27
Woodcott. Hants 8B 20
Woodcroft. Glos 4D 18
Woodcutts. Dors 4H 9
Wood Dalling. Norf 7G 39
Woodditton. Cambs 6C 30
Wood Eaton. Staf 8G 35
Woodeaton. Oxon 2C 20
Wood End. Bed 5H 29
Wood End. Herts 1L 21
Wood End. Warw
nr. Bedworth 3L 27
nr. Dordon 2L 27
nr. Tanworth-in-Arden 4K 27
Woodend. Cumb 5L 45
Woodend. Nptn 7D 28
Woodend. Staf 7K 35
Woodend. W Sus 5F 10
Wood Enderby. Linc 3K 37
Woodend Green. Essx 1B 22
Woodfalls. Wilts 3K 9
Woodfield. Oxon 1C 20
Woodfields. Lanc 4E 40
Woodford. Corn 4B 6
Woodford. Devn 6K 5
Woodford. Glos 4E 18
**Woodford**. G Lon 4L 21
Woodford. G Man 1G 35
Woodford. Nptn 4G 29
Woodford. Plym 6H 5
Woodford Green. G Lon 4M 21
Woodford Halse. Nptn 6C 28
Woodgate. Norf 8G 39
Woodgate. W Mid 3H 27
Woodgate. W Sus 5G 11
Woodgate. Worc 5H 27
**Wood Green**. G Lon 4K 21
Woodgreen. Hants 4K 9
Woodgreen. Oxon 2A 20
Woodhall. Inv 2B 58
Woodhall. Linc 3K 37
Woodhall. N Yor 6H 47
Woodhall Spa. Linc 3J 37
Woodham. Surr 7H 21
Woodham Ferrers. Essx 4D 22
Woodham Mortimer. Essx 3E 22
Woodham Walter. Essx 3E 22
Woodhaven. Fife 5H 67
Wood Hayes. W Mid 1H 27
Woodhead. Abers
nr. Fraserburgh 7J 81
nr. Fyvie 2G 73
Woodhill. N Som 6C 18
Woodhill. Shrp 3F 26
Woodhill. Som 3B 8
Woodhorn. Nmbd 3F 54
Woodhouse. Leics 8C 36
Woodhouse. S Yor 1B 36
Woodhouse. W Yor
nr. Leeds 4L 41
nr. Normanton 5A 42
Woodhouse Eaves. Leics 8C 36
Woodhouses. Ches W 2D 34
Woodhouses. G Man
nr. Failsworth 7H 41
nr. Sale 8F 40
Woodhouses. Staf 8K 35
Woodhuish. Devn 6M 5
Woodhurst. Cambs 4L 29
Woodingdean. Brig 5L 11
Woodland. Devn 5K 5
Woodland. Dur 3J 47
Woodland Head. Devn 6G 7
Woodlands. Abers 6G 73
Woodlands. Dors 5J 9
Woodlands. Hants 4M 9
Woodlands. Kent 7B 22
Woodlands. N Yor 2M 41
Woodlands. S Yor 7C 42
Woodlands Park. Wind 6F 20
Woodlands St Mary.
W Ber 6M 19
Woodlane. Shrp 7E 34
Woodlane. Staf 7K 35
Woodleigh. Devn 7K 5
Woodlesford. W Yor 5A 42
Woodley. G Man 8H 41
Woodley. Wok 6E 20
Woodmancote. Glos
nr. Cheltenham 1H 19
nr. Cirencester 3J 19
Woodmancote. W Sus
nr. Chichester 5E 10
nr. Henfield 4K 11
Woodmancote. Worc 7H 27
Woodmancott. Hants 1C 10
Woodmansey. E Yor 4H 43
Woodmansgreen. W Sus 3F 10
Woodmansterne. Surr 8K 21
Woodmanton. Devn 7K 7
Woodmill. Staf 7K 35
Woodminton. Wilts 3J 9
Woodnesborough. Kent 8K 23
Woodnewton. Nptn 2H 29
Woodnook. Linc 6G 37
Wood Norton. Norf 7G 39
Woodplumpton. Lanc 4D 40
Woodrising. Norf 1F 30
Wood Row. W Yor 5A 42
Woodrow. Cumb 7G 53
Woodrow. Dors
nr. Fifehead Neville 4F 8
nr. Hazelbury Bryan 5F 8
Woods Eaves. Here 7A 26
Woodseaves. Shrp 6E 34
Woodseaves. Staf 7G 35
Woodsend. Wilts 6L 19
Woodsetts. S Yor 1C 36
Woodsford. Dors 6F 8
Wood's Green. E Sus 2C 12
Woodshaw. Wilts 5J 19
Woodside. Aber 5J 73
Woodside. Brac 6G 21
Woodside. Derbs 5A 36
Woodside. Dum 4E 52
Woodside. Dur 3K 47
Woodside. Fife 7H 67
Woodside. Herts 3K 21
Woodside. Per 4F 66
Wood Stanway. Glos 8J 27
Woodstock. Oxon 2B 20
Woodstock Slop. Pemb 4G 15
Woodston. Pet 2J 29
Wood Street. Norf 7K 39
Wood Street Village. Surr 8G 21
Woodthorpe. Derbs 2B 36
Woodthorpe. Leics 8C 36
Woodthorpe. Linc 1M 37
Woodthorpe. Notts 5C 36
Woodthorpe. York 3C 42
Woodton. Norf 2J 31
Woodtown. Devn
nr. Bideford 3D 6
nr. Littleham 3D 6
Woodvale. Mers 6B 40
Woodville. Derbs 8M 35
Woodwalton. Cambs 3K 29
Woodwick. Orkn 7C 88
Woodyates. Dors 4J 9
Woody Bay. Devn 1F 6
Woofferton. Shrp 5D 26
Wookey. Som 1D 8
Wookey Hole. Som 1D 8
Wool. Dors 7G 9
Woolacombe. Devn 1D 6
Woolage Green. Kent 1J 13
Woolage Village. Kent 8J 23
Woolaston. Glos 4D 18
Woolavington. Som 1B 8
Woolbeding. W Sus 3F 10
Woolcotts. Som 2J 7
Wooldale. W Yor 7K 41
Wooler. Nmbd 7G 61
Woolfardisworthy. Devn
nr. Bideford 3C 6
nr. Crediton 5H 7
Woolfords. S Lan 4J 59
Woolgarston. Dors 7H 9
Woolhampton. W Ber 7C 20
Woolhope. Here 8E 26
Woolland. Dors 5F 8
Woollard. Bath 7E 18
Woolley. Bath 7F 18
Woolley. Cambs 4J 29
Woolley. Corn 4B 6
Woolley. Derbs 3A 36
Woolley. W Yor 6M 41
Woolley Green. Wilts 7G 19
Woolmere Green. Worc 5H 27
Woolmer Green. Herts 2K 21
Woolminstone. Som 5C 8
Woolpit. Suff 5F 30
Woolridge. Glos 1G 19
Woolscott. Warw 5B 28
Woolsery. Devn 3C 6
Woolsington. Tyne 5E 54
Woolstaston. Shrp 2C 26
Woolsthorpe By Belvoir.
Linc 6F 36
Woolsthorpe-by-Colsterworth.
Linc 7G 37
Woolston. Devn 7K 5
Woolston. Shrp
nr. Church Stretton 3C 26
nr. Oswestry 7B 34
Woolston. Som 3E 8
Woolston. Sotn 4B 10
Woolston. Warr 1E 34
Woolstone. Glos 8H 27
Woolstone. Oxon 5L 19
Woolston Green. Devn 5K 5
Woolton. Mers 1C 34
Woolton Hill. Hants 7B 20
Woolverstone. Suff 8H 31
Woolverton. Som 8F 18
Woolwell. Devn 5H 5
**Woolwich**. G Lon 6M 21
Woonton. Here
nr. Kington 6B 26
nr. Leominster 5D 26
Wooperton. Nmbd 7H 61
Woore. Shrp 5F 34
Wooth. Dors 6C 8
Wooton. Shrp 3F 26
Wootton. Bed 7H 29
Wootton. Hants 6L 9
Wootton. IOW 6C 10
Wootton. Kent 1J 13
Wootton. Nptn 6E 28
Wootton. N Lin 6H 43
Wootton. Oxon
nr. Abingdon 3B 20
nr. Woodstock 2B 20
Wootton. Shrp
nr. Ludlow 4C 26
nr. Oswestry 7B 34
Wootton. Staf
nr. Eccleshall 7G 35
nr. Ellastone 5K 35
**Wootton Bassett, Royal**.
Wilts 5J 19
Wootton Bridge. IOW 6C 10
Wootton Common. IOW 6C 10
Wootton Courtenay. Som 1J 7
Wootton Fitzpaine. Dors 6B 8
Wootton Rivers. Wilts 7K 19
Wootton St Lawrence.
Hants 8C 20
Wootton Wawen. Warw 5K 27
**Worcester**. Worc 6G 27
Worcester Park. G Lon 7K 21
Wordsley. W Mid 3G 27
Worfield. Shrp 2F 26
Work. Orkn 8D 88
Workhouse Green.
Suff 8F 30
**Workington**. Cumb 2J 45
**Worksop**. Notts 2C 36
Worlaby. N Lin 6H 43
World's End. W Ber 6B 20
World's End. W Sus 4L 11
Worlds End. Hants 4D 10
Worlds End. W Mid 3K 27
Worldsend. Shrp 2C 26
Worle. N Som 7B 18
Worleston. Ches E 4E 34
Worlingham. Suff 3L 31
Worlington. Suff 4C 30
Worlingworth. Suff 5J 31
Wormbridge. Here 8C 26
Wormegay. Norf 8C 38
Wormelow Tump. Here 8C 26
Wormhill. Derbs 2K 35
Wormingford. Essx 8F 30
Worminghall. Buck 3D 20
Wormington. Glos 8J 27
Worminster. Som 1D 8
Wormit. Fife 5G 67
Wormleighton. Warw 6B 28
Wormley. Herts 3L 21
Wormley. Surr 2G 11
Wormshill. Kent 8E 22
Wormsley. Here 7C 26
Worplesdon. Surr 8G 21
Worrall. S Yor 8M 41
**Worsbrough**. S Yor 7A 42
Worsley. G Man 7F 40
Worstead. Norf 7K 39
Worsthorne. Lanc 4G 41
Worston. Lanc 3F 40
Worth. Kent 8K 23
Worth. W Sus 2K 11
Wortham. Suff 4G 31
Worthen. Shrp 1B 26
Worthenbury. Wrex 5C 34
Worthing. Norf 8F 38
**Worthing**. W Sus 5J 11
Worthington. Leics 7B 36
Worth Matravers. Dors 8H 9
Worting. Hants 8D 20
Wortley. Glos 4F 18
Wortley. S Yor 8M 41
Wortley. W Yor 4L 41
Worton. N Yor 7H 47
Worton. Wilts 8H 19
Wortwell. Norf 3J 31
Wotherton. Shrp 1A 26
Wothorpe. Pet 1H 29
Wotter. Devn 5H 5
Wotton. Glos 2G 19
Wotton. Surr 1J 11
Wotton-under-Edge. Glos 4F 18
Wotton Underwood.
Buck 2D 20
Wouldham. Kent 7D 22
Wrabness. Essx 8H 31
Wrafton. Devn 2D 6
Wragby. Linc 2J 37
Wragby. W Yor 6B 42
Wramplingham. Norf 1H 31
Wrangbrook. W Yor 6B 42
Wrangle. Linc 4M 37
Wrangle Lowgate. Linc 4M 37
Wrangway. Som 4L 7
Wrantage. Som 3B 8
Wrawby. N Lin 7H 43
Wraxall. N Som 6C 18
Wraxall. Som 2E 8
Wray. Lanc 1E 40
Wraysbury. Wind 6H 21
Wrayton. Lanc 8E 46
Wrea Green. Lanc 4B 40
Wreay. Cumb
nr. Carlisle 7J 53
nr. Penrith 3C 46
Wrecclesham. Surr 1F 10
**Wrecsam**. Wrex 4B 34
Wrekenton. Tyne 6F 54
Wrelton. N Yor 7E 48
Wrenbury. Ches E 5D 34
Wreningham. Norf 2H 31
Wrentham. Suff 3L 31
Wrenthorpe. W Yor 5M 41
Wrentnall. Shrp 1C 26
Wressle. E Yor 4E 42
Wressle. N Lin 7G 43
Wrestlingworth. C Beds 7K 29
Wretton. Norf 2C 30
**Wrexham**. Wrex 4B 34
Wreyland. Devn 7G 7
Wrickton. Shrp 3E 26
Wrightington Bar. Lanc 6D 40
Wright's Green. Essx 2B 22
Wrinehill. Staf 5F 34
Wrington. N Som 7C 18
Writtle. Essx 3C 22
Wrockwardine. Telf 8E 34
Wroot. N Lin 7E 42
Wrotham. Kent 8C 22
Wrotham Heath. Kent 8C 22
Wroughton. Swin 5K 19
Wroxall. IOW 7C 10
Wroxall. Warw 4L 27
Wroxeter. Shrp 1D 26
Wroxham. Norf 8K 39
Wroxton. Oxon 7B 28
Wyaston. Derbs 5K 35
Wyatt's Green. Essx 4B 22
Wybers Wood. NE Lin 7K 43
Wyberton. Linc 5L 37
Wyboston. Bed 6J 29
Wybunbury. Ches E 5E 34
Wychbold. Worc 5H 27
Wych Cross. E Sus 2M 11
Wychnor. Staf 8K 35
Wychnor Bridges. Staf 8K 35
Wyck. Hants 2E 10
Wyck Hill. Glos 1K 19
Wyck Rissington. Glos 1K 19
Wycliffe. Dur 4K 47
Wycombe Marsh. Buck 4F 20
Yr Wyddgrug. Flin 4M 33
Wyddial. Herts 8L 29
Wye. Kent 1G 13
Wyesham. Mon 2D 18
Wyfold. Oxon 5D 20
Wyfordby. Leics 8E 36
The Wyke. Shrp 1F 26
Wyke. Devn 6H 7
Wyke. Dors 3F 8
Wyke. Shrp 1E 26
Wyke. Surr 8G 21
Wyke. W Yor 5K 41
Wyke Champflower.
Som 2E 8
Wykeham. Linc 7K 37
Wykeham. N Yor
nr. Malton 8F 48
nr. Scarborough 7G 49
Wyken. Shrp 2F 26
Wyken. W Mid 3A 28
Wyke Regis. Dors 8E 8
Wykey. Shrp 7B 34
Wykin. Leics 2B 28
Wylam. Nmbd 5E 54
Wylde Green. W Mid 2K 27
Wylye. Wilts 2J 9
Wymering. Port 5D 10
Wymeswold. Leics 7D 36
Wymington. Bed 5G 29
Wymondham. Leics 8F 36
**Wymondham**. Norf 1H 31
Wyndham. B'end 5J 17
Wynford Eagle. Dors 6D 8
Wyng. Orkn 2E 86
Wynyard Village. Stoc T 3B 48
Wyre Piddle. Worc 7H 27
Wysall. Notts 7D 36
Wyson. Here 5D 26
Wythall. Worc 4J 27
Wytham. Oxon 3B 20
Wythenshawe. G Man 1G 35
Wythop Mill. Cumb 2L 45
Wyton. Cambs 4K 29
Wyton. E Yor 4J 43
Wyverstone. Suff 5G 31
Wyverstone Street. Suff 5G 31
Wyville. Linc 7F 36
Wyvis Lodge. High 6E 78


## Y


Yaddlethorpe. N Lin 7F 42
Yafford. IOW 7B 10
Yafforth. N Yor 6M 47
Yalding. Kent 8C 22
Yanley. N Som 7D 18
Yanwath. Cumb 3D 46
Yanworth. Glos 2J 19
Yapham. E Yor 2E 42
Yapton. W Sus 5G 11
Yarburgh. Linc 8L 43
Yarcombe. Devn 5M 7
Yarde. Som 2K 7
Yardley. W Mid 3K 27
Yardley Gobion. Nptn 7E 28
Yardley Hastings. Nptn 6F 28
Yardley Wood. W Mid 3K 27
Yardro. Powy 7M 25
Yarhampton. Worc 5F 26
Yarkhill. Here 7E 26
Yarlet. Staf 7H 35
Yarley. Som 1D 8
Yarlington. Som 3E 8
Yarm. Stoc T 4B 48
Yarmouth. IOW 7A 10
Yarnbrook. Wilts 8G 19
Yarnfield. Staf 6G 35
Yarnscombe. Devn 3E 6
Yarnton. Oxon 2B 20
Yarpole. Here 5C 26
Yarrow. Nmbd 3M 53
Yarrow. Bord 7A 60
Yarrow. Som 1B 8
Yarrow Feus. Bord 7M 59
Yarrow Ford. Bord 6B 60
Yarsop. Here 7C 26
Yarwell. Nptn 2H 29
Yate. S Glo 5F 18
**Yateley**. Hants 7F 20
Yatesbury. Wilts 6J 19
Yattendon. W Ber
Yatton. Here
nr. Leominster
nr. Ross-on-Wye
Yatton. N Som
Yatton Keynell. Wilts
Yaverland. IOW
Yawl. Devn
Yaxham. Norf
Yaxley. Cambs
Yaxley. Suff
Yazor. Here
Yeading. G Lon
Yeadon. W Yor
Yealand Conyers. Lanc
Yealand Redmayne. Lanc
Yealand Storrs. Lanc
Yealmpton. Devn
Yearby. Red C
Yearngill. Cumb
Yearsett. Here
Yearsley. N Yor
Yeaton. Shrp
Yeaveley. Derbs
Yeavering. Nmbd
Yedingham. N Yor
Yeldersley Hollies.
Derbs
Yelford. Oxon
Yelland. Devn
Yelling. Cambs
Yelsted. Kent
Yelvertoft. Nptn
Yelverton. Devn
Yelverton. Norf
Yenston. Som
Yeoford. Devn
Yeolmbridge. Corn
Yeo Mill. Devn
**Yeovil**. Som
Yeovil Marsh. Som
Yeovilton. Som
Yerbeston. Pemb
Yesnaby. Orkn
Yetlington. Nmbd
Yetminster. Dors
Yett. N Lan
Yett. S Ayr
Yettington. Devn
Yetts o' Muckhart. Clac
Yielden. Bed
Yieldshields. S Lan
Yiewsley. G Lon
Yinstay. Orkn
Ynysboeth. Rhon
Ynysddu. Cphy
Ynysforgan. Swan
Ynyshir. Rhon
Ynyslas. Cdgn
Ynysmaerdy. Rhon
Ynysmeudwy. Neat
Ynystawe. Swan
Ynys-wen. Rhon
Ynyswen. Powy
Ynys y Barri. V Glam
Ynysybwl. Rhon
Ynysymaerdy. Neat
Yockenthwaite. N Yor
Yockleton. Shrp
Yokefleet. E Yor
Yoker. Glas
Yonder Bognie. Abers
Yonderton. Abers
**York**. York
Yorkletts. Kent
Yorkley. Glos
Yorton. Shrp
Yorton Heath. Shrp
Youlgreave. Derbs
Youlthorpe. E Yor
Youlton. N Yor
Young's End. Essx
Young Wood. Linc
Yoxall. Staf
Yoxford. Suff
Ysbyty Cynfyn. Cdgn
Ysbyty Ifan. Cnwy
Ysbyty Ystwyth. Cdgn
Ysceifiog. Flin
Yspitty. Carm
Ystalyfera. Neat
Ystrad. Rhon
Ystrad Aeron. Cdgn
Ystradfellte. Powy
Ystradffin. Carm
Ystradgynlais. Powy
Ystradmeurig. Cdgn
Ystrad Mynach. Cphy
Ystradowen. Carm
Ystradowen. V Glam
Ystumtuen. Cdgn
Ythanbank. Abers
Ythanwells. Abers


## Z


Zeal Monachorum. Devn
Zeals. Wilts
Zelah. Corn
Zennor. Corn
Zouch. Notts



PEFC
PEFC/18-31-103
PEFC Certified
This product is from sustainably managed forests and controlled sources
www.pefc.it



Copyright of Geographers' A-Z Map Company Ltd.

The representation on the maps of a road, track or footpath is no evidence of the existence of a right of way.

No reproduction by any method whatsoever of any part of this publication is permitted without the prior consent of the copyright owners.

# CALL OF THE BLUE

To Dylan
with my warmest
regards - Think blue &
enjoy the oceans, and don't
forget they truly need you
P. Hamilton
NHM NOV '18

# CALL OF THE BLUE

## PHILIP HAMILTON

PHILIP HAMILTON
photography

**PHOTOGRAPHY BY PHILIP HAMILTON**
TEXT IN COLLABORATION WITH TOM HOOPER

Photos © Philip Hamilton 2018
Text © the authors 2018

ISBN 978-1-911300-51-9

British Library Catalogue in Publishing Data

A CIP record of this publication is available from the British Library

*CALL OF THE BLUE* IS SPONSORED BY

**The Claude and Sofia Marion Foundation**

Biotherm (L'Oréal Group)

MSC Foundation (Mediterranean Shipping Company)

*Funding to support this book has been provided by Clément Perrette and by Philip Hamilton himself. Profits from sales of the book will be given to ocean conservation organizations.*

Produced by Paul Holberton Publishing
89 Borough High St, London SE1 1NL
WWW.PAULHOLBERTON.COM

Designed by Laura Parker
Copy edited by Paul Holberton and Diana Davies
Printed by E-Graphic Srl, Italy

**FRONT COVER** Silky sharks gracefully patrolling the deep blue

**FRONT ENDPAPERS** Eagle rays flying in formation over a reef full of pelagic life

**FRONTISPIECE** A school of redtail butterflyfish move in loose formation above the reef

**PREFACE** A reef wall carpeted in colourful soft coral, anthias and moorish idols completes the picture of a busy coral reef

**FOREWORD** Underwater among mangrove roots – a vital nursery habitat for juvenile fish species

**PAGE 10** The Galapagos penguin is the most northern species of penguin

**PAGE 12** The author and photographer, Philip Hamilton

**CALL OF THE BLUE** A fin whale disappearing into the blue horizon

**BACK ENDPAPERS** The sight of marine life carrying the scars of human activities is jarring. With fishing gear set amidst so much of our coastlines, inevitably much more remains unseen

**BACK COVER** A true oceanic wanderer, the loggerhead turtle

# CONTENTS

# PREFACE

To fly over the earth is to observe the omnipresence of the oceans. To breathe is to feel that they bring us to life. The oceans are as varied and complex as the sky's shades of blue – the clarity of the white sandbars, the transparency of the lagoons, the intensity of the oceans' depths or even the whiteness of the waves that break against our shores. The oceans strive to hide their wealth but betray themselves through their beauty. I used to think of them as unvarying and monotonous, but I discovered them to be varied and rich. While directing the film *Planète Océan*, with my co-director Michael Pitiot, I met many of those who make the marine world accessible to all. Scientists, photographers, underwater directors and sailors bring us the huge diversity of seascapes – from coral citadels visible from space to the invisible world of plankton. The oceans need witnesses, for others to tell of their fragility. Philip Hamilton gives them a voice in *Call of the Blue*.

When I was born, there were two billion human beings on the planet. Today there are nearly 7.5 billion and yet we are still as close to the ocean. We maintain intimate relationships with the sea which often go back to childhood memories. Whether we feel fascination or fear, no one remains indifferent to the sea. Almost one out of two people live less than 100 kilometres from the coast, and one out of seven have fish as their only source of animal protein. I have seen what the sea brings us and how we depend on it. Whether it's oxygen, climate, energy, food or medicine, the ocean is the motor of our planet. And yet, the warnings are there and make my head turn. The alarm bells rung by scientists are real, the oceans are beginning to falter. One out of three species of fish is threatened by industrial fisheries, pollution now seems a permanent issue, sea water is getting warmer and acidifying from our greenhouse gas emissions, the world's climates are changing. The infinite ocean

is showing its limits. From Antarctica to the Pacific Islands, no corner of the oceans remains untouched by human activity. Our consumer society is placing unbearable pressure on our oceans.

The ocean faces its greatest challenge, that of being the common resource for all humanity. One world, a single resource to share between 7.5 billion people. The oceans belong to no one, therefore to everyone, and so to who ever gets there first .... When rules do not exist, will common sense be enough? Will we meet the challenge of not systematically sawing off the branches beneath our feet? After having met thousands of people from all over the world for my films, I deeply and sincerely believe in our capacity to act. We no longer have the time to look back, we are in an era of solutions, innovations, engagement, action and solidarity.

Our oceans, our world, needs a revolution: that of morals and ethics.

**YANN ARTHUS-BERTRAND**

Photographer, journalist, reporter and environmentalist. Author of *Earth from Above*

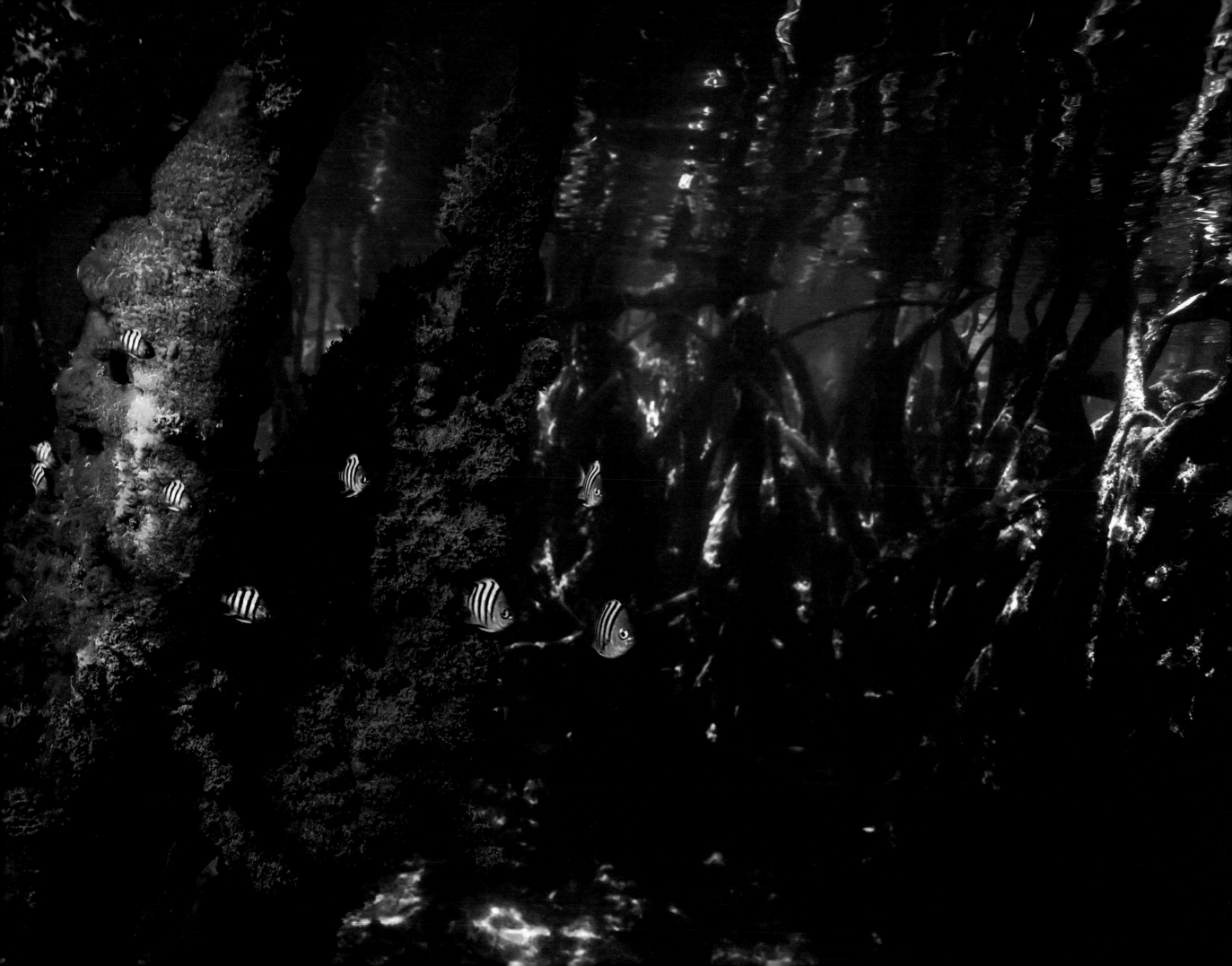

# FOREWORD

Because there are oceans, there is life. Oceans regulate our climate, feed us, underpin our economies, and even provide the air we breathe.

Philip Hamilton's journey has taken him to all corners of the planet. He has managed to capture both the majesty and the rich diversity of our oceans as well as the sobering reality that befalls life below the surface.

As highlighted by many of the ocean Guardians and Experts featured in this book, mounting pressures from overfishing, pollution, rising temperatures and acidification mean that the future of our blue planet is very much in the balance. Forecasts predict that, without significant changes, more than half of the world's marine species may stand on the brink of extinction by 2100.

There is still time, however. Oceans are resilient and they will recover if given space and protection. The world currently protects 8% of the oceans. This is a start but there is now an urgent need to expand marine protected areas to ensure the health of ocean biodiversity and the continuation of its critical ecosystem services which underpin all life above and below the surface.

The importance of work like Philip's is that it helps us re-focus, it helps ensure that the spotlight remains fully and firmly on what is at stake – the ocean life that inspires and sustains us. *Call of the Blue* is a vivid and powerful reminder of the ocean treasures we must continue to fight for.

**INGER ANDERSEN**

Director General of the International Union for Conservation of Nature (IUCN)

# INTRODUCTION

NATURE has no nationality, frontiers or borders, no flag, no religion or race and yet, despite its extraordinary beauty, we humans abuse and exploit it, regrettably sometimes beyond repair. When in North America or Western Europe we pollute the waters of the Atlantic, deep and cold currents take the toxins and waste south to the most remote places in Antarctica, where isolated animals that have never seen man have been found to have metals and plastic in their bodies. Effectively we are spreading pollution like a plague, just under our noses. Yes, nature has no frontiers or borders … the same way hurricanes or earthquakes hit indiscriminately, ocean devastation spreads around and fast. Evidently, faced with such a reality the response needs to have no borders, a unique coordinated approach will be required, and, if it doesn't come from supranational agencies and governments, it will have to involve a global cultural change and resources from the largest and wealthiest corporations. As marine biologist and explorer Sylvia Earle says, 'With every breath you take you are connected to the ocean' – there is no way out, we are all on it together.

In the last 50 years, 50% of coral reefs have disappeared, 90% of large fish in the ocean are gone and many species are on the brink of collapse. Not surprisingly, the oceans are in desperate need of help. As a quick reminder, the oceans are home to more than 90% of the planet's species, they generate more than 60% of all oxygen, and they absorb most of the planet heat and its carbon dioxide. If that weren't enough, oceans feed a third of the world's population. At the time of printing this book, only an estimated 2% of all global philanthropic and charitable donations go to protect the environment. Of this, only a tiny fraction goes towards supporting and safeguarding our main source of life, the oceans. All the while, rich governments spend billions sending vessels to Mars and the poorest countries question nature's needs while confronted with poverty, the next political election, corruption and strong corporate lobbying. Unfortunately, despite recent efforts and the establishment of almost 5,000 marine reserves, less than 1% of the ocean is under protection, while the other 99% is open for grabs and greed. Even if tomorrow we protect 5%, migratory species that travel thousands of miles can still be exploited almost anywhere. Close to half of the world's population live within 100 kilometres of the sea and about 97% of the world's fishermen live in developing countries, with fishing as their main source of food and income. Seabed exploration for mining purposes is growing rapidly, and its territory accounts for more than 50% of our planet. Licenses for mining the ocean's floor are being granted even though we have little idea of the nature of the deep sea, and we may be destroying habitats and wildlife we have yet to discover and protect.

Exploiting our oceans' reserves and polluting them beyond mend is not only against most religions and beliefs, as well as the United Nations Human Rights charter, but is also failing our future generations.

The French-Canadian astrophysicist Hubert Reeves once wrote:

*Humanity is the most insane species. In principle a 'unique and super intelligent' species but it worships an invisible God while slaughtering visible nature, without even realising that this nature it slaughters is the invisible God it worships.*

I have had the privilege to visit some of the most amazing locations in the world for their vibrant marine life. This book is the culmination of five years' work to

capture the beauty, magnificence and diversity of our oceans. When I started underwater photography many years back my intention was to share it with friends and hang some beautiful pictures on a wall. Unfortunately, given what I have witnessed over the last 30 years at sea, I find I can't share the lovely photos without raising the alarm. The message had to change and the audience had to be greater, unlimited, and global, matching the size of the problem. Large marine animals have survived five mass extinction events millions of years ago; however, many of them are now at the brink of disappearing for good. Can we keep trawling the seas? Use long lines and modern technology to wipe out their inhabitants? Fish for tuna while the by-catch is greater in mass and annihilates a number of species? If pioneer photographers and explorers managed to influence the US government in 1872 to create and protect Yellowstone Park and many subsequent land reserves, I want to believe that today with modern social media and new underwater equipment we can again spread the word and influence policy-makers about the importance and beauty of the oceans. It has never been easier to spread a campaign, to start a movement. The power of visual communication is evident and

unquestionable. However, we need to remain alert and vigilant, since the vast exchange of beautiful nature and wildlife images via social media sometimes tends to distract us from the reality, creating an illusion, a dangerous mirage.

By presenting only the beautiful photos I'm not trying to deceive myself, hiding the problems and pretending that everything is perfect out there – I'm just avoiding passing on a message with no hope that will get no audience. A single photo can be the most powerful conservation tool.

I have moved around the world all of my life and have witnessed the many changes the oceans have suffered, but also some rare improvements. As a photographer, I am drawn to places in our ocean that are the best protected and managed, but I have also visited whole regions where the oceans have been exhausted or where the pollution is unbearable.

There is a gap between the best and the worst that has driven me to seek the insight and knowledge of people around the world. Working with scientists, fishermen and conservationists I have seen a common thread in people who have been drawn to the sea and spent their lives as protectors, harvesters, educators and researchers. Their interests may sometimes conflict and their world-views and aspirations may differ, but they all share a deep connection and knowledge. The voices in this book describe fundamental shifts and declines that are being witnessed in our own lifetime, and highlight the challenges that we face in continuing to use the sea as a source of our food and a sink for our waste. But there are also stories of hope – small places where life is bouncing back as communities have organized themselves to protect their own futures.

There is no doubt that there are a multitude of threats to marine life, but equally I have been amazed by the resilience of the marine environment and the optimism and commitment of those who are driven to ensure that it is protected for future generations. When you combine the skills of our scientists, conservationists and fishermen together with trust and understanding between governments, corporations and society a great deal is possible. I wouldn't have started this project if I didn't believe in humanity and our power and ability to find solutions when they are really needed. It is undeniable that the oceans could not only provide a substantial percentage of global food, but, well managed, could generate all the energy the world requires – only if corporations could think beyond next quarter results and politicians beyond the next election.

Each photo in this book has a strong association for me – a memory of the place and the feeling of being in the water. My experiences around marine life have been amazing, sometime even overwhelming. Attempting to capture nature's perfection in a photograph can prove haphazard, surprising and even dangerous. The challenges are numerous – finding the right sea conditions, water clarity and light, then maybe marine life decides to participate. As any professional photographer will tell you, securing the shot is often the culmination of weeks of patience and persistence. Nature may, or may not, provide the opportunity, and I am grateful for whatever I get.

I'm truly convinced that a small gesture from everyone can make huge positive changes in the environment, and as the old African proverb says: 'If you think you are too small to make a change, it means that you have not yet spent the night with a mosquito in your room'.

**PHILIP HAMILTON**

# CALL OF THE BLUE

CALL OF THE BLUE brings together a collection of modern-day explorers, sailors, freedivers, film-makers and conservationists who talk about their lives, passions and exploits on, in or under the oceans. What they all have in common is a profound love and respect for the ocean, inspired by their first trips to the beach, the stories of previous generations of explorers and seafarers, and a relationship that has been shaped by their own voyages and experiences. Many of them have been close to losing their lives in the sea, they have felt the primal fear of being alone on wild oceans and isolated in its depths. Those who were initially driven by a thirst for adventure or competition have developed and broadened their relationship to a love for the environment and a deep concern for the future of our oceans. The reasons for their devotion range from the joy of solitude, the necessity of self-reliance, the unpredictability of their journey, the sight of vast expanses and the privilege of a glimpse into the lives of ocean creatures. They share a strong sense of optimism that recovery of our oceans is possible, but this is tempered by a tough realization that our action will have to be transformative and far-reaching.

The marine biologists that have been part of *Call of the Blue* have their own sense of what is happening across the marine world, which is based on years of careful observation. From the life of a seahorse off the coast of eastern Australia to the trans-oceanic wanderings of a blue whale – they talk about what they have learned about the species that they have chosen to follow. *Call of the Blue* explores many different facets of the people that study the oceans. A marine biologist is the archetypal dream career – a life spent at sea observing dolphins, tagging sharks and photographing whales – and none of those who share a passion for the natural world are immune from a love of the animals that they study. Watching and recording the gradual dismantling of the life, beauty and diversity of the oceans is a torturing experience for scientists, burdened with the knowledge of what is happening but at the same time unable to provide easy fixes and straightforward answers that are palatable enough for politicians or tangible enough for society. There is a sense of urgency in answering critical scientific questions about the sea, but there is also a growing feeling that dedicated conservation work is beginning to pay off, with humpback whale populations

bouncing back and communities mobilizing to protect and restore their coastal domains.

*Call of the Blue* demonstrates the best of our seas with beautiful images of the most pristine locations and stories of positive, focused people who are driven to ensure that they stay that way. We are determined that this book is not to become an epitaph of what we once had, but rather to encapsulate what is precious and shine a spotlight on what people around the world are doing to keep it so. The scale of the problem feels insurmountable and beyond the grasp of any one nation, let alone any individual, to resolve. Yet what we are showing here is the way that the efforts of individuals and communities can inspire and drive change. Our own optimism comes from the knowledge that not only do groups of committed people representing the oceans exist, but that they are growing in strength and number. We have called on some of them to speak within this book about their own journeys and inspiration.

# CORAL REEFS AND COASTAL WATERS

CORAL REEFS are living landscapes of intricate shapes created by generations of coral polyps. These are anemone-like animals which, over tens of thousands of years, build hard structures around themselves, fusing their calcium carbonate skeletons together into enormous colonial structures. The beauty of a reef comes from the complexity of its structure. Different coral species form themselves into distinct shapes – rounded boulders with maze-like ridges, enormous rows of overhanging plates, or delicate branches. Reef-building corals inhabit a central band within the Pacific, Indian and Atlantic Oceans between the tropics of Capricorn and Cancer, in areas where the water is clear, shallow and warm. Because of a lack of nutrients in the surface waters, tropical oceanic regions are comparatively barren and unproductive. Coral polyps live in a symbiotic relationship with zooxanthellae, tiny plant cells that live within the coral tissue, feeding the coral by generating (and sharing) energy from the sun. Reef-building corals also feed using stinging tentacles to catch zooplankton floating in the water column, but the vast majority of their nutrition comes from their zooxanthellae, which is why they are restricted to the shallow, clear waters of the tropics where sunlight is strongest.

Coral polyps secrete a limestone skeleton which fuses them together in colonies, and over multiple generations these skeletons grow to form a reef structure. The fastest growing branching corals can extend by 20 cm a year, whereas the more rounded 'massive' corals only grow a couple of millimetres in a year. Some of the biggest living coral boulders have been dated to over 5,000 years old. Charles Darwin was the first naturalist to recognize the different forms of reef; he published his theories in *The Voyage of the Beagle*. Darwin's description of the three principal coral reef types remains valid to the present day. Fringing reefs skirt closely around islands and continental coastlines, creating shallow tidal lagoons. Atoll reefs form around islands that have since subsided and disappeared, leaving a circular braid of small islets with a deep inner lagoon. Barrier reefs form much further offshore, where they are separated by deep lagoons. The most famous example is the Great Barrier Reef in Australia, but there are others, such as the Meso-American reef that stretches from Mexico to Honduras in Central America.

ABOVE Sponges create the most incredible architecture in the coral reef landscape

PREVIOUS The anemonefish and anemone have a symbiotic relationship –
both benefit from their partnership

Sea fans waving in the current

A healthy reef is an intricate and complex seascape of valleys, caves, crevices and overhangs created by corals and shaped by the animals and oceans around them. Watching life on a reef is endlessly rewarding – bustling like a busy market, as hundreds of fish go about their daily business of finding food, defending territory, avoiding being eaten, seeking comfort in a crowd or looking for a mate. It can appear chaotic until you begin to recognize the characteristic behaviours of different species – farmer damsel fish tending and defending napkin-size territories of the reef; trumpet fish and squirrel fish hiding in caves and overhangs; herds of surgeon fish busily grazing on tufts of algae; bright parrot fish scraping chunks of coral to get at the algae within them; and an array of bright butterfly fish, with distinctive yellow, white and black markings, feeding on tiny reef invertebrates. Predatory fish such as snappers and groupers loiter above waiting for an opportunity to dart in and seize a fish momentarily venturing too far from safety. Jacks rely on their speed to pick out prey; moray eels gape threateningly from their holes in the reef, coming out at night to hunt.

Reefs are oases of marine life that provide food and shelter for a huge diversity of crabs, lobsters, worms, sponges, sea squirts and fish, which in turn provide food for other reef animals. The multitudes of different animals that make their home on a coral reef are part of a delicate equilibrium. On a healthy reef, there is little room for vacuums; as soon as a space is created it is filled; sick animals are eaten and the nutrients recycled through a complex web of scavengers occupying every niche in the ecosystem. Some creatures work together for mutual benefit. Cleaner wrasse, found in the Indian and Pacific Oceans, pick off bits of dead skin and parasites from larger fish that assemble at cleaning stations. Reef fish scientist Dr Isabelle Côté has recorded how one species of blenny mimics the colour and behaviour of cleaner wrasse but, instead of removing dead skin or parasites, takes bites out of the skin, upsetting the basis of trust on which cleaning stations operate.

Corals live on a knife-edge, inhabiting and thriving in the shallow ocean where they can be exposed to the open air by low tides and pounded by waves. There is slow-motion competition for sunlight and space on the reef. Fast-growing branching corals may be able to outgrow their slow-growing rivals, but they are more easily broken apart than their slower-growing, more solid-shaped cousins if the reef is hit by big waves. Corals can use long stinging tentacles to try to fend off their neighbours and secure their own living space. Over decades, centuries and millennia, conditions on a reef change, allowing different species to thrive and overtake their rivals. Even the same coral species can vary their growth form and skeleton according to the environment in which they grow. As one of the first reef scientists to spend long periods underwater, Dr Charlie Veron from the Australian Institute of Marine Science was the first to observe this. He spent many years unpicking the mistakes of the many historical taxonomists who had given multiple names to the same species, causing a considerable upset in museums around the world as their order was turned upside down. Charlie Veron, often called 'the godfather of coral', has been studying corals on the Great Barrier Reef in Australia and around the world for the last fifty years, naming over a third of the species:

*Diving has been the means through which I can access the reef environment and observe the wider context of the corals that I am studying and collecting.* [CONTD PAGE 31]

An incredibly diverse scene of hard and soft corals: each individual
will be fighting for space and light on the shallow reef

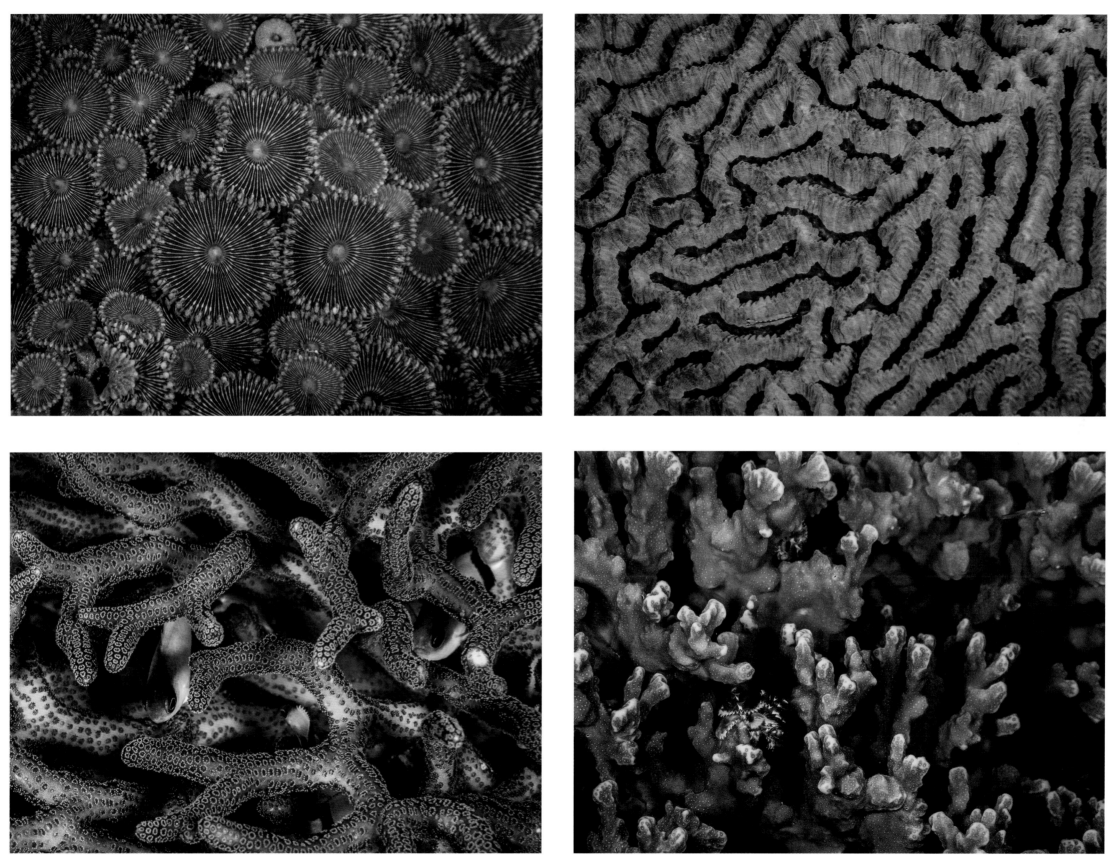

Beauty in shape and form

FACING AND ABOVE Coral reef formations could almost be mistaken for a forest floor

Sea urchins perform an essential cleaning role on the reef,
picking off the thin strands of algae that grow on the corals

27

At dusk you can see the soft corals awakening

Tube worms, anemones and soft corals extend from the reef and feed
on plankton that drift past

*I have had the opportunity to dive and explore the entirety of the Great Barrier Reef over the last 50 years. Most memorable of all are the occasions when I can sneak out to dive on my own on a reef during a full moon. At night, the reef is noisy, busy and surreal, corals have outstretched tentacles, parrotfish are asleep in their mucous cushion and sharks are out hunting. I use a torch to find a good spot, and then turn it off, lie back and relax.*

The modern story of corals and coral reefs is mostly not a happy one. The diversity and productivity of reefs are both their strength and their weakness. They are not only valuable biologically, they are also a source of food for over 400 million people. Coastal societies are directly dependent on reefs, and for millennia established their own equilibrium within the reef ecosystem. Over recent decades, as human populations have grown and new commercial links and markets have developed, fishermen have tended to exploit a resource to the point where it can no longer replenish itself. Isabelle Côté reflects that she has spent a large part of her career documenting the gradual decline of the numbers and diversity of fish on coral reefs, but she recognizes that many species of fish are equipped to survive change and will still be present after corals are gone:

*You can't ignore or be indifferent to the changes that you see on coral reefs. I feel a responsibility to make my work more applied and to try to find solutions to the problems we face.*

Corals reproduce through spawning, producing vast numbers of tiny larvae, a lucky few of which will survive long enough to settle out of the water column and form new colonies of their own. Coral reefs are connected through ocean currents that distribute and share larvae to islands and reefs downstream. In this networked system, reefs around islands and atolls that have suffered a natural disaster can be replenished and recover. The same principle works for reefs that have suffered from human impacts, but only up to a point: if nowhere is left fallow, then the system can fail. Warning signs at a global level were not spotted until relatively late, as scientists were often too focused on what was happening to individual species or reefs. Mark Spalding is a scientist who has a more global perspective, piecing together knowledge of what is happening from thousands of reefs across the world. As part of the team that put together the first global *Reefs at Risk* report in 1998, he remembers the sense of shock at the scale of human impact across the

world. An update to this report in 2013 found that 60% of reefs are currently at risk and predicts that by 2050 all coral reefs will be in danger. No reef has been completely untouched by the impact of humans, and only a few remain in a pristine state. Even the Great Barrier Reef, one of the best protected and most studied areas of ocean in the world, has been suffering from a combination of different human pressures. Populations of crown of thorns starfish, a species of echinoderm that feeds on corals, have exploded across the reef, benefiting from nutrient-rich water running off from farms in Western Australia. More intense cyclones and heavy rainfall have also taken their toll and over the last 30 years the Great Barrier Reef has lost more than half its coral.

One of the biggest problems faced by reefs is coral bleaching. This happens when water temperatures rise even just slightly above their normal summer high. The coral animals become stressed and eject the zooxanthellae that they rely on for most of their nutrition. Without their zooxanthellae, coral polyps are translucent, revealing their white calcium carbonate skeletons – this is why the phenomenon is called 'bleaching'.

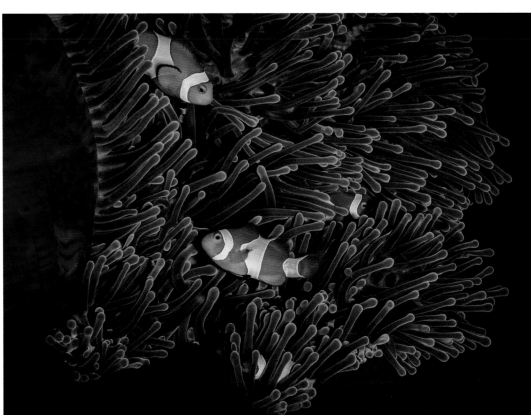

Most male anemonefish cohabit with a single female

Cleaning their eggs with their mouths and ventilating oxygen for them with their
fins – anemonefish take their parenting role very seriously

Sometimes, corals can recover from bleaching, but if the high temperatures persist for too long, they die. Once dead, their white skeletons are swiftly overgrown by algae, and the variety of life on the reef that relies on healthy corals starts to dwindle. The bleaching of corals has become one of the most visible and well-understood impacts of climate change. Dr Mark Spalding was on a research expedition to the Seychelles in 1998, which planned to survey some of the most pristine and amazing reefs in the world. Instead, his team were witnesses to the world's first mass bleaching event. Reefs and atolls across 1500 km of ocean were bleached white or were already dead and overgrown with algae:

*For the first time, scientists were grappling with the long-term implications of such a significant event and we were left wondering whether this could be the beginning of the end for coral reefs. Many bounced back surprisingly quickly, although others have never recovered. It is possible that those sites which were already suffering from the impacts of fishing or pollution were simply tipped into an irreversible decline by the added stress of the bleaching.* [CONTD PAGE 44]

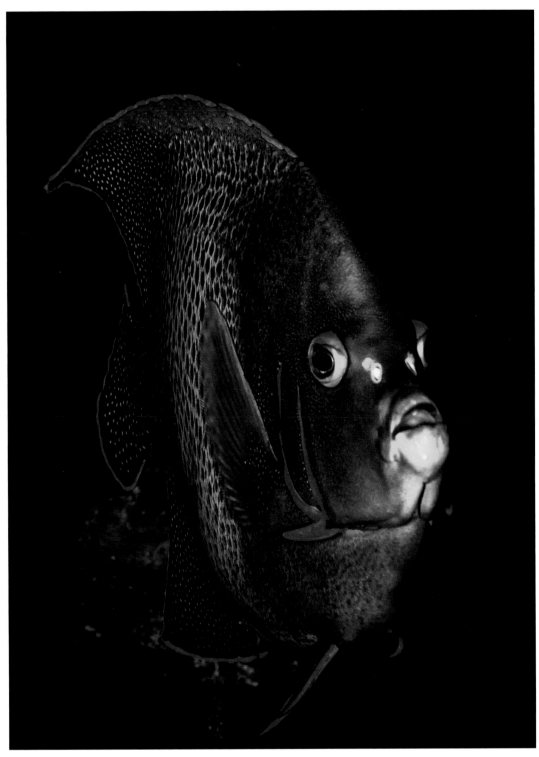

The vibrant colours of an angelfish become almost luminescent at night

Lyretail anthias can change sex, the dominant female changing colour and pattern in transforming to male

Warty frogfish lie motionless, attracting their prey with a lure before striking

Valentin's sharpnose puffer is highly poisonous, and the blacksaddle filefish (often found nearby) have evolved to mimic the toxic puffer

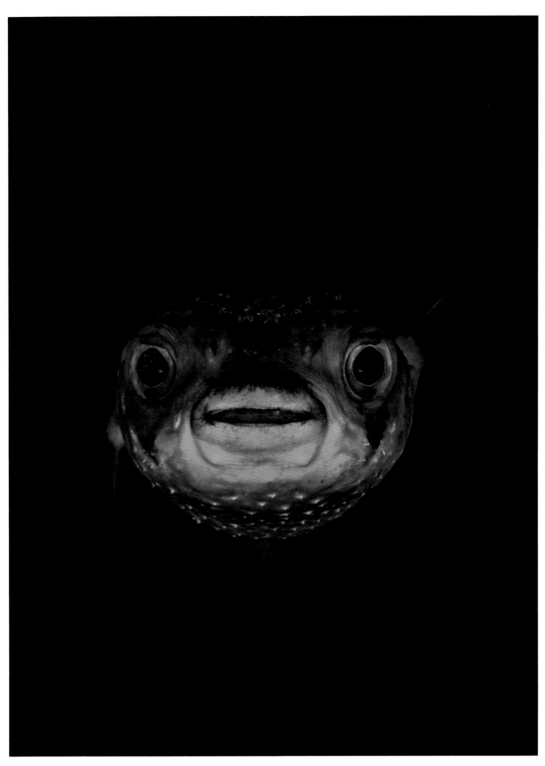

THIS PAGE To deter predators, the porcupine fish can inflate its body to nearly
twice its natural size by swallowing water

FACING The complex structure of the coral branches provide shelter to the small
inhabitants of the reef

Native to the Indo-Pacific, lionfish are voracious hunters feeding on other fish from coastal mangroves down to a depth of over 300 m. They disorientate their prey by blowing a jet of water at them before swallowing them whole

Moray eel are one of the few species to have a second set of jaws,
contained in their throat

LEFT Sex change in groupers is a one-way street. When too few males are available during spawning, dominant females will change sex so that by the following spawning season the ratio is balanced out

RIGHT A potato grouper hovers motionless in a coral cave while two striped cleaner wrasse get to work picking off pieces of dead skin and parasites

The first global mass bleaching event was alarming for scientists, by nature and necessity cautious of what they infer and predict, but the level of understanding has improved over the 40 years since that time. Rising sea surface temperatures are exacerbated regionally by the El Niño-Southern Oscillation, periodic shifts in the ocean and atmosphere that are associated with extreme weather. These seasonal events bring high pressure and extended periods of clear skies that increase sea temperatures that are already elevated. The bleaching between 2014 and 2016 was the worst global bleaching event in history, affecting huge tracts of the Maldives, Great Barrier Reef, Red Sea and Caribbean. A quarter of the coral on the Great Barrier Reef and 90% along the coast of Florida are now dead. Australian reef scientist Ove Hoegh-Guldberg recognized that this first bleaching event was not a one-off, and further research led him to predict the demise of many of the world's coral reefs over the coming decades. He was met with huge amounts of scepticism and criticized for being alarmist, but, twenty years on, we are seeing reefs bleaching and dying all over the world. [CONTD PAGE 54]

GUARDIAN **Ken Nedimyer** is the founder of the Coral Restoration Foundation. Since 2007 he has planted over 35,000 corals in reefs around the Caribbean.

The undersea world of Jacques Cousteau arrived on our screens in the 1960s, almost at the same time as colour television was being widely adopted across America. Until then, I don't think we had any real conception of the vibrant beauty of a coral reef. I had kept tanks of freshwater fish in my bedroom since I was a boy, and dreaming of the mystery and challenge of exploring the ocean and seeing all of these different animals was almost too much for a young boy to stand. On my first trip to the Florida Keys, aged 13, I bought a mask and some fins from a ten-cent store and dived on a field of elkhorn coral that stretched beyond sight. I was mesmerized at the expanse, the complexity and the beauty. Six years later I was at university studying marine biology and I moved permanently to the Florida Keys when I graduated.

There wasn't much work around for a young graduate, so I set myself up to collect and sell live reef fish for the aquarium trade. I would be underwater for hours each day, carefully selecting the fish I wanted and then bringing them slowly and carefully to the surface. I looked after them in my own system of tanks, before they were packed up and sent around the country. I have run this business with the help of my wife and children for over forty years, living off a small and selective take from our coral reefs.

As someone who was diving on the reefs every day, you notice changes. You could see that the coral was dying, places of incredible beauty were just fading away. Carysfort Reef, the site in Key Largo where I had first dived as a young boy, was now completely dead. The biggest turning-point was in 1998, when we had a huge bleaching event that left large tracts of the reef dead. There was almost nothing left. Someone had to do something – but what could we do?

I knew how to grow coral artificially. As part of my business I was licensed to grow live rock on two offshore sites in the Florida Keys. Live rock is formed from the limestone skeletons of dead coral and the porosity of the stone makes it an ideal natural filter for aquariums. In 1996, conditions must have been just right because we had a couple of staghorn corals settle and start to grow on our live rock. Together with my daughter, I started a project to see if we could grow pieces of staghorn coral back. Branching corals like staghorn coral grow fast, but storms, sharks and turtles can also cause breakage. Since they had settled and grown on my own live rock, federal law allowed us to gather up the pieces and start growing them on artificial structures.

The next challenge was to find somewhere we could test to see if these new pieces of coral would survive and grow on the reef itself. Eventually we got permission to plant some of our corals on to an area of the reef damaged by a boat grounding. We 'planted' six pieces, using an epoxy cement to glue them in place on the bare rock. We monitored these corals carefully, diving on the site every month to measure their progress, and to our delight they were all thriving and growing nicely.

When we started the coral farm our goal was to sell them to make money, but after we saw how well the transplanted corals did on the reef we changed our focus and decided to scale up the nursery and grow a boatload of coral for restoration work. I am now running seven coral farms, and we are on track to plant 35,000 corals in sites across the Florida Keys and Caribbean this year. We snip off pieces of coral from our own growing stock in the same way that you might take a cutting of a fruit tree. We then hang these new pieces on fibreglass frames like Christmas decorations. Here in shallow, clear water we let them grow until they are about a year old and ready

> *The elkhorn and staghorn corals that we are growing are the survivors from decades of adverse conditions, able to withstand the high water temperatures, and the smothering and pollution that caused so many others to die.*

for planting. The process is intensive, so we have a team of staff and volunteers who help to nurture the corals, keep them healthy and get them ready for transport and planting.

For a few years I was financing the operation out of my own pocket. Now we are set up as our own non-profit organization, and we have been able to channel resources from conservation organizations to support coral restoration programmes in countries around the Caribbean. Every time we start in a new country we have to prove ourselves again, overcoming scepticism that corals can't be grown in these particular conditions. Some people seem to think that our aim is to restore the

world's coral reefs by hand, but that isn't the case. What we are trying to do is to preserve the genetic diversity and resilience of the species that we have, and plant enough of them so that they can successfully reproduce and reseed downstream reefs. The elkhorn and staghorn corals that we are growing are the survivors from decades of adverse conditions, able to withstand the high water temperatures, and the smothering and pollution that caused so many others to die. I hope this sort of artificial selection of the fittest will give us some breathing space to boost natural recovery and improve the chance that they will reproduce naturally.

I can blink and my mind can go forward a few years, and I will imagine hundreds of plate-size corals growing on some of the reefs where we are replanting corals. Some in the scientific community think that we are not doing our homework, but the results speak for themselves – our corals are thriving and multiplying in reefs all over the Caribbean. Everything we are doing right now is about buying time to try to get us to a point where temperatures stop rising and conditions stabilize. I know that I am only helping to solve a small part of a much greater problem, but this is what I know how to do.

There are still some incredible places that I go to in the Keys, and some have managed to hold on to expansive areas of elkhorn coral – that's all I need to make me feel fulfilled.

A juvenile batfish, which will completely transform in shape and colours
as it develops to adulthood

A lionfish hunting along a reef

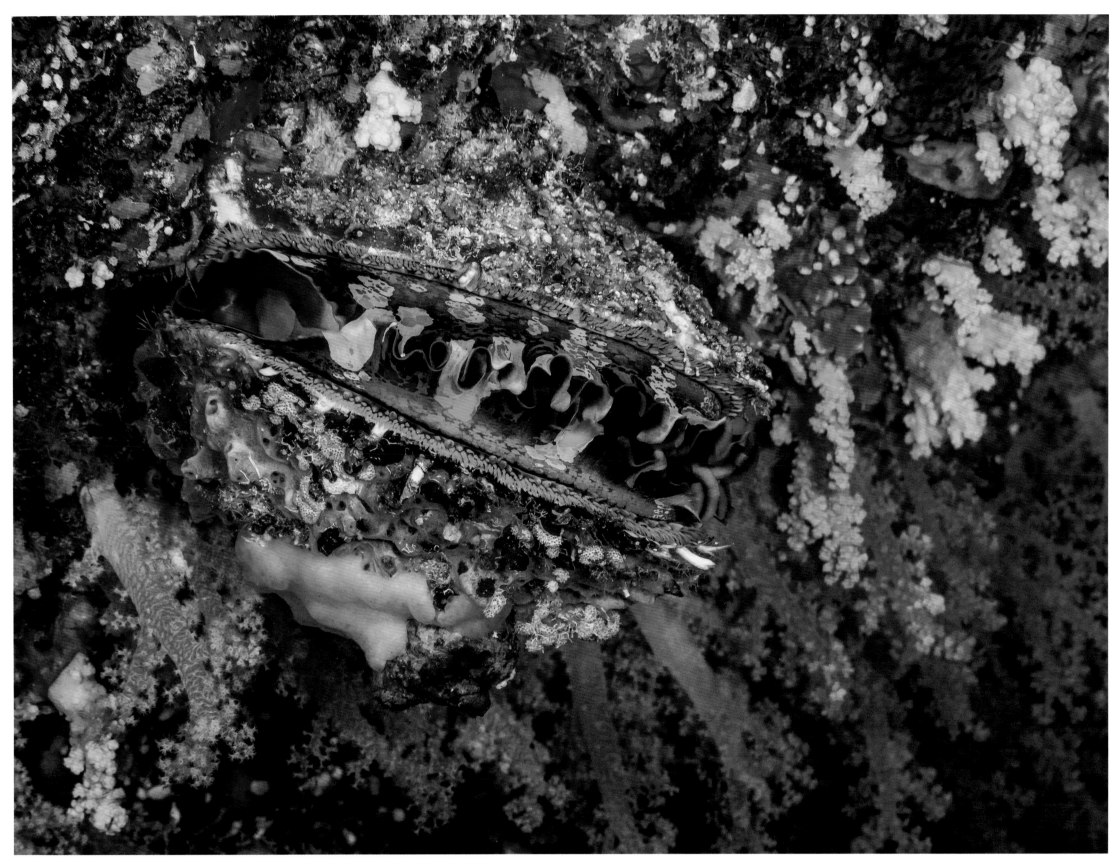

A bivalve attached to a reef wall and surrounded by beautiful soft corals

A giant clam displaying the iridescent blue algae that grow around the opening of its shell

CLOCKWISE FROM TOP LEFT Clown triggerfish, Red Sea clownfish,
leaf scorpionfish and cuttlefish

52

Spiny lobster emerge from their holes at night

Indo-Pacific schooling bannerfish sometimes seem to dance in the most extraordinary co-ordinated movements

It is looking extremely likely that these bleaching events will increase in frequency and severity the world over.

Having spent 11 years studying in Canada and the USA, David Obura returned home to Kenya to set up an organization that would help understand the impacts and vulnerabilities of coral reefs in the western Indian Ocean. Kenya is a country that has seen its population quadruple over the last forty years, placing ever increasing burdens on coastal resources. His own inspiration comes from seeing how the people of Phoenix Islands, a remote Pacific archipelago, have a huge pride in their ocean and a strong commitment across their society to make sure it is protected. In the waters off the East Coast of Africa there are still some remote areas of incredible diversity and abundance, and David is hoping that a collaboration of countries and organizations can create their own Phoenix Islands. He believes that the fundamental goal of humanity should be to keep ecological systems functioning, and to try and retain them in as good a state as possible even as they inevitably change into something different.

Scientists working on coral reefs recognize the need to communicate simple and uncomplicated truths, but are sometimes at a loss as to how to talk about the

gravity of the situation without creating a message too bleak to energize action. Charlie Veron has borne witness to the steady decline of the places he loves best, and in his seventies struggles with the role he is forced to play as a defender of the Great Barrier Reef:

*The outcome of my research on climate change has robbed me of much of the enjoyment I once had in working on reefs, because I now have a clear idea of what lies ahead. I'm reluctant to talk about climate change and the future of coral reefs, for it's hard to see the bright side, and hope is an essential need for just about everybody.*

As always there are caveats and uncertainties, there are local success stories and some reefs that are thriving; but on a global scale reefs are declining and are forecast to get worse. David Obura thinks that scientists know enough to make accurate predictions of how our seas are going to change and what is necessary to protect them:

*Globally, I do not think we are going to retain coral reefs as we used to know them. Undoubtedly there will be some isolated fantastic reef sites, but they will not be part of a global system.*

A dense shoal of striped eel catfish

GUARDIAN **Miranda Krestovnikoff** is a natural history television presenter, zoologist, author and diver specializing in the coasts and marine life of the British Isles.

I am a complete and utter water baby. I feel a joy, excitement and a continual sense of wonder when I am in water. It is difficult to know why (or where it came from) – I just have a sort of uncontrollable urge when close to water to fling myself into it. I grew up in Buckinghamshire, which is about as far from the sea as it is possible to get in England, but I managed to immerse myself in the nature and adventure that was around me, spending a great deal of time at the top of a copper beech tree in the garden and wandering in the local woodland.

I had idyllic beach holidays, and plenty of rummaging around in rockpools, but, as a child, I never had the opportunity to learn to dive; it just wasn't something that was very accessible 20 years ago. When I left home, I headed straight for the dive club at Bristol University and had my first open water dive off Skomer Island in Wales. I can still remember the excitement of getting into the water and the joy of being able to breathe without surfacing. We were in only six metres of water, swimming through a seaweed garden with spider crabs and small wrasse.

I am a huge fan of diving in the UK, and if I never dived abroad again I wouldn't really miss it. I love enthusing people about the underwater life we have around our shores. The vibrancy of an unspoilt reef is enthralling – you don't perhaps find the colours you get in the tropics, but it is nonetheless fascinating; marine life doesn't have to be brightly coloured to be interesting. I was on Lundy Island recently and could have stared at the reefs there for hours; the rocks were festooned with jewel anemones and sea fans and the crevasses between the rocks concealed giant lobsters hiding away. Diving with a dolphin or a seal is a thrill, but I am honestly as happy watching tom-pot blennies with their busy inquisitiveness.

I love the fact that, from the shore, the sea appears to be a monochrome expanse, but if you just put your head below the water there is a whole new dimension of colours, movement and shades. Just off our shoreline is a completely unknown, hidden world. I know that I am lucky to have the opportunity to explore it, and I would love to encourage as many people as I can to have a look at what is below the surface of the sea. To understand our environment and our place within it, we need to spend time in it. A woodland or a garden is a start, but the oceans provide a unique opportunity to be immersed in a completely wild environment. It is so important for children to be able to play, explore and dream; to pick up a crab and feel the brush of seaweed. Without this recognition or connection it is difficult to generate a sense of care and responsibility.

We gain so much from the sea, yet we give little back in return. There has been terrible damage and misuse, but of course so few people really know the extent of the damage. Protected areas are being established around the whole of the UK and I hope that these will allow wildlife to recover and re-establish. I had the opportunity to dive

> *Out of sight is out of mind and never more so than when a piece of litter dips beneath the water surface; gone from sight but remaining in the water system for many, many years.*

in Loch Carron on the east coast of Skye, a unique site home to acres of flame shell beds. Just recently there has been news of a scallop dredger which has ripped its way through the reef causing untold damage to the fragile environment – dead spider crabs, smashed sea urchins and flame shells in pieces. A single pass of a fishing trawler like this and it will take decades for the seabed to recover. Protected areas will help to restore our wildlife, but we need to make sure that they are really operating effectively and halting the most damaging forms of fishing and human activity.

Plastic pollution is a massive and growing problem that we need to solve quickly if we are going to avoid drowning in the sea of litter that already exists and clear up the seas for the next generation. Out of sight is out of mind and never more so than when a piece of litter dips beneath the water surface; gone from sight but remaining in the water system for many, many years. Somehow, seeing a piece of plastic underwater is more shocking than on land, because it seems so out of place – artificial and alien. There are such simple steps that we can take to avoid using cotton buds, plastic straws and single-use plastic bottles, luckily there are great organizations such as Neptune's Army in Pembrokeshire, which has been making a sterling effort to remove rubbish from the seabed and help restore it to a more natural state.

That said, I am eternally optimistic. If I can persuade a few more people to spend more time underwater and discover what I get so excited about, and hopefully voice their support for stronger protection for our waters, then we will be able to continue to experience the pure, wild joy of our oceans. I feel I owe it to the sea for the wonderful experiences and memories that it has given me in 20 years of diving. I still feel like a kid when I get my diving kit on. A forward roll and I'm into zero gravity and the potential of discovering something new and different becomes real once more.

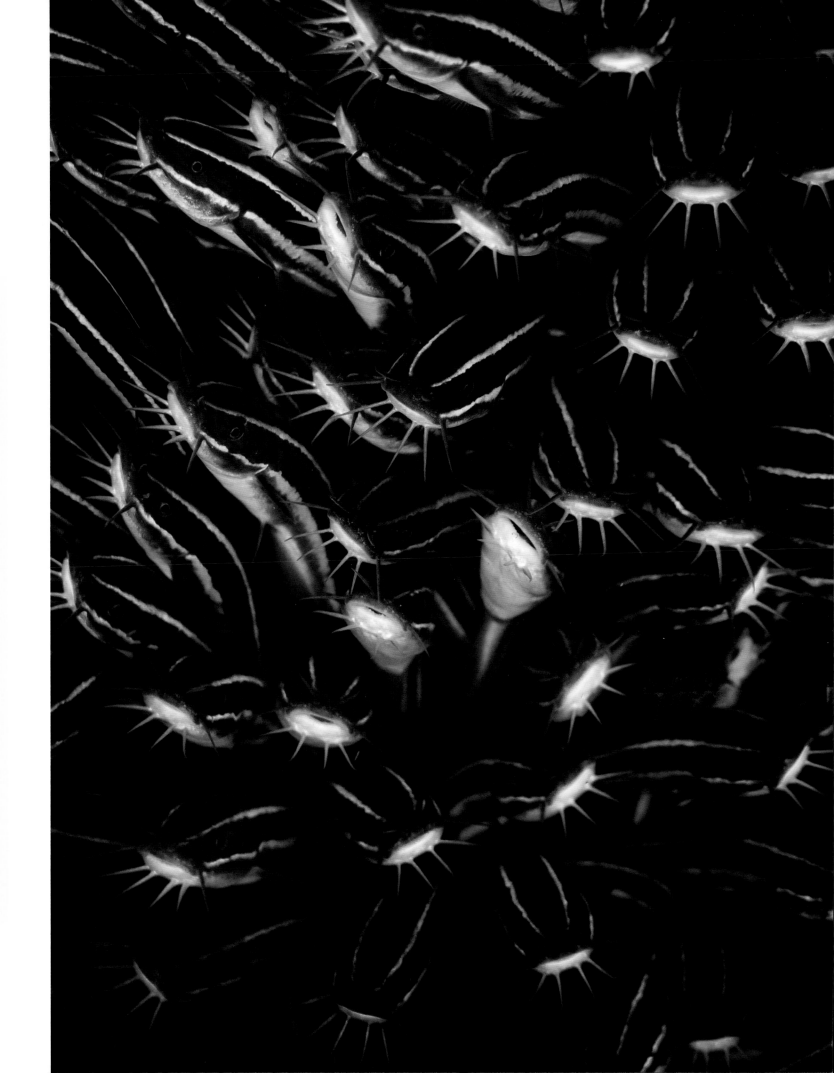

The mandarin fish is among the most striking of reef fish – it is one of just two species in the world that can produce its own blue colouring. It has a protective mucus coating that is both toxic and foul-smelling

No one should mistake the statement of this unwelcome news as an epitaph or a signal that we should give up and walk away; what is at stake is how well we can help coral reefs manage the pressures of the next half century, and whether we are able to hold on to small pockets of life. That is the reality. The challenges we face to protect reefs – and the people that depend on them – as they contend with multiple challenges will be enormous. The role of governments and the international community is to think about how they can reduce the vulnerability of people and increase the resilience of coral reefs to climate change impacts by removing as many other causes of stress as possible. This role needs to be taken seriously to help us prepare for our future. With his global perspective Mark Spalding provides reassurance that:

*The world will be changed, not doomed.*

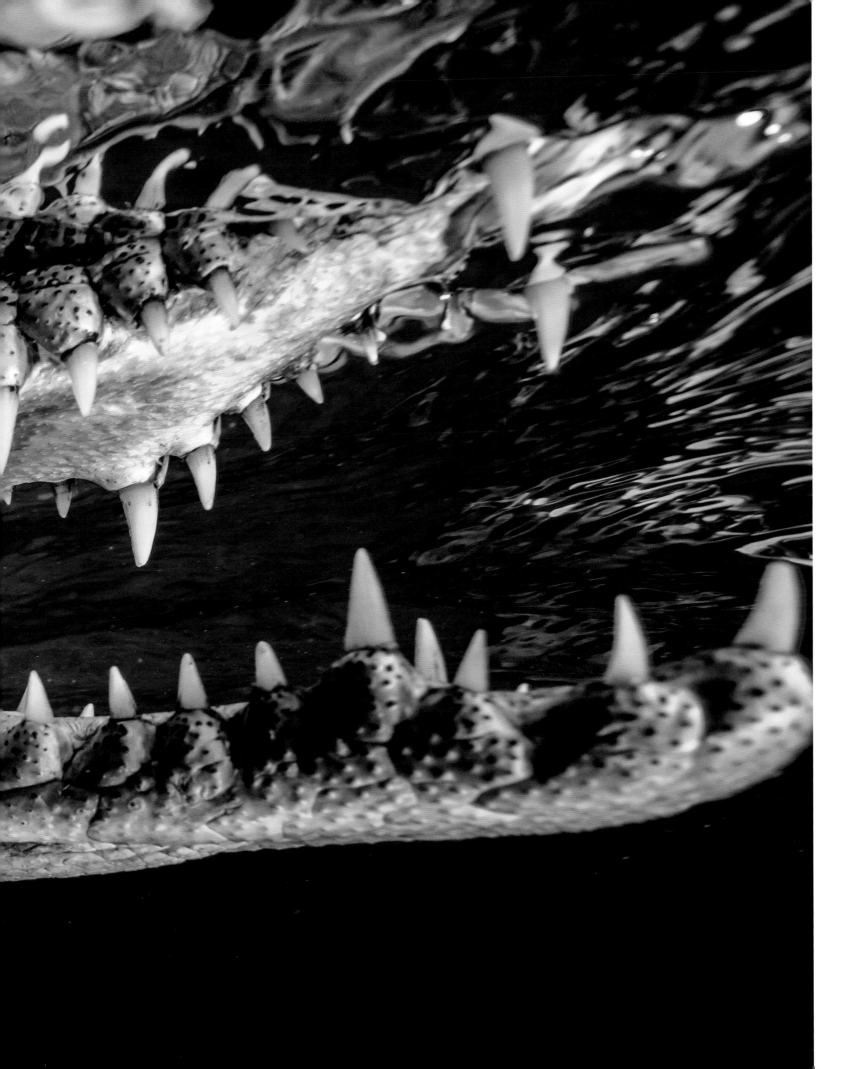

The American crocodile is one of the larger crocodile species but it feeds on small prey, such as fish, small mammals and birds

## Coastal waters

Our coastlines are where the oceans are at their most productive and diverse. Here the shallow waters are energized by the sun and shaped by the ceaseless force of the waves and the constant movement of tides. In temperate climates, each creature of the marine life of these dynamic coastlines finds its own niche, creating distinct societies that rely on each other for food or shelter. As the tide recedes, animals left behind in the rockpools have to be hardy enough to survive dropping oxygen levels and the gradual increase in temperature and salinity before the sea returns again. Scientists have identified clear zones that are characterized and occupied by different groups of animals that change as the seabed gradually deepens.

Forests of kelp fringe underwater coastlines of North America, Europe and Asia, creating a three-dimensional habitat for thousands of different species. Kelp is an algae that thrives in cold, nutrient-rich water, anchoring itself to the rock and growing upwards in ribbons towards the surface. Where rivers meet the sea, the organic-rich, black mud of estuaries are a stomping ground for birds that search for the countless small hidden invertebrates. The rising tide brings in other foraging fish, and molluscs such as oysters and

While photographing crocodiles, you cannot afford to be distracted for a second –
they are much more likely to try to eat you than sharks are

mussels draw in water to trap tiny plankton to feed on.

In tropical climates, coastal habitats are dominated by mosaics of coral reefs, seagrasses and mangroves, ecosystems that support and benefit each other. Reef-building corals create lagoons that provide shallow, sheltered water for seagrasses. In return, seagrasses bind the sediments that would otherwise smother the coral polyps. Seagrasses are underwater flowering plants that form dense meadows, trapping carbon from the atmosphere in the sediment beneath their roots. Often called the 'lungs of the sea', they are one of the most productive ecosystems in the world, found in all continents except Antarctica. Animals such as the dugong and green turtle feed directly on the grasses, but they are also the basis of an ecosystem that provides shelter for fish and invertebrates that in turn are a source of food for others. For many coral reef species, it is the seagrasses that provide the nursery grounds – a shelter for the tiny larvae among the leaves and roots. The decomposing leaves are the source of nutrients for micro-organisms, and they too are sought after as food by many species of animals.

Mangrove forests are found throughout the tropics, covering vast expanses of shallow coastlines and estuaries. Over 50 species of mangrove occupy different bands of coast, some preferring shoreline habitat and others occurring further inland, providing a protective barrier for coasts from the actions of waves and storms. The roots are both straws and struts, radiating out from the base of the tree and plugging down into the sediment. This complex network is a host for encrusting barnacles, oysters and sponges and a shelter from predators for many species of young fish and crustaceans, while their canopy provides habitat for nesting coastal birds.

Palaeontological evidence suggests that shellfish were one of the last additions to the diet of our hunter-gatherer ancestors. Since early humans migrated out of Africa 90,000 years ago, the coast has become increasingly essential to the lives and diet of growing settlements across the world. The Mediterranean has been a source of food for millennia, and archaeological records show how much this environment has changed as pressure from humans has grown. Surviving mosaics display huge groupers being caught by fishermen using harpoons close to the shore. A species of red mullet was

so rare and sought after that in Roman times it was only allowed to be eaten by the imperial family. As recently as two or three generations ago, sharks and large groupers were a common daily catch for Mediterranean fishermen. The magnitude of fishing in the last 60 years has put an end to this cycle of sustainability. Now, almost all of the fish eaten in the Mediterranean is imported; even 'local' delicacies such as the octopus are often imported from East Africa. The Medes Islands off the coast of Costa Brava in Spain are one of the few areas of the Mediterranean that are protected from fishing and this is now one of the very few places where you can still see large groupers.

Zafer Kizilkaya had travelled to some of the world's most amazing wildlife areas as a National Geographic photographer, but when he returned to his homeland of Turkey he was staggered by how impoverished the Mediterranean Sea had become. He was part of a small group involved in the rehabilitation of an abandoned monk seal pup. Once she had recovered, the group started to look for somewhere reasonably pristine to release her. The only possible place was Gökova Bay. At 1300 km², it is the biggest bay in Turkey, with a well-protected coastline, but the marine environment had

been completely destroyed by overfishing. There were around 200 families making their living from fishing around the bay, relying to a large extent on shrimp and white grouper. Since both of these species had virtually disappeared, many people were starting to change jobs and look for work elsewhere.

After establishing the Mediterranean Conservation Society, Zafer started talking to the local community about the idea of a protected area, showing them examples from places that he had visited such as Apo Island in the Philippines:

*There was initially quite a lot of resistance to some of these sites which were still used for fishing, but I was saying to them 'What have you got to lose? It can't get any worse!' Within a year, I had agreement to establish six no-fishing zones.*

There was no capacity within government to manage or enforce these sites, so a group from the local community was trained and provided with uniforms. Zafer emphasizes that they were encouraged to use 'soft power' – warning and educating people rather than fining them. The speed and recovery inside and outside these sites has been incredible. Since 2013 the income

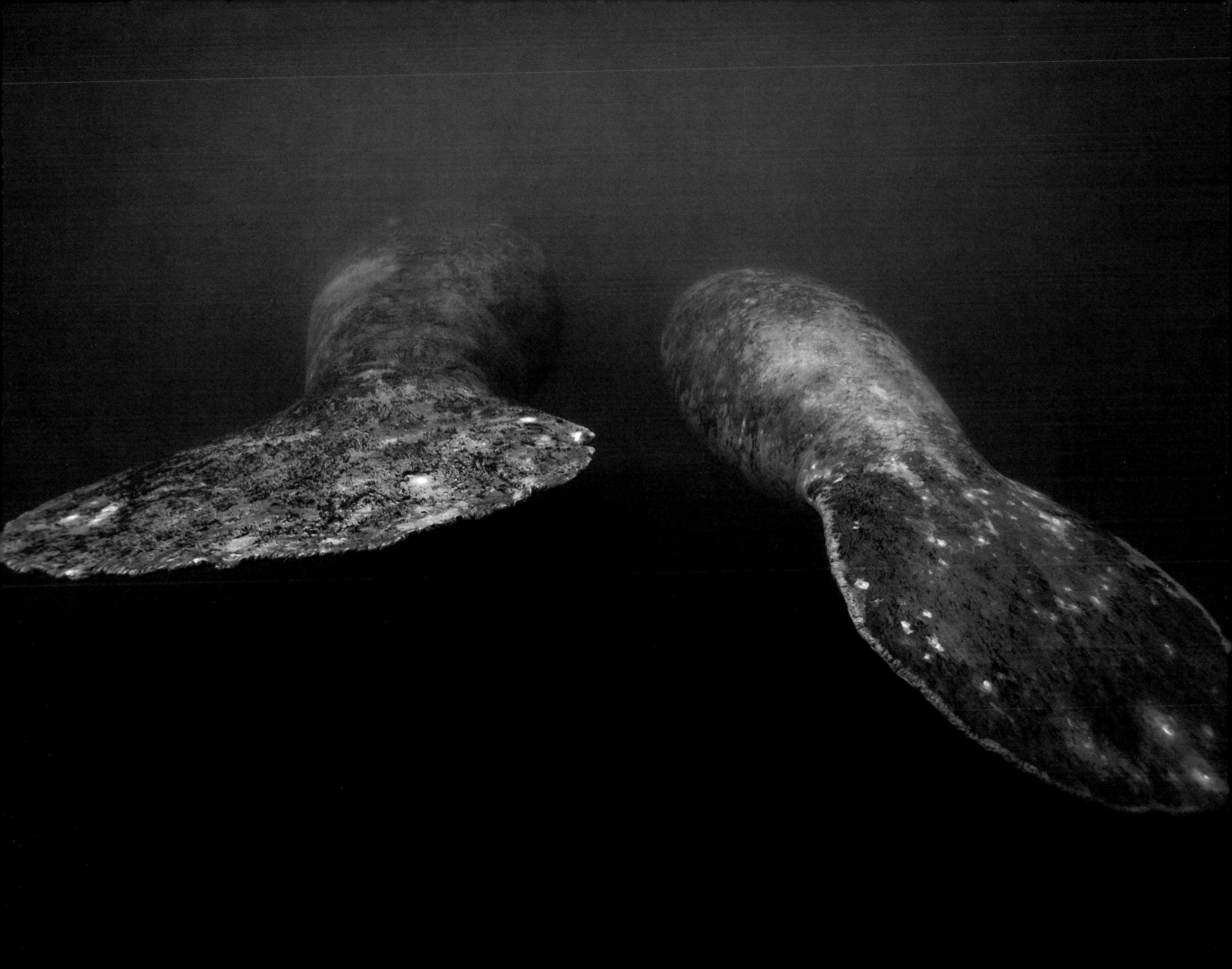

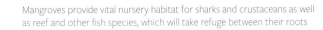
Mangroves provide vital nursery habitat for sharks and crustaceans as well as reef and other fish species, which will take refuge between their roots

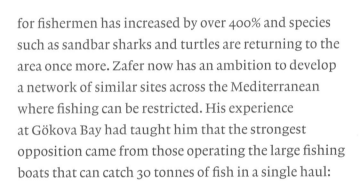

for fishermen has increased by over 400% and species such as sandbar sharks and turtles are returning to the area once more. Zafer now has an ambition to develop a network of similar sites across the Mediterranean where fishing can be restricted. His experience at Gökova Bay had taught him that the strongest opposition came from those operating the large fishing boats that can catch 30 tonnes of fish in a single haul:

*These boats only employ three people, yet that same amount of fish could provide a livelihood for a whole community. Coastal communities need to ensure that economic benefits are shared across society, and not monopolized for short-term economic gain.*

Forty per cent of the world's population live within 100 km of the coast; many of them belong to some of the poorest communities in the world, hugely reliant on what they can catch from the sea. Coral reefs are incredibly productive systems, and sea food in shallow lagoons and reef edges is accessible and easy to catch. Trying to balance the needs of people with measures to protect and sustain marine resources has proven a huge challenge for society. Madagascar and Haiti are

**GUARDIAN Jo Royle** is an ocean-racing and expedition sailor, conservationist and campaigner against the abuse of plastics, for protected areas and for sustainable fishing.

From a young age, I have been inexplicably drawn to the ocean. I was very ill as a child, often in a wheelchair or in a hospital bed and struggling with reading and writing, but I loved to be by the sea and go sailing with my dad. I grew up on the Dart Estuary in England, and spent my holidays and weekends building boats and taking them out on voyages and adventures around the coast. It felt great; this was something that I was naturally good at. On a boat you are a self-contained community, responsible for everything around you and learning from your own mistakes. Everyone has their different goals and interests, but pretty early on I had a clear impression that life was precious, and I didn't want to sit in front of a computer. I wanted to get out there and have adventures.

I was trained by Trevor Vincett, the most natural, confident seaman that I have ever come across. He had been a fisherman and then ran a company delivering yachts around the world. Straight out of university I joined him on my first Atlantic crossing from Dartmouth to Antigua. My aim was simply to spend as much time at sea as I could and take opportunities as they came along. It wasn't easy, people too often saw a young girl and gave me stewardess jobs. I love the independence and multi-faceted nature of life at sea, not just the sailing, but the cooking, sail-making and patching up fibreglass. For a few years, I was a sponsored ocean-racing skipper, but a search for something more adventurous drew me down into the Antarctic, taking expeditions to South Georgia and the Antarctic peninsula.

South Georgia is an island in the South Atlantic and one of the most remote spots on the planet, over a

> *Eight billion tonnes of plastic are littering our seas, circling around the oceans in vast gyres like a toilet that never flushes. No plastic that has ever been produced has yet degraded, and our legacy is likely to remain in the fossil record for millennia to come.*

thousand kilometres from the Falkland Islands. It is a place that I had dreamed of visiting for years and in 2003 I led a small expedition sailing across the South Atlantic from the UK to circumnavigate and explore the island. It is spectacularly rugged, with steep-sided mountains and huge colonies of king and macaroni penguins as well as thousands of albatross and petrels that feed in the highly productive waters. Walking around a headland on the south of the island I came to a small cove that was piled with plastic debris. It was staggering – how could we, as intelligent human beings, allow ourselves to have such a far-reaching impact on a land that doesn't even seem to belong to the human race? This encounter changed my life. I had to understand why pristine oceans were being polluted with plastic and what impact it was having on the ocean.

I was contacted out of the blue by David Rothschild, who asked me to partner him on a project to build a recyclable boat and sail it across the Pacific to raise awareness of the Pacific Garbage Patch. I joined him in California, spending two years trialling and developing the technologies that would be used for the boat. We used 12,000 recycled plastic bottles, a glue made of cashew nuts and sugar and a recyclable resin structure. I skippered a crew of five across the Pacific from San Francisco to Sydney. The voyage was tough – we had no idea whether the structure would hold together and we were severely tested in the tail end of a hurricane as we approached Australia. When I look back, what I am most proud of was the design process rather than the voyage itself –

we really wanted to show how you could develop a product that could be entirely stripped down and used again, as all plastic should be.

I have learned to appreciate the qualities of plastic; but there is a fundamental misunderstanding of our relationship with a durable product that is used for a disposable purpose. Eight billion tonnes of plastic are littering our seas, circling around the oceans in vast gyres like a toilet that never flushes. No plastic that has ever been produced has yet degraded, and our legacy is likely to remain in the fossil record for millennia to come.

My work is so disconnected from the sea now. As things are becoming more and more critical I have a constant unease that what I am doing is not tackling the right issue or talking to the right people or at the right level. The problems keep building and multiplying, but you have to remain optimistic. The only real solution is a big shift in the human relationship with the natural world. I am a believer in humanity. Look at what we have created and overcome. There are many things that are within our grasp, but change is not going to come from governments. It is going to come from businesses and people doing the right thing.

ABOVE Australian sea lions warming themselves in the shallows

FACING The playful and agile Galapagos sea lion will dive down to 200 m to find fish

Endemic to Southern and Western Australia, the Australian sea lion is endangered. Its complex breeding cycle makes population recovery or even maintenance difficult

among the poorest countries on earth, yet here two organizations are proving that conservation can work for people, improving fish catches and demonstrating a remarkable recovery of marine life.

In Haiti, faced with extreme poverty, people have resorted to overfishing, and mangrove forests are being cut down to make charcoal. Marine biologist Dr Jean Wiener returned to his home country refusing to believe that restoring the reefs was a lost cause. He has spent the last decade helping fishermen to see the potential of protected areas and strengthening community associations so that they can look after their own resources and futures. He recognized that the best thing he could do for Haiti's reefs was to try and reduce the impact from fishing, an impact which had left the reefs almost completely lifeless. Jean focused his attention on two densely populated areas of the country which faced many challenges of poverty and had limited options for livelihoods. The recovery of coastal ecosystems will take many years, so he is setting up activities such as beekeeping, algae farming and oyster production, which can provide sustainable incomes in place of fishing. Haiti's first two Marine Protected Areas were created in 2013; they include

Marine iguanas are the only reptiles to feed exclusively on algae. After their foraging excursions in the cold sea, they will bask in the sun to warm up

some areas that will be off-limits to fishing. But Jean is careful never to forget that he is dealing with people who need to be able to catch and grow food to eat every day:

*My promise to the communities is that I will never ask them to give up something without trying to provide something greater in return. As the reefs start to recover and the fish return, it will be critical that we continue to enforce and look after these areas with the help of local communities. Ultimately it is down to the people in these communities to want to nurture this new opportunity.*

In south-west Madagascar, Dr Alasdair Harris and his organization Blue Ventures have spent the last 15 years working with Vezo communities, helping them discover how they can both catch more fish and provide benefits for conservation. Working closely with the village of Andavadoaka in south-west Madagascar, Blue Ventures gained the trust of the community and supported them through a transformation in the way their reefs were managed. A small area of reef was set aside as a temporary fishery closure, where fast-growing species such as octopus could propagate

quickly in size and number. Following the closure period, fishermen started to see significant increases in their catches. Neighbouring communities wanted to replicate the approach and, with 25 villages in the region, a large managed area called 'Velondriake' was set up, covering 800 km² of coastal habitats. Within this area, some zones may be permanently closed to fishing, while others may be opened seasonally; but ultimately these communities will witness the economic benefits of their actions. This approach has given rise to a new movement of locally led marine conservation in Madagascar – areas of coast and ocean within which communities set aside diverse management interventions. Over the last decade, 117 such areas have been created around Madagascar alone; and more around the Indian Ocean are being set up. Alasdair is proving that small organizations working closely with communities can deliver lasting results:

*We have helped communities discover for themselves what is possible, how some simple steps towards fisheries management and strong community cohesion can quickly provide greater fish catches as well as benefits for conservation.*

# WORDS FROM THE EXPERTS

*In a logical, uncomplicated, unselfish world it would be easy to see that we need to stop damaging nature, and in turn, harming people*—Mark Spalding

**Jean Wiener** started the Foundation for the Protection of Marine Biodiversity in Haiti in 1992 to protect and restore the marine wildlife there. He has provided environmental education and alternative livelihoods for fishing communities, and worked with them and the government on legislation to establish eight Marine Protected Areas:

*I am a trained marine biologist, but most of my life has been focused on helping people to meet their basic needs so that they can then take care of reefs, mangroves and fisheries. There is nowhere in the world that you will meet a hungry conservationist – people know that what they are doing is not sustainable, but they have no choice when it comes to finding food to eat. I recognized that the best thing we could do for Haiti's reefs was to reduce the impact from fishing, which had left them almost completely lifeless. For the last decade our role has shifted towards helping fishermen to see the potential of protected areas by providing education, strengthening community associations, and talking about how we might protect our resources and futures. I am proud of what has been achieved in the last 25 years; and I like to believe that we will be able to restore a few perfect places that my kids and grandkids can enjoy, as I did when I was a boy. This is my dream. Maybe it is naïve. You could say I was the fool that didn't realize it was impossible, so he did it.*

**Zafer Kizilkaya** set up a network of six marine reserves in Gökova Bay in Turkey. These have become one of the Mediterranean's greatest success stories, with benefits for biodiversity and local fishing communities:

*Change needs to come from civil society. We are a small organization with a goal to help communities and humanity, rather than look for profit or material gain. To make a positive change you need to work directly with fishermen and support the wider health and education needs of the community; then you can start to talk about conservation. In my lifetime, I have seen huge changes, but I have also shown what is possible when you are single-minded and persistent. There is a huge sense of momentum and optimism for how this model can be replicated across the Mediterranean. Biodiversity is something that touches my heart – the idea of unique species that have evolved over millions of years and are here now for us to see is an amazing concept. For me this is reason enough to do whatever we can to protect them.*

**Alasdair Harris** is the Executive Director of Blue Ventures, an organization that helps local communities in Madagascar and beyond to catch more fish and at the same time provide benefits for conservation:

*Our focus on working closely alongside communities and having a team with an entrepreneurial culture that is ready to try new ideas and take risks has been an important part of our success. The necessity of understanding people and market forces applies just as much in the world of conservation as it does in business. Solving the combined challenge of overfishing and climate change is an urgent issue for the world, and we are proving that small, flexible, 'guerrilla' organizations working closely with communities can deliver lasting impacts. Time is running out to protect marine biodiversity and we have to be single-minded in our mission to do better; the conservation sector has to do more than simply document the collapse of our ecosystems. There is an overwhelming need for urgent action to address the immense challenges that our oceans are now facing. It is this sense of urgency, which can be both compelling and often also frightening, that has always been my overriding motivation.*

**David Obura** is a marine scientist specializing in climate change and coral reefs. He is a Director of CORDIO (Coastal Oceans Research and Development – Indian Ocean), an organization that provides research and support for communities and governments to help them understand and prepare for future changes:

*The key question is how can we communicate our findings so that people understand the links between their actions and their impact on the world. I have been fortunate enough to work in the Phoenix Islands in Kiribati, Micronesia, where millennia of ocean-based culture have instilled people with huge pride in the quality of the oceans and reefs, and strong commitment to protect them. By contrast, I realized that most African traditional culture is land-based, and population density was historically so low that there was never any issue of resources being limited. The consequence is that there is very little appreciation or understanding of the limitations of marine systems, and experiences of sustainable ocean resource use are not well integrated within our cultures. Our modern governments, too, are led by terrestrially minded people. In the 21st century there is an urgent desire for more wealth in East Africa, and governments are increasingly looking to the sea as the next frontier. My fear is that there will be a huge increase in exploitation, but with insufficient forethought about how we can properly manage our resources.*

**Mark Spalding** is a Senior Scientist at The Nature Conservancy, Honorary Research Fellow at the University of Cambridge and Chief Science Adviser to the Government of the British Indian Ocean Territory. He has mapped the condition, conservation and value of reefs and mangroves on a global scale:

*In a logical, uncomplicated, unselfish world it would be easy to see that we need to stop damaging nature and, in turn, harming people. I used to believe that, with enough information, people would come to see the world as I see it and stop damaging the reefs and oceans on which we all depend. Now I recognize that changing minds is best done through a myriad of different approaches. One is simply to help get people into nature – as the world becomes more urbanized there is less and less recognition of the existence and importance of nature in our lives. To remain credible, scientists must be clinically honest about what they report, but in marine science there are rarely simple and uncomplicated truths. This can make it difficult to pick out the signal from the background noise, leading scientists to drown urgent and compelling messages to society in scientific caveats.*

**Isabelle Côté** is a Professor in Marine Ecology at Simon Fraser University, British Columbia, where she specializes in fish behaviour. She has spent a decade studying cleanerfish on reefs across the world and more recently has focused her attention on the impacts of invasive lionfish in the Caribbean:

*My favourite thing to do, bar none, is watching fish underwater. The first time I went snorkelling, I couldn't help but wonder why fish were doing what they were doing. I have now spent so much time watching fish that I can immediately interpret a lot of their behaviour – I can see the courtship, the defence of territory, the squaring up to opponents and stalking prey. The redlip blenny is my favourite fish in the whole world. I spent eight months just watching and recording the behaviour of a small group of blennies on a reef in Barbados. I knew all these fish – which mates they liked, which were the good dads and which damselfish troubled them. On a reef, there is so much going on around you. Even when snorkelling out to the site just before dawn I could see the regular changeover between 'night fish' and 'day fish'; I got to know which patch of reef belonged to which fish.*

**Peter Sale** is an expert on corals and reef fish, having worked in Hawaii, Australia, the Caribbean and the Middle East. He is the author of *Our Dying Planet*, an ecologist's view on humans and their place in the world:

*There are still places on the Great Barrier Reef that are in good shape, but when I dive there I find that I have to keep my mouth shut, rather than ruin the enthusiasm of those who are experiencing what is for them a new, and wonderfully rich environment, but to me is just a ghost of what I once knew. Naturalists may try hard to appear dispassionate and objective, but they are prone to become enraptured by their subjects. I find that I can be talking about coral reefs, and suddenly discover tears in my eyes. In a way, I am proud to know that this emotional connection runs so deep, but it is painful when I consider that the place I love best has only got worse in my lifetime. I get depressed from time to time by silly things; by the stupidity and selfishness of politicians and the fact that environmental news is still second-class, just a filler at the end of a broadcast; but I am also inspired by people who stand up so bravely and strongly to protect and defend the places that are important to them. I do still have faith that we will somehow beat the odds and find a way to solve these most intractable and multi-headed of human challenges.*

**J. E. N 'Charlie' Veron** is a coral taxonomist, ecologist and the former Chief Scientist at the Australian Institute of Marine Science. He has described over a third of the world's coral species and written the definitive publications of the world's corals:

*My career could have been very different; I had completed my PhD on dragonflies and had been offered a great job to study locusts in Canada, but I had also applied for a job as a research scientist on the Great Barrier Reef with James Cook University. At the time there were growing threats to the Great Barrier Reef from companies that wanted to mine and extract oil, and this was something that I felt strongly about. To my astonishment I was offered the job and started my new career as the Great Barrier Reef's first research scientist, without ever having attended a single lecture on marine biology. On the day I started, the Head of Department pointed out towards the reef and told me to 'go out there and just do something', and this was the only job description I was ever given. I decided to try and map the coral community types and work out the dominant species, but before long I discovered that the formal species descriptions were a labyrinth of errors. One of the requirements for my new job (and possibly the reason why no-one else applied) was that I had to dive, and this was clearly not something that any other taxonomist had done before me. Corals vary their growth form and skeleton according to the environment where they grow, so the same species can look completely different in a colony in the shallow reef crest and one in the deeper water of the reef slope. I knew I was going to have to start from scratch and unpick the mistakes of dozens of historical taxonomists who had given multiple names to the same species. My theories caused quite a lot of upset among scientists, outraged that a novice was dabbling in taxonomy.*

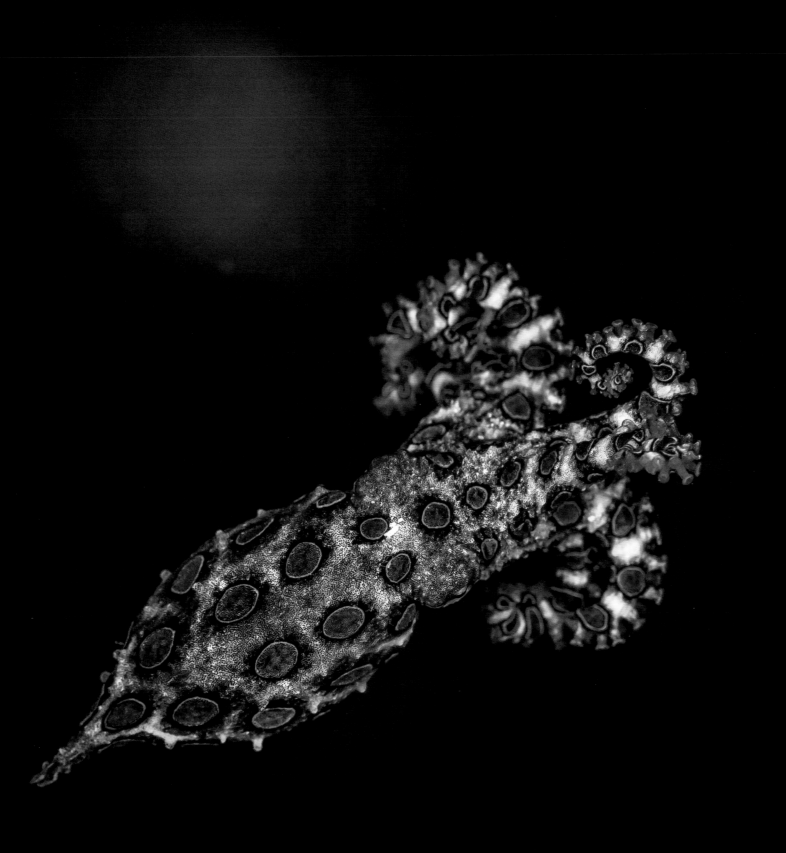

# HIDDEN OCEAN

MUCH OF THE LIFE in our oceans remains unseen, blending into the background and hidden within the structure of our reefs or lost among countless expanses of the deep ocean. Our eyes and our attention are inevitably drawn to the large and beautiful animals, but, as we have sometimes discovered to our cost, the very small often have an importance in the ocean ecosystem than is greater than we would have expected. The huge variety and forms of life in our ocean still remain unknown and uncounted, and, as scientists acknowledge, there is a vast amount of ocean unexplored and animals yet to be seen or described. Counterbalancing a photographer's eye for the beautiful and spectacular, in this book we provide a fleeting spotlight for some of those animals that remain hidden – small, camouflaged or lying deep on the ocean floor.

New Zealander Dr David Pawson has always had an interest in life in the oceans that is out of reach, but the opportunity to explore the deep ocean is frustratingly fleeting: 'We are constantly having to make decisions on what to collect or photograph, knowing that we may never see that species again.' During his 50 years working with the Smithsonian Museum in Washington, he has discovered over 200 echinoderms, a group of species encompassing starfish, sea urchins and sea cucumbers. David has concentrated much of his research in the deep ocean, working from submersibles hundreds of metres beneath the surface. Across the vast areas of permanently dark sea bed, 90% of all animal weight is made up by ordinary looking sea cucumbers playing an extraordinary role in the deep ocean. As they scavenge for food, they engorge themselves with mud and, in the process of oxygenating the sediment as it passes through their intestines, make the seabird habitable for other deep-sea animals.

In shallow water rocky habitats, some sea urchins cover themselves with bits of shell or pebbles. It often seems that these animals are trying to disguise themselves, and indeed some are, but mostly they do this to reduce damage from the sun's ultra-violet light. Other species gather pieces of seaweed as their personal larder so that they can roll a piece down towards their mouth whenever they need to eat. David and his team have found that there are a few species living in the deep sea that also cover themselves. [CONTD PAGE 90]

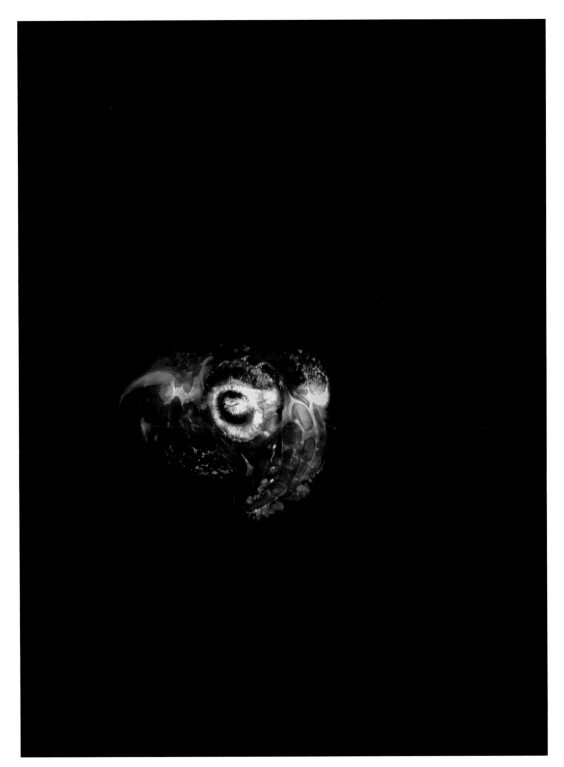

ABOVE Bobtail squid have a symbiotic relationship with bioluminescent bacteria that match the light radiating from above, silhouetting the squid when viewed from below

min. size

PREVIOUS The pygmy seahorse is a tiny (less then 2 cm), extremely well-camouflaged animal living in gorgonian corals. Its body matches the colour and texture of the coral

The cryptic crinoid shrimp is perfectly camouflaged against its crinoid host

max. size

Translucent Sarasvati anemone shrimp

 max. size

The tiny orang-utan crab is part of the decorator crab family,
found predominantly on bubble coral

 max. size

The Denise pygmy seahorse stays in the same coral for its entire life

 max. size

Sarasvati anemone shrimp grow no longer than 2.5 cm

max. size

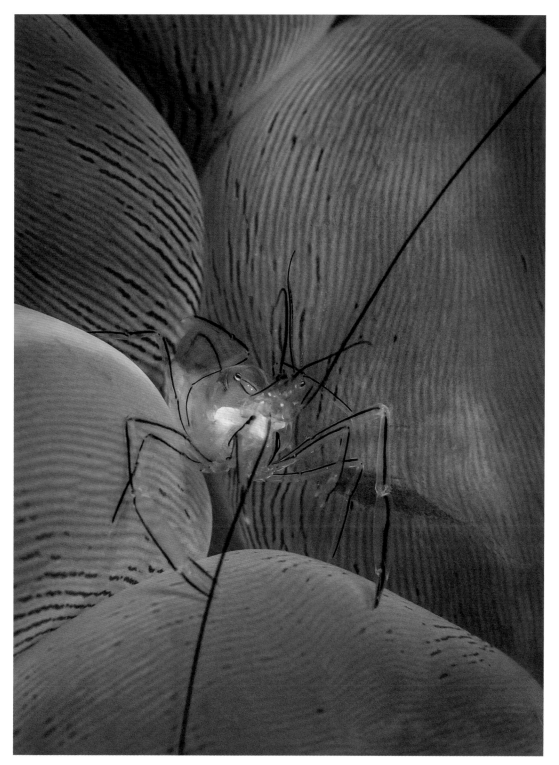

The bubble coral shrimp charms prospective customers to its cleaning station
by waving its long antennae

max. size

An Anker's whip coral shrimp mimics the texture of the whip corals
on which it lives

max. size

We still have no idea why they would do this when there is no sunlight, no need for camouflage, and the topknot of debris that these animals carry does not consist of any food. Urchins play a significant role in maintaining the balance in their ecosystem. As herbivores, they garden their way through reefs feeding on tiny tufts of algae that grow on top of the living corals. Without the urchins grazing the young plants, the algae gradually smother and weaken the corals, making them more susceptible to events such as hurricanes. This became particularly obvious in the Caribbean Sea, where an urchin species named *Diadema* almost died out following a widespread viral infection. These urchins are now gradually recovering and returning to many parts of the Caribbean and, alongside them, the corals have started to regrow.

Competition for food, space and creating offspring within the oceans is constant, and the balance can be upset through natural or human causes. In enough numbers, even a small species can have huge impact. Without predators, urchin populations can overgraze coastal habitats to the point of them becoming barren and devoid of life. Likewise, David has witnessed large swarms of crown-of-thorns starfish eating their way through coral and quickly devastating large areas of reef. Huge efforts and large amounts of money have gone into trying to cull them, using volunteers armed with poison syringes, but over the years it now appears that these sea stars have an effect similar to forest fires on land – they are devastating for a short period, but they never kill off 100% of the corals. Over time, corals can come back, and the reef can be healthier and more diverse.

Marta Pola is a Professor at the Universidad Autónoma of Madrid in Spain and has been enraptured with nudibranchs since she first saw one through a microscope as an undergraduate:

*Their colours and shapes are so amazing, but there is much more to them than just their beauty. They have an amazing capacity to defend themselves with tiny spines or to fight back with toxic chemicals if they are threatened.*

Nudibranch means 'naked gills', and they are among a group of molluscs that have lost their shell, relying on camouflage or natural toxins to defend themselves. They can use chemicals gathered from their prey, storing them up on the sides of their body so that their flesh becomes toxic to eat. Marta has been studying the diet of nudibranchs and is particularly fascinated by their teeth. Some nudibranchs feed on each other or are cannibalistic among their own species. In this contest, size matters – if one is bigger than the other then the smaller one is eaten, but if they are the same size, then mating is a much more likely outcome. Marta has dived all over the world and described over 70 new species. Many are only a few millimetres in length, so a search across the seabed can be painstakingly slow, although some species can grow as long as your arm. They can also surprise her: 'once we were resting on an island off Mozambique waiting for the next dive when suddenly, after a wave left the shore, the sand turned blue with the colour of thousands of blue dragons.' Naming, studying and understanding the biodiversity of marine life is critically important to Marta, because it indicates that there is still so much more for us to know in this world that is unravelling around us, 'if incredibly beautiful animals such as nudibranchs are still unknown, what can we expect for those species that do not catch our eye?' [CONTD PAGE 97]

A tiny xeno crab on whip coral. The name comes from the Greek 'xenos', meaning strange: little is known about this species

max. size

A mushroom coral ghost shrimp

max. size

Common ghost goby on coral

A goby has made a home on the coral, neighbouring a Christmas-tree worm

LEFT The porcelain anemone crab regularly cohabits with clownfish, which seem to tolerate its presence as long as it does not lay eggs

RIGHT To ensure the survival of their young, male yellowhead jawfish will protect newly laid eggs in their mouths until they hatch

Kike Ballesteros is a field naturalist based at the Centre d'Estudis Avançats de Blanes in Spain. While he specializes in seagrass and seaweed ecology, he has a deep understanding of marine invertebrates and has witnessed the gradual changes that have taken place in the Mediterranean over the last 50 years. Kike has been able to identify key invertebrate species, including urchins, as natural indicators of the health of coastal ecosystems. These species are particularly vulnerable to human threats and are often the first to disappear. Canaries of the sea, their disappearance warns marine biologists that particular attention and protection are needed in these habitats. He reminds us that it is through patient and careful observation that we are able to develop a deep understanding of what is occurring in our oceans: 'even after a whole life dedicated to the study of the oceans I always notice new things in almost every dive.'

Scientists specializing in seahorses also spend a large proportion of their time crawling around searching for their subjects. British naturalist Richard Smith has spent hundreds of hours underwater studying the pygmy seahorse, a group that remained unnoticed and undescribed until 1969. [CONTD PAGE 103]

There are over 833 known species of blenny across the world's oceans

A Klausewitz's blenny perched in a coral crevice

Brown-banded pipefish are related to seahorses and sea dragons.
A male and female will remain together for life

Degrave's cleaner shrimp has only recently been described as a new species

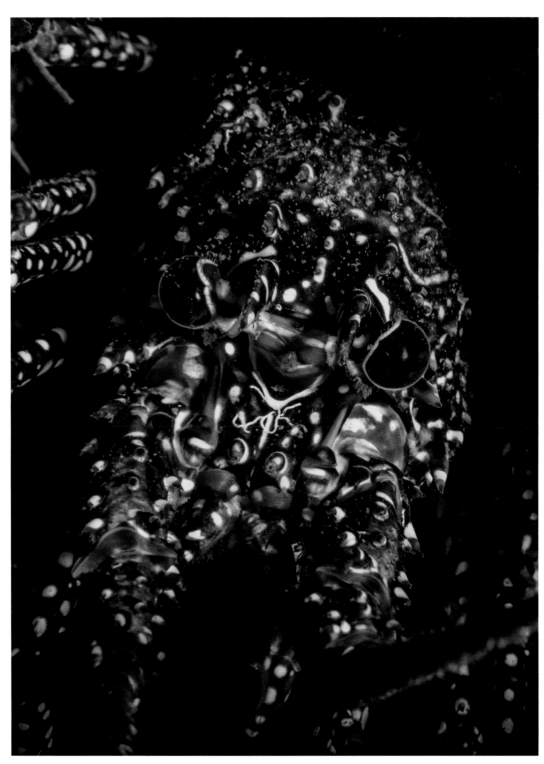

Spiny lobsters are one of the few invertebrate species that can
use the earth's magnetic field for navigation

Competing for space on the reef

Ghost pipefish, up to 12 cm long, vary in colour or, as in this case, may be transparent.
They float motionless with their mouths down and are very difficult to spot

The red night shrimp uses its large eyes to hunt in the darkness at depth

The fragile Degrave's cleaner shrimp

Since then seven species have been found living around the Great Barrier Reef, Indonesia, New Caledonia, Papua New Guinea and the Philippines. Some species spend their lives on specific gorgonian corals, others are known from a single bay in Indonesia. Richard's love for the small and hidden animals in the sea developed on one of his first research trips, and he is determined to change the perception that small animals are just a side-show. During his expeditions to Indonesia and the Philippines, he encourages the divers he leads to observe small areas of coral carefully and wait for the creatures behind the camouflage to be revealed.

Seahorses are fantastically well camouflaged fish, developing spines and nodules that perfectly match their favoured sponge, coral or seagrass home. Like the octopus and cuttlefish, they use chromatophore cells in their body to change colour so that they blend in with their surroundings to avoid predators or disguise themselves when they are hunting throughout the day. Inching themselves towards small shrimps and larvae until they are within striking range, they then inhale their prey in an instant. Seahorses form long-lasting partnerships, renewed each day by a slow-motion courtship dance. For a few days before mating the pair perform a pre-dawn ritual dance, ensuring they are both ready to reproduce. Unique and spectacular in the animal kingdom is the passing of the eggs from the female to the male's protective brood pouch, where they are fertilized and developed before hatching. The male ejects perfectly formed miniature seahorses in bursts from his pouch, and from here on they are on their own. Seahorses will mate many times through the season in their pairs. However, Richard Smith has witnessed females mating with two different males and then observed the males trying to strangle each other. So it seems that their lives are not without some aggravation.

The seahorse has been strongly embedded in our culture; it has remained a source of intrigue and fascination through the centuries. Often portrayed in Greek and Roman myths pulling the chariot of Poseidon or Neptune, its scientific name *hippocampus* means 'horse monster'. An animal with the head of a horse, a tail that can wrap tightly around objects like a monkey and a male pouch that provides a nursery for growing embryos is an almost incredible combination of exotic traits. Fragile and vulnerable to environmental change, they rely on the delicate fronds and branches of sponges, gorgonians and seagrasses to provide something that they can curl their tails around. Seahorses are poor swimmers, so they rarely range more than a few metres from their chosen home, using a small, fluttering dorsal fin to propel them upright through the water. If their habitats are destroyed, they are immediately exposed to predators and, unable to swim against currents, are swept away from their homes.

Dr Sarah Foster has spent her entire career at Project Seahorse, focusing her efforts on helping governments find ways to stop destructive fishing techniques that are having a devastating impact on seahorses and countless other species. Spending a year knee-deep in bycatch, the so-called unwanted 'trash' of biodiversity left over from shrimp trawlers in the Gulf of California, Mexico, she has seen first-hand the destructive power of trawling. Trawler boats drag large fishing nets through the water, often destroying in the process delicate sponges, sea-fans and other living structures on the seabed that are critical for providing a camouflaged and protective home for much marine life.

Coleman or fire urchin shrimp are normally found in pairs. Here they clear a place
to live in the toxic fire urchin, where they will feed on parasites, algae and plankton

Look carefully and you may spot a bubble coral shrimp tucked away between the polyps

Fishing for smaller species such as shrimp requires using nets with smaller gaps (mesh). The smaller the mesh, the less selective the catch. Countless unwanted species may be accidentally caught – referred to as bycatch. Some may be discarded back in the sea or turned into food pellets on shore for aquaculture and agriculture, feeding fish and pigs. As seahorses are swept up, they are picked out from mounds of marine life dumped on deck before being dried and exported. An estimated 15–20 million seahorses are traded across south-east Asia every year. Even if demand completely evaporated, that number will still be killed every year, which is why seahorses have been included on the Convention on the International Trade in Endangered Species of Wild Fauna and Flora (CITES) since 2002. This global agreement has opened doors to organizations such as Project Seahorse, enabling Sarah to have conversations with countries about what they are doing to reduce the impact of trawling, and to help governments develop a fishing industry that does not have such catastrophic human and environmental costs. [CONTD PAGE 114]

**GUARDIAN Frank Pope** is an author and conservationist. He is Chief Executive of the research and conservation organization 'Save the Elephants' and former Ocean Correspondent for *The Times*.

My father is a classicist who took the family on long trips to various ruins across Italy and Greece, which was a pretty effective inoculation against my following in his footsteps. But it did mean that one day, aged 16, I was sitting on a small boat off the Italian coast staring down through 55 metres of clear blue water watching archaeologists excavate an Etruscan shipwreck off the Island of Giglio (more recently famous for the wreck of the *Costa Concordia*). It was like an underwater crime scene, divided up by yellow and black grids busy with divers working away with measuring tapes, cameras and bubbling air-powered excavators.

At the time all I wanted was adventure, and marine archaeology was full of it – the drama of a sunken shipwreck with the intrigue of science and the deep allure of the ocean. There was urgency, too. Developments in fishing technology meant that trawlers were scraping ever deeper and more remote parts of the seabed and wrecks that had lain untouched for millennia were being exposed and torn to pieces. We were working on ships that had been hidden for hundreds of years to reveal the history of the sailors, their technology, and their time. But I was becoming aware that something else was also being lost at sea, something even more precious. At the start of a series of surveys in Mozambique we would sit down for

dinner with tables overflowing with lobsters and people would fight over the precious potatoes; a few years later it was all potatoes and people fighting over a couple of small lobsters. Those same changes that I was seeing on the table, I was also noticing underwater – the numbers and variety of fish were declining and there were no more octopus hiding within the timbers of the ship.

The turning point for me was a big project to recover a cargo of ceramics from a trading vessel that sank off the coast of Vietnam in the 15th century. It was a deep wreck that required expensive saturation diving equipment to work on, and the area was notorious for sudden typhoons, but the prize was a forgotten golden age in Vietnam's history. To finance the work the archaeological director had made a Faustian pact with a businessman; the deal

> *… all I wanted was adventure, and marine archaeology was full of it – the drama of a sunken shipwreck with the intrigue of science and the deep allure of the ocean.*

went wrong, and they tore each other's ambitions to pieces amid a maelstrom of corruption and back-stabbing.

I turned to writing, initially telling the story of the Vietnam wreck and subsequently obtaining a job at *The Times* as the world's first Ocean Correspondent. My pitch to the editor was to ask how they could call themselves a global newspaper when they did not have someone reporting on 73% of the planet. I saw the ocean as a

dramatic frontier that was going to generate a lot of stories – humankind had outgrown the continents and with the aid of new technologies was increasingly looking to the sea for food, energy, and adventure. As a journalist you are always looking for the untold tales. We have been telling stories about the sea for thousands of years – fables of sea monsters, shipwrecks and storms. If you can't get people interested in these stories, then I don't think you have much hope. The bigger challenge is how to forge a link between the sea and the world's increasingly urban populations. My position gave me incredible access to the most fascinating people in marine science, exploration, and geopolitics. They too were excited that someone on the inside of the media was speaking up for the sea and for a few years I felt like I was at the heart of a lot of interest around the ocean.

Things changed again when I met my wife Saba Douglas-Hamilton and she introduced me to elephants. Now my days are spent trying to reveal the world of these land-whales and secure them a future. Scientists need producers to provide the structure within which they can work, and they need help to communicate their stories and this is what I've become. After witnessing the difficulties faced by scientists studying marine mammals, I find that studying elephants allows an amazingly deep insight into the complexity of their consciousness, and of their society.

The sea continues to intrigue and fascinate me, and I'm still drawn to it. One fix is to go snorkelling with my family along the coast of Kenya – I see my children

open up like flowers in the same way they do when we
are camping in the bush, their eyes wide with excitement
behind their facemasks as they see the kaleidoscope of
fish around a coral head. Part of me mourns, though. The
thriving coral reefs I knew when I was younger are now
rare, and more are disappearing. If we're not careful our
children won't even know what has been lost. Snorkelling
in dazzling blue and clear waters in Turkey recently I
could see no sign of life – there was not a fish or plant in
sight, and yet still there was a stark, ascetic beauty to the
scene. I wonder if the Amazon turned into Death Valley,
would our minds salvage a sense of rugged charm?

My hopes and fears for the future revolve around
humans. The people we are working with in Northern
Kenya have a culture that has co-evolved with the wide
array of large and often dangerous mammals that they've
lived alongside for millennia. But change is coming fast
there, as with the rest of the planet. The challenge is
how we can forge a link between the wild – especially
that mysterious 73% covered by water – and the world's
increasingly urban and dissociated human population.
For all of our technological prowess our brains still pulse
with competition, greed and tribalism. The question is
whether humans can evolve and adapt fast enough to
retain enough of the living planet to sustain us, and build
more co-operative societies that take into account all life,
not just human life. It will take a seismic shift. It's a scary
thought, but inspiring too.

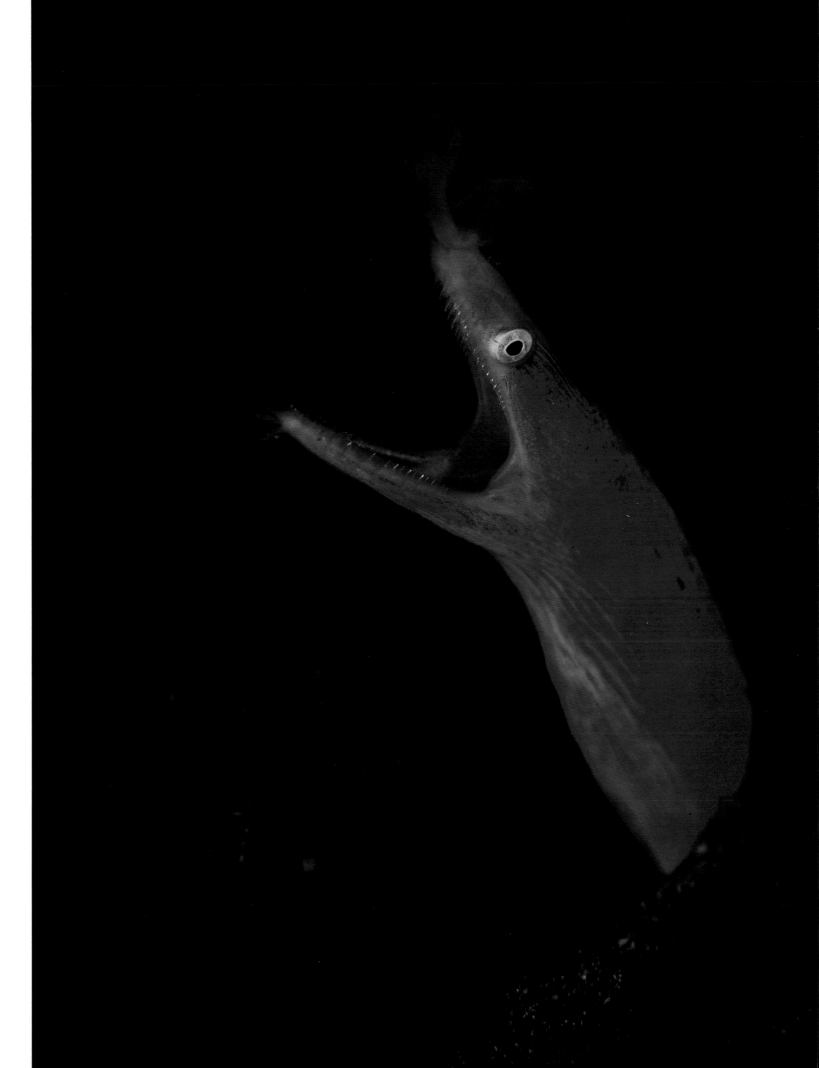

This fish is actually perched on the rock – it is one of several species that lack a swim bladder

Mantis shrimp have more complex eyesight than any other species, seeing ultraviolet and polarized light, too

One of the most valuable species in traditional Chinese medicine,
the common seahorse is threatened by extinction

The bottom-dwelling lizard fish has a mouth full of sharp teeth,
even on the tongue

The Barbigant's pygmy seahorse is no longer than a human fingernail

It takes careful observation to spot pygmy seahorses among the soft coral

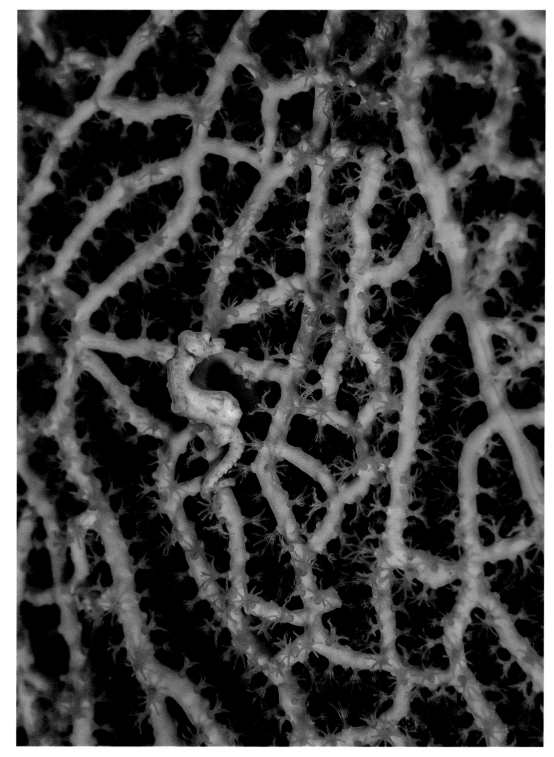

Like all the seahorses, the male Denise pygmy seahorse carries and cares
for the eggs before and after they are fertilized

Pygmy seahorses are the only species to have a single gill opening
on the back of their head

Weedy seadragons are one of the most ornately camouflaged sea creatures, resembling the seaweed in which they live. Larger than any seahorse species, they can measure up to 45 cm in length

Australian seahorse biologist David Harasti has spent thousands of hours in the water, determined to identify every species, no matter how small or indistinct. His first seahorse encounter was with the White's seahorse, one of only two species of seahorse in the world that is officially listed as endangered. The species was thought to be at risk because it is found in a few estuaries along the coastline of New South Wales in Australia, but no one really knew how the population was faring. David spent the next four years carefully monitoring the populations, ultimately concluding that numbers were declining and highly vulnerable to human impact. As the coastline was being developed, their natural habitat was disappearing. It is rare to have a marine species where there is something you can physically do to help it recover, but the principle of 'if you build it, they will come' does work perfectly for seahorses. They are a species that like to gather together, so one pioneer will ultimately attract other settlers until you have a whole colony. In the Port Stephens Great Lakes Marine Park, David tried sticking some old tree branches in the sand around the estuary, and within a few days many of them were occupied by seahorses. [CONTD PAGE 122]

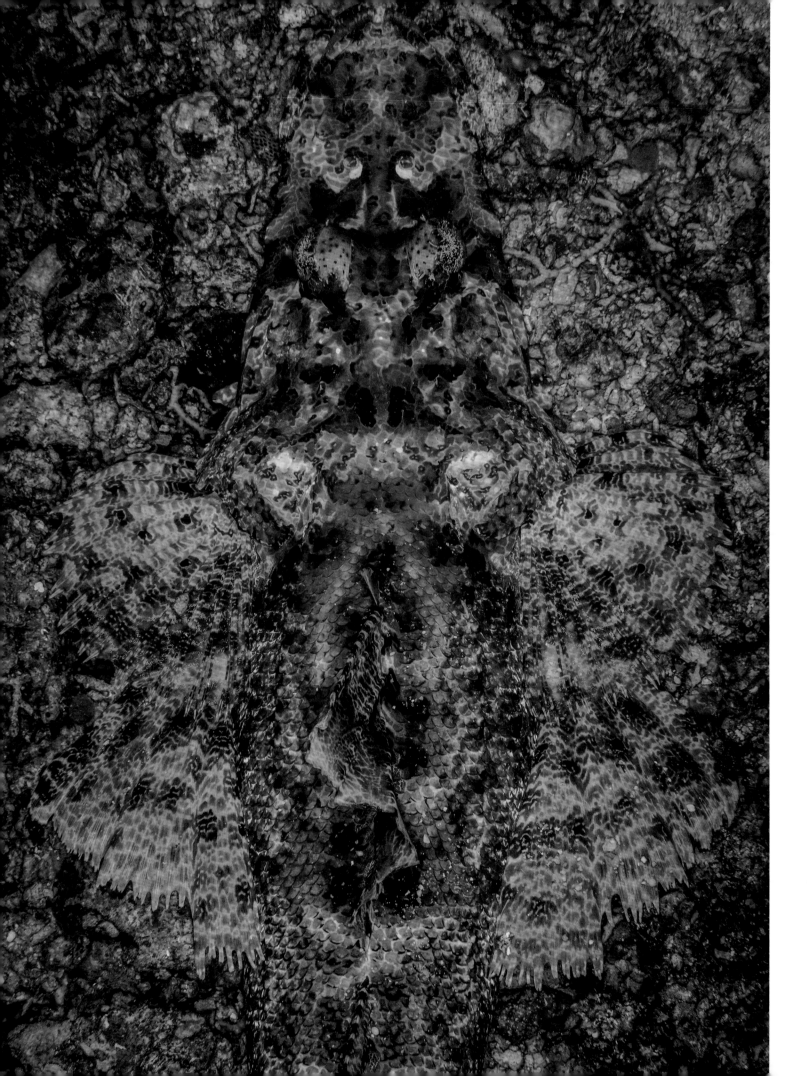

**GUARDIAN** **Doug Woodring** is the co-founder of Ocean Recovery Alliance, a non-profit organization dedicated to help corporations and society solve the problem of plastic pollution in our oceans.

I was brought up in California and spent a great deal of time outdoors, camping and swimming. After studying economics, my first job was in Japan, where I was a trader for one of the world's biggest seafood companies. We would forward sell six months in advance, and then have to find the stocks somewhere to make good on the contract. As fish stocks dwindled we were looking further and further afield for smaller and smaller pockets of fish. What made me mad was not just the degree of illegal fishing; but the scale of legal fishing. I have spent enough time working in business and finance to recognize that the free market economy fails our natural resources, and governments are too intertwined to act with enough authority.

I first heard about this island of garbage in 2008, a place in the Pacific where currents had corralled and concentrated a vast expanse of floating plastic. Why was no one talking about it? More to the point why was no one doing anything about it? Together with Mary Crowley, a sailor, and George Orbelian, a surfer, we raised the money for one of the first expeditions to properly research the extent of the plastic. In that first research trip for what

had become known as Project Kaisei, scientists were shocked to discover plastic in every single one of over 100 water samples taken along a 1,700 mile track. We know that 80% of this plastic comes from land, but much of the debris sinks, so we have little idea of the scale of impact on life in the deep ocean.

Shortly afterwards I founded Ocean Recovery Alliance, an organization that has allowed me to focus efforts on removing plastic pollution in our sea – surely one of the most intractable issues of our times. We focus on bringing the right people together to solve the problem and raising awareness in parts of the world that have never considered plastic pollution to be their priority or even to be of interest. We can achieve all that we've done because my background allows me to be the conductor and interlocutor between sports, business, governments and environmental organizations. This broad collaboration across sectors of society is necessary when it comes to solving a problem of this scale and complexity.

The developing world doesn't have the resources to cope with the scale of this problem, and governments don't seem to have the capacity or courage to step in. When economies are just trying to survive, when people are greedy, and when there is corruption, the barriers become too great. In a perfect world, an enlightened leader would put in place the laws and regulations – yet in the real world, there are too many holes in the system and too many vested interests. It is not my role to be judgmental and to criticize companies for not doing more; our approach has to be about getting the right organizations together and helping to find the right economic incentives and design solutions. Hopefully the companies will realize their responsibility to the communities they serve, that they shouldn't be making things worse from the after-life of their products.

Companies need to focus on the potential of their products to create positive value for the environment and communities rather than seeing them simply as a resource or a market. Many companies are already

> We know that 80% of this plastic comes from land, but much of the debris sinks, so we have little idea of the scale of impact on life in the deep ocean.

highly engaged in how they can reduce waste, and I hope that this will ultimately create a tipping point in which it becomes accepted practice to recover most of the waste from materials they sell. Our Plasticity Forums are now taking place around the world to harness new ways to reduce waste created from our growing global consumption patterns. The Plastic Disclosure Project is one way that we are encouraging companies to think about their plastic footprint and to focus on how they can use the raw material more efficiently or to reduce waste through improved product design.

The free market economy is structured in a way that ignores the impact of business on the environment and society. Companies look for the quickest, cheapest path to manufacture and sell a product. They never factor in the cost of their impact on air, water or society. If our environment is going to continue to provide for us into the future, then we need to start pricing in these impacts.

Most of our manufacturing and recycling systems are not designed for the complexities of plastic. It is immoral to export waste to the developing world when they don't have the technology to properly cope with it. We need a new plastic economy where there are capable communities, municipalities and facilities to deal with waste products all over the world. People are receptive and aware, but they don't always know what they should do. Our Global Alert Platform System is a way for people to identify and share problems of trash across coastlines and river systems anywhere in the world.

I get excited about trying to solve problems on a grand scale, but it is the little things that frustrate me most. We are being blinded by convenience and herded into choices for things that we don't need – wrappings, straws, stirrers and products that are disposable, yet made from highly durable material.

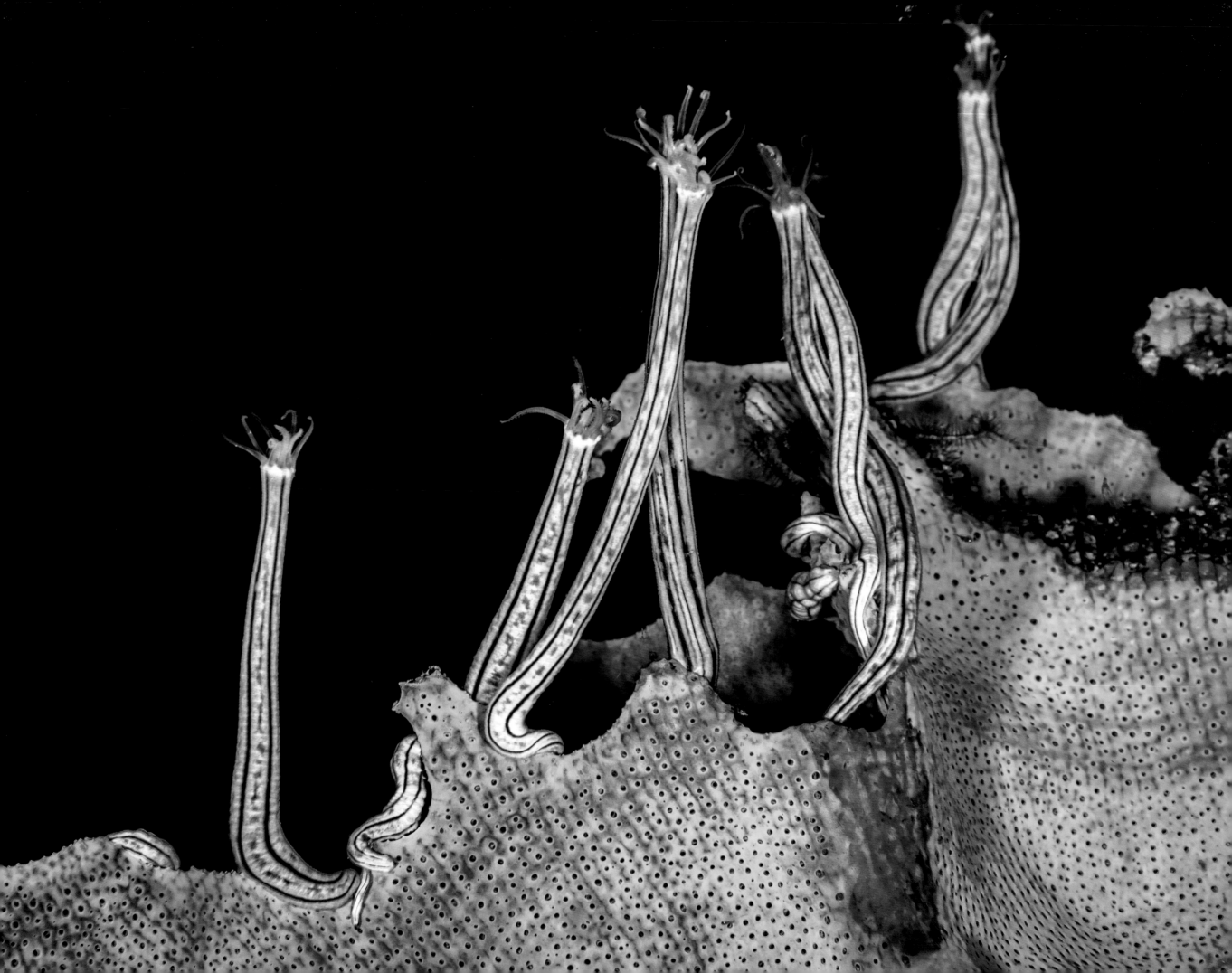

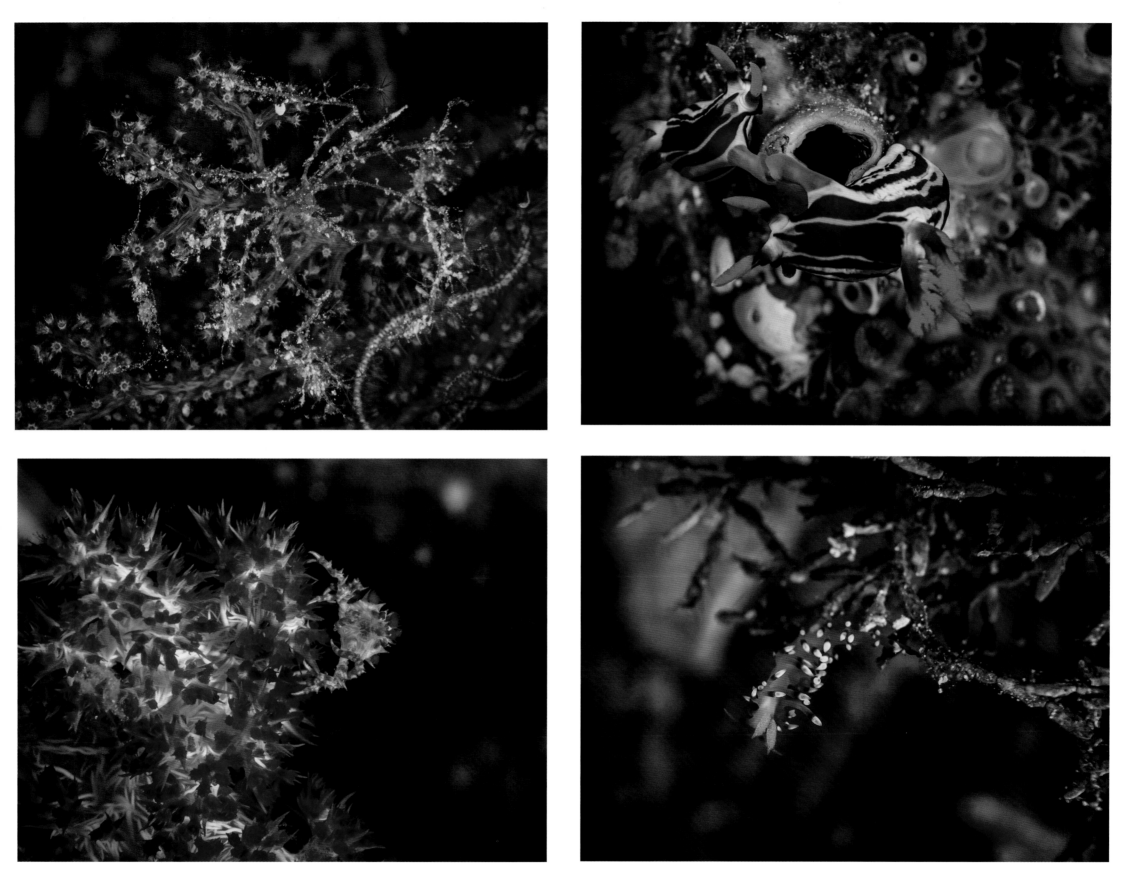

FACING Lambert's worm sea cucumbers live in groups on sponges, sifting food from the water

THIS PAGE Nudibranchs, from the Greek 'naked gills', are well known for their exuberant colourations and shapes. (BOTTOM LEFT) The candy soft coral crab not only mimics the colour of the coral on which it lives, but will also attach polyps to its carapace

CLOCKWISE FROM TOP LEFT Sea urchins crawl slowly across the reef with their tube feet, grazing on algae; hard table coral serves as a refuge for many small fish species; if provoked, the colours of the highly venomous blue-ringed octopus go bright to warn any predators of their toxicity; a spiny lobster over soft coral

A jewel anemone hermit crab, which can grow up to 7 cm. Sea anemones,
fixed haphazardly on their gastropod shells, are actively hosted by hermit crabs

He has now built a more permanent network of simple seahorse hotels using ropes wrapped around metal frames:

*Seahorses do not need much to survive, and they do not move very far, so once they have found their happy place in the ocean, they can live in that one spot throughout their lives.*

The more that the life and stories of seahorses are shared the better, and both David Harasti and Richard Smith recognize the significance of their role in championing the very small. Many creatures of our shallow seas remain unseen: they are just part of the background, species known only to specialists and taxonomists, yet seahorses are also representatives, emissaries of the unknown and unseen that are gradually being eroded from our seas. The beauty and individuality of a seahorse means that it gets noticed, when so many other species are amalgamated in our minds as life at the seabed. In this sense, seahorses are the most visible reminder of how countless other species are faring. Yet they are an animal that would prefer to remain invisible.

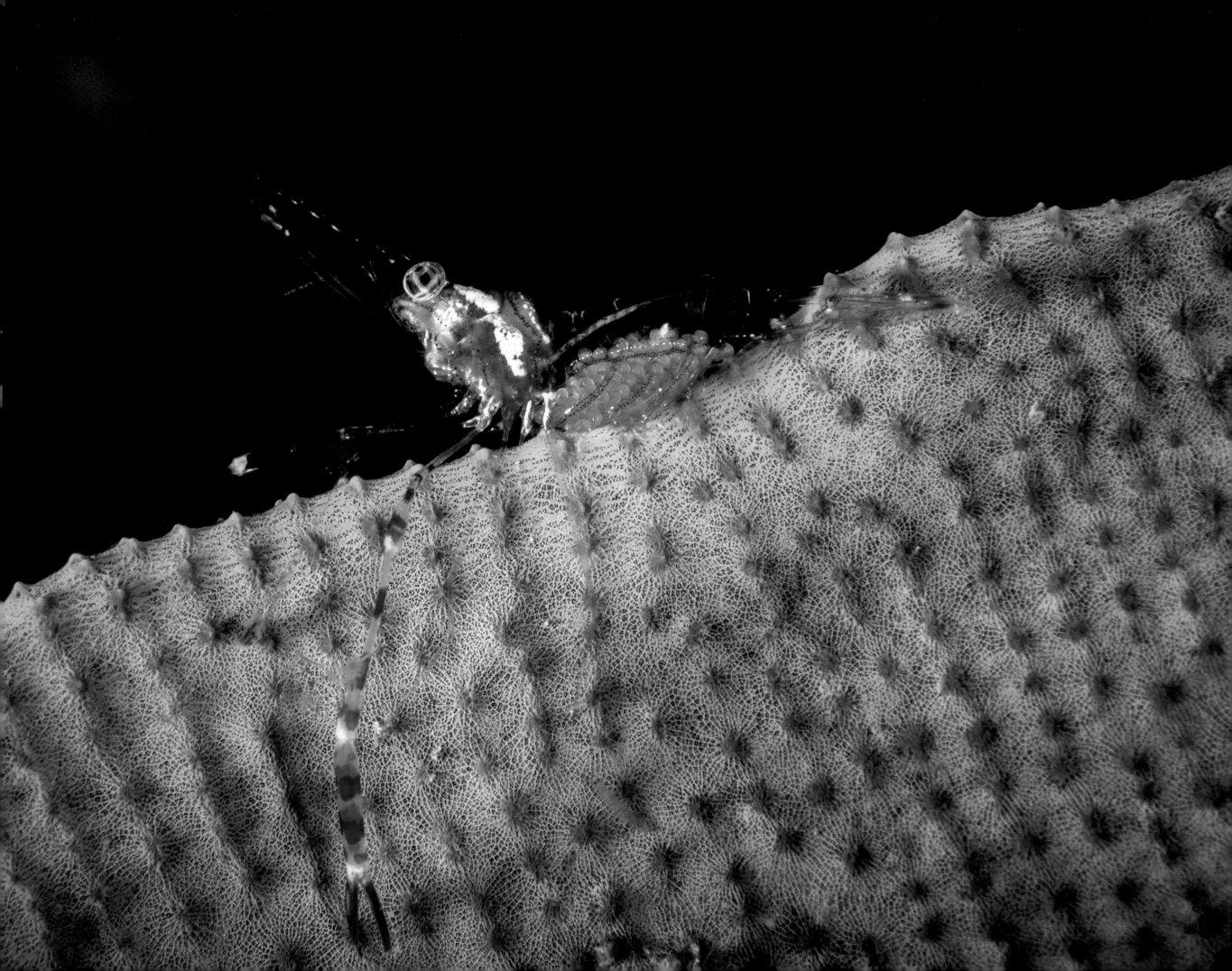

# WORDS FROM THE EXPERTS

*An awful lot of attention is spent on the big things. Cryptic animals often have lives that are as interesting and complex as those large marine mammals and sharks that attract most of the attention from divers, scientists and conservationists*
—Richard Smith

**Richard Smith** is an underwater photographer and expert in pygmy seahorses. He leads dive expeditions around the world to share his passion for the smaller and more cryptic reef animals:

*I can spend entire dives just searching and watching a few square metres of reef – I have missed at least two whale sharks that have swum past me while I'm focusing on something much smaller, but equally interesting. I am fascinated in the small and hidden species because so little is known about them, and they open up much more opportunity for new knowledge and discovery. To many people, these cryptic animals are just part of the background or the mush that is left at the end of a fishing trawl. I aim to change this perception.*

**Sarah Foster** is the programme manager for Project Seahorse. Based in Vancouver, Canada, she works with communities and governments across the world to reduce the impact from fishing:

*I have spent a great deal of time working with governments to find ways to stop destructive fishing and reduce bycatch. It's a huge challenge for us, as the organizations and companies behind this fishing are extremely powerful. We need to do a better job of making other people aware, building up a sense of urgency and drawing together the power of people to support our cause. The thought that we could lose such incredible places on my watch is terrifying and sickening, but it also fires me up to show up each day and get to work. Conservation is slow and incremental, sometimes a problem seems immovable, and then we get a sudden shift. I am incredibly motivated by being part of a community of organizations all working towards the same goal and by the thought that my two young sons deserve to grow up into a world as beautiful as the one I have known.*

**David Harasti** is a fisheries research scientist for the Port Stephens Great Lakes Marine Park. He is an expert on the White's seahorse and has spent thousands of dives studying them:

*I tagged over 1000 individuals and then studied them over a decade, observing and recording their behaviour, their diet, how long they lived and how dependent they are on a very small area of territory. I was on familiar terms with over 50 different individual seahorses; each in its own special place with its tail curled around a tiny holdfast. Over a period of three years, I watched one pair that I nicknamed 'Grandpa and Goldilocks' grow up and grow old together, producing many new generations of offspring. I would really encourage people to take the opportunity to put on a mask and see what is under the surface. I have learned so much simply by being there and observing what is going on around me, certainly more than I ever picked up by reading books.*

**David Pawson** is Senior Research Scientist Emeritus and Curator of Echinoderms at the Smithsonian Museum of Natural History in Washington, DC:

*I have made about 150 deep sea dives in little submersibles, exploring and collecting samples from the deep seabed in many parts of the Caribbean and eastern Pacific. In our dives around the Bahamas we discovered over 200 species of echinoderms, many of them new to science. Manned submersibles are wonderful platforms for deep-sea science, but the battery power means we have very limited time on the seabed. We are constantly having to make decisions on what to collect or photograph, knowing that we may never see that species again. There are more than 100 million square miles of deep sea floor on our planet, but we have properly explored only about 50 square miles. Even seemingly featureless abyssal planes are still hiding fantastic secrets, and we have barely touched the surface.*

**Marta Pola** is a professor at the Universidad Autónoma in Madrid, Spain, and an expert on nudibranch taxonomy and biology:

*It was not until I went on a field trip with my invertebrate class that I met my first sea slug through the lens of a stereoscope. I had no idea what it was but I decided that I wanted to spend the rest of my life studying those creatures. I have since worked in countries all over the world diving and slowly picking my way over the seabed looking for nudibranchs. I hope to be able to continue describing, naming and discovering the hidden biodiversity of these creatures that are small in size, but huge in their interest.*

**Enric 'Kike' Ballesteros,** author of *Marine Wildlife of the Mediterranean*, is a field naturalist with a huge range of global knowledge from seaweeds to invertebrates:

*I have been part of the scientific team for National Geographic's Pristine Seas expeditions for the last five years and have had the opportunity to dive in some of the most remote and pristine areas of the planet. I am hugely proud to be part of this great team and to know that my work has helped to mobilize governments to protect over four million km of oceans. We have discovered that these more untouched locations are dominated by predator species such as sharks, groupers and jacks in numbers that we did not think were possible to sustain. To me, ocean conservation matters not only because it provides tangible assets to humanity, but because it is a source of emotions; and emotions are what make us human. My affinity to the oceans is as strong now as it was when I was a boy; but this connection comes not through study, but through experiencing some of the strongest and most inspiring moments of my life – free diving with penguins and flightless cormorants in Isabella island, Galapagos; being wrapped by a school of great amberjacks in Desventuradas Islands, Chile; witnessing spawning events of bumphead parrotfish in Palau or watching a whale shark swimming across an endless school of red snappers in Cocos, Costa Rica.*

# SEA TURTLES

SEA TURTLES are a curious and ancient link between land and sea. Their evolutionary lineage may not extend as far back as sharks, but they have been living in our oceans for over 120 million years. The impact of an asteroid 10–15 km across at Chicxulub on the tip of the Yucatan peninsula brought global devastation 66 million years ago, leading to the extinction of dinosaurs and three-quarters of animal and plant life on earth. Alongside crocodiles, sea turtles were the only large four-limbed aquatic animals to survive, ultimately evolving into the seven species that are alive today – green, hawksbill, olive ridley, Kemp's ridley, flatback, loggerhead and leatherback, each with its own distinct ecology and natural history. Except for polar regions, turtles are found throughout the world's oceans, often migrating across whole ocean basins as they seek food and return to their birthplace to mate and lay eggs. Once the eggs hatch the turtle hatchlings emerge from their nests and hurry towards the surf, and spend the rest of their lives at sea. Nesting females return to the vicinity of the beach where they were born to lay successive clutches of eggs. The sight of a female turtle digging out a nest alone on a beach at night feels unworldly; the tears in their eyes were thought to have been shed for their unborn young, but the more prosaic reality is that the secretions rid their bodies of excess salt.

Traditionally green turtles have been hunted for food and hawksbill turtles for the beautiful translucent plates covering their shells. This hunting still persists today, albeit to a much lesser degree. However, turtles increasingly face new threats from coastal development, fisheries, pollution and global climate change. Successful conservation is inextricably linked to human use of resources and the way the benefits are shared among present and future generations. Despite local and international protection measures hawksbill turtles are struggling to recover from high levels of past exploitation for their shells. Demand for shell still exists, driving an illegal trade especially from the Caribbean and South East Asia. Green turtles were named for the green colour of the fat and cartilage that was scraped from inside the shell, dried and exported to Europe for turtle soup. An estimated 42,000 turtles of all species are still intentionally caught each year around the world, but the scale of impact from hunting is only a small proportion of the number that are accidentally caught in fishing gear. The use of

PREVIOUS Adult loggerhead turtles can carry across the ocean hundreds of species and 37 types of algae attached to their shell, creating a small and safe ecosystem that also provides food

LEFT AND RIGHT An adult hawksbill turtle. On the left, it is feeding on a sponge, followed closely by two French angelfish waiting to pick at the remains

escape devices on trawling nets has helped reduce the problem, but, since they are wide-ranging species, the principal threat comes from entanglement in gill nets and accidental capture in long lines. Both hawksbill and green turtles play a critical role in the balance and health of marine habitats. When hawksbill turtles feed off the sponges on a reef it allows space for the slower-growing corals to thrive, increasing the reef's richness and biodiversity. Grazing green turtles help to keep seagrass beds from becoming overgrown with encrusting organisms, which enables the leaves and roots to get access to sunlight and nutrients.

When Jeanne Mortimer arrived in the Seychelles in 1981, she was tasked with conducting a national survey of sea turtle populations and developing a sustainable management plan for the future. Over a period of three years, she travelled to almost every island in the country, and spent 18 months in the outer islands, living and working with small communities who were salting fish, catching turtles, and tending coconut plantations. In those days it was still legal to kill hawksbills and remove their shells for export to Japan or for use in the curio trade. Adult male green turtles could be legally harpooned at sea, and adult

females were illegally captured on the beaches. Healthy males were shipped alive back to the capital, Mahé; and weak males and any captured females were butchered on site for local consumption, or their meat salted and dried. Understanding the life history of the turtle enabled Jeanne to highlight the precarious situation of populations in the Seychelles:

*the people believed that the resources were infinite, that they were a gift from God, but it was clear to me that there was no chance of sustaining the rate at which they were being taken.*

Records of females returning to beaches are among the most reliable indicators of population status, but the fact that turtles may take twenty to forty years to become sexually mature can mask signs of over-exploitation. If nesting females are heavily fished it can take a quarter century or more to detect a decline in the numbers coming back to the beach. If too many eggs are harvested, then it can take even longer before a decline is evident. Meanwhile, the lives of young turtles remain largely unknown. Jeanne Mortimer initially struggled to convince Seychellois fishermen and government decision-makers to protect turtles, since it was locally

thought that they were only migratory visitors and were more likely to be caught in East Africa. When some individuals were tracked using satellite tags their movements told a different story. Most female hawksbills remained within 200 km of their nesting beaches. The migrations of individual green turtles were more variable – some moved less than 10 km from the beach where they nested, whereas others migrated thousands of kilometres. Through working together with the government and beach-front hotel operators, and conducting public awareness campaigns in the schools and on television, Jeanne has helped to reduce hunting pressure, create an appreciation for the economic value of live turtles as a tourist attraction, and enhance protection around the islands.

Much of a sea turtle's life remains a mystery; once they leave the beach as hatchlings they are rarely seen during the first few years of their life. For many years numbered plastic or metal tags, clipped to an adult turtle's flippers, were the primary tool that would enable researchers to gain an insight into the health of turtle populations, as well as broadening our understanding of the frequency with which females come to the beach to nest, how quickly they grow and

GUARDIAN **Leonor Varela** is an actress based in Los Angeles who has been actively supporting global efforts to protect our oceans.

I feel a deep sense of belonging to the sea. Whether I am surfing, diving or just sitting on the beach I always find inspiration, courage and ultimately a stronger sense of myself when I am by the sea. Experiences from my childhood are still so vivid for me – the joy, danger and freedom of exploring and discovering the coastlines around Chile. Our childhood experiences of the sea are such important memories. These are moments when families come together to relax and have fun in a huge playground where children can feel free. On holiday in Northern Chile, my brother, sister and I were once caught in strong currents that pulled us out into rough seas. We held on to each other and managed to get safely back to shore. These experiences and emotional connections have inspired me to become actively involved in ocean conservation.

This summer I am heading to the Juan Fernández Islands with Professor Enric Sala and the National Geographic Pristine Seas team. These islands in the Mar de Juan Fernández, nearly 700 km from the Chilean coast, were the home of Alexander Selkirk, the real-life sailor who was marooned for four years and later fictionalized as Robinson Crusoe. The islands were badly affected by a tsunami in 2010 and a plane crash a year later. They are a protected marine park because of the incredible importance of their turtles and marine mammals. The Chilean government has just announced that 11,000 km² of the Mar de Juan Fernández is to be given even stronger protection. This trip is a unique opportunity for me to learn more from the marine scientists, and in turn I hope that I can help them to convey the importance of protecting these remaining ocean jewels to audiences back at home.

In 2016 I was on Easter Island with the Rapa Nui people. This is one of the most remote islands on earth, and must be one of the most beautiful places that I have ever seen. I was there with the organization Oceana to learn more about how a protection area could help to preserve marine life around the island and the local fishery. The plans would allow local people to fish out to a limit of 50

> *The sea used to seem so big – a limitless expanse where we could catch as many fish and throw away as much of our rubbish as we wanted.*

nautical miles from shore but would prevent any fishing from this point out to 200 nautical miles. I could see that there was still unease among the community about what a protected area could mean. While there was the potential to secure their own fishing grounds and resources, people were also scared that they would be giving up their independence and losing their offshore fishing grounds. I could feel their passion and strong feelings, but I believe a compromise is possible. Ultimately, however, this is a decision that they will need to reach themselves.

As an actress I am in a a unique position to help people become more aware of overfishing, illegal fishing, coral bleaching and ocean acidification, and why these pose a threat and how they can be confronted and solved. Even if people haven't had the chance to experience the sea for themselves, my aim is to give them a sense of the magic and beauty that I have always felt. Now more than ever it is important for people to get involved, to act in a more organized and determined way. Changes to our oceans are already causing huge hardship to communities around the world, and I believe we must confront the problems that are already leaving people increasingly vulnerable.

The sea used to seem so big – a limitless expanse where we could catch as many fish and throw away as much of our rubbish as we wanted. We now know that the sea's resources are stretched beyond capacity. This is a global problem, but one that can be solved through a collective desire to change our behaviour. Humans are capable of incredible acts of kindness, bravery and selflessness – but, when it comes to sharing the sea, we seem to forget about the impact we are having and the link between our actions and their consequences. It makes me furious that we are having to cope with the impact of problems that are so avoidable – but I continue to be driven by my hope for the future.

*For whatever we lose (like a you or a me)*
*It's always ourselves we find in the sea*
(E.E. CUMMINGS)

how faithful they are to a particular beach. Once an
identifiable turtle was subsequently caught or seen
returning to a beach, the details of the sighting were
sent to the research institute involved. The principal
drawback with flipper tags is that live records were
inevitably biased towards females returning to beaches
where scientists were working, and dead records
tended to point towards areas where turtles were being
actively hunted.

Since the 1990s scientists have been able to benefit
from the development of satellite technology to track
adult sea turtles, giving us a much richer picture of
their movements. Turtles have been tracked moving
around entire ocean basins, to return once more to the
vicinity of where they hatched. They are most likely
orientating themselves using the earth's magnetic
field, but they will also use a range of other sensory
cues from the water and sky around them. Ascension
Island is a remote, volcanic island with the second
largest population of green turtles in the Atlantic
Ocean. Annette Broderick has been studying these
populations for the last 20 years, recording their
nesting behaviour and migrations.

*Females come to the island to nest every three to four years, navigating across two thousand miles of ocean from the coast of Brazil. Our work with satellite tracking shows that the turtles are approaching the island from downwind, which would suggest that smell plays an important part in helping them navigate back home to such a tiny spot in the ocean.*

The resurgence of green turtles in some parts of the Atlantic is a sign of success, but other species are still struggling to rebound from a combination of threats on land and in the sea. With intensive efforts to protect nesting turtles and their habitats, some localized populations of green turtles have now started to recover. The question is beginning to arise whether hunting should be allowed once more, and when it is acceptable for populations to lose their status as globally threatened. Annette Broderick believes that the recovery of these populations is a real success story and conservationists should be open to the idea that turtle harvests could be re-established in locations where populations have recovered:

*In the Turks and Caicos Islands, fishermen are living hand to mouth and are suffering from declines in catches of lobster and*

Loggerhead turtles are omnivorous, using their powerful jaws to crack into the shells of gastropods as well as feeding on sponges, worms, crustaceans, sea cucumbers and starfish

*conch. Turtles can provide an alternative subsistence catch. If people are hungry, it is difficult to demand that biodiversity should be protected solely for the enjoyment and benefit of tourists. Biodiversity needs to demonstrate its worth, otherwise who is going to pay for it?*

The first few hours of a turtle's life are by far the most precarious. In a clutch of 100 eggs, the chances of just one making it through to becoming an adult are slim. As they crawl out of the sand and scuttle down towards the sea they are picked off by crabs and birds; in the shallow coastal waters they are easy prey for snappers, groupers and sharks. After the initial dash to the water's edge, the turtles disappear to unknown parts of the ocean until they return once more as young adults to breed. Scientists are just gaining small insights into this period that they call 'the lost years'. Acoustic pingers transmit an electronic signal and are now small enough that they can be attached to hatchlings as they emerge from the nest. Rebecca Scott tracked leatherback hatchlings in Gabon for their first few hours in the ocean, following them in a boat as they swam into deeper water and were carried away in multiple directions by coastal currents which fluctuate

GUARDIAN **Sheldon Whitehouse** is an American lawyer, politician and Junior Senator for Rhode Island. He was one of the founder members of the US Senate Oceans Caucus and a campaigner for climate change action. He is a keen diver and sailor; the sea has played an important role in his life. He has become one of the most active politicians in the Senate in driving forward action on climate change and protection for the oceans.

I'm from Rhode Island, the Ocean State, where our economy and our way of life depend on a healthy ocean and vibrant coast. The docks of Galilee and Point Judith are home to fishermen whose families have been making their living from the sea for generations, and our beloved Narragansett Bay is a resource for businesses and families from Providence to Newport. Rhode Island's Coastal Resources Management Council is now telling us that for planning purposes we need to face the possibility of nine to twelve vertical feet of sea level rise along Rhode Island's shores by the end of the century. That invasion of our shores by a rising ocean will leave Rhode Island's map unrecognizable.

The oceans face a myriad of hazards to their functioning and survival, from pollution to exploitation and climate change. Warming, acidifying, and rising seas are a clear and present danger to many aspects of our Rhode Island way of life, and to coastal communities around the world. Sea-level rise now threatens to remake our coastline, swallowing low-lying land, widening existing inlets, eroding beaches, and stranding higher shorefronts as new islands. The oceans, and the wildlife that call them home, don't care about political boundaries. Marine debris leaves the shores of Asia and washes up in Alaska; fish caught with forced labour on the high seas can end up in grocery store shelves in your neighbourhood; mercury released from coal-fired power plants in the United States can accumulate in tuna served in Europe.

Countries must work together to protect our common natural heritage of marine resources, whether in deterring pirate fishing or improving waste management on land to prevent non-degradable debris from ending up in the sea. Our oceans and coasts are notoriously underfunded and under-researched, and consequentially, sometimes misunderstood and mismanaged. Coastal communities must deal with immediate threats, while also planning

> *We are approaching the point of no return on climate change and the next three years are likely to be the last chance to limit global warming to safe limits in this century.*

for future sea-level rise, increased storm severity, shifting fisheries stocks, acidifying waters, and changing coastlines. The private sector has become increasingly engaged in a number of issues facing the marine environment. Private technology companies are developing advanced satellite and vessel tracking software to support efforts to identify and stop pirate fishing. The plastic industry has also been engaged in understanding and reducing the flow of trash from land into the ocean. We must significantly increase our investments in understanding the marine environment so we can manage and conserve ocean resources.

In 2011, Senator Lisa Murkowski started a bipartisan Senate Oceans Caucus, which now has 36 members. The Caucus supported the Senate's approval of four international agreements to curb 'illegal, unreported, and unregulated fishing' and the treaties enabling legislation. Oceans Caucus is also leading the charge on the Save Our Seas Act, a bipartisan bill aimed at reducing the flow of plastic waste into the oceans.

More broadly, we must address climate change. Virtually every person on the Republican side who has thought through the climate change problem has come to the same solution: a fee on greenhouse gas emissions. I introduced the American Opportunity Carbon Fee Act with Senator Brian Schatz, which would make polluters pay a fee to cover the costs of their emissions and return every dollar to the American people. Climate change was once a bipartisan concern. But since the Supreme Court's 2010 Citizens United decision lifted limits on corporate spending on political campaigns, fossil fuel companies and their allies have funnelled millions of dollars of

dark money into lobbying and campaign efforts to sway the political tides against climate action. Opponents of climate action relish operating in the dark. Their slimiest work, to undermine science and deny the harmful effects of carbon pollution on human health, natural systems, and the economy, is done by hidden hands, through the front groups they fund. These front groups intentionally poison public understanding and productive dialogue by promoting the fabrication that there is scientific debate about whether climate change exists. However, there is hope. We just need to acknowledge peer-reviewed science, the expert assessments of our military and national security communities, and the business case for climate action so many American companies are making.

We are approaching the point of no return on climate change and the next three years are likely to be the last chance to limit global warming to safe limits in this century. The United Nations Environment Programme warns us that unless reductions from carbon pollution from the energy sector are taken swiftly, it will be nearly impossible to keep warming below two degrees and avoid widespread catastrophe. I urge you all to do what you can to take action – organize an event in your community, join an environmental group, do a beach clean-up and help to support the work of conservation and science. The multiples of every action counts. My hope is that ultimately the climate denial machine will be exposed and dismantled; my fear is that by the time we get there, the sand will have run out of the hourglass.

LEFT AND OVERLEAF The pointed bird-like beak which gives the hawksbill its name is used to tear into sponges growing on coral reefs

RIGHT Juvenile green turtles take shelter in shallow coastal waters to avoid predation from tiger sharks

through the days and seasons. Juvenile loggerheads have been found living in clumps of floating sargassum weed as they voyage on oceanic gyres, but, beyond this, scientists still have little idea of where turtles spend the first two decades of their lives.

The beaches of northern Cyprus are hugely important as nesting sites for green and loggerhead turtles. In 1992, Brendan Godley and Annette Broderick gathered a few students and organized an expedition to survey the turtle populations. The programme has grown and continues more than 25 years later, with over 1,200 students having taken part in the project since its inception. The principal threat to the turtles nesting on these beaches is from stray dogs and foxes that dig down to the eggs. Volunteers patrol the beaches through the night, and position a mesh cage to protect newly laid clutches. Until recently, beaches in the north of Cyprus remained largely undeveloped. New hotels need to be very carefully designed and located so that the beaches remain dark and undisturbed, to prevent females being discouraged from laying on these beaches. Artificial lights can also lead hatchlings in the wrong direction, slowing their progress to the sea and making them more vulnerable to predators. The fact that so much coastline

142

Resting green turtles can hold their breath for up to seven hours

Much of a turtle's first years of life is spent out in the open ocean, a period referred
to as the 'lost years' as very little is known about this part of their life cycle

Green turtles take special care of their carapace, scraping algae off on rocks or letting cleaner fish remove parasites

in the Mediterranean has been developed means that the remaining isolated and undeveloped beaches are critical for the future of these turtle populations.

Plastic pollution and climate change pose further serious risks. The temperature of the nest influences whether hatchlings will emerge male or female (a trait that is common to turtles, alligators and crocodiles). When the sand remains at its normal temperature of approximately 29°, there is an even split between the sexes, but just a two-degree increase will lead to exclusively female hatchlings, with obvious potential consequences for future populations. The leatherback is one of the fastest declining species of turtle, with their numbers in the Pacific Ocean falling by 90% in the last two decades. As a species that migrates across vast distances during its life, they are more difficult to protect and more prone to entanglement in fishing gear or being caught on longlines. Floating plastic litter can resemble jellyfish (the principal prey for leatherbacks), and if eaten this can become stuck in the digestive system, causing the animal to starve and die. The full impact of plastic debris in the sea remains unknown, and we will need to keep a careful eye on leatherback numbers.

The global picture of turtle conservation is mixed. Some species are responding well to intensive measures to protect their nesting and breeding sites. In other parts of the globe, populations are declining, sometimes worryingly quickly and often due to a combination of impacts from fishing and loss of nesting sites. Nesting turtles are very wary of disturbance on beaches and will retreat if there is too much noise and activity. Although remote stretches of beach are diminishing, with careful supervision research teams can bring tourists and locals on to the beach to observe turtles as they lay their eggs. 'There is something incredibly alluring and magical about a turtle emerging from the sea and crawling up the beach,' says Annette Broderick, who recognizes the opportunity to connect people to a sea creature. Scientists working on nesting beaches in proximity to humans see that the more they know about a species the more story there is to tell, which in turn generates greater interest and awareness. Rebecca Scott says:

*I feel it is my duty to talk to as many people as possible about my work and to share the excitement of discovering more about the lives of turtles. The popularity of turtles helps us connect people with other less well-known species and habitats.*

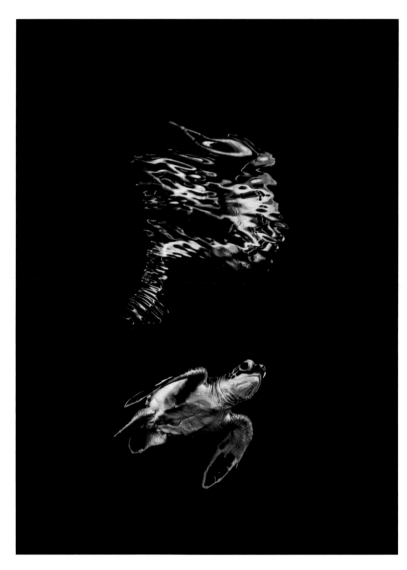
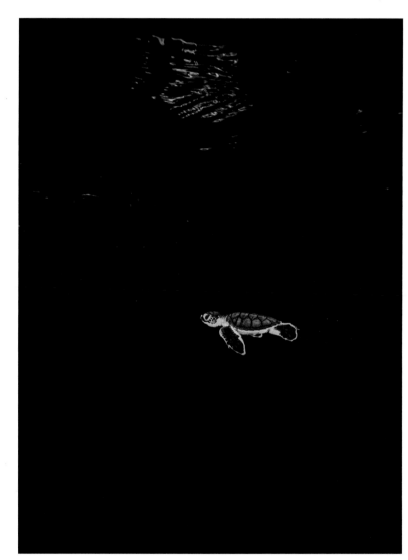

Using the moon to guide them, turtle hatchlings make a dash to the open ocean, where they will spend the first few years of their life

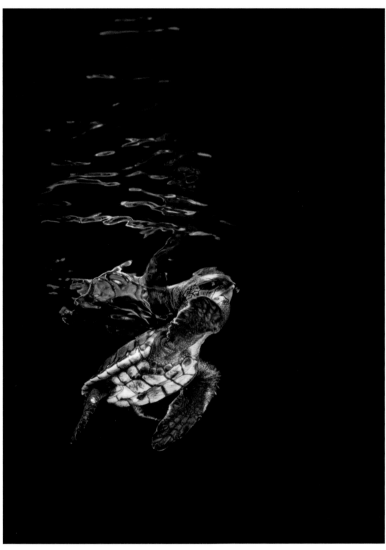

# WORDS FROM THE EXPERTS

**Annette Broderick** is Professor of Marine Conservation at the University of Exeter, specializing in the ecology and conservation of sea turtles:

*Sea turtles are long-lived species, so you need to accumulate many years of data before it is possible to infer trends. Conservation is a human science, it is about people and how they live and use resources – it can never be just about the animals. My objective is to provide information that can help us use our resources sustainably.*

**Brendan Godley** is Professor of Conservation Science at the Centre for Ecology and Conservation at the University of Exeter. Together with Annette Broderick he has been running the Marine Turtle Conservation Project in Cyprus since 1992:

*We have generated a huge body of knowledge about these turtles – their migration, breeding and populations. Each individual that comes ashore is tagged or recorded, so we know that some of the turtles we tagged in 1992 are still coming back to nest on the same beaches. The increase in green turtle populations in Cyprus is a cause for optimism, particularly when the Mediterranean Sea faces so many other environmental pressures.*

**Jeanne Mortimer** has been studying sea turtles around the world for over 40 years. She is based in the Seychelles, where she has set up and co-ordinates a network of turtle monitoring and protection programmes across the world:

*The Seychelles comprises some 115 islands and enormous marine areas of banks and coral reefs that remain rich in wildlife. I travelled to the Seychelles for the first time in 1981 and I was privileged to spend extensive periods on remote atolls such as Aldabra and Cosmoledo, living with small groups of fishermen without radio contact or communication with the outside world. During the nights, I walked the beach to tag and measure nesting turtles and then I would be out again at dawn to count all the turtle tracks from the night before. I wanted to know the size of the turtle populations, how many were being killed each year, and what the resource meant to the people.*

**Rebecca Scott** is a marine ecologist at the Future Ocean Cluster of Excellence, GEOMAR Helmholtz Centre for Ocean Research, in Kiel, Germany. She has spent the last ten years studying sea turtle migration patterns globally:

*Sea turtles are a perfect model to study migration since the females come to the beach to lay eggs and are docile enough for us to attach satellite transmitters. Scientists have been able to benefit from the development of satellite technology to track large animals like adult sea turtles. If we have a better understanding of where turtles are going through their lives, then we can be more targeted about our conservation efforts. It is fascinating to think that sea turtles can travel thousands of kilometres, but large parts of their journey remain a mystery.*

# WHALES AND DOLPHINS

THE 'SAVE THE WHALES' CAMPAIGN was a huge part of a counter-cultural movement that put pressure on governments to act to ban industrial whaling in the 1970s. Roger Payne is both a scientist and a musician; he recognized that to save an animal you first have to get people to fall in love with it. When he heard the haunting, lingering underwater refrains of humpback whales, he knew that this was his opportunity. Humpbacks in the Atlantic region spend the winter months primarily on banks to the north of the Dominican Republic, passing by the island of Bermuda when migrating back to their feeding grounds. The first recordings of humpback song were a mystery to the US Navy acoustics engineer who first heard them. In the engine-room of a wooden minesweeper, Roger was invited to listen to these strange sounds and knew immediately that they came from humpback whales. He convinced the US Navy to let him have the recordings and spent six months intensively listening to the sounds. He realized that the whales were stringing together complex phrases in rhythmic and tonal patterns – in other words, qualities that we would attribute to songs and singing. The next summer Roger chartered his own boat and sailed

offshore from Bermuda with a hydrophone to make his own recordings and spent the next two years travelling the world, playing the songs to anyone who would listen. An album of whale song sold over 100,000 copies and the production of a flexible vinyl record that accompanied a *National Geographic* magazine led to a further 12 million recordings being distributed around the USA. For many people, the connection with the songs was real – melancholic and poignant. The true meaning is of course indecipherable, but in capturing the plight of the whale it sparked a global campaign.

The scientists who work with whales are people who have spent much of their careers out at sea learning about the lives of the cetaceans around their coasts. With each new generation of scientists, the extent of our knowledge of whales has grown, but much more is needed if we are going to ensure that cetaceans can continue to recover from centuries of exploitation. Whale research initially focused on gathering catch data for commercial whaling, using observations from whaling ships to build up a picture of populations and migration routes. Discovery tags had been in use since the 1930s – fired into the whale with a shotgun. These tags were only retrieved if the whale was caught and

ABOVE The humpback whale travels up to 25,000 km per year, living off its fat reserves as it migrates from the food-rich polar waters to subtropical waters to breed and give birth

Over the last 40 years populations of humpback whales have been gradually recovering – a fantastic example of what international co-operation and conservation can achieve

killed, and, as commercial whaling drew to a close, a new method was needed to track whale movement. Roger Payne started to build his own photographic catalogue of individual humpbacks, focusing on the distinct pattern of markings on the underside of their tail flukes, a project that has grown into shared global catalogues through which scientists can identify individuals and match movements that reveal their extraordinary migrations between the tropics and the poles. As whales have returned to our oceans, scientists have been able to study their ecology and behaviour – the close-knit cultures of sperm whales and the intricate social lives of bottlenose and spotted dolphins. These insights have come through spending countless hours out at sea watching whales, but our knowledge is still patchy – we are mostly limited to studying whales in coastal areas that can be accessed in small boats and our insight is still mostly based on what they are doing at the surface.

In the spring of 2005, biologist Christie McMillan was working as a whale-watching guide out of Port McNeill on Vancouver Island, Canada. They had been following a pod of orcas, when there was a much larger blow ahead of the boat. It had been half a century since humpbacks were regularly seen in these waters, but that season two females and their calves spent the whole summer season feeding in waters around north-eastern Vancouver Island. Over the following years, the number of humpbacks feeding in this area each summer has risen to 91. Around the globe, commercial whalers hunted over 200,000 humpbacks before bans were put in place by the International Whaling Commission. The bounce-back of humpback whales over the last 30 years has been one of the great global marine conservation success stories. A new whale-watching industry has grown up alongside, often located in the same whale hunting ports, but taking a new generation of people to experience the world's largest mammals at the surface of the sea. In the waters around Vancouver Island on the west coast of Canada, Christie McMillan and her colleagues have recorded over 300 individual humpbacks. Every time an individual is sighted it adds multiple new layers of knowledge about its movement, growth and diet. Christie has known some of these individuals since they first arrived as calves with their mothers, before migrating back to tropical waters. Sharing data with scientists across the Pacific has shown how the animals from northern Vancouver are predominantly travelling to waters off Hawaii before returning once more to feed in the summer. After travelling thousands of miles humpbacks will focus on restoring the energy lost during their long journey. Humpbacks often hunt co-operatively, working together to herd shoals of fish into tight balls by blowing bubbles to create an artificial net, before sharing their joint catch. A more docile fishing technique has also been observed more recently by Christie and her team, where the whales float motionless at the surface with their mouths open, using their long flippers to push the fish towards their mouth. They have called this 'trap feeding' and have recorded how others have gradually adopted this new behaviour by mimicking members of the pod.

Similar identification techniques were also developed for orcas as part of research commissioned in British Columbia in 1970 to understand the orca population and to observe whether the numbers that were being killed by fishermen or caught for displays were truly sustainable. An orca can be distinguished by the saddle markings and a combination of nicks, cuts and dorsal fin characteristics on its left-hand side. [CONTD PAGE 171]

A close encounter with a huge male sperm whale is an experience
that lasts in your memory for a lifetime

ABOVE AND OVERLEAF Parenting is shared among mature females,
who will protect and nurture their young

GUARDIAN **Louie Psihoyos** is a photographer, Oscar-winning film-maker and Executive Director of the Oceanic Preservation Society.

As a kid, I loved painting and drawing pictures of birds, animals and the natural world around my home in Iowa, USA. Photography was even better: this was a way that I could create these same pictures instantly. I had seen a *National Geographic* magazine in my mum's hair studio and read an article about Easter Island that blew my mind. Here was adventure and excitement that I wanted to be part of. A photographer wanting to work for the *National Geographic* is a bit of a cliché, but that is what I set out to do. I studied photojournalism at the University of Missouri, worked for several newspapers including the *L.A. Times* and *Dubuque Telegraph Herald*. I tried to get a job with the *National Geographic* first as an intern, and then by winning six of the seven categories in the College Photographer of the Year Award. I realized the power of photography when we were given an assignment in college to photograph an animal that was about to be euthanized. Every one of the dogs that I captured was saved and rehomed. I wanted to use my photographs to change the way people thought, and found a niche in covering some of the more unexpected aspects of our world.

The first article I wrote at the *National Geographic* was about coal mining in Powder River in Montana, a story of the transformation of agricultural communities to mining. It was one of the first black-and-white photo essays to be published for 20 years. In the early 1980s the *National Geographic* had a circulation of 11 million in the USA, and most of these readers would pass it on to three or four others, so our stories were reaching 44 million people. Our potential to influence and engage was enormous. I did three assignments on extinction, sowing a seed for the disquiet I was increasingly feeling about the rate at which humans were pushing animals and plants into oblivion.

I had learned to dive at university and a whole new, beautiful underwater universe had then opened up for me.

> *Since the film* [The Cove] *was released in 2009, the number of dolphins killed has fallen from 23,000 a year to fewer than 6,000, and many countries have now banned captive dolphins in displays.*

Many years later I met tech entrepreneur Jim Clark, when I photographed him and his yacht, *Hyperion*. He asked me

to teach him to take great photos and we became regular dive buddies, taking dive trips to some of the most remote and amazing places on the planet. Over the years, when we returned to some of our favourite places we found that they had degraded – the coral had bleached and the large fish and sharks had become scarcer. It was in the Galapagos, when we witnessed fishermen longlining illegally in a protected area, that Jim said, 'Someone should do something about this!' I replied, 'Why not us?'

I had a good nose for a story and an eye for film-making, and Jim provided the financial backing, but also the courage to go out and do something unusual. Together we formed the Oceanic Preservation Society, with big ambitions and a modest logo: 'We're not trying to save the world, just 70% of it.'

I came across Ric O'Barry when he had been barred from speaking at a marine mammal conference. He told me about the slaughter of dolphins at Taiji and invited me to come and join him. First, I had to take a three-day crash course in film-making and then I flew out to Japan for the first time. This was the start of a three-year project to make a film about Ric's campaign to stop the slaughter of dolphins and the capture of young females for dolphinariums around the world. When we started to make the film – *The Cove* – I wasn't sure what the story

was going to be, but with the huge political and security obstacles we had to overcome just to get in and film in this fishing village, it became obvious that this was the most exciting narrative – described later as a cross between *Flipper* and *The Bourne Identity*. We used cameras hidden in rocks and freediver Mandy-Rae Cruickshank to deploy underwater cameras. Since the film was released in 2009, the number of dolphins killed has fallen from 23,000 a year to fewer than 6,000, and many countries have now banned captive dolphins in displays.

Film producers mostly see an audience as bums on seats, ten dollars of revenue for the films that they make. I look at an audience and see hearts and minds on seats. First you need to reach the hearts, then you can change the minds. If we are going to effect a change, then we need to change their hearts, but how can you tell a story about the extinction of species on our planet, yet still give people hope? The next film I made, *Racing Extinction*, tells the story of how humans are causing the extinction of animals at 1,000 times the normal rate. We are currently heading towards the sixth mass extinction, and the first to be caused by a single species – humans. It is difficult for people to get their heads around some of the numbers involved, or even to connect extinction and their own behaviour. In the film, we show the last male O'o bird in

Hawaii, singing a song for a female that will never come. It is hard not to share a sense of empathy and desolation for this bird, emblematic of what is happening every day across the planet, but which we can all do something about. In order to achieve the snowball effect of societal change you need to hit a minimum threshold of 10% – a boiling point for the spread of ideas. I hadn't forgotten about the power of images, and we projected wildlife images 300 metres tall down the side of the Empire State Building in New York, across the UN building during the

> *In order to achieve the snowball effect of societal change you need to hit a minimum threshold of 10% – a boiling point for the spread of ideas.*

climate change conference and on to St Peter's Basilica in the Vatican City.

Everyone needs to become an actor in solving this crisis; whatever it is you do, you have a skill or a connection or an ability to do something positive or to change your behaviour. I hope that people will feel a little more empowered to do something, even just one little thing in their lives that will help to avert a crisis for humankind. We all have a fear of speaking out, of being made to feel foolish, but I know that I can't sit back and do

nothing – I can't watch this crisis unfold without raising my voice. Change does happen, and it can happen very quickly when the public and government act together.

> *Everyone needs to become an actor in solving this crisis; whatever it is you do, you have a skill or a connection or an ability to do something positive or to change your behaviour.*

I look back on my time as a *National Geographic* photographer as a walk in the wilderness: I was telling great stories and informing people, but I had no sense that I was changing their world views, perceptions or habits. With film, you have 90 minutes to tell a dramatic story with voices, characters and music, which would be impossible with still images. I feel that film is the most powerful weapon in the world – a weapon of mass construction. This is the most important time in history to be human, and I think the next few years will define whether we are on the path to greatness or oblivion.

THIS PAGE End of the day – mother and calf sleep vertically, at 15 m deep

FACING The sperm whale's tail – the fluke – is the largest of any whale species

The same research also established some cornerstone knowledge of orcas and their culture – their matriarchal societies and clearly distinct 'resident' populations that feed on fish and the 'transient' populations that feed on warm-blooded mammals.

Filipa Samarra has been studying orcas in Iceland for the past decade. Unlike the populations in British Columbia, these orcas live in much looser societies, coming together to hunt and feed, then dispersing once more. Both Norwegian and Icelandic orcas feed almost exclusively on shoals of herring, working together to round the fish into a dense ball and stunning them with slaps of the tail. Filipa and her team from the Icelandic Orca project spend the summer seasons observing and recording the behaviour of a core group of about 250 individuals. Photographs shared with researchers in Scotland have so far revealed that at least 16 individuals from Iceland have migrated to Scottish shores, where they preyed on seals. Most orca populations specialize in feeding on either fish or marine mammals like seals; switching between prey is rare. The reasons for this are still unclear, but one possible answer is that herring populations are notoriously volatile, so, when you feed

on such an unpredictable species, it makes sense to have an alternative strategy up your sleeve.

Footage of orcas barrelling up a stony beach to snatch sea-lion pups have become some of the most iconic wildlife scenes. The beach is on the Valdes Peninsula in Argentina, and, for a few weeks every year, one group of orcas comes to a narrow rocky channel that allows them to get access to the beach at high tide. Mel is the most famous of the Patagonian orcas, often playing a starring role in these documentaries, and clearly identifiable from a bent dorsal fin that was the result of a gunshot wound in 1977. Miguel Iñíquez has been studying orcas for over 30 years, but every so often he notes that they remind him how little he knows. There are often many people on the beach watching and filming the sea-lion hunts. Miguel has observed Mel capture a sea-lion pup and then release it unharmed, only to catch and kill another one a few minutes later, taking it out to deeper water and then 'spy-hopping' with the prey in his mouth as if showing off his catch.

Unlike the humpback and orcas, blue whales rarely show signs of any curiosity towards humans, as they feed and travel across vast ranges. Blue whales

are true long-limbed, oceanic wanderers, hugging the continental shelves, seamounts and the highly productive frontal areas, rich in zooplankton. In the North Atlantic there are two distinct groups: one in the east Atlantic that is found between Mauritania in West Africa and Norway, while the west Atlantic population ranges between West Greenland and the Carolinas and offshore seamounts. Many are found along the shelf off Nova Scotia and the Gulf of St Lawrence in Canada. Richard Sears has been studying the western population for more than 40 years, but admits that we still have only limited snapshots into their lives: 'My big ambition is to find out what blue whales are doing in the North Atlantic – where are they travelling between, where are they giving birth and what routes are they following?' Richard and his team from the Mingan Island Cetacean Study have had some success using satellite tags that are attached to the blubber on the back of a whale using a specialized air gun. Each tag unit costs $3,000 and they rarely stay attached for more than a month, so our knowledge of their movements is still frustratingly elusive. The tracks show that these individuals headed out to the edge of the continental shelf, but then the signals

GUARDIAN **Buzzy Kerbox** is a professional surfer and waterman from Oahu, Hawaii, and one of the pioneers of tow-in surfing.

I was nine years old when my family moved from Indianapolis to Kailua, eastern Oahu. I had come across the first Beach Boys album cover when I was on holiday and thought that surfing looked cool, so I organized a surf lesson on Waikiki beach. By age eleven, I was taking every chance to surf, and starting my journey as the water sports professional, or 'waterman', that I wanted to become. For a few years I travelled round on the global competition circuit and I was ranked in the top ten in the world in the late 1970s, winning the 1978 World Cup on Sunset Beach.

The era of big-wave tow-in surfing started when I was exploring Hawaii's outer reefs with fellow surfers Darrick Doerner and Laird Hamilton in my small Zodiac inflatable boat. On our first attempt we were just playing with the waves at Phantoms and dropped into a 15-foot wave that almost caught up with us. It would have flipped the boat with the engine blazing and could have been really nasty. Next time we came out with a bigger engine. Once we had got the hang of weaving in and out of the breaks, we tried pulling each other on to waves on our boards. We knew we had unlocked something amazing – we were catching scores of waves every day in complete solitude just around the bay from some of the most congested surf zones in the world. We moved around to explore other giant waves at Backyards, and then ultimately to the discovery of Jaws (Peahi) on the north shore of Maui. I've ridden a 60-foot wave here that was like snowboarding down a shuddering mountain. Unlike beach surfing, tow-in surfing is a team sport that requires trust and communication between the surfer and the

> *I love being out on the ocean, but I try to seek out solitude and serenity .... I can paddle out into the wild ocean for miles with just dolphins for company.*

jetski driver, who needs to have the skill and experience to come down the wave to pick you up in the surf before the next set comes in. Wipe-outs can be horrifying – you are held down for a minute or more, swimming disorientated in liquid space. I try to stay relaxed and focused, waiting for the moment to swim up and get a breath.

Big-wave surfing was not something I continued to pursue. I felt that we had conquered the Everest of waves, and it was not something that we had to go back to.

A friend had just died surfing the pipeline on Oahu, I was married with two kids, and my wife was pregnant with our third child. That was the point at which I started backing off on the throttle. I just didn't feel it was fair to be out there pushing the limits just for fun. Twenty years ago I set up my own surf school, creating a job that would allow me to continue as a waterman, but without the huge risks and global travel. I am not someone who runs the business from an office, I teach everybody myself. The best part is introducing people to that first ride and seeing their faces as they come off the wave. For me, it is just great that there are more people who are enjoying the purity of the energy of the ocean.

I love being out on the ocean, but I try to seek out solitude and serenity. If you are competing for waves with 30 other guys then it takes the fun out of the experience. Stand Up Paddleboarding opened up a whole new ocean for me; I can paddle out into the wild ocean for miles with just dolphins for company. I have spent a lifetime in the water travelling the world in pursuit of the freedom and excitement that comes from riding waves. Surfing is something that I love to do, but I really can't explain why. I have been lucky and feel blessed that things have happened well for me and enabled me to spend my life on the ocean.

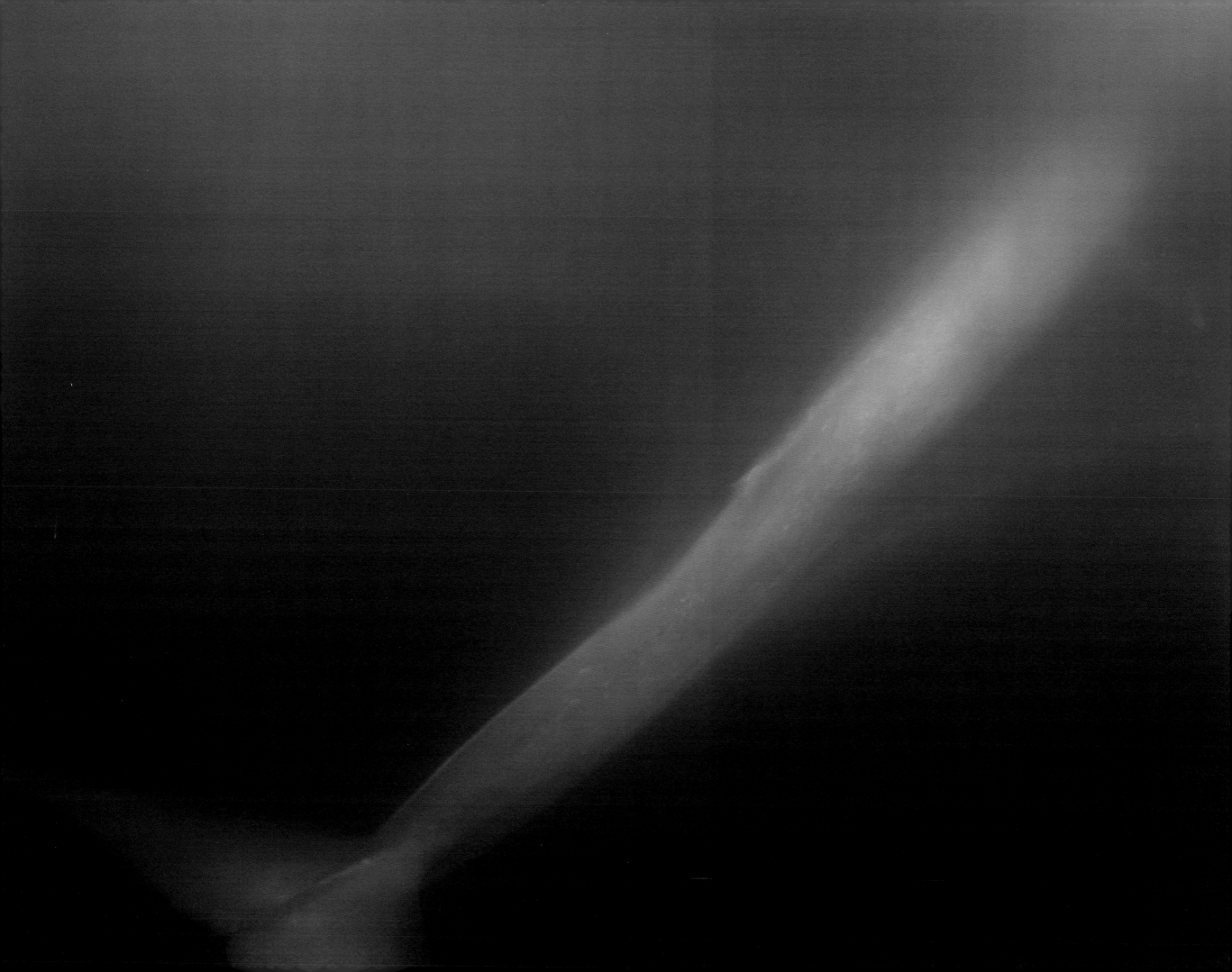

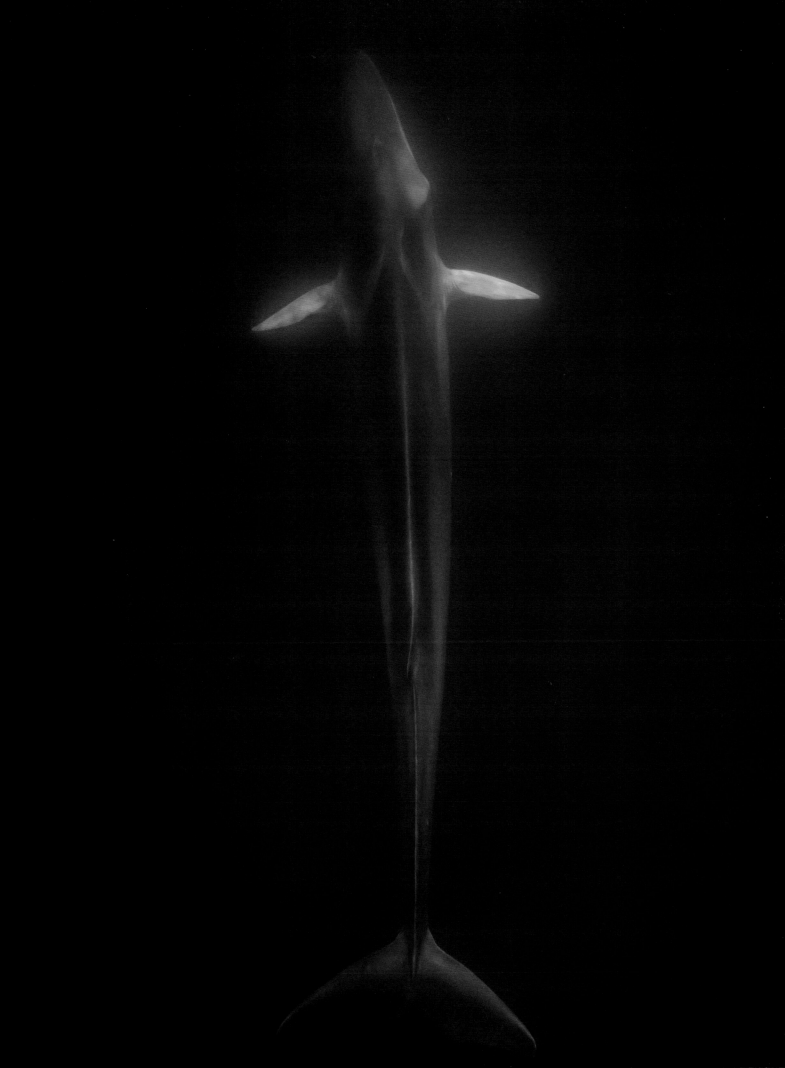

disappeared. Where they are ultimately going is still unknown. From a catalogue of over 1,200 individual blue whales that Richard has for the North Atlantic, only two have been spotted in both the Gulf of St Lawrence in the west and the Azores Islands in the east, showing that the interaction between these groups appears to be limited.

Blue whales are mostly solitary animals, but they will come together where food is plentiful. They are dependent solely on krill for their diet, travelling long distances to coincide with seasonal blooms across the ocean. We cannot predict how these areas might be altered by climate change in the future – they might become weaker and less productive or they might move entirely. The north-west Atlantic blue whale population is not growing as fast as the north Pacific population, and their future remains uncertain. Numbers are estimated to be between 300 and 600 individuals and only 23 calves have been seen in the last 40 years. Blue whales come into the St Lawrence estuary to feed, which brings additional concerns about impacts from boat strikes and an ecosystem that it is still highly polluted.

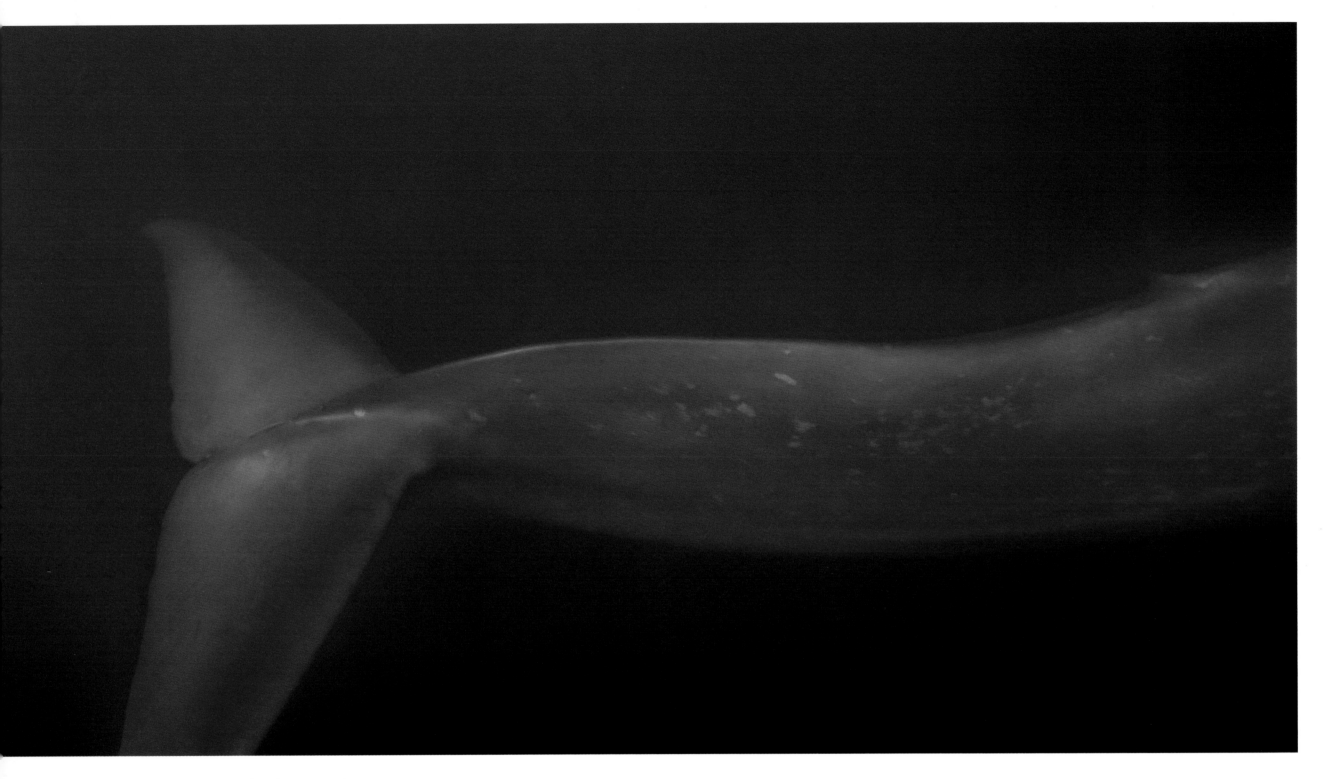

No lens or camera can transmit the mighty presence and majesty
of the largest animal that ever lived

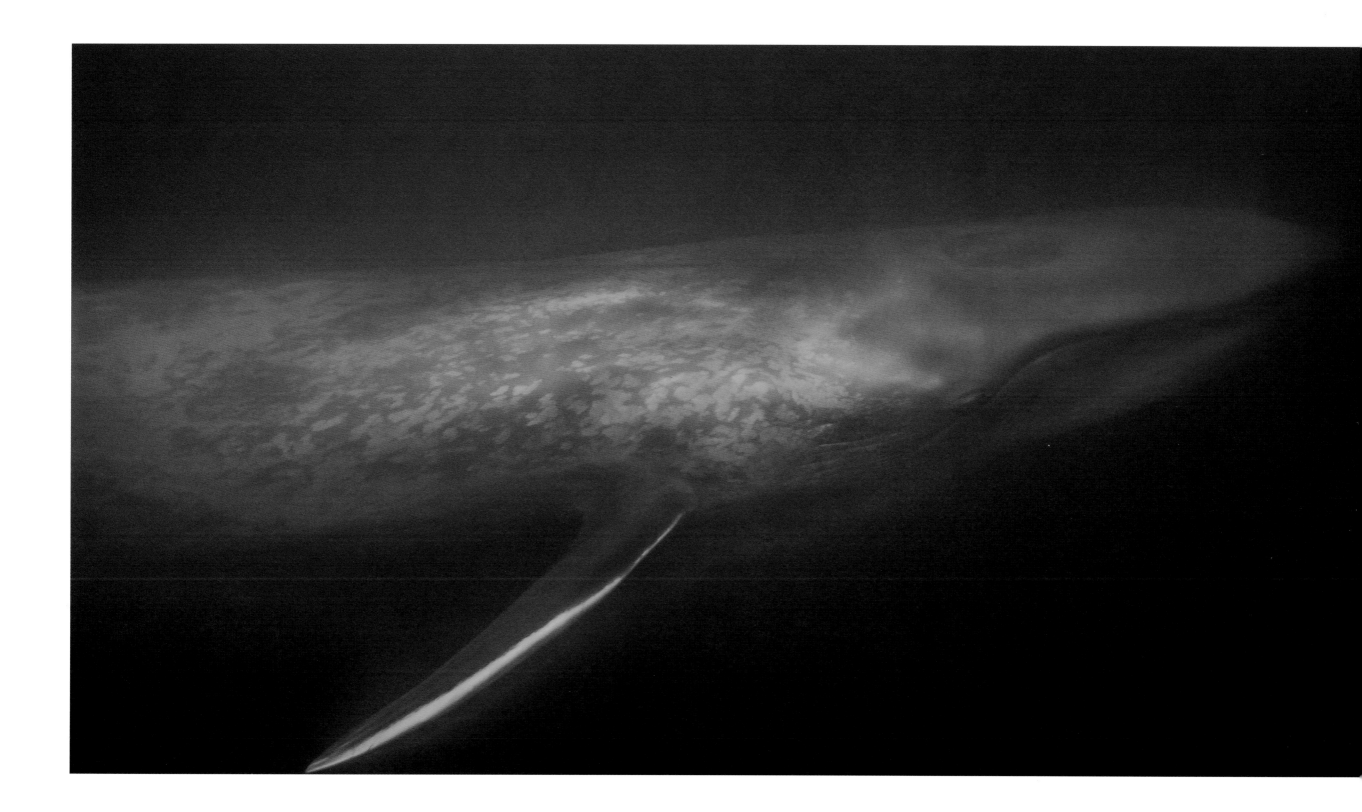

In 1997, whale biologist Peter Gill was reading a report of a research cruise that had been surveying waters off the coast of southern Australia. Buried deep within the document were records of numerous blue whale sightings, something unprecedented in this part of the world. Peter persuaded a friend to take his yacht out there to seek them out, and within a day they had found them. This region is known as the Bonney Upwelling, an area of nutrient-rich water drawn up from the deep that supports the phytoplankton – the plant-like plankton that are fed on by swarms of krill, in turn attracting blue whales. From this first encounter has blossomed a project seeking to understand why this smaller subspecies of blue whale, the pygmy blue whale, was gathering in this location through summer and autumn. This pygmy subspecies can still grow to a length of 24 metres and are thought to be more numerous than their larger cousins. Leading mostly solitary lives, they will come together to feed and breed, the males exhibiting vocalizations similar to the song of the humpback whale as a means to attract a mate. The female will gestate for 10–12 months before giving birth to a calf, nursing it for up to a year on milk that is rich in fat and nutrients. After a year, the calf will be weaned and will start to hunt on its own.

Compared to humpbacks or southern right whales, blue whales have only a thin layer of blubber on which to rely for their food reserves, so they need to keep moving from one productive area to another, following seasonal blooms of krill. Each season Peter and his team from the Blue Whale Study are on the water using photo identification to study how whales interact with each other, how long they remain in one area and the extent to which they are moving between different areas. After leaving southern Australia an individual might wander as far west as Madagascar or down to the sub-Antarctic. There is good evidence that some of these blue whales are travelling up to Indonesia to breed, and many have also been sighted in another productive feeding ground in western Australia. Beyond this, their movements remain unknown.

Whales bring insight into what is happening in our deep oceans. The sperm whale is an animal of extremes. It has the most powerful sonar system and the biggest brain in the natural world; they descend deeper than almost any other mammal in search of food. Their diet consists mostly of deep-water squid, and they eat up to 3% of their body-weight every day. They live for most of their lives in family units of about six to nine animals. These groups are based around females that will suckle each other's young, socialize and defend themselves communally. The males tend to be more solitary, leaving the family unit when they reach maturity to head towards more productive polar waters. Hal Whitehead spends a quarter of every year on his boat *Balaena* watching, listening and recording the behaviour of sperm whales at study sites in the Galapagos and Dominica in the Caribbean:

*Through my work I hope we can perhaps understand that extraordinary animal, the sperm whale, as well as perhaps our own cultures, better; I also think that we need to understand how our actions are impacting on sperm whales. There are still threats from the growing impact of ocean noise, ship strikes, the huge quantity of garbage that we put into the ocean, as well as accumulation of chemicals in their bodies.*

Sperm whales are a species that were hit hard by over two centuries of whaling activities that saw fleets pursue them in oceans around the globe. [CONTD PAGE 185]

GUARDIAN **William Trubridge** is a world record-holding freediver. He runs a freediving school and annual competition at Dean's Blue Hole in the Bahamas and is at the forefront of a campaign for the protection of the Hector's and Maui dolphin in New Zealand.

When I was 18 months old my parents sold our house in the UK, bought a boat and sailed out across the Atlantic and the Pacific Oceans to New Zealand. The boat was my home for three years and the ocean was my playground and classroom. My passion and love for the oceans goes all the way back to the experiences I had as a young boy – swimming among reefs that were alive with life and colour. By the time I was eight years old I was diving down to 15 metres and challenging my brother to see who could fetch the deepest stones from the seabed. I have always liked to challenge and test myself; and when I discovered that there was a competitive element to freediving I left New Zealand for the Caribbean and became hooked.

Freediving is a sport where you hold your breath and go as deep as possible. I hold records in two disciplines: 124 metres in the 'free immersion' category where you pull yourself along a weighted rope; and 102 metres for the 'constant weight – no fins' category where you swim downwards with no external assistance. I have trained for years to be able to reach these depths, preparing my body for the physiological challenge and my mind for the mental challenge. I train and compete at Dean's Blue Hole

on Long Island in the Bahamas. The dark-blue, circular pool just off the beach plunges downwards and opens out like an hourglass to a depth of 202 metres – making it the world's deepest sinkhole.

Descending from the clear, sunlit surface I swim downwards. After 30 metres I become negatively buoyant and can begin to glide through a silent water column. Light begins to fade after about 40 metres and I continue to drop down into the darkness for two minutes. My heartbeat has slowed, blood is flowing into my core and I can feel the pressure growing around my body. Once I reach my target depth, I begin my return to the surface, drawing out the long strokes of my arms and legs as I fight the need to breathe for a further two minutes. Each time I do a dive, I put myself through an intense psychological experience, but to succeed I must remain calm and focused, shutting out the voices of doubt and fear. One of the legends of freediving, Umberto Pelizzari, said, 'the SCUBA diver dives to look around, the freediver dives to look inside'. As I dive, I am having both a conversation with myself and with the ocean that is enveloping me to retain the serenity that I need to succeed.

When I was preparing to be the first person to descend to 100 metres – a distance known as a hectometre – I stumbled across the Hector's dolphin and learned about the threats it faces from fishing nets and trawlers. This species is only found in New Zealand's waters and is among the world's smallest marine dolphins. Over the last 40 years their population has fallen to only 7,000 remaining individuals. A closely related subspecies, the Maui dolphin is only found off the west coast of the North Island and 50 individuals are known to remain. The

> *Descending from the clear, sunlit surface I swim downwards. After 30 metres I become negatively buoyant and can begin to glide through a silent water column. Light begins to fade after about 40 metres .... My heartbeat has slowed, blood is flowing into my core and I can feel the pressure growing around my body.*

situation is critical and the only solution is an immediate and complete ban on commercial and recreational fishing in the coastal areas where they live.

There is an outcry from people across the world for these dolphins to be protected; but equally the fishing industry protest that they must continue earning a living. This is not a vendetta against fishermen, but against a technique that is indiscriminate and threatens the survival of an iconic species. If I were in their shoes, and if the decision was between going bankrupt and causing the extinction of a species, I am confident that I would go and find something else to do. Using traps and lines is not just the only way to avoid the accidental capture of dolphins, but also a way for us to reduce the impact on fish stocks – in other words a way to ensure a sustainable future for our fishing industry.

I think that New Zealand's global reputation as an untouched paradise is unwarranted. It has the same landmass as Japan, but a population that is 5% of the size, so of course there is less human impact and large areas of wilderness. But there are also rivers which are unswimmable due to the dangerous levels of pollution and there have been many examples of unsustainable and destructive fishing. The protection of these dolphins,

> *This is not a vendetta against fishermen, but against a technique that is indiscriminate and threatens the survival of an iconic species .... Using traps and lines is ... the only way to avoid the accidental capture of dolphins*

our fish and our environment could come from the government with a swipe of the pen, but the measures that they have put into place so far are superficial and will do little to stop these declines.

There is undoubtedly a romantic side to my relationship to the sea. It has been a constant and profound presence in my life. When I leave the coast, I feel a longing to return. The sea has given me so much, it only feels natural now to give something back.

A historic worldwide population that may have been originally over 1.5 million was decimated year after year. The primary value of sperm whales was the spermaceti liquid within the head, which was used in a wide range of applications from lamp oil to soap, cosmetics and as a lubricant for cars. Hunting reached its peak after the Second World War when 25,000 were being taken each year, until fossil oils gradually took over. Hal Whitehead reflects that 'whaling was the oil industry of its day. Oil from the sperm whale literally lubricated the Industrial Revolution.'

One of the most closely studied groups of cetaceans must surely be the pods of spotted dolphins in the Bahamas that have been followed by Denise Herzing for the last 30 years. Most of the early dolphin research was focused on using captive dolphins, but Denise was determined to observe the lives of dolphins in their own environment, an approach used most famously by Dr Jane Goodall with chimpanzees and Dian Fossey with gorillas. One resident group of spotted dolphins from the shallow, clear waters of the Bahamas proved to be uniquely curious and for the most part willing participants in the research. Starting her research for the first time, Denise slipped into the ocean about

40 miles offshore from Grand Bahama. Out of the blue two dolphins appeared, swimming side by side, scanning her with clicks of sound. Over the next 30 years, Denise came to know each member of that community as if they were her family.

In turn, Denise has learned how to behave in dolphin society. Through trial and error, she has become aware of the messages she may be sending through her body language. Whenever she joined a pod of moving dolphins during her research, they would give her a position at the back of the group, but if she broke out of formation, there would be jittery turns and backward glances. Some individuals have their own unique way of greeting her, and, in time, this customary behaviour would be passed on to their offspring. At the start of every field season, Denise feels a mixture of excitement and concern over which animals have remained and which have been lost to tiger sharks or old age. Following the devastating hurricanes in 2005, the community experienced its greatest losses, and longer-term ecological changes and crashes in fish stocks have meant that the dolphins have now dispersed from their homeland. Denise is proud to have contributed to new insights in our

understanding of dolphins but believes that, in comparison to the scale of human impacts on oceans, conservation efforts are just a sticking plaster:

*It annoys me when I hear people talking about 'maintaining a percentage of a population' when I know that each dolphin has an individual character and a place within that society. If we give nature a break, it is pretty good at looking after itself, but I suspect we will lose some high-profile species in the next couple of decades; some populations are so vulnerable and confined to such a narrow area that any further human or natural disasters could mean extinction. It will be a hard lesson for humans to swallow and will be a real test for what we are prepared to lose before we question our behaviour to the point where change becomes a necessity.*

In Hurghada in Egypt, swimming with dolphins has become one of the most popular tourist activities. This pod of Indo-Pacific bottlenose dolphins comes to the shallow reef to socialize and sleep. They swim slowly over the reef with one eye closed, heading towards the surface every two or three minutes to breathe. The story of regular interaction with humans began when a three-year-old female dolphin was isolated from

her pod following a shark injury. Solitary dolphins are more social, and interact more confidently with people, and she developed a bond with some of the regular diving instructors she encountered. When she eventually re-joined the rest of her pod, she started to bring other members to interact with people, showing an incredible level of trust towards humans. Diving companies used this opportunity to sell a dolphin encounter experience to tourists. With growing competition between dive operators to get more people closer to the animals, the dolphins are spending less time on the reef and drawing away from the crowds.

Swiss marine biologist Angela Ziltener had been leading tourists as part of a collaborative research project on the dolphins, and she became gradually more concerned about the disturbance to their natural behaviour. Dolphins, like orcas, use sound to communicate as well as for navigation and hunting. With increasing noise from boats, dolphins struggle to hear one another and catch prey. Angela decided to set up her own organization to study this human impact and to find ways to protect them. Operators were earning a huge amount of money from these tours and for a long time they resisted

GUARDIAN **Ric O'Barry** was formerly a trainer of dolphins for the *Flipper* TV series, but for nearly 50 years he has been an activist and campaigner against dolphin captivity.

My first experience of dolphins was not until I was in my early twenties. I had spent five years in the Navy and was working for treasure-hunter Art McKee in the early 1960s. We were off the coast of the Bahamas when we saw a pod of spotted dolphins. The rest of the crew had all leapt out of the water fearing that the dorsal fins were sharks, but I jumped in. I realized that they wanted to play with me, and out in the wild ocean this interaction was completely on their terms.

Art helped me to get a job at the Miami Seaquarium, where I was initially helping to capture dolphins and collect live fish for the aquaria from around the Caribbean. I took on a role feeding sharks and dolphins, became an understudy to the dolphin trainers, and ultimately found myself in charge of training the dolphins in the shows. There had already been a *Flipper* film, and I became involved as the trainer when they started a pilot for the TV series. The stories revolve around a father, a ranger in a marine sanctuary, and his two sons, who tame a bottlenose dolphin that helps to protect the park, extract people from scrapes and catch various baddies, all through clicks and nods of the head. There were five dolphins that played the role of Flipper – the most commonly used were Kathy and Susie. There was a section of the Seaquarium that was exclusively for me and the five dolphins, and we lived right there on set. These were good times; I had my misgivings and sometimes questioned the rightness of what I was doing, but I didn't want to spoil the party.

The show wrapped up after four years, and when the spotlights faded I fell into a bit of a void. The moment I decided to commit my life to freeing dolphins was when Kathy died in my arms at the Seaquarium. After years in captivity, Kathy decided that she did not want to live any longer and sank to the bottom of the tank. Dolphins need to make a conscious effort to come to the surface to

> *The moment I decided to commit my life to freeing dolphins was when Kathy died in my arms at the Seaquarium. After years in captivity, Kathy decided that she did not want to live any longer and sank to the bottom of the tank.*

breathe. The day after Kathy died I was in jail in Bimini in the Bahamas, where I had tried to release a dolphin from a cage. I have since rescued and rehabilitated dolphins all over the world. I had spent ten years capturing and training dolphins and I have since spent 46 years releasing dolphins and campaigning against their capture for displays and aquaria.

There are still dolphins doing displays and kept in aquaria in numerous places and it is a multi-billion-dollar industry. In the Caribbean, the marketing is slick, bright and colourful, and the growing cruise market provides tens of thousands of eager customers every year. Audiences think they are seeing smiling dolphins; I see a spectacle of dominance and brainwashing. These are animals that naturally live in complex family groups, hunt, play and travel up to 40 km a day – and we want to keep them in a chlorinated box, reduce them to circus clowns and then sell this to the public as educational. When parents take their children to see a dolphin show, they are being taught to think that this is normal.

My strategy is simply to stop people buying tickets to dolphin shows. Social change must come from people, not governments, because governments listen to corporations, not people.

The film *The Cove* has changed everything. It showed the huge amount of suffering and cruelty inflicted as pods of dolphins in Taiji, Japan, were driven towards the shore, and individuals separated from their pod and dragged on to boats or butchered in the water. I have been to Japan every year since I first volunteered to go in 1979. I have sat for days on my own in the rain gathering video evidence and been threatened many times by the local fishermen. Last year I was arrested in the airport and marched out to spend 20 days in a detention centre. It's humiliating, but if it keeps the issue in the news then it's worth it.

Wherever a dolphin is in trouble in any part of the world, my phone will ring and I will do my best to get there and do something about it. My main adversaries for

the last 40 years have been the powerful interests behind the dolphinarium shows. My heart goes out to fishermen who capture dolphins to make a living, but they need to find an alternative – and where possible we will try to

> These are animals that naturally live in complex family groups, hunt, play and travel up to 40 km a day – and we want to keep them in a chlorinated box, reduce them to circus clowns and then sell this to the public as educational.

help them do that. What the fishermen in Taiji are doing is not part of a traditional culture – it has only happened on a large scale since 1969. The incentive is obviously the huge amount of money that they make from catching live dolphins. I am not a natural activist and the daily conflict in my life is wearing and dispiriting. But what keeps me going is the knowledge that fewer dolphins now suffer cruel and degrading lives – my passion and determination are as strong as ever.

Before we started, no one took dolphin captivity seriously. I used to have to justify and explain the problem to every journalist I met. People are catching on and things have improved across the globe. They don't capture dolphins any more in the USA, while Seaworld is halting its performing dolphin shows and will eventually stop keeping the animals in captivity. We are winning, but there is more than a lifetime's work still to do.

calls to change, but eventually she succeeded in setting up two areas around Hurghada where boats are restricted, protecting the dolphins from boat noise and overcrowding. Organized whale-watching tourism seems like the perfect solution for people to witness incredible natural spectacles and support local economies which have a vested interest in making sure they are protected. However, the experience of Hurghada clearly demonstrates how human competitiveness and greed can easily destroy the foundation on which that solution is built. Making money from watching whales and dolphins in the wild is of course preferable to hunting them for their blubber or capturing and training them to perform in tanks. It starts to become a problem, though, if cetacean populations are harmed by these activities. If they are less able to socialize, communicate and feed, then wildlife watching becomes an additional problem for the whales.

Whale watching has been rapidly growing in many countries that are tapping into a growing need for tourist experiences and encounters. Sri Lanka has some of the world's largest gatherings of sperm whales and blue whales, which remain year-round in the same region of the northern Indian Ocean. Operators offering whale-watching experiences have grown rapidly since 2008, and a throng of boats now surround herds, competing to get their passengers right in the middle of the action, irrespective of the disturbance to the whales. If whale watching is to survive without harming whales then it has to be tightly regulated and controlled. Erich Hoyt is now advocating that more whale watching is done from land:

*We have exploited the fact that cetaceans are curious about us and not as elusive and skittish as terrestrial animals and birds. The 'encounter driven' element of the business and the desire to please guests means that many operators are becoming increasingly aggressive and focused on the needs of people rather than wildlife.*

Whales have undoubtedly benefited from protection from hunting, but for many species their re-establishment is increasingly coming up against oceans that are busier and more crowded. In Patagonia, Miguel Iñíquez organizes annual surveys to look for whales and dolphins that have been stranded on the beach. They examine the dead animals for disease or injury, which can help to show whether there are emerging or long-lasting threats to populations. In some cases, the cause of death is obvious; the scarring on Commerson's dolphins shows clearly that they have been drowned by fishing gear. As oil companies have started to survey new areas of ocean we have seen a growth in the number of beaked whales that have been washed up dead on beaches. This is a group of whales that spends much of its time in deeper water and is much more susceptible to the deafening sound of seismic survey and military sonar. Seismic airguns are used for oil exploration, producing rapid, continuous and explosively loud blasts of air that have the potential to disorientate or damage the hearing of animals in the vicinity. Loud noises in the ocean are one of the possible causes of mass strandings of whales around the world and Miguel has worked with the companies to try to encourage them away from areas where we know animals are feeding and migrating.

The steady growth of many whale populations is one of the world's most precious success stories, but scientists are still understandably wary about the future. Will growing numbers of humpbacks have

Atlantic spotted dolphins have been extensively studied in the Bahamas, and have been shown to have sophisticated communication and social interaction. Their gestation period is 11 months, and the mother will take care of the calf, with the help of the other mothers, for at least five years

enough to feed on when they return to the colder northern and southern latitudes? Will blue whales be able to seek out new sources of krill? The answer to these questions is that we don't really know. Climate change will undoubtedly test the adaptability of species. Scarcity of food may lead to low birth rates or whales moving to unexpected parts of the world in search for food, or it may simply mean that whale numbers start to decline. As Arctic ice melts, orcas have been observed moving further north using newly melted passageways to target slow-moving species such as bowhead, narwhal and beluga. In the Aleutian Islands in the Canadian Arctic, the loss of baleen whales due to hunting in the 1960s led to orcas switching prey, targeting Stellar's sea lions, and then moving on to sea otters. With declines in sea otters, the numbers of sea urchins grazing on the kelp forests steadily grew. The dense strands of kelp are a vital nursery habitat for fish and the loss of this habitat caused commercial stocks to collapse and many fishermen to go bankrupt. This story reinforces the need for us to remember that the ocean is one linked system, and that our impacts can reverberate all the way through it.

The empathy that people have for whales is strong; stories of strandings and whales in trouble will captivate and concern. People want to help and to know that the animal is going to be all right. The invisible impacts from fishing-gear entanglement or seismic surveys are more remote and out of sight and therefore it is more difficult for people to perceive and care about them. We recognize our close ancestry with whales and dolphins, their intelligence, magnificence and close social bonds. Our growing knowledge of the sophisticated culture and society of whales reinforces the fact that our concerns should be conservation as well as welfare. We do not lack scientific knowledge, nor strong mandates and clear courses of action. What we still do not have is the opportunity to put on the brakes, to call for a time-out while we evaluate ourselves and our impacts. As one of the most visible residents of global oceans from the tropics to the poles, and encompassing species that feed on zooplankton, fish and mammals, whales are watchkeepers for the health of our seas. If whales are doing well, then there is a good chance that everything else is in good shape, too.

# WORDS FROM THE EXPERTS

*I love the mystery of blue whales, they are the planet's biggest animal, their huge blows are easy to spot from a boat, and yet they can just vanish. Blue whales are rare beasts, almost mythical. They have no home territory, and their migration patterns are largely unmapped and unknown*—Peter Gill

**Christie McMillan** is the Co-Founder and Research Director at the Marine Education and Research Society based in Port McNeill in Canada. Her research focuses on how to reduce human threats on cetaceans:

*We are based in Port McNeill, a small town on the north end of Vancouver Island, in a region where native Canadians have lived off the ocean for millennia and that is traditionally important for fishing and logging. Many members of the community are closely involved in our research, providing financial support, helping to collect data, sharing photos and reporting sightings. The area is designated as a provincial marine park and a growing number of people are now visiting to experience the amazing wildlife. It is really important to engage with people in these communities, and to work together to raise awareness and mitigate the threats like entanglement in fishing gear and boat collisions. If scientists start to talk about losing hope, then I worry that people will not be motivated to change their behaviour for the sake of protecting wildlife. Our mission is to inspire people about whales so that they are motivated to take action.*

**Roger Payne** is a scientist, musician and founder of Ocean Alliance. He was one of the first people to record humpback whale song and was one of the leaders behind the save the whale campaigns of the 1970s. He has spent many years in remote parts of Patagonia researching southern right whales:

*My sound recordings of humpback whales took my career from science to campaigning globally against commercial whaling, working with others to pressure governments to ban whaling. Once we had secured the global moratorium on whaling in 1982, I returned to my life as a whale researcher, living as close to them as I could. I took my wife and children with me into the field in Patagonia and we lived for years in a place we built a few yards from the high tide line, in a remote bay where our nearest neighbour was 10 miles away. It was in this environment that my children grew up, and it gave them a deep understanding of nature that has become part of their adult lives. At night the whales would come so close to our house that their breathing would awaken us – as lovely an interruption to sleep as can be imagined. A whale's great size must give it great confidence; very little must disturb or worry it. To a whale, humans probably seem to be just a part of the background. Once, while swimming in the shallows in Patagonia, I came across a female southern right whale. Her eyes were closed and she appeared to be asleep. When I approached, she opened an eye, looked me over, and closed it again—as if saying; 'when you've seen one of these, you've seen them all'. It was the greatest compliment a whale has ever paid me.*

**Angela Ziltener** is a Swiss zoologist and Research Associate at the University of Zurich. She is the Founder of Dolphin Watch Alliance, an organization that studies and protects a population of Indo-Pacific bottlenose dolphins around Hurghada and El-Gouna in Egypt:

*Humans want to interact with dolphins; there is a thrill from being in the water with an intelligent mammal. Considering the amount of disturbance to their lives, it seems incredible to me that dolphins are so tolerant. I have had over a thousand dives with these dolphins, and these moments are so intense. As a scientist you are trying to remain analytical and objective, but the emotional experience sometimes makes it really hard. The dolphins recognize me as an individual, encouraging me to interact with them by bringing me pufferfish or pieces of seaweed. I'm just there as a passive observer, but of course I wonder what they think I am. As I swim alongside them I can feel the eddies in the water from their movement. Their trust in me is so complete that their eye is closed on the side where I am swimming.*

**Peter Gill** is an expert on the pygmy blue whale of Southern Australia, and Honorary Research Fellow at Deakin University. He is the founder and Chief Executive of the Blue Whale Study, an independent not-for-profit research and education organization aimed at understanding and protecting blue whales and their feeding habitat:

*A vital part of my work is the time that I spend talking to young people about the blue whales, the Bonney Upwelling and the amazing sea life that is just off their coastline. There is no point in being a scientist sitting in an ivory tower, we have to draw people into our work. Each year I take on a small group of students to give them a few days of hands-on experience observing and recording whales from our boat. In ten or twenty years time, I want young people to feel they have a responsibility for these whales and can stand up and defend them. I want to do whatever I can to ensure that blue whales have a good chance of being around for a few million years.*

**Filipa Samarra** is a Post-Doctoral Fellow with the Marine and Freshwater Research Institute in Iceland. She is the Lead Scientist on the Icelandic Orca Project, which researches the behaviour and foraging ecology of orcas:

*My research is based in the Vestmannaeyjar Archipelago (Westman Islands) in the south of Iceland. The more I learned, the more questions I had about this population, so for the last ten years I have continued my research on Icelandic killer whales, spending the summer season photographing and recording behaviour from land and sea. Understanding the behaviour of killer whales within such a large and dynamic system is difficult and we will need a few more seasons of data before we can begin to see any emerging patterns. We need to continue to gather data about the condition and health of this population to see if there is a need for protection measures, but I worry that by the time we have gathered enough data to be sure about what is happening it will be too late to do anything about it. My work only tells a very small part of the story, and I sometimes question whether what I do is meaningful, but ultimately I want to help people become more interested in their world.*

**Miguel Iñiguez** has been the Argentine delegate for the International Whaling Commission since 2002 and is the Founder of the Fundación Cethus, an organization researching and promoting the conservation of cetaceans in the Argentine Sea:

*Originally, all I wanted to do was research, but I have recognized that helping communities to learn and understand is as important if we are going to ensure that cetaceans are valued and protected. My aim to spend the majority of my career observing and recording whale behaviour was ultimately confounded by my growing involvement with the International Whaling Commission. I now act as a stand-in delegate for Argentina, spending nearly five months a year travelling to different meetings. There are still some countries that are taking whales commercially, but there is strong dialogue between the two sides and conservation plans have been agreed that will help our most threatened species. The sea is becoming more depleted of life, and human impacts are reaching further and deeper. Whales are the flagships for the wider marine environment, and, if we can't hold on to them, I think there is very little hope that the rest of the ecosystem could survive.*

**Richard Sears** founded the Mingan Island Cetacean Study in 1979 to study the seasonal migrations and habitat use of cetaceans in the Gulf of St Lawrence:

*Our job is to observe oceans and try and piece together their behaviour from tiny glimpses of their lives on the surface of the water. There are often some universal truths in cetacean behaviour that we can all recognize, and in many scenarios I can fairly confidently predict what a whale is going to do next; but I also love it when they surprise me. Some animals don't want to have anything to do with us and they will slap their tail as we approach; others will be incredibly curious and interactive with us. If the animals are moving quickly looking for patches of food, then they make it clear that they have more pressing interests. On other days the same animal could be much more relaxed. With the knowledge we have now, our experience at sea is so much richer, we know the histories of many individual fin, blue and humpback whales that come each season to the Gulf of St Lawrence. My fundamental interest is to learn more about these species, but at the same time I want our knowledge and observations to be used to help protect those species that are not doing so well.*

**Denise Herzing** has spent three decades observing Atlantic spotted dolphins underwater in the Bahamas. She is an affiliate Assistant Professor in Biology at Florida Atlantic University and the founder and Research Director of the Wild Dolphin Project, a long-term research programme studying their behaviour, communication and habitat:

*Keeping a research organization going for thirty years has been really tough; the responsibility of raising money, dealing with weather, and keeping the boats and operation going every year is a constant pressure for me. Now, I need to find a way to make sure that this work continues into the future and to find people who are prepared to devote their lives to the sea and the dolphin research. Everyone thinks they want to be a cetacean researcher until they discover what it is really like! It is a tough life in hard physical conditions, but the rewards from dolphins and strong bonds within the crew have kept me coming back for more. I am a strong believer that good biologists and ecologists need to spend time in the field; it is here that you learn about yourself, your subjects and making your own discoveries and insights. Spending my life in the ocean is hard, physical work, but every day I am at sea the wild, dynamic environment restores and reinvigorates me.*

**Hal Whitehead** is a Professor at Dalhousie University in Nova Scotia, Canada, and has been studying whale behaviour for over 40 years. Every year he returns to his study sites in the North Atlantic and Galapagos on his boat *Balaena* to study behaviour, ecology and population biology of sperm whales and northern bottlenose dolphins:

*With a small group of researchers we set off on two- to three-week trips on a 40-foot sailing yacht, returning to our sites off the island of Dominica in the Caribbean and in the Galapagos in the Eastern Pacific. We search for the whales using hydrophones and then follow them, listening to their clicks, recording their behaviour and collecting samples of faeces from the water. From these observations we learn about how they interact with each other in a three-dimensional space. From our own societies we understand how we share information and learn from each other. This allows us to build up a human culture which influences the way we share information, customs and ideas, and ultimately to develop complex machines. Sperm whales too have a complex culture that influences their feeding, movement, play, songs and social conventions. In the Galapagos Islands we found two clans of sperm whale who lived in the same area, but had different ways of moving, socializing and communicating with each other.*

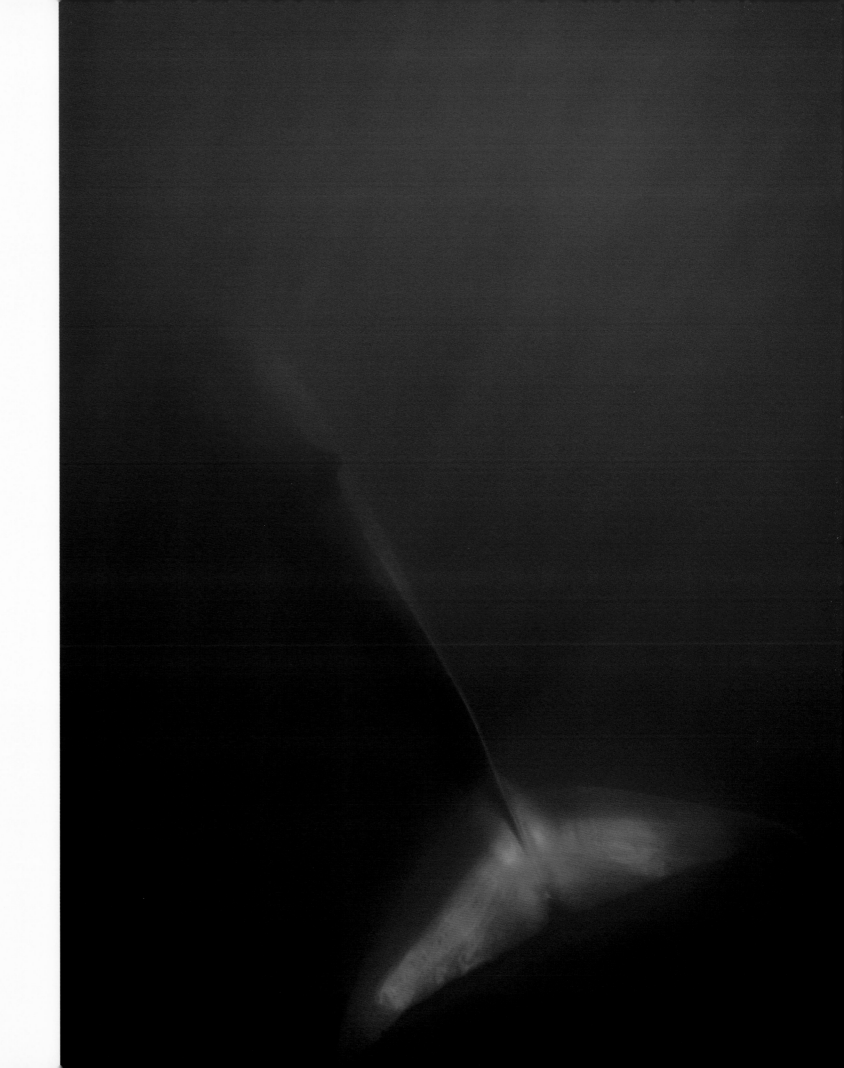

**Erich Hoyt** is a research fellow with Whale and Dolphin Conservation in the UK. He has written more than 20 books and hundreds of articles on cetaceans and many other subjects:

*My idea of protected areas for whales goes back to British Columbia in 1980. We were fighting for a reserve at Robson Bight, an area that was important for killer whales. A logging company was going to boom logs across the bay where the whales fed, rested, played and carried on a cultural behaviour in which they rubbed their bodies on pebbles along the shallow shoreline. We created a popular movement, drawing in scientists to provide evidence and credibility, and ultimately Robson Bight was protected. Still, we didn't ask for anywhere near enough. Back then there were only a few marine protected areas, so in hindsight we were naïve about the sort of scale needed. In recent decades, there have been huge efforts to protect the oceans, but I realized that cetaceans were still not getting into the picture. We needed a tool that could identify the most important parts of the ocean for cetaceans and help put them on the road towards becoming protected areas. Over the last few years a growing number of scientists have joined efforts to create Important Marine Mammal Areas, or IMMAs, across the world's oceans.*

# SHARKS

SHARKS INSPIRE AWE AND FEAR in equal measure, shadowing our minds like no other species on land or sea. They are one of the most ancient animals on the planet, having survived through millions of years. Their long existence in our oceans intensifies the wonder that we feel towards them. Indeed a proper understanding of sharks is possible only within the context of the vast expanse of time that they have existed on the planet. They have been able to evolve and adapt in virtually every aquatic environment – shallow reefs, deep beneath the Arctic and in estuaries and mangroves. Sharks are highly specialized and perfectly suited to each of the environmental niches that they occupy, and they have developed incredible adaptations for camouflage, hunting, energy preservation and reproduction.

Shark biologists inevitably become advocates for their protection, recognizing through their own observations that our seas have been rapidly depleted. The shark specialists that we feature in *Call of the Blue* have a shared ambition to use their scientific understanding to improve the conservation of sharks – to design better protected areas, reduce the numbers caught in fishing gear and safeguard the few remaining global hotspots where sharks aggregate.

The human relationship with sharks has evolved within a few short decades; gradually, we are overcoming the imaginary monsters created in film and beginning to understand the incredible realities of the lives of sharks. Fear is one route towards love and understanding. For many, seeing the film *Jaws* has inspired a love of the ocean, yet that film could also reinforce a deep-rooted unease when swimming in the dark ocean. Mikki McComb-Kobza saw the film at a young age, and it instilled in her a fear that took over her life, but ultimately shaped her life's work and passion:

*I thought sharks were everywhere, under the bed and in the carpet. I would sit cross-legged at the kitchen table, so my legs wouldn't get bitten off, and I swam in the pool as if my life depended on it. I channelled my obsession into learning more about them and eventually discovering for myself that they were not the monsters that were portrayed in the film.*

Our understanding of shark behaviour has increased massively, and we are gradually leaving

ABOVE AND FACING Oceanic whitetip sharks range across vast areas of ocean in search of prey, often accompanied by a troop of pilot fish waiting to snap up any leftovers

PREVIOUS The silky shark is a highly mobile migratory species that becomes active and inquisitive at dusk

202

behind the perception that they are all killing machines hunting humans to eat. The lazy taglines of journalists who describe all sharks as 'man-eaters' or the cliché of people being lost in 'shark-infested waters' are gradually being replaced by a better understanding of their behaviour and recognition of sharks as fascinating, ancient and highly adapted creatures.

We have not yet completely broken out of our association of sharks with danger and adrenalin. In parts of the world this remains the primary marketing material that encourages over 100,000 people a year into a cage to experience great white sharks. The water is chummed with a soup of blood and mashed fish, attracting sharks and manipulating their behaviour so that they become more frenzied and aggressive in response. Without chumming, the chances of tourists seeing a shark would be remote, yet what they are seeing is a poor representation of their behaviour. It remains disputed whether the increase in cage diving has led to a rise in the number of attacks on surfers and spearfishermen, but the practice has now been banned in the Cayman Islands, Florida, Hawaii and South Africa. [CONTD PAGE 210]

GUARDIAN **Paul de Gelder** is an author, motivational speaker, former member of the Royal Australian Navy Clearance Diving Force and shark attack survivor.

The oceans have always played a big part in my life and my Dad had taught me to swim before I could walk. As I grew up, the ocean was where I would escape to swim, surf and muck about. My Grandad would take me spearfishing in a drop off along Flinders beach: we swum out to where the sea was so deep you had no idea what was lurking beneath you. Years later, when I was in the Navy, I heard that great white sharks were commonly seen there. I have always been afraid of sharks; it is the fear of the unknown and the primeval terror of being eaten alive. Watching *Jaws* and the *Pirhana* films etched some pretty convincing ghosts in my imagination, but it never stopped me getting in the water.

My life started to unravel when we had to move away from the sea to Canberra. I lost an interest in swimming, life and learning. This part of my life isn't what I want to talk about here, but I ended up spending my time drinking, stealing and fighting. Eventually things boiled over and I was kicked out of my home and ended up becoming a bouncer at a strip club, selling drugs and living off benefits and pot noodles in a house with no beds or electricity. I knew I had to do something drastic, and joining the infantry seemed like the best way out of this rut. I went on to become a Navy Clearance Diver, passing a gruelling series of selection tests followed by years of specialist training to work in the most extreme underwater conditions, clearing explosives or launching covert attacks.

It was a good decision, the best I have made in my life. I learned a hell of a lot about myself from my time in the forces – I stopped being afraid of failure and learned how to sort myself out in pretty much any situation.

On the morning of 11 February 2009, I was part of a Navy exercise in Sydney Harbour to test a new sonar defence system. I had dived here hundreds of times, and had never seen a shark. I had taken over from another guy, just swimming in a wetsuit on the surface, when I felt a massive whack in my leg; I looked down to see the head of a huge bull shark with my leg in its teeth. Fear and

> *I looked down to see the head of a huge bull shark with my leg in its teeth. Fear and adrenalin kicked in and I tried to push it off ...*

adrenalin kicked in and I tried to push it off, but my arm just felt pinned by my side, I hadn't realized my hand was also in its mouth. I was punching it on the nose with my other hand trying to get free. The attack probably only lasted an instant; it started gnawing at me and dragging me underwater and then I was released and struggled up to the surface and thrashed my way back towards the boat. I was hauled out of the water and passed out. The rescue was already well under way and the speed with which I was stabilized and in surgery no doubt saved my life.

I spent two months in hospital and had my leg and arm amputated. The physical and psychological recovery took much longer. As a Navy Clearance Diver I had a great sense of pride and commitment to my job. Sitting in a

hospital bed without an arm and leg, I was staring down the barrel of losing any sense of fulfilment. Every day we are mobilized by our jobs, sports, passions and loves and I thought I had lost these. If I were going to survive I had to find a new purpose in a new life. The first thing I did when I had my stitches taken out was to go surfing – the sea has the capacity to wash away stresses, calm you down and make you feel better about everything, but don't imagine for a second that recovery was as simple as a dip in the sea; I struggled for months to rebuild my strength and confidence.

From the moment I woke up in hospital I have never held a grudge against the shark. After my encounter people kept calling for sharks to be culled, to be cleared out of the sea. The issue rumbles on every time there is a shark attack in Australia. My argument is that the sea is their domain; we're the ones trespassing in their territory. I was invited to join a United Nations conference on shark finning and started reading up about what was happening to sharks across the world and how millions were being caught to end up in soup. It seemed to me that humans should know better and this movement to protect sharks was something that was necessary. I was asked to do a shark documentary, where I was to swim with grey nurse sharks in an aquarium. I remember feeling more comfortable just looking at the tail. Since then I've worked my way up to diving with reef sharks, bull sharks and great white sharks. I'm at peace with it now.

My story is no bigger or better than anyone else's, it is just a bit different. My life is good because I am helping other people overcome their own obstacles and giving

my voice to shark conservation. My own happiness comes from offering a helping hand or a pat on the back to other people. I have spent time counselling and helping other victims of shark attacks. I think I can offer a unique perspective as a shark attack victim, but I also show them how they can adapt and overcome their fear. I give talks in schools too; if I can help children look after themselves, treat people better and protect our wild things, then that

> *Every time I leave the surface for a dive, a calm comes over me; I feel at peace, away from the rush of the world and in the presence of beautiful, alien animals.*

makes me happy. So far only 42 kids have fainted when I start talking about my injuries. You never know how challenges you face through life will change you or what opportunities will present themselves; my two biggest fears used to be sharks and public speaking!

Every time I leave the surface for a dive, a calm comes over me; I feel at peace, away from the rush of the world and in the presence of beautiful, alien animals. I think being underwater has the same attractions as being in wilderness – no more concrete, wi-fi or traffic and all that crap we get caught in. There are times when I curse the shark that, in just a few mad seconds, completely altered the course of my life, but it has never stopped me going back into the ocean. The chances of being attacked by a shark were a million to one, and what's the possibility of that happening twice? So, I figure I'm good to go.

The experience of diving with sharks that have not been artificially attracted is completely different. On the Island of Guadeloupe on the Pacific Coast of Mexico, biologist Mauricio Hoyos has championed an experience where divers can see the same species of shark, but in a different light – serenely patrolling and mildly curious of the divers watching them. Our perception of sharks has been skewed by our own behaviour towards them, creating monsters for tourists that perpetuate a sensationalist myth. The point is important for conservation – people will not protect sharks if they see them as monsters. The public perception of sharks has changed a great deal; there used to be outrage that dolphins were caught in tuna nets, but little was said about sharks. Now there are campaigns across the world to pressure governments to put in place tough measures to stop shark finning, longlining and the global trade in shark fins.

For many years, no one was standing up for sharks in the same way that they were for whales and dolphins. Through the 1990s fleets of fishing vessels and trading networks were being set up to service the growing demand for shark-fin soup in China, and few people were showing concern. The turning-point seems to have come at the turn of the millennium, as scientists started recording reefs and whole ocean basins where sharks were virtually absent. Sharks have lived through five global mass extinction events, yet their future is threatened by the massive demand for their fins to add texture to soup. The number being fished cannot possibly be sustained, and more has to be done nationally and internationally to stop this trade and find better alternatives for fishermen. The story for sharks now is whether protection and conservation measures can be put in place quickly enough, and whether they can be enforced effectively and for long enough to allow shark populations to recover. International concerns over the sustainability and welfare of sharks has meant that demand for shark fins is waning, but the tradition of eating shark-fin soup is strongly ingrained in some cultures and continues to drive shark fishing across the globe.

The pressure on shark populations in the seas around Central America has been considerable, with exploitation driven by demand for meat and for shark-fin soup in Asian countries. Yet when shark conservation scientist Rachel Graham talks to the fishermen about these dramatic declines, many blame anything and anyone for this sudden disappearance: 'they will say that weather is driving them offshore, migration patterns have changed or that there is too much pollution in the water.' In order to change these mindsets and perceptions, Rachel has realized that you must start from within communities:

*We have spent countless days out on boats with fishermen, who are central and core to our team, catching and tagging sharks; sharing the same boat, getting stuck into the work and chatting about daily life, work, fishing and girlfriends. This close collaboration helps to put us in other people's shoes, and in turn these fishermen have become some of the strongest advocates within the community for protection of sharks and rays. I am doubly proud that many of our scientists and team members are women: they are role models in many societies where these sorts of careers are not considered or valued as an option.*

Protection measures have been put in place to ban shark fishing across the whole territory of Palau, the Maldives, the Bahamas and Darwin and Wolf Islands in the north of the Galapagos archipelago. [CONTD PAGE 218]

Schools of scalloped hammerhead sharks

GUARDIAN **Kevin Huang** is a first-generation Canadian immigrant from Taiwan, who is helping Chinese communities in Vancouver, Canada, move away from shark-fin soup and embrace sustainable seafood.

My parents came from Taiwan seeking better opportunities, but like many immigrants they gravitated towards their own people, living in a bit of a cultural bubble in Vancouver. I am a first-generation Chinese Canadian, who took a different approach, immersing myself in English media and education. Many of my friends shared a desire to be less distinguishable from the predominant European ethnicity. It was not until I went back to Taiwan for the first time in my early twenties that I realised how 'white' I had grown. I went back because I wanted to reconnect with my cultural heritage. As I looked back into the history of Chinese Canadians I understood more about why communities such as ours find that they have to stick together and support each other.

I grew up eating a lot of fish and seafood, and seafood has huge cultural importance for Chinese people. I could peel shrimp before I could use chopsticks. As I grew up, I learned more about the industrialization of fishing fleets, the decimation of the shark populations and the destruction of mangroves and coastlines through the rapid development of shrimp farms. I found that environmental movements in Canada were very white and privileged and there was a strong tone of racism around the shark-fin campaigns – blaming and shaming Chinese people for the demise of shark populations around the world. We all make individual choices about what we buy and what we eat, but we do this on the basis of what we have learned, what our peers are doing and where we feel comfortable and secure.

In 2009 I founded SharkTruth with a fellow Chinese Canadian, Claudia Li. We wanted to lead a more positive campaign that would help protect sharks without demonizing people and cultures. We wanted to undo some of the myths that had grown up around shark-fin soup, not only in the eyes of the diners, but also as propagated by some of the other campaigners. Serving shark-fin soup at Chinese weddings is a tradition that is born out of generosity. Having worked hard and saved money for very special occasions, people wanted to give their friends and family the very best that they could afford. Shark fin was always an expensive, difficult-to- obtain commodity for many rural Chinese, but as we became richer it became more accessible to more people. The impact on shark

> *We wanted to lead a more positive campaign that would help protect sharks without demonizing people and cultures.*

populations became lost in the spate of capitalism and economic growth in China over the last 30 years.

The 'Happy Hearts Love Sharks' Wedding Contest was born out of a need to find a positive and empowering way to bring about change. Wedding couples who went 'fin free' at their weddings were entered into a contest to go swimming with whale sharks. This campaign alone has prevented over 80,000 bowls of soup being served, but more importantly it demonstrated how a positive message can be embraced and talked about in an optimistic context. Over the last ten years, campaigns to stop shark-fin soup being eaten grew from individual restaurants to hotel chains and whole cities and states; but for us it became uncomfortable when the issue became more xenophobic and aggressive – campaigners were standing outside restaurants telling the diners that they were disgusting. This approach was neither acceptable to us, nor likely to have a positive impact.

We have now widened our scope to include communities where environmental issues and cultural traditions meet. We recognized that changing tradition to fit with modern society needs to be done through a cohesive group of people who are motivated to solve this problem from within, rather than seeking to make people change by force. We need to help communities understand the impacts they are having and present solutions that work. Chinese people have lived in Canada for over 150 years, migrating to work on the railway or in search of better lives. Canada celebrates its multiculturalism, but it is not good at talking about the issues of the past. As we expand our work, we have learned more about class, society and race and how these have become ingrained in our food, media, sport and daily lives. Since Chinese food systems in Canada are often outside mainstream media and environmental cultures, the work that many restaurants and suppliers are doing to source sustainable seafood and improve their environmental footprint has gone unnoticed and uncelebrated. Our families came to Canada to give us a better quality of life – a place where we could have clean water, clear air and access to food. We are carrying on this lineage from our elders to create a place that can sustain us for many generations into the future.

Ensuring that there is no illegal fishing in such vast areas creates its own enforcement challenge and poaching undoubtedly continues. Longlining can devastate a spawning aggregation or resident reef population in just a few days, so these nations need to ensure that they are using satellite monitoring systems and fast patrol vessels to tackle the problem. In August 2017, the Ecuadorian authorities captured a boat leaving the Galapagos Islands with over 300 tons of shark destined for Chinese markets. Rachel Graham sees an increasing number of international conventions, plans of action, quotas, regional agreements, and even national legislation to protect sharks and rays, but in reality she believes there is still a chasm between what is written on paper and what is happening at sea and within communities:

*The nuts-and-bolts work of conservation may not be glamorous nor is it a quick fix – it is just a steady, repetitive combination of monitoring wildlife and building support from within communities to create the foundation for lasting conservation.*

Sharks are at the top of the food chain across our oceans and play a vital role in maintaining a healthy and balanced ecosystem by preying on fish and other animals that may be old, weak or diseased. The huge declines have taken place in just a few decades, a snap of the fingers in geological time-scales. When a top predator is missing from an ecosystem, the whole community suffers with knock-on impacts across the food chain. The loss of sharks on reefs in Jamaica has caused an increase in predatory fish such as snappers and groupers that feed on 'grazers' such as surgeon and parrot fish. Without these 'grazing' species to pick off the tufts of algae from the corals, these are gradually being smothered by the growing algae. As the corals die they are no longer able to support the rich and diverse communities of reef fish.

Understanding movement and migration is a critical component of shark ecology and key to protecting them. Tagging involves attaching electronic transmitters to the dorsal fin, or surgically implanting them within the shark. Tags transmit data to satellites whenever the shark breaks the surface or to a receiver fixed to the seabed. Yannis Papastamatiou has tracked thousands of sharks in the Atlantic and Pacific Oceans using these methods:

*In some ways, shark behaviour is similar to that of humans. We know that humans live in a house, leave their houses in the morning and then come back in the evening. Similarly, many sharks occupy a core area during the day, which they leave at night and come back to in the morning.*

Michelle Heupel tracked juvenile black tip sharks off the coast of Florida, their movements revealing how they use different parts of a bay through the day and through their lives. The experiments also revealed how finely tuned these sharks were to their environment, able to detect small physical and chemical changes in the water:

*A few hours before a hurricane hit the coastline, we saw how they were all moving out into the safety of deep water. They were all juveniles, so it must have been instinctive rather than learned behaviour. In other parts of the world, I have seen sharks leave areas after there has been flooding and then return once salinity returns to normal.*

Research expeditions are heading to some of the few remaining remote islands and oceanic atolls where shark populations remain healthy. [CONTD PAGE 228]

The thresher shark has a tail that can be as long as its body and uses it as a weapon to stun prey

The most feared of all marine animals, the great white shark has no known
natural predators other than orcas

Great whites live mostly in tropical and temperate waters including the
Mediterranean Sea, and are most abundant around large colonies of seals,
sea lions and cetaceans

Blue sharks patrol cooler temperate waters, hunting across the open ocean

The sleek, iridescent beauty of blue sharks in the open ocean

Galapagos sharks are sometimes seen among big schools of scalloped hammerheads

The National Geographic Pristine Seas expedition to Tristan da Cunha in the South Atlantic used baited underwater video cameras to identify and count shark populations around this remote volcanic island. The results revealed large numbers of large female and juvenile blue sharks, one of the most heavily fished sharks in the world. Studies from these expeditions have also revealed that large populations of sharks go hand in hand with vibrant ecosystems. Dr Michelle Heupel is part of the Global FinPrint project that is using similar technology to look at shark populations at over 200 sites around the world. In countries where sharks are well protected, such as Australia or the Bahamas, a large number of sharks are seen on camera. Alarmingly, in some parts of the oceans around Jamaica and Malaysia sightings are incredibly rare or not recorded at all.

Sharks are an exhilarating topic for any classroom, and shark biologists are great for drawing a crowd. Mikki McComb-Kobza delights in sharing her childhood curiosity and wonder for sharks, using her enthusiasm to generate wider interest in seas and the environment around them.

[CONTD PAGE 239]

Silky sharks have an extremely acute sense of hearing
and can detect prey at great distances

Dusky sharks migrate thousands of kilometres between the poles in the summer
and to the equator in the winter

Silky sharks are known to display a contorted 'threat' posture to warn
divers to stay clear. These silkies are apparently undisturbed

GUARDIAN **Regina Domingo** was inspired to dedicate her life to marine conservation by an island called Cocos. She has since set up Nakawe, an organization that is on the front line of conservation efforts to protect the future of sharks in Central America.

I have been infatuated by the remote Pacific Island of Cocos ever since I first saw a documentary about it. Cocos lies 550 km to the south west of Costa Rica and was designated a World Heritage site in 1987. Jacques Cousteau called it one of the most beautiful islands in the world. I was captivated by his films, but it was the images of huge shoals of hammerhead sharks that enthralled me – I needed to get to this island, and I needed to do something to help protect it.

I grew up by the sea near Barcelona and I became a diver and volunteer at a local rescue centre for turtles and dolphins. My father was a sled-dog musher and I was one of the first girls to race in long-distance competitions in Alaska, Norway and Finland.

I secured my first trip to Cocos to work as a volunteer ranger – it was as beautiful as I had imagined, a truly magical place. The marine life was incredible, with so many tuna, sharks, jacks and mantas it felt like Nature was having a party. I fell in love with an island, and I felt more complete than ever before in my life. As I spent longer on Cocos, however, I realized that it is under huge pressure from the fishing fleets that come in search of its sharks, tuna and other fish. We were pulling out longlines every day, filling whole warehouses full of illegal fishing gear. These fishermen wait just outside the park boundary and slip inside to set their nets, knowing that their chances of being caught are slim.

I spent time travelling and working as a dive guide and skipper in Panama, Mexico and Tonga, and I was seeing similar scenes there too – amazing, remote places that were suffering from illegal fishing and scarred by plastic pollution. There are thousands of organizations dedicated to marine conservation, yet it is not enough – we are still failing. I wanted to do something more.

I set up my organization, the Nakawe Project, in 2014. Nakawe is the goddess of the Earth and mother of all plant and animal life for the Huichol people of the Wixarika indigenous culture in Mexico. I had no experience in running a charity and people thought I was crazy, but we now have a small team campaigning to combat illegal shark fishing in Central America. From the moment I open my eyes in the morning to the moment I go to sleep, I am constantly thinking about how I can work more effectively, reach more people and take more action. This experience has allowed me to meet many amazing people who give everything that they can to help.

Our campaigns have shown Costa Ricans the close connection between community and national pride and the sharks that live in the seas. Every time I go to the market I see sharks for sale – protected species such as hammerheads, silky and thresher. Our research has shown that over 3,000 tonnes of sharks are being consumed locally every year. Many people don't even know they are eating sharks, or that sharks are endangered. I also wanted to target the fishing communities and find out where the boats were coming from, where the sharks were

> *Every time I go to the market I see sharks for sale – protected species such as hammerheads, silky and thresher .... Many people don't even know they are eating sharks, or that sharks are endangered.*

being caught, and where they were being exported to. Our film *Game over Fishing* has taken over two years to make and is designed to open Costa Ricans' eyes to the extent of the illegal fishing that is destroying their heritage.

Too many people spend their time thinking about how they can be rich, famous or more beautiful. I would like to see a global movement of people fighting to protect nature and the places that inspire them. I want to move the right people and inspire others in the same way that Cocos touched me.

She draws on her own research into the evolution of hammerhead shapes: the greater surface area within the head gives hammerhead sharks an enhanced ability to detect and find prey buried in sand or mud. These supremely sensitive smell and electrical sensors are also used to navigate across oceans, following well-established routes between seamounts as they migrate to mate and find food. Some of Mikki's students have become more involved in her research, helping to design and build a laser device that can measure the length of great white sharks from the safety of a cage. In Belize, Rachel Graham is taking schoolchildren into the water to meet sharks, an activity that might be a bit unnerving for their parents, but the success of this programme is proof that an opportunity for children to experience wildlife creates life-long advocates and enthusiasts. Gradually there is a new generation of people who are seeing sharks for their amazing senses and abilities, and as a species that is in need of protection rather than one to be feared and hounded.

The chances of someone being bitten by a shark are incredibly small, but equally the idea that there is no such thing as a dangerous shark is obviously not true.

[CONTD PAGE 244]

The crested bullhead shark is a nocturnal and bottom-dwelling species.
The form of its mouth allows it to eat sea urchins and other small invertebrates

Galapagos bullhead shark are endemic to the Galapagos and islands off Peru

ABOVE Blacktip reef sharks remain within a small reef territory for much of their adult life

FACING The sand tiger shark is docile but a stealthy nocturnal hunter,
its pointed and protruding teeth perfectly designed to grab and hold its prey

A wobbegong or carpet shark rests under a table coral.
Its shaggy beard mimics the branching coral above

A wobbegong or carpet shark camouflaged in the night reef

Yannis Papastamatiou cautions:

*It comes down to knowing the animal, how to behave around it and to know when it's time to get out of the water. Keep an eye on them and make it clear that you know they are there.*

Lauren Smith has dived with many shark species, and tells of an amazing encounter with an oceanic white tip off Cat Island in the Bahamas in which an individual white tip headed straight towards her, maintaining eye contact all the way until it turned at the last minute to brush past her:

*When I am in the water I am completely calm and focused, thinking only about the animal in front of me and nothing else. No matter how attuned you think you are to sharks, they will always be a wild animal and we should never forget that we are in their domain.*

Working with sharks is undoubtedly a huge privilege for scientists: the animals have such highly tuned senses and they are so finely adapted to their environment, but equally there is the burden of knowledge of the extent of our impact on them. [CONTD PAGE 253]

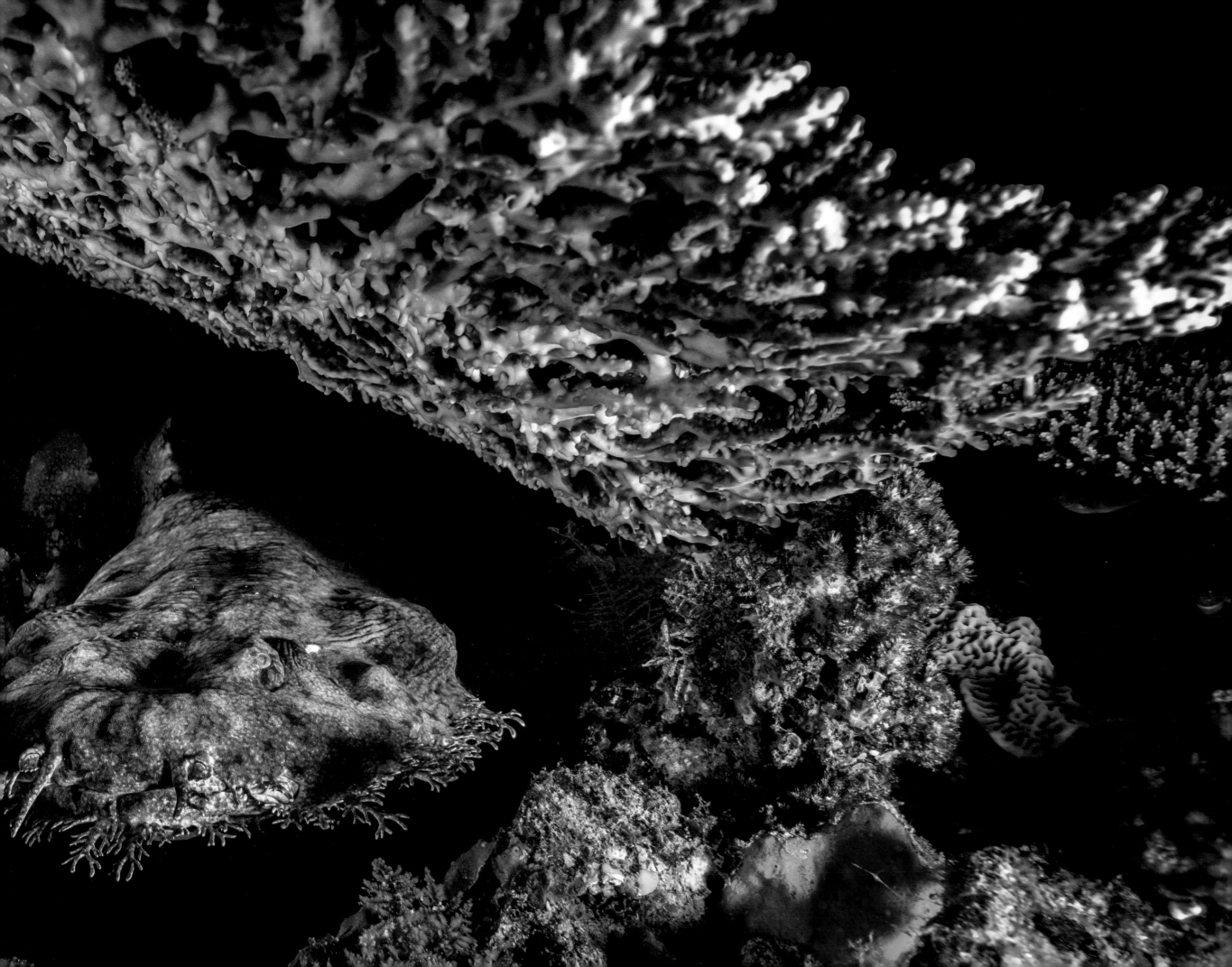

During mating, the male nurse shark grabs the female's pectoral fin with his
mouth to try to immobilize her

GUARDIAN **Paul Rose** is an explorer and television presenter. Formerly Base Commander of the Rothera Research Station in Antarctica, he is currently the Expedition Leader for National Geographic Pristine Seas Expeditions.

I grew up in Elm Park, in east London, a long way from the sea. I have always had an inexplicable and overwhelming desire to be outside, and would drag my mattress out on to the balcony to sleep at night as often as I could. We went to the coast for our holidays, and I did get to spend a bit of time in the countryside, but mostly I remember feeling claustrophobic as I grew up. On my television set I was watching Jacques Cousteau and Hans Haas having incredible adventures in exotic locations. My ultimate hero was the character Mike Nelson in the television series *Sea Hunt*, every week having adventures and rescuing pilots from crashed jets and surviving underwater knife fights, and of course all the beautiful women were falling in love with him. There was no doubt in my mind that I wanted to be a diver, and all I had to do was escape school with at least one qualification.

My experience at school was not a happy one – I was only ever good at sports and metalwork. When I was 14, our Geography teacher took us on a field trip near Merthyr Tydfil in Wales, taking me outdoors, out of the classroom and into the mountains. As we got closer to Wales our teacher became less of a teacher and more of a mountain enthusiast, transforming into a smiling, cagoule-wearing, inspiring man. I remember sitting on the back step peeling potatoes, and thinking, 'Wow, I'm alive'. I couldn't do geometry or trigonometry, but I could

do night navigation with a map and compass; it all made sense to me when it was real. If I were put in charge of the country for the day I would make sure that children spent at least half their time outdoors.

Diving defines me. The most important thing I have ever done was my first dive at Chesil Beach in Dorset. I had made my own wetsuit, cutting out the neoprene and taping the seams in yellow, just like the Cousteau diving team. We were in clear water, just off the beach and I can still feel the moment I rolled into the water, the water rushing through the holes in my wetsuit.

When I left school, I started off working as a panel beater for Ford Cars in Dagenham, but I was taking every opportunity I could to dive and get qualified as an outdoor instructor. I moved to the USA to work for

> *I urge young explorers to get out there and stand on it, walk around it, swim in it, touch and feel it, climb it, wiggle underneath it, get cold, hot, lost, eat whatever comes, be frightened and exhilarated and share it with others.*

Johnson Outboards, started teaching diving at schools, and then became an instructor and ultimately Director of the US Navy SCUBA diving programme at the Great Lakes Naval Training Centre. Seeing my son dive at the age of six was a reminder for me of the thrill of being able to breathe and see underwater, something I wish we could open up for many more people.

I spent the next decade of my life working with the British Antarctic Survey, spending every summer season

in this incredible, remote environment. We have so much to learn about the environment under the ice, but also the history of humanity contained within deep ice cores provides an incredible record on long-term climatic and atmospheric changes. I started off as a field assistant and ultimately became the Commander of the Base at Rothera. Every dive was a world first: we were seeing places that no one had ever dived, and finding many species that were unknown to science. Diving among moving ice is really tricky – icebergs can shift quite quickly and close off your exit. We were doing a dive to recover a lost piece of equipment and, as we rose off the bottom, we banged our heads on a huge iceberg that had been blown right on top of us. We had to leave our line and swim round all of these upside-down contours until we headed blindly upwards inside a fissure. With incredible luck we emerged back on the surface to greet an ashen-faced boat crew!

I have the sort of brain that can translate complex ideas into simple logistics and practical actions; and I think that's where the broadcasting work comes in. Since I left Antarctica I have had some incredible opportunities to make programmes about the sea, and to try and get across why people should care about ocean issues and help to change their perceptions and habits. For the BBC I organized expeditions to each of the world's oceans, travelling the world with a team of 25 people and two tonnes of equipment. It was an incredible opportunity to observe some of the strangest marine creatures and demystify some of the more hidden aspects of the oceans. We had an incredibly rare encounter with a six-gill shark, one of the most primitive sharks still living today – a relic from the Jurassic period and almost never seen in shallow

water. I was diving at night in the Straits of Messina, between Italy and Sicily, with a couple of tuna heads strapped to my belt. I could hear the nightclub music and racing motorbikes on the shore. This was our third attempt, and I was already towards the end of my dive at 37 metres when out of the dark came two green eyes heading straight for me – a six-gill shark! It stayed with me for a few minutes, before I had to leave and return to the surface.

I am really proud of a series I made about the underwater world around Great Britain. I think there is a common perception that you have to go to the tropics or the Arctic to see anything interesting, but we saw incredible wildlife during this series. One of the highlights for me was snorkelling with ten basking sharks just offshore in Cornwall. We discovered that if you stayed quite still they would approach really close – it is a truly incredible experience to have a 10-metre-long fish brush past you.

For the last few years I have been the Expedition Leader for the National Geographic Pristine Seas expedition. This has been an incredible opportunity to get out to some of the most remote and least explored oceanic islands to try to inspire action and create protected areas. The impact so far has been incredible with governments putting in place new marine reserves such as Ascension Island, Pitcairn and Rapa Nui (Easter Island). I have had amazing experiences in my life, but just because I have made these journeys doesn't mean that no one else can! I urge young explorers to get out there and stand on it, walk around it, swim in it, touch and feel it, climb it, wiggle underneath it, get cold, hot, lost, eat whatever comes, be frightened and exhilarated and share it with others.

Lemon sharks prefer shallow waters close to fringing mangroves,
targeting the fish that use them for nursery grounds

The determination of scientists to provide better understanding of sharks and more compelling cases for their protection is clear. There is a strong sense of positivity and optimism alongside a recognition that knowledge and understanding are key to their protection; but equally there are no illusions that, for some species, time is running out. No one is giving up; no one feels that this is not a cause worth fighting for; but all share a sense that there are shocks to come and that measures for the protection of sharks and the wider marine environment will have to be far-reaching and comprehensive. The passion, commitment and determination of so many people working to champion shark science and conservation are not in question. What remains unanswered is whether governments can provide the leadership, and society the backing and support.

## Whale sharks

The whale shark is the largest fish in the ocean, growing to lengths of up to 20 metres, yet much of its life remains hidden. It is difficult to believe that a fish so large could be so elusive – we still have little idea where they breed or give birth and our best guess is that they take at least three decades to become sexually mature. Whale sharks are found across the tropical oceans, but there are hotspots around the world where they are drawn to nutrient-rich waters that form the first step in a chain of ocean productivity that leads to blooms of microscopic phytoplankton. This in turn attracts the zooplankton and finally the whale sharks that feed on it. Oceanographic conditions may provide year-round sources of food; or whale sharks may (with an uncanny timing) arrive on reefs or isolated seamounts to feed off a glut of food from a fish-spawning event.

Each whale shark has a pattern of spots and stripes across its back, mimicking dappled sunlight or small schools of fish, helping to camouflage young sharks from potential predators. These markings are as unique as a human fingerprint and can be used by researchers to identify each individual shark as it returns to feeding spots or voyages the world.

Scientists began by sharing and comparing photos by post; now there are databases and software that can automatically recognize markings, and sharks can be instantly identified as they appear in different locations. The global database has enabled scientists to learn more about how long they may stay in one location, or migrate across ocean basins, and about how fast they grow.

Over the last ten years, Jim Hancock and the team at the Maldives Whale Shark Research Programme have observed 310 individual sharks in 5,000 sightings. The use of photo identification has shown how these sharks spend many years living and feeding around the archipelago, but where they come from or where they go to breed is still a mystery. In the Maldives, the shallow reefs and sandy atolls drop off steeply to the seafloor 4,000 metres below. Whale sharks are diving down to depths of several hundred metres, where they are most likely feeding on plankton and then returning to shallow water, cruising slowly in order to gradually recuperate and warm up their bodies.

The vast majority of known aggregations comprise juvenile males; sightings of female whale sharks are rare and pregnant females and very young whale sharks are almost unheard of. The Gulf of California in Mexico and an isolated island in the Galapagos chain are two of the few places where pregnant females have been seen. Dení Ramírez Macías knows that the Gulf of California is an important nursery ground, but populations fluctuate so it is difficult to get a sense of what is normal:

*Some years there were none, and now they are seen all year round. The same juveniles are returning year after year to coastal waters in Bahía de Los Ángeles, Bahía de la Paz and San Luis Gonzaga. The numbers have doubled to more than 120 individuals, perhaps indicating that they are moving in from other areas in search of food.*

Starting out as a scientist in Mozambique and feeling overwhelmed at how little was known about whale sharks, Simon Pierce first tried to establish why the sharks were coming to this part of the East African coast. He pieced together clues from water samples, satellite images of surface temperatures and maps of the seafloor. The island of Madagascar funnels the equatorial current into deep channels and around seamounts that form huge eddies over 300 km

The largest fish, the whale shark, feeding on some of the smallest prey – zooplankton

across. Close to the coast of Mozambique, the seabed plunges steeply, forcing up water rich in nutrients and laden with plankton. The use of satellite tags is a development that provides a more detailed picture of the movements of a small number of individuals. Experiences from tagged sharks in Indonesia show that migration and movement are highly variable, and scattered in many directions – some whale sharks ventured hundreds of kilometres out into the Pacific Ocean, and others remained close by, meandering along the coastline. Simon Pierce sees the same tagged shark, Rio Lady, every year at Isla Mujeres in the Yucatan peninsula, her voyages taking her 7,000 miles into the mid Atlantic and back again.

The whale shark is one of the most threatened of all fish, with populations declining by 80% over the past two decades. In the past whale sharks had been targeted in some countries for their meat, fashionable in Taiwanese restaurants as 'tofu shark'. Fisheries in India, the Philippines and Indonesia were catching hundreds of sharks a year, but the stocks soon became exhausted and much stricter regulations were put into place. The fins do not have the same gelatinous properties that are prized for shark-fin soup, but their

huge dorsal fins are sought as trophies to be pinned to restaurant walls. The principal threats to whale sharks are from accidental capture in fishing nets and from collisions with ships and fast-moving boats, but these losses remain largely hidden and unrecorded. As a species that has a vast range, there is a greater likelihood of encountering fishing gear and becoming entangled in nets, where they will starve and become asphyxiated. They are a slow growing, late maturing species that only gives birth to one pup at a time, so the population remains vulnerable to small and persistent losses.

When a species ranges over such vast distances it is vital that conservation is internationally co-ordinated; there is no point in having strict protection in one country while they are still being hunted elsewhere in the world. Management and enforcement cost time and money, and governments are reluctant to put regulations in place unless they know there is a clear need and a benefit. The impact of coastal gill nets and shipping traffic is now much better understood, and measures can be taken in locations which are known to be important for aggregations. In the Maldives, a country highly dependent on income from tourism,

the capture of whale sharks has been restricted since 1965, and fully protected across the archipelago since 1995.

The protection of whale sharks in the Gulf of California remains a constant battle between developers and conservationists. This narrow spit of water is hugely important for its marine biodiversity and is home to many migratory species. Measures have been put in place to protect marine life, but these have been hampered by powerful fishing interests and tourism development. For Dení Ramírez Macías, this means a constant battle to ensure that critical feeding grounds for whale sharks are protected from the clearing of mangroves and development of marinas and golf courses:

*People in Mexico are becoming more aware and proud of the amazing marine life in our waters and this will help us ensure that species such as whale sharks remain something we can cherish long into the future.*

The Mexican government is keen to protect whale sharks and is putting in place measures to reduce the impact from gill nets and introduce new

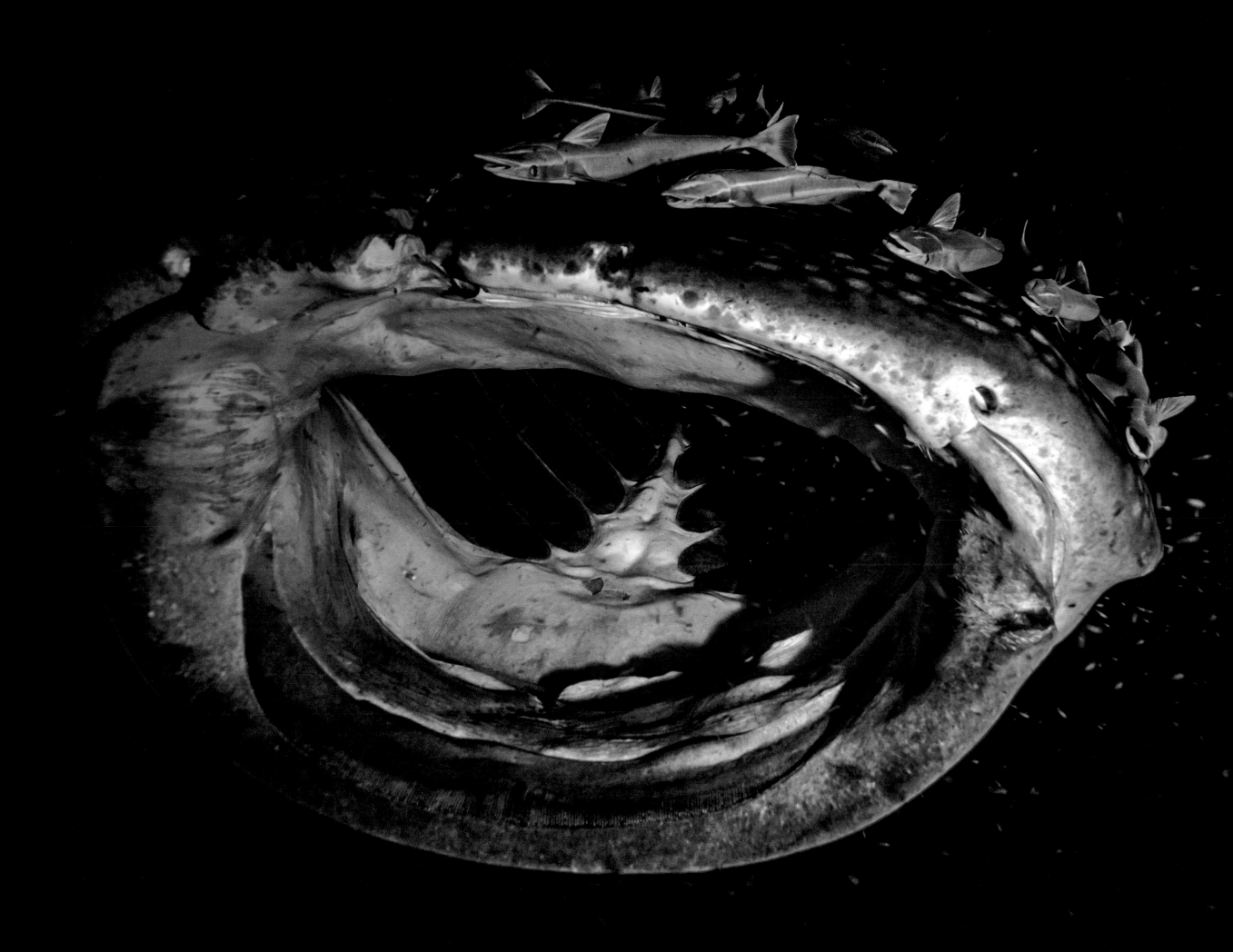

The remoras that hitch a lift from whale sharks bring no known
benefits and can sometimes cause real injuries

A whale shark silhouetted against scalloped hammerheads in the distance

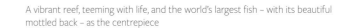

A vibrant reef, teeming with life, and the world's largest fish – with its beautiful mottled back – as the centrepiece

protected areas for whale sharks at Quintana Roo on the Yucatan Peninsula and Bahía de Los Ángeles in the Gulf of California.

Whale shark tourism around the world has grown enormously in the locations where they aggregate to feed. Ningaloo Reef in Western Australia was among the first to develop tours to swim with whale sharks, and tourism is developing rapidly in Belize, the Maldives, Mozambique and Indonesia. One of the biggest aggregations in the world was discovered only a few years ago off the Island of Mujeres in the Gulf of Mexico. A total of 600 were counted from the air, swimming in tight formation to hoover up vast amounts of eggs from spawning bonito tuna. This 'Afuera' event has become a huge tourist attraction and its short season is also a busy time for operators from the resorts of Cancun. In La Paz on the tip of the Baja peninsula, Dení Ramírez Macías watched the number of operators grow rapidly until there were over 100 different operators:

*At one point there were as many tourist boats as there were whale sharks; if there are only a couple of individuals around, it can be chaos with boats aggressively trying to secure space around the shark.*

She has been putting pressure on the government to limit the number of licences and ensure that operators are properly trained, so that they know how to approach sharks with minimal disturbance, developing a code of practice to make sure that boats are approaching slowly and are not crowding and disturbing any one individual.

There is a similar problem in the Maldives, where Jim Hancock and the team from the Maldives Whale Shark Research Programme have been trying to put in place better management and ensure that operators are trained and tourists educated:

*On an average day, a single shark will have 30 people swimming around it, and I have seen cases where there are 25 boats and 150 people in the water around a single shark. The best approach is to make sure that guests are taken into the water educated on how they should interact with the shark and encouraged with a sense of responsibility and empathy for an animal that is recuperating from time feeding in deep cold water.*

The economic importance of whale sharks helps to focus minds and ensure that they are protected from fishing, but the increased pressure from boats and tourism poses a new challenge as the numbers of tourists wanting to experience whale sharks continue to grow.

As scientists race to learn more about whale sharks, old threats fade away and new ones emerge: tourism may once have been seen to be the way for fishermen to find the new livelihoods that kept whale sharks alive, but now the popularity of swimming with whale sharks itself needs to be managed. Governments may act if there is international pressure, but too often the measures are superficial or inadequate and populations continue to decline. Globally, whale sharks are now endangered, but there are pockets of hope: populations are growing and, if we can connect and scale them up, then even ocean-ranging animals such as the whale shark can thrive. The work of researchers to build community support for our biggest fish is paying off; the challenge for the future is ensuring that growing pressure from tourism does not stifle this hard-won success.

# WORDS FROM THE EXPERTS

**Mauricio Hoyos** specializes in the great white and hammerhead sharks of the Gulf of California and islands of Guadalupe. He leads work to ensure that white shark tours are responsible and works with coastal fishermen to reduce the numbers of young sharks being captured:

*The great white shark spends a great deal of its life in coastal waters, and the females and young are particularly vulnerable to fishing nets when they come to shallow waters to give birth. Tourists are paying a huge amount of money for the experience of diving with sharks, so we need to find better ways of sharing this money more widely with fishing communities. The fishermen who border the Sea of Cortez have limited resources and are having to travel further and further to catch less and less. They are not seeing the benefits from the tourists coming to dive, so there is little justification for them to change their ways. When we talk to them, we try to learn more about the challenges that they have and how we can find options that can reduce the pressure on fishing and help them at the same time. Conservation needs to consider the realities of poverty and livelihoods – if not, it is doomed to failure.*

**Mikki McComb-Kobza** is the Executive Director of the Ocean First Institute in Colorado, USA, and an expert on shark physiology. She leads research and an outreach programme offering experiential education for young people to engage with marine science and sharks:

*Finding the way to becoming a shark biologist was a struggle for me; I wasn't sure if I was cut out to be a scientist, and living in Colorado, 1,000 miles from the sea, didn't help. For a time, I worked for an insurance claims company, sitting in an office cubicle with walls covered in pictures of sharks, dreaming of the life I really wanted. Eventually I made the leap and moved to the Florida Keys to become a diving instructor. Being a scientist has been the greatest adventure of my life. You have the opportunity to explore, observe and think about things with an open mind. I have to be creative in solving problems and try to make sense of my data and observations. There are disturbing stories out there, but people respond much better if you talk positively and practically about what they can do. I want to be able to keep bringing people to a place of hope and action.*

**Yannis Papastamatiou** is a marine biologist and Assistant Professor at Florida International University. He co-leads the Predator Ecology and Conservation Lab, specializing in shark and ray ecology, biology and behaviour:

*In terms of shark populations and conservation we need to look on a species-by-species basis; some really need urgent help and some localized populations are doing fine. A blanket statement that sharks are endangered or are recovering is false. Conservation and management cost money, so we need to make sure that we focus our efforts where they are really needed. We are starting to get a reasonable picture of which species need help and beginning to figure out how quickly they grow, how often they reproduce and how vulnerable they are. There is hope, and we need to keep up with the research and make sure that it is communicated well. It is great that we have so many people engaged and interested and as scientists we are getting better at talking about our work outside of our academic circles. I do feel that if we continue with concerted and targeted efforts we can make a difference. Sharks are not a lost cause; we are nowhere near to getting the job done, but we need to try and celebrate and build on the successes that we have had.*

**Rachel Graham** is the Founder and Executive Director of the Belize-based MarAlliance, an organization which undertakes research with small-scale fisheries and builds community support to protect sharks and rays:

*It's clear that we don't have time to waste – we are losing species and populations faster than we can generate champions to protect them, so we need to expand efforts to create more sites and make the survival of the large marine wildlife relevant for fishermen and their families. Twenty years ago, I was regularly seeing Caribbean reef sharks or bull sharks on Belize's reefs – now I am lucky if I see a nurse shark or a stingray. These changes have occurred in my own lifetime. Whole populations are simply disappearing. I dream of seas that are filled with thriving populations of sharks and rays, where every time I go snorkelling or diving I see wild populations of sharks that are not habituated to come in for feeding. What really motivates me on tough days is the thought of what our seas would be like if people weren't helping to protect our oceans.*

**Michelle Heupel** is an expert on the ecology and movement of sharks and other predatory fish at the Australian Institute of Marine Science, Queensland, Australia:

*The best part of my job is the thrill of discovery and the opportunity to share new knowledge with people. This is the fundamental drive behind science; and inevitably, as you learn more, further questions emerge. My job is to get answers to these questions and deliver information to help people make good decisions about how they manage society, resources and our environment – because I obviously want people to protect sharks. The loss of huge numbers of sharks in our oceans is undoubtedly bad news: we need everything in our marine systems, every species plays a part and nature doesn't make spares. We can't fix everything, but it is not all lost yet. We need to keep going, do better and try to find ways to give people solutions. As a scientist I have a role in this and a drive to make a contribution that is meaningful.*

**Lauren Smith** is a diver, photographer and shark biologist specializing in shark sensory and immune systems. She runs Saltwater Life, an educational initiative promoting enjoyment, appreciation and conservation of the ocean:

*One of my favourite experiences with sharks was diving over a seamount in the Azores to see blue sharks. They are a shy but curious species and would cautiously gain confidence and get closer to me throughout the dive. I was captivated by their sleek shape and graceful motion through the water. Back on the boat, I was shocked to learn that there was a high likelihood of these sharks ending up caught on a longline in these very same waters where hundreds of people come to visit the incredible megafauna, notably whales and sharks. Sometimes I wonder if the environment needs to get worse before it gets better. There is no doubt in my mind that changes will need to be far-reaching if they are going to have any impact. The incentives need to come from government, the change from fishermen and sea users, and the support from the public.*

**Dení Ramírez-Macías** is a conservation biologist and Director of Whale Shark Mexico. She has been studying the shark populations off Mexico and has led efforts to help protect them and their habitat. Recently she started to study in Peru in collaboration with Oceánica Perú:

*I work in eight different sites around the Gulf of California with a research boat and a team of scientists and volunteers. Using photo identification, we are studying where the animals are moving and how long they are staying in different areas. Our research continues to try and understand more about the movements and life history of whale sharks and how they are being impacted by human activities. People in Mexico are becoming more aware and proud of the amazing marine life in our waters and this will help us ensure that species such as whale sharks remain something we can cherish long into the future. I enjoy every day on the ocean and I know I am doing the right thing with my life.*

**Jim Hancock** is a marine biologist and co-founder of the Maldives Whale Shark Research Programme, an organization that conducts whale shark research and community awareness projects around the archipelago:

*Whale sharks have been a protected species in the Maldives since 1995, and there is full recognition of their value to tourism. Yet the main threat to whale sharks now comes from the growing pressure of tourism and boat traffic. In one sense this is great, as more people are having the opportunity to have an encounter with an amazing animal, but too many tourists are motivated solely by the opportunity to get a selfie and are crowding the animal oblivious to the stress they are causing. If whale sharks are touched or disturbed, then they will return to deeper water and possibly not return to their optimum body temperature. The best approach is to make sure that guests are taken into the water educated about the way they should interact with the shark and encouraged to develop a sense of responsibility and empathy for an animal that is recuperating in the warm, shallow waters.*

**Simon Pierce** is a co-founder of the Marine Megafauna Foundation, where he is a Principal Scientist. His research focuses on the population ecology and conservation of threatened marine species, particularly the whale shark, around the world:

*Anything I can do to help protect species is better than nothing. If we know a species is in trouble then we need to gather together enough information to know how we can mobilize efforts to protect it. There are great success stories from protected areas in Galapagos and Komodo, where animals are coming back. I am sure that these positive stories encourage people to recognize that their actions can have a real impact and that, if we can scale up these small success stories to a large scale, then ecosystems can recover. Too often those of us working in conservation can feel paralysed by the size and complexity of the problems that we face, so watching a population recover is a great feeling.*

# MANTAS
# AND RAYS

I HAVE FOLLOWED AND SWUM WITH MANTAS *in oceans across the world. They are one of a very select number of animals that seek out interaction with humans. Their movements completely transfix me as I follow their playful loops and meandering circles – like Kaa the snake in* The Jungle Book*, they can hypnotize me to the point where I lose my sense of space and time. What other animal can transmit such love?*—Philip Hamilton

When you are in the water with manta rays there is a sense that you are being watched as much as you are watching; they will seek out human interaction, sometimes approaching divers and circling round them playfully. Tracking the slow-motion undulations of these enormous rays gliding through clear water is a mesmerizing experience. Our five ray researchers have many stories of interactions – most notably those occasions when mantas hover placidly while embedded fish hooks and fishing line are removed from their bodies. This behaviour distinguishes mantas as capable of a very sophisticated level of awareness. We know that mantas have the largest brains of all fish, but we still have little insight into what they sense and perceive.

The oceanic or giant manta (*Manta birostris*) is more nomadic and larger than the reef manta (*Manta alfredi*), and these two species are distinguished from other devil rays (mobulids) by the large paddle-like structures on their heads, which are used to funnel plankton into their mouths. Like whale sharks, mantas swim with their mouths open to draw in seawater and filter out zooplankton through a fine mesh in their throats. It seems incredible that such a large and charismatic species should remain so overlooked until recently. Scientific knowledge of the natural history of mantas and our insight into the extent of their exploitation have grown rapidly. Within the last twenty years amateur and professional scientists and conservationists have come together to secure global protection for these threatened species.

Dr Andrea Marshall is widely known as the 'Queen of Mantas'. A marine biologist from California, she was one of the first people to undertake a detailed study of mantas, which led to the official distinction of two separate species in 2008. She has built up a photographic record of over 650 individuals from her field station in Tofo, Mozambique:

*We seek knowledge about mantas because we are curious, but also because we inevitably need to understand how humans are impacting on them and how we can direct global and local conservation efforts. If you have no information about where mantas live or whether their populations are growing or declining, it is impossible to focus resources on protecting them.*

Most of the mantas that Andrea sees in Tofo are reef mantas, and over 80% of them are female. This group stays close inshore for much of their lives, leaving for an unknown destination when it is time to give birth. Andrea's familiarity with the group enables her to recognize different personalities: some are shy and are reluctant to come close, others like to be tickled with bubbles or to circle around the diver. Each one has a unique pattern of spots and patches on its underside, and Andrea visualizes each shape into a name that identifies them – Dracula, Tristar and Bleeding Heart are among many that are instantly recognizable. The use of characteristic markings to identify individual species began with humpbacks and orcas and has become well established as a tool to share individual sightings around a global community of manta researchers. Once you can recognize individuals,

you are able to build a picture of their movements and the overall population size in a region.

Just off the coast of Ecuador around the Isla de la Plata, diving instructor Michel Guerrero had discovered huge numbers of oceanic mantas in the late 1990s. They were coming close to shore between June and October when the Humboldt current brings in cold, nutrient-rich water that produces one of the most productive ecosystems in the world. With a basic camera, Michel and a small group of local divers started to photograph the mantas that they encountered. Newly accessible digital cameras enabled amateur and professional researchers to gather their own records of individual mantas. To build a more global picture, scientists started to connect, sharing databases of photographs and observations and looking out for individuals that might be migrating across oceanic regions. The use of satellite tags has only just started to reveal the scale of some of these voyages: one individual tracked by Andrea Marshall travelled over 1,000 km, from Mozambique to Durban in South Africa. The tags also show at what depths the mantas are swimming and how much light is in the water, providing a small insight into the factors which might be influencing their behaviour.

Diver and film maker Erick Higuera had been diving in the Sea of Cortez and in the Revillagigedo Islands on the Pacific coast of Mexico since 1997, witnessing a steady decline in the numbers of sharks and mantas that he was seeing. Over six years Erick built up his own database of photographs and through this he was able to piece together the migration of oceanic mantas as they moved between different areas in search of food, visited cleaning stations or gathered at mating grounds. Cleaning stations are an important part of a manta's itinerary, and there are well established underwater pinnacles around the Revillagigedo Islands where mantas approach and hover while a small shoal of clarion angel fish pick off parasites and bits of dead skin, in a mutually beneficial arrangement. In Mozambique the work is split between a more specialist team of sergeant major fish to clean inside the mouth and butterfly fish attending to bite wounds. During the mating season males start turning up at cleaning stations knowing that this is where they will be finding females. Receptive females release a sexual pheromone scent, and males will approach, hovering over the female's back and shadowing her movements. In most cases, the males are rejected or a chain of males

THIS PAGE Mobula rays, including mantas and devil rays, have cephalic lobes which protrude from the side of their heads. They work as an extra pair of limbs moving in and out to funnel prey into their mouths

FACING Three reef mantas gliding effortlessly over a coral reef – these species prefer shallow atolls and reefs to the open ocean

273

may be led on a procession, mimicking each turn, flip and bank in an elegant linear dance known as a 'mating train'. Eventually a single, persistent chosen male will mate, biting on the female's wing and then flipping his body underneath her. Around Isla de la Plata, Michel Guerrero has discovered males with blood on their claspers and females with fresh scars on the tips of their fins, which suggests that this region could be an important mating area. Around the globe we still have very little idea where mantas are breeding and giving birth, so these new insights are hugely significant.

The manta ray makes a really poor meal for humans: it is not pleasant to eat, but it has been targeted by fishermen for food when there is little else to fish. As a slow-moving, large animal it is easy to spear or catch in a net. Mantas are also vulnerable to accidental capture in nets that hang in vast quantities throughout coastal waters. Like their closely related shark cousins, mantas have to keep swimming to maintain a flow of oxygen-rich water over their gills, making them vulnerable to entanglement and suffocation in these nets. The exploitation of manta rays really started to escalate when a new market opened up for the use of gill plates in traditional Chinese medicine. Gill plates are the

delicate feathers of cartilage circling the mouth of a manta ray and are used to filter out tiny zooplankton from the water. Its medicinal properties are promoted by charlatan practitioners who claim it can reduce toxins in the blood and treat asthma, chicken pox or cancer. The market in manta products is worth $10 million a year, despite there being no proven medicinal value nor any evidence of historic use. Concern among manta researchers was growing, such was the number of mantas that were turning up in markets across Sri Lanka, Thailand, Indonesia and the Philippines. Growth of the fishery has been driven by middlemen and retailers with an eye for profit, resulting in overfishing and collapses in populations across the Pacific and Indian Oceans.

The odds are often stacked against people working in conservation who are trying to counter both huge social, commercial and political pressures to exploit resources and the poverty of fishing communities who have few other economic options. Populations of mantas are extremely vulnerable to fishing since they reproduce so slowly; manta females take 15 years to reach maturity and will only produce a pup every four to six years. The population of mantas across the

Inhambane province in Mozambique declined by 80% between 2005 and 2011, and subsistence fishermen continue to target an estimated 20–50 a year. This number cannot be sustained. Andrea Marshall and her team from the Marine Megafauna Foundation work closely with fishermen to help them understand the impact of fishing and find different alternatives:

*My strategy is to work closely with communities in a small number of carefully selected projects, targeting and orchestrating research and community work to maximum effect. Now these communities are demanding stronger regulation from government to protect mantas.*

In Ecuador, Michel Guerrero could see that local fishermen were targeting the smaller devil rays for export; they knew the numbers were declining, but there was little incentive to stop. They caught bigger rays, too, but this was something they tried to avoid because the larger rays would damage their nets. The only way to stop the decline was a complete ban on fishing of all manta and devil rays, and Michel and his group from Proyecto Mantas Ecuador pushed the Ecuadorian government hard for a new law.

Mantas feed on zooplankton, which they filter through their gill rakers

**GUARDIAN Catherine Yrisarri** is a film-maker who has covered stories of climate change all over the world.

At 23, I started working for *National Geographic* and was sent out on assignment in northern Alaska to cover a story of the Inupiat whalers. We were camped out on the ice-shelf asleep when the ice cracked and our tent almost fell into the freezing waters of the Arctic Ocean. It was one of the first years since the Ice Age that the ice-shelf went from being perennially frozen to melting into the ocean each spring. The white ice-cap that covers the surface of the earth and deflects the hot rays of the sun is becoming increasingly smaller and, in turn, the ocean absorbs more heat and the water temperature rises exponentially. These changes will affect the fragile reef ecosystems, migration patterns, storms — everything.

I became a film-maker because I wanted to help scientists translate complexity so that a broader audience could feel connected. We are standing on the brink of the loss of a 300 million-year-old ecosystem and I ask myself constantly: how can I speak about this to communities that can't see past the need for food, shelter, security and employment? People can become burdened by the scale of the challenge, and overwhelmed by the complexity of what needs to be done. It's like having a camera in hand while watching a train careening out of control. Do you put it down to try to stop the train or just let it roll? I have felt visceral heartbreak from the madness of following

what I like to call 'my wild love of this world'. And it is that – love – that is the driver behind it all – that strange beauty found in places unreachable.

I gravitate to places of such spectacular beauty yet on the brink of disappearing – landscapes laced with receding glaciers at the headwaters of the Amazon River, coral reefs bleached and furred up by algae, and ancient forests ripped from their roots. The discovery of coral reefs for the first time was like opening up a second life; it was phenomenal to realize that this entirely new world existed. The huge expanses and vast depths in a world where you must carry your own air to breathe inevitably drives a sense of curiosity. I like sometimes to rewind in my mind the moments that take my breath away.

> *I like sometimes to rewind in my mind the moments that take my breath away ... the pull of South Pacific Ocean currents, swimming fiercely to keep up with these graceful, behemoth manta rays.*

I scroll through sunsets and the pull of South Pacific Ocean currents, swimming fiercely to keep up with these graceful, behemoth manta rays. I think about my first dive and seeing tiny neon purple and gold shrimp and electric blue nudibranchs and simply feeling my heart explode at their mere existence on this earth.

I have recently packed my bags and left New York City to return home to Colorado. It felt in some ways like a defeat, in others a relief. I've spent the last months in the comfort of my home examining the most tragic consequences that humanity faces: from dying children in Somalia to the deforestation of the Amazon and the wildfires ripping through the American West. It's sunk me at times. And now I am left to reflect: if I feel so devastated on a daily basis telling these stories, I wonder how the world feels hearing them?

I go back to my mental 'flip book of wonder': the creatures that make my heart leap and the stillness I find when it is just me and an ocean. That is what lights everything in my heart, coupled with my community and dear friends. It is in that where my favourite farmer philosopher Wendell Berry's final poetic lines resonate: 'For a time I rest in the grace of the world, and I am free.'

Ultimately, when we put down our cameras we are all left understanding what truly pulls our hearts; it's from that place that we can take a small step forward toward our values. Until now I have focused on the most dramatic and tragic things that have infected our minds, but on a philosophical level I think we need to go back to what connects us, what motivates us and sparks our hearts. As a film-maker I continue to seek ways to reignite curiosity, understanding and reverence for the natural world through showing the beauty of what we have, hope for the future and solutions for how to get there.

Two remoras hitching a ride on top of a giant oceanic manta ray.
While they may increase the drag for the swimming mantas, they help
to remove parasites and dead skin

The fishermen were not happy initially, but four
years later Michel has started to see Mobula rays
on his dives again. Our knowledge is still patchy
but, as the oceanic manta is known to migrate huge
distances throughout its life, protection has to be
secured globally if it is to be meaningful. Michel used
the momentum he had built with the fisheries ban to
push the Ecuadorian government to lead a proposal to
have oceanic mantas included within the Convention
on Migratory Species, a measure that would ensure all
116 signatory nations would have to protect the giant
manta and its habitats. After this success, Ecuador
partnered with Colombia to seek further protection
for the manta through the Convention on the
International Trade in Endangered Species (CITES) for
both reef and oceanic manta. Despite some opposition,
both mantas have now been included on a list of species
which have severely restricted controls on their trade.

Also pushing hard to secure this protection was Guy
Stevens from the Manta Trust together with Andrea
Marshall from the Marine Megafauna Foundation, and
a coalition of organizations who had been building up
support from around the world to persuade nations to
back the inclusion of manta rays. Guy had started his

work in the Maldives, sharing manta sightings with other researchers so that he could co-ordinate research efforts around the world; this network grew into the Manta Trust, an organization formed in 2011.

Sanctuaries for mantas have now been established to help protect them in many parts of the world, with varying levels of success. There are many strong incentives to protect manta populations, but often conservation measures are not effectively implemented or enforced. To ensure compliance, it is essential to provide realistic alternative livelihoods for fishermen who previously relied on catching mantas for their income. Indonesia, for example, now has the world's largest sanctuary for mantas, covering 5.8 million km² of sea. Guy Stevens recognizes that Indonesia does not have the capability or the manpower to enforce this vast area across 17,000 islands so, in Lamakera on the Indonesian Island of Solor, the Manta Trust has helped to retrain and support fishermen to become tourist guides:

*Pride is an important motivation. For many men the hunting of a manta is a rite of passage; but equally there is pride in showing people an ocean that you have protected.*

[CONTD PAGE 288]

GUARDIAN **Roz Savage** was the first woman to row across the globe's three great oceans, driven by a need to highlight awareness about the environment and take control of the life she wanted.

At the age of 32 I had a degree, a good job as a management consultant, a nice house and a red sports car. But I was doing a job I didn't like, to buy stuff I didn't need. I sat down and wrote two obituaries of my life – the one I wanted, and the one I was heading for – and I didn't like what I saw. How would I feel if I reached the end of my life and had not done everything I could to lead the life I wanted? I began to put myself back on a different course, leaving behind a secure job and the trappings of my former life. You could say I jumped out of the aeroplane first, then started thinking about how to make my own parachute!

This transformation of my life led to an appreciation of simplicity and an understanding of the custodial relationship that humans have with the earth. I felt appalled that I had never thought about the environment before. I travelled in the Peruvian Andes, where people worship the spirit of the glaciers, yet they had seen them retreat by half over the last 30 years. I decided I wanted to raise awareness of environmental issues, but I needed to do it in a way that was confident and empowering, rather

than evangelical and patronizing. I had found my mission but not yet my project.

I knew that inside me was an adventurer fighting to get out. I loved reading about people with huge amounts of courage who were climbing up mountains, trekking to the Poles and rowing across oceans – but they all seemed to have enormous beards, and I did not seem to fit the image. This myth was exploded for me when I heard the story of how Dan Byles rowed across the Atlantic with his 53-year-old mother, Janice Meek, who at the time was the oldest person to row any ocean. I formed in my mind a very clear goal. I would become an ocean rower in order to provide a platform on which to talk about the environment. I wanted a physically adventurous project that would test me, something that would take me out of my comfort zone. A couple of years later, as I was rolling around my cabin in an Atlantic storm, I had to remind myself that getting outside my comfort zone would, by definition, be uncomfortable.

It had taken me 14 months to find the sponsorship and prepare myself physically and mentally; now I just had to row 3,000 miles from the Canary Islands to Antigua. That year, 2005, was one of the worst years for weather in the Atlantic. I caught the tail end of one of many hurricanes and I faced some brutal conditions. For the first two weeks, I was petrified and overwhelmed by the scale of the challenge that I had set myself. It is the psychological

challenge, the doubts and fears that are the hardest to overcome – when you are alone and afraid you have to find a way to keep body and soul together. I just counted the strokes and celebrated each small achievement. There were so many times when I wanted to give up, but ultimately you realize that you cannot be terrified indefinitely. My motivation to continue and finish was ultimately greater than my fear.

I have since spent a further 400 days at sea, rowing one oar-stroke at a time, to cross the Pacific Ocean from San Francisco to Papua New Guinea. Then I traversed the Indian Ocean from Western Australia to Mauritius. In a small boat on a big ocean, it is very clear who is boss. We live our lives insulated from the natural world, but at sea you feel incredibly humble and vulnerable to the power of nature. There is a purity and simplicity to life on the ocean. It is the mundane moments that I tend to think about most, like brushing my teeth while looking up at the stars of the Milky Way. Finding complete solitude in this world is a rare and precious thing.

The other thing that struck me was how small the world is. I travelled most of the way around the world at walking pace, so it seems incredible that our planet can still support 7.5 billion people. What I have achieved and what I have seen at sea has given me a platform from which to talk about our own narrative with the

environment that sustains and supports us. We seem to imagine that we're separate from nature, rather than realizing we are part of it. I hope we can create a new positive story for humans in the 21st century that is wiser,

> *In a small boat on a big ocean, it is very clear who is boss …. you feel incredibly humble and vulnerable to the power of nature. There is a purity and simplicity to life on the ocean.*

more far-sighted and focused on genuine happiness, rather than excessive consumerism. I feel encouraged when I see signs that we are shifting towards a new narrative of being good global citizens, rather than just consumers. My experience on the ocean has changed my own 'inner story' about who I am and what I am capable of, and for this I am always grateful.

I turn 50 this year. I have found happiness in what I do, rather than in what I own; I have come to appreciate how little I need to make me happy. A boat is a perfect illustration of the importance of careful resource use – all we have on our voyage is what we carry. I have been in situations that are truly terrifying but what scares me even more is that we might not wise up in time to see what we're doing to our beautiful and precious earth.

Mantas can launch themselves several metres out of the water, potentially using the noisy breaches as a form of communication during courtship displays

Remoras have left attachment marks on the manta, like dusty footprints

The reef manta, *Manta alfredi*, was named after Alfred, Duke of Edinburgh (1844–1900),
who was the first British royal to visit Australia, where these mantas are found

However, the long-term viability of this new relationship will only succeed if the revenue generated is equitable and shared. As a stopgap some of the fishermen are involved as researchers or in taking tourists to watch hunting re-enactments.

In countries where fishing is the only means of livelihood, it is vital that nature pays for itself. A study by the Manta Trust and WildAid showed that manta tourism globally generates $140 million a year, whereas targeted fishing generates $5 million. It feels strange to argue for the conservation of a majestic species on the basis of cold, hard economics, but the figures are quite compelling as a means to persuade governments and communities that it is in their interests to protect mantas. Manta diving tourism is big business in Indonesia, the Maldives, Australia, Mozambique, Mexico and Hawaii. It is an incredible experience for the diver, and lucrative for the diving industry and local economies when retraining is provided.

While local and global conservation measures have made huge progress in our knowledge of mantas and on reducing fisheries impacts, it is the threats from climate change which could have the most significant impact on mantas in the future. Guy Stevens has

The Chilean devil ray is the only Mobula species with a ventral pattern;
all the others have white bellies

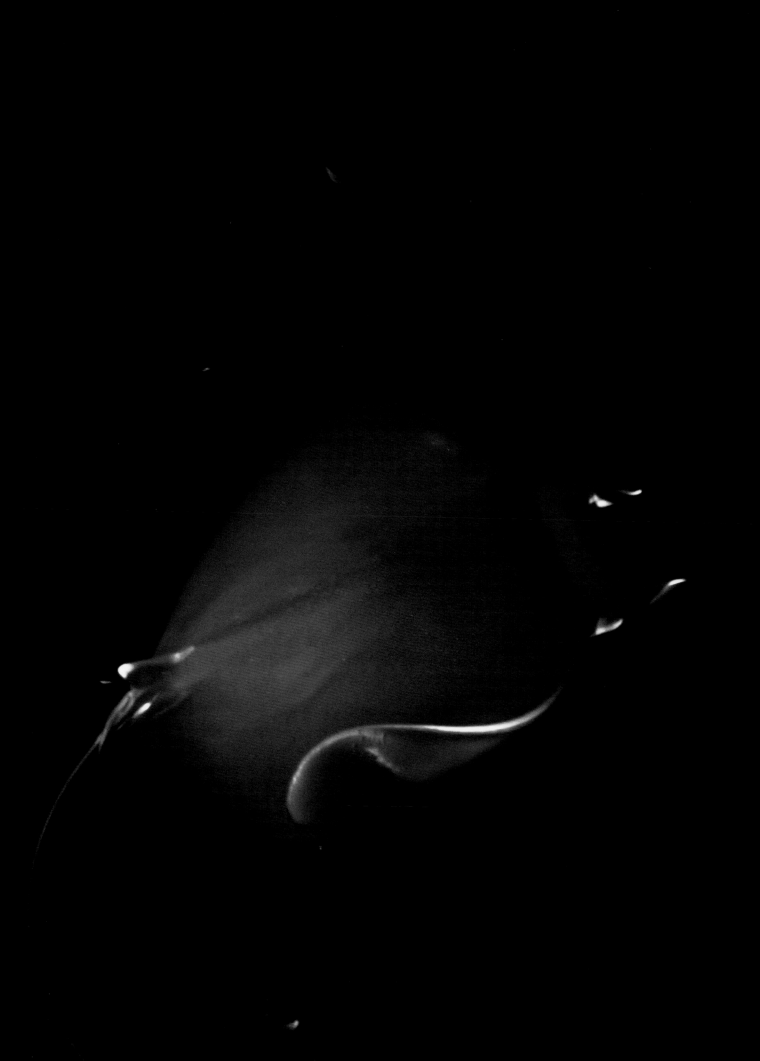

recorded changes in wind patterns that may alter the strength and location of currents and upwelling across our oceans:

*We have seen a massive and inexplicable fluctuation in the levels of productivity in the Maldives over the last decade. Both fishermen and climatologists are noticing these changes in current and weather patterns – despite all the protection and knowledge that exists on the Maldives, these are shifts that may have far reaching implications for mantas.*

Mantas are a pan-tropical species that need both international and local protection. Key global protection measures have been secured and thriving dive tourism means that there is a clear incentive to keep mantas alive, but protecting a wide-ranging species is challenging. What stands out in these stories is the extraordinary level of collaboration between researchers across the world, sharing data and sightings to build an understanding of their populations and movements and record where threats are coming from. Working on the front line of manta conservation must sometimes be dispiriting, with small organizations coming up against seemingly intractable problems

LEFT Eagle rays have longer tails than other ray species, measuring over three times their body length, and are equipped with from two to six venomous spines, used in defence

RIGHT Witnessing a formation of spotted eagle rays 'flying' together is one of the most beautiful underwater spectacles

of desperate fishermen, insatiable desires for exotic products and greedy commercial enterprises. The combination of international agreements and local protection secured by this small, but forceful group of people provide a real hope that mantas have a future.

## Rays

Rays have evolved to occupy every major aquatic habitat on the planet, from the Arctic to the tropics, from shallow freshwater rivers to the deep ocean. Throughout these habitats, they have developed a diverse range of body shapes and ways of finding food. Dr Owen O'Shea has focused his research on stingrays, a group that have a venomous barb at the base of their tail and are found around the tropics and sub-tropics. Stingrays, like sharks, have a skeleton made of cartilage and lack the swim bladder that other fish would use to maintain their buoyancy in the water. They spend their lives close to the seabed, where they feed on buried crustaceans, molluscs and other invertebrates, using their powerful 'wings' to uncover them and then their powerful grinding jaws to crush shells and outer skeletons. Popular perception of stingrays can often be conflicted – the case of the famous

Australian conservationist Steve Irwin, who was fatally injured by a stingray, is well known, but on the other hand hundreds of thousands of tourists interact with gentle stingrays that are drawn towards the sandbanks in the Cayman Islands.

Many species of ray play important roles in maintaining the integrity of the ecosystem in which they live, and Owen is convinced that the importance of stingrays has been underestimated. In the muddy, soft sediment areas of mangrove that fringe the Ningaloo Reef in Western Australia there are countless rounded depressions in the mud that had been carved out by rays as they search for prey, creating new microhabitats for invertebrates to exploit. Studying rays around Ningaloo, the second largest reef in Australia, Owen was struck by the way populations of rays were living together without seeming to compete with each other. Within a chaotic and highly competitive environment rays seemed to have established a very distinct niche.

Now based in the Bahamas, Owen has been working on the yellow ray, the southern stingray and the Atlantic chupare stingray for the last five years. Information on the chupare stingray is so minimal that it was only officially described as being an inhabitant

297

FACING Marbled stingrays are characterized by their beautiful mottled pattern. They are found in sandy, shallow bays of the Indo-Pacific

THIS PAGE Though different ray species may overlap geographically, they feed on separate prey, so as not compete with one another

LEFT Like the reef manta or the whale shark, the spotted eagle ray has distinctive patterns across its wings, which are used by scientists and divers to distinguish individuals

RIGHT Eagle rays use their snout and wings to help uncover buried prey. They have special plate-like teeth which enable them to crush the hard shells of molluscs

of the Bahamas in 2018 and almost nothing is known about its life history:

*Through my research I wanted to understand what influences the movements and use of space by these rays, highlighting potential areas that play important roles in their life history. I think if we have an insight into some of these key species, then we are better equipped to protect them.*

As more knowledge is built up about their life history, Owen is confident that we will be able to put in place more effective measures to protect rays and the ecosystems that support them. During his career, he has introduced thousands of school children, young scientists and adults to rays, involving them in his work as he catches and tags them around the shallow waters of the Bahamas. Enabling people to be part of research and to work closely with an incredible animal is something valuable that a scientist can offer, changing perceptions about an animal that is often misunderstood.

# WORDS FROM THE EXPERTS

*When you look into the eye of a manta ray and wonder what it's thinking, you always*
*get the feeling that it's looking back at you and pondering the same question—Guy Stevens*

**Owen O'Shea** is the Executive Director and Principal Research Scientist at the Centre for Ocean Research and Education (CORE) and an expert on the ecology of the stingray:

*As an island nation, the sea has always been part of the lives of people in the Bahamas and perhaps to a certain extent it fades into the background. Taking school children out into the ocean is a hugely important part of what we do. I will ask a classroom 'Who is afraid about what we are going to do today?' and everyone puts their hand up. By the end of the day we have given them an opportunity to see rays up close, to see how large and prominent its eyes are, the barb on its tail and the tiny spines that are on its back. The immersive experience is transformative. Seeing an animal in front of your eyes is one way we can change what people think and feel about the ocean on their doorstep.*

**Erick Higuera** is an underwater film-maker, professional cameraman and a passionate advocate for protection of the waters around the Baja Peninsula and the islands of Socorro and Revillageged:

*I feel as if I have a deep connection with mantas and I take huge pride in showing people around these places. My films are now being broadcast around the world, and I hope that they will help people to realize that we need to protect marine life in order to share it with future generations, especially people in Mexico who are often completely unaware of the rich marine life that lies around our coasts. I have spent so much of my life at sea, it sometimes feels that I am a stranger on land. These waters are also my home and I remain passionate that they must be protected. It sometimes seems like a huge burden to carry, but as soon as I break the surface into the liquid kingdom problems and stress melt away.*

**Andrea Marshall** is affectionately known as the 'Queen of the Mantas'. She co-founded the Marine Megafauna Foundation and now directs its global manta-ray research programme, which focuses its efforts on the science-based conservation of manta rays across the world:

*When you work with a species as charismatic as mantas, the emotional bond for scientists and conservationists is obviously strong. I have studied some of these groups for over 15 years, witnessing their birth and development into adults, so it hits me hard to see an animal that I know really well lying on the beach as part of a fisherman's haul. I'm never going to leave these guys. I will do everything I can for their protection. I want to pass on a positive message about what is possible in conservation – the recovery of mantas is a success story that I want to share.*

**Michel Guerrero** and his team at Proyecto Mantas Ecuador discovered the largest aggregation of manta rays off the coast of Ecuador. He runs a diving centre and leads research and scientific programmes through Fundación Megafauna Marina del Ecuador:

*The oceanic mantas around the coast of Ecuador are now well protected – with the international measures and local marine reserves their future is as assured as it ever could be. My dive business provides me with the means to spend at least half of my time on manta research and conservation and I want to keep discovering more about this population and their movements around the region. We know that they are a species that migrates across ocean basins so it is vital that we keep working to secure real protection around the world. The mantas that we have here in Ecuador seem to be truly unique, interacting with divers in a way that fills you with joy, as if they are folding into your soul.*

**Guy Stevens** is the founder of the Maldivian Manta Ray Project and the co-founder of the Manta Trust. He is an expert on manta ecology and author of *Manta: Secret Life of Devil Rays*:

*There is a cruel irony in the fact that mantas accept humans as being harmless to them – indeed they recognize our ability to help them. I have had had mantas hover placidly beneath or above me while I pull hooks and lines out of their bodies. Very few marine creatures have such a high level of understanding, and this unusual empathy and intelligence is a great way for us to engage people with them. I think we have turned the corner on manta conservation by addressing targeted fisheries and the gill plate trade. I am optimistic that humans are caring; we just need to overcome the apathy and focus on providing positive ideas. There are setbacks of course, and it is depressing when politics has such a short-term horizon and is so inward-looking. Nature is resilient and can bounce back, it is just a question of how much we lose along the way. My biggest fear is that future generations will not be able to have their own encounters with these animals.*

# FUTURE OCEAN

OUR RELATIONSHIP *with the ocean is currently not a healthy one. We take the good stuff that we want – the fish, the minerals and the oil – and these products become the basis of our economies – and then we throw back our waste into the very place where we take the resources we need. The real challenge is doing something about it.*
—Ussif Rashid Sumaila

An ocean with a future for us all has to be one from which we take no more than the surplus on offer, not take as much as we are able to extract. This objective appears to be obvious and attainable; yet achieving it, considering the vastness of the area, seems like an impossibility. In order to protect and manage our resources and biodiversity with care, we need to control our excesses and our increasing technical ability to reach further and with greater consequence into our oceans. Our modern lives allow us easily to forget how reliant we are on natural systems to grow our food and provide clean water; and ignore how these systems have suffered as we take too much and give back too little. Within city limits we can maintain an illusion that we live without nature – energy, food and water are there for us to tap into from unseen sources. More than ever before we are connected to each other, but we have a tin ear for what is happening in the natural world. Humans have lived off the continuous replenishment of resources for hundreds of thousands of years, the very definition of sustainability. The gradual decline of marine life is the result of a multitude of small incremental changes over vast areas. Throughout history people have understood the need to hold something back to allow stocks to recover and to survive when times are lean, and different communities around the world have generated their own stories and taboos to ingrain these traditions into common practice. The last half century has seen the development of international markets and new technologies that have gradually eroded these customs, leading to increasing competition for smaller shares of the catch, classically expressed as 'too many boats catching too few fish'. An open fishery rewards those who are greedy – those who take what they can as fast as they can, while others (and future generations) lose out. There is no incentive to cut back, because you can't be sure that someone else won't take advantage. Solving the problem often depends on a serious collapse of the system, which of course makes the restoration even more challenging.

ABOVE Sailfish can swim up to 30 km/h when chasing their prey,
using their large sail-like dorsal fin to herd schools of fish

PREVIOUS The surface-dwelling mahi-mahi, also known as dorado
or dolphinfish, is much sought after by sport fishers

Tarpon, themselves predators, are a favourite target for anglers

## Fishing

The story of the collapse of the Newfoundland cod fishery is one that exemplifies the tragedy of the commons – people fishing competitively and taking quantities that are beyond the means of nature to replenish. The fishing grounds off the east coast of Canada, 'the Grand Banks', were the richest in the world, exploited by European fishermen since the 15th century. For 400 years the supply of cod that could be salted and dried was seemingly limitless, attracting fishermen from across Europe and America. The development of fishing technology and large distant-water fleets in the 1950s led to a quadrupling of the catch and a gold-rush mentality that ultimately led to the inevitable bust, with numbers falling by more than 60% within a decade. In 1977, Canada joined other countries to adopt a 200-mile exclusive economic zone that gave them control of their own fisheries, but the government continued to invest in more fishing boats and gear, putting even more pressure on the dwindling stocks. Small-scale fisheries and co-operatives could see that their catches were getting smaller, while scientists were calling on the government to reduce the size of the overall share or quota that could be caught. By 1992, the main fish stocks had collapsed and the whole

cod fishery was closed, putting 80,000 people out of work.

Bonnie McCay has spent her career studying fishing communities and how fish stocks are exploited and shared. Working on Fogo Island off the coast of Newfoundland in Canada, she watched a devastated community come together to save livelihoods and homes by forming a co-operative and building boats that could target different fish stocks. In Bonnie's mind what happened in Newfoundland was not a tragedy of the commons, but a tragedy of mismanagement that led to a tragedy of the commoners – of people dependent on common rights to the natural resources:

*None of the Newfoundland fisheries is 'open access' any longer, and they are tightly regulated by the government, which consults closely with representatives of the fisheries. As I looked at the way in which people were managing their own fisheries I was impressed by the extent to which they insisted that they were part of their own governance, jointly looking after their own resource.*

Fishing on the island of Fogo continues today, catching and processing shrimp and crab; but despite

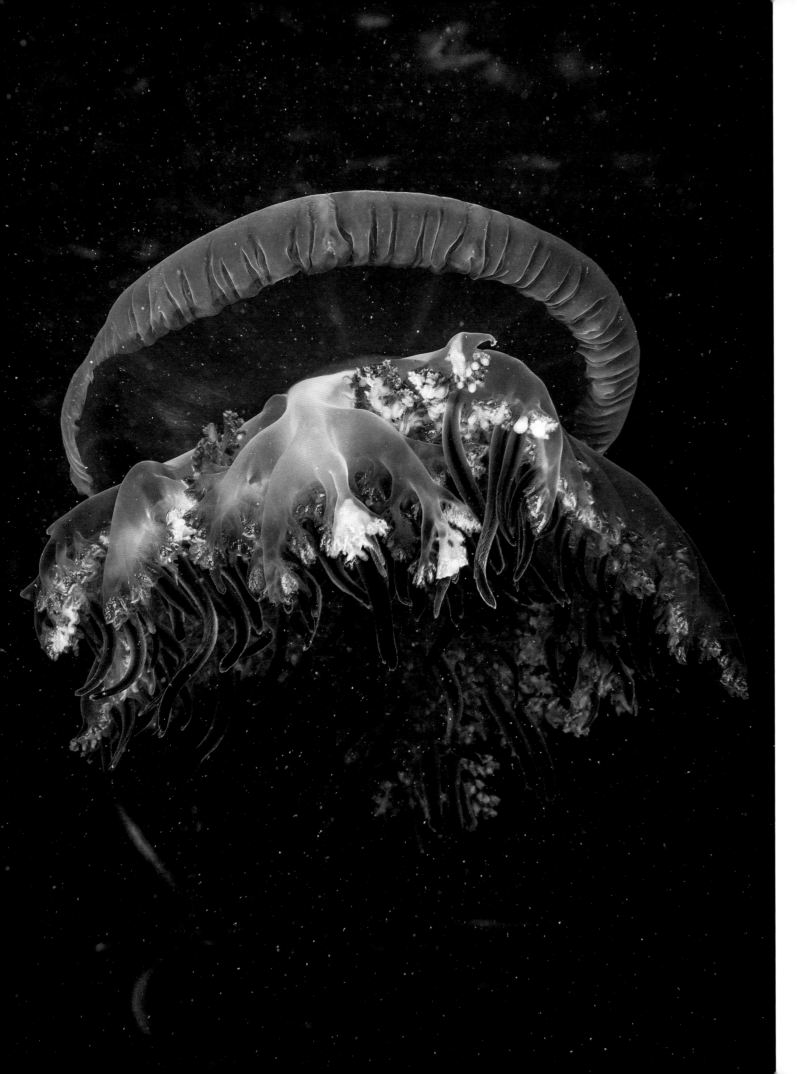

LEFT The upside-down or *Cassiopeia* jellyfish has the same algae in its tentacles as corals, exposing them to the sun to generate energy from photosynthesis

OVERLEAF The Portuguese man o' war is not a single animal but a whole colony of organisms forming a sail-like gas-filled bladder to drift across the sea

the continued moratorium on cod fishing, the stocks have shown no sign of recovery.

Fishermen are now able to work across the world's oceans, and nations pursue access agreements that can remove vital resources from under the noses of local fishermen. Hundreds of millions of people in coastal areas and islands throughout the world are completely dependent on the seafood that they catch to survive. They are the most vulnerable to dwindling fish stocks, having no alternative livelihoods or source of food. Ownership of fish stocks has become highly political; too often the emphasis is on economic protection rather than ecological needs or future benefits. In some parts of the world, public money in the form of subsidies is used to support fishing, damaging the environment and undermining long-term economic prospects and food security. In many cases, if the public money stopped then so would the fishing and, if the fishing were to end, political support would evaporate. Ussif Rashid Sumaila has been studying the natural and human elements of fishing across the globe. To him, the use of public money makes no sense:

[CONTD PAGE 311]

319

GUARDIAN **Conrad Humphreys** is an ocean racing skipper, adventurer and environmentalist.

We lived a stone's throw from the sea in Exmouth in Devon where I had my first introduction to sailing at our local sailing club. During the 1980s, Exmouth Sailing Club went through a golden period of junior sailing, producing some of the best Cadet class sailors in the country. By the age of 12 I was training four times a week and racing every weekend. My mum realized that there was some talent and started taking me to national events and selection trials in a donated VW Beetle. I went on to win a Junior World Championship in 1989 and began to create a name for myself in the world of sailing.

Aged 19, I was invited to join a group of buccaneering adventurers and racers training for the Whitbread Round the World Race; I arrived in Uruguay penniless and completely unsure of what I had got myself into. I ended up sailing with the Ukrainian team, spending nine months racing around the world often having to manage the fatigue and friction that sparked between a crew with few common values. Picking a route further south meant cutting distance and picking up the big southern storms that would push us around the world. Surfing down

huge Southern Ocean waves at 30 knots in black night is exhilarating and addictive. Covering 400 miles a day at 55 degrees south made me feel invincible – I wanted to do more of this, but as a skipper, not as a member of the crew. My opportunity came in the BT Global Challenge. Over a year of intense selection trials, the 180 of us who had applied were whittled down to 12 skippers. I was given a team of 30 volunteers, and I had five weeks to select and train a winning crew. We won four out of the seven legs of the race, setting a new record from Cape Horn to the Cape of Good Hope and I became the youngest winning skipper in the history of the race.

My ocean racing career up to that point had all been aimed at getting myself to the Vendée Globe race; the

> *Surfing down huge Southern Ocean waves at 30 knots in black night is exhilarating and addictive. Covering 400 miles a day at 55 degrees south made me feel invincible.*

longest and toughest race in any sport. I secured my place by racing solo across the Atlantic in the 2004 Transat race from Plymouth to New York. That year there was a

huge storm in the North Atlantic, with many boats being dismasted and capsizing in the race. I made it through, but towards the finish I fell into a heavy sleep, dreaming that my manager was at the helm. I woke to find that the wind had picked up and I was in a strong gale with too much sail up; I dashed out onto the deck naked and half asleep, pulling down the canvas as quickly as I could. This small mistake cost me 40 miles, but coming fifth was good enough to get me to the Vendée start line later that year.

Setting off from Sables d'Olonne in France, the first four weeks of my Vendée race had gone well and I was lying seventh in a field of 19. Then, 400 miles west of Cape Town, I smashed into something just under the surface of the water breaking one of my rudders. Race rules meant that I couldn't have any outside assistance or leave the boat, so I had to replace the rudder on my own at anchor in South Africa. By the time the work was done I was in last place and 2,000 miles behind the leaders. Each day around the Southern Ocean, I was clawing back miles from the rest of the field, pushing myself and the boat to our limits. I have always had a constant critical voice in my head, chastizing myself for not doing things better, not being prepared, or not being quick enough to make sail changes. After my rudder had been damaged, I started to enjoy

myself more and relish being out in the ocean. I found that I had grown into the isolation, it forces you to find resolve you didn't know you had. When you are part of a crew, you

> Most of us who sail just love being on the ocean, but the language around environment and environmentalism has been constantly negative. Sport can be a powerful means to engage people in something positive and active, and this is where the Blue Project came from.

are used to the voices and morale boosts from people who pick you up and encourage you; but on your own you've got to pick yourself up and drive yourself on.

Rounding Cape Horn and on my way home, the hydraulic rams controlling my keel both failed, leaving the boat dangerously unstable. I lashed them in place as best as I could, but I still had 4,500 miles to go to the finish line. I was tired and the grinding of the bearings was deafening and gut-wrenching; I wasn't sure if the boat was going to last and I slept fitfully for the last two weeks of the race. Finishing at all was a miracle, but I felt proud that I had fought back through the field into seventh

place, somehow keeping the boat together. I would not see myself as a practical or resourceful person; but I don't get flustered and keeping this boat working for the preceding three months had taught me that I can figure things out and find a way through. In the years following the race I had a complete sense of peace and comfort in my abilities.

My life has been most heavily influenced and inspired by two people: Jacques Cousteau and Sir Peter Blake, courageous adventurers, ocean pioneers and conservationists. Most of us who sail just love being on the ocean, but the language around environment and environmentalism has been constantly negative. Sport can be a powerful means to engage people in something positive and active, and this is where the Blue Project came from. Starting in 2011 we organized an annual 'Blue Mile' event for people to swim, row or paddle together that would help raise money for organizations working in marine conservation. I think these annual events have helped to energize people around causes such as climate change, and water and plastic pollution.

Joining the crew for the Mutiny voyage was probably the most reckless thing I have done in my life. For a television documentary we were recreating the route that Captain Bligh took in 1789 when he was cast adrift from

the Bounty, sailing in an exact replica of the ship's seven-metre launch. I was using traditional instruments to navigate the boat across thousands of miles of ocean from Tahiti to the Great Barrier Reef and through the Coral Sea to East Timor. I was the only professional sailor and had to train and guide the crew of nine through the very basics of knots and managing the sails. Living and sleeping so close to each other with very limited water and a ration of two ships biscuits a day was a real test of survival and our ability to hold ourselves together to reach our destination.

The Island Trust is a UK charity that introduces young people to the joy, adventure and freedom of sailing a traditional boat. On behalf of the Island Trust I bought the replica Bounty launch from the programme's producers and I am now taking it around to schools; it is a fantastic way to bring the story to life and encourage children to think about history, survival and the oceans. I have witnessed how learning to sail and navigate a wooden boat can transform the lives of vulnerable young people as they experience the joy and freedom of a voyage at sea. These emotions are as strong for me now as they were when I was a ten-year-old sailing a dinghy in Exmouth.

*Subsidies are what enable fishing vessels from the European
Union to go to West Africa to fish, forcing local fishermen to
pick over the remains, unable to catch enough to make a living
or pay for school fees. Public money should be used for social
purposes, not as a perverse incentive to destroy the foundation
of a resource.*

Global fisheries were once seen as an infinite source of
food, but the catch has now stalled and is falling, despite
the increased effort that is taking place. Rashid Sumaila
reminds us that 'we take roughly 110 million tonnes
of fish and seafood out of the ocean every year, that is
the equivalent of about 110 million mature cows. What
other kind of system could sustain an annual removal
of biomass of this size?' One of the greatest barriers to
implementing sustainable and well-managed fishing
is the short-term nature of political cycles. When the
economic pain is felt among potential voters and the
benefits are far off into the future, many political leaders
feel that fisheries management is a problem best left
to someone else. Rashid comes across this challenge
in many different countries and in response he tells
politicians to think about what they want their legacy
to be and what they want to be remembered for.

The co-operatives of the Pacifico Norte region of
the Baja Peninsula in Mexico are a model that Bonnie
McCay thinks should be shared with the rest of the
world: 'These co-operatives have successfully managed
highly valuable stocks that have been exhausted in
almost every other place that they are found.' Along
an arid and sparsely populated stretch of the coast
there are ten fishing co-operatives that have rights to
fish for abalone, lobster and other key species, each
occupying an area of between 500 and 1,000 km². They
own their boats, fishing gear and processing plants and
each fisherman is obliged to be part of the decisions
when the fishing season opens how much should be
harvested each year. Being at the table means that you
are able to craft regulations that make sense to you
and to ensure that there is a future for your children.
Bonnie also discovered that there was strong support
between each co-operative, recognizing that currents
transport the lobster larvae, which in turn means that
they are all dependent on each other for their future.

Boats are now able to range across the globe catching
fish in other countries' waters without their knowledge,
causing a wake of destruction and leaving local
fishermen severely deprived. We know that the amount
of fish being caught illegally and under the radar is vast,
potentially as much as 50% of the officially reported
catch. We need to change the economic equation
to make it less profitable for people: with better
surveillance there is a greater probability of their being
caught, and with penalties that really bite we can make
the potential gains seem much riskier. This new frontier
of fishing in areas that are outside national jurisdiction
presents a new problem, but also an opportunity for
governments. 'High seas' are areas of the ocean that are
outside any one nation's Exclusive Economic Zone, a
vast area covering 60% or 219 million km² of our ocean,
yet ten wealthy nations are currently taking most of the
fish in these areas that are meant to be the property of
the whole world. Ussif Rashid Sumaila is promoting the
need to protect our high seas as a fish bank, allowing
some fish stocks time to grow and fertilize coastal
countries all over the globe:

*When I first presented this idea, people were quite affronted,
but slowly more and more people are beginning to think that
closing the high seas to fishing may not be a bad idea. In fact,
the first high seas marine protected area, in the Ross Sea,
Antarctica, was implemented in 2017.*

GUARDIAN **Siddharth Chakravarty** has spent much of his adult life on the sea as a merchant sailor and a skipper on ocean protection campaigns. He is now an advocate for human rights in the fishing industry.

As a child I would listen in awe to my grandfather's stories about his life. He went to sea in 1939 as part of the first batch of Indian cadets in Colonial India. Later in life he was a pilot on the Hooghly estuary in Calcutta, notorious for its shifting sandbanks. I wanted to experience these great voyages and visit ports on the other side of the world, and joined as a deck officer on merchant ships straight after I had finished school. I spent the next ten years ferrying timber, petroleum and chemical products around the world.

In 1983 the world's worst industrial disaster at Bhopal killed over 16,000 people and continued to affect more than five million people over the next three decades. The wind direction that night was the only thing that kept the gas away from where I was sleeping a few miles away. Twenty-five years later I was in the middle of the Pacific Ocean on a chemical tanker carrying a similar cargo, my vessel chartered by the very company that had shrugged off all responsibility for Bhopal. It was a wake-up call for me to examine where my life was heading.

I signed up with Sea Shepherd as a volunteer in 2011 and stayed on as a first mate for patrols in the Mediterranean to monitor blue-fin tuna fishing along the coasts of North Africa. This was my first interaction as a conservationist and it soon became a way of life for me. For the next five years I became an integral part of the organization, leading various campaigns against poaching in the high seas. In 2014 we started a campaign to target the illegal fishing of Patagonian toothfish, also known as icefish or Chilean seabass. This fish lives in the deep southern oceans and is hugely sought after for the prices it can fetch in markets. The extent of illegal fishing in the 1990s nearly collapsed some fisheries, and nations with their own fishing interests in the southern

*Illegal, unreported and unregulated fishing costs the oceans $ 12–23 billion annually. The ills and malpractice that we see in fishing has been driven by greed and dwindling catches.*

oceans have been scrambling to put proper enforcement into place. A few pirate vessels still persist in fishing – they are well known to the authorities, but there are limited resources with which to catch them. One of the most notorious is the *Thunder*, a vessel that has been registered in more than six different countries with as many different names. I was the captain of one of two Sea Shepherd vessels that followed her for over 110 days from the waters of the Antarctic, around Cape Horn and up the coast of West Africa. She tried to ram us on more than one occasion. Having travelled more than 10,000 miles she was scuttled off the Island of São Tomé e Príncipe. We rescued the crew, but much of the evidence went down to the bottom of the sea with her.

Having witnessed the disregard for law and human rights on campaigns with Sea Shepherd, questions about the crew began to arise in my mind. For example, how does an Indonesian fisherman on a Taiwanese fishing vessel in the Pacific Ocean access his rights when he has a job grievance? I wanted to understand a business model that is based on the availability of cheap migrant labour, and how this drives overcapacity in fishing effort and the resulting deterioration in the health of the oceans. My ambition is to further the work being done internationally in restoring ocean health by looking at solutions through the lens of human rights and social justice. I have chosen to use my experience to build an empowered community of fishermen that will reduce the availability of cheap labour, tackle exploitative labour practices and thereby undercut profit margins and decrease overcapacity.

Illegal, unreported and unregulated fishing costs the oceans $12–23 billion annually. The ills and malpractice that we see in fishing have been driven by greed and dwindling catches. Our demand for seafood is pushing communities to the edge and enabling the destruction of our seas and the trafficking and abuse of people. In the race to fish the last of what is left, the real price is being paid by humans who are forced to work in inhumane conditions. The mechanization of industrial fishing fleets, and the role they play in providing cheap protein to the masses, has meant that nations with the ability to subsidize their fishing industry will send their vessels to distant waters to fish. This has led to widespread and unchecked misuse of the ocean's resources.

Abuses within the garment and construction industry have diminished through consumer pressure, but at the moment there is little prospect of change in the fishing industry. I don't want to see a police state at sea, but I think we need a fundamental change in how fisheries are governed. I would question whether we are that hungry for seafood that we are prepared to look away from the destruction of the environment, harvesting of endangered species and inhuman treatment of people.

## Protected Areas

Debates continue around the globe on how we can best protect the oceans, how we can safeguard species that migrate over huge distances and how we can make sure that people are not losing livelihoods. Reducing the scale and extent of human impact through protecting parts of our ocean provides a breathing space for ecosystems. The challenge is how to balance the short-term economic effects on people with the longer-term ecological benefits that will follow from a more productive ocean. There are now well-established trends for the recovery of areas that are protected from human impacts, but every location is different, and it is impossible to predict exactly how things might change. Kirsten Grorud-Colvert has focused a great deal of her work on communicating what we do know about how protected areas and reserves work. It can be difficult for scientists to enter debates about marine reserves; decisions that are likely to impact on humans are inevitably emotionally charged, and scientific research can easily be misunderstood or taken out of context. However, Kirsten emphasizes that we don't have time for a perfect understanding: 'Protection is an imperative now.'

In the last few years there has been a transformation in attitudes, and the number of protected areas established around the world has gathered pace over the last quarter of a century. Kirsten Grorud-Colvert cautions that a rush to meet global targets inevitably leads to false hope and expectation, reminding us that 'our efforts should be spent on finding and protecting areas that have real ecological value and then ensuring they are properly enforced'. Tundi Agardy agrees that we need to put in place collaboratively and carefully designed plans to share and manage space at sea – an approach that is less splashy, but arguably more effective in tackling the most pressing conflicts. Tundi has spent a career working on protected areas across the globe but is uneasy about a situation in which the needs of conservation have been pitted against fishing communities and people who want to eat fish:

*I've lost faith in protected areas as the panacea that they were once thought to be. I thought that they were going to be more systematically used, much stronger in terms of their protection and more enthusiastically embraced by decision-makers and the public at large.*

Tundi Agardy sees a situation in which the conservation of wildlife will have been marginalized to a special interest, as an inconvenience to the expansion of our new 'blue economies'. Conservation has been running to catch up, trying to find the right language and mechanisms to protect marine wildlife and systems for politicians and the public. She believes that conservation organizations have failed to articulate clearly what they are trying to achieve: 'Fundamentally we need to understand what the problem is we are trying to solve first, and then craft the solution that is needed to fit.' One of the greatest problems for conservationists and scientists is to articulate how the sea provides for and benefits humans in multiple different ways. Tundi worries that so many of these benefits are hidden from view and from our consciousness, unrecognized and undervalued:

*If we see the world around us solely as a resource for the taking, then we are unlikely to consider the importance of protection and judicious use – the arena becomes competitive, a race to exploit without thought for how future generations could benefit.*

LEFT A huge school of sardines race for refuge behind my body as they are chased by a hungry sailfish

RIGHT Barracudas hunting a bait-ball

## Plastics

Jennifer Lavers's photograph of a plastic-strewn beach on Henderson Island, one of the world's remotest islands, was shared around the world. This island is part of the Pitcairn group in the South Pacific, yet it acts like a giant net for the vast amounts of plastic floating in the water and has the highest density of plastic waste anywhere in the world. Jennifer calculated that the island has an estimated 38 million pieces of debris, around 18 tonnes in total, with more arriving every day: 'All I could hear at night was the scuttle of rat feet and all I could see in the day was plastic tossing in the surf.' She recalls how the incredible coverage threw her life into a tailspin; she received thousands of e-mails, all of them offers of help to clean up, yet not one offered to change consumer habits, talk to a politician or lobby a company:

*You just can't clean up 8 million tonnes of rubbish, as my friend Heidi Taylor from the Tangaroa Blue Foundation says – 'if all we do is clean up, that is all we will ever do'.*

Jennifer Lavers is a seabird scientist, someone who has worked in some of the most isolated parts of the planet and who recognized early on in her career that

**GUARDIAN Nick Moloney** was the first person to compete in the three great global sailing challenges – the Whitbread Trophy, the Jules Verne Trophy and the Vendée Globe.

I grew up 500 metres from the water's edge in Ocean Grove, Australia. My Mum doesn't even swim, but my Dad was really keen and we would go out sailing on the nearby estuary. I was a surfer before I was a sailor – the ocean on our doorstep was my playground and all I could think about through school. Before I was ten, I was helping out at a place on the Barwon River which rented small sailing dinghies; if it was quiet the owner would let me take a boat out on my own. I headed out to the sandbanks, listening to the sound of the water with my ear pressed to the gunnel, mesmerized by the fact that this movement was wind-driven.

Every December a flotilla of yachts races from Melbourne to Hobart in Tasmania across the Bass Strait. With my Dad we would watch the tiny, triangular sails disappear over the horizon and listen to their calls on a VHF radio. Here was an adventure and something that I desperately wanted to be part of. My parents were concerned that I would never make a living from being a sailor and petrified that I would want my own boat – something that was well beyond their means.

By the time I was a teenager, I was winning dinghy races in Australia and more opportunities started to come my way. I joined a crew to challenge for the America's Cup in San Diego. This is one of the most prestigious sailing

events in the world, but ultimately not for me – it's too much about the technology, money and politics. I wanted the adventure and the wild oceans.

The Jules Verne Trophy is awarded for the fastest navigation of the globe. The trophy is in the maritime museum in New Zealand. Standing in front of it I set myself three circumnavigation goals – the first in the Whitbread Race (now known as the Volvo Ocean Race), the second for the Jules Verne Trophy and the last for a solo attempt in the Vendée Globe.

In the Whitbread race of 1997 I was competing with ten other boats in a series of nine legs around the world. We were chasing the storms, looking for a slingshot that would propel us further down the track. The power and intensity of the ocean were off the scale, but this race taught me about how to push a boat to its limits. I was ecstatic to be out in the ocean. If you fall overboard you know the chances of being recovered from the sea are remote. You feel vulnerable as you battle through huge ocean storms with water pouring all over the deck, but among the crew these are all realities we share so everyone looks out for each other.

In the Mini Transat of 1999 I was one of an 80-strong flotilla of six-metre sailboats racing from France to Guadeloupe in the Caribbean. As the race was starting there was a huge storm in the Bay of Biscay and conditions were horrific. Eighteen skippers had been rescued and one was fighting for his life. I was not coping well, and my boat had taken a battering. A huge wave flipped my boat over, breaking my arm and ripping my harness off.

I was held under the boat unable to get back to the surface. I could have let go of the boat, but I would have been lost to the ocean. I held on to the keel, inhaling water, losing

*Alone at sea you are in survival mode, your mind is in a permanent state of anxiety .... I am a risk taker, and I knew people could die at sea, but I never thought it could happen to me.*

consciousness and at the point of drowning. My body must have brought the boat around into wind and it slowed enough for me to pop-up and scramble back on board.

When I look back I realize I was completely unprepared mentally for this race. Alone at sea you are in survival mode, your mind is in a permanent state of anxiety, so you have to learn to manage yourself and your routines. I am a risk taker, and I knew people could die at sea, but I never thought it could happen to me. This experience left me with deep emotional scars – voices that taunted me that I was going to fall off the boat again. The sea had been a place of carefree adventure for me, and I worried that I'd never find the same relationship again.

You can either face your demons or walk away and I still had two goals left to achieve. In 2001, French skipper Bruno Peyron asked me to help coach a team for an attempt at the record for non-stop circumnavigation around the globe – the Jules Verne. I wasn't going to be left behind, so I joined the team of 12 Frenchmen setting out on a 15-metre, 20-tonne catamaran. We broke the

record by 7 days, circling the globe in 64 days, and I got my name on the magnificent floating trophy.

The Vendée Globe is one of the most difficult challenges on the planet, an emotional and mental struggle as you race solo around the most remote and inhospitable oceans. As soon as the sponsorship deal was signed my heart sank. I was petrified, overcome by the prospect of the solitude of a journey across some of the most isolated and dangerous oceans on the planet. But fear is also a trigger, a reason to get up and do something. I was going to be the first person to achieve all of these sailing goals and this had been my driver for the last ten years. Back home in Australia, my father was dying of cancer and I was questioning what I was doing out in the middle of the ocean. I was hit by a freak storm in the southern ocean, hurricane force winds that turned the sea into a wild cauldron. All I wanted to do was to get out of there, to be back home with my family. Heading up towards home in the Southern Atlantic my keel was torn off and my race ended by my being towed into Rio de Janeiro. Ten months later I came back to complete the leg between Brazil and France and finish what I had started. The race had ended my sailing career, but on this final Atlantic crossing I rediscovered a connection to the oceans that I had lost – it wasn't about chasing storms any more, just a journey across the ocean.

My relationship with the sea is now back to where it was when I was mucking about in dinghies on the Barwon River in Australia. The ocean has given me the greatest life of all, and for that I am grateful.

plastics was a problem that was affecting the lives of vast numbers of seabirds, but going unnoticed. Jennifer was working on the Frigate Shoals, in the North Western Hawaiian Islands, a breeding colony for many species of seabirds including the black-footed and Laysan albatross. The Laysan albatross (named after the island 300 km to the north west) has become the poster child for seabirds and plastics, with photographs showing decomposing chicks with stomachs full of lighters, bottle caps and other pieces of debris. Albatross range over thousands of miles in search of food, and tracking them by satellite positioning shows that they are predominantly heading north to the Bering Sea around Alaska. What alarmed Jennifer was the knowledge that this area must be the source of the plastics and that it is an area also used by vast numbers of seabirds:

*Seabirds are declining faster than any other bird group. The proportion being impacted by plastic is going up and up; clearly, they are not coping. We have helped to provide protection on land, reducing threats from invasive predators, but we seem powerless to do anything to prevent them from eating pieces of plastic.*

GUARDIAN **Robert Swan** is a Polar explorer, environmental leader and the first person to walk to both the North and the South Poles.

The film *Scott of the Antarctic* grabbed me when I first saw it aged eleven – it was the most unbelievable story of courage and commitment that left an indelible mark on my mind. The graves of those explorers are now cairns of snow and rock, but their bodies are encased within the ice where they died. In their sleds they were still carrying nearly 20 kilos of rock samples; their dedication to their scientific mission came at a terrible cost to themselves.

I was the youngest in a family of seven, so it was easier to see how short life is. Looking at my globe, I became obsessed by these two white fingers that were sticking up from the bottom of the world and I wanted to find my way into history. If you don't execute your dream early on, then it will remain a dream. At the age of 29 I set out with fellow explorers Roger Mear and Gareth Wood to walk 900 miles to the South Pole. For 70 days we walked for nine hours a day, each towing a 160 kg sled. It was the longest unassisted march in history. As far as possible, I was keen to replicate the conditions of the Scott expedition, so we had no dogs, depots, air support or communications, and we navigated using a compass and sextant to bring us to the Amundsen-Scott South Pole station. We celebrated briefly and then learned that our ship, the *Southern Quest*, had been crushed by pack ice just a few minutes before our arrival. We were flown back to New Zealand and I then

spent a further year raising the money and organizing another ship to remove all traces of our expedition – a commitment I had made to our expedition patron, Jacques Cousteau. Three years later I completed the second part of my goal with a walk to the North Pole with a team of eight people from seven different nations. We reached the North Pole on 14 May 1989, making me the first man to walk to both the North and South Poles.

The world is a small place and all the great adventures have now been undertaken. When the world has been photographed by satellites, we can no longer call ourselves explorers. I am a traveller in the footsteps of others, a survivor. Most of the people I met said that I was going to fail and that I was most likely going to die. Polar expeditions are a war of attrition, you could make a mistake on day three that could kill you a month later. I would rather reach the Poles than come back without having achieved my goal – I was either going to get there or die. The fear I carried was one of failure, that I would let people down by not completing our mission.

I had huge debts at the end of these expeditions and no prospect of being able to dig my way out. John Mills, the actor who played Captain Scott in the film, told me that I had to talk my way out of debt; and I spent a weekend with him learning how to stand up and speak to people. This is the engine room of what I do now; I tell people about how I survived my expeditions and how we all need to mobilize ourselves to ensure that we can continue to survive on Planet Earth.

When I was undertaking the polar expeditions, scientists at the British Antarctic Survey had only just recognized the extent of the damage to the ozone layer that we were walking beneath. The impact on the ozone layer badly damaged our skin, and changed the colour of my eyes. This was a huge shock, and a recognition in my mind of the potential scale of human impact.

Antarctica is the only place that we all own. The 1991 Antarctic Environment Protocol came into force in 1998 and it is signed by 34 nations. It designates Antarctica as a natural reserve devoted to peace and science until 2041, when new terms will have to be negotiated. Jacques

> As far as possible, I was keen to replicate the conditions of the Scott expedition, so we had no dogs, depots, air support or communications, and we navigated using a compass and sextant ...

Cousteau gave me a 50-year mission to make sure we have the sense to leave Antarctica protected and unexploited. He urged me to engage young people in the issues of climate change and promote the use of renewable energy. My first action was to organize the removal of rubbish from the Russian base on King George Island, Antarctica. It took eight years to raise the money, plan and execute the mission and it involved 35 young people from 25 nations. Together we removed 1,500 tonnes of metal and shipped it to be recycled in Uruguay.

The biggest existential threat to Antarctica is from the changing climate and the use of fossil fuels around the world, so this is where I have focused my attention. The ice is melting in the Arctic at such a rate, I may well be the last person able to walk to both Poles. When we were heading towards the Arctic, unseasonable melting of the ice meant that we nearly drowned as the ice began to disperse. Back in the UK, I started giving talks about how the world was being destroyed, how the ice-caps were melting and pristine areas were being filled with rubbish, but no one was listening to me; people felt powerless and overwhelmed. I learned to inspire commitment by blowing people's socks off with positivity and action. Young people don't want more information, they need to see inspiration and leaders living and acting by example. Every year I go to Antarctica with young people from all over the world, to galvanize their interest, leadership and commitment.

My commitment to Antarctica will remain all my life. I want to continue to inspire governments, educators, businesses, investors and individuals to take concrete and measurable actions to shift the way we think about and use energy. Future heroes will come from business and industry as they innovate new ways to look at the environment as a business opportunity. I am travelling once more to the South Pole with my son using only renewable technology to power us. At my age it will be hard, but it is the best way I can think of to make people change the way they use energy.

Erik van Sebille is another scientist who has been accidentally and somewhat reluctantly drawn into the study of plastics in the ocean. Understanding the nature of the problem and how to solve it inevitably means that we need different scientific skills that can help us find out where plastic is coming from, where it is going and how it is impacting different species and systems. Erik's speciality is on the movement and interconnectivity in the oceans which help us predict where plastics will be interacting with vulnerable ecosystems. Knowing where plastic comes from is an important tool for attributing blame and responsibility back to the source countries; knowing where plastic is going is necessary for showing us where problems are likely to arise in the future.

Erik had never seen plastic in the open ocean during many months spent at sea on research cruises:

*When people talk about 'garbage patches' in our oceans, there is a false perception that there are floating islands of plastic litter that can be cleaned up. The plastic in the surface layer is tiny, hardly visible to the naked eye. I would call it more of a soup.*

Floating on the surface of the ocean are a few hundred thousand metric tonnes, but the amount

332

The bluefin tuna sometimes travel long distances in company with yellowfin and big-eyed tuna

entering the ocean each year is eight million tonnes. Once pieces of plastic are broken up and crushed into tiny pieces, they sink to the ocean floor quite quickly. Erik is leading a team of scientists looking for the 99% of plastic that is missing: 'Somewhere hidden in the ocean are millions of tonnes of plastic, but we don't know whether it is on the ocean floor, on coastlines or inside animals.'

There is a growing sense of alarm among the scientists who are looking into how plastics are entering the food chain. Everywhere they search for plastic, they find it – seabirds, oysters, fish and whales have all been found with plastic in their bodies. So far, there is no evidence that eating affected fish or seafood can harm humans, but what really concerns Erik is the potential there is for a link showing how humans can be harmed by eating fish with plastic in their bodies. The rule of thumb is that the smaller a piece of plastic is, the more harm it does. Only a few animals might eat a plastic bag, yet there are numerous species that could potentially eat a tiny plastic fibre or plastic nurdle. Microbeads are tiny pieces of plastic granules that are added to cosmetics. More than a third of fish in the English Channel were found to be contaminated

with microbeads. Under pressure from environmental organizations governments in Europe have now banned the manufacture and sale of these products.

The profile of the plastic problem has transformed in recent years, and there is growing political momentum for solving our relationship with plastics that we use just once and throw away. As well as stopping what is coming into the ocean, there is the challenge of cleaning up the vast quantities that are already floating on it. A young Dutch inventor, Boyan Slat, has risen to the challenge and led the Ocean Cleanup, a project that will install a floating array of V-shaped barriers across the oceans. As the floating plastic is carried on oceanic gyres, it flows into these barriers, gradually being concentrated until it can be collected and recycled. Boyan remembers diving in Greece and seeing plastic bags all around him. When he asked why they couldn't be cleaned up he was told it was impossible, an unsolvable problem. It was the sheer absoluteness of that statement that has driven him to seek a technological answer that could work on a vast scale. 'The problems we face today are the side effects of things that people didn't think about. We can use technology to work with nature to solve the big challenges of our time.'

## Lionfish

The story of lionfish in the Caribbean is a cautionary tale for humanity – an example of how quickly our ecology can unravel and a reminder of why we need to keep a careful eye on what is happening to our sea. Lionfish are a beautiful fish armed with a beautiful array of poisonous fins. They are naturally found in the Indian and tropical Pacific oceans but were discovered off the east coast of Florida in the mid 1980s. Most likely released as unwanted pets by aquarium owners, they found themselves in a warm tropical sea, began to breed and dispersed around the Caribbean Sea. The invading lionfish are a problem that can never be solved and the impact on Caribbean ecology and economy has been devastating – there are fewer fish for fishermen to catch; and less colour and life on the reef that would attract tourists to come diving or snorkelling. Lad Akins at the Reef Environmental and Education Foundation (REEF) was watching lionfish appear more and more frequently around Florida and the Bahamas through the 1990s, but it was not until 2005 that he realized that the situation was serious:

*The pace at which lionfish have spread across the Caribbean is truly frightening. This issue was on no-one's priority list and on noone's radar, so we had to do a huge amount of work just to make people aware that there was a problem at all. We realized that with our networks of divers across the Caribbean we were in a great position to mobilize tens of thousands of divers to collect data so we could understand the scale and speed at which lionfish were spreading.*

Lionfish are voracious predators and, because they are not recognized as a threat by other fish on the reef, they are able easily to approach and eat small reef fish, consuming such vast numbers that they can quickly change the balance of a reef system. Nor are they targeted as a potential prey, so predators like sharks, eels and grouper are not naturally controlling their populations. The next challenge for Lad was to find ways to solve the problem. Lionfish are very difficult to target using conventional fishing gear, so spearfishing underwater is currently the most effective way to remove them. Organizations around the Caribbean are now racing to try to keep the lionfish under control. Lad is philosophical accepting that once the lionfish were released the spread was inevitable, 'No matter how fast we reacted, I think the problem would still have unfolded; we could never have stopped it.' He believes that humans need to continue to innovate and to think of smart ways to solve the problem, or at least curtail the worst impacts to the ecology of a whole region.

## Our future ocean

Overwhelmingly there is a nervousness about what the future might bring, a recognition that we have stood on the tail of the monster, and the realization that we are not quite sure of the outcome. The question for society as a whole is how to maximize the economic benefits without damaging ecosystems, but the irony is that the economic potential of our fisheries is not fully realized because it is so poorly managed. Ussif Rashid Sumaila's research has shown that if we were to allow fish stocks to recover then we could sustainably catch 10 million more tonnes, increasing the global annual value by over 50 billion dollars. He points out that many of us are cushioned from the impacts of dwindling stocks through alternative markets and different sources of protein. For hundreds of millions of people there is no other choice. There is the moral dimension too – climate change is pushing fish to lower latitudes, away from the tropical coasts where people are much more dependent

on these catches for their livelihood and protein. What should these communities do if there are no more fish for them to catch?

Around the world, the most exciting changes are occurring at a local level, breaking down corrosive cycles of increasing exploitation. Communities are taking back control of their reefs through strong leadership and carefully crafted negotiations. Ultimately our oceans, and our own future, depend on whether they are something we truly cherish. Our lives and behaviour impact on the sea in a multitude of ways and what happens next is up to us. Our relationship now, inevitably, must be one in which we balance the excess of what we take with our ability to restrain our needs. There are no other examples in our lives where we can expect only benefits without investing time in caring, nurturing and restoring. Enjoyment and responsibility go hand in hand and are not mutually exclusive; in fact, they reinforce each other. We can either be crushed by the magnitude of the problem or buoyed up by the opportunity and huge scale of ambition required to solve it. The combination of many small actions has brought us to where we are; a similar multitude of collective changes can indeed rescue us.

# WORDS FROM THE EXPERTS

**Lad Akins** is Director of Special Projects at Reef Environmental Education Foundation (REEF). He is an inductee in the Scuba Diving Hall of Fame, and has been recognized as Oris Sea Hero and National Oceanic and Atmospheric Administration (NOAA) Environmental Hero for his conservation efforts, including the fight against invasive lionfish in the Caribbean:

*It is great for divers to be able to feel that they are putting their skills to good use and are helping protect against lionfish impacts. We now organize and promote annual lionfish 'derbies' throughout the region and a cookbook is helping lionfish become the Caribbean's new delicacy. As a conservationist, it feels strange to be encouraging people to kill a fish, and in the early years we were often confronted by people asking why we were catching these fish, but this was a great opportunity to talk about what we were doing and the dangers of releasing things that don't belong to our shores. The scale and severity of environmental problems can feel overwhelming, but the mobilization of people in a multitude of roles to solve this problem is also hugely empowering and motivating.*

**Bonnie McCay** is an anthropologist and Emeritus Professor at Rutgers University in the USA, where her research focuses on how humans use and share resources in the sea:

*I think that Newfoundland too has a positive future, and the collapse of its cod fishery has raised some fundamental questions about who really owns the fish and how responsibility can come with rights. I would like to see governments managing people, fisheries and biodiversity as if they were one system. Human use of the sea is widening and intensifying. In heavily industrialized regions across Europe, South East Asia and North America we are seeing rapid growth in shipping, offshore wind, oil and gas exploration and, among all of this development, whales need to be able to continue to migrate and communicate and fish to spawn and grow. I am not very good at being patient and I am anxious to know that we are properly looking after our seas. We are getting there, so I suppose that makes my glass half full.*

**Ussif Rashid Sumaila** works in the nexus between the natural and the human elements of fisheries across the globe. He is the Director of the Fisheries Economics Research Unit and the Ocean Canada Partnership at the University of British Columbia, Canada, and has worked with the United Nations, other intergovernmental organizations, NGOs and several governments worldwide:

*We need to find ways to reduce economic pressure on individual fishers, so that they can think long term. If our fish stock were given an opportunity to recover and if they were then properly managed, we could sustainably catch 10 million more tonnes, increasing the global annual value by over 50 billion dollars. There is an imperative for us to act urgently, populations are growing alongside growing living standards with expectations of access to resources. The question for us as scientists and for society as a whole is how can we maximize the economic benefits without damaging ecosystems? The tragedy is that climate change is pushing fish away from the tropical coasts, where people are much more dependent on these catches for their livelihood and protein.*

**Kirsten Grorud-Colvert** is an Assistant Professor at Oregon State University, where she is primarily interested in what happens when we protect the ocean and how to communicate this information effectively:

*I am an optimist. I like to focus on where I see progress being made, and where I can contribute to best effect. There is no doubt that there are some scary things happening in the sea, but I have enormous respect for the ocean and the way it has proven resilient in the past. What I can do is continue to try and share with others the importance of protecting these places.*

**Tundi Agardy** is a marine conservationist, specializing in how the protection of the sea can be most effective in the context of human use. She is the Founder and Executive Director of Sound Seas, a marine conservation policy group based in Washington, DC:

*I do think there is great hope for the future – we have the ability to get it right. A strategic approach is required where we look at what our natural systems need to survive, understand the context, engage closely with users and look for a balanced outcome for how space at sea is used by humans. Human use is mostly concentrated in the areas of coast and the nearshore. This is where conservation efforts need to be focused, looking for the synergies and trade-offs that can work with the grain of economic needs. An integral part of this plan would be to include a range of protected areas to make sure that all marine life is breeding, growing and ultimately thriving.*

**Jennifer Lavers** is a Lecturer in Marine Science at the Institute of Marine and Antarctic Studies at the University of Tasmania, Australia. She is an expert on the impact of plastic pollution on seabird populations:

*I first came across the plastics when I was working in Frigate Shoals in the North Western Hawaiian Islands. The nests of the albatross colonies here were littered with decomposing bodies of chicks with stomachs full of lighters, toothbrushes and other pieces of plastic debris. My work took me to Australia, where I was studying the flesh-footed shearwater, a species that was being accidentally caught on tuna longlines in huge numbers in their feeding grounds in the Tasman Sea and North Pacific. I was focused on the fisheries, but in the back of my mind I was also looking for more evidence of impacts from plastic. Sure enough, when I went to one of their principal breeding colonies at Lord Howe Island, 600 km offshore from the east coast of Australia, I saw plastic debris scattered among the trees inside the nesting colony. This was the point I knew that my role was to help show the world how plastics are impacting on seabirds across our oceans. For thousands of years humans have relied on seabirds as a sentinel species, helping fishermen spot shoals of fish or explorers find land on ocean voyages; now they are telling us that the health of the oceans is in trouble and their survival is in doubt.*

**Erik Van Sebille** is an oceanographer at the University of Utrecht's Institute for Marine and Atmospheric Research in the Netherlands. As an expert on ocean currents, he leads and coordinates the European Union-funded Tracking of Plastics in Our Seas Project:

*Plastic is a great material – lightweight, durable, waterproof, versatile and cheap, but also very hard to get rid of. It is a material that has no value to humanity after use. We fundamentally need to find a way to make ex-plastic valuable. We will never have a plastic-free ocean again, this is just not possible. What we should be looking to do is manage what we have created. The amount of plastic in our ocean is atrocious and shameful, but so far we have not seen too many signs of harm at an ecosystem level. This doesn't mean there isn't a problem, there is still hope; but since we know that plastic production is forecast to rise exponentially, if we don't do something soon then we will face a tsunami of plastic.*

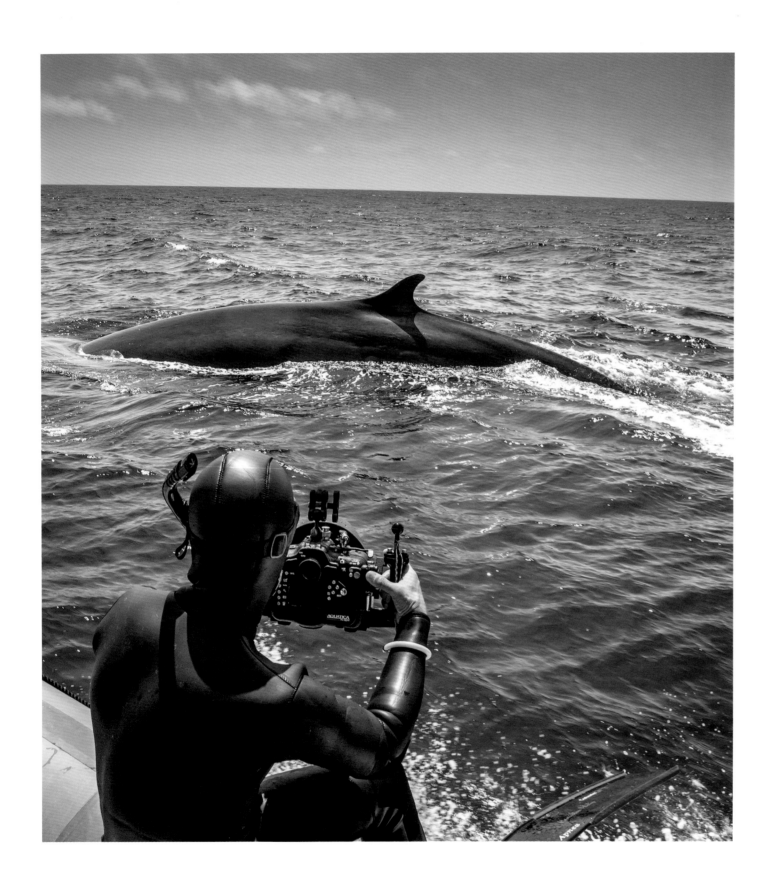

# MAKING *CALL OF THE BLUE*

**Y**OU MIGHT BE A LITTLE SURPRISED THAT you didn't get to read about some exotic locations or wild places, and I feel somehow cruel that you won't be able to pick your next diving vacation from this book. But there are so many important things to talk about that I decided to leave all geography and national borders aside.

The three hundred photographs of *Call of the Blue* were selected from a first set of almost a hundred thousand; after taking out any trace of 'human presence' and selecting the most relevant and beautiful photos I ended up with three thousand. From there it was like having to pick one out of ten of your own children, so by the end I was inviting friends and family to help me with the choice. It took time. I always try to keep my photography as pure and faithful as possible. I do not have Photoshop and have never used it. So many pictures were discarded just because I did not want to twist reality; many others stayed because, despite not being perfect photographs, they captured something essential of what it is to be underwater.

In what follows, I will try to give you a better understanding of what is behind a good underwater photograph but, in a nutshell, you need expertise and good equipment – and for the best shots all the stars

have to be aligned. For this book alone I spent hundreds of hours underwater making multiple trips around the world. I had many frustrating and unproductive journeys across oceans but I also had unforgettable encounters, though not all of these translated into beautiful photographs.

The complications of underwater photography are numerous and easy to imagine. Moving subjects, poor visibility and choppy seas make it very difficult. One can end up disappointed even after hours underwater. That perfect photo that you were after might have to wait another full year for conditions to be right again.

In certain aspects underwater photography is similar to land photography, in that a subject and proper framing are always required. However, that crucial component, lighting, is usually a huge challenge. We lose the colours (red, yellow, orange are the first to disappear as you go down) but you also lose lots of light: even on a sunny day at 50 metres there is little light left.

The water column that separates you from the subject not only absorbs the light, making your image blur, or less neat at best, but also it usually contains particles and residues that your camera will find hard to focus behind, and lastly it also brings 'backscatter'. To minimize the water column you have to get closer to the wild life – and this is the biggest challenge. To get a proper shark shot is like getting within a metre of a lion on land. In so many cases wildlife will not allow you to get that close. Bubbles, noise, your size, colours – they all cause fright. Hence some of my best shots come from freediving, which for me became mandatory to learn if I wanted to get close to many more species. Although I learned to dive to 30 metres on one breath, while photographing I rarely go down below 20 metres and normally keep my computer depth alarm at 15 metres. This is very important when following cetaceans and pelagic life underwater, because often, when you are behind the camera and have already equalized your ears, you may not notice the speed of your descent. If you are distracted or delay the ascension because of that famous last shot, you may never make it back to the surface.

It is only freediving (or with the large, cumbersome closed-circuit rebreather) that you can approach wildlife almost unnoticed. Sometimes when scuba diving I need to hide behind rocks or coral heads, hold my breath and let the animal approach (this is certainly not recommended by scuba training schools: it is dangerous and at the least gives you headaches due to $CO_2$ retention in your system under pressure).

On the other hand, the really expensive strobes and lights we use, which can blind you on land, under water get absorbed so much that they only give you, at best, an effective range of two metres. The fastest strobes will recharge within a second, but that is already too late when working with fast animals, so you need to be patient and learn when to take the shot. The converse is also true: when working on macro photography, where your subject is normally within one metre, your flash can blow the image and can even kill fragile and tiny animals.

Underwater the subject is most of the time a difficult one: it can be fast-moving, huge in size (whale) or tiny (shrimp or pygmy seahorse), it can be dangerous (croc) or poisonous (blue-ring octopus); the colour could be a challenge, too, since a silver tarpon will reflect most of your light and blow the picture, a black frogfish will absorb it all and give you back a flat picture, making it hard to detect its features. Some can be shy (thresher shark), others inquisitive (tuna or longimanus). If you hide behind a sardine bait-ball, sharks, whales, dolphins and sailfish can easily hit you unintentionally. Some animals are in the deep ocean and almost unreachable. Other species bother you while you are working on your chosen subject; we have all been stung by 'invisible' jellyfish or even got krill in our ears. Marine animals

The author under a manta ray. Photo courtesy of William Drumm

can also travel very fast: I registered a fin whale I was working with at 16 knots once – so freediving with it proved impossible. In a way there is no easy or perfect model, but if I had to pick one it would have to be a slow-moving manatee in shallow crystal water on a sunny day. Needless to say, for the best chance of success you need to know the species well before setting out to photograph it.

Other considerations would include noise and bubble from other divers, not to mention that they might get into your frame (that is why I tend to dive alone). The fact you can't really change a lens underwater is sometimes very unfortunate; however, when conditions are right I tend to carry two cameras, one attached to my waist, though this makes it harder to swim against currents.

A zoom will have no use really: it might get you a souvenir photo but nothing very good. Only proximity to the subject and the right lens, with the right lighting, can secure great photographs. To that end, as well as my three Canon cameras (5D Mark II, 5DS and 5D Mark IV), I take with me a number of lenses (EF17-40, EF16-35, EF100 Macro and EF8-15 Fish-eye), underwater housings from Aquatica, and Ikelite DS161 strobes.

At night, not only will you have no depth of field beside a macro shot, but also if you use lights you will usually attract quantities of krill and particles.

One of the main issues is water clarity, cleanness. Water is sometimes full of plankton and is green, sometimes just murky. You can be at the right place, with the friendly subject willing to play ball, but the water will not let you get the shot you were after. Water visibility could be three to five metres and you might be working on a 25-metre whale. It becomes an impossible task. Frequently you find huge currents and thermoclines underwater (notably in the zones where large pelagic and sharks tend to be); unfortunately these, too, blur your images and reduce visibility.

Last but not least, there is the cost involved. Underwater photography equipment is expensive, and diving and chartering boats are well beyond the reach of many; in certain cases you even need government or other authorities licencing. Sometime you pay two weeks licence and charter a boat and then, such are the weather and sea conditions, you only get in the water on two or three days. It can be still worse, if, when you do get the chance to jump in the water, the animal is not there or the visibility will not allow you to take a decent picture.

In sum, I try to be grateful to nature and accept happily everything I get – storm, rain, rough waters and also that exceptional encounter that will keep me motivated and hopeful until my last days.

The author working around a bait-ball while freediving. Photo courtesy of Jordi Chias

# CLOSING WORDS: THE CONSERVATIONISTS

*The fate of human existence is dependent on a bountiful sea. I lost my leg to a shark, but an ocean void of them is much more frightening than any attack*—Mike Coots

THERE IS UNTOLD VALUE in working with young people, and little as rewarding as seeing a child discover something that they are truly excited to learn about. It is vital to capture that spark in youth, cultivate it through hands-on experience, new knowledge, and facilitate access to the possibilities for their future. Even when living thousands of miles from the nearest ocean kids can naturally form a connection with the sea and develop their own sense of ownership and responsibility towards it.

We each get to decide what kind of difference we want to make, and I would challenge anyone who thinks that they can't influence a change for the better. Wherever your talents lie, you have something to give to the ocean. If you make a good argument you can debate and lobby for vital ocean policy; if you're a journalist you can write about it; if you're an artist you can make your statement through creative expression.

We have reached the point where we need all hands on deck to help drive solutions forward and properly deal with issues negatively impacting our oceans. Our stewardship of the ocean is not a political issue; this is something that affects all of us personally – people we love, those we take care of, family, friends, our children. The realization of what needs to be done is a big deal, and can be scary and disheartening at times. Moving forward requires young and brilliant minds to come on board and join the fight. Each new generation brings fresh perspective, energized ideas and most importantly an untarnished optimism and inspiration that we all need to sustain and encourage. But the future of our oceans does not rest on one generation alone, we are tethered together in our responsibility to one another. We must not give up on searching for those pieces of hope and must work jointly for the best possible outcome for our blue planet.

**MEHGAN HEANEY-GRIER**

American champion freediver, adventurer, marine conservationist and television presenter, passionate about empowering young people to become water stewards and ocean leaders

GROWING UP HUMAN, I adopted the usual biases against fish – prejudices that have unfairly relegated them to the dim end of the vertebrate spectrum. How wrong I was! Not only has science put to rest the malevolent myth that fish do not feel pain, we now know that they can be intelligent, emotional, even Machiavellian. Among their achievements, fish have personalities, they plan, recognize, remember, court, play, parent, innovate, manipulate, collaborate, communicate with gestures, keep accounts, show virtue, form attachments, possess culture, fall for optical illusions, use tools, learn by observation, form mental maps, and pay attention to their audience. We need a sea-change in our view of fish, and it can't happen too soon.

**JONATHAN BALCOMBE**

Author of *What a Fish Knows, Pleasurable Kingdom* and *Second Nature*. Formerly Director of Animal Sentience with the Humane Society Institute for Science and Policy, he teaches a course on animal sentience for the Viridis Graduate Institute, and serves as an Associate Editor for the open-access journal *Animal Sentience*

# CLOSING WORDS: THE PROFESSORS

*Call of the Blue has connected so many global guardians of the sea – the world's leading specialists in their field. The result is a rich and colourful work of art*—Michael Braungart

From the creation of planet earth 4.5 billion years ago, it took around one billion years for the first plant cells to appear. After another billion years the oceans evolved primitive colonies of single-celled organisms. It took a further billion years to create multicellular plants, where myriad cells in each plant started to play their specified roles within a more complex pattern of life.

Up until then, all of evolution happened in the ocean. Dying algae were sedimented and mineralized at the bottom of the ocean where they sequestered toxic materials. By producing food and oxygen, plants provided the conditions necessary for animals to appear by creating the ozone layer, protecting the land from ultraviolet light. So, after three billion years of paving the ground for animals, the first primitive animal cell entered the scene.

Human civilization has brought about a wonderful technical and cultural development, the very late newcomer of billions of years of evolution. And living within nature we see societies of people loving one other, helping each other, playing Bach and curing cancer. The side effect from the evolution of civilization, however, is that we are increasingly trespassing the boundaries of what nature can spare. We are systematically allowing forests, soils, bottoms of seas and coral reefs to become deserts again. We are going backwards. As if our 3.5 billion-year evolution were being played in reverse.

We may walk in a forest or look at nature from a window, but we forget that the largest part of our world, the birthplace of nature, is hidden from most of us –the oceans. How do we relate to them as we live our lives?

Modern science has helped us model a sustainable world where nature on land and seas is pure and healthy again, and constant innovations help us increase the quality of civilized life within sustainability constraints. A society can now be designed, in very real terms, so that all sectors – fisheries, forestry, agriculture, energy, traffic, industry – and the infrastructure of our societies are sustainable together. Furthermore, science has given us methods by which leaders at all levels in society, and from public as well as private sectors, can systematically enter and monitor transitions towards compliance with such constraints. And finally, modern science has shown us that such journeys are easier, more fun, more economic and more dignified than any other alternative.

On this dangerous path towards greater ecological and social problems, we are moving deeper into a 'funnel' of declining resources and purity to sustain life, and we are losing trust between people at many levels. This moment in human history is when we need trust more than ever to solve our ecological problems. How can we reverse destruction? Could we search for stories that help us understand the mechanisms of destruction so that we can avoid them in the future? There is no better story than the emergence of all life from our oceans.

This book is precisely about this, opening our eyes and hearts to something we really love from deep within us. We are in danger of contemplating how much we loved it only after having lost it.

**KARL-HENRIK ROBÈRT**

One of Sweden's foremost cancer scientists and founder of The Natural Step, a framework which sets out the system conditions for sustainability

I AM NOT SOMEONE WHO WORKS CLOSELY with the oceans, yet when I came to think about them specifically for *Call of the Blue* I realized that the increasing human impacts on the ocean are among the best examples of two of the 'four laws of ecology' that were first put forward by Barry Commoner in 1971:

1. Everything is connected to everything else.
There is one ecosphere for all living organisms and effects on one part of it can affect everything else. Emissions from carbon dioxide go into and warm the atmosphere, which warms the oceans, which bleaches and destroys coral reefs, which are among the most diverse ecosystems on earth. The oceans also absorb the carbon dioxide, turning them more acidic, with as yet uncertain and potentially devastating effects on shellfish and other ocean life.

2. Everything must go somewhere.
There is no 'waste' in nature and there is no 'away' into which things can be thrown. Currently some eight million tonnes per year of plastic, 'thrown away' by humans, find their way into the oceans. Some of the effects on larger creatures are obvious – whales with plastic bags in their guts, seabirds and fish strangled in netting, drinking straws in the nostrils of turtles. The long-term effects of the micro-particles of plastic that are now ubiquitous in food chains are still unknown, but they certainly are not 'away'.

Humanity today seems little closer to learning and paying attention to these laws than it was nearly five decades ago when Barry Commoner first articulated them. These are truths that we have known about for quite some time, yet somehow we have managed to ignore them or just hope that somehow the oceans are so large they will be OK. Or we may get fixated on a small component of the problem such as drinking straws, and tell ourselves that banning them will solve the problem, when in reality we need a complete reorganization of how we make, use and re-use all plastics, and much else besides.

There is always hope, and it is certainly very positive that there are some signs that we seem to be waking up to our impact on planetary systems and biodiversity and the need for action and change. Yet public interest is often fleeting – too often the demand is for a quick fix, before attention moves on to something else. To fix our environmental problems we need to put long-term measures into place, and keep our eye on the ball every step of the way. Will governments show leadership and determination to follow through? Time will tell, but the extent to which oceans can contribute to our future prosperity while maintaining their integrity depends completely on how willing we all are to acknowledge the scale of the challenge.

**PAUL EKINS**

Professor of Resources and Environmental Policy at University College London, Deputy Director of the UK Energy Research Centre and Adviser to Government on sustainable energy and environmental policy

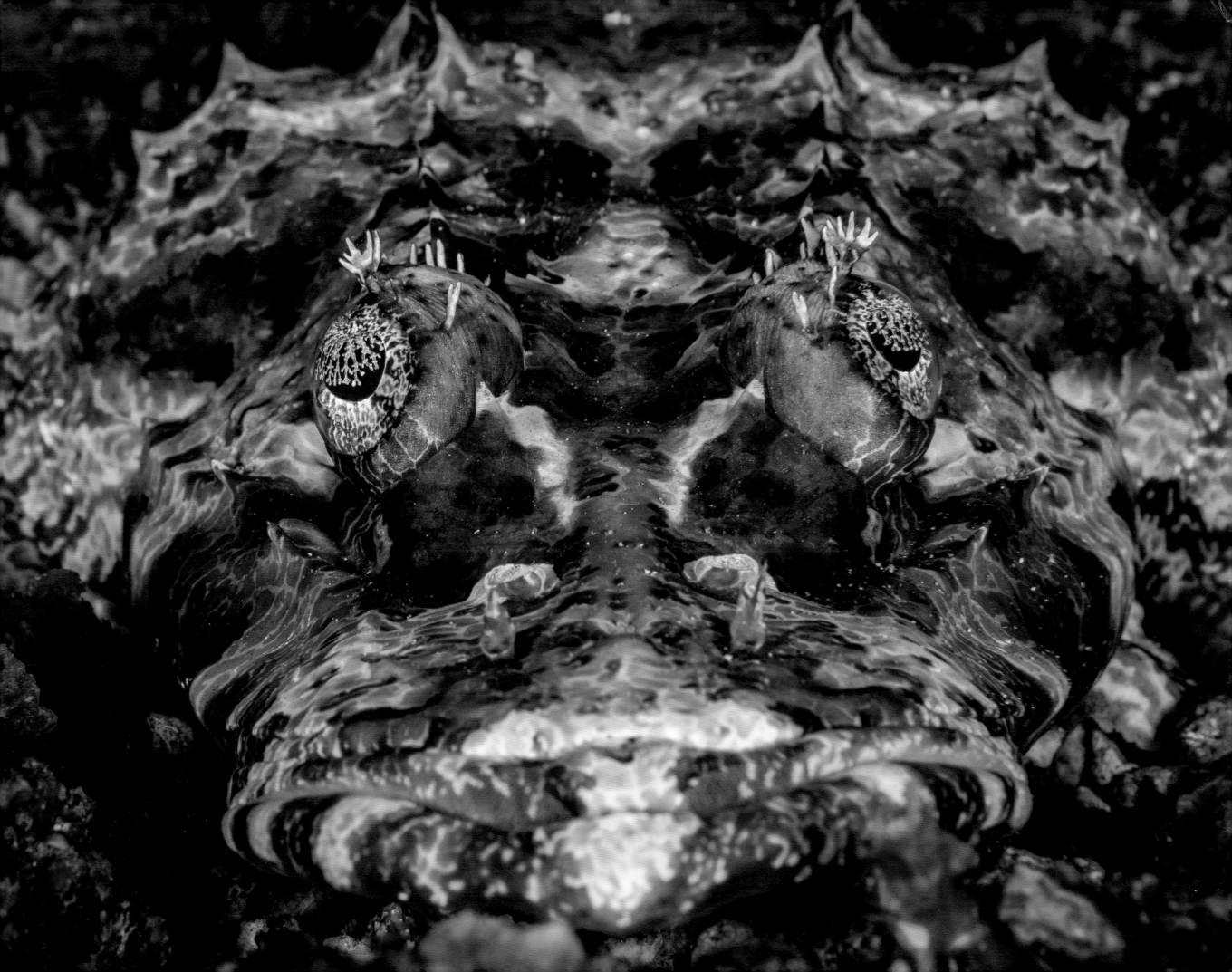

# ACKNOWLEDGEMENTS

Thank you to all the amazing ocean Guardians and Experts who took time to share their 'call of the blue' – their stories, wisdom and lives spent with the ocean: Tundi Agardy, Lad Akins, Kike Ballesteros, Stefanie Brendl, Annette Broderick, Sid Chakravarty, Isabelle Côté, Paul De Gelder, Regina Domingo, Sarah Foster, Peter Gill, Brendan Godley, Rachel Graham, Kirsten Grorud-Colvert, Michel Guerrero, Jim Hancock, David Harasti, Alasdair Harris, Michelle Heupel, Denise Herzing, Erick Higuera, Mauricio Hoyos, Kevin Huang, Conrad Humphreys, Miguel Iñiguez, Buzzy Kerbox, Zafer Kizilkaya, Miranda Krestovnikoff, Jennifer Lavers, Andrea Marshall, Bonnie McCay, Mikki McComb-Kobza, Christie McMillan, Nick Moloney, Jeanne A. Mortimer, Ken Nedimyer, Ric O'Barry, David Obura, Owen O'Shea, Yannis Papastamatiou, David Pawson, Roger Payne, Simon Pierce, Marta Pola, Frank Pope, Louie Psihoyos, Dení Ramírez-Macías, Ussif Rashid Sumaila, Paul Rose, Jo Royle, Peter Sale, Filipa Samarra, Roz Savage, Rebecca Scott, Erik Van Sebille, Richard Sears, Lauren Smith, Richard Smith, Mark Spalding, Guy Stevens, Robert Swan, William Trubridge, Hal Whitehead, Sheldon Whitehouse, Jean Wiener, Doug Woodring, Charlie Veron, Catherine Yrisarri and Angela Ziltener.

Many thanks, too, to Guardians Eric Blais, David Diley, Pascal von Erp, Katie Linczenyiova, Enrico Villa, Jane Walker and Howard Wood for sharing their experiences and wisdom with us – their contribution and inspiration is throughout the book. I am enormously grateful to Nicola Chadwick, Rob Enever, Gemma Hooper, Tara Hooper, Louise Lieberknecht, James Masters, Joana Smith, Vanessa Smith, Yorgos Stratoudakis, Claire Wallerstein, for their insight, knowledge and time spent reviewing the writing, and to the artist Jo Maynard for contributing the book's tailpiece.

I cannot thank Tom Hooper enough. Over the last two years he has spent long days conducting interviews, and writing and shaping chapters. His patience and motivation know no limits. Special thanks, too, to Jessica Rudd for her overall contribution – drafting, interviewing, researching and editing.

Thanks must also go to the freediving safety team, camera assistants, spotters and diving buddies that sometimes accompanied me: Robert Gitz, Christopher Hamilton, Nicholas Hamilton and Clement Perrette.

Thank you Nancy and Greg Saichin for your help selecting the 'finalists' among several thousand photos.

Finally, no words to thank my biggest supporter, my partner in life, Denise Hamilton. Without her little could have been achieved.

---

PAGE 344 The mandarinfish produces 'cyanophores' – blue-pigmented, light-reflecting cells – to achieve its vibrant colouring

PAGE 345 The spectacular, slow-moving leafy seadragon likes to camouflage itself around kelp-covered rocks and sea grass

PAGE 347 The juvenile crocodilefish is entirely black, but as it ages it becomes mottled, its colouring varing in intensity according to its surroundings

FACING With its distinct truncated shape, the ocean sunfish looks like half a fish. Its back fin never grows but folds into itself, creating a rounded rudder

OVERLEAF Oil painting courtesy of Jo Maynard. 50% from the sale of this painting will be donated to an ocean conservation organization www.artbyjomaynard.co.uk